PHILOSOPHICAL FOUNDATIONS OF CRIMINAL LAW

PHILOSOPHICAL FOUNDATIONS OF CRIMINAL LAW

Edited by

RA DUFF

and

STUART P GREEN

OXFORD
UNIVERSITY PRESS

OXFORD
UNIVERSITY PRESS

Great Clarendon Street, Oxford, OX2 6DP,
United Kingdom

Oxford University Press is a department of the University of Oxford.
It furthers the University's objective of excellence in research, scholarship,
and education by publishing worldwide. Oxford is a registered trade mark of
Oxford University Press in the UK and in certain other countries

First Edition published in 2011
First published in paperback 2013

Impression: 1

British Library Cataloguing in Publication Data
Data available

ISBN 978–0–19–955915–2
978–0–19–967367–4 (pbk.)

Printed in Great Britain
on acid-free paper by
Ashford Colour Press, Gosport, Hampshire

PREFACE

....

We gratefully acknowledge the help given by a number of people in the planning, writing, and production of this volume. Alex Flach of Oxford University Press suggested the idea to us, and helped us throughout the process, as did his colleagues in the Law Department at the Press; thanks are also due to Steinvör Thöll Árnadóttir for very valuable editorial assistance. A small group of colleagues—Markus Dubber, Kim Ferzan, Doug Husak, Sandra Marshall, Paul Robinson, and Bob Weisberg— spent a day (hosted and funded by the Paul M Hebert Law Center at Louisiana State University) discussing the shape and structure of the planned volume—though they cannot be blamed for the shape that it actually took. The Rutgers School of Law, Newark, hosted and funded a workshop at which preliminary drafts of the papers were discussed: grateful thanks are due to the commentators who started off the discussion of each paper—Vera Bergelson, Michael Cahill, Michelle Demspey, Adil Haque, Kyron Huigens, Youngjae Lee, Alice Ristroph, and Ekow Yankah. Finally, of course, thanks are due to the authors: for their work in drafting and redrafting; for their patient, constructive responses to editorial suggestions and requests; and for the illuminating and stimulating papers that appear in this volume.

RAD
SPG

Contents

....

PART I CRIMINAL LAW AND POLITICAL THEORY

PART II THE SUBSTANCE OF CRIMINAL LAW

PART III PROCESS AND PUNISHMENT

PART IV   ACROSS BORDERS AND INTO THE FUTURE

LIST OF CONTRIBUTORS

Larry Alexander is the Warren Distinguished Professor of Law, University of San Diego.

Andrew Ashworth is the Vinerian Professor of English Law at the University of Oxford.

Mitchell N Berman is Richard Dale Endowed Chair in Law, Professor of Philosophy (by courtesy), University of Texas at Austin.

Richard Dagger is E Claiborne Robins Distinguished Chair in the Liberal Arts, University of Richmond.

Donald A Dripps is a Professor of Law at the University of San Diego.

Markus D Dubber is Professor of Law, Faculty of Law, University of Toronto.

RA Duff is a Professor Emeritus in the Department of Philosophy, University of Stirling, and a Professor in the Law School, University of Minnesota.

Kimberly Kessler Ferzan is Professor of Law, Rutgers University, School of Law—Camden and Associate Graduate Faculty, Rutgers-New Brunswick Department of Philosophy.

Stuart P Green is Professor of Law and Justice Nathan L Jacobs Scholar, Rutgers School of Law, Newark.

Adil Ahmad Haque is Assistant Professor of Law, Rutgers School of Law, Newark.

Mireille Hildebrandt is an Associate Professor of Jurisprudence at the Erasmus School of Law, Rotterdam, and a senior researcher at Law Science Technology and Society (LSTS) at the Vrije Universiteit Brussels.

Douglas Husak is Professor of Philosophy and Law, Rutgers University.

Nicola Lacey is Senior Research Fellow at All Souls College, Oxford, Professor of Criminal Law and Legal Theory, University of Oxford.

Matt Matravers is Professor of Political Philosophy and Director, Morrell Centre for Toleration, University of York.

Michael S Moore is Walgreen University Chair, Professor of Law, Professor of Philosophy, Professor in the Center for Advanced Study, and Co-Director of the Program in Law and Philosophy, University of Illinois.

Alice Ristroph is Professor of Law and Eileen Denner Research Fellow at Seton Hall University School of Law.

Paul Roberts is Professor of Criminal Jurisprudence, University of Nottingham.

Kenneth W Simons is Professor of Law and The Honorable Frank R Kenison Distinguished Scholar in Law, Boston University School of Law.

Victor Tadros is a Professor in the School of Law, University of Warwick.

Malcolm Thorburn is Associate Professor of Law and Canada Research Chair in Crime, Security and Constitutionalism at Queen's University, Canada.

Christopher Heath Wellman is Professor of Philosophy at Washington University in St. Louis and Professorial Fellow at CAPPE, Charles Sturt University.

Peter Westen is Frank G Millard Professor of Law, Emeritus, University of Michigan.

Lucia Zedner is Professor of Criminal Justice, Faculty of Law, University of Oxford and Conjoint Professor, Faculty of Law, University of New South Wales.

TABLE OF CASES

Table of Statutes, Codes, and Charters

INTRODUCTION: SEARCHING FOR FOUNDATIONS

RA DUFF AND
STUART P GREEN

THE title of this volume, *Philosophical Foundations of Criminal Law*, might seem to beg at least two important questions. First, does the criminal law have foundations? Second, if it does, is it the responsibility of philosophy to construct, or to excavate, those foundations?

Talk of foundations implies that the criminal law has an ordered, stable structure, whose basic or foundational elements can be discovered; to call those foundations philosophical is also to imply that they are a matter of reason. But, critics will argue, the criminal law (indeed, law generally) is not like that. It is certainly not a matter of reason, if that is taken to mean that it is grounded in coherent principles or that it displays a rational structure of consistent rules or doctrines. Nor can it claim the security or stability that foundations are supposed to provide, since it is grounded in and determined by nothing more stable than the shifting sands of historical contingencies—of political, social, and economic forces. What an understanding of the structures, the development, and the bases of criminal law therefore requires is not (just or primarily) the metaphysical explorations, conceptual analyses, or rational reconstructions that may be offered by different types of philosopher, but the more empirical and interpretive skills of the historian and the sociologist. They have more chance of explaining criminal law—what it means, how and to what ends or with what effects it functions—by explaining how it has developed, and by identifying the historical and social factors that have made it what it is, and that have created the conflicts that it embodies. To understand the criminal law, or to identify whatever foundations it might have, we must attend to its history and to its social and political context, not to the rational (re)constructions of philosophers.[1]

Such critics might find symbolic support in the explanation of this volume's title, since it was indeed a matter of historical contingency rather than of rational or prin-cipled reflection. Oxford University Press asked the editors if they would like to organize a volume to follow in the steps of *Philosophical Foundations of Tort Law*,[2] and that gave us our title: no deeper or philosophically more ambitious meaning is to be found. To understand our choice (if it was a choice) of title the reader must therefore look not to philosophical theory, nor to a conception of criminal law as having 'philosophical foundations', but to the contingencies of publishing history and to the marketing concerns that help to drive that history. So, too, critics will argue, an understanding of criminal law requires attention not (just or primarily) to the abstractions of philosophical inquiry, but to the messy contingencies of its history—more precisely, of the histories of the very different systems of criminal law to be found in our contemporary world.

We will resist this criticism. This is not because we think that philosophical inquiry is *the* key to understanding criminal law, or that philosophical inquiry can isolate itself from other disciplines such as history and sociology. There is indeed no such thing as *the* key, in part because there is no unitary goal of 'understanding criminal law'. Different understandings are gained through different disciplinary perspec-tives, and although they cannot be isolated from each other, each has its own distinc-tive character; theorists should aspire, not to develop some all-embracing theory that could count as *the* theory of criminal law, but rather to explore the theoretical insights that emerge from different disciplinary (and cross-disciplinary) inquiries, and the extent and character of the connections between them.

What, then, should emerge from a philosophical approach to criminal law? What kind of understanding should it offer? What kinds of foundation should concern it? Such questions could be adequately answered only through a thorough discussion of the wide range of very different approaches and methods that might count as

---

[1] Extreme versions of such criticisms were pressed by proponents of Critical Legal Studies (eg M Kelman, 'Interpretive Construction in the Substantive Criminal Law' (1981) 33 *Stanford Law Review* 591, and 'Trashing' (1984) 36 *Stanford Law Review* 293). For more recent, less radically nega-tive (and for that reason more interesting) critiques see eg L Farmer, *Criminal Law, Tradition and Legal Order* (Cambridge: Cambridge University Press, 1996); N Lacey, 'Contingency, Coherence and Conceptualism', in Duff (ed), *Philosophy and the Criminal Law* (Cambridge: Cambridge University Press, 1998), 9, and '"Philosophical Foundations of the Common Law": Social not Metaphysical', in J Horder (ed), *Oxford Essays in Jurisprudence, 4th Series* (Oxford: Oxford University Press, 2000), 17; AW Norrie, *Crime, Reason and History* (2nd edn; London: Butterworths, 2001).

[2] DG Owen (ed), *The Philosophical Foundations of Tort Law* (Oxford: Oxford University Press, 1995).

'philosophical'—a discussion on which we will not embark here. A further closely related question is whether philosophers should seek to develop a 'theory' of criminal law—and, if so, what kind of theory that should be, and what it should be a theory of. As far as that question is concerned, we can usefully start with the traditional distinction between analytical, or expository, and normative, or censorial, jurisprudence—between a focus on what criminal law is, and a focus on what it ought to be.[3]

Expository jurisprudence, if it is to claim to be philosophical, cannot of course be simply a matter of describing the content and the operations of existing legal systems: it must delve beneath the surface, to articulate the structures that inform that content and underpin those operations. Some would talk now of an enterprise of conceptual analysis that explicates the meanings of legal concepts (concepts that can of course be understood only in the contexts in which they are used); some would talk of a related enterprise of discerning the logic, or the logical structure, of the criminal law; others, with larger metaphysical ambitions, would talk of discerning the real nature of criminal law.[4] Censorial jurisprudence, by contrast, is focused not on the structure or content of existing systems of law, but the aims, values, and principles that *should* structure a system of criminal law (one key question for any such theorist will of course concern the grounds for such normative claims, and their relationship to the analytical or expository).

It is easy enough to state this distinction between analytical and normative jurisprudence, but we should not suppose that it can be sharply drawn, for two reasons.

First, an analytical approach cannot avoid normative engagement. This is not just because what we are trying to analyse is itself a normative institution—one that centrally involves the authoritative creation and application of normative judgments; it is because anything more ambitious than an unstructured, piecemeal description of that institution (and philosophical analysis must be more ambitious than that) will inevitably involve an attempt at more or less radical rational reconstruction—an attempt whose failure would be just as instructive as its success, since it would show the institution to lack any rational structure. As critical theorists rightly remind us, our criminal law is not the carefully crafted product of a divinely inspired creative moment, but the messy outcome of the variegated, shifting forces that determined its historical development. The challenge is to make sense of this set of practices—a

[3] See J Bentham, *An Introduction to the Principles of Morals and Legislation* (1789; ed Burns and Hart, Oxford: Oxford University Press, 1996), ch 19 on 'expository' as against 'censorial' jurisprudence (he comments there on 'local' as against 'universal' jurisprudence, and remarks that, given the diversity of laws, in both content and form, expository jurisprudence can claim universal application only if it confines its attention to 'terminology' or 'the import of words'). For a more contemporary discussion of the distinction between analytical and normative (or 'descriptive' and 'prescriptive') jurisprudence, see DN Husak, *Philosophy of Criminal Law* (Totowa, NJ: Rowman & Littlefield, 1987), 20–6.

[4] See recently MS Moore, *Placing Blame: A General Theory of the Criminal Law* (Oxford: Oxford University Press, 1997): conceptual analysis, on Moore's view, is at best a somewhat uncertain guide to the underlying metaphysics that it is the proper task of philosophical inquiry to uncover.

sense that must be a normative sense, given their normative character: to discern a normative structure that expresses coherent principles and values, and that is adapted to the pursuit of identifiable ends. This is not to say that a rational reconstruction must produce a normative structure that is free of all conflict: once we recognize the reality of conflicting, incommensurable values, we must recognize that conflicts or 'contradictions', even those between which only uneasy compromize rather than definitive resolution is possible, need not mark a rational deficiency in the system in which they are found; they might instead mark the way in which the system is sensitive to the plurality of values.[5]

The task of rational reconstruction, as so far described, is not (yet) fully Herculean, since it does not involve the construction of a political theory:[6] but it is proto-Herculean, since its completion requires the reconstruction of a complete system of criminal law. Inevitably, such reconstruction will require construction rather than mere excavation, blurring the always less than sharp distinction between 'discovery' and 'creation'. It will also require some substantial theory of mistakes: not only will particular judicial decisions turn out to be inconsistent with the doctrines, principles, and rules that rational reconstruction shows to be at least implicit in the system of law; the same will be true of statutes, of doctrines, and of principles or slogans that many might see as entrenched features of our law.

However, the task of rational reconstruction must become more fully Herculean than this, since it cannot attend only to what is strictly internal to the law.[7] Analysis or reconstruction that attends only to what the law itself (insofar as we can even separate 'the law itself' from what lies beyond the law) offers can reveal conflicts or inconsistencies between this aspect of the law and that, and *might* sometimes also be able to show that one of those aspects must be classed as a 'mistake', since the aspect with which it is inconsistent lies closer to the centre of the law's structure;[8] but both the interpretation of the doctrines or principles involved, and the determination of what should count as a mistake, will often need to look beyond what is strictly internal to the law, to some set of moral or political values that we can suppose the law to be intended to embody. What counts as making normative sense at all must depend in part on such underlying values, and any attempt to decide which reconstruction makes better normative sense must appeal to such values. The reconstructive theorist can try still to remain detached—to identify the political and moral values that make best sense of a particular legal system without either endorsing or criticizing

---

[5] See further DN MacCormick, 'Reconstruction after Deconstruction: A Response to CLS' (1990) 10 *Oxford Journal of Legal Studies* 539; RA Duff, 'Principle and Contradiction in the Criminal Law', in Duff (ed), *Philosophy and the Criminal Law*, 156.

[6] See RM Dworkin, *Law's Empire* (London: Fontana, 1986), esp chs 7–10.

[7] See J Tasioulas, 'Philosophy, Criticism and Community' (2009) 26 *Journal of Applied Philosophy* 259; V Tadros, 'Law, Strategy and Democracy' (2009) 26 *Journal of Applied Philosophy* 269.

[8] Compare WV Quine, 'Two Dogmas of Empiricism' (1951) 60 *Philosophical Review* 20, on the 'web of belief' and the ways in which propositions are more or less revisable.

those values (though there are questions to be asked about how far such a detached view will be able to judge what makes *best* sense); but what is being reconstructed is now an account of what the law ought to be—even if it is an account of what the law ought to be from a particular normative perspective.[9]

Second, an approach that is avowedly normative from the start must still engage with the analytical or descriptive, since a normative theory of criminal law must be a theory of what can be recognized as criminal law, as a particular kind of human practice. Normative theorists might argue (any normatively plausible theory will have to argue) that our criminal law must be more or less radically reformed if it is to claim legitimacy; some might argue that it cannot achieve legitimacy, and must therefore be abolished:[10] but such arguments must be grounded in an understanding of what it is that is to be reformed or abolished, and of what would count as a radical reform as distinct from abolition. That much is true even for theorists who aspire to a universalist normativity that would generate an account of the basic principles or aims of 'criminal law' as such, whenever and wherever it exists, since that would still need to be an account of what can be recognized as criminal law: a universalist normative account of what criminal law ought to be needs a correspondingly universalist analytic or descriptive account of what criminal law is. An engagement with the analytical and descriptive is, however, even more important for theorists who eschew such universalist ambitions.[11]

One question that arises, when we look beyond our own local systems and recognize the very diverse forms that criminal law can take, is whether we should aspire to an analytical or descriptive universalism—one more substantial than Bentham thought possible.[12] There must of course be some substantive features of a practice that warrant describing it as a system of criminal law: as, that is, both a system of law, and a system of criminal law in particular, as distinct from other kinds of legal regulation. But should we hope to specify the necessary or defining features that any practice must display if it is to count as a system of criminal law; or should we rather say that what connects the many very different instances of criminal law is a matter of family resemblance rather than of common defining features? Is it, for instance, an essential feature of anything that is to be classed as a criminal law that what is criminalized is portrayed as morally wrong; or that it provides for the punishment

[9] Compare J Raz, *The Authority of Law* (Oxford: Oxford University Press, 1979), 153–9, on 'detached normative statements'.

[10] Some 'abolitionists' argue that we should abolish not just criminal punishment, but criminal law itself as a distinctive legal practice: eg N Christie, 'Conflicts as Property' (1977) 17 *British Journal of Criminology* 1; L Hulsman, 'Critical Criminology and the Concept of Crime' (1986) 10 *Contemporary Crises* 63.

[11] This is an issue on which the editors are divided: compare Green's comments in this volume (at 354), and SP Green, 'The Universal Grammar of Criminal Law' (2000) 98 *Michigan Law Review* 2104, with RA Duff, *Answering for Crime* (Oxford: Hart Publishing, 2007), 6–11.

[12] See n 3 above.

of those who commit what it criminalizes?[13] Or could we find, or imagine, practices which we should count as criminal law, but which lack those features?

But even if a modestly substantive analytical or descriptive universalism is plausible, this does not guarantee, and need not lead us to, a normative universalism. More precisely, it need not lead us towards the kind of top-down universalism which grounds itself in a set of a priori principles revealed by a practical reason operating independently of any particular, contingent human practices or cultures: towards a universalism that aspires to declare, from such a view from nowhere in particular, what criminal law ought to be or to do wherever and whenever it operates. To eschew that kind of universalist ambition is to insist that normative theorizing cannot be independent of the historical (and geographical) contingencies of the practices to which it is to apply. The point is not just that we must recognize the historically contingent character of those practices (no one would deny that): it is that normative theorizing is itself inextricably rooted in its historical and cultural context. Any normative theorizing must begin from where we, the theorizers, are, within our particular context; nor can we sensibly aspire to break free from all such contexts, to take a God's eye view or a view from nowhere, and articulate a universal normative theory of what the criminal law, as such, ought to be.[14] But it does not follow that we cannot aspire to rational normative theorizing about, or to a rational critique of, criminal law; nor does it follow that such critique and theorizing must be limited to the very local setting of a particular legal system. To suppose the former would be to show oneself to be a 'disappointed metaphysical absolutist' for whom 'reason' could be real only if it was a priori;[15] to suppose the latter would be to ignore the possibility (one that a moment's reflection shows to be often actualized) that different traditions and forms of thought might be sufficiently closely connected to permit rational mutual discussion and argument.

To deny the possibility of a priori normative theorizing is to insist that such theorizing is possible and intelligible only within some human practice. That practice, that 'form of life', provides the 'we' of and to whom we talk when we talk of what 'we' should believe or say or do—the 'we' with whom theorizing constitutes a conversation; it provides the language in which such conversations can take place. That 'we', however, expands as we come to realize the porous character of the boundaries between different practices or forms of life, and the possibilities of discussion and dialogue between them. When legal theorists ask what the criminal law ought to be, they cannot but be asking and arguing about 'our' criminal law: but the temporal and cultural scope of that 'our' is open for exploration and extension, including

---

[13] Which raises, of course, the question of what counts as 'punishment'.

[14] See, eg, Lacey, 'Contingency, Coherence and Conceptualism'.

[15] JM Finnis, 'On "The Critical Legal Studies Movement"', in J Eekelaar and J Bell (eds), *Oxford Essays in Jurisprudence, 3rd Series* (Oxford: Oxford University Press, 1987), 145, at 160, on proponents of 'Critical Legal Studies'.

expansion through other legal traditions. Furthermore, a theoretical normative engagement with the criminal law must, as we have already noted, include engagement with the moral and political values that it must claim to embody: this opens up further possibilities for rational normative theorizing, in the familiar realms of moral and political philosophy. If we take this kind of bottom-up approach, which begins from where (a relatively limited) 'we' are now, we need not abandon all universalist ambitions: we could still aspire to work towards some set of aims or values that, we can claim, should inform any system of criminal law. But, first, such an approach requires a close attention to the analytical or descriptive dimension of theorizing, since it must be grounded in a detailed understanding of the characters (and contexts) of the systems of criminal law with which we are dealing. Second, we must not assume in advance that such universalist aspirations will be fulfilled or fulfillable: we might discover that the differences, not just between the systems of criminal law but between the political and social structures in which they are embedded, run too deep for us to be able to sustain any claims about what criminal law should be or do at all times in all places. Perhaps the most that we can hope to achieve, through normative philosophical theorizing, is to articulate a series of conceptions of criminal law (as distinct from *the* concept of criminal law);[16] to identify the ways in which they conflict (as well as the ways in which they agree, as they must agree if they are to count as competing conceptions of criminal law); to articulate the political and moral values on which they depend, and so locate them within the debates and disagreements that surround such values; and ask ourselves what is in the end no longer a philosophical question—whether we can make any of these conceptions our own. That is not to say that anything goes: some suggested conceptions might be rejected as not conceptions of criminal law at all; others might be rejected as beyond the bounds of 'reasonable'—bounds that are themselves, of course, always controversial. It is to suggest, however, that philosophers need to be modest in their claims about what philosophical theorizing can achieve.

This leads us to a further question about normative criminal law theorizing (as about any other kind of normative theorizing): what kind of 'theory' should it aspire to produce? Should it, in particular, aspire to articulate a tidily consistent set of goals, values, and principles, even if that set is local rather than universal, by which we can say that the, or at least our, criminal law should be structured? Or should we instead recognize that criminal law (like other human practices) cannot be theorized in that way—that we must either adopt a different conception of 'theory', or abandon any ambition to theorize criminal law? What is at issue here is not the 'critical' theorists' charge that the criminal law is a site not of reason and principle, but of unreason and contradiction: it is, rather, a matter of what would count as rationalizing the criminal law—as showing if not that it is, then at least how it could be, a rational practice

---

[16] See Dworkin, *Law's Empire*; see also WB Gallie, 'Essentially Contested Concepts' (1956) 56 *Proceedings of the Aristotelian Society* 167, on 'essentially contested concepts'.

that is appropriately structured by principles and values.[17] We can clarify this question by noting the two spectra along which theoretical accounts of criminal law can be distinguished: one runs from complexity to simplicity, the other from neatness to messiness.

Complexity and simplicity belong to the underlying conceptual architecture of criminal law: how complex must that architecture be if it is to display, or how simple can it be whilst still displaying, the significant features of a substantive criminal law? Should it, for instance, distinguish 'offences' from 'defences'; or can we do all that we need to do by analysing the elements of an offence?[18] If it should distinguish offences from defences, what distinctions (if any) should we draw among defences: should we, for instance, distinguish justifications from excuses; should we add further categories, of exemptions,[19] or of warrants?[20] Should it, for another instance, distinguish different species of mens rea (and, if so, which—and should it do so across all offences); or can we capture all that we need to capture by talking simply of one kind of fault—'insufficient concern', perhaps?[21] A simple theorist will argue that the criminal law's normative structure is adequately captured by a rather simple architecture, and that the distinctions and complications introduced by more complex theorists are unhelpful, unnecessary, and distorting. Complex theorists will in turn accuse simplifiers of procrustean distortions—of twisting, and so misrepresenting, significant features of the criminal law to make them fit their (over-)simple architecture:[22] we need these complexities, they will argue, if we are to do justice to the logic of the criminal law.

The spectrum from neatness to messiness is quite different: although simpler theorists are more likely also to be neater, neatness and simplicity are different qualities—as are messiness and complexity. A theory is neat to the extent that it captures all of criminal law within some coherent, integrated, non-conflictual structure of goals, principles, and concepts: the structure might be very complex, but it fits together into a systematically coherent whole. A theory is messy (and portrays the criminal law as messy) to the extent that it denies the possibility of such neatness—to

---

[17] See J Gardner, 'On the General Part of the Criminal Law', in Duff (ed), *Philosophy and the Criminal Law*, 205.

[18] Contrast G Williams, 'Offences and Defences' (1982) 2 *Legal Studies* 233, 'The Logic of "Exceptions"' (1988) 47 *Cambridge Law Journal* 261, with G Fletcher, *Rethinking Criminal Law* (Boston: Little, Brown: 1978), 552–79, 683–758. For other defences of the distinction's importance, see K Campbell, 'Offence and Defence', in IH Dennis (ed), *Criminal Law and Justice* (London: Sweet & Maxwell, 1987), 73; J Gardner, 'Fletcher on Offences and Defences' (2004) 39 *Tulsa Law Review* 817; V Tadros, *Criminal Responsibility* (Oxford: Oxford University Press, 2005), ch 4.

[19] See eg J Gardner, 'The Gist of Excuses' (1998) 1 *Buffalo Criminal Law Review* 575; J Horder, *Excusing Crime* (Oxford: Oxford University Press, 2004), 8–10, 103–6; Tadros, *Criminal Responsibility*, 124–9.

[20] See Duff, *Answering for Crime*, 271–7.

[21] See L Alexander and KK Ferzan, with SJ Morse, *Crime and Culpability: A Theory of Criminal Law* (Cambridge: Cambridge University Press, 2009); also Alexander and Ferzan in this volume.

[22] Compare Hart's objections to Austin's account of law: HLA Hart, *The Concept of Law* (2nd edn; Oxford: Oxford University Press, 1994), chs 2–3.

the extent that it posits different goals for the criminal law, for instance, that are incommensurable or non-integratable; or to the extent that it portrays certain kinds of conflict, between goals, values, or principles, as an inevitable feature of the criminal law; or to the extent that it denies the possibility of drawing clear or sharp distinctions between different categories or dimensions.

There are two kinds of messy theory, parental and Etonian. The parental theorists regard messiness, as parents might regard their children's messiness, as a defect that is regrettable but incurable; critical theorists' comments on the 'unreason' of the criminal law might reflect this view. Etonian theorists accept, or even celebrate, messiness as an ineliminable feature of the world to which theorists must do justice:[23] messiness (of the right kind and in the right circumstances) is a virtue rather than a defect, and is no threat to rationality; a theory, and the practice that it theorizes, must be as messy as is the world with which it has to deal.

Neat theorists regard messiness as a defect. If there is conflict between different goals or principles or values, there must also be a procedure for resolving those conflicts if the law is to attain the kind of principled rationality to which it should aspire—and to which it must at least come close if it is to claim our respect or allegiance. If distinctions cannot be clearly and sharply (even if complicatedly) drawn, they are not real, or have no place in a rational theory of criminal law. Messy theorists (of the Etonian sort) regard the right kind of messiness as a necessary virtue, and criticize neat theorists for distorting the rich and detailed diversity of the world to fit their rigid structures. Conflict is ineliminable in our world of different, conflicting, and irreconcilable values between which only uneasy compromise rather than reconciliation is possible;[24] precision and the tidy exactitude after which neat theorists yearn is unavailable in the realm of human action and value: an adequate theory must be true to that messy reality.

In their different ways, Bentham and Kant (in the *Grundlegung*) were paradigm examples of neatness. For Bentham, if we are to take the felicific calculus seriously, we have available a single criterion of value, a measurable final good to which all human institutions should be instruments: complex though the calculations of utility must be, the underlying structure is both simple and neat.[25] For the Kant of the *Grundlegung*, the structure of moral thinking is equally, though differently, neat: we judge the permissibility of any proposed course of action by identifying its maxim, and determining whether the agent can universalize it. Aristotle, by contrast, is a

---

[23] 'Eton mess' is a dessert that is much prized in some quarters.

[24] A familiar theme of one kind of contemporary liberal theorizing: see eg I Berlin, *Four Essays on Liberty* (Oxford: Oxford University Press, 1969); T Nagel, *Mortal Questions* (Cambridge: Cambridge University Press, 1978); S Hampshire, *Morality and Conflict* (Oxford: Blackwell, 1983).

[25] 'Intense, long, certain, speedy, fruitful, pure—Such marks in pleasures and in pains endure. Such pleasures seek if private be thy end: If it be public, wide let them extend. Such pains avoid, whichever be thy view: If pains must come, let them extend to few' (Bentham, *An Introduction to the Principles of Morals and Legislation*). Compare also the aspirations to neatness displayed by economic theorists of law.

paradigm of one kind of messiness: although he held to such a strong version of the unity of value that any apparent ethical conflict could be dissolved by the clear perception of the *phronimos*, and was thus a neat rather than a messy theorist on the issue of conflict, he insisted that ethics as a normative discipline should seek only such precision as 'the subject matter admits of', which is far less than we might seek in science or logic. The theorist must 'be content…to indicate the truth roughly and in outline',[26] while the *phronimos*, the paragon of practical wisdom, must rely not on the application of neat principles, but on a perception of the inevitably messy particularities of each situation.[27]

How do such other disciplines as history and sociology bear on philosophical theorizing, as thus understood? At a minimum, as Herodotus was the first to point out, they can generate a suitable caution in the theorist: they remind us both that what 'we' do 'here' is not done by others elsewhere, and that what we do here was not always thus; what we might take to be unchangeable features of any (civilized) human society turn out to be rather recent features of certain specific societies. They also remind us that things are not always as they might appear to the hasty eye: that meanings and functions are not always evident, and that the way in which an institution presents itself might not always give a true picture of its aims or work-ings. They are also a source of alternative interpretations: rational reconstructers might find other possible purposes and principles in the history or sociology of an institution. They also remind normative theorists, of course, of the factual character of that which they seek to theorize; and when it comes to proposing reforms, they can help theorists to recognize what is or is not feasible, at what kind of cost—as well as reminding them of the unintended consequences that can flow from principled reform.

None of this is to say, however, that such other disciplines should undermine nor-mative philosophical theorizing, or that they render it otiose, impossible, or point-less. They remind us of its limits—limits that its proponents should already have recognized; of the need for caution and some humility; of the concrete realities, context, and history of the institutions that we theorize; of the ways in which such theorizing can be frustrated by the recalcitrance of the world and of the human agents who try to apply it: but such reminders serve to improve, not to undermine, normative theorizing.

Our aim in the discussion over the last few pages has not been to lay down a deter-minate account of what philosophical theorizing about criminal law must amount to or involve; it has rather, more modestly, been to indicate the different forms it can take, and the different kinds of theory it can aspire to develop. This was also intended

---

[26] Aristotle, *Nicomachean Ethics* (trans Ross) I.4.

[27] JS Mill was also a messy theorist, even in *Utilitarianism*, at least as compared with Bentham: once he insisted that we must attend to the 'quality' as well as the 'quantity' of pleasures, he made impossible any neat Benthamite felicific calculus.

as a modest defence of the title of this book, by showing that an exploration of 'the philosophical foundations of criminal law' need not have the kinds of grandiose ambition that critics might rightly reject as unwarranted—that it need not aspire to produce the kind of neat, a priori, universal theory of criminal law that is, arguably, an illusory grail. The explorations in which the contributors to this volume were asked to engage are foundational in the sense that they aim to uncover and to illuminate the deeper structures—conceptual and normative—of criminal law; they are philosophical in the sense that they deploy familiar philosophical techniques both of analysis and of normative theory. The aim of the volume as a whole is not to reveal the truth, analytical or normative, about criminal law, or to reveal the structure that criminal law must have. It is rather to reveal and to explore some of the foundational questions that the institutions of criminal law raise: to work down through some of the salient doctrinal and normative debates in contemporary criminal law theory, to reveal the deeper and broader philosophical questions and problems that they reveal, and to suggest fruitful ways in which those questions and problems can be approached. We do not expect that the contributions in this book will settle many, or any, of those questions or problems, although they certainly recast some of them, and show that some existing debates and controversies might be misdirected or based on assumptions that should be questioned: but we hope that they can help to set the terms and direction of philosophically informed criminal law theory for the next decade or more. The book is thus 'foundational' in relation to the questions that it raises and clarifies, to the approaches to those questions that its contributors explore and develop, and to the further debates and inquiries that it hopes to provoke among criminal law theorists.

This is an apt time for a volume of this kind, for at least two reasons. First, the role and the scope of the criminal law in contemporary nation states have in recent years come under increasingly intense theoretical scrutiny, and more acute political pressure. That political pressure bears partly on penal policy (perhaps most obviously, at least in Britain and the United States, on the role of imprisonment), and on aspects of the criminal process (most obviously on criminal trials and their proper structure). It bears on the content and structure of substantive criminal law: for instance, in the ways in which new and ever broader offences are created, capturing conduct ever more remotely connected to the relevant mischief,[28] and the ways in which the Presumption of Innocence has been progressively eroded by broad offence definitions, shifts in burdens of proof, and the use of strict liability.[29] It bears on the role that criminal law plays in relation to other types of state regulation and

---

[28] For some examples, see DN Husak, *Overcriminalization: The Limits of the Criminal Law* (Oxford: Oxford University Press, 2008), 33–45. In English law, offences related to terrorism provide clear illustrations of this expansionist tendency: see eg Terrorism Act 2000; V Tadros, 'Justice and Terrorism' (2007) 10 *New Criminal Law Review* 658.

[29] See AJ Ashworth and M Blake, 'The Presumption of Innocence in English Criminal Law' (1996) *Criminal Law Review* 306; W Stuntz, 'The Pathological Politics of Criminal Law' (2001) 100 *Michigan*

control—in, for instance, the ways in which governments anxious to find more effective ways of controlling undesirable conduct or of warding off perceived threats make increasing use of systems of 'administrative' regulation, or of provisions for the preventive detention or constraint of those thought to be dangerous, or of various hybrid civil-criminal proceedings.[30] The theoretical scrutiny has come partly from radically critical theorists—from, for instance, advocates of restorative justice and other kinds of non-criminal practice who urge us to turn away not just from criminal punishment, but from criminal law itself, with its focus on wrongdoing;[31] and from those influenced by 'critical legal studies' who argue that any attempt to make rational normative sense of the criminal law is doomed to failure.[32] It also comes from theorists who, whilst committed to the idea(l) of criminal law, wonder whether our existing institutions of criminal law are 'a lost cause', or look with increasing despair on their unprincipled growth and abuse;[33] and, in a different way, from philosophical theorists who bring the insights of political and moral philosophy, and of philosophy of mind and action, to bear on criminal law in ways that can cast new light on its normative structures, whilst also putting into question many of its traditional doctrinal assumptions.

The second reason why the time is apt for such a volume is that philosophy of criminal law is booming: the last couple of decades have seen an impressive increase in the amount of interesting, good work being produced by both established and newer scholars. This is due, in significant part, to the way in which more legal academics have become more aware of the need for legal theory to engage with other disciplines (philosophy, but also sociology, history, and politics), and have also become better versed in those other disciplines; and in part to the way in which those working in other disciplines that bear on law (notably philosophy) have also become more aware of the need to engage seriously with legal doctrines and practices, rather than theorizing about them from the outside. The result has been a significant growth in philosophical work that takes both the law itself, and other disciplines that bear on

---

Law Review 506; V Tadros and S Tierney, 'The Presumption of Innocence and the Human Rights Act' (2004) 67 *Modern Law Review* 402.

[30] See AJ Ashworth and L Zedner, 'Defending the Criminal Law: Reflections on the Changing Character of Crime, Procedure, and Sanctions' (2008) 2 *Criminal Law and Philosophy* 21; 'Preventive Orders: A Problem of Under-Criminalization?' in RA Duff, L Farmer, SE Marshall, V Tadros, and M Renzo (eds), *The Boundaries of the Criminal Law* (Oxford: Oxford University Press, forthcoming, 2011), and in this volume; also RA Duff, 'Perversions and Subversions of Criminal Law', in Duff et al, *The Boundaries of the Criminal Law*.

[31] See n 10 above.

[32] See n 1 above.

[33] See eg AJ Ashworth, 'Is the Criminal Law a Lost Cause?' (2000) 116 *Law Quarterly Review* 225; IH Dennis, 'The Critical Condition of Criminal Law' (1997) 50 *Current Legal Problems* 213; Stuntz, 'The Pathological Politics of Criminal Law'; DA Dripps, 'Terror and Tolerance: Criminal Justice for the New Age of Anxiety' (2003) 1 *Ohio State Journal of Criminal Law* 9.

the law, seriously, whilst reaching new levels of theoretical sophistication and depth. The essays in this volume exemplify this growth, and strengthen it.

A word should be said about the planning and organization of this book. One possibility would have been to start with a systematic conception of the key foundational philosophical issues in criminal law, and then commission authors to write essays on specific issues within that conception, thus securing an organized and thorough coverage of (what the editors took to be) the central terrain of philosophy of criminal law. We decided against that way of proceeding: in part because we were not confident that we could agree, with each other or with contributors, about just what the key or central issues are (that is itself a central meta-issue in philosophy of criminal law); but primarily because the best way to secure interesting, groundbreaking work is to select interesting, original authors and invite them to write on what interests them, leaving them a (relatively) free hand in choosing their topics. This is what we did: the result of this strategy is that there are some obvious gaps in the topics discussed in the volume (we leave it to readers to work out their own lists of key missing topics), but we believe it is vindicated by the interest and quality of the essays. In the remainder of this Introduction, we provide a brief survey of the essays and their interrelationships.

The essays in this volume traverse a wide range of topics that defy any neat categorization. Many essays deal with multiple topics, but for present purposes we have grouped the essays into four broad thematic clusters, covering different aspects of the philosophy of criminal law. The first cluster involves threshold questions about the methods of theorizing about the philosophical foundations of criminal law, about the purposes and proper scope of criminal law, and about criminalization. The second and largest cluster deals with the substance of criminal law, including questions about the ascription of criminal responsibility, about offences and defences, and about action and intent. The third cluster focuses on the relationship between criminal law and criminal process, and on the question of punishment. The final cluster discusses some recent developments that pose new challenges to criminal law theory: the growing importance of international criminal law, and the implications for criminal law of new technologies.

1 CRIMINAL LAW AND POLITICAL THEORY

For the last few decades, one preoccupation of Anglo-American criminal law theorizing, which reflects the prevalence of retributivist ideas, has been with the question of how the norms of criminal law are or are not like those of everyday morality. Many of the chapters in this volume continue down that path, offering fresh insights on the meaning of retributivism; the role of intent, motive, and character judgments in defining responsibility; and the best way to formulate offence definitions in accordance with moral norms. But the book also reflects a new theoretical turn toward a broader conception of criminal law theory, one rooted not just in moral theory but also in express consideration of history, political theory, and social theory.

The chapters by Malcolm Thorburn, Richard Dagger, and Matt Matravers are all, in their own ways, exemplary of such an approach. Thorburn argues that criminal law scholars have tended to draw too close an analogy between the system of criminal law and that of private morality. In place of such a 'legal moralist' account, Thorburn offers what he calls a 'public law' account of the criminal justice system, which he says does a better job of explaining and justifying the coercive aspects of criminal law, its liberty-respecting aspects, and various doctrinal issues concerning justification defences. Dagger, for his part, offers a specifically 'republican' theory of criminal law, one, he says, that reflects the public nature of criminal wrongs, the development of the criminal law historically, and the public nature of the criminal law as a cooperative, self-governing enterprise. And Matravers, following a parallel path, looks to contractarian theory for a principled grounding for criminal law, arguing that a Rawlsian perspective has more to offer here than Rawls himself allowed, and exploring the implications for our attitudes towards those who commit crimes of Rawls' idea that we must agree 'to share one another's fate'.

Two other chapters that expressly seek to broaden the focus of criminal law theory are those by Markus Dubber and Alice Ristroph. Dubber is broadly concerned with how we should conceive of the inquiry into the foundations of criminal law, whether legal, philosophical, historical, genealogical, or political. He argues that we cannot hope to develop a foundational account of the criminal law without an account of what, if anything, legitimizes the state power that underlies the criminal law, an inquiry, he says, that has mostly escaped the attention of American thinkers both at the time the nation was founded and in the years since. Ristroph contends that criminal law theory has been too narrowly focused on the responsibility of the *offender* for his criminal acts, and seeks to show how other key players in the system—including legislatures, police, prosecutors, and courts—share responsibility for the system of criminal law and how it chooses to treat its subjects.

Antony Duff's chapter is also concerned with the proper basis of criminal responsibility: with its grounding in political community. In a liberal democracy we are paradigmatically criminally responsible, he argues, as citizens to our fellow citizens. This focus on citizenship, however, generates concerns about how non-citizens are treated under the law, and about the possibility of exclusion from citizenship: Duff suggests that such concerns can be met, but that they highlight some of the challenges faced by a liberal criminal law.

2 THE SUBSTANCE OF CRIMINAL LAW

The second cluster of chapters returns the focus to the content and structure of the substantive criminal law, while offering some strikingly new approaches to a host of issues that have occupied theorists in recent years. First among them is the proper basis for criminal responsibility and liability. For example, can we say whether, analytically or normatively, criminal responsibility is focused on choice, or action, or character? Illustrative here is the contribution from Nicola Lacey, who argues that judgments about an offender's character, central to pre-modern conceptions of the criminal law, have experienced a resurgence in contemporary criminal law, as is evident in phenomena as diverse as sex offender notification requirements, laws relating to terrorism, evidentiary rules regarding presumptions, and the practice of offender profiling. This leads Lacey to conclude that the criminal conviction itself increasingly implies a judgment of bad character, and to relate such practices to a broader, extra-doctrinal explanation rooted in the context of various political, economic, and social considerations.

Also central here is an examination of the psychological concepts that structure our understanding of criminal fault, including the centrally important concepts of intention and motive, which are explored by Michael Moore and Victor Tadros, respectively. Both concepts have a life outside the law, of course, and Moore and Tadros draw on that life to illuminate their role in the criminal law. Moore is interested in the role that intention plays in defining the most serious forms of criminality. He argues that the criminal law as it now exists presupposes what is essentially a 'folk psychology' of intention, and he proposes as an alternative a more nuanced and complex conception of intention that would take into account recent developments in philosophy of mind, cognitive science, and moral psychology. Tadros, for his part, is interested in the role that motive plays, or ought to play, in judgments of culpability. Taking on the conventional view that motivation is relevant, if at all, only if there has first been a determination that the defendant has caused harm, Tadros argues that motives should be given a more significant role in determining what is wrong—specifically, that an act can be wrong *in virtue of* the motivation with which it was performed.

Another problem that has bedevilled criminal law scholars in recent years is that of how to formulate the norms that define the substantive criminal law. This is the focus of the chapters by Kenneth Simons and by Larry Alexander and Kim Ferzan. Simons is interested in the degree of specificity we should employ in deciding how to formulate the norms that inform both the general and special parts. He contrasts what he calls the 'particularist' approach with a 'generalist' approach, and compares their relative ability to track underlying moral norms and political values, whether thick or thin, neat or messy, descriptive or normative, intuitionist or pluralistic. Alexander and Ferzan believe that contemporary criminal codes do a poor job of capturing what it is that makes state punishment truly deserved. They propose a radical rewriting of criminal codes, which would eliminate negligence as a basis for criminal liability, abolish liability for incomplete attempts, and replace detailed offence definitions and hierarchically arranged mens rea terms with a streamlined standard according to which people would be subject to deserved punishment when they show 'insufficient concern for others', defined as risking harm to others for insufficiently good reasons.

The extent to which the criminal law should be concerned with preventing risky behaviour is also taken up by Andrew Ashworth and Lucia Zedner, and by Peter Westen. Ashworth and Zedner are interested in the ways in which the law criminalizes the creation of risks of harm, and offer a catalogue of various kinds of criminal offence that are primarily concerned with preventing the creation of risk. But they also highlight the protections that the criminal law provides, through the criminal process, for those suspected of creating risks, and the ways in which such protections are undermined by the use of 'civil preventive orders' that effectively bypass the criminal law. As for Westen, his focus is on offences that punish offenders who engage in risky behaviour that never in fact causes any harm. He argues that the problem of punishing actors for risks that in some sense do not exist must be solved not by thinking of risk as a form of probability—that is, the factual likelihood of harm—but rather in terms of counterfactual events that a judge or jury fear *could have* occurred and, had they done so, would have produced the same kind of harm that the offence at issue is designed to prevent. The problem of such offences, he contends, is therefore closely related to the problem of criminalizing impossible attempts.

Two other chapters, by Douglas Husak and by Stuart Green, deal in very different ways with what might loosely be regarded as the theory of criminal defences. Husak offers a critical analysis of what he says may or may not be a de minimis 'defence' to criminal liability, using this somewhat obscure doctrine to shed light on more overarching issues such as the appropriate limits of criminalization, the proper exercise of prosecutorial discretion, and the distinction between offences and defences and between justification and excuse. And Green, in his contribution, is concerned with the problem of imposing criminal liability on offenders who are themselves victims of serious economic, social, or political injustice. He argues that the extent to which such offenders deserve to be punished will vary from case to case, depending on the type of crime the offender has committed, the type of deprivation to which he has been subjected, and the circumstances of the crime victim.

3 Process and Punishment

While philosophers have had much to say about the substantive criminal law and about punishment, and quite a lot to say about issues concerning criminalization, they have had considerably less to say about the criminal process that connects (alleged) crime to punishment. The chapters by Paul Roberts and Donald Dripps, included in the third cluster, help to correct that relative neglect by bringing process back into the frame as an essential dimension of the criminal law as a set of institutional practices. Roberts seeks to broaden the canon of criminal law theory to include a consideration of criminal evidence. He describes four rival approaches to evidence law theory—which he calls doctrinal-conceptualist, epistemological, legal-institutional, and normative—and demonstrates both its convergences with, and divergences from, criminal law theory. Dripps, in his chapter, takes on the relationship between substance and procedure in criminal law, arguing, as do various other contributors, that it must be explained with reference to competing conceptions of underlying political and moral theory. Particularly concerned with the ways in which a system of criminal procedure is meant to implement the goals of substantive criminal law, he offers three models—which he calls rationalism, pluralism, and reductionism—and explores the extent to which they should be viewed as mutually compatible or incompatible.

Mitchell Berman then takes on an issue that has been much more at the forefront of criminal law theory, though he does so in a novel way. Berman argues that the traditional distinction between consequentialist and retributive justifications for punishment is no longer accurate because retributivism has increasingly 'morphed' into an account that rests on a justificatory structure that is itself consequentialist. Retributivism, he says, or at least some forms of retributivism, is thus more correctly understood as a subtype of consequentialist justifications for punishment.

4 Across Borders and into the Future

The trio of chapters that concludes the volume seek to push criminal law theory beyond the realm of both domestic law and current technology. Two of the contributions, by Christopher Wellman and Adil Haque, deal with criminal law in the international context. Wellman asks what rationale there is for international criminal court jurisdiction over crimes that do not cross international borders. He argues that states have a unique ability to realize the important aims of punishment, but that they are entitled to a monopoly in this area only when they are in fact able and willing to realize these aims. Where states are unable or unwilling to protect their own citizens' human rights, their claim to sovereignty is lost, and international institutions like the International Criminal Court may justifiably step in. Haque is similarly interested in extending the use of conceptual tools used to theorize about domestic criminal law to the context of international criminal law. His particular concern is with envisioning the moral norms applicable to killings that occur in the midst of armed conflict, of both civilians and combatants, whether directly participating in hostilities or not, and with evaluating the consistency of such norms with the law in these areas.

In the final chapter in the volume, Mireille Hildebrandt, looking to the future, is concerned with two criminal law-related problems that might be posed by developing technologies. The first is that of human beings who become so entangled with the 'smart' technological environments in which they work that it becomes hard to view them as distinct, autonomous, and responsible individuals. The second is the problem of computer-related technologies that become so self-aware and autonomous that they arguably take on the attributes of moral agency that is presumably a prerequisite for criminal liability.

Between them, these chapters attest to the flourishing condition of contemporary criminal law theory. More importantly, they offer new directions for future work in this area, and highlight some of the pressing issues that criminal law theorists need to address—issues that directly concern the proper role, scope, and structure of the criminal law in the contemporary world.

PART I

CRIMINAL LAW AND POLITICAL THEORY

2

CRIMINAL LAW AS PUBLIC LAW

MALCOLM THORBURN[*]

1 INTRODUCTION

WHEN trying to make sense of an institution that causes as much hardship as our system of criminal justice, it is perfectly natural to ask what good we mean to bring about through all this suffering. Indeed, this question has been the central focus of both major schools in punishment theory for centuries. Utilitarians suggest that this hardship is ultimately worthwhile because it prevents more harm than it causes (through deterrence,[1] rehabilitation,[2] etc). Most retributivists suggest that punishing

* Thanks to the Social Sciences and Humanities Research Council of Canada and to Borden Ladner Gervais LLP for financial support for work on this chapter; thanks to audiences at a conference on the philosophical foundations of criminal law at Rutgers Law School (Newark), and especially to my commentator, Vera Bergelson, at that event, and to audiences at faculty workshops at Cornell Law School, Brooklyn Law School, the Syracuse University College of Law, and McGill University Faculty of Law for helpful questions and discussion; thanks to Antony Duff, Larissa Katz, and Arthur Ripstein for invaluable comments; and thanks also to Alison Barclay and Noémi Paquette for excellent research assistance. Responsibility for all this chapter's shortcomings lies solely with the author.

[1] This is the mechanism emphasized by mainstream utilitarians, such as Jeremy Bentham and HLA Hart.

[2] The rehabilitative ideal had widespread currency, especially in the United States. It was at the root of the American indefinite sentencing schemes so prevalent in that country until quite recently. But it has been in precipitous decline in recent years. See FA Allen, *The Decline of the Rehabilitative Ideal: Penal Policy and Social Purpose* (New Haven: Yale University Press, 1981). Sometimes, 'rehabilitation' was taken to import a wholesale theory of re-education, as in the theory of Lady Barbara Wooton, *Social Science and Social Pathology* (London: George, Allen and Unwin, 1959).

the guilty is itself an important good to be pursued.[3] The problems associated with both views are all too familiar and I don't mean to rehearse them here. The point for my purposes is simply to note that both approaches take it for granted that the way to justify the workings of the criminal justice system, if that can be done at all, is to display its value as a tool for pursuing some independently identifiable good.

But not all institutions can be justified by reference to the goods they bring about. Take the family. Within this institution, there are some clearly defined roles (parent, child, sibling, etc) and there are appropriate ways for occupants of each role to relate to others. One of the most important ways for members of a family to relate to one another, of course, is to show love and concern for them. If one were to ask 'what is the point of showing love and concern for a family member?' the answer would involve much more than just the goods one meant to bring about by doing so. Instead, the answer would identify the intrinsic value of standing in these sorts of familial relationships to others, how occupying these sorts of roles makes our lives richer, etc. Given that it is valuable to occupy these various family roles and to stand in familial relations to others, it follows that there is value in acting in accordance with the demands of those roles, whatever they might be. So if we are asked to justify the practices characteristic of a parent or sibling, we would not simply identify any goods that acting in this way would bring about; instead, we would simply point out that these practices are part of what it means to play our part in an institution that is intrinsically valuable.

Two of the most influential criminal law theorists of recent times—Antony Duff and John Gardner—have suggested that we should pursue a justificatory strategy of this sort for the institutions of criminal justice. For both Duff and Gardner, the core of the criminal justice system is the trial, for it is here that we can see most clearly the intrinsic value of the roles and relationships that matter in the criminal justice system. In a criminal trial, they argue, we are simply doing in a somewhat more formal way what we do privately all the time. When someone commits a moral wrong, we feel the urge to demand an explanation from her: did you really do what I think you did? Can you justify what you did? Do you have any excuse for your conduct? And so on. We don't necessarily think that any further good will come of asking these questions; we simply feel that it is appropriate in these circumstances to demand an explanation and, if asked, we feel that it is appropriate to provide one. The reason why we undertake this exercise—both the questioning and the answering—is that it is part of what it means to relate to one another as responsible moral agents. Answering for your wrongdoing is just what responsible moral agents do. To give up this practice would be tantamount to giving up our conception of ourselves and of our fellows as responsible agents.

---

[3] Michael Moore, the most famous retributivist today, put the point as follows: 'what is distinctively retributivist is the view that the guilty receiving their just deserts is an intrinsic good.' M Moore, 'Justifying Retributivism' [1993] 27 *Israel Law Review* 15, 19. Though my own account could be seen as a brand of retributivism, I mean to distance my account from those such as Moore's.

My point here is not to endorse Duff and Gardner's account of the criminal justice system. Instead, I mean to endorse one aspect of their project—the idea that we may justify a set of practices by showing that they are required to be true to a set of roles and relationships that we take to be intrinsically valuable—while rejecting the particular way that they go about justifying the practices of the criminal justice system. The trouble with Duff and Gardner's account, I believe, is that they too quickly assume that the practices of the criminal justice system are nothing more than formalized versions of the private practice of calling others to account for their moral wrongdoing. As a result, they very quickly try to re-shape the criminal justice system to make it fit the contours of ordinary morality. They are thereby committed to the view that legitimate criminal wrongs must all be moral wrongs and that criminal justifications should track the structure of moral justifications. Most controversially, they argue that the practice of criminal punishment, insofar as it is justifiable at all, is nothing more than a formalized, institutionalized version of the sorts of things that private people are entitled to do to one another in response to moral wrongs, as well.[4]

Duff and Gardner's new-fangled legal moralism cannot succeed, I believe, because it is premised on trying to turn criminal justice into something that it is not. There are three important differences between the state-dominated practices of criminal justice and the private moral practice of calling one another to account that make it impossible for us to think of one as nothing more than a scaled-up version of the other. First, the criminal justice system is generally thought to be legitimately coercive in a way that our private practices never are. As John Locke put it, 'Every man is entitled to admonish, exhort, and convince another of error, and lead him by reasoning to accept his own opinions. But it is the magistrate's province to give orders by decree and compel with the sword.'[5] Second, because of the uniquely coercive and state-dominated nature of the criminal justice system, it is thought to be necessarily subject to liberal principles that respect our individual freedom to arrange our private affairs as we see fit—that grant us what Jeremy Waldron calls a 'right to do wrong'[6] in such matters. And third, the legal moralist view just does not fit with existing doctrine: criminal wrongs and justifications in the common law world do not even approximately follow the contours of moral wrongdoing and justification.[7]

---

[4] J Gardner 'Introduction', in *Punishment and Responsibility* (2nd edn; Oxford: Oxford University Press, 2008), l: 'It is very common for one estranged spouse to punish the other, for example, by preventing him or her from spending time with his or her children, fully intending that this should be a terrible experience. I know of no reason to think that such punishment is "sub-standard or secondary" as compared with, say, imprisonment by the courts.'

[5] J Locke, *Letter on Toleration* (1689), 19.

[6] J Waldron, 'A Right to Do Wrong' (1981) 92 *Ethics* 21.

[7] M Berman has previously pointed this out in 'Justification and Excuse: Law and Morality' [2003] 53 *Duke Law Journal* 1.

In this chapter, I propose a different way of justifying the practices of the criminal justice system—a position I call a 'public law account' of criminal justice. I call it a 'public law' account because it conceives of the operations of the criminal justice system, insofar as they are legitimate,[8] as concerned with the basic question of public law: when the use of state power is legitimate. Like the new legal moralism of Duff and Gardner, my account is an attempt to justify the workings of the criminal justice system by demonstrating that they are just what is required for us to be true to a set of roles and relationships that have intrinsic value. But the relevant roles and relationships for criminal justice are not those we understand from ordinary morality. Rather, they are the legally defined roles—such as private citizen, police officer, judge, etc—that we take up within a larger constitutional order that, I shall argue, we could not abolish without abandoning necessary preconditions for our moral life.[9]

The advantages of this approach are several. First, because the liberal constitutional order is concerned with protecting our liberty rather than with guiding our moral choices, it is consistent with a less moralistic criminal justice system than the one Duff and Gardner feel impelled to endorse. Second, because the relations in the constitutional order are set out in terms of the rightful use of coercion, the public law account has the resources to explain when the state is justified in using coercive force toward its citizens. This means that we are able to provide an account of criminal justice that does not have to explain away the centrality of coercive state power. And finally, because Anglo-American criminal law doctrine is fundamentally concerned with the requirements of liberal constitutionalism rather than the enforcement of morality, we find that the public law model is a much better fit with existing doctrine than the moralist alternative.

2 THE RISE OF LEGAL MORALISM

2.1 Hart's false promise

The legal moralist positions of Duff and Gardner that have come to play such an important part in criminal law theory in recent years are best understood as part of a longer historical development. Thirty years ago, the criminal law theory world in which

---

[8] In what follows, I do not always make this qualification explicit. I hope that it will be clear from context when I am talking about the structure of legitimate criminal law according to the public law model rather than simply the structure of whatever criminal law doctrine we happen to have in a particular time and place.

[9] What Michael Oakeshott calls our 'personae'. M Oakeshott, 'The Rule of Law', in *On History and Other Essays* (Oxford: Basil Blackwell, 1983).

contemporary legal moralism was born was dominated by the writing of HLA Hart.[10] For centuries before Hart, the philosophy of crime and punishment consisted largely in a war of attrition between utilitarian and retributivist accounts. Retributivists insisted that theirs was the only account that could show why particular individuals deserved to be punished. Utilitarians countered that the reasons for punishment proffered by retributivists were little more than primal instincts for revenge;[11] the only adequate account of punishment, they insisted, would have to show that it was part of a larger strategy that promoted the general welfare. To this, the retributivists replied that the utilitarian account of punishment was morally indefensible: it was nothing more than a strategy for using the censure and punishment of particular individuals as instruments for the promotion of policies they might not share. And on it went.

In his famous essay, 'Prolegomenon to the Principles of Punishment', Hart promised to resolve the dispute by finding the value in each approach and putting each in its proper place.[12] Hart claimed that what he called the 'General Justifying Aim' of the institution of punishment as a whole was likely to be utilitarian, but the principles by which we distribute punishment to particular individuals must be 'retributivist'. By this, Hart meant that the decision whether or not to punish a particular individual ought never to be determined solely by considering the beneficial outcomes it would bring about. Instead, we ought to be sure that the accused was given fair notice of the prohibition and that he was also given a fair chance to avoid committing the offence. Only if the accused chose to commit the offence despite the fair notice and the fair opportunity to avoid doing so should we punish him, for only then could we say that he was truly given a fair chance to avoid punishment and made a meaningful choice to bring it upon himself.

For many years, Hart's account was thought to be a workable resolution to the long-standing dispute between retributivists and utilitarians. But eventually, the weakness in Hart's argument became clear. Although Hart claimed to have given due regard to both sides in the debate, his position was really a fundamentally utilitarian one, for, as John Gardner points out, '[t]he only Hart-approved reason in favour of punishing the guilty (or anyone else) is the reason given by punishment's general

---

[10] As Gardner notes in the introduction to the new edition of *Punishment and Responsibility*, vii, a 'survey [of] subsequent work in the field that either developed or reacted to Hart's thinking...has proved unfeasible. There is a vast amount of subsequent work in the field—by philosophers, lawyers, and policymakers—and, directly or indirectly, it has all either developed or reacted to Hart's thinking'.

[11] Hart famously said of retributivism that it 'is uncomfortably close to human sacrifice as an expression of religious worship'. HLA Hart, *Law, Liberty and Morality* (Oxford: Oxford University Press, 1962), 65. Sanford Kadish echoes this sentiment in 'The Criminal Law and the Luck of the Draw' (1994) 84 *Journal of Criminal Law and Criminology* 679, 698–9: 'I find positive retributivism to be a principle unworthy of our allegiance.... Why is it good to create more suffering in the world simply because the criminal has done so?'

[12] HLA Hart, 'Prolegomenon to the Principles of Punishment' (1959–60) 60 *Proceedings of the Aristotelian Society* 1, 3–4.

justifying aim, viz that future wrongdoing is thereby reduced.'[13] Hart's principles of distribution, which he claimed would ensure that punishment was only imposed upon the deserving, were nothing more than side-constraints on the imposition of punishment. That is, they were mechanisms to ensure that no *further* injustice was done by punishing those who were not given fair notice of the prohibition or who did not have a fair opportunity to avoid offending, but they did not offer any positive rationale to the individual who was about to suffer censure and punishment. Despite Hart's protests to the contrary he simply provided another utilitarian contribution to the ongoing punishment theory debate.

2.2 The moralist resurgence

Over the past 30 years, Antony Duff has led a movement to replace Hart's utilitarian-ism as the dominant theory of criminal justice with a sort of legal moralism. Duff's new moralism should not be confused with the rather different 'legal moralist' posi-tion championed by Patrick Devlin in the 1960s, however. Devlin's brand of legal moralism was not really concerned with the enforcement of morality for its own sake; rather, his central objective was to use the criminal law as a way of preventing societal collapse. This, he believed, required that the criminal law enforce broadly shared moral convictions about right and wrong, whether or not those convictions were in fact morally sound. A society without some shared set of moral convictions, he thought, was doomed to collapse. The main point of Devlin's legal moralism, then, was simply to enforce some sort of shared societal norms not for their own sake but only as a way of fostering social cohesion.[14]

The advocates of the new moralism such as Duff and Gardner, by contrast, take morality very seriously on its own terms. Indeed, for Duff, the project from the very beginning has been 'to explore the implications of the Kantian demand that we should respect other people as rational and autonomous moral agents'.[15] And it is on precisely these grounds that he attacks Hart's utilitarian account. He puts the point most succinctly, as follows:

If we are to justify maintaining a system of criminal law, as a particular type of legal institution, we must explain why the state should regulate certain kinds of conduct by

---

[13] Gardner continues: 'To mount an adequate defence of punishment one must show how an already committed wrong is a reason...for P to make D suffer. Hart's defence of punishment does not meet this adequacy condition.' 'Introduction', in HLA Hart, *Punishment and Responsibility* (2nd edn; Oxford: Oxford University Press, 2008), xxv.

[14] P Devlin, *The Enforcement of Morals* (Oxford: Oxford University Press, 1965). Ronald Dworkin once remarked, '[w]hat is shocking is not [Lord Devlin's] idea that the community's morality counts, but his idea of what counts as the community's morality'. R Dworkin, 'Liberty and Morality', in his *Taking Rights Seriously* (Cambridge, MA: Harvard University Press, 1977), 255.

[15] RA Duff, *Trials and Punishments* (Cambridge: Cambridge University Press, 1986), 6.

defining them as wrongs...Part of that explanation will consist in an account of why this approach is consistent...with the respect that is due to those whose conduct the state seeks to regulate...[16]

And on that score, Duff argues, the utilitarian account of punishment fails entirely. The only way to satisfy this demand is to re-think the nature of the criminal justice enterprise from the ground up.

Rather than thinking of the criminal justice system as a delivery mechanism for punishment, Duff suggests that we should think of the procedures of criminal law—especially the trial—as ends in themselves.[17] If we do so, then it becomes possible to conceive of the criminal justice system as simply another manifestation of our ordinary moral practices of holding one another to account for moral wrongdoing and, thus, as an essential part of our shared moral life, crucial to our claim of being responsible moral agents.[18] John Gardner nicely draws the parallel between the criminal justice system and our extra-legal moral practices with the following rhetorical question: 'Doesn't the criminal justice system attempt, in its inevitably clumsy way, to institutionalize certain moral practices, including the practice of punishment with its familiar relationships to wrongdoing and guilt, that already exist quite apart from the law and its institutions?'[19]

Duff even goes so far as to suggest that the criminal justice system is just a mechanism for calling people to account, eliminating almost entirely the usual role given to legislative choice in crafting the scope of criminal prohibitions. He argues as follows:

[W]e should not see the criminal law as *prohibiting* the conduct that it defines as *mala in se*—as offering the citizens content-independent reasons to refrain from such conduct. We should see it instead as *declaring* such conduct to constitute a public wrong properly condemned by the community, for which the agent is answerable to the community through a criminal process.[20]

---

[16] RA Duff, *Answering for Crime* (Oxford: Hart, 2009), 87–88.

[17] The role of punishment for Duff is but a communicative add-on to the trial. If an accused is found guilty of a crime, then the proper way to communicate appropriate moral censure (which itself is required in order properly to communicate respect for the offender) might be to take measures to allow the offender to undergo penance for the wrong he committed and to try to re-establish his position within the community. I discuss Duff's highly original view about the place of punishment in the criminal justice system in 'The Models of Criminal Justice: Deterrence, Accountability and the Rule of Law' (forthcoming, *University of Toronto Law Journal*).

[18] This point was made most famously in the philosophical literature by Peter Strawson in his essay, 'Freedom and Resentment' (1962) 48 *Proceedings of the British Academy* 1, 25. As he put it: 'Our practices do not merely exploit our natures, they express them.'

[19] 'Introduction' in Hart, *Punishment and Responsibility*, xlix.

[20] RA Duff, *Punishment, Communication and Community* (Oxford: Oxford University Press, 2003), 64. John Gardner does not share Duff's opinion on this point, however. In a recent article responding to my earlier work on justification defences, Gardner makes clear his 'exclusive legal positivist' leanings: 'Inasmuch as they call for moral judgment in their application (and they invariably do) the legal norms that supply justification defences in the criminal law should always be read, like all other legal norms that call for moral judgment in their application, as elliptically investing authority in someone

Indeed, given that we are dealing with genuine, freestanding moral wrongs, Duff argues, it would be disrespectful for us *not* to call our fellow citizens to account for their genuine moral wrongdoing. The only ones we do not bother to call to account for their conduct are those whom we believe to be incapable of explaining their conduct: small children, animals, and the insane. John Gardner puts the point even more strongly, as follows: 'if they are basically responsible, all wrongdoers have an *interest* in being punished. Since all rational beings want to assert their basic responsibility, all else being equal they cannot but welcome whatever contributes to that assertion.'[21] So for Duff and Gardner, the core of the criminal justice system is the trial, and the trial should be understood as the mechanism through which a political community calls its members to account for their failures to live up to its standards and provides them with the opportunity to respond to allegations against them by denying the allegation, by providing an answer (by way of justification or excuse), or by confessing wrongdoing.[22]

On the new legal moralist account, criminal punishment not only cedes centre stage to the trial, it actually fades away from the picture almost entirely. It is not surprising, then, to find that both Duff and Gardner admit to a sort of scepticism about the possibility of ever justifying the element of punishment in the criminal justice system. Antony Duff tries to re-define criminal punishment as a sort of non-coercive, communicative process designed to bring about what he calls 'secular penance'.[23] And John Gardner admits to a sort of scepticism about justified punishment. His best defence of the practice of criminal punishment is that it is justified on the same grounds as private acts of 'punishment' with perhaps some added reasons in favour of punishment such as the displacement of private instincts for revenge.[24] He puts his point as follows:

The criminal law (even when its responses are non-punitive) habitually wreaks such havoc in people's lives, and its punitive side is such an extraordinary abomination, that it patently needs all the justificatory help it can get. If we believe it should remain a fixture in our legal and political system, we cannot afford to dispense with or disdain any of the various things, however modest and localized, which can be said in its favour ... [T]o the extent that any of them lapse or fail, the case for abolition of the criminal law comes a step closer to victory.[25]

to determine their application by exercising such moral judgment.' J Gardner, 'Justifications Under Authority' (2009) 23 *Canadian Journal of Law and Jurisprudence* 71, 74.

[21]   J Gardner, 'The Mark of Responsibility' (2003) 23 *Oxford Law Journal* 157, 192.

[22]   Duff also considers other possible answers such as denying the jurisdiction of the court, pointing to a statute of limitations, or alleging abuse of process that would warrant a stay of proceedings. Duff, *Answering for Crime*, ch 8.

[23]   Duff tries to re-define punishment as a form of 'secular penance' in *Punishment, Communication and Community*, 175–94.

[24]   Gardner's justification of punishment is what he calls 'aggregative'. That is, insofar as it can be justified at all, we should simply add up all the reasons in favour of punishment in the hope that they might be weightier moral reasons than the ones against: 'The real, problem to put it another way, is not that the Hartian defence of punishment is too mixed but that it is not mixed enough.' Gardner, 'Introduction', in *Punishment and Responsibility*, xxix.

[25]   J Gardner, 'Crime: In Proportion and in Perspective', in *Offences and Defences* (Oxford: Oxford University Press, 2007), 214–15.

The new legal moralist project seems to come very close to eliminating the place of legitimate coercion in the criminal justice process altogether.

Duff and Gardner are only two of the best-known legal moralists today. There are many others who do not provide any comprehensive account for why criminal law doctrine ought to follow the structure of moral theory, but simply *assume* that this is so, without explanation, and proceed accordingly. The point for my purposes, however, is not the details of these positions but simply to note how they have reoriented criminal law theory. Because the Duff-Gardner version of legal moralism conceives of the criminal process as simply a formalized version of private practices of calling to account, they say that the structure of criminal law doctrine should follow quite closely the moral status of the accused's conduct. Unless there is some overriding reason to do things otherwise in a particular case, they assume that criminal law wrongs are moral wrongs; criminal law justifications are moral justifications; and criminal law excuses are moral excuses.

2.3 Legal moralism and criminal wrongs

Once we turn from theoretical considerations about the justification of the criminal process to the business of explaining actual criminal law doctrine, things become a good deal more complicated for legal moralists. For the fact is that criminal wrongdoing does not track moral wrongdoing even remotely closely. So long as we are simply arranging our own affairs—rather than determining the affairs of others—Anglo-American criminal law does not concern itself with our moral wrongdoing. For example, even though almost all plausible moral theories would require us to make easy rescues,[26] there is no general duty to rescue in criminal law. The criminal law leaves it up to us what to do with our money and our bodies.[27] And it is not generally a crime to engage in immoral acts per se[28] on our own or with others so long as we have their valid consent.[29]

---

[26] Utilitarians see this as the easy case. They sometimes extend this reasoning even to quite difficult rescues. Eg P Singer, 'Famine, Affluence and Morality' (1972) 1 *Philosophy and Public Affairs* 229. Immanuel Kant would insist that we have a perfect *moral* duty to make easy rescues. See EJ Weinrib, 'The Case for a Duty to Rescue' (1980) 90 *Yale Law Journal* 247.

[27] The conditions under which the criminal law imposes any positive duties are notoriously few. One of the most egregious examples is the American case of *People v Beardsley* 150 Mich 206, 113 NW 1128 (Mich Sup Ct, 1907) in which it was held that even though the accused owed a moral duty to provide his mistress with reasonable medical care for a morphine overdose, he was under no legal duty to do so.

[28] Of course, there are plenty of immoral acts that are crimes. But, I shall argue in section 4 below, they are best understood to be crimes not because they are immoral but for other reasons.

[29] There are, of course, counter-examples to this claim such as the English case of *R v Brown* [1993] 97 Cr App R 44, HL in which the House of Lords refused to recognize as valid the consent given to particularly cruel forms of sado-masochism. We might also add the Canadian case of *Jobidon v The Queen* [1991] 2 SCR 714 in which the Supreme Court of Canada held that the law will not recognize

The legal moralists, of course, are well aware of these concerns and they have well-rehearsed answers to these challenges. John Gardner seeks to explain the law's reluctance to interfere in our private affairs by recourse to the harm principle;[30] and Duff (together with Sandra Marshall) suggests that we may explain most of these concerns by refining the notion of moral wrongdoing to what he calls 'public wrongs'.[31] It might be possible to adjust the claims of legal moralism through one or more of these mechanisms to fit better with the structure of criminal law offences, but the question remains whether the scope of the adjustments, and their seemingly ad hoc nature, makes legal moralism less plausible as an account of criminal wrongdoing. To some extent, the only way to show the weakness of moralism on this score is to offer up a better alternative (a challenge I shall take up later in this chapter).

2.4 Legal moralism and criminal justification

Legal moralism is not simply a theory about criminal wrongdoing; it is also a theory about justification defences in criminal law. Following the logic of legal moralism, Antony Duff insists that it is a 'plausible presumption that the concept of justification should function in legal thought in at least roughly the way that it functions in extra-legal moral thought...'.[32] And it is for this reason, too, that John Gardner feels that he is able to slide between moral and legal conceptions of justification with ease: 'Our interest,' he writes, 'is in the ordinary phenomenon, that of justification, which still plays a major role in the thinking of most criminal courts...'.[33]

Since there is widespread agreement among legal moralists that justification defences should mirror the structure of moral justification, most of them have simply taken this point for granted and moved on to an area where there is genuine

---

as valid any consent given to an assault causing bodily harm within the context of a street fight. It is noteworthy, however, that these were both forms of extreme violence that could result in permanent injury. As I shall suggest in section 4 below, however, there are different reasons for prohibiting such conduct than simply its immorality.

[30] J Gardner, 'Justifications and Reasons', in his *Offences and Defences*, 119. But, as Bernard Harcourt has pointed out, the precise meaning of the harm principle is notoriously unclear—perhaps to the point of being altogether useless as a limit on the scope of the criminal law. B Harcourt, 'The Collapse of the Harm Principle' (1999) 90 *Journal of Criminal Law and Criminology* 109.

[31] RA Duff and S Marshall, 'Criminalization and Sharing Wrongs' (1998) 11 *Canadian Journal of Law and Jurisprudence* 7.

[32] Duff, *Answering for Crime*, 266.

[33] Gardner, 'Justifications and Reasons', in *Offences and Defences*, 94–5. Gardner makes it clear that although an exclusive legal positivist, he still insists that the law ought to have a certain structure: 'One part of the law that I have often reflected upon in this (you may say) conspicuously moralistic way has been the part relating to criminal defences. Here—and this is no coincidence—the law makes particularly pervasive calls for officials to make moral judgments concerning allegedly illegal actions.' J Gardner, 'Justification Under Authority' (2010) 23 *Canadian Journal of Law and Jurisprudence* 71, 73.

disagreement: viz, what is the best moral theory of justification? Theorists of a utilitarian persuasion such as Paul Robinson incline toward a 'balance of harm' approach to justifications.[34] When we cause harm to prevent a greater harm, Robinson argues, 'due to the special circumstances of the situation, no harm has in fact occurred'.[35] John Gardner and Antony Duff, borrowing heavily from George Fletcher, argue for a distinctively non-utilitarian account of justification.[36] According to Gardner, when we say that something is morally wrongful, we are simply saying that there are strong moral reasons not to do it. When we say that something is justified, we do not thereby suggest that it is no longer wrongful. Indeed, it is precisely because it *is* wrongful that it calls for justification. A justification does not undo the wrongfulness of the act, Gardner argues; instead, it simply provides strong countervailing reasons in favour of doing the act.

But does either account of justification fit existing Anglo-American criminal law doctrine? Absolutely not. The main purpose of the next section is to show that the settled doctrine of justification defences in the common law, just like the structure of criminal wrongdoing, is concerned with the protection of jurisdiction, both public and private, rather than with the identification of moral wrongs. Although my overarching concern is with rival accounts of criminal law *as a whole*, I focus on justification defences here for two reasons. First, justification defences appear to present the strongest case in favour of the legal moralist view. Since justification defences permit individuals caught in extraordinary circumstances to do things that they are not normally permitted to do, they might seem to provide proof that criminal law is primarily concerned with the demands of morality rather than with the allocation of jurisdiction. If I am able to show that a jurisdictional account of justifications is possible, this will make the rest of the account a good deal easier to make. Second, I believe that justification defences are not only consistent with the protection of jurisdiction; they are, in fact, crucial devices for giving effect to claims of jurisdiction in difficult circumstances. Developing the jurisdictional account of justifications, I believe, will allow us to make sense of a great many other features of criminal law doctrine that have hitherto been left unexplained. After I have developed this account of the structure of criminal offences and defences in section 3, I will return in section 4 to the justification of the criminal justice system as a whole and show how the 'public law' account of criminal law, unlike legal moralism, is focused on the question of jurisdiction.

[34] Michael Moore, too, adopts this 'balance of evils' approach to justification even though he would resist categorization as a utilitarian. He makes this clear in M Moore, *Placing Blame: A General Theory of Criminal Law* (Oxford: Clarendon Press, 1997), 66.

[35] PH Robinson, 'A Theory of Justification: Societal Harm as a Prerequisite for Criminal Liability' [1975] 23 *UCLA Law Review* 26, 272.

[36] J Gardner, 'Fletcher on Offences and Defences', in *Offences and Defences*, 141; RA Duff, 'Rethinking Justifications' (2004) 39 *Tulsa Law Review* 829. Although Duff remains anti-utilitarian in his theory of justification, he now subdivides the territory into justified and warranted conduct. Duff, *Answering for Crime*, 267ff.

3 CRIMINAL LAW AND JURISDICTION

3.1 Necessity: the paradigmatic justification

The necessity defence—sometimes called the defence of 'lesser evils'—is often referred to as 'the paradigmatic justification'.[37] In the American Model Penal Code, it is simply referred to as 'justification generally'.[38] Its existence is often taken to be proof positive of the truth of the legal moralist position. According to the moralist view, the criminal law is concerned with moral wrongdoing, so it is appropriate that morally justified conduct should also be treated as justified in criminal law. When things become difficult, the necessity defence appears to allow us to ignore claims of jurisdiction as mere legal technicalities that get between us and doing the morally right thing. But that reading of the necessity defence, I believe, is deeply misguided. Across Anglo-American criminal law—indeed, even under the Model Penal Code—the defence of necessity is centrally concerned with questions of jurisdiction.

Consider the famous English case of *Southwark London Borough Council v Williams*.[39] In that case, the council in charge of the public housing for the London borough of Southwark left much of it vacant for long periods of time even though there was an 'extreme housing shortage' in London at the time. Noticing that the public housing was left vacant, a number of homeless families decided to seek shelter there. They entered peaceably and did not cause significant damage to the property (indeed, some of the squatters made considerable repairs to the property).[40] The council, noticing that the property was occupied without its permission, brought an action for the immediate eviction of the families from the public housing. The squatters claimed that their occupation of the public housing was justified on

[37] I borrow this expression from L Alexander, 'Lesser Evils: A Closer Look at the Paradigmatic Justification' (2005) 24 *Law and Philosophy* 611. I do so because this is the one point on which I am in agreement with the standard style in criminal law theory: necessity is indeed the paradigmatic justification (though not when conceived of as a defence of 'lesser evils'). I should point out that notwithstanding this common assumption among criminal law theorists, the necessity defence—at least as it relates to private citizens—is considered to be an excuse in Canadian criminal law (*R v Perka* [1984] 2 SCR 232) and it has an unclear status in English criminal law (*R v Dudley and Stephens* [1884] 14 QBD 273, DC; *Southwark London Borough Council v Williams* [1971] 2 WLR 467; but see also *Re A (Children) (Conjoined Twins: Surgical Separation)* [2000] 4 All ER 961, CA).

[38] American Model Penal Code (1962), s 3.02.

[39] *Southwark London Borough Council v Williams* [1971] 2 WLR 467, 467 (per Lord Denning). It should be noted that this was not a criminal law case. Nevertheless, the nature of the claim of necessity is the same—a point that is borne out by the fact that this case is frequently cited as good precedent on the necessity defence in criminal law cases.

[40] One defendant testified that 'so that we could live together as a family, we, therefore, on the 10th September, 1970, squatted in 38 Harders Road in the Borough aforesaid, a house in which the floor boards had been ripped up, window sashes smashed, and the toilet concreted up. Since we have moved in, we have repaired all these' (*Southwark London Borough Council v Williams* [1971] 2 WLR 467, 468).

grounds of necessity. On almost any plausible moral theory, the squatters' claim would surely have succeeded. Their reason for squatting was a very weighty one: that it was necessary in order for themselves and their families to live under humane conditions. The reason against their squatting was rather thin: simply that the council had not granted them permission to do so. Nevertheless, the Court of Appeal for England and Wales insisted that, however *morally* justified the squatters' decision was to move into the vacant housing, it was simply not their decision to make. Citizens must defer to the public officials whose job it is to make decisions about how best to use public housing. Lord Denning stated: 'They must appeal to the council, who will, I am sure, do all they can. They can go to the Minister, if need be. But... [w]e cannot allow any individuals, however great their despair, to take the law into their own hands and enter upon these premises.'[41]

Next, consider the case of concerned citizens engaged in civil disobedience to prevent others from carrying out serious harm. Consistently, courts deny them a justification defence on the grounds that, however noble their actions, some decisions are simply not up to ordinary citizens to make. If we disagree with our government's military or other policies, then the proper course of action is to appeal to public officials to change their minds.[42] This is usually captured in the requirement that the actor must have 'no legal alternatives to violating the law'.[43] Whether or not we are right about the morality of the situation, it is simply not within our jurisdiction to decide such matters. And, of course, the same is true when individuals try to usurp the jurisdiction of other private actors, as well, no matter how noble their motives. Robin Hood, who takes property from the rich (who may not even notice its absence) and gives it to the poor (who may need it desperately), is still treated as a thief by Anglo-American criminal law. The doctor who performs a blood transfusion against a competent patient's will commits a criminal assault even if it is necessary to save her life and her reasons against it are trivial or even silly. The question of whether or not to accept a blood transfusion is in the patient's jurisdiction, not the doctor's, no matter how morally superior the doctor's view of the matter might be.[44] Once again, the criminal law's focus is on the allocation of jurisdiction rather than

---

[41] *Southwark London Borough Council v Williams* [1971] 2 WLR 467, 473.

[42] See eg *United States v Schoon* 955 F 2d 1238 (US Ct of Apps (9th Cir), 1991); *State v Cozzens* 490 NW 2d 184 (Sup Ct of Neb, 1992); *State v Warshow* 410 A 2d 1000 (Sup Ct of Vt, 1979). See also: *R v Morgentaler et al* [1985] 22 CCC (3d) 353: 'With respect, the defence of necessity is not premised on dissatisfaction with the law.'

[43] *United States v Schoon* 955 F 2d 1238 (US Ct of Apps (9th Cir), 1991) 1239–40. It is also captured in the Model Penal Code's language in s 3.02(1)(b) and (c) which limit the defence to cases where 'neither the Code nor other law defining the offence provides exceptions or defences dealing with the specific situation involved; and a legislative purpose to exclude the justification claimed does not otherwise plainly appear'.

[44] In the words of Justice Cardozo (*Schloendorff v Society of the New York Hospital*, 211 NY 125, 129 (NY Ct of Apps, 1914)): 'Every human being of adult years and sound mind has a right to determine what shall be done with his own body.'

on the morality of particular acts. No matter how virtuous our conduct, the law will not grant us a justification if we are usurping someone else's authority to do it.

The *Williams* case and the case of civil disobedience are both failed claims of criminal law justification—where someone tries to usurp another's jurisdiction on the grounds that he is doing the morally justified thing. Put together, they seem to suggest that no matter how strong the moral justification for our actions, the law requires us *never* to interfere in matters that are outside our jurisdiction; they seem to preclude the possibility of anyone *ever* successfully claiming a criminal law justification. But if that is so, then it seems that the criminal law of justifications can no more be squared with a concern for jurisdiction than it can with legal moralism. The key to reconciling a concern for jurisdiction with the necessity defence—indeed, with justification defences generally—is to consider how it might be possible to justify interfering in another's jurisdiction. The only way we could render such interfering consistent with the victim's claim of jurisdiction, I argue, is by introducing the idea of assuming another's jurisdiction pro tem.[45]

Consider, once again, the case of the doctor who believes that the best course of action for his unconscious patient is to perform a blood transfusion. Should the patient have made clear her desire never to have a blood transfusion under any circumstances, then the doctor would have no right to perform the transfusion—the patient has decided not to accept a transfusion and it is her decision to make. But if she is unconscious and has simply not made her wishes clear on the matter either way, then the doctor is in a very different situation. Now, it is simply unknown what the patient's wishes might be—her jurisdiction has not been exercised one way or the other on this matter. Of course, there is a default presumption against interfering with a person's body without her consent, but it is a default presumption, nothing more. And in this case, there is a pressing situation: the patient will suffer irreparable harm (possibly even death) should she not receive the blood transfusion. In a case where the failure to make any decision will result in irreparable harm and where the primary decision-maker's wishes are unknown, the criminal law (indeed, the law more generally) will then permit someone else to make that decision in her stead. But this is not because the law considers that getting to the 'right answer' is more important than the proper allocation of jurisdiction. Rather, it is simply because the whole point of allocating jurisdiction is to allow it to be exercised; where the party to whom it has been allocated is simply unable to do so, then the best way to approximate her exercise of jurisdiction is to allow someone else to stand in her place. Indeed, even when the patient is unconscious, the law does not allow just anyone to take charge of the situation. It still proceeds according to the logic of jurisdiction and looks for the party with the best claim to make decisions

---

[45] I first set out this idea in an earlier article, 'Justifications, Powers, and Authority' (2008) 117 *Yale Law Journal* 1070.

on the behalf of the patient: first her next-of-kin and second, only if next-of-kin are unavailable, the doctor.

It is important to highlight two key points here. First, the transfer of jurisdiction is not required by some other value that trumps the allocation of jurisdiction, but by the very principle of jurisdiction itself. We are not letting the doctor decide the matter *instead of* the patient. Rather, we are allowing the doctor to make the decision *in the name of* the patient. And second, the party who assumes another's jurisdiction pro tem bears special responsibilities that the party to whom it belongs does not. The patient, when deciding whether or not to accept a blood transfusion, may decide the matter on whatever grounds she likes, no matter how trivial or how silly. But when the doctor makes this decision in her stead, he is required to do so as a good steward of her interests: reasonably and considering only her best interests (subject, of course, to any clear wishes that she might have expressed). That is, we scrutinize the wisdom of the doctor's choices carefully when he decides for his patient, but that is not because he must show that his choice is morally justified *tout court*. Rather, it is because the only grounds on which he is entitled to make a decision on the patient's behalf is that he is acting as her steward, deferring to whatever choices she has made explicit, and deciding reasonably in her best interests on questions where she has been silent.

3.2 Private justifications and public power

Now, this account of the doctor's private necessity claim might seem reasonably satisfying, but it does not yet explain the workings of the justifications that are the focus of most debate in criminal law theory circles. The necessity claims that have attracted the most interest among criminal law theorists concern individuals who assume a form of public jurisdiction rather than the private jurisdiction of another person: for example, where citizens burn down buildings to create a firebreak,[46] break into a house in order to save the occupant from asphyxiation from a gas leak,[47] and so on. In cases such as these, one individual does not simply make a decision in place of another. Rather, he makes a decision that is usually thought to be within the state's jurisdiction: it is usually up to state fire department officials to decide how to prevent the spread of a wildfire, and it is usually up to police or other emergency response officials to decide how best to deal with a gas leak.[48]

---

[46] K Greenawalt, 'The Perplexing Borders of Justification and Excuse' (1984) 84 *Columbia Law Review* 1897.

[47] Duff, 'Rethinking Justifications', 829.

[48] This, of course, raises deep issues about the legitimacy of contracting out core government services. I address some of these questions in 'Rethinking the Night-watchman State?' (2010) 60 *University of Toronto Law Journal* 425.

Although these public emergencies look quite different, the same jurisdictional logic is at work here as in the cases of private necessity. In public emergencies, the state may be in a situation very much like that of the unconscious patient: although it might have a preference about what to do, it is unable to communicate that preference before irreparable damage is done. This is the case where a fire or a gas leak occurs in a remote area and no properly authorized state officials are available to deal with the situation. In cases such as these—and *only* in cases such as these—the criminal law allows private citizens to take it upon themselves to decide what is the best course of action. Private citizens are precluded from taking the situation into their own hands in any case where the state is in a position to take care of it. A private citizen who tries to take matters into her own hands when state officials are available to take charge of the situation is branded a vigilante and treated as a criminal without justification.[49] This is the meaning of the 'no legal alternative' requirement in the justification of necessity: if the party whose jurisdiction it is, is able to decide how to deal with the situation, then others must not interfere no matter how morally worthy their plan of action might be.

Once we have re-conceived of the rationale of the necessity defence in the manner sketched above, we may agree with the legal moralists on at least one point: necessity is the paradigmatic justification. But because necessity is not concerned with the balance of reasons for and against a course of conduct, but rather with the appropriate circumstances under which to allow one party to exercise another's jurisdiction, this also means that we should think of other justification defences quite differently. I have argued elsewhere that self-defence and citizen's arrest are cases, like necessity, where an irreparable harm will be done unless jurisdiction is exercised, but the party to whom that jurisdiction belongs is unable to do so.[50] In both cases, the power invoked by the citizen (to use force to protect himself or to apprehend a fleeing felon) belongs to the state.[51] As with necessity generally, it is only in situations where the appropriate state official is unavailable to discharge his duties that ordinary citizens are entitled to act in self-defence or to make a citizen's arrest.

---

[49] Of course, there are situations where officials are available in the sense that they are physically proximate and aware of the situation but the citizen might still be entitled to take action. In cases where it is absolutely clear that the officials are unwilling to perform their legal duties, the law might also grant a justification to a citizen who takes matters into her own hands. Thanks to Antony Duff for pressing me on this point.

[50] Thorburn, 'Justifications, Powers, and Authority'.

[51] The use of force against others is not part of our private jurisdiction to decide what shall happen to ourselves and to our property. Rather, these matters concern the enforcement of the law and the protection of the just allocation of jurisdiction from attempts at usurpation. Max Weber's famous formulation of this point is: 'The state is that human community that lays claim to the *monopoly of legitimate physical violence* within a certain territory...' M Weber, 'The Profession and Vocation of Politics', in P Lassman and R Speirs (eds), *Political Writings* (Cambridge: Cambridge University Press, 1994), 310–11 (emphasis in original).

4 THE POLITICAL MORALITY OF CRIMINAL LAW

4.1 Justifying state power

Our analysis of claims by private parties to be exercising public powers does not answer all our questions about justification defences; it only changes the focus of debate. Now, we come face to face with the problem with which this chapter began: how might we justify the exercise of public power through the criminal justice system? This question, difficult though it is to answer, moves our debate about the nature and justification of the criminal justice system to the right plane of debate: most claims of criminal law justification are directly concerned with the justified exercise of coercive power by the state.[52] It should come as no surprise that legal moralists virtually ignore the many ways in which the criminal law regulates public power. Since their core idea is that there is nothing importantly different about the criminal justice system and extra-legal moral practices of holding one another to account for moral wrongdoing, it is convenient for them to leave aside the area of criminal law doctrine where our theory of the state plays a crucial role.[53] Early work on justification defences such as George Fletcher's *Rethinking Criminal Law* and Paul Robinson's *Criminal Law Defences* at least catalogued the justification defences available to public officials (before going on the spend the bulk of their time dealing with 'private' justifications).[54] But more recent works in criminal law theory have done away even with this preliminary treatment of public law justifications, going directly to justifications claimed by private citizens. The law of self-defence and necessity have both been subject to numerous detailed treatments in criminal

[52] With due deference to Alan Brudner, *Punishment and Freedom* (Oxford: Oxford University Press, 2009), 192, n 10, I do not claim that all claims of justification are claims to act in the name of the state. As indicated above, there is an important class of justifications (which includes the claim of parents to act in the name of their children) that are fundamentally private.

[53] It is somewhat surprising, then, to see one criminal law theorist who puts political theory front-and-centre of his account doing the same thing. In his recent book *Punishment and Freedom* (Oxford: Oxford University Press, 2009), 192, Alan Brudner writes: 'The primary division is between justifications claimed by public officials and those claimed by private agents. In the former category belong the legal authority to search, arrest, detain, punish (and penalize), and the public necessity to violate property or to override constitutional rights in general...I say little...about this class of justifications for my topic is the limit on the state's penal authority posed by the justified use of normally unlawful force by private agents. Thus, I deal here only with private justification: self-defence, defence of others, defence of property, and justificatory private necessity and duress.'

[54] GP Fletcher, *Rethinking Criminal Law* (Oxford: Oxford University Press, 1978); PH Robinson, 'Criminal Law Defenses: A Systematic Analysis' (1982) 82 *Columbia Law Review* 199.

law theory but the justified use of force by police officers seems to have been all but forgotten.[55]

Although legal theorists might have forgotten about justifications for the use of force by public officials, those who work in the criminal justice system have not. As John Kleinig points out, '[p]olice are not generally exempt from criminal and civil law, or from the regulatory power of the legislature'.[56] Every day, police officers throughout the common law world rely on justification defences in order to render their conduct permissible. Without such justifications, a great deal of police conduct would constitute criminal offences: arrests would be criminal assaults, searches would be trespasses, imprisonment would be unlawful confinement, execution would be murder, and so on.[57] And, as AV Dicey reminds us, the principles of the rule of law tell us that, without a valid justification defence, public officials should expect criminal conviction for engaging in criminal conduct in the same way as private citizens.[58] He writes:

[E]very official, from the Prime Minister down to a constable or a collector of taxes, is under the same responsibility for every act done without legal justification as any other citizen. The Reports abound with cases in which officials have been brought before the Courts, and made, in their personal capacity, liable to punishment, or to the payment of damages, for acts done in their official character but in excess of the lawful authority.[59]

Although Dicey might have been overstating to say that the reports 'abound' with cases in which officers are brought forward on criminal charges for the use of excessive force when making an arrest, for trespassing when making an illegal search, and so on, such cases do exist.[60] One of the leading cases on justification defences in England, *R v Dadson* is a case of just this sort.[61] Dadson was a police officer who shot a fleeing felon without being aware at the time that the man he was shooting at was in fact a felon. Since he was unaware of the justifying reason for his actions, the officer was denied a claim of justification and, without a valid justification defence, he was

---

[55] One salutary exception to this trend is Hamish Stewart's 'The Role of Reasonableness in Self-Defence' (2003) 16 *Canadian Journal of Law and Jurisprudence* 317. I should add, of course, that my claim is only that criminal law theorists have forgotten them. Criminal procedure scholars as well as criminologists spend much of their time discussing the conditions under which the use of police power is justified.

[56] J Kleinig, *The Ethics of Policing* (Cambridge: Cambridge University Press, 1996), 225.

[57] MD Dubber, 'A Political Theory of Criminal Law: Autonomy and the Legitimacy of State Punishment' (MS, 15 March 2004) <http://ssrn.com/abstract=529522>.

[58] The scope of criminal law justifications open to police officers is growing, especially in the area of undercover operations. See EE Joh, 'Breaking the Law to Enforce It: Undercover Police Participation in Crime' (2009) 62 *Stanford Law Review* 155.

[59] AV Dicey, *An Introduction to the Study of the Law of the Constitution* (8th edn; Indianapolis: Liberty Fund Inc, 1982), 124.

[60] In the United States, where most of these cases seem to be tied to questions of race, most such cases arise under s 20 of the USC, dealing with the denial of an individual's civil rights. See eg *Screws et al v US* 325 US 91 (1945).

[61] [1850] 2 Den 35, 169 ER 407.

convicted of intentionally causing grievous bodily harm. The same requirement for police officers to offer a valid justification applies in Canada. In early cases such as *Frey v Fedoruk*[62] and more recent cases such as *Langlois and Bédard v Cloutier*,[63] the Canadian courts have consistently held that the assault element of an arrest is a crime unless the person performing it has a valid justification defence of lawful arrest.

It is clear, then, that police officers and other public officials require justification defences to render much of their quite routine conduct permissible. But on what grounds can officials make their claims of justification? So far, we have seen that claims of justification have all been concerned with the conditions under which it is appropriate for one party to exercise another's jurisdiction. In the private context, we considered the case of the doctor who must decide whether or not to perform a blood transfusion on an unconscious patient; in the public context, we considered the case of the citizen who must decide whether to destroy a home in order to create a firebreak when state officials are unable to take care of the wildfire. In both cases, I argued, the party making the decision about what to do is not the one to whom the jurisdiction belongs originally. Jurisdiction belongs to the patient herself in the first case and to the state in the second, but the party acting out of necessity is entitled to do so because of the pressing need for that jurisdiction to be exercised by *someone* under the circumstances.

When looking for the grounds of justification open to state officials, it is helpful to consider an analogous case among private justifications. Although private justifications concern individuals who are only temporarily unable to exercise their own jurisdiction (such as the unconscious patient), there are others who are unable to exercise their own jurisdiction as a long-term condition. Take the case of minor children.[64] Like the unconscious patient, minor children are unable to exercise their jurisdiction over themselves, but unlike the unconscious patient, minor children are *generally* unable to do so. So although the law permits parents to exercise that jurisdiction on behalf of their children for similar reasons as it permits the doctor to make decisions for his unconscious patient, it would be somewhat misleading to call the situation of childhood as such an 'emergency'. Nevertheless, the same logic applies: parents are entitled to make decisions on behalf of their minor children, but they are not entitled to make decisions based on all available moral reasons; rather, they are required to act only in the best interests of the child, even if that means sometimes ignoring the significant moral claims of others when acting on the child's behalf.

How does the case of parents and children help us to justify state coercion in the criminal law? Drawing the connection requires one further step. Children are

---

[62] [1950] SCR 517.

[63] [1990] 1 SCR 158.

[64] Of course, there are others: the mentally disabled, those suffering from psychiatric disorders, etc.

unable to exercise their jurisdiction over the entire period of their legal minority, so they are in need of someone to stand in a position to exercise it for them for the long term. But there are others who are also incapable of exercising their jurisdiction over the long term for quite different reasons. Consider the corporation. It is a legal person distinct from both shareholders and directors, but it cannot act on its own behalf. Instead, the directors of the corporation are given fiducary powers to act in the corporation's best interests. By similar logic, state officials are fiduciaries of the people as a whole. In all fiduciary contexts, those who exercise another's jurisdiction on the latter's behalf are entitled to do so only insofar as they may be seen as acting *in the name of* the latter. In the corporate context, this means that insofar as someone purports to be acting in the name of the corporation, he must be acting reasonably and in the best interests of the corporation—discharging his duties of loyalty and care. And loyalty to the corporation sometimes means that we are required to disregard certain weighty moral reasons for action.[65]

The right of state officials to act on behalf of the citizenry as a whole, then, can be understood in terms of the justification of necessity in the same way as the right of corporate officers to act in the name of the corporation. Although the right to decide questions of collective concern belongs to the citizenry as a whole, the citizenry are—like the shareholders of a corporation taken one by one—incapable of exercising that jurisdiction for themselves. State officials are entitled to make decisions on behalf of the citizenry because they make it possible for the citizenry as a whole to exercise its jurisdiction insofar as they act as the stewards of the citizens' jurisdiction. Courts often say that public officials owe a fiduciary duty to the public in whose name they are exercising public power.[66] They have also insisted that the right of public officials to engage in otherwise prohibited conduct is constrained by constitutional rights-protection documents such as the Bill of Rights in the United States and the *Charter of Rights and Freedoms* in Canada. Once again, these considerations are treated by legal moralists as questions that have little to do with the internal structure of criminal law doctrine. But the understanding of the necessity defence in terms of jurisdiction gives us reason to think otherwise. The point is that, given the state officials' special place as fiduciaries of the people as a whole, they are constrained in what they may do beyond the ordinary rules that might govern the conduct of individuals

---

[65] This goes beyond the sorts of partiality that is sometimes thought to play a part in moral thinking. Here, directors are absolutely precluded from acting on *any* reasons other than the best interests of the shareholders.

[66] *Driscoll v Burlington-Bristol Bridge Co* 86 A 2d 201, 221–2 (Sup Ct of NJ, 1952) per Vanderbilt CJ: 'As fiduciaries and trustees of the public weal they are under an inescapable obligation to serve the public with the highest fidelity. In discharging the duties of their office, they are required to display such intelligence and skill as they are capable of, to be diligent and conscientious, to exercise their discretion not arbitrarily but reasonably, and above all to display good faith, honesty and integrity... These obligations are not mere theoretical concepts or idealistic abstractions of no practical force and effect; they are obligations imposed by the common law on public officers and assumed by them as a matter of law upon their entering public office.'

toward one another. The jurisdictional conception of the necessity defence helps to explain why both constitutional rights guarantees and public law norms impose important constraints on the ability of public officials to claim justification on the grounds that they are discharging the duties of their public office.[67]

4.2 Public law and political theory

Anglo-American criminal law doctrine of both criminal offences and justification defences exhibits a clear focus on the protection of jurisdiction from usurpation. Criminal wrongs are all concerned with attempts to usurp either the private jurisdiction of another person or the public jurisdiction of the people as a whole; and the logic of justification defences is best captured through the idea that what might at first look like a usurpation of another's jurisdiction is, in fact, a valid act on behalf of the party to whom the jurisdiction rightly belongs. This understanding of both offences and justification defences is clearly at odds with the legal moralists' focus on the moral wrongness or justification of the accused's conduct. It also provides the outlines of an alternative account of how we might be able to go about justifying the operations of the criminal justice system.

At the outset of this chapter, I suggested that the new legal moralists were right to try to justify the practices of the criminal justice system by showing that they are the ways we must act in order to live up to a certain conception of ourselves. The trouble with the moralist account, I suggested, was that the conception of ourselves simply as responsible moral agents was not the right one upon which to found a theory of criminal justice, for three reasons: because it imports an illiberal conception of the role of the criminal law; it is unable to justify the use of state coercive force through the institutions of criminal justice; and it fits very poorly with the structure of Anglo-American criminal law doctrine. But there is another conception of ourselves that, I believe, is one that we should be just as unwilling to jettison but which will allow us to justify a liberal and coercive criminal justice system that looks very much like the one we see in operation throughout the common law world. It is the

---

[67] The point is not that some defendants are to be treated differently from others in the criminal courts in virtue of their offices. Rather, the point is that some conduct is properly to be understood as the conduct of the people as a whole acting through a particular individual. A successful claim of justification of this sort simply establishes all the necessary conditions for saying that one's conduct was really undertaken on behalf of the people as a whole. Thus, contrary to what John Gardner suggests, everything turns on the fact that they were the powers of public officials. Gardner, 'Justifications Under Authority', 71, 97: '[E]very defendant comes before the criminal court simply as an ordinary person, unencumbered and unenhanced by any robes or seals or badges of office[.] Of course it is true, as we saw, that occasionally the criminal law must recognize people's legal powers (eg, their power to arrest) as part of the process of determining whether their prima facie crimes were justified...But...nothing turns, for the criminal law, on the fact that they are the powers of public officials.'

conception of ourselves as free and equal moral agents—the conception that is at the heart of modern theories of liberal constitutionalism.[68]

The best way to make sense of this conception of ourselves and its demands is to consider how law and the state might be required in order to solve a particular sort of moral problem about life in community with others. The problem is this: if I am operating in a world without law or state, my choice to lead my life according to the demands of morality has a deeply morally unsatisfying result. For although I would like all my actions to be deeply moral, there is something about the context within which I perform those actions that undermines that possibility. For when I decide unilaterally to act according to the demands of morality, I find myself in a situation vis-à-vis others that is deeply unequal. I am committed to acting according to moral principles but I have no assurance that anyone else will. So, far from acting according to principles that treat the moral worth of all persons equally, my actions actually undermine my status as an equal to those among whom I live. The only option available to me in the state of nature is to impose moral constraints upon myself without any assurance of similar constraints on others. Put another way: in the state of nature, there is simply no morally acceptable course of action open to me.

Liberal constitutionalism offers a solution to this problem through the creation of law and the state. In a world without either of these, I simply do not have the tools at my disposal to act morally without undermining my claim to equal moral status with others. But in a world with a state that has effective power and that can make a legitimate claim to acting on behalf of us all, I can get around this problem. The state guarantees us all that we can focus on the morality of our own choices without having to worry about whether this will undermine our status as moral equals of those around us. As we focus on the morality of our choices, the law focuses on each person's jurisdiction—the set of issues that it is up to them to decide—and the state promises to enforce the limits of jurisdiction in the name of us all.

According to this picture, the state (through its officials) is not concerned with the moral rightness of our conduct *tout court*. Just as before, it remains up to each of us to make sure that we act morally. The state's concern is with ensuring the conditions within which it is even possible for us each to make moral choices without thereby undermining our own status as the equal of those around us. The state does so (through its officials) by patrolling the boundaries of each person's jurisdiction, using coercive force to resist any attempt to usurp the jurisdiction of others. The use of force by state officials in resisting attempts to usurp another's jurisdiction are not justified because it would be morally right conduct if performed by a private

---

[68] TRS Allan, *Constitutional Justice: A Liberal Theory of the Rule of Law* (Oxford: Oxford University Press, 2001); E Fox-Decent, 'The Fiduciary Nature of State Legal Authority' (2005) 31 *Queen's Law Journal* 259; D Dyzenhaus, *The Constitution of Law: Legality in a Time of Emergency* (Cambridge: Cambridge University Press, 2006); MD Walters, 'Written Constitutions and Unwritten Constitutionalism', in G Huscroft (ed), *Expounding the Constitution: Essays in Constitutional Theory* (New York: Cambridge University Press, 2008).

party; indeed, when private parties attempt to do the same things, they are branded as vigilantes and criminals. Rather, the use of force by state officials is justified insofar as it sets out the necessary preconditions to a life in community with others as free and equal moral agents.

5 CONCLUSION

The 'public law' account of the criminal justice system I sketch here satisfies each of the three considerations that Duff and Gardner's new legal moralism does not. Unlike their account, it recognizes that state coercion is a central aspect of the criminal justice system—something quite different in kind from the sort of thing that private parties are entitled to use against one another as 'punishment' for perceived moral wrongdoing. It is based around the fundamental distinction between the right of private parties to criticize one another for moral wrongdoing and the state's right to use coercive force to resist criminal wrongs ex ante and to punish criminal wrongdoers them ex post facto. Second, because it is focused entirely on the protection of jurisdiction—both the private jurisdiction of each person to decide how to use his body and property as he sees fit and the public jurisdiction of the state to deal with the preconditions of individual freedom through binding laws and coercive enforcement—it fits nicely with the widely shared liberal conception of criminal law. And third, as we have seen from our review of Anglo-American criminal law doctrine, the 'public law' account fits much more neatly with existing doctrine than does it legal moralist rival.

3

REPUBLICANISM AND THE FOUNDATIONS OF CRIMINAL LAW

RICHARD DAGGER[*]

ESTABLISHING the philosophical foundations of criminal law is less a matter of excavation than of reconstruction. Neither criminal law nor law in general is the product of an architect's design, which careful digging in the right places will reveal, but something that has emerged, evolved, and developed over the centuries. Codifiers and constitution drafters have played parts in this development, to be sure, but their efforts have had less to do with excavation than with the reconstruction of the criminal law. That is, their aim typically has been to clarify the form and improve the substance of the law as it has come down to them in order to approximate more closely the law as they think it ought to be. To carry out these tasks, however, the codifiers and drafters must have some sense of what law can and ought to be—some theory, however implicit and inarticulate it may be, of the law. To articulate such a theory is to provide a rational reconstruction of the law.

Rational reconstruction thus aims to discover the reason or logic inherent in the law despite its irregular development over time and the various courses it takes

* I am grateful to Jeffrie Murphy, Alice Ristroph, Mary Sigler, and the editors for their helpful comments on an earlier draft of this chapter.

from one place to another. In the case of criminal law, rational reconstruction must account for the leading features of criminal law and point the way to its reform or further development. Such a reconstruction, in other words, should lead to a theory that will have, in Antony Duff's terms, both an analytical and a normative dimension. The theory must not only account, analytically, for the typical operations and aspects of criminal law but also take a position, in its normative dimension, on 'what it [criminal law] ought to be (and whether it ought to be at all)'.[1]

My purpose in this chapter is to make a case for the republican tradition in political philosophy as a theory that can provide this rational reconstruction of criminal law. I claim no originality in this regard, as others have found the underpinnings of criminal law and law more generally in republicanism. John Braithwaite and Philip Pettit advance 'a republican theory of criminal justice' in their *Not Just Deserts*, for instance, and Antony Duff suggests that republicanism provides a basis for criminal law in his recent writings.[2] I shall argue, like Duff, not that republicanism is superior to every possible competing theory, but that it offers a reconstruction of criminal law that is both rational and plausible. In particular, I shall try to show that republicanism can help us to make sense of three important features of criminal law: first, the conviction that crime is a public wrong; second, the general pattern of development of criminal law historically; and third, the public nature of criminal law as a cooperative enterprise. To begin, however, I must explain what I take republicanism to be and why it is a proper place to look for a rational reconstruction of criminal law.

1 REPUBLICANISM, BRIEFLY CONSIDERED

Whether one thinks the republican tradition a likely place to look for a rational reconstruction of criminal law will depend in large part on how one conceives of the relationship between political and legal philosophy. A quarter of a century ago Jeffrie Murphy complained that philosophers of law often forget 'that the philosophy of law is a part of social and political philosophy and not merely of moral philosophy... [I]n addition to considering the intrinsic moral merits and demerits of a legal practice,

---

[1] RA Duff, 'Theories of Criminal Law', *Stanford Encyclopedia of Philosophy* (<http://plato.stanford.edu>; posted 14 October 2002), §1. See also M Moore, *Placing Blame: A Theory of Criminal Law* (Oxford: Clarendon Press, 1997) on why 'descriptive theories of an area of law are also evaluative theories', 15–18, at 18.

[2] J Braithwaite and P Pettit, *Not Just Deserts: A Republican Theory of Criminal Justice* (Oxford: Clarendon Press, 1990); RA Duff, 'Toward a Theory of Criminal Law?' (2010) 84 *Proceedings of the Aristotelian Society*, Supp Vol, 1–17, and *Answering for Crime: Responsibility and Liability in the Criminal Law* (Oxford: Hart Publishing, 2007), 49–53.

such as punishment, philosophers of law must also see such practices in terms of the general problems of social and political philosophy—particularly the problems of the nature and justification of the state and its coercive power'.[3] Murphy is right, in my view, and emphatically so where criminal law is concerned. The determination of what counts as a crime, the prevention of crimes, the proper treatment of those charged with crimes, the conviction and subsequent treatment of criminals—all these are matters typically entrusted to political authorities. One might argue that no one *should* entrust these powers to political authorities, or that no one is truly justified in claiming political authority, but to advance such arguments is in itself to engage in political philosophy.

The republican tradition's place in political philosophy should not disqualify it, then, from consideration as a theory of criminal law. But what is republicanism? As I see it, the fundamental elements of republicanism, today as in classical Greece and Rome, are *publicity* and *self-government*.[4] That is, republicans believe that government is a public concern—the *res publica*—rather than the personal business or property of some ruler or ruling class; and public concerns are the province of self-governing citizens who will seek to enjoy liberty under and through the law. Understood in this way, republicanism is not sharply different from some other traditions of political thought, including the liberalism to which Murphy and many other philosophers of law claim adherence. John Locke, John Stuart Mill, and other exemplars of liberalism maintain that government is a public concern and citizens should enjoy liberty under law, just as republicans do. There is, however, a difference of emphasis, best captured in the republican claim that liberty is not so much a matter of freedom *from* the law as of freedom *by* or *through* the law.[5] To put the point another way—and to do so while allowing for the possibility of a liberal republicanism or republican liberalism—we may say that liberals tend to worry about protecting the privacy of individuals from unwarranted intrusion,

---

[3] J Murphy, 'Retributivism, Moral Education, and the Liberal State' (1985) 4 *Criminal Justice Ethics*, 3–11, at 4. For a general consideration of the connection between the philosophy of law and political philosophy by an author who deplores 'the artificial boundary' between the two, see J Waldron, 'Legal and Political Philosophy', in J Coleman and S Shapiro (eds), *The Oxford Handbook of Jurisprudence and Philosophy of Law* (Oxford: Oxford University Press, 2002), 352–81, at 381. For a contrary view, at least with regard to the philosophy of punishment, see M Davis, 'The Relative Independence of Punishment Theory', in Davis, *To Make the Punishment Fit the Crime: Essays in the Theory of Criminal Justice* (Boulder, CO: Westview Press, 1992), 18–41.

[4] The remainder of this section draws on my 'Republicanism and Crime', in S Besson and JL Marti, *Legal Republicanism: National and International Perspectives* (Oxford: Oxford University Press, 2009), 148–50. For a somewhat fuller sketch, see my 'Republicanism', in G Klosko (ed), *The Oxford Handbook of the History of Political Philosophy* (Oxford: Oxford University Press, 2010).

[5] Philip Pettit is fond of quoting in this regard the 17th-century republican James Harrington's disparagement of Thomas Hobbes's conception of liberty, which Harrington took to be an untenable 'liberty or immunity *from* the laws' ; see, eg, J Braithwaite and P Pettit, *Not Just Deserts*, 59 (emphasis in original).

while republicans worry more about the need to promote active and responsible citizenship.

That republicans are committed to the importance of publicity and self-government has been evident since at least the first century BCE, when Cicero set down his definition of the republic. The 'commonwealth [res publica]', he wrote, 'is the concern of a people, but a people is not any group of men assembled in any way, but an assemblage of some size associated with one another through agreement on law and community of interest'.[6] According to another classical definition, a republic is the empire of laws, not of men. Both of these definitions focus on the rule of law because law limits the rulers' ability to impose their will or whims on their subjects; when everyone is subject to the law, no one is subject to the arbitrary, unchecked power of another. As an empire of laws, the republic protects the public interest and promotes the liberty of its citizens, who will be free to govern themselves because they are free from the grip of those who would dominate them.

In terms recently made familiar by Philip Pettit, the rule of law helps to secure people from both *imperium* and *dominium*.[7] Security from *imperium*—that is, arbitrary power in the hands of those who control the state or government—has been the principal concern of republican theorists through the centuries, but Pettit is surely right to point out the need for security also from *dominium*—that is, arbitrary power in the hands of private individuals. This double security also connects with the republican emphasis on the common interest or public good. Exactly what constitutes the common interest or public good is a point on which republicans will often disagree among themselves. They agree, however, that a political society is a shared or common enterprise that must proceed according to rules, as Cicero's definition indicates. One aspect of the public good, then, will be the need to protect and preserve these rules and the bonds that hold the members of this enterprise together. Another aspect is the need to respect citizens not only as public persons but also as individuals with personal interests. As Mortimer Sellers says: 'Republicanism is the theory that law and government exist to serve the public good, *including the public interest in protecting private interests against each other*, but also against the state.'[8] Protecting private interests against one another is thus a way of securing liberty from *dominium*. It is also the point at which crime becomes relevant to republicanism.

To be sure, crime is not the only way in which one person may exercise arbitrary power over another. There is *imperium*, of course, and one virtue of the criminal law is that its provisions for procedural justice help to protect citizens from various kinds of unwarranted coercion by those holding political office. There are also

[6] Marcus Tullius Cicero, *On the Commonwealth and On the Laws* J Zetzel (ed) (Cambridge: Cambridge University Press, 1999), 18.

[7] P Pettit, *Republicanism: A Theory of Freedom and Government* (Oxford: Oxford University Press, 1997), esp 112 and 130.

[8] MNS Sellers, *Republican Legal Theory: The History, Constitution and Purposes of Law in a Free State* (New York: Palgrave Macmillan, 2003), 72 (emphasis added).

forms of *dominium* that may be quite lawful—the husband who browbeats his wife, for example, or the landowner who bends her tenants to her will. Other forms of *dominium*, such as defamation of character, may be matters for tort rather than criminal law.[9] Yet crime is surely one of the most common and persistent ways in which some people wield arbitrary power over others. Like the unchecked ruler, the criminal interferes with our ability to govern our own lives. By stealing my property or robbing me of the use of an eye or arm, the criminal also leaves me less free to go about my life—less free not only because of the loss of the property, eye, or arm, but also because of the fear and insecurity I now feel.[10] Nor do I need to be the direct victim for crime to make me less free by being less secure or feeling more vulnerable. The fact that others in my vicinity have become victims could be enough to raise my insurance rates, send me to the locksmith or private protection agency, and change the routes I take as I go about my business.

Crime, in short, is a threat to a republic insofar as it threatens the rule of law and interferes with the ability to be self-governing. To say this, of course, is to presume that murder, rape, robbery, and the other offences we commonly call crimes are not really torts—private wrongs inflicted by some individuals upon other individuals, to be settled by lawsuit in civil court. But that is exactly what republicans presume. As they see it, the standard criminal offences are not matters to be settled by private agreement or arbitration but wrongs deserving of public condemnation and punishment. Crime certainly harms and threatens the persons and property of private individuals, but it also tears at the sentiments that make a sense of common life, under law, possible. Crime is a fitting subject for republican concern, then, because dealing with crime is an important part of the public's business. For that reason, the public should play a part in passing laws that define what crimes are, that provide for agencies to protect its members from crime, and that establish just procedures for treating those accused of committing crimes, including the proper treatment of those found guilty.

Crime is also a very real threat from the republican point of view. Republicans share a persistent worry about the likelihood of corruption, and corruption breeds, among other things, crime. Ambition, avarice, the desire for luxury and ease—these and other temptations to criminal and other kinds of vicious conduct may be held in check or redirected, but republicans see no reason to believe they can be eradicated. Republicans celebrate civic virtue, but they do so largely because they know that such virtue is not to be taken for granted. Putting the public good ahead of one's private interests is a virtue that republicans believe most people can achieve, but they

---

[9] I venture a republican explanation for classifying defamation as a tort rather than a crime in 'Republicanism and Crime', in S Besson and JL Marti, *Legal Republicanism: National and International Perspectives* (Oxford: Oxford University Press, 2009), 162–5.

[10] On this point, see GP Fletcher, 'Domination in Wrongdoing' (1996) 76 *Boston University Law Review* 347–60, at 347. But cf FM Lawrence, 'Comment: The Limits of Domination' (1996) 76 *Boston University Law Review* 361–70.

also fear that most people can as easily put their private interests ahead of the public good—and ahead of the personal interests of others. For republicans, therefore, finding ways to deal with crime is definitely part of the public's business. But can republicanism help with the problem of defining crime?

2 Crime as the Public's Business

Jaded lawyers and legal theorists sometimes say that the definition of 'crime' is simply a matter of legislative action—that is, what makes something criminal is that the relevant legislature declares it to be so. There is, of course, more than a grain of truth to this way of defining 'crime', but there are also reasons to find it unsatisfactory. The problem, as one influential commentator complains, is that this definition 'is simple, circular, and largely useless'.[11] In particular, it is of no use to the legislators who must decide whether to declare certain acts or activities criminal, for they will find no guidance in the statement that a crime is whatever they collectively say it is. What legislators want to know is *how* they should vote, not what the outcome will be when all of their votes are counted. Like the people they represent, in other words, legislators need to have some sense of independent standards for regarding some acts as criminal and others as not. Who would conclude, for example, that murder is not really a crime, but brushing one's teeth more than twice a week is, simply because a legislature passes laws to make the former legal and the latter criminal? The standards will seldom be as clear and uncontroversial as they are in these far-fetched examples, but the conviction that such standards are to be found—and that there is something more to the definition and determination of crime than legislative *fiat*—is widespread and deeply rooted. Why else would apparently intelligent and reasonable people think it worthwhile to draft and revise such documents as the Model Penal Code? Presumably they believe they have found independent standards, or criteria embedded in the law as it has come down to them, that make some acts and activities fit candidates for the designation 'crime' and others not.

Unsatisfactory as it is, however, there remains an important truth in this 'simple, circular, and largely useless' definition of crime, for it points to the connection between public action and the criminal law. When a legislature declares certain acts

---

[11] J Dressler, *Understanding Criminal Law* (4th edn; Newark, NJ: LexisNexis, 2006), 1. But cf HL Packer, *The Limits of the Criminal Sanction* (Stanford, CA: Stanford University Press, 1968), 18–19: 'the definition of crime is inescapably tautological. Crime is whatever is formally and authoritatively described as criminal... [C]rime is conduct capable of incurring consequences formally termed criminal.'

or activities to be criminal, it takes a public stance by means of political action; or when a judge or jury declares an act or activity to be an instance of a common-law crime, the judge or jury issues a public pronouncement. We may not always approve of these legislative or judicial stances on these matters—we may even protest, para-doxically, that these decisions make a crime of something that in its essence is not, and surely *ought not* to be, a crime—but the point is that the decisions have, *ceteris paribus*, the force of law. Crimes are not only wrongs but *public wrongs,* and 'public' in the twofold sense that they both require the attention of the law and are different from the *private wrongs,* such as torts and breaches of contract, to which the law also must attend. That is why it is the proper business of legislatures and courts to decide what is to be deemed a public wrong—a crime.

Etymology is not especially illuminating in the case of 'crime', but it does tell us something about the nature of crime as public wrong. According to the *Oxford English Dictionary,* 'crime' derives, by way of Old French, from the Latin *crimen,* meaning 'judgement, accusation, offence'; or, as the *Oxford Latin Dictionary* defines *crimen,* 'An indictment, charge, accusation'. In *The Data of Jurisprudence,* William Galbraith Miller also suggests a connection between *crimen* and the Greek κρίνω, which Liddell and Scott's *Greek-English Lexicon* translates as 'decision, judgement'; 'decree, resolu-tion'; 'legal decision'; 'matter for judgment, question'; 'law-suit'; 'judging, judgment'.[12] What is most striking about these definitions, from the modern perspective, is that the forebears of the English 'crime' apparently referred to an accusation brought or a judgment rendered against someone, and not, as we would expect, to the wrongful act that the accused or judged supposedly committed. How this shift occurred is not clear, but Miller's conclusion seems apt: 'The mere trial, the accusation, the very sus-picion is a stigma—*crimen,* a charge, becomes *crimen,* a crime.'[13] Such a conclusion is consistent, at least, with the *Oxford Latin Dictionary's* fourth definition of *crimen* as, with references to Ovid and Seneca, a 'misdeed, crime'.

Less striking, but more important for present purposes, is the way that the Latin and Greek ancestors of 'crime' invoke public activity. To bring an indictment or an accusation against someone is to call him to account; to seek a judgment against that person, or to pass judgment on him, presupposes that at least one other person is in the position of judging. Something official or public takes place, in short. The office in question may be only loosely defined, and in the ancient world it would have been concerned as much with what we now think of as religion, morality, and cus-tom as with politics or law. Nevertheless, calling to account and passing judgment were, and are, actions that involve more than the putative offender and victim, as the aggrieved party must appeal to some standard—and typically to some third party in at least a quasi-official position—for a judgment against the accused. In this sense,

[12] WG Miller, *The Data of Jurisprudence* (Littleton, CO, 1980 [1903]), 193. Henry Liddell and Robert Scott, *A Greek-English Lexicon,* vol I (rev edn; Oxford: Clarendon Press, 1948).
[13] Ibid 193–4.

crimen was, as crime continues to be, concerned with wrongs that were not simply private or personal matters. What etymology suggests, in sum, is that the concept of crime emerged not from an attempt to identify wrong or wrongful conduct as such but from attempts to provide a public, formal response to certain kinds of activities already identified as wrong. Extending Miller's comment, it seems that '*crimen*, a charge, becomes *crimen*, a crime', because the public charges brought against certain wrongdoers led eventually to the conclusion that their activities were wrongs for which one would face a public charge and judgment.

But what have these considerations to do with republicanism? The answer is to be found not in etymology but in the rational reconstruction of which I wrote earlier. 'Crime' and 'republic' both relate to matters of *public* concern—implicitly in the former case, as we have seen, but explicitly in the case of *res publica*. The classical republican thinkers—including at least one, Cicero, who had considerable experience of criminal law—thought that the public business encompassed far more than accusing and passing judgment, but they certainly included these actions among the proper concerns of republican citizens and officials. More generally, they conceived of the republic as a common enterprise, under law, in which citizens were to enjoy freedom through self-government. If the republic truly was to be an empire of laws rather than of men, as we have seen, then it was necessary to identify those wrongs that threaten the public enterprise and to pass judgment on those who commit them. Defining crime, then, is as important to the public's business as the apprehension, conviction, and punishment of criminals.

This conclusion may seem to be neither surprising nor compelling. Apart from the anarchists, one might ask, who does not take crime to be an important part of the public's business? Even monarchies and other non-republican regimes have systems of criminal law in which acts and activities called 'crimes' are defined, condemned, and punished as public wrongs. Why, then, should we look to republicanism for a rational reconstruction of criminal law?

The republican response to this challenge has two aspects. The first consists in pointing out that monarchies, juntas, and authoritarian regimes of various sorts can only have systems of criminal law insofar as they rely, albeit implicitly and perhaps parasitically, on the republican ideal of the empire of laws. If King Rex, to borrow Lon Fuller's famous example, is to rule through law rather than whim or sheer will, there are certain things he must and must not do—make his pronouncements public, for example, and not command his subjects to do what they cannot possibly do.[14] In other words, laws must at least carry the appearance of satisfying Thomas Aquinas' definition of law as an 'order of reason for the common good by one who has the care of the community, and promulgated'.[15] The more difficult it becomes to see even the

---

[14] L Fuller, *The Morality of Law* (rev edn; New Haven, CT: Yale University Press, 1969), 33–8.

[15] T Aquinas, *On Law, Morality, and Politics*, trans RJ Regan (2nd edn; Indianapolis, IN: Hackett, 2002), 15 (*Summa Theologica*, I-II, Q. 90, Art 4).

appearance of reason, authority, promulgation, or a concern for the common good in the ruler or rulers' pronouncements, the less likely it is that those subject to these pronouncements will believe themselves to be subject to the rule of law.[16]

The second aspect of the republican response is simply to proceed to develop a republican reconstruction of criminal law in the expectation that its value thus will become clear. For example, the republican might try to show that a theory of criminal law grounded in the desire to be free from *imperium* and *dominium* is not merely plausible but powerfully illuminating, both analytically and normatively. That, indeed, is what Pettit has tried to do.[17] I shall proceed in a different way here, however, by looking more directly to the reconstruction of the *foundations* of criminal law. In doing so, I shall make use of the familiar idea of the state of nature.

3 THE STATE OF NATURE, THE 'SELF-HELP' MODEL, AND LAW'S POTENTIAL

Republican thinkers typically have not resorted to state-of-nature or social-contract arguments. In general they have begun, like Aristotle, by conceiving of men and (more recently) women as political or social beings, which leaves little reason to investigate a supposedly natural condition in which law and government do not exist. Jean-Jacques Rousseau is an exception to this rule, however, and I believe that we can learn something from his example.[18] But I also take it that appeals to the state of nature and the social contract can illuminate important aspects of political and legal philosophy even when they are not presented as historically accurate accounts of how political and legal authority came to be—or adequate justifications, for that matter, for claims to such authority.[19]

Rousseau conceives of the state of nature in his *Discourse on the Origin of Inequality* (1755) less in the 'what if' fashion of Thomas Hobbes than in a 'how it must

---

[16] I return to this point in section 4 below, with reference to HLA Hart's 'internal aspect' of law.

[17] J Braithwaite and P Pettit, *Not Just Deserts: A Republican Theory of Criminal Justice* (Oxford: Clarendon Press, 1990); also, inter alia, P Pettit, 'Republican Theory and Criminal Punishment' (1997) 9 *Utilitas* 59–79.

[18] For an explication of the republican (or republican-liberal) aspects of Rousseau's political thought, see ch 6 of my *Civic Virtues: Rights, Citizenship, and Republican Liberalism* (New York: Oxford University Press, 1997).

[19] For a recent example of the illuminating use of the idea of the social contract, see BC Zipursky, 'Philosophy of Private Law', in J Coleman and S Shapiro (eds), *The Oxford Handbook of Jurisprudence and Philosophy of Law* (Oxford: Oxford University Press, 2002), esp §4, 'A Contractarian Model of Private Rights of Action in Private Law'.

have been' manner. That is, Hobbes presents the state of nature as the 'solitary, poore, nasty, brutish, and short' condition in which the men and women of his day would find themselves were there to be—perhaps as the result of a civil war—no political or legal authority over them.[20] Rousseau, by contrast, proceeds in an anthropological rather than hypothetical manner, asking what the state of nature must have been like, and how political and legal authority might have arisen out of it. For present purposes, how Rousseau answers these questions is less important than his general approach. We need not follow him, for example, when he suggests that human beings in the state of nature were originally little more than brute animals wandering about the fields and forests, each living a solitary existence save for the occasional satisfaction of natural urges that led to pregnancy and childbirth. In contrast to this view, which has social life and sentiments developing only as people slowly come to recognize the benefits of cooperation, it seems more plausible to think that humans have always lived in groups of some kind—families, clans, or tribes, if not societies or polities. Nor is Rousseau's famous account of the foundation of civil society, at the beginning of Part II of the *Discourse*, as persuasive as it is provocative:

The first man who, having fenced off a plot of land, thought of saying 'This is mine' and found people simple enough to believe him was the real founder of civil society. How many crimes, wars, murders, how many miseries and horrors might the human race have been spared by the one who, upon pulling up the stakes or filling in the ditch, had shouted to his fellow men, 'Beware of listening to this impostor; you are lost, if you forget that the fruits of the earth belong to all and that the earth belongs to no one!'[21]

Such an account is plausible only if one takes the existence of property relations as the defining feature of civil society. Even then, as Aristotle and many others have argued, there is at least as much to be said for private property as Rousseau says against it here. Indeed, Rousseau himself endorses an essentially Lockean justification of private property in his *Social Contract* (Bk I, ch 9).

Why, then, should we take Rousseau's approach to the state of nature as a model when we look for the foundations of criminal law? The answer has two parts. First, suitably modified, Rousseau's 'how it must have been' approach provides a helpful way to think about the gradual *emergence* of criminal law, and law in general, over time. Second, it also tells us something about the potential of criminal law, and law in general, as a force for good that is vulnerable to manipulation and ideological distortion.

Concerning the first point, a suitably modified account of the emergence of criminal law would take something like the following form. In the original state of nature, as it must have been, men and women lived in small groups, clinging together from

---

[20] T Hobbes, *Leviathan* (1651), Book I, ch XIII.

[21] Jean-Jacques Rousseau, *Discourse on the Origins and Foundations of Inequality among Men*, in A Ritter (ed) and J Conaway Bondanella (trans), *Rousseau's Political Writings* (New York: WW Norton & Co, 1988), 34.

affection and for the sake of survival. Other groups of people would have threatened them, however, and rivalries, jealousy, and sheer selfishness occasionally must have disturbed every group's harmony, so that it became necessary not only to join in defensive efforts but also to find ways to deal with those who harmed or wronged other members of the group. There were also probably some misdeeds—violations of a deeply shared belief, perhaps—that seemed to wrong no one as an individual but the group as a whole. In this state of nature, individuals presumably tried to set things right by acting on their own. You hit me, so I hit you back; you maimed my brother, so I maim you or your brother in return. In clans or groups that included many families, the retaliation or retribution would be not so much an individual as a familial matter; in even larger groups, it would be a clan-based matter. In this fashion, the idea of a crime as something more than an individual offence—as a public wrong—must gradually have emerged.

Crucial to this emergence would have been the dissatisfaction with the blood feuds and vendettas that grew out of private acts of vengeance. In some cases rough and informal standards for meting out retribution may have served to keep the violence in check, but the obvious problem with private vengeance is that it is as likely to incite bitterness, enmity, and further violence as it is to leave all parties feeling that justice has been done. Whether a grievance is slight or truly significant is a matter the parties can easily disagree about, as are the questions of whether the offence was real or merely imagined, intended, or accidental. So too is the question of whether a retaliatory act is in or out of proportion to the original harm or wrong. For these reasons, private vengeance would produce unending feuds and escalating violence as it drew more and more people into the conflict—or in some cases left the weak to nurse their grievances as they cowered before the strong. One need not conclude that the state of nature would thus become a catastrophic state of war—a conclusion that Hobbes and Rousseau shared—to believe that people caught up in feuds and vendettas would eventually come to perceive the desirability of some better way to try to set matters right. This better way would necessarily consist of some means of defining and dealing with offences too serious simply to leave to the individuals directly involved to settle among themselves. Such is the story that Aeschylus' *Oresteia* trilogy tells in dramatic form, with Athena founding a system of laws to quell the spiralling violence of blood feuds. In John Locke's terms, in place of the state of nature, where everyone has the right to punish offenders, the rule of law would provide 'an established, settled, known... standard of right and wrong', a 'known and indifferent judge, with authority to determine all differences according to the established law', and an enforcement agency 'to back and support the sentence when right, and to give it due execution'.[22] In short, one need not resort to the social contract, as Locke did, to imagine how something like criminal law, and the rule of law in general, could have emerged from a state of nature as a response to these defects.

[22] J Locke, *The Second Treatise of Government*, §§124, 125, 126.

I say 'something like criminal law' here because it is conceivable that the public system of dispute resolution that emerges from a state of nature will resemble a system of civil rather than criminal law. If all that matters is finding a way to end blood feuds and vendettas, then public arbitration may be sufficient. In fact, historical scholarship on the origins of law suggests that something of this sort is what happened. According to James Q Whitman, 'our dominant model of the origins of law and the state' is what has come to be called the 'self-help model'.[23] In Whitman's capsule version, this model comprises:

four fundamental stages in the early development of law and the state. Stage one is the stage of the state of nature. This is a stage of ordered vengeance and vendetta. In this first stage, clans and/or individuals exact vengeance, in a systematic and rule-governed way, when injured by other clans and/or individuals; in particular, they exact *talionic* vengeance, seeking, in the famous biblical phrase, 'an eye for an eye, a tooth for a tooth'. In stage two, the early state emerges. This early state does not, however, attempt to prevent violence. Rather, it sets out to supervise the existing system of vengeance. Thus, the early state assumes a kind of licensing power over acts of talionic vengeance, requiring that injured parties seek formal state sanction before avenging themselves. In stage three, the early state itself begins to function as an enforcer, taking vengeance on behalf of injured clans; in [Max] Weber's phrase, the early state of stage three monopolizes the legitimate use of violence. Only in stage four does the early state at last move to eliminate private violence. In this fourth stage, the early state institutes a system of 'compositions', substituting money damages for talionic vengeance.[24]

So described, the self-help model is consistent in its broad outlines with the Rousseauvean account. There are important respects, however, in which the Rousseauvean account differs from the self-help model. To begin with, the two differ with regard to the question of how orderly the 'ordered vengeance and vendetta' of stage one, the state of nature, truly was; but I think a resolution may be found, following Rousseau, by conceiving of the state of nature in a more dynamic fashion than 'stage one' of the self-help model suggests. That is, the model's first stage would have occurred later in the course of the state of nature than the beginning point of the 'how it must have been' account. In addition, the model's first stage depicts 'clans and/or individuals' exacting vengeance '*in a systematic and rule-governed way*', before 'the early state emerges' in stage two.[25] This seems to presume some sense of a community—of being part of a *public*—that underpins this system of rules for exacting vengeance. Those who do wrong and those who suffer wrongdoing are not completely alien to one another, in other words, but members of a public insofar as they accept this system of rules as something that applies to all of them. In this respect, the Rousseauvean account, with its picture of societies forming before civil society forms, complements the self-help model.

[23] JQ Whitman, 'The Origins of Law and the State: Perversion of Violence, Mutilation of Bodies, or Setting of Prices?' (1995–96) 71 *Chicago-Kent Law Review* 41–84, at 41.

[24] Ibid.

[25] Ibid (emphasis added).

Whether this system of rules would be likely to produce 'a stage of ordered vengeance and vendetta' in the absence of a state, as the self-help model indicates, is, however, a point at which the model and the Rousseauvean account appear to be at odds. Indeed, there seem to be two interpretations of the self-help model in this regard. According to one interpretation, the state emerges, in effect, when a group of entrepreneurs seizes the opportunity to take control of the already existing system of 'ordered vengeance and vendetta' in order to advance the entrepreneurs' interests. According to the second interpretation, the state emerges in response to some defect or deficiency in the already existing system, the most likely of which is the tendency of the system of 'ordered vengeance and vendetta' to break down when there are no public institutions to maintain it. This second interpretation is more in keeping with the Rousseauvean, republican account of the emergence of criminal law, as I have previously suggested, but there is also room, as we shall see, for elements of the first interpretation in that account.

Despite these differences, the 'how it must have been' story of the emergence of criminal law seems broadly consistent with the self-help model. But is the self-help model itself altogether satisfactory? Whitman and others maintain that it is not.[26] The key word here, though, is 'altogether'. The critics agree that the model is sound in important respects, and those respects seem to be those most salient to the 'how it must have been' account of the emergence of law and legal authority. As Whitman acknowledges: 'Some sort of vengeance or vendetta system *must* lie somewhere in the background of our earliest sources; the evidence for the partial truth of the model is too powerful to be thrown out.'[27] But there is also another aspect of the self-help model that is problematic, at least from the standpoint of a rational reconstruction of *criminal* law. According to Whitman's description, the early state moves 'to eliminate private violence' in stage four, but it does so by instituting 'a system of "compositions", substituting money damages for talionic vengeance'.[28] So described, however, the early state seems to have instituted a system of civil rather than criminal law, as there is no suggestion that condemnation or punishment attached to the 'money damages' the early state apparently imposed. In this respect, again, the Rousseauvean account provides a useful supplement to the self-help model. On that

[26] In addition to Whitman's 'The Origins of Law and the State', see WI Miller, *Eye for an Eye* (Cambridge: Cambridge University Press, 2006), esp 25.

[27] 'The Origins of Law and the State', 43 (emphasis in original); also 82: 'The idea that some kind of private vengeance order lies in the background of the archaic codes is too plausible, and too revealing, to be abandoned. It must surely be correct that the authorities that erected the bronze tables and the diorite steles upon which the early codes are inscribed meant, *in part*, to meddle in a system of vengeance' (emphasis in original). To be sure, Whitman goes on to say (82), 'The most attractive starting hypothesis is that the codes that have come down to us were produced not in the course of a typically nineteenth-century campaign to clamp down on violence, but in a much more alien archaic effort to control the marketplace and to deal with the problems of body mutilation in a world of sympathetic magic and ritually-ordered social hierarchy.'

[28] 'The Origins of Law and the State', 41.

account, those charged with enforcing the law will have the authority to express the public's condemnation of lawbreakers and to punish them for their crimes.

There is reason, then, to regard the Rousseauvean sketch as a plausible account of the gradual emergence of criminal law, and law in general, at least in broad outline. But what of the second reason for taking Rousseau's *Discourse on Inequality* as a model? That is, what does this approach reveal about the potential of criminal law?

In brief, the 'how it must have been' account indicates that criminal law has the potential to protect interests, both private and public, and to promote autonomy. Insofar as criminal law works to secure people against the wrongdoing of others, it protects their interest in health, safety, and property, among other things. In doing so, moreover, it promotes their autonomy, both in the sense of their freedom to go about their business and in the stronger sense of self-government. Criminal law requires a sense of *publicity*—that is, of being part of a body politic under the rule of law. Criminal law proscribes and punishes certain acts and activities that it some-how identifies as public wrongs. But the 'it' that identifies, proscribes, and punishes these wrongs is not criminal law itself, but the public, or some person or persons acting in the name of the public. To be sure, monarchs, dictators, and function-aries sometimes talk as if their word is law, but in doing so, as I indicated earlier, they are trespassing on the presumption that law is a public rule of conduct—an 'order of reason', to recur to Aquinas's definition, for the common good enacted by those in authority and promulgated. Criminal law is a public responsibility, in other words, that presents an opportunity for members of the public to participate in self-government by helping to give definition and force to the law—an opportunity that republicans would have us seize and preserve.

Rousseau's *Social Contract* (1762) is apposite here, especially as it appears to present a picture of the 'passage from the state of nature to the civil state' very dif-ferent from the one he set out seven years earlier in the *Discourse on Inequality*. This passage, he now says:

produces a most remarkable change in man, by substituting justice for instinct in his con-duct, and giving his actions the morality they previously lacked. Only when the voice of duty succeeds physical impulse and right succeeds appetite does man, who had until then con-sidered only himself, find himself compelled to act on different principles and to consult his reason before listening to his inclinations. Although in this state he denies himself several of the advantages he owes to nature, he gains others so great—his faculties are exercised and developed, his ideas are extended, his feelings are ennobled, his whole soul is so uplifted—that if the abuses of this new condition did not often degrade him beneath the condition from which he emerged, he would constantly have to bless the happy moment that tore him away from it forever, and made a stupid and shortsighted animal into an intelligent being and a man.[29]

---

[29] A Ritter (ed) and J Conaway Bondanella (trans), *Rousseau's Political Writings* (New York: W W Norton & Co, 1988), 95 (Bk I, ch 8).

In the course of this remarkable transformation, people give up the 'natural liberty' of the state of nature, 'which is limited only by the strength of the individual', in order to enjoy 'civil liberty'—freedom under law—and 'moral liberty, which alone makes man his own master, for impulsion by appetite alone is slavery, and obedience to the law that one has prescribed for oneself is liberty'.[30]

'Moral liberty' is thus the kind of self-government that is possible in the civil state, under the rule of law, but not in the state of nature. There is clearly much to be said for Rousseau's position here, taking 'moral liberty' to be equivalent to 'autonomy' and recognizing that an autonomous person must be self-*governing* rather than simply at liberty to do as he or she pleases. There is also an obvious problem, however. For how is one to obey 'the law that one has prescribed for oneself' while living under laws that others also have had a voice in making? This, indeed, is the problem that Rousseau sets himself in the *Social Contract*: 'To find a form of association that defends and protects the person and possessions of each associate with all the common strength, and by means of which each person, joining forces with all, nevertheless obeys only himself and remains as free as before.'[31] Whether Rousseau's solution to the problem is satisfactory, or even coherent, is a question we need not take up here. What is clear is that his and any plausible response to the problem he sets must rest on an understanding of freedom as 'moral liberty', autonomy, or the freedom of self-governing citizens who have a voice in the making of the laws under which they live. It must rest, that is, on a broadly republican understanding of politics and law.

There is also a second problem to consider here, however, and it is one to which Rousseau pointed in the *Discourse on Inequality*. This problem is that potential is not always realized. That means, in this case, that we cannot simply take for granted that the gradual emergence of law according to the 'how it must have been' account has led, or necessarily leads, to a just or republican society in which everyone enjoys civil and moral liberty. According to Rousseau's analysis, the social contract that established the civil state was a bad bargain for all but the rich and powerful, who persuaded the poor and weak to surrender their natural liberty in order to replace the 'right' of the strongest with known and settled laws—laws that have been settled by agents of the rich and powerful. 'Such was, *or must have been*, the origin of society and laws', Rousseau declares, 'which gave new fetters to the weak and new powers to the rich, irretrievably destroyed natural liberty, established forever the law of property and inequality, made clever usurpation into an irrevocable right, and, for the benefit of a few ambitious individuals, henceforth subjected the whole human race to labor, servitude, and misery'.[32] In this respect, the Rousseauvean account clearly has something in common with the interpretation of the self-help model that links

---

[30] Ibid 96 (Bk I, ch 8).
[31] Ibid 92 (Bk I, ch 6).
[32] Ibid 44–5 (emphasis added).

the emergence of the state to the entrepreneurial efforts of a few to take control of what had been a private system of vengeance and vendetta.

What Rousseau presents, then, is a contrast between law's potential and its perversion. Law is the public's business, and life under the rule of law promises freedom from domination—the freedom to be a self-governing member of a self-governing citizenry. That is the law as it ought to be, however, and too often the law as it is, through manipulation by the powerful and ideological distortion, falls far short of what it ought to be. In the case of criminal law, this means that the definition and interpretation of what counts as a crime, and the enforcement of the law's proscriptions, may be largely in the hands of some dominant individuals or groups. It also means that social conditions may make it extremely difficult for many people to live within the law. Crime entails liability to punishment on virtually all definitions of 'crime', but the justice of punishing those who seem driven by circumstances to break the law is hardly obvious. 'The justice of the punishment depends', as the British Idealist TH Green observed, '...not merely on...maintaining this or that particular right which the crime punished violates, but on the question whether the social organization in which a criminal has lived and acted is one that has given him *a fair chance of not being a criminal*'.[33]

The question for a republican theory of criminal law, then, is whether it can point the way toward fulfilment of the law's potential and away from its perversion. To that question I now turn.

4 CRIMINAL LAW AS A REPUBLICAN PRACTICE

The foregoing pages have demonstrated, I hope, that there is a connection between criminal law and the republican concern for publicity. They have also established that a republican 'how it must have been' explanation of the criminal law's emergence provides a plausible reconstruction of the historical foundations of criminal law. But what of the *philosophical* foundations of criminal law? How adequate is this republican account in this respect?

---

[33] TH Green, *Lectures on the Principles of Political Obligation*, §189 (Ann Arbor, MI: University of Michigan Press, 1967), 190 (emphasis added). Anatole France's famous remark about the law forbidding the poor as well as the rich from sleeping under bridges, begging, and stealing bread is also pertinent here, as is, in the recent philosophical literature, Jeffrie Murphy's widely cited 'Marxism and Retribution' (1973) 2 *Philosophy and Public Affairs* 217–43. For a helpful exploration of related issues, see Stuart Green's contribution to this volume, 'Just Deserts in Unjust Societies: A Case-specific Approach'.

To answer this question, it may help to turn to an eminent philosopher of law who is far more likely to be considered a liberal than a republican. That philosopher is HLA Hart, and he is relevant here because of his depiction of the rule of law as a cooperative practice—in his terms, 'a joint enterprise according to rules'.[34] In *The Concept of Law*, Hart gives the following account of law as a practice that is both cooperative and coercive:

The facts that make rules respecting persons, property, and promises necessary in social life are simple and their mutual benefits are obvious. Most men are capable of seeing them and of sacrificing the immediate short-term interests which conformity to such rules demands...On the other hand, neither understanding of long-term interests, nor the strength or goodness of will, upon which the efficacy of these different motives towards obedience depends, are shared by all men alike. All are tempted at times to prefer their own immediate interests and, in the absence of a special organization for their detection and punishment, many would succumb to the temptation...[E]xcept in very small closely-knit societies, submission to the system of restraints would be folly if there were no organization for the coercion of those who would then try to obtain the advantages of the system without submitting to its obligations. 'Sanctions' are therefore required not as the normal motive for obedience, but as a *guarantee* that those who would voluntarily obey shall not be sacrificed to those who would not. To obey, without this, would be to risk going to the wall. Given this standing danger, what reason demands is *voluntary* co-operation in a *coercive* sytem.[35]

What Hart calls 'a special organization for [the] detection and punishment' of those who break the rules that protect 'persons, property, and promises' is usually called the state or government; or, if the emphasis is on the word 'special', some branch(es) of the state or government. Those terms will suffice, but republicans will prefer, for reasons to appear shortly, to call the (comprehensive) entity the polity, commonwealth, or, of course, republic. For now, however, the important point is to understand how a system of laws is a cooperative practice or enterprise.

To say that a legal system is a cooperative practice is to point out, first, that no system of laws can rely entirely on coercion. It is doubtful that even the most thoroughgoing dictatorship, in which the dictator's every wish is an enforced command, can rest entirely on coercion. Anyone who thinks that *laws* cannot be reduced to the commands of the powerful will have all the more reason to believe that a system of laws must depend upon the general cooperation of those to whom the laws apply. For these people, as Hart argues, the law will have the *internal aspect* characteristic of social rules, so that 'some at least must look upon the behaviour in question as a

---

[34] HLA Hart, 'Are There Any Natural Rights?', in AI Melden (ed), *Human Rights* (Belmont, CA: Wadsworth, 1970), 70; originally published in (1955) 64 *Philosophical Review* 175–91.

[35] HLA Hart, *The Concept of Law* (2nd edn; Oxford: Oxford University Press, 1994), 197–8 (emphasis in original).

general standard to be followed by the group as a whole'.[36] In the case of a system of laws, the 'behaviour in question' will consist in taking the laws as rules by which members of the group must guide their conduct—that is, obey the law. By doing so, the members of the group may enjoy the benefits of the rule of law, benefits that would be unavailable to them if there were not sufficient cooperation in the form of obedience to the law.

Obeying the law is sometimes burdensome, however, which points to the second respect in which a legal system is a cooperative practice. Cooperation often entails restraint or sacrifice, and the temptation to avoid doing one's cooperative part is sometimes quite strong—for some people, it seems, frequently so. The temptation is especially strong when one recognizes that it is possible to be a free rider, thereby enjoying the benefits of others' cooperation without bearing one's full share of the burdens of the cooperative practice. Coercion and the threat of coercion are thus necessary, as Hart says, to ensure that 'those who would voluntarily obey will not be sacrificed to those who would not'.[37] In some circumstances, such as the small and close-knit societies Hart mentions, the sense of solidarity will be powerful enough to make the threat of sanctions for non-cooperation almost unnecessary. But those circumstances are rare, and probably growing rarer; and even when they do obtain, the threat of coercion must still be present.

These points should be familiar enough to require no further elaboration here. There is a sense, however, in which the rule of law is a distinctive kind of cooperative practice, and something does need to be said in that regard. To put it succinctly, a system of laws is a *super-* or *meta*-cooperative practice.[38] In other words, the legal order is not only a cooperative practice; it is a cooperative practice that enables people to engage in other cooperative practices. The members of a car pool, for example, are engaged in a cooperative practice that provides them with benefits that they produce for themselves by taking in turns the burdens of picking up and driving those who are sharing the ride. But in order to produce these benefits for themselves, they must also be able to take advantage of benefits provided by the legal order, such as the traffic laws that make it possible for them to drive in relative safety to the workplace, school, play group, or other destination. Unless they live in a libertarian utopia, wherein every inch of their journey takes place on privately owned roads governed by the owners' regulations, they must rely indirectly on the law as a meta-practice if their car pool is to be the joint venture for mutual benefit that they want it to be.

A further implication of this way of thinking about a system of laws is that such a system is necessarily *political*. As a meta-practice, the legal system must establish laws that make it possible for people to engage in other cooperative practices and to

---

[36] Ibid 56.

[37] Ibid 198.

[38] In what follows I develop some sketchy remarks in my 'Punishment as Fair Play' (2008) 14 *Res Publica*, 259–75, at 269.

go about their individual lives. Laws by themselves are not sufficient, however. The members of the car pool need not only traffic laws but traffic signals and roads on which to drive, and these require the collection and expenditure of funds. They also require that decisions be made as to where roads are to be built, what kind of roads they should be, and where the signals should be placed, among other things. What is necessary, in short, is a political order operating under the rule of law.

In a political order of this kind, the political order itself will be a cooperative practice—or, more properly, a meta-cooperative practice. The laws in such an order will be the terms of fair cooperation, or of what the members take to be the terms of fair cooperation. Laws will thus need to be promulgated, and cooperation will need to be encouraged, but the laws themselves will become matters of debate and the products of public decisions. 'What laws do we need?' thus becomes a vital question, as do the related questions of who should make these laws, who should enforce them, and who should apply and interpret them. There is also, finally, the question of how to hold those who make, enforce, and apply the laws accountable to the public—that is, to those who have not only duties but rights as members of the cooperative meta-practice that is the political order.

Conceiving of the legal order as a cooperative practice, in Hartian fashion, thus has a number of significant implications. One is that the legal order is also a political order, with the further implication that the philosophy of law—including the philosophy of criminal law—is entangled with political philosophy. Other things being equal, those who commit crimes threaten the rule of law, and it is necessary to find ways to prevent them from doing anything more than merely posing a threat, and then to punish them on those occasions when the preventive efforts fail. What kinds of actions really do threaten the meta-practice, and should therefore count as crimes, are not always obvious, however. Robbery, rape, murder, and other standard examples of crime clearly threaten the meta-practice, as we can hardly expect people to think and act as participants in a cooperative enterprise when they believe themselves to be in constant jeopardy from those who are supposedly fellow members of the polity. So do offenses that directly threaten the rule of law itself, such as suborning witnesses and other forms of obstruction of justice. But what of flag burning, say, or drug use? Or what of so-called Bad Samaritan laws, according to which those who fail to intervene in or even report a criminal act when they could do so safely are themselves guilty of a crime?[39] Decisions that affect the members of the polity will have to be taken in these and many other cases, which is to say that the definition of crime must in this way be a public or political matter.

Yet another implication of conceiving of the legal *cum* political order as a cooperative practice is that the connection to republicanism becomes more evident. So conceived, the need for what Hart calls a 'special organization for [the] detection

---

[39]   See, eg, J Dressler, 'Some Brief Thoughts (Mostly Negative) about "Bad Samaritan" Laws' (2000) 40 *Santa Clara Law Review* 971–89.

and punishment' of those who would not respect 'persons, property, and promises' is clear. Such an organization, as I said earlier, is usually called a (branch of the) 'state' or 'government'. To the extent that these terms imply that faceless, nameless functionaries are the ones who make, enforce, and apply the laws, however, these terms are less satisfactory than terms such as 'polity', 'commonwealth', or 'republic'. The latter all convey that the law is a matter of public concern—a crucial part of the public's business. Such must be the case if the legal *cum* political order is a meta-practice, for then the terms of fair cooperation will be of vital importance to the government of their lives. That means both the ability to govern their individual lives, free from interference when possible, and the ability to govern their lives collectively through the making of laws, whether directly or indirectly by the election of legislators. Conceived as a meta-cooperative practice, in short, the rule of law implies the two leading features of republicanism—that is, publicity and self-government. That is the republican potential implicit in the law, at any rate, even if that potential is far from realized in actual systems of law, criminal and otherwise.

A final implication is that the conception of the legal *cum* political order as a cooperative practice helps to clarify the *communicative* aspect of the criminal law. According to some philosophers, legal punishment is, among other things, an attempt to communicate to those who break the law the wrongness of their actions, with the aim of bringing them into the fold or restoring them to the community whose standards they have violated. In *Punishment, Communication, and Community*, for example, Antony Duff develops a 'communicative theory' of punishment, 'according to which punishment should be understood as a species of secular penance that aims not just to communicate censure but *thereby* to persuade offenders to repentance, self-reform, and reconciliation'.[40] Similarly, Herbert Morris's paternalistic theory of punishment 'relies essentially on the idea of punishment as a complex communicative act...'; moreover, Morris takes a 'communicative component' to be 'a defining characteristic of punishment' that 'in part distinguishes it from mere retaliation or acting out of revenge...'.[41] But what, we may ask, gives some of us the right or authority to communicate our standards in this way? We may grant that punishment of lawbreakers is a way of communicating the society's, community's, or polity's displeasure with them, but punishment is typically an especially harsh and unpleasant form of communication. As such, it requires more of a justification than, say, a remonstrance or mere expression of disapproval does. Such a justification may be found, however, in the offender's violation of the laws comprising the meta-practice that, *ceteris paribus*, supplies him or her with benefits through the cooperative restraint of others. As part of that practice, we give some of our members

[40] RA Duff, *Punishment, Communication, and Community* (Oxford: Oxford University Press, 2001), xviii–xix (emphasis added).

[41] Both passages quoted from H Morris, 'A Paternalist Theory of Punishment', in A Duff and D Garland (eds), *A Reader on Punishment* (Oxford: Oxford University Press, 1994), 7; originally printed in (1981) 18 *American Philosophical Quarterly* 263–71.

the authority to detect and punish those who do not respect the 'persons, property, and promises' of the other members of the practice—that is, the other members of the polity, commonwealth, or republic. Insofar as the offender enjoys the benefits of the meta-cooperative practice without fully contributing to their provision by bearing his or her share of the burdens of obeying the law, then the offender in effect justifies the rest of us in punishing him or her. In Rousseau's terms, the offender wants to 'enjoy the rights of a citizen without wanting to fulfill the duties of a subject, an injustice that would bring about the ruin of the body politic, were it to spread'.[42] That is why the polity is justified in communicating its censure to the offender by means of punishment. How severely to punish, or whether a mere remonstrance will be sufficient, is a judgment that will have to vary with the severity of the crime and other circumstances; but the *authority* to punish rests on the polity's commitment to the meta-practice of law.

For these reasons, I believe that republicanism supplies a plausible philosophical as well as historical reconstruction of the foundations of criminal law. The account sketched above is too brief to be fully satisfactory, of course, and some parts of it are surely controversial. The justification of punishment that follows from conceiving of the legal *cum* political order, for example, is the oft-criticized reciprocity or fair-play theory. Whether the critics are right, though, remains a matter of dispute.[43] In any case, I believe that it should now be clear that republicanism provides the materials for a coherent philosophical account of the foundations of criminal law with considerable appeal. That this account draws heavily on HLA Hart's conception of law as a cooperative practice suggests that republicanism is capable of attracting wide support. Two worries remain, however, and I now turn to them in concluding this chapter.

5 CONCLUSION

These two worries stem from the suspicion that republicanism may not be an altogether benign approach to either politics or law. When it is taken to provide the underpinnings for criminal law, there is therefore cause for concern that the power of the law will be employed in ways that are inimical to individual liberty and rights. In particular, there is the worry that taking criminal law to be the public's business will lead to some kind of majoritarianism or populism that will declare unpopular

---

[42] Rousseau, *On the Social Contract*, Conaway Bondanella (trans), *Rousseau's Political Writings* 95 (Book I, ch 7).

[43] I respond to the critics in 'Playing Fair with Punishment' (1993) 103 *Ethics* 73–88, and the previously cited 'Punishment as Fair Play'.

acts and practices to be criminal; and even if the majority is held in check, there is the further worry that republican regimes will impose the pursuit of virtue on people who simply want to go about their lives without harming or being harmed by others.

In the space remaining, I cannot hope to set out a fully adequate response to these worries. I can, however, indicate how such a response would proceed. With regard to the first worry, the response is simply the denial that republicans are committed to any kind of straightforward majoritarianism or populism. Indeed, one of the complaints against republicans is that their tendency to exalt the virtues of the arms-bearing, property-owning citizen has led them to be insufficiently appreciative of democracy and of the importance of women to public life. Contemporary republicans have taken pains to meet this objection, but in doing so they have also made it plain that the neo-republican commitment to democracy is not a commitment to the unchecked, unqualified rule of the majority. Not only do constitutionalism, mixed government, and separation of powers remain as important to neo-republicans as to their forebears; they are now supplemented by attempts to devise 'contestatory' and deliberative forms of democracy.[44] Republicans do believe that crime is very much a part of the public's business, to be sure, but they do not hold that crime is simply whatever the majority declares it to be. To take such a position would be to surrender the republican commitment to self-government.

That leaves us, though, with the second worry. Republicans place considerable emphasis on virtue, it may be said, and the desire to cultivate virtue among the citizenry could easily lead to the abuse of the criminal law. Although he does not expressly refer to republicanism in this regard, Jeffrie Murphy's concerns about attempts to use the law, and punishment in particular, to promote virtue are surely apposite. In brief, his concern is that such attempts are illiberal, with liberalism understood to be an ideology that is 'basically *fearful* of government (because of its potential to impose a uniform vision of the good life) and tolerates government only as a kind of *umpire*, an agency to make sure the basic ground rules that preserve individual moral autonomy—such as the rules of toleration—are observed'.[45] Taking liberalism thus understood as his baseline, Murphy then goes on to say:

It is hard indeed to see how any very strong or interesting program of coercive state moral education and improvement is consistent with this outlook—whether carried out explicitly

---

[44] For 'contestatory democracy', see P Pettit, *Republicanism: A Theory of Freedom and Government* (Oxford: Oxford University Press, 1997), 277, and, inter alia, his 'Republican Freedom and Contestatory Democratization', in I Shapiro and C Hacker-Cordón (eds), *Democracy's Value* (Cambridge: Cambridge University Press, 1999). For republicanism and deliberative democracy, especially with regard to criminal law, see JL Martí, 'The Republican Democratization of Criminal Law and Justice' and R Gargarella, 'Tough on Punishment: Criminal Justice, Deliberation, and Legal Alienation', both in Besson and Martí, *Legal Republicanism*, 123–46 and 167–84 respectively.

[45] Murphy, 'Retributivism, Moral Education, and the Liberal State', 8; also R Dworkin, 'Liberalism', in S Hampshire (ed), *Private and Public Morality* (Cambridge: Cambridge University Press, 1978).

in the public schools or in some indirect and symbolic way via criminal punishment. To see such programs as representing a compelling state interest is, I think, simply to abandon the liberal theory of the state.[46]

What is there to say in response to this worry? Those who see a sharp distinction between republicanism and liberalism might well grasp the nettle here and accept that abandoning liberalism is the price to pay for using schools and criminal punishment to promote virtue—a price well worth paying, in their view. For those who deny, as I do, that republicanism and liberalism either can or should be sharply distinguished from each other, a more conciliatory response is appropriate. The key point here is that the kind of virtue that republicans want to promote—the kind that they fear too many liberals have taken for granted—is *civic* virtue.[47] Republicans do want to make people better, in other words, but they want to make them better citizens; and this means, among other things, that they want people to be better observers of 'the rules of toleration' and the other liberal 'ground rules' that Murphy takes to be necessary to the preservation of 'individual moral autonomy'. They also want to foster the conditions under which men and women will be citizens who are willing to do their part in maintaining the cooperative practice that is the rule of law—and who can thus set aside the temptation to violate the person, province, and property of others.[48]

These worries, then, should not deflect us from the project of developing the republican theory of criminal law. Such a theory will take criminal law to be a cooperative, communicative practice that is itself part of the meta-practice of the polity. As such, it will be necessary to determine what activities threaten the existence of the practice as a whole and the interests of its cooperating members, what steps are necessary to prevent these activities, and what measures are to be imposed on those who nevertheless engage in them. In other words, what activities are to count as crimes, how are crimes to be prevented, and how are criminals to be punished? The answers to these questions will for the most part be the standard answers—rape, murder, robbery, and assault must be crimes, for example—and in other cases the answers will vary with the circumstances of the polity. At the most general level, however, the answer will always be the response to this question: what kinds of activities should we proscribe as threats to our republic, should we be fortunate enough to inhabit one, and to ourselves as self-governing citizens?

---

[46] Murphy, ibid 8.

[47] It may be worth noting here that Kyron Huigens, who advanced a republican *qua* virtue theory of criminal law in 'Virtue and Inculpation' (1995) 108 *Harvard LR* 1423, subsequently abandoned republicanism in favour of virtue (or 'aretaic') theory simpliciter: Huigens, 'On Aristotelian Criminal Law: A Reply to Duff' (2004) 18 *Notre Dame J of Law, Ethics & Public Policy* 465, at 483.

[48] To borrow terms from Braithwaite and Pettit, *Not Just Deserts*, 69.

4

POLITICAL THEORY AND THE CRIMINAL LAW

MATT MATRAVERS[*]

1 INTRODUCTION

THIS chapter asks what contractarian political theory can tell us about the place of the criminal law, and of criminals, in a liberal society. It begins by distinguishing two forms of contractarian thinking: one owed to the mutual advantage tradition of Hobbes; the other to the impartialist tradition of Kant. The argument is that both can underwrite a system of criminal law, and of punishment, for similar reasons.

However, at this point the traditions diverge. The mutual advantage tradition allows—indeed, commends—the transmission of natural inequalities into just out-comes. The Kantian tradition, in particular in Rawls, does not. Instead, it posits a position of fundamental equality from which, in distributive justice at least, we move only when, in Rawls's language, we agree 'to share one another's fate'. Much

* Earlier versions of this chapter were given to the UK ALPP Conference at York and to a gathering of lawyers and philosophers at Rutgers. I am grateful to Matt Kramer, Antony Duff, and Stuart Green for their invitations to try out some of these ideas, and to the audiences on both occasions for construc-tive comments. I am also grateful to Antony and Stuart for written comments. I am sure I have not met all their objections, but I have made so many changes (and, I hope, improvements) in response to their comments that I have not noted each one. The first inklings of the ideas discussed in this chapter were batted back and fore with my colleague, Sue Mendus, to whom (as ever) I am indebted.

of the argument then concerns whether it is possible to (and whether there is reason to) apply this Rawlsian insight to the retributive sphere and what it would mean to do so.

The argument proceeds at a high level of both abstraction and generality. To some extent this is inevitable, it seems to me, given that political theory tends to operate at some distance from the immediate and practical and given that it is probably right to do so. Political theory tends to generate general, abstract principles that may well not be fine grained enough to answer the question of whether we should do X or Y when confronted with that choice of policy options.[1] Nevertheless, the chapter concludes with some reflections on the attitude citizens should take to one another and to the criminal justice system that they reflectively endorse in the contract.

2 THE CRIMINAL LAW IN A LIBERAL STATE

2.1 Methodological preamble

One method of inquiry into the philosophical foundations of the criminal law, or (only slightly) more modestly into the place and nature of the criminal law in a liberal state, is to ask what people would agree to in some hypothetical choosing situation (that is, to invoke contractarianism). Contract theory is often alleged to hide substantive normative commitments in itself—and has variously been criticized as sexist, speciesist, and normatively individualistic—but contract theory, suitably understood, need not be any of these things; it all depends on the specification of the choosing situation and of those who do the choosing.[2]

I have argued elsewhere that rational, self-interested choosers could endorse rules of cooperation as moral norms, but in order so to do they would (given certain

---

[1] This is not to say that particular political theorists have not contributed to specific policy debates; clearly they have. However, to use the techniques of critical rational inquiry to examine questions of what we should do differs from deriving what we should do from some abstract political theory. Brian Barry is a useful case in point. His *Culture and Equality* and *Why Social Justice Matters* both offer specific policy proposals. These are said to 'satisfy the reasonable rejectability test' as developed in his more theoretical *Justice as Impartiality*. This claim can be disputed, but even if it is true, it does not mean that these are the only policies that could satisfy the contractarian test (and Barry does not claim that they are). See BM Barry, *Justice as Impartiality: Volume 2 of A Treatise on Social Justice* (Oxford: Clarendon Press, 1995); *Why Social Justice Matters* (Cambridge: Polity Press, 2005); *Culture and Equality: An Egalitarian Critique of Multiculturalism* (Cambridge: Polity Press, 2001).

[2] A particularly useful account of constructivist theorising in general is in BM Barry, *Theories of Justice: Volume 1 of A Treatise on Social Justice* (Hemel Hempstead, Herts: Harvester-Wheatsheaf, 1989), 262–84.

plausible background factors obtaining) also have to endorse a system of punishment.[3] The function of the system of punishment would be to address an assurance problem (parties can only be expected to endorse constraints on their pursuit of self-interest if they can be assured that others will do so too); to communicate to the offender the significance of the commitment to morality (both individual and general); and, where necessary, to educate the offender so as to enhance his ability to engage with others on moral terms. Rationality does not compel persons to endorse the rules of cooperation as moral, it cannot compel acceptance of the system of punishment, but it does not undermine this rationale for these practices.

Clearly, the particular form of contractarianism I defend contains substantive normative and methodological commitments, and these are of course not uncontroversial.[4] However, for present purposes, I intend to try to work with general (I hope), plausible, and less controversial claims in order to develop an account of some aspects of the criminal law that could be accepted at least by most liberals. To give just one example of the kind of consensus with which the paper tries to work, consider the (some would say special) need to justify social arrangements to those individuals who do worst under those arrangements.

According to the contractarian position I defend, it makes no sense to think that justification is owed to others. Rather, the (primary) problem of morality is how to justify to oneself moral constraints on the pursuit of one's self-interest. According to the much more common liberal contractarianism of, for example, Rawls, Barry, and Scanlon, the issue is what we owe and can justify to each other.[5] This dissimilarity reflects a fundamental difference between my argument and that of liberal egalitarians about the nature and scope of morality. Nevertheless, on both accounts it is plausible to think that there is something special about those who do worst under any given set of social arrangements. For on both accounts there is some set of social arrangements, which could be otherwise, under which some persons do worse than others. It seems natural to think, from the one perspective, that some justification needs to be offered to these people in particular,[6] and, from the other, that the problem of justifying to oneself a commitment to constrain the pursuit of one's self-interest in accordance with norms that are part of a set of social arrangements

---

[3] See M Matravers, *Justice and Punishment: The Rationale of Coercion* (Oxford: Oxford University Press, 2000).

[4] Some of the more controversial commitments are usefully brought out, and subject to criticism, in R Shafer-Landau, 'Matt Matravers, Justice and Punishment: The Rationale of Coercion' (2004) 114 *Ethics* 361.

[5] David Gauthier usefully compares the ideas of justification to self and to others in his 'Political Contractarianism' (1997) 5 *Journal of Political Philosophy* 132.

[6] Of course, Rawls goes further than this and gives the worst-off group a special status and the equivalent of a veto on the agreed set of social arrangements, but whether he is justified in doing so is a moot point. Whether he is or not, throughout *A Theory of Justice* it is clear that Rawls thinks that there is a special need to justify inequalities to those who do worse out of them. See JB Rawls, *A Theory of Justice* (Cambridge, MA: Harvard University Press, 1971).

under which one does worse than others, will be particularly acute. As the argument proceeds, more will have to be said about these two forms of contractarianism, not least when they recommend different determinate answers to pressing legal and political problems.

The reference (in the previous paragraph) to the fact that social arrangements could be otherwise hides one substantive commitment. This is to the claim that contractarianism builds on natural facts about us and the world, but that these facts are normatively 'inert'. That is, natural facts themselves are (in Rawls's words) 'neither just nor unjust', and they do not dictate the shape of agreed social arrangements. Rather, we must recognize that 'the social system is not an unchangeable order beyond human control but a pattern of human action'.[7] That system can be just or unjust and it is up to us which it is. For example, the fact that human beings normally feel pain is not in itself just or unjust, right or wrong. It is just a fact about the psychophysical make-up of human beings. But a set of institutions that needlessly allows the inflicting of pain on some set of human beings may well be unjust and, insofar as it is, and we reflectively endorse it in a contractarian thought experiment, we are complicit in that injustice.

I take it that this constructivist commitment need not be shared by all contractarians. For example, a theorist could invoke contractual thinking merely as a heuristic device and use the contractors as means to reflect on the innate moral order of the universe as given by God. Thus in stipulating it as a commitment I am ruling out certain forms of natural law theory (and certain understandings of such things as 'wrongs in themselves'). However, I do not think this is particularly significant. There are other forms of natural law theory that could fit the proposed contractual scheme, but even if that were not the case, the constructivist commitment is something that is shared by those whose liberal dispositions are the target of this chapter.

It is worth making one final remark about the use of contract theory in this chapter. It might be thought that if the argument is going to rely on either shared, uncontroversial, premises, or premises that are explicitly spelt out so as to make differences between contractual accounts transparent, then it could proceed without any reference to 'contract'. The argument would simply move from premise to conclusion. What then is the purpose of the language of contract? Of course, this is a common question asked of contract theory and a line of criticism with impeccable philosophical credentials has it that talk of contracts is (at best) little more than unnecessary window dressing.[8] The answer, the best account of which is given by Samuel Freeman, is that contract theory describes a form of rational reflection. Anyone, at any time, can 'enter' the contract simply by thinking in the manner described in the construction of the hypothetical choosing situation. That person then reasons

---

[7] All quotations from Rawls, ibid 102.

[8] D Hume, 'Of the Original Contract', in D Hume, *Essays—Moral, Political and Literary* (EF Miller ed; Indianapolis: Liberty Classics, 1987).

from premise to conclusion; in the rhetoric, she 'chooses' principles of justice (or whatever). The notion of contract captures two ideas: first, that if the choosing situation is properly constructed then every person entering the contract and thinking in this way ought to be able to acknowledge the conclusions as both right and 'theirs'. Second, each agrees only on the understanding that others do, too. As Freeman puts it, 'the *mutual acknowledgement* of principles...warrants the term "agreement", and the *mutual precommitment* involved might just as well be called a "contract"'.[9]

2.2 Contractarianism and the criminal law

As noted above, I have argued elsewhere that we can—taking up the standpoint of self-interested agents engaged with one another for mutual advantage—reflectively endorse a system of criminal prohibitions, enforcement, and punishment. This is true, too, for Kantian-inspired contractarianism. The reason is that when we 'contract' to live together on moral terms—or terms that bind us together as citizens in a well-ordered society—we do so on the basis that others do so, too, and that we can be reasonably assured of their compliance with the terms of agreement. The state's enforcing of the law—in relation to, for example, taxation—allows each person reflectively to endorse her commitment to the scheme of social cooperation.

As stated, it may not be immediately clear why the assurance problem requires *criminalization* rather than just *regulation*. The short version of the answer is that it does not. However, if the arrangements endorsed by the contracting parties are to be stable and are to avoid some of the well-documented failures of mutual advantage theory, then the parties must affirm the principles by which they agree to be governed as having the imperatival force of moral principles. It is this that makes it a theory of morality rather than of mere cooperation.[10]

---

[9] S Freeman, 'Introduction: John Rawls: an Overview', in S Freeman (ed), *The Cambridge Companion to Rawls* (Cambridge: Cambridge University Press, 2003), 1, 19, original emphasis. These ideas—that by reflective endorsement we commit to social arrangements that we endorse as 'ours'—will be important in what follows.

[10] I believe the above description is sufficiently broad to encompass theories in both the mutual advantage tradition (which includes Hobbes, Gauthier, and the account I defend above) and the Kantian tradition (of Kant, Rawls, Barry, and Scanlon). Differences between the traditions emerge as soon as one digs deeper, in this case, into the nature of the endorsement of the principles as moral. In *A Theory of Justice*, justice and goodness are said to be congruent, so one has reason to endorse the primacy of reasons of justice (relative to prudential reasons of short-term advantage) because to do so is one's good as a free, rational being. This is the account with which Rawls became disillusioned, and in *Political Liberalism* the parties endorse the principles from within their own comprehensive views in an 'overlapping consensus'. In Barry, the contractors are motivated by a sense of justice, which amounts to a recognition of the special place that should be accorded to reasons of justice in practical deliberation. The mutual advantage tradition finds it harder to ground the imperatival force of agreed principles given that the contract is built around the idea of advancing individual contractors' interests. For Gauthier, what makes his theory an account of *morals* by agreement and not *rules*

Failure by one person to adhere to the rules, then, is a moral failure in relation to all others. Moreover, on this account, it is a particularly damaging failure since the scheme works only to the degree that all contractors are willing to make the necessary commitment, which itself depends on their being assured that others will do so too. The appropriate response to such a failure, then, is one of condemnation and not simply of correction. In condemning the offender, the state reasserts the moral value of the agreed principles and reminds the offender of his agreement to abide by those principles. At least, that holds for those who agree to contract by reflectively endorsing the principles as principles that rightfully govern their pursuit of their own advantage. The need to address the assurance problem, and recognition of the prudential reason of agents, underpins an account of hard treatment. The recognition of the moral commitment of the parties to the construction of the community underpins the account of censure and condemnation.

This contractual account of the criminal law is clearly sketchy. The degree to which the procedure can generate precise answers as to the content and scope of the criminal law is an interesting question, but one which I am not going to pursue here. Obviously, given the types of beings that we (human beings) are, the content of the criminal law will concern wrongful harms of certain kinds, and given the kinds of community in which we currently exist, it will also cover certain economic and social spheres. The question I want to pursue concerns the justification of the system as a whole, its relationship to ideas of desert, and the attitude participants should have to one another (including to those who are punished).

3 Contractarianism and Natural (Dis)advantages

Consider the position of those who are born deaf. Presume (plausibly) that modern societies make deafness more of a disadvantage than it would be under other more simple social arrangements. On the account of contractarianism based on mutual advantage, the critical question for the deaf and the hearing is whether mutually advantageous cooperation is possible and, if so, under what conditions.

by agreement is the idea that it can be rational to adopt a disposition (constrained maximization) such that one is disposed to keep agreements even where immediate self-interest might better be served by free-riding. On my account, rationality cannot quite deliver that, so what is required is an 'existential leap' on the part of the contractors see Barry, *Justice as Impartiality*; D Gauthier, *Morals by Agreement* (Oxford: Oxford University Press, 1986); Matravers, *Justice and Punishment*; Rawls, *A Theory of Justice*; J Rawls, *Political Liberalism: Expanded Edition* (New York: Columbia University Press, 2005).

For the mutual advantage theorist, each contractor must advance his interests through cooperation relative to the baseline of non-cooperation. What this may mean is that no mutually advantageous 'deal' can be done, in which case those left outside cooperation are left 'beyond the pale'—the protection of—morality.[11] Where a deal can be done, the bargaining solution will reflect the unequal starting points of the parties and, in this sense, natural advantage and disadvantage will be transmitted through the bargain into the outcome. For many, this is one reason why the mutual advantage tradition in contractarianism is flawed (and worse[12]). For its critics, the job of justice is (at least in part) to protect the weak not least by negating the effects of natural inequalities. This is, of course, at the heart of Rawlsian contractarianism.

As already noted, for Rawls the fact that some people are born, for example, deaf is 'neither just nor unjust'. What can be just or unjust is the social system given the fact that some people are hearing and others deaf. For Rawls, a just social system will not reflect, but will neutralize, natural advantages and disadvantages. 'In justice as fairness', as Rawls memorably puts it, we 'agree to share one another's fate'.[13] That is to say, for Rawls the question of whether the hearing would advance their interests by excluding the deaf from cooperation is not relevant. In reflecting on principles of justice, we realize the morally arbitrary nature of natural (dis)advantages and commit to live together in a well-ordered society. We initially share one another's fates—in this example, we share the fate of the deaf—by excluding knowledge of all personal information in the choosing situation (that is, by imposing the veil of ignorance on the parties in the choosing situation). By doing this we recognize the morally arbitrary nature of natural starting points and ensure that those (unequal) starting points are not automatically transmitted into unequal outcomes (even in the case where allowing natural inequalities to be reflected in the outcome of the contract would be to the advantage of some of us).[14]

Rawls's account of the moral arbitrariness of both social and natural (dis)advantages underpins his radical account of equality of opportunity. If justice requires equality of opportunity, then we should ignore natural (dis)advantage just as we

---

[11] Gauthier (in)famously describes 'animals, the unborn, the congenitally handicapped and defective' as beyond the pale of a morality tied to mutual advantage. See Gauthier, ibid 216.

[12] Will Kymlicka (eg) describes the mutual advantage tradition as not supplying an alternative theory of morality, but 'an alternative morality', and Brian Barry characterizes the position as 'morally pathological'. See Barry, *Justice as Impartiality* and W Kymlicka, 'The Social Contract Tradition', in P Singer (ed), *A Companion to Ethics* (Oxford: Blackwell, 1991).

[13] Rawls, *A Theory of Justice*, 102.

[14] Those who are suspicious of Rawls's (methodological) individualism sometimes baulk at the centrality he accords to ideas such as 'fraternity' and to his invoking (here) of the idea of 'sharing' one another's fate. However, it needs to be remembered that the language of self-interested rational choice is relevant in Rawls only once the original position (the choosing situation) is defined. The characterization of the original position—including the thick veil of ignorance—reflects deep moral convictions (particularly a commitment to fundamental equality).

ignore social (dis)advantage. In general terms, this gives rise to Rawls's non-desert based principles of distributive justice (in which legitimate expectations replace desert), which ensure equality in the distribution of basic rights, equality of opportunity, and inequalities in the distribution of social and economic goods only insofar as those inequalities maximally benefit the least well off.[15]

What this means for deaf and naturally disadvantaged people is something like this: they are, of course, included in the contract and thus are entitled to the protections of the first principle (that is, to equal basic liberties). They are also entitled to equality of opportunity when it comes to the chance to enjoy social and economic inequalities. Quite what this means in practice will be complicated, but the idea is clearly that opportunities should be made available to all wherever it is reasonable to do so. Despite these protections, it may well be that some of those who are naturally (and/or socially) disadvantaged still end up in the economically worst-off group. However, if that is the case, they do not do so because they are less able or less deserving. Rather, there are inequalities in the system—inequalities that allow others to do better than them—only because those inequalities maximally benefit the position of the worst off. In this sense, too, we share one another's fates in that natural features of persons play a role in distribution that is constrained by the system as a whole. If the talented do well it is only because by doing well they benefit the worst off.

What is the relevance of this to questions about the criminal law? On one account, none, because retributive justice (broadly conceived) is different from distributive justice and the arguments in the one sphere do not translate into the other.[16] However, I have argued elsewhere that this is not the case: the same concerns should underpin our analysis of the basic structure whether in relation to retributive or to distributive justice.[17] I will not rehearse that argument here, but I hope that the discussion of the examples that follow will make the case seem plausible (even if not proven).

Allowing that Rawls's broad approach can be applied in the retributive sphere means departing from Rawls's own assumptions of ideal theory and full compliance. It also means applying his account to a question to which he thought it did not apply. That is, one cannot be true to the text and ask what the persons in the original position would choose in relation to criminal justice because Rawls did not believe the question to be one appropriately dealt with in this way.[18] We can depart from Rawls whilst borrowing from his account, though, which is the project here. This

---

[15] See particularly Rawls, *A Theory of Justice*, §48.

[16] This is the argument of Rawls himself and Samuel Scheffler: S Scheffler, *Boundaries and Allegiances: Problems of Justice and Responsibility in Liberal Thought* (Oxford: Oxford University Press, 2001).

[17] See M Matravers, 'Mad, Bad, or Faulty: Desert in Distributive and Retributive Justice', in C Knight and Z Stemplowska (eds), *Responsibility and Distributive Justice* (Oxford: Oxford University Press, forthcoming).

[18] Thus, to ask what a Rawlsian theory of punishment would be like, and to try to answer that question by trying to apply Rawls's theory directly, strikes me as (at best) an invitation to perform intellectual contortions of a quite demanding kind and (at worst) a straightforward mistake. That is not to say

means avoiding the details, but hanging on to the moral commitments that drive the theory.

The place to start, then, is with the construction of the original position. As with natural inequalities and all other personal factors, one's disposition to criminal behaviour would be included in the veil of ignorance (that is, it would not be known to the contracting parties). I have argued above that the contracting parties would have reason to choose—reflectively to endorse—a system of criminal law. What the veil of ignorance adds to that is that one will not know one's risk of falling foul of that law, either because of a disposition to criminal behaviour or because of circumstance, or for that matter mistake (on your part or on that of the system). As a risk-averse contractor, then, one has reason to choose a system in relation to criminal behaviour that is, in the words of the sometime UK Prime Minister Tony Blair, 'tough on crime and tough on the causes of crime'. That is, one will choose a system of criminal law (for the reasons given above), but surround that system with protections—including, but going beyond those of equal legal rights, etc—that reduce the prospect of one being subject to punishment (this will hold even where punishment only affects the offender, but will be even more important given the 'spillover' effects that punishment has on family, friends, job prospects, etc, in the real world).

Clearly this account needs to be unpacked, and there will be those who will have already baulked at being asked to consider natural facts such as talent or disability together with a disposition to criminal behaviour, but it is worth pushing on a little further before considering possible criticisms.

Recall, for the Rawlsian liberal egalitarian, natural facts are what I called morally inert, or what Rawls calls morally arbitrary. This means that we begin with a conception of the members of the society as fundamental moral equals and design the basic structure on that basis. Once the basic structure is in place, our ordinary social practices continue, but on the basis of the principles chosen to govern that structure. 'Thus', as Rawls puts it:

> it is true that as persons and groups take part in just arrangements, they acquire claims on one another defined by the publicly recognized rules. Having done various things encouraged by the existing arrangements, they now have certain rights, and just distributive shares honor these claims. A just scheme, then, answers to what men are entitled to; it satisfies their legitimate expectations as founded upon social institutions.[19]

Put more informally, the argument is this: 'natural' people (so to speak) differ in being more or less talented and in things such as their gender and skin colour. In deciding the principles of distribution of rights, political liberties, and economic and social goods, these things are arbitrary because none is connected to a pre-justicial notion of moral worth. Therefore, they do not figure in the principles of distribution.

---

that nothing interesting results. Eg, see S Dolovich, 'Legitimate Punishment in Liberal Democracy' (2003–04) 7 *Buffalo Criminal Law Review* 307.

[19] Rawls, *A Theory of Justice*, 311.

However, once those principles are in place, the principles may (for reasons of, for example, efficiency) encourage the talented into well-remunerated professions such as brain surgery (one does not want a talentless brain surgeon). In that case, the trainee brain surgeon will develop an expectation that her training, if successful, will be rewarded and that expectation is legitimate.[20]

To apply this to the criminal law, then, would be to insist that inert natural facts ought not to dictate the shape of the principles of (retributive) justice. However, once these principles are in place, such facts may well play a role in where, within the scheme, a given person ends up. Just as the talented (and socially lucky) will tend towards the better-off groups—not because justice requires rewarding the talented, but because rewarding the talented maximally benefits the least well off—those who are disposed to break the criminal law (for whatever reason) will tend towards the group who are punished, but again not because justice requires principles that punish those who act on such a disposition, but because only by punishing them will the system provide the assurance needed to be stable.[21]

Extending Rawls's argument in this way is something for which one can find some encouragement in the text. After all, Rawls famously denies the connection between justice and moral desert. He writes, in a passage that follows directly from that quoted above: 'but what they [persons taking part in just arrangements] are entitled to is not proportional to nor dependent upon their intrinsic worth. The principles of justice that regulate the basic structure and specify the duties and obligations of individuals do not mention moral desert, and there is no tendency for distributive shares to correspond to it.'

It seems to me that the argument offered above is plausible and is, indeed, one that Rawls should have left open. However, as already noted, and as the reference to 'distributive shares' in the last quotation makes clear, Rawls is explicitly committed to the claim that distributive justice is not 'somehow the opposite of retributive justice'.[22] By this, Rawls seems to mean that principles of retributive justice can legitimately refer to the pre-justicial moral worth of the person (or the person's actions), and thus these features of the person are not morally arbitrary.[23] This is a common

---

[20] The legitimacy of this claim is disputed by some including GA Cohen (see GA Cohen, 'Incentives, Inequality, and Community', in S Darwall (ed), *Equal Freedom: Selected Tanner Lectures on Human Values* (Ann Arbor: The University of Michigan Press, 1995), 331–97).

[21] The account offered in the last few paragraphs owes a great deal to a discussion with Jo Wolff at the UK ALPP Conference. What is remarkable is the degree to which the position recalls Rawls's justly famous defence of rule utilitarianism in 'Two Concepts of Rules'. In short, the overall purpose of the system of punishment is given (primarily) by the need for assurance. Once established, the rules governing the application of punishment are retributive. See J Rawls, 'Two Concepts of Rules', in JB Rawls and S Freeman (eds), *Collected Papers* (Cambridge, MA: Harvard University Press, 1955 (1999)).

[22] Rawls, *A Theory of Justice*, 314.

[23] It should be said that Rawls writes of retributive justice in different ways in different places. Sometimes, he comes close to the post-justicial legitimate expectations view described here. Consider the following passage (235): 'A Legal system is a coercive order of public rules addressed to rational persons for the purpose of regulating their conduct and providing the framework for social

response and, if the argument above is to have any plausibility, something needs to be said about the (dis)analogy I am drawing between distributive and retributive justice (and so between, for example, the case of the talentless person who ends up in the worst-off group and the person disposed to break the criminal law who ends up being punished).

I have argued so far that we might think of 'sharing each other's fate' in the retributive sphere in a way that is analogous to the way in which we do that in the distributive sphere. Retributive questions are asked in the original position, and the people in that position do not know their tendency to disobey, or the likelihood that they will fall foul of, the criminal law. They have reason to choose a system of criminal law, but they also have reason to surround that system with protections that will reduce the likelihood of their being punished. Perhaps more radical than that is the suggestion that just as those who do well or badly in distributive terms can only be properly thought of in terms of legitimate entitlement and not desert—one does well because by doing well one maximally benefits the least well off and one does badly only because positions of relative disadvantage exist only so that the least well off can be as well off as possible—so those who are punished are punished not because they (pre-justicially) deserve it but because they are entitled to it under a just scheme in which punishment has some other, non-desert based, rationale.

For some—as we have seen, including Rawls—this position is unsustainable. One version of the objection can be captured if one thinks of one way in which the position of the talentless person who ends up in the worst-off group and the person disposed to criminal behaviour who ends up punished seem disanalogous. In addressing the talentless, it is not just Rawls who might hold that there is something objectionable in saying, just like that, 'the explanation and justification for your being worse off than others is that you are talentless'. However, in the case of the punished, it seems enough to say 'the explanation and justification for your being punished is that you broke the law'. The difference seems to be one of responsibility. According to a well-established liberal position, it is not justifiable to hold people to account, and to make them pick up the burden, for things over which they had no control. The talentless did not choose to be talentless, but the criminal, ex hypothesi, did choose to break the law.

According to one reading of Rawls, 'moral arbitrariness' depends on not being responsible. So, factors such as one's height, intelligence, and talents are morally arbitrary because they are unchosen. On this reading, it is thus because they are unchosen that these features of people are hidden from the view of the people in the original position by the veil of ignorance. If so, and if criminal behaviour is chosen, then one's tendency to criminality would have to be known to the people in the

co-operation. When these rules are just they establish a basis for legitimate expectations. They constitute grounds upon which persons can rely on one another and rightly object when their expectations are not fulfilled.'

original position and thus would be excluded from the realm in which we share one another's fates.

Although there is some textual evidence for this view, it is not Rawls's.[24] Rather, for Rawls the veil of ignorance captures the commitment to the idea that persons are fundamentally equal. Moral desert as a basis for justice is rejected because there is no sensible way of moving from desert to distributive outcomes (an argument that seems to me to be at least as plausible in the case of retributive judgements as distributive ones).

Nevertheless, the responsibility sensitive position is so widespread that it is worth considering its application here before, finally, considering how and in what ways we share the fate of others in the retributive sphere.

3.1 Responsibility and natural (dis)advantage

Consider someone who is disabled, but not visibly so, who enters a two-storey building and asks that the janitor come out to activate the elevator. The janitor may well ask why he should be inconvenienced, but on being told of the disability he would presumably accept that the person has good reasons for needing the elevator and would act accordingly. Contrast this with an agent predisposed to aggression. The case here is more complicated. Assume the agent to have assaulted someone as a result of a perceived (or real) minor slight. In this case, we hold the agent responsible. If the agent explains that he is genuinely incapable of acting otherwise—he has a disorder such that he loses control over himself completely—then that judgement is revised. However, if his explanation is that he is simply the kind of person who is quickly angered and acts on that anger, then we do not think that an excuse. The agent is the subject of our reactive attitudes and is held responsible for his aggressive act.

According to mainstream compatibilist accounts, in both cases the principal actors act for reasons, but the disabled person has good reasons, and reasons that underwrite his not fully bearing the costs of his disability. The aggressive individual also acts on reasons, but it on the basis of so doing that he is rightly held to account and asked to pick up the bill for his actions.

Now, one strategy in response to this might be to deny that compatibilism can do the work asked of it. One might here appeal to the (mis)reading of Rawls that has it that all features of individuals are unchosen and so undeserved up to and including the reasons on which we act. If so, mainstream compatibilism does not adequately justify our reactive attitudes and the practices of blaming and punishing (as well as praising and rewarding) that are associated with them. Compatibilism, arguably,

---

[24] See my M Matravers, *Responsibility and Justice* (Cambridge: Polity Press, 2007).

shows that some form of responsibility is compatible with the truth of 'the causal thesis', but it is a hollow form of responsibility when what we seek is something much more robust to underwrite those practices.[25] Although interesting, I want to put this response to one side.

The second response admits the relevance of responsibility, but only after the system of justice is established. This is, of course, simply to return to the entitlement system commended by Rawls in relation to distributive justice. After all, the student who works hard to be a brain surgeon acts responsibly and is rightly praised. He is not, though, rewarded directly because of his talents (including the talent of working hard), but because the system that rewards people like him maximally benefits the worst off. The reason for this, as we have seen, is not because of some incompatibilist premise that Rawls failed to make explicit. It is that there is no justification for allowing inequalities in natural facts (or social luck) to be reflected in the principles of justice. The initial position of equality is fundamental. Stepping away from equality can be justified in some cases—not in matters of basic rights, but in the economic realm—but on the grounds of advancing the position of the worst off and not on grounds of moral desert. Even were we to attempt to find some proxy for moral desert such as the willingness to engage in conscientious effort, we would be defeated since even that, Rawls notes, is as much to do with one's upbringing as one's natural talents.[26]

4 'SHARING ONE ANOTHER'S FATE' IN RETRIBUTIVE JUSTICE

To recap: I have argued that if we extend Rawls's arguments about the irrelevance of natural starting points and the social lottery from distributive to retributive justice two important things result. First, and unlike the mutual advantage tradition, we exclude the possibility of placing some—the congenitally dangerous, say—outside the protection of justice. Since to do so might well be mutually advantageous for those who remain, I take this to be an initial aspect of what it is to share one another's

---

[25] See eg G Strawson, 'The Impossibility of Moral Responsibility' (1994) 75 *Philosophical Studies* 5; and for a discussion Matravers *Responsibility and Justice*, ibid. The phrase 'the causal thesis' is taken from (but possibly not original to) Scanlon to capture the claim that 'all our actions have antecedent causes to which they are linked by causal laws of the kind that govern other events in the universe'. TM Scanlon, *What We Owe to Each Other* (Cambridge, MA: Harvard University Press, 1998), 250.

[26] Rawls, *A Theory of Justice*, 102.

fate; it is to include all—whatever their ability (or inability) to contribute to the social product. Second, the justification for the system of punishment as a whole will lie primarily in its providing the necessary assurance to make contracting (reflective endorsement) possible. Once in place, the system of criminal law and punishment will give rise to legitimate expectations that the system must honour. The arrangements that give rise to these expectations will be responsibility-sensitive (since it is only by punishing only the guilty that the purposes of the system can be achieved) such that those who are punished can be told that they are being punished because of their actions against a background in which a great deal is done to mitigate natural, and eliminate social, causes of crime. However, in reply to the question of why there should be a system of punishment at all, the answer does not appeal to moral desert—to the idea that the system exists to give pre-justicially deserving people the suffering they deserve—but to the overall good achieved by the system including the good of the person being punished.

I take it that this is the analogue of the scheme of distributive justice in which all (citizens) are included and in which unequal positions only exist to achieve an overall outcome (the best position for the worst off group). Thus, in response to the question of why a given person should be less well off than someone in another position, an explanation can be given in terms of that person's talents, abilities, hard work, and their resulting ability to do 'the various things encouraged by the existing arrangements'. However, asked why unequal positions exist at all (which allow rewards for those things that are encouraged), the answer does not appeal to moral desert, but to the overall position of the least well off. In this sense, too, we share one another's fate.

However, the idea of 'sharing one another's fate' also seems to have a personal dimension that is missing from the above analysis. What, it might be asked, is it to view one another in this light in the retributive domain? To focus on this it might be worth posing a challenge. Recall the disabled person asking for a lift at some inconvenience to the janitor. Given his disability, it is reasonable to ask for the lift and (given certain background facts) it is reasonable that the 'cost' of the lift is somehow shared. More generally, we share the fate of the disabled by paying into general taxation some of which is then spent in providing them with support, ensuring equal opportunities, where reasonable, etc. Compare this, then, with someone predisposed to aggression who enters the building and asks the janitor to take a beating so that he can relieve his aggressive tendencies. Clearly, here, we do not think that the janitor (or anyone else) should comply. Sharing one another's fate must not be reduced to this.

The question of general taxation, though, is more difficult. Obviously, we do not think that we should pay into general taxation to support lifestyles that are criminal or aggressive. However, we do think that it is a reasonable use of general taxation to support those who have fallen foul of the criminal law to rebuild their lives.

Moreover, as I have already argued, we think it is a reasonable use of general taxation to reduce the social causes of crime, and to provide early intervention for those who seem to be set on a path of criminality.

These things, I think, speak to a way in which we share the fate of others at a personal level. Underpinning the position is a sense of the contingency of natural starting points, upbringing, and social arrangements. And this is the final sense of sharing one another's fate that I wish to consider.

It is, as already noted, an aspect of the constructivist position that social arrangements could be otherwise, and that in reflectively endorsing them we together take responsibility for them. It is, of course, also the case that a given set of social arrangements—even a just set—will suit some more than others. This is in part simply a matter of circumstance. For example, given some technological advances, certain skills will become redundant and those who have cultivated those skills will find their relative position in the market reduced. Other skills may, for contingent reasons, be rare and so their market value enhanced. This does not mean that we should not admire the holder of some rare skill, but it does surely mean that our, and her, attitude to her place in the market should be tempered by an awareness of the role of chance and contingency. We do not have to think of ourselves as entirely the hand-maidens of fate to appreciate nevertheless that things could easily be, or have been, different even in a just world.

I take it that the same is true in the retributive sphere. Of course, here choice is more important. The existence of other people with similar skills alters one's market position and that is something that is out of one's control (at least in the first instance). The decision to commit a criminal act is different. And yet, even in a just world, the path that leads to criminality is one that is strewn with contingent features. The modern world provides for many people a confusing, fast-paced, highly stressed environment. It creates criminogenic opportunities and provides temptations in the form of highly valued goods. This is not unjust; it is (as the colloquial saying has it) 'just life'. This does not, on the Rawlsian inspired account offered above, negate responsibility, but it does alter the attitude we have to those who find the temptation to act criminally too strong. If so, then perhaps we should endorse Scanlon's view that whilst there are circumstances in which we can justifiably blame and condemn people, our attitude when we do so 'should not be "You asked for this" but rather "There but for the grace of God go I"'.[27] If so, then the final sense of sharing one another's fate is not to think of criminals as different from the rest of us—as 'them' as against 'us'—but instead as just like us only perhaps less fortunate in either their natural (dis)advantages, their social upbringing, or their 'fit' with the world that surrounds them.[28]

[27] Scanlon, *What We Owe to Each Other*, 294.

[28] Interestingly, Rawls himself hints as such a possibility when he writes towards the very end of *A Theory of Justice* (576) that there may be some for whom 'being disposed to act justly is not a good'. If

5 Concluding Remarks
(or Two Caveats)

The position for which I have argued in the bulk of this chapter flows, I believe, fairly naturally from its Rawlsian origins. For those who are repulsed by the mutual advantage tradition's transmission of natural inequalities into just outcomes, and/or for those who are impressed by Rawls's deep sensitivity to chance and contingency, the argument should have some attraction. However, for others, the conclusions, far from being compelling, may take the form of a *reductio*. If this is what Rawls leads to, they may say, then so much the worse for Rawls. This chapter does not take a position on this. As noted above, my own commitments are to the mutual advantage tradition, which I believe must incorporate something of the personal dimension of sharing one another's fate described above, but in which the scope of who counts as a relevant 'other' is constrained by their ability to bring something advantageous to the contract.

For those who are convinced—or for whom the argument has at least some purchase—the pressure comes from a different direction. The position requires one to face up to the consequences of chance and contingency—not just in the ways in which they affect us directly, but in that even a just world is one that disadvantages some—whilst maintaining individual responsibility for actions. This strikes me as difficult to do, and the step from 'there but for the grace of God go I' to thinking responsibility irrelevant to justice is a short one.[29]

there are many such people, Rawls writes, then 'penal devices will play a much larger role in the social system'. But, of these people, he adds, 'one can only say: their nature is their misfortune'. The emphasis on not seeing offenders as 'them' to be contrasted with the law-abiding 'us' is emphasized throughout Duff's writing.

[29] It is important to note that this is not an argument about doing (retributive) justice in a (distributively) unjust world. That is, of course, an important topic, but the point here is that even a just world is one that is chosen (or reflectively endorsed) and is one in which some people will fare less well than others. Social structures—even just ones—turn some natural facts into social disadvantages. That is no one's fault, but it is something that on the Rawlsian account we all share. In this very loose sense, we can be thought (non-culpably) complicit in crime even while we hold the criminal responsible. If so, I think we can learn from the 'doing justice in an unjust world' literature particularly with respect to the attitude we should take to criminal institutions (and criminals). We should always be hesitant about punishment and its justification and when we use it we should always be conscious of a different way the offender and the social world could have been. If this sounds to some readers like bleeding heart liberalism, then Rawlsians should make no apology for that. Even without distributive injustice, this is a realm in which 'we can say that the hearts of bleeding hearted liberals have good reason to bleed': V Tadros, 'Poverty and Criminal Responsibility' (2009) 43 *Journal of Value Inquiry* 391, 413.

5

FOUNDATIONS OF STATE PUNISHMENT IN MODERN LIBERAL DEMOCRACIES: TOWARD A GENEALOGY OF AMERICAN CRIMINAL LAW

MARKUS D DUBBER*

THE search for foundations of criminal law can be a worthwhile project, even an
important one, both theoretically and practically. Whether it makes sense to limit

* I am grateful to Antony Duff and Stuart Green for many helpful comments and suggestions,
as well as to Lindsay Farmer, Angela Fernandez, and the participants in a workshop at Universidad
Torcuato di Tella (Buenos Aires).

this project to a search for *philosophical* foundations is another question. The philosophicalness of the foundational inquiry either undercuts it or adds nothing to it, depending on what one means by 'philosophical'. It undercuts the foundational inquiry if philosophical is taken to imply an ahistorical, if not unhistorical, mode of inquiry because the search for foundations is essentially, and importantly, also historical. If philosophical simply means theoretical, or perhaps conceptual, then it adds nothing to the inquiry, except perhaps an aspiration somehow to reach beyond, or beneath, empirical historical research, whatever that would be.

The point of a foundational project, as I envision it, would not be historical in the sense of capturing *wie es wirklich gewesen*, nor descriptive, no matter how rich— and richly conceptual—that description might turn out to be, but functional, and, ultimately, critical. The point of an inquiry into the foundations of criminal law, on this account, is to enable and to facilitate critical analysis of the legitimacy of state punishment.[1]

Section 1 considers various ways of conceiving of an inquiry into the foundations of criminal law. Section 2 explores the distinction between modes of foundational inquiry by considering the significance of the *Rechtsgut* principle in German criminal law science, on one hand, and in the jurisprudence of the German Constitutional Court, on the other. Section 3 presents preliminary remarks on an inquiry into the foundations of American criminal law.

1 PHILOSOPHICAL, HISTORICAL, GENEALOGICAL

Initially, it may be helpful to think of the foundational inquiry I have in mind as walking the line between historical and philosophical searches for foundations. If we need a name for this inquiry, we might call it *genealogical* (or, if you prefer, historical-philosophical). One doesn't have to be a Foucauldian (or Nietzschean) to appreciate the attempt to carve out an alternative to what Foucault called the antiquarian and metaphysical searches for foundations, which really simply are sharpened versions of historical and philosophical modes of inquiry.[2] Foucault—channelling Nietzsche— has a very specific, and somewhat elusive, view of what genealogy is, or rather does, that we can safely ignore, and leave to the Foucault scholars, because it doesn't affect

---

[1] See M Dubber, 'Historical Analysis of Law' (1998) 16 *Law & History Review* 159.
[2] See M Foucault, 'Nietzsche, Genealogy, History', in P Rabinow (ed), *The Foucault Reader* (New York: Pantheon Books, 1984), 76.

and may even obscure the main insight: that what we might call a functional, and what Foucault calls 'effective', inquiry into the foundations of criminal law, be it labelled history or philosophy (or genealogy, or anything else), has a point, namely to facilitate, and in fact to enable, the critical analysis of the practice of punishment as an exercise of the law power (*Rechtsmacht*) of the state.[3]

In the end, it makes no difference whether this inquiry is labelled historical, philosophical, or genealogical, theoretical, practical, or even legal or political; what matters is the point of the exercise, which is as central to the enlightenment's critical project as the threat and infliction of penal violence by the state upon its constituents is facially inconsistent with the *raison d'être*, and the legitimatory foundation, of the liberal state under the rule of law (*Rechtsstaat*). Put another way, if the state's penal power isn't subjected to foundational critique, the critical analysis of state power has failed to tackle its most important, and most difficult, task.

This project, though sweeping in scope, is also limited, even parochial, in several senses and it is important to be aware of its limitations, lest the search for foundations of criminal law become a timeless and spaceless exercise in unintentional metaphysics. The first limitation is *legal*, the second *political*, for lack of better words.

The search for foundations of criminal law is, first and foremost, a search for foundations of a particular system of (criminal) *law*, which defines the *subject* of inquiry. In most cases, the subject of inquiry is the searcher's domestic ('own') criminal law system, though this is not always made explicit. It is, of course, possible, though quite difficult, to analyse critically a 'foreign' criminal law system or, less tricky, to take a comparative approach to the critical analysis of the criminal law system with which one is most familiar, using comparison to unearth and highlight features of the system under analysis that otherwise might remain hidden in plain view.[4] This comparative method, though potentially useful, is not a prerequisite; one may identify systemic foundations for use in critical analysis through immanent inquiry.

At the same time, the *method* of inquiry, including its tools and purpose, must be identified, once again limiting the project's scope. The method of inquiry is less limited in scope, yet still parochial. The foundational *political* inquiry I have in mind is essentially an enlightenment project. It is limited to those political systems that profess a commitment to enlightenment ideals of legitimacy, where of course these ideals themselves are subject to critical analysis, along with their manifestation in particular state practices. I consider the concept of personal autonomy, or self-government,

---

[3] On the contrast between the law power (*Rechtsmacht*) of the state and its police power (*Polizeimacht*), see below. These two powers correspond to two, more familiar, conceptions of the state, the law state, or state under the rule of law (*Rechtsstaat*), and the police state (*Polizeistaat*). Criminal law (*Strafrecht*), rather than criminal police (*Strafpolizei*), then, is a particular aspect of the state's law power, rather than its police power.

[4] On different forms and uses of comparative analysis in criminal law, see MD Dubber, 'Comparative Criminal Law', in M Reimann and R Zimmermann (eds), *Oxford Handbook of Comparative Law* (Oxford: Oxford University Press, 2006), 1287.

to lie at the core of the enlightenment critical project in all spheres of ethical life, including morality and politics.[5] Others may disagree, both about the centrality of autonomy and about the specific contours of the concept of autonomy itself. In my view, autonomy is both a formal and substantive concept that refers to both a mode of inquiry (or structural principle) and to a particular concept of the personhood that is presupposed by that mode of inquiry: critical self-analysis by persons through an exercise of some capacity for autonomy presupposes that persons possess—or are thought to possess—that capacity.[6] In this way, autonomy is both the means of the inquiry and its end, which is then used to subject other, less basic, components of the legal system in question to critical analysis, formally and substantively.

It may of course be possible to launch a different foundational inquiry, one that seeks out the foundations of a different cluster of political systems—and the penal power of the state (or who- or whatever holds governmental power) within them—that are not defined by their commitment to enlightenment ideals. Theocratic regimes, or other authoritarian systems, including totalitarian states, characterized by the radical inequality between governor and governed, may be found to have certain organizing principles, or at least common features or dogmas, though their essential heteronomy precludes meaningful *critical* analysis in light of these norms.[7] (Of course, the absence of principles itself would prove illuminating.) At any rate, here, too, a comparative approach may prove helpful, at a more abstract level, using these alternative systems as points of contrast and reference, even if the analysis of a radically different system on its own terms would prove difficult. Insofar as the enlightenment evolved as a critique of these political systems, the boundaries between historical and contemporary ('philosophical') analysis will blur; the enlightenment's critical project, in this sense, cannot be fully appreciated without reference to the modes of state power it arose to critique in the first place.

It is important to recognize, then, that the historical and the philosophical inquiry into foundations, or rather the historical and philosophical aspects of the genealogical inquiry into foundations, are both distinct and complementary. Historical inquiry into foundations of penal practice extends beyond the enlightenment; at the same time, enlightenment principles, which guide philosophical analysis, cannot be understood without reference to the practices that preceded the enlightenment.

---

[5] For a historical perspective, focusing on moral critique, see JB Schneewind, *The Invention of Autonomy: A History of Modern Moral Philosophy* (Cambridge: Cambridge University Press, 1998).

[6] For a useful overview of distinctions among various concepts of autonomy, and their interrelationship, see J Christman, 'Autonomy in Moral and Political Philosophy', in EN Zalta (ed), *Stanford Encyclopedia of Philosophy* (2003), <http://plato.stanford.edu/entries/autonomy-moral/>.

[7] Examples may include theoretical and, especially, programmatic writings on National Socialist criminal law. See eg G Dahm and F Schaffstein, *Liberales oder autoritäres Strafrecht* (Hamburg: Hanseatische Verlogsanstalt 1933) [*Liberal or Authoritarian Criminal Law*]; G Dahm, 'Verrat und Verbrechen,' (1935), 95 ZStW 283 ['Treason and Felony']; F Schaffstein, 'Das Verbrechen als Pflichtverletzung', in K Larenz (ed), *Grundfragen der neuen Rechtswissenschaft* (Berlin: Junker und Dünnhaupt Verlag, 1935), 108 ['Felony as Violation of Duty'].

Obviously, the power and practice of discipline, in households large and small, long precedes the enlightenment, and its history informs the power and practice of contemporary punishment. Even if the enlightenment generated a radically new, even revolutionary, conception of punishment that does not proceed from and reassert the essential superiority of the punisher vis-à-vis the punished, the power and practice of *discipline* did not disappear as a matter of fact from the realm of private, or public, governance, simply through the emergence of a new set of legitimacy requirements (most notably that punishment remain consistent with the equal autonomy of all persons).

In this context, it may be helpful to distinguish between a search for foundations and one for origins. The genealogical inquiry into foundations is also, but not exclusively, historical. Founding moments are significant not because they put in stone a static state of affairs, but insofar as they frame and facilitate a continuous process of creation and action. If we pursue the foundational metaphor a little further, while foundations precede the construction of the building, what matters more is that they set basic parameters for, and also make possible, its existence. Foundations are both part of the structure, and distinct from it. More than one superstructure may be compatible with a single foundation, yet some are more compatible with it than others, and some are altogether incompatible. The price for erecting a superstructure that does not fit its foundation, and even exceeds it, is instability and ultimately collapse under strain. It is possible to change the superstructure, not only by adding to it, internally or externally, but also by rebuilding it, even from the bottom up; changing the foundation is not impossible, but with greater effort, and at greater cost.

Foundations, unlike origins, are not discovered as one might discover the origin of a river by following it upstream. Foundations are made (by Founders' Generations, Founding Fathers, and the like), and may be rediscovered—remade or reconstructed—even if the superstructure above them has been lost, or has been obscured over time. Genealogical inquiry does not presuppose some external reality that awaits discovery through historical or philosophical inquiry; it is not an empirical science, even though it sifts through manifestations of human activity to unearth its fundamental layer, itself a manifestation of human activity.

Here genealogical inquiry is usefully distinguished from the pursuit of the study of state action in the form of law, and more specifically criminal law, as legal science. Legal science, as it was practised in the United States in the late nineteenth and early twentieth centuries and is still pursued in Germany, is an empirical science, in the pursuit of facts about what (the) law is.[8] American legal science used the

---

[8] On German criminal legal science, see MD Dubber, 'The Promise of German Criminal Law: A Science of Crime and Punishment' (2005) 6 *German Law Journal* 1049. More recent work in social science of law ('law and society', 'law and economics', etc) does not treat the study of law itself as a science, but merely applies external scientific methods (sociological, psychological, economic) to law as an object of study (like other social phenomena or human communal activities or institutions, such as playing games or running a gang, or a business).

laboratory of law libraries filled with reports of appellate court opinions to distill doctrinal facts about what the law is. German criminal legal science continues to rely on, and to refine, discoveries of ontological facts about what criminal law (and notably 'crime') is, which are then claimed to generate a comprehensive doctrinal system: Such discoveries include, for instance, the 'ontological structure of criminal conduct' (*ontologische Handlungsstrukur*), which has been found to require intentionality (*Finalität*, literally 'finality') and to account for the relationship between act and omission, and the structure of criminal liability, notably the distinction between unlawfulness and guilt (or responsibility) in its doctrinal manifestation of the distinction between justification and excuse.[9]

By contrast, genealogical inquiry in criminal law is best thought of as seeking to rediscover foundations that are *legal* and, ultimately, *political*, rather than ontological, and therefore susceptible to philosophical discovery: criminal law is regarded as a political act, as one instance of a mode of state governance ('law') that manifests state power. As a political act, its foundations are political, ie located within the project of state government as a whole. As political, the foundations of criminal law are also man-made (or, rather, person-made) and therefore subject to discussion and agreement, to disagreement and critique, both actually (see Habermas) and constructively (see Kant's and Rawls's thought experiments). Certain commitments may be so basic as to be beyond, or beneath, negotiation, but they remain commitments nonetheless, though as foundational their compromise, or outright rejection, will draw the political project as a whole into question, by weakening ('compromising') or even destroying its foundation.

2 CRIMINAL LAW SCIENCE AND POLITICAL LEGITIMACY

This distinction between philosophical and political foundations of criminal law may be illustrated by a dispute about the relative significance of basic tenets of German criminal legal science, as discovered by German criminal law scientists (ie German criminal law professors), and principles of German constitutional law, as promulgated by the German Constitutional Court in light of the German Basic Law. The dispute arose, or at least emerged, in a well-known judgment in which

---

[9] See eg E-J Lampe, 'Zur ontologischen Struktur des strafbaren Unrechts', in T Weigend and G Küpper (eds), *Festschrift für Hans Joachim Hirsch zum 70. Geburtstag* (Berlin: Walter de Gruyter, 1999), 83.

the Constitutional Court upheld the constitutionality of the incest provision in the German Criminal Code.[10] The result is less significant than the reasoning, in the course of which the Court brushed aside a fundamental tenet of German legal sci-ence, the *Rechtsgut* principle, as constitutionally irrelevant, and instead insisted on applying the standard flexible and deferential means-ends proportionality analysis of German constitutional law that the Court had developed over the six decades of its existence.[11]

As discovered by German criminal law science, the *Rechtsgut* principle declares— subject to considerable variation among different versions of the principle, a fact that is significant in its own right but which we'll ignore for present purposes—that the criminal law may only be employed to protect a *Rechtsgut* (law good), and that only certain objects qualify as a *Rechtsgut*.

Standard constitutional analysis under the general rubric of proportionality, by comparison if not contrast, looks to see whether the statute under review pursues a legitimate purpose and does so in a reasonable way, with the legislature enjoying considerable leeway on both ends and means. The Court, then, saw its job in the incest case simply as coming up with a list of purposes, any or all of which could be reasonably considered legitimate (which they could) and then checking whether the statute could be seen as reasonably related to this purpose or these purposes (which it could). In the Court's view, the *Rechtsgut* concept did not enter into the analysis.

In one reading of the case, it pitted one doctrinal system (of constitutional law) against another (of criminal law). In this light, the German Constitutional Court and German criminal law professors/scientists are engaged in the same type of project: as German criminal law scientists ponder the *Sein* of crime, German Constitutional Court judges— along with German *constitutional* law professors/scientists—ponder the *Sein* of constitution (or of dignity, liberty, 'twoness in oneness',[12] etc).

Alternatively, and for our purposes more helpfully, the case can be seen as setting up a contrast between, on one hand, a political inquiry into the legitimacy of state power by subjecting an exercise of that power through penal law to scrutiny in light of basic constitutional principles,[13] and, on the other, an application of the results of

---

[10] BVerfGE 120, 224 (26 Feb 2008).

[11] For a more detailed discussion of this case, see MD Dubber, 'Moral Police and Constitutional Law' (2011) 61 *U Toronto Law Journal* ___ (Symposium on Constitutionalism and the Criminal Law).

[12] See [1993] *BVerfGE* 88, 203 (Second Abortion Decision) (relationship between mother and embryo); cf H Weinkauff, 'Der Naturrechtsgedanke in der Rechtsprechung des Bundesgerichtshofes' (1960) NJW 1689.

[13] See eg A Brudner, *Punishment and Freedom* (Oxford: Oxford University Press, 2009) (criti-cal analysis of the legitimacy of state punishment as a matter of political and constitutional theory). Constitutional law, of course, also can block critical analysis of the legitimacy of state power rather than facilitate, and reflect, it, particularly in legal systems with written constitutions. For instance, the American law of criminal procedure is both over-constitutionalized and, at the same time (and not coincidentally), under-theorized. Rather than providing the doctrinal means for inquiries into the legitimacy of various procedural institutions and practices, American constitutional criminal procedure obscures these inquiries by instead becoming entangled in superficial doctrinal matters

a philosophical inquiry into the nature of *Rechtsgut* conducted by expert criminal law scientists without reference to these constitutional principles.

Of course, other—political, rather than ontological, phenomenological, or metaphysical—approaches to *Rechtsgut* theory are easily imagined. After all, the *Rechtsgut* principle could be said to derive from an account of state power in a liberal democracy committed to the manifestation of *Recht*, or right, understood as the recognition of the equal personhood of state constituents based on their shared capacity for autonomy, or self-government. It is true that such an account of the *Rechtsgut*, though theoretically straightforward enough, would fly in the face of the actual origins, development, and deployment of the concept, which was driven by an effort to expand, or at least to reflect the expansion of, the scope of criminal law beyond the manifestation and protection of personal right.[14] What matters at this point, however, is not whether a political account of *Rechtsgut* is ultimately convincing, but whether it is possible. In fact, traces of a political account of *Rechtsgut* can be found in recent contributions to German criminal legal science, as well as in the dissenting opinion in the German Constitutional Court's incest judgment, authored by Judge Winfried Hassemer, (not so) coincidentally a leading German criminal law professor and critical contributor to the *Rechtsgut* literature.[15] To take a further step, it should be possible to integrate a political account of *Rechtsgut* into the political account of constitutionality developed by the German Constitutional Court (or any other such account), by establishing (rather than simply asserting) the *Rechtsgut* concept's constitutional status.

Nonetheless, it is significant that German criminal legal scientists have made few, if any, serious efforts either to constitutionalize the *Rechtsgut* principle or even to recognize its political foundation within some account of the legitimacy of state power,

---

revolving around the interpretation of the specific (and very sparse) constitutional provisions in question, notably the 4th, 5th, and 6th Amendments to the US Constitution. See M Dubber, 'The Criminal Trial and the Legitimation of Punishment', in RA Duff et al (eds), *The Trial on Trial* (Oxford: Hart Publishing, 2004), 85, 85–8.

[14] See generally MD Dubber, 'Theories of Crime and Punishment in German Criminal Law' (2006) 53 *American Journal of Comparative Law* 679. The concept first emerged in the early nineteenth century as a positivistic challenge to PJA Feuerbach's theory of crime as a violation of subjective right (*Recht*), which could not account for morals and public order offenses, incidentally including incest, among (a great many) others. JMF Birnbaum, 'Über das Erforderniß einer Rechtsverletzung zum Begriffe des Verbrechens' (1834) 15 *Archiv des Criminalrechts (Neue Folge)* 149. The competing conceptions of crime as violation of, and threat to, (objective) goods (*Güter*), rather than (subjective) rights (*Rechte*) were then combined in the late nineteenth century into the concept of *Rechtsgut* and placed at the heart of Karl Binding's highly influential theory of criminal law, where the state's right to punish was 'nothing but the right to obedience of the law' and *Rechtsgut* had morphed into 'anything that the legislature considers valuable and the undisturbed retention of which it therefore must ensure through norms'. K Binding, *Handbuch des Strafrechts*, vol 1 (Leipzig: Duncker und Humblot, 1885), 169.

[15] See eg W Hassemer, *Theorie und Soziologie des Verbrechens* (2nd edn; Frankfurt/Main: Europäische Verlagsanstalt, 1980).

apart from its standing as a constitutional legal norm. There are several explanations for this failure, including sociological ones having to do with status relationships between professors and judges, particularly politically appointed judges (as opposed to professional judges who rise through the judicial bureaucracy, such as judges on the German Supreme Court) and the general decline in status among German professors in general.

In the present context, the most notable explanation derives from the sense that *Rechtsgut* is a philosophical, rather than a political, concept that is open to ontological inquiry by experts in the science of criminal law—ie (German) criminal law professors.[16] As such, the *Rechtsgut* is not only beyond the discretion, but beyond the grasp, of Constitutional Court judges—or, for that matter, of constitutional law professors. They must content themselves with consulting the discoveries of those experts who can appreciate the 'ontological or Dasein-related' aspects of *Rechtsgut*.[17] Note, however, that there is nothing about the concept of *Rechtsgut* that would mark it as an exclusively *criminal* legal concept; this limitation, and the claim to criminal law professors' particular expertise in all things *Rechtsgut*, instead reflects the limited, and generally apolitical, approach to the concept of *Rechtsgut* (from *Recht* to *Gut* to *Rechtsgut*) in German criminal law science.[18]

It is tempting, though perhaps facile, to dismiss this ontological-scientific inquiry into foundations of criminal law for any number of reasons, including that it is self-serving, undemocratic, obscurantist, and anachronistic.[19] But what matters here is not whether the ontological search for foundations is worthwhile or (re)commendable, but what constitutes it and more precisely, what distinguishes it from the sort of genealogical *political* inquiry I have in mind. Similarly, it doesn't make a difference whether the political inquiry into foundations of criminal law takes the form of the sort of hands-off constitutionality analysis favoured by the German Constitutional Court or of an attempt to ground the *Rechtsgut* in foundations of legitimate state power. What matters is to get a sense of the genealogical project, of its point and method, in contradistinction to other foundational projects, historical or philosophical.

---

[16] On remaining ontological foundations of German criminal law science, see MM Hernández, 'Über die Verknüpfungen von Strafrechtsdogmatik und Kriminalpolitik', in B Schünemann et al (eds), *Festschrift für Claus Roxin zum 70. Geburtstag* (Berlin: Walter de Gruyter, 2001), 69, 89.

[17] D Spinellis, 'Die Strafbarkeit der "sexuellen Belästigung" nach griechischem Recht', in B Schünemann et al (eds), *Festschrift für Claus Roxin zum 70. Geburtstag* (Berlin: Walter de Gruyter, 2001), 1467, 1469.

[18] As purely descriptive, positivistic accounts, such as those of Birnbaum and Binding, of course are not meant to play a role in critical analysis in the first place.

[19] For a recent attempt to make sense of German criminal law scholarship's self-conception as science, see Urs Kindhäuser, 'Die deutsche Strafrechtsdogmatik zwischen Anpassung und Selbstbehauptung: Grenzkontrolle der Kriminalpolitik durch die Dogmatik?' (2009) 121 ZStW 954.

3 GENEALOGICAL FOUNDATIONS OF AMERICAN CRIMINAL LAW

An inquiry into the foundations of American criminal law in particular, be it historical, philosophical, or genealogical, faces another challenge, aside from clarifying the nature and function of the foundational inquiry at stake. Defining the subject of the foundational inquiry, however framed, encounters the same difficulty faced by any discussion of 'American criminal law'. The risk is that one indeterminacy is replaced by another; while it is difficult to speak non-metaphysically about foundations of criminal law, period, it is only slightly less difficult to speak sensibly about foundations of American criminal law, which in the end may prove to be simply another artificial construct assembled, or presupposed, for the sake of theoretical inquiry.[20]

In an important sense, American criminal law no longer exists, if it ever did. Despite an ever-growing body of federal criminal law, criminal law in the United States remains primarily a state matter. Unlike in other modern liberal democracies, including, say, Germany and Canada, there is no single national criminal code (not even one as antiquated and unsystematic as Canada's nineteenth-century Stephen Code). The closest thing there is—and perhaps ever has been—to a body of American criminal law is, ironically, an unenacted model code drafted by a private organization of lawyers, judges, and academics devoted to law reform, the American Law Institute's Model Penal and Correctional Code, conceived in the interbellum period during the 1920s and 1930s and drafted between 1952 and 1962 under the directorship of Herbert Wechsler of Columbia.[21]

In a way, the Model Penal Code is very much *not* 'American criminal law', both because no American jurisdiction adopted it in its entirety (nor was it designed to be adopted in toto, rather than to provide reform-minded legislatures with a blueprint for criminal law reform—not unlike other optimistic and progressive how-to manuals of the time, such as Norval Morris and Gordon Hawkins's *Honest Politician's Guide to Crime Control*[22] or, less explicitly, Herbert Packer's *Limits of the Criminal Sanction*[23]) and because it was specifically intended as a *model* code, ie, as a model for comprehensive criminal law reform, in contrast to the ALI's efforts in

---

[20] Consider (eg) the construct 'Anglo-American' criminal law, which is at best a convenient shorthand and at worst a gross over-simplification that blocks the sort of careful comparative cross-systemic inquiry that might reveal noteworthy similarities and differences. See Dubber, 'Comparative Criminal Law', 1287.

[21] On the history of the Code project, see SH Kadish, 'Codifiers of the Criminal Law: Wechsler's Predecessors' (1978) 78 *Columbia Law Review* 1098; MD Dubber, 'Penal Panopticon: The Idea of a Modern Model Penal Code' (2000) 4 *Buffalo Criminal Law Review* 53.

[22] N Morris and GJ Hawkins, *The Honest Politician's Guide to Crime Control* (Chicago: University of Chicago Press, 1970).

[23] HL Packer, *The Limits of the Criminal Sanction* (Stanford, CA: Stanford University Press, 1968).

other areas, notably torts and contracts, where *Restatements* of the law were deemed sufficient. The Model Code, then, emphatically was not what American criminal law is, or was, but what it should be—or at best, what it could be at its very best. At any rate, since the Model Code was not adopted everywhere, or in fact anywhere, with many states following it substantially, others less so, and some (along with the federal government) not at all, it does not reflect American criminal law as it is today, in the sense of the sum of disparate bodies of state (and federal) criminal law based on separate (state and federal) criminal codes and separate bodies of (state and federal) case law.

Ideally, then, the foundational inquiry would focus on a body of criminal law that is recognizably distinct, such as the criminal law system of any of the states or, more problematically, the federal government—or, more interestingly, on American *military* criminal law (as codified in the Uniform Code of Military Justice) or even the criminal law of Native American tribes, which raise intriguing questions about the origin, nature, and scope of sovereignty and therefore of the power to punish (and, more specifically, the power of criminal law, ie the power to make and impose criminal norms, and to inflict sanctions for their violation). Perhaps it is enough, and for present purposes it will have to be enough—not least because American criminal law scholars have shown little interest in producing reasonably systematic or at least comprehensive *contemporary*, never mind historical, accounts of any particular system of American criminal law[24]—to acknowledge the diversity of American criminal law systems, to point to the Model Penal and Correctional Code as the closest available approximation of a system of American criminal law (at least *de lege ferenda*) and at any rate to shift the task from a genealogy of American criminal law to one of American criminal laws. By abstracting from the diversity of present American criminal law—as a collection of criminal law systems that is usefully compared to the systems that would constitute 'European criminal law', if that term were used in this sense (rather than as the criminal law of the European Union, analogous to federal criminal law in the United States)—one can set out to trace the genealogy of that collection of criminal law systems often labelled 'American criminal law', a task that presumably will result in the discovery of foundational commonalities at some point in the not too distant past.

This way of proceeding is not unfamiliar in American legal and political discourse, as the United States, like France, continues to view itself in light of a certain foundational moment, or moments (depending on what significance is attributed to the Civil War). The difficulty with this approach is not so much formal, or methodological,

---

[24] For some exceptions, from the casebook literature, see PW Low, *Federal Criminal Law* (2nd edn; New York: Foundation Press, 2003); N Abrams, SS Beale, and SR Klein, *Federal Criminal Law and Its Enforcement* (5th edn; St Paul, Minn: West Publishing, 2006); M Moskovitz, *Cases and Problems in California Criminal Law* (Cincinnati, Ohio: Anderson Publishing Company, 1999); SF Shatz, *California Criminal Law: Cases and Problems* (2nd edn; Newark, NJ: LexisNexis, 2004); MD Dubber, *New York Criminal Law: Cases and Materials* (New York: Aspen, 2008).

as substantive. The common foundational moment in American legal and political history—signified by the Revolution, the Declaration of Independence, and the US Constitution (including the original Bill of Rights)—did not concern itself with the foundations of criminal law as a manifestation of the state's power to punish. The common foundation of 'American criminal law' thus is an absence, which is to say two things: first, that there was no foundational moment of American criminal law as such; and, second and related, that the foundations of American criminal law, such as they are, precede the foundations of American law and politics. Few doubt, at least in the United States, that the late eighteenth century generated a new, distinctly American, ideal of government, a new political science and, less clearly, a new concept of law, or at least of the significance of law (Thomas Paine's 'THE LAW IS KING!'), however ill-defined the concept of law remained. It did not, however, produce a new ideal of criminal law.

In other words, the foundational moment of American law was not the foundational moment of American criminal law. What is distinctive, and in this sense foundational, about American criminal law during the foundational moment of American law instead is the very fact that there is no foundational moment of American criminal law. The Enlightenment's comprehensive critique of law and politics identified punishment as an instance of state power that was in particularly dire need of legitimation, not relegitimation in light of new ideas and principles, but legitimation for the very first time after millennia of unquestioned, and unquestionable, penal might (*Strafmacht*), understood as the hard essence of sovereignty.

The Enlightenment did not merely produce new answers to the question of why the state has a right to punish, but posted the question for the very first time, and with great urgency. Punishment was no longer beyond legitimation as a manifestation of the sovereign subject's authority over the objects of government. Now viewed as a particularly direct and prima facie illegitimate violation of the very rights the state existed to manifest and protect, punishment desperately required legitimation in terms of the fundamental principle of legitimacy, autonomy, or self-government, which in the political sphere reflected the capacity for autonomy that defined the equal personhood of all state constituents. Only a system of penal power that respected all persons as such, ie as beings with a capacity for autonomy, could hope to survive the Enlightenment's comprehensive critique.

In the United States, by contrast, the traditional conception and system of penality survived the foundational and constitutional moment essentially undisturbed. The foundations of the state's penal power remained not only unchallenged, but unexamined, and unnamed. In occasional, off-hand, references to the source of that power, courts, or commentators, when moved to state the obvious, might remark that the power to punish was one, if a particularly obvious, instance of the state's comprehensive and discretionary power to police, ie the power to safeguard and maximize the public welfare in all of its myriad aspects.[25] The police power in turn was defined by its very undefinability, as amorphous and unquestionable as sovereignty itself, which was transferred unchanged from 'the king' to 'the people', an intentionally apersonal construct that obscured the nature of sovereignty rather than altering it, thereby complicating its critical analysis rather than facilitating it.[26]

Here, I think, it is useful to differentiate the distinction among branches of government from the fracturing of sovereignty itself. The division among governmental functions—legislative, judicial, executory—or the 'separation' of the attendant powers to perform these functions, is neither essentially democratic nor monarchic. The sovereign acts through all state actors, no matter what function they perform; and the police power, as an essential feature of sovereignty, is exercised by all branches of government. Police power, like sovereignty, is an attribute of state governance, not of any particular 'branch' or 'department'.

The search for the foundational moment of American criminal law, as a manifestation of the state's power to police, then is a search for the foundational moment of the concept of police or, more fundamentally still, the concept of sovereignty it embodies. Sovereignty, however, is always already there, complicating a search for its foundations, if not making it altogether impossible. Moreover, insofar as sovereignty is by its nature beyond critique, it resists genealogy in the present sense, ie as the search for tools for critical analysis of the legitimacy of state institutions. Still, as a historical and conceptual matter, it is possible to investigate the foundations of the power to police, and the attendant concept of sovereignty.

As I have argued at length elsewhere,[27] the underlying concept of sovereignty as the nature of political power is grounded in the ancient concept of householdership, ie the power of the householder (*oikonomos*) to govern his household (*oikos*).[28] The police power is the modern manifestation of that power, which emerged as the mode of governance was transferred from the micro household of the family to the macro household of 'that great family, the State', in Rousseau's phrase[29] or, 'the individuals of the state, like members of a well-governed family', in Blackstone's.[30] The police power is the mode of governing the state as a matter of 'political economy',

[25] See eg *Foucha v Louisiana*, 504 US 71, 80 (1992); *Sutton v New Jersey*, 244 US 258 (1917); CE Laylin and AH Tuttle, 'Due Process and Punishment' (1922) 20 *Michigan Law Review* 614; WR LaFave and AW Scott, Jr, *Substantive Criminal Law* (2nd edn; St Paul, Minn: West, 1986), § 2.10; see generally MD Dubber, *The Police Power: Patriarchy and the Foundations of American Government* (New York: Columbia University Press, 2005).

[26] See MD Dubber, 'The State as Victim: Treason and the Paradox of American Criminal Law', in M Kremnitzer and K Ghanayim (eds), *Offences Against the State* (forthcoming 2011).

[27] MD Dubber, *The Police Power: Patriarchy and the Foundations of American Government* (New York: Columbia University Press, 2005).

[28] See K Singer, 'Oikonomia: An Inquiry into Beginnings of Economic Thought and Language' (1958) 11 *Kyklos* 29.

[29] JJ Rousseau, *Discourse on Political Economy* (1755).

[30] W Blackstone, *Commentaries on the Laws of England* vol 4 (Oxford: Clarendon Press, 1769), 162.

ie, as a matter of resource management of the body politic, composed of human, and other (animate and inanimate) resources; it is, simply, 'the power to govern men and things'.[31]

Locating the foundation of the police power in ancient Greece not only helps to elucidate the inner structure of police as a mode of governance, but also makes clear that the police power cannot be regarded in isolation, but must be seen in contrast to, and in tension with, another mode of governance rooted in Athenian political life. From the very beginning, the concept of *oikos* was contrasted with the concept of *polis*, a contrast that often, somewhat misleadingly or at least blandly, is put in terms of the distinction between private and public.[32] Whereas the *oikos* was governed by the *oikonomos* (or, less politically, the *despotēs*, lord, master), the *polis* was governed by the *politikos*.[33] The *oikos* was essentially *heteronomous*, characterized by other-government; the *polis* was essentially *autonomous*, characterized by self-government. The *oikos* was defined by the radical distinction between governor and governed, between *oikonomos* and *oikos*, the subject and object of government; the *polis* was defined by the radical equality of governor and governed, of *politikos* and *politikos*, who would govern himself and others as himself.

Each sphere of governance is worthy of analysis by itself, in an effort to define its scope and contours, its structure and mode of operation. Initially, however, it is worth considering the interaction, and interrelation, of the two. While the spheres of governance were distinguished carefully (more carefully by some, notably Aristotle, than others, Plato), they were also complementary and connected through the personal unity of the *oikonomos* and the *politikos*—the *politikos* in the *agora* was the *oikonomos* at home. Other-government at home qualified men for self-government in city life; the capacity for (political) autonomy was evidenced by the capacity for (domestic) heteronomy. Public equality presupposed private inequality, the *polis* presupposed the *oikos*. While the two spheres of government were seen as complementary, it could not be said that *oikos* presupposed *polis*. Historically, and conceptually, the family preceded the city, *oikonomika* preceded *politika*, and heteronomy preceded autonomy. Anxieties triggered by the prospect of collapsing the distinction between the two spheres, at least since Aristotle, have tended to concern the elimination of the political, rather than the oeconomic, sphere, which is regarded as a reversion to a pre-political state of affairs, historical or not, with the development of the notion of equality and self-government being seen as a more recent phenomenon, if not accomplishment (or discovery).

---

[31] License Cases, 46 US (5 How) 504, 583 (1847); see M Dubber, '"The Power to Govern Men and Things": Patriarchal Origins of the Police Power in American Law' (2005) 52 *Buffalo Law Review* 1277.

[32] See eg DB Nagle, *The Household as the Foundation of Aristotle's Polis* (Cambridge: Cambridge University Press, 2006); J Roy, '"Polis" and "Oikos" in Classical Athens' (1999) 46 *Greece & Rome, Second Series* 1.

[33] For an interesting discussion, see A Virtanen, 'General Economy: The Entrance of Multitude into Production' (2004) 4 *Ephemera* 209.

It is fruitful, I think, to see the distinction between police and law in light of the ancient distinction between *oikonomika* and *politika*. The concept of police, or of political economy, then, appears as a comprehensive and systematic attempt to break down the distinction between private and public modes of governance through the expansion, or if you prefer the transfer, of household governance from the micro family to the macro family of the state. Domestic, or familial, economy becomes political, or state, economy. The state as a whole is now regarded as a ('great') family, as heteronomous resource management spills over into the public sphere.

The tension between *oikonomia* and *politika*, however, remains; it is, in fact, sharpened as it is transferred onto the macro level of state governance. Whereas heteronomy and autonomy once co-existed as the appropriate modes of governance for the private and the public sphere, respectively, now both stand in direct tension at the state level, as police and law, and as the police (or welfare) state (*Wohlfahrtsstaat*) and the law (or justice) state (*Rechtsstaat*). Heteronomy and autonomy are brought into direct contrast at the same level of government, in the same political sphere, as the objects of governance are both and at the same time radically different than (and inferior to) the subject—from the perspective of police—and identical with (and equal to) it—from that of law.

The critical analysis of state punishment makes this tension between police and law, between heteronomy and autonomy, particularly visible. From a police perspective, state punishment is not so much obviously legitimate as it is obviously in no need of legitimation. *Naturally*, the sovereign-householder is empowered to wield penal discipline as a tool of human resource management in whatever circumstance and in whatever manner he sees fit. Without the power to discipline, he would lack the power to police, and without the power to police he would be no sovereign. The connection between the police power and sovereignty was so tight, and so unquestionable, that American federalism—a topic that, unlike the legitimacy of the power to punish, did attract considerable attention during the foundational period of American law and politics—rested on the insistence that the states must retain the power to police and, to drive home the point, that the national government must *not* have the power to police. Depriving the states of their police power would have meant stripping them of their sovereignty and simply incorporating them, as points of delegated power, into a unitary national state.

Within the police realm, then, the legitimacy of state punishment is, quite literally, a non-issue. The legitimacy challenge of state punishment only emerges if one shifts into the realm of law. Suddenly, state punishment appears no longer as a quintessentially sovereign act of state, but as the intentional infliction of violence upon a person. From the perspective of police, punishment is an act of heteronomy through which the superior subject of government inscribes his very superiority onto the body of its object, and as such is beyond reproach. It is precisely this conception of punishment that could not withstand critical analysis from the perspective of law. Legal punishment, punishment under the rule of law (not of police), cannot be essentially heteronomous. Legal punishment instead must be autonomous, of persons by persons for persons.[34]

Incidentally, what is often portrayed as the second constitutional moment in American legal and political history, triggered by the Civil War, also did not reach the issue of the legitimacy of state punishment. When Lincoln called for government of the people, by the people, for the people, the 'people' did not include criminal offenders as passive ('of') or active ('by') citizens, nor as beneficiaries ('for'). The Thirteenth Amendment to the US Constitution abolished slavery and involuntary servitude except as criminal punishment, and late nineteenth-century prison law, such as it was, considered incarcerated felons as rightless 'slaves of the state'.[35]

During the (original) American foundational moment, if questions of criminal law attracted the attention of the Founding Fathers living, and making, that moment at all, which was rare enough, they concerned the expedient use of the criminal sanction rather than the prior question of its legitimacy. So the contributors to the Federalist papers can be seen exploring the use of penal discipline to suppress internal rebellion, which they treated as a problem of public political health (ie of health police), with Hamilton insisting on the need for 'punishment for disobedience',[36] notably 'the disorderly conduct of refractory or seditious individuals'.[37] Penal sanctions, he explained, were required to remove those 'seditions and insurrections...that are, unhappily, maladies as inseparable from the body politic as tumors and eruptions from the natural body'.[38] The Bill of Rights, of course, did end up addressing itself to some issues in the penal process, but the relevant provisions, too, presumed the existence and legitimacy of a system of state punishment and were content to regulate the pre-trial and trial process of investigation (search, seizure, confrontation, jury, etc), ie the stage of the penal process before the classification of its objects as 'offender' (or 'felon') rather than as mere suspects or defendants.[39]

There was one notable, but ultimately only apparent, exception to the general failure to recognize, never mind to address, the question of the foundations of the state's power to punish in the course of the comprehensive analysis of the

---

[34] The focus of this chapter is not on any particular account of the philosophical foundations of criminal law, but on the foundational project in general. For recent citizen-, rather than person-, based theories of state punishment and criminal law, see, eg, RA Duff, *Answering for Crime* (Oxford: Hart Publishing, 2007); C Brettschneider, 'The Rights of the Guilty: Punishment and Political Legitimacy' (2007) 35 *Political Theory* 175; G Jakobs, 'Bürgerstrafrecht und Feindstrafrecht' (2004) 5 *HRR-Strafrecht* 88; M Pawlik, *Person, Subjekt, Bürger* (Berlin: Duncker und Humblot Verlag, 2004); see generally M Dubber, 'Citizenship and Penal Law' (2010) 13 *New Criminal Law Review* 190.

[35] *Ruffin v Commonwealth*, 62 Va 790, 796 (1871).

[36] A Hamilton, Federalist No 15, pp 73, 78; A Hamilton, Federalist No 21, p 106.

[37] A Hamilton, Federalist No 16, pp 81, 85.

[38] A Hamilton, Federalist No 28, pp 146, 146.

[39] On the pointlessness of procedural 'protections' in the face of an unconstrained and unconsidered substantive penal regime, see eg HM Hart, Jr, 'The Aims of the Criminal Law' (1958) 23 *Law and Contemporary Problems* 401, 431; see also M Dubber, 'Toward a Constitutional Law of Crime and Punishment' (2004) 55 *Hastings Law Journal* 509.

foundations of American law and government during the American *Gründerzeit*.[40] Thomas Jefferson, having returned to Virginia after his work on the Declaration of Independence, drafted a criminal law bill (or rather, more modestly, a 'Bill for Proportioning Crimes and Punishments in Cases Heretofore Capital') as one of his contributions to a general revision of Virginia law in light of 'our republican form of government'. '[N]ow that we had no negatives of Councils, Governors & Kings to restrain us from doing right', Jefferson set out to 'correct[]' the law of Virginia 'in all it's [sic] parts, with a single eye to reason, & the good of those for whose government it was framed'.[41]

Jefferson's criminal law bill is worth a closer look because it captures the founding generation's lack of interest in criminal law, and notably the foundations of and legitimation of criminal law. Jefferson picked up criminal law only after the committee member who had originally been assigned the topic (George Mason) resigned. The closest thing to a 'leading principle[]' that the committee's brief consideration of criminal law yielded was the 'lex talionis'. By far the most original, and potentially foundational, part of the bill was its preamble, which is worth reproducing in full:

Whereas it frequently happens that wicked and dissolute men resigning themselves to the dominion of inordinate passions, commit violations on the lives, liberties and property of others, and, the secure enjoyment of these having principally induced men to enter into society, government would be defective in it's [sic] principal purpose were it not to restrain such criminal acts, by inflicting due punishments on those who perpetrate them; but it appears at the same time equally deducible from the purposes of society that a member thereof, committing an inferior injury, does not wholly forfiet [sic] the protection of his fellow citizens, but, after suffering a punishment in proportion to his offence is entitled to their protection from all greater pain, so that it becomes a duty in the legislature to arrange in a proper scale the crimes which it may be necessary for them to repress, and to adjust thereto a corresponding gradation of punishments.

And whereas the reformation of offenders, tho' an object worthy the attention of the laws, is not effected at all by capital punishments, which exterminate instead of reforming, and should be the last melancholy resource against those whose existence is become inconsistent with the safety of their fellow citizens, which also weaken the state by cutting off so many who, if reformed, might be restored sound members to society, who, even under a course of correction, might be rendered useful in various labors for the public, and would be living and long continued spectacles to deter others from committing the like offences.

And forasmuch the experience of all ages and countries hath shewn that cruel and sanguinary laws defeat their own purpose by engaging the benevolence of mankind to withhold prosecutions, to smother testimony, or to listen to it with bias, when, if the punishment were

---

[40] For a more detailed analysis of the bill, see MD Dubber, '"An Extraordinarily Beautiful Document": Jefferson's Bill for Proportioning Crimes and Punishments and the Challenge of Republican Punishment', in MD Dubber and L Farmer (eds), *Modern Histories of Crime and Punishment* (Stanford, CA: Stanford University Press, 2007), 115.

[41] T Jefferson, *Autobiography* (1821).

only proportioned to the injury, men would feel it their inclination as well as their duty to see the laws observed.

Here Jefferson comes closer than anyone in the founding generation to formulating the challenge of the legitimacy of state punishment in the new self-governing republic. Since the state's purpose is to safeguard the 'lives, liberties and property' of its constituents, it has the right (and even the duty)[42] to 'restrain such criminal acts'—which are defined as 'violations on the lives, liberties and property' of their fellow state constituents—'by inflicting due punishments on those who perpetrate them'. Yet, not every criminal offender (ie violator of others' fundamental rights) by his criminal act 'wholly forfiet[s] the protection of his fellow citizens'. Those who inflict 'inferior injury' and have good rehabilitative prospects 'might be restored sound members to society'. Others, whose 'existence is become inconsistent with the safety of their fellow citizens', are 'exterminate[d]', if only as the 'last melancholy resource'.

This is not much of an account of the foundation of state punishment, but it does indicate at least an attempt to connect the institution of state punishment to the state's *raison d'être* in the new republic, its 'principal purpose'—safeguarding the rights of its constituents. The legitimacy of punishment is not problematized, but taken for granted; still Jefferson at least states the obvious in terms that would be open to the possibility of critical analysis: the question may have an obvious answer, but it remains a question. Punishment is not simply dismissed as beyond legitimation as a—and in fact the most visible—manifestation of state sovereignty.

This is as far as it goes. While Jefferson grants that some offenders may retain their status as state constituents, provided their deficiency (in their capacity for autonomy—they are not governed by themselves, but are under 'the dominion of inordinate passions') is treatable through penal reform, others are 'cut off' from the body politic, much as the seditious 'tumors' and 'maladies' that in the Federalist were thought to require penal intervention as a matter of public health. Even the reformable offenders are kept alive as public resources, or 'long-continued spectacles'.[43] Recall that the notion of penal servitude survived even the abolishment

---

[42] On the duty to punish, see K Günther, 'Is there a Responsibility to Protect By Criminal Law?' (2011) 61 *U Toronto Law Journal* ___ (Symposium on Constitutionalism and the Criminal Law).

[43] Capital offenders, too, might serve as public spectacles, as in the case of those convicted of duelling, who were hanged, and, if they were the challenger, had their body gibbeted after death; the removal of their corpse, for good measure, was declared a misdemeanour and 'the officer' instructed to 'see that it be replaced'. Sec VI. In another bill, Jefferson set out in greater detail what he had in mind for those convicted of non-capital offences: '[M]alefactors...shall be employed to row in the gallies of the commonwealth, or to work in the lead mines, or on fortifications or such other hard and laborious works, for the behoof of the commonwealth, as by the Governor and Council, in their discretion, shall be directed: And during the term of their condemnation...shall have their heads and beards constantly shaven, and be clothed in habits of coarse materials, uniform in color and make, and distinguished from all others used by the good citizens of this commonwealth...' A Bill for the Employment,

of slavery in the Thirteenth Amendment, some seven decades later. Exterminating the useful offender would be a waste of human resources; excessive punishment is bad resource management. At the margins, extreme disproportionality in fact may not merely be imprudent, but—as 'cruel and unusual', in the familiar words of the Eighth Amendment, copied from the English Bill of Rights of 1689, which itself drew on Magna Carta—may manifest a basic unfitness for the job of householder, on the ground that 'the heart is wrong'.[44]

When penal discipline is clearly inconsistent with proper householding—ie safe-guarding and maximizing, in other words, managing resources—it may suggest that it is not penal discipline at all; instead it is an acting-out on the part of the governor/ householder who, in the guise of heteronomous household rule, in fact displays the very incapacity for rule—of himself and others—that marks the objects of his power as objects. As a slave to his passions (his malice, cruelty, etc), he has revealed himself (as measured through prudential devices such as the rule of thumb or the depriva-tion of life or limb) as unfit to govern, and as fit to *be* governed instead.[45] And so the limitation on the state's power to punish (as laid out in the Eighth Amendment and its—very similarly worded—state analogues) emerges as rooted in the same police paradigm that Jefferson's preamble cannot, in the end, transcend.[46]

It is of course unfair to subject Jefferson's short preamble to his short Virginia criminal law bill to prolonged critical analysis. It is the closest thing to a recognition of the idea of new foundation of criminal law in the new republic that the founding generation produced. It could well have been developed into a more comprehen-sive account of the new criminal law in light of the fundamental principles that drove the revolution. And such a comprehensive account, rather than Jefferson's brief comments in the preamble, would then be the proper object of sustained criti-cal analysis. But no such comprehensive account materialized. The preamble is not only brief, and ambiguous in its recognition of the enormity and the importance of the task of legitimating criminal law *as law* as part of a project that viewed itself as a radical reconsideration of the fundamentals of state power, it also had no impact whatsoever.

Jefferson's contemporaries ignored it; Jefferson scholars ignored it; and, what's most telling, Jefferson himself ignored it, not just in general and later on, but in the very bill to which the preamble is attached. The bill itself bears virtually no trace of the preamble's approach to the problem of state punishment in the new republic. The bill instead is a haphazard collection of unconsidered restatements of common law punishments, as described by Lord Coke, whom Jefferson greatly admired. The

---

Government and Support of Malefactors Condemned to Labour for the Commonwealth, in JP Boyd et al (eds), *Thomas Jefferson, Papers*, vol 2 (Princeton, NJ: Princeton University Press, 1950), 513.

[44] *United States v Clark*, 31 F 710 (EDMich 1887).
[45] See Dubber, '"An Extraordinarily Beautiful Document"', 115, 122–4.
[46] See generally ibid 115.

lex talionis—true to Jefferson's rendition of the Virginia law revision committee's brief discussion of criminal law—makes several appearances, both in the text of the bill and in the copious footnotes, which contain so many quotes from Anglo-Saxon dooms that the editor of Jefferson's papers had to enlist the services of an Anglo-Saxon scholar. Ducking, whipping, and the pillory appear as sanctions, as does castration or, in the case of a female offender, 'cutting thro' the cartilage of her nose a hole of one half inch diameter at the least' (for 'rape, polygamy, or sodomy'), along with poisoning (as talionic punishment for poisoning) and maiming (for maiming).

Jefferson did spend a lot of time on the criminal law bill, not on its substance, but on its form. He created two versions of the bill, with ornate marginalia in the style of his admired Coke. So eager was Jefferson to adopt a Coke look that he adopted Coke's spelling by, for instance, changing the spelling of 'forfeit' to 'forfiet' (see above).[47] In the end, Jefferson used the criminal law bill as an elaborate, and time-consuming, calligraphic exercise, practising and displaying his superb penmanship.[48] The best that can be—and has been—said about the bill by the few Jefferson biographers and editors who have paid attention to it is that it is an 'extraordinarily beautiful document'.[49]

In hindsight, Jefferson's modest preamble to his universally ignored (and never enacted) criminal law bill for the state of Virginia turns out to have been the (first and) last best chance for engagement with the foundations of American criminal law.[50] The foundational moment had passed, to be invoked but never repeated. The second constitutional moment of the Civil War and its immediate aftermath did not, and could not, create a new republic, nor critique the foundations of law and politics with the original radicalism of the revolutionary period and its Founding Fathers. At any rate, it did not generate a fundamental revision of American criminal law in light of basic principles of legitimacy. Instead, the Civil War period served to cement the pre-revolutionary view of penality as beyond critical analysis and, specifically, constitutional scrutiny. In this way, the Thirteenth Amendment abolished slavery while at the same time reaffirming, in the constitution itself, the essential aconstitutionality of the state's penal power.

---

[47]   JP Boyd et al (eds), *Thomas Jefferson, Papers* vol 2 (Princeton, NJ: Princeton University Press, 1950), 504.

[48]   Ibid 505; cf D Malone, *Jefferson and His Time* vol 1: *Jefferson the Virginian* (Boston: Little Brown and Company, 1948), 269–70.

[49]   Ibid 269–70.

[50]   Edward Livingston's ambitious, and also unenacted, criminal codes were an exercise in codification, and more particularly the application of Bentham's 'great principle of utility!'; they did not undertake a critical analysis of the legitimacy of state's power to punish in a republic based on the principle of autonomy, but instead sought to categorize and, perhaps, to rationalize the exercise of that power in various doctrinal contexts. See Kadish, 'Codifiers of the Criminal Law', 1098; E Livingston, *The Complete Works of Edward Livingston on Criminal Jurisprudence*, vol 1 (New York, 1873).

American criminal law doctrine, if not its foundations, did not come in for a comprehensive reconsideration until the 1950s, when the American Law Institute turned its attention to the subject. (The ALI first dealt with criminal procedure, in 1930; World War II intervened before it could attend to substantive criminal law.) The project was headed up by Herbert Wechsler, who in 1937 had published a progressive criminal law manifesto in a two-part article co-authored with his Columbia colleague Jerome Michael, entitled 'A Rationale for the Law of Homicide'.[51] Though drafted in the 1950s and early 1960s—and completed in 1962—the Model Penal and Correctional Code reflected the programme set out in 'A Rationale', which both recognized the lack of serious interest in criminal law as a subject of study, or reform, in the United States (thus necessitating a model code, rather than a restatement) and set out to 'rationalize' the subject in light of the progressive ideas of the day.[52] This meant reconceiving criminal punishment as peno-correctional treatment, replacing woolly notions of malice and intent with scientific inquiries into dangerousness, and constructing the penal system as a system for the identification and treatment of abnormally dangerous offenders. The Model Penal and Correctional Code thus had four parts, the first two of which (the Penal Code) were devoted to the modernized version of the traditional rules of criminal liability, reconceived as preliminary judicial diagnoses of dangerousness leading to preliminary 'sentences', and the latter two (the Correctional Code) concerned themselves with the individualized professional diagnosis and treatment of that dangerousness as it manifested itself in specific offenders.[53]

The Model Penal Code had no patience for what it considered anachronistic and pre-scientific notions like autonomy or the will (as evidenced, for instance, by its refusal to define voluntariness requirement for criminal liability so as not to 'inject into the criminal law questions about determinism or free will'[54]). Its treatmentist approach fits more comfortably with the police paradigm of human resource management (by the state of abnormal individuals) than with the law paradigm (of equal respect for the dignity of persons as endowed with a capacity for autonomy). At any rate, the Model Penal Code did not set out to derive an account of criminal law from the foundations of law and politics. The ALI is not a body of Platonian statesmen, or Founding Fathers, but a group of legal professionals, founded in 1923 'to promote the clarification and simplification of the law and its better adaptation to social needs, to secure the better administration of justice, and to encourage and carry on scholarly and scientific legal work'.

---

[51] J Michael and H Wechsler, 'A Rationale of the Law of Homicide' (Parts I & II) (1937) 37 *Columbia Law Review* 701, 1261.

[52] See Dubber, 'Penal Panopticon', 53; MD Dubber, *Victims in the War on Crime: The Use and Abuse of Victims' Rights* (New York: New York University Press, 2002), 128–47.

[53] See M Dubber, *Criminal Law: Model Penal Code* (New York: Foundation Press, 2002), ch 1; Dubber, 'Penal Panopticon', 53.

[54] *Model Penal Code and Commentaries* § 2.01, at 215 (1985).

The Model Code project, then, cannot be seen as a foundational moment in American criminal law. It was successful within the scope of its ambition—it triggered widespread reform of American criminal codes and provided American criminal law teaching and scholarship with a common, if artificial, platform. It did not, however, facilitate the critical analysis of the legitimacy of state punishment. The Model Penal and Correctional Code took the sovereign's penal power for granted and, from that assumption, proceeded to devise the most sensible (and practically palatable) system for its exercise.[55] Ironically, it had virtually no effect on the terms of criminal law discourse. While its rules—notably its taxonomy of mental states—reshaped criminal law doctrine, their underlying treatmentist rationale was ignored, no matter how explicitly and systematically that rationale was set out, as early as 1937, and applied throughout the Penal Code (parts 1 and 2) and the Correctional Code (parts 3 and 4). (In fact, the Correctional Code, which makes up the second half of the Model Code, has been ignored in its entirety, even though, from the Code's treatmentist perspective, the Penal Code makes no sense without the Correctional Code since it functions as the gateway to the latter, by producing the rough and penologically amateurish preliminary diagnoses that are fine-tuned under the regime set out in the Correctional Code.)

To ignore does not mean to reject. The point is that the Model Penal and Correctional Code neither sought nor produced nor stimulated an inquiry into the foundations of criminal law. To the extent it relies on systematic considerations that go beyond, or beneath, concerns of good housekeeping (such as clarity, consistency, or even rationality, narrowly construed), ie to the extent it presented itself as working out the treatmentist program sketched in 'A Rationale' (and other publications of the period, not only in the United States), the Model Code had no impact, or rather it appeared to make no difference that it chose to present itself in this way, rather than in any other.

4 CONCLUSION

And so the genealogy of American criminal law goes nowhere. American criminal law remains without foundations and, what's more, without an inquiry into its foundations. This absence of foundations helps account for the phenomenon of the War on Crime, which recently has morphed into a War on Terror, without any noticeable systematic resistance in the form of foundational principles that required

---

[55] Herbert Packer called this the drafters' 'principled pragmatism'. HL Packer, 'The Model Penal Code and Beyond' (1963) 63 *Columbia Law Review* 594.

engagement. Doctrinal rules about 'mens rea' and 'actus reus', for instance, are but ancient broadsheets blowing in the wind of imminent threats to the authority of the sovereign or the welfare of the household under its/his control. Anachronistic slogans are no match for the rhetoric of emergency.

Of course, the genealogy of American criminal law as an inquiry into founda-tions that may serve as the point of reference for critical analysis is not empty if one broadens the scope of the inquiry from criminal law, to law, and eventually to state government in general. Then the task of critical analysis becomes one more of application than of excavation, or reconstruction. The philosophy of criminal law would then be concerned with the question of how a system of criminal law might manifest the fundamental principle, or principles, of legitimate state power, in other words, what criminal law *as law* would look like. Even though this strikes me as a worthwhile endeavour, the genealogy of American criminal law, narrowly speak-ing, remains significant if only because the critical analysis of a particular system of law must have an account of its absence. It is a meaningful, and arguably distinctive, feature of American criminal law that it has escaped critical analysis in light of foun-dational principles for so long and that the legitimacy of state punishment attracted no attention at the very foundational moment which is to serve as the basis for its belated critique, when so many other exercises of state power were scrutinized with great enthusiasm (taxation!).

With all this talk about the absence of an inquiry into the foundations of criminal law as law, one might get the sense that the police model not only represents the real-ity of American penality but also that it has been showered with sustained attention. That sense would be mistaken. It is one thing to point out that police is essentially discretionary, undefinable, and ultimately alegitimate; it's another to say that the police model is inconsistent with serious analysis, period. The absence of compre-hensive treatments of penality as *police* is not a necessary feature of the police model. And yet there can be no talk of a well-worked-out project of American criminal police. American penal police, then, is not only essentially discretionary, but the sovereign in fact has exercised that discretion without systematic guidance.

The police sovereign, of course, is not bound by principle, or legitimacy con-straints, to develop, recognize, or follow guidelines of any kind. But that is not to say that choosing to guide its discretion in this way would be inconsistent with its sovereignty. After all, even the ancient Greeks had their studies of *oikonomia* (as an art, rather than a science), Florence had Machiavelli's *The Prince*, seven-teenth- and eighteenth-century German and French rulers had their police science (*Polizeiwissenschaft*) and their police treatises (for example, Delamare's *Traité de la police* (1705–1738)), and slaveholders in the American antebellum South had their plantation manuals.[56] In legal academe, the economic analysis of law has shown

---

[56] See JA Bush, 'Free to Enslave: The Foundations of Colonial American Slave Law' (1993) 5 *Yale Journal of Law and the Humanities* 417, 426.

little, if any, interest in imagining an efficient system of crime control (occasional programmatic efforts, notably by Richard Posner, notwithstanding[57]), which is not to say that American state officials would be inclined to accept the guidance of whatever systems of, or approaches to, criminal police might be generated. In the end, the foundations of American criminal police no less require attention than do the foundations of American criminal law.

[57] Eg RA Posner and TJ Philipson, 'The Economic Epidemiology of Crime' (1996) 39 *Journal of Law and Economics* 405.

6

RESPONSIBILITY FOR THE CRIMINAL LAW

ALICE RISTROPH

EVERY crime is a collective endeavour. Social factors often influence the acts of individual offenders, but that is not the collective aspect of crime emphasized here. Even if we cannot identify social factors that led to a given offender's act, even if we believe in free will and are convinced that this criminal has acted on it, his crime is still a collective endeavour. This is so because the very category crime is distinctively political. Political here refers to the public and collective enterprise—the polity—and law is a dimension of the political rather than an alternative to it. Perhaps sin is pre-legal and pre-political, but crimes take place only in the context of a political community that has established a legal system.[1] As an illustration, consider the difference between killing and murder. Death is at least conceptually independent of the law, as are killing and being killed.[2] But murder is a legal construct, and the construction of law is a public, collective enterprise. Indeed, the Latin word *crimen* referred not to the offender's action but to the public one—to the accusation and judgment. Even once the English word crime began to be used to refer to the prohibited act,

---

[1] 'For sin indeed was in the world before the law was given, but sin is not counted where there is no law.' Romans 5:13 (English Standard Version).

[2] I say at least conceptually independent, because as legal regulation reaches more areas of human conduct, legal definitions of death become increasingly important and may supplant extra-legal understandings.

it remained important to distinguish crime from sin and to emphasize, again, the political, constructed character of crime.[3] The maxim *nullum crimen sine lege* is not simply a preference for the notice afforded by clearly drafted criminal statutes; it is a reminder that crime literally does not exist in the absence of law. And law is inevitably a collective endeavour.

A theory of crime, or criminal law, thus needs to be attentive to the collective entity that makes crime. Criminal law theory needs political theory. This point has been made before, most often with respect to justifications of punishment, but it bears re-emphasis. There is a difference between the claim that wrongdoers should be punished and the claim that the state should punish them; a properly political theory must address the latter claim.[4] But punishment is not the only dimension of criminal law that involves the collective enterprise. We need accounts of the process by which crimes qua crimes come into being and the political consequences of bringing them into being. It is not just punishment, but also criminalization, policing, and prosecution that need to be subject to the analytical and evaluative scrutiny of political theory.

Nowhere has criminal law theory been less attentive to political collectivities, and more focused on the individual, than in its discussions of responsibility. 'Criminal responsibility' has almost always been characterized as a question about the individual offender.[5] The dominant paradigm, I think it is fair to say, is what Arthur Ripstein has called 'the agency conception of responsibility', an umbrella term that includes various theories concerned with the circumstances in which 'a deed or consequence is attributed to the agency of its author'.[6] An agency conception may encompass some empirical inquiries related to causation, so that an offender is responsible for harms she causes but not for those she does not cause. More often (but not exclusive of the causal inquiries), responsibility has been theorized as a normative concept: to say someone is responsible is to make a normative judgment about that person. Whether the normative judgment is dependent on various empirical claims is a

---

[3] T Hobbes, *Leviathan* (Richard Tuck ed; Cambridge: Cambridge University Press, 1996), 201.

[4] 'Just because the offender might deserve punishment, it does not follow—without an appropriate theory of state power—that the state should assess the degree of deserved punishment and use its power to impose it on the offender. The quick assumption that the state is entitled to punish offenders who "deserve" it is one of the unfortunate banalities of criminal law in our time.' G Fletcher, *The Grammar of Criminal Law: American, Comparative and International, Volume 1: Foundations* (New York: Oxford University Press, 2007), 153.

[5] '[W]hy is modern legal theory apparently so preoccupied with individual responsibility? The individualism of modern criminal law theory is one of its most remarked upon features, and an increasing amount of space is given over to the analysis and specification of the conditions of individual liability.' L Farmer, *Criminal Law, Tradition, and Legal Order: Crime and the Genius of Scots Law 1747 to the Present* (Cambridge: Cambridge University Press, 1997), 141. For a critique of the individualist approach to criminal responsibility, see A Norrie, *Punishment, Responsibility, and Justice—A Relational Critique* (New York: Oxford University Press, 2000).

[6] A Ripstein, 'Justice and Responsibility' (2004) 17 *Canadian Journal of Law & Jurisprudence* 361, 361–2.

matter of ongoing dispute. As neuroscientists and psychologists present new evidence about the factors that influence human decision making, some scholars argue that we must rethink criminal responsibility, while others maintain that criminal responsibility is a moral concept indifferent to medical science.[7] Notably, both sides of this debate assume that the key questions for criminal responsibility are questions about the individual offender—her acts, her brain, her self-control, her moral blameworthiness. Responsibility is a matter of agency, but the only agent visible to most theories of criminal responsibility is the wrongdoer herself.

But if we keep in view the political character of crime, it is clear that responsibility for crime is a question of collective responsibility. Members of a political entity develop and enforce the criminal law, and those acts of public agency need the theorist's scrutiny. When one agent is held responsible, some other agent or group of agents is doing the holding. And a theory of criminal law must consider *those* exercises of agency: the choices to criminalize, to prosecute, and to punish. In other words, an account of criminal responsibility must not rest with attributions of responsibility for individual criminal acts; it must address collective responsibility for the criminal law itself.

There are other ways, beyond making and enforcing the criminal law, in which a community or a state might be said to be collectively responsible for crime. A state that knowingly fosters, or even just permits, criminogenic conditions is arguably complicit in subsequent offences.[8] A complete account of criminal responsibility should address this form of collective responsibility as well. But the responsibility of greatest interest in this chapter is not analogous to complicity. The claim is not that the state caused the offender to act in a particular way. The claim is that the state designated this act as a crime and chose to prosecute and punish it. For these public acts, there is collective responsibility. That responsibility should be part and parcel of any theory of criminal responsibility.

I develop these claims further in three sections. First, I identify some of the distinctive inquiries and methods of a political theory of criminal law. I then turn to the concept of responsibility and offer a revisionist, or perhaps rehabilitated, account of criminal responsibility. On this account, the accused individual does not stand isolated as the responsible agent; instead, criminal responsibility is also a matter of the public and collective agency exercised throughout the processes of criminalization, prosecution, adjudication, and punishment. In a concluding section, I connect my examination of responsibility for the criminal law to questions about responsibility for other forms of bureaucratic violence. In the criminal law, as in other contexts

---

[7] Stephen Morse, who takes the view that neuroscientific research is largely irrelevant to the criminal law, describes some of the major points of contention in a recent article. SJ Morse, 'Thoroughly Modern: Sir James Fitzjames Stephen on Criminal Responsibility' (2008) 5 *Ohio State Journal of Criminal Law* 505.

[8] Eg, V Tadros, 'Poverty and Criminal Responsibility' (2009) 43 *Journal of Value Inquiry* 391, 404–5.

where state officials regularly authorize and use physical force, decisions and actions are often fragmented across complex bureaucratic structures. Tracing responsibility in such contexts is not easy. I do not solve the puzzles of political responsibility here, but I do seek to show that those puzzles should be part of an inquiry into criminal responsibility.

1 POLITICAL THEORY AND THE CRIMINAL LAW

What does it mean to offer a political theory of criminal law? Some preliminary methodological observations may clear the ground, though to offer them is to risk fuelling petty disciplinary squabbles, and maybe also omphaloskepsis. But given that much criminal law theory, and theories of criminal responsibility in particular, tend to obscure the political context of the criminal law, the methodological preliminaries may be worth these risks.

Political theory is a capacious field with uncertain boundaries. Judith Shklar once described 'the most obvious task of political theory' as 'the elucidation of common experience, the expression of what is inarticulately known to groups of people at any time'.[9] Her description implies an element of contingency in political theory—it is a form of knowledge, but knowledge particular to place and time. To be sure, in the history of political thought one finds no shortage of claims of universal and eternal truth. But the enterprise of political theory involves a continual re-examination of those claims. On many accounts, theorizing is an activity, an effort to understand some observed spectacle or phenomenon.[10] (Michael Oakeshott suggests an etymological connection between theory and theatre: both terms are related to the Greek *thea*—something seen, a spectacle, an occurrence.[11]) *Political* theory presents a puzzle in that the spectacle of politics is not clearly determined a priori. That is, when we say what is and is not political, we are already engaged in the activity of theorizing.

---

[9] J Shklar, *Legalism: Law, Morals, and Political Trials* (Cambridge, MA: Harvard University Press, 1986), 28.

[10] 'The traditional meaning of theory, etymologically tied to "seeing" (theoria), has modeled the activity of the theorist on the solitary act of grasping an object within a field of vision.' SK White, 'Pluralism, Platitudes, and Paradoxes: Fifty Years of Western Political Thought' (2002) 30 *Political Theory* 472, 477.

[11] M Oakeshott, 'What Is Political Theory?', in *What Is History? And Other Essays* (Exeter: Imprint Academic, 2004), 391, 393.

Whether the apparent contingencies of political theory should be remedied with essentialist claims, or instead embraced as an opportunity, is itself a matter of dispute within the field.[12] I believe I can bracket that dispute for now, for there seems to be sufficient consensus on the content of 'the political' for purposes of theorizing criminal law in a twenty-first-century liberal democracy. Whatever else political theory is concerned with, it is definitely concerned with collective coexistence—with how large groups of human beings do and should live together. For centuries, the question of collective coexistence has presented questions about the collection of institutions and offices we commonly refer to as the state. Political theory seeks to examine the state, to explain its functioning, and to justify or critique its exercises of power. The state does not exhaust the inquiries of political theory, but it is a central focus.

The focus on the state is especially important when we consider the criminal law and the institutions of punishment. Accordingly, as several scholars have emphasized, a political theory of punishment requires attention to the specific question whether and why punishment is a legitimate exercise of state power.[13] But the potential contributions of political theory to criminal law extend far beyond the question of the justification of punishment. Indeed, as I have argued elsewhere, political theory may teach us that in a liberal state, punishment simply can't be fully justified; it always retains a trace of the rule of the stronger that is inconsistent with liberal principles of consensual rule.[14] Beyond the question of justifying punishment, criminal law poses other puzzles for the political theorist. What processes and structures generate and sustain the criminal law? How does the criminal law, in turn, distribute power across individuals and institutions?[15] What are the political consequences of various principles of criminal liability,[16] or of various distributions of the penal power? And importantly, if punishment cannot be fully justified and yet cannot or will not be abandoned, what account can we give of its normative status?

---

[12] Compare Oakeshott ('[The political theorist's] only hope of achieving a better understanding of what he has identified as politics lies in being able to resist the temptation to question the limits he has imposed upon himself.') with Wendy Brown: '[P]olitical theory is a fiction, constituted by invented distinctions and a range of rivalries and conceits, all of which are mutable and puncturable and vary across time and place…To identify political theory's contrived nature, however, does not reduce or devalue the enterprise; rather, it helps set the stage for considering the possibilities and challenges it faces in a particular time and place.' W Brown, 'At the Edge' (2002) 30 *Political Theory* 556, 557.

[13] N Lacey, *State Punishment: Political Principles and Community Values* (London: Routledge, 1988); G Binder, 'Punishment Theory: Moral or Political?' (2002) 5 *Buffalo Criminal Law Review* 321; J Murphy, 'Does Kant Have a Theory of Punishment?' (1987) 87 *Columbia Law Review* 509, 510–11.

[14] A Ristroph, 'Respect and Resistance in Punishment Theory' (2009) 97 *California Law Review* 601, 619–22.

[15] On this question, see M Thorburn, 'Justifications, Powers, and Authority' (2008) 117 *Yale Law Journal* 1070.

[16] On this question, see VF Nourse, 'Reconceptualizing Criminal Law Defenses' (2003) 151 *University of Pennsylvania Law Review* 1691.

These sorts of questions encourage us to think of criminal law not as a natural phenomenon with fixed parameters, but as a political artifact. A political community makes, sustains, alters, and applies its own criminal law. How does this happen, and what are the consequences? From this perspective, the key normative issue is not, or at least not only, a question about justifying the criminal law. We should study also responsibility for the criminal law. Indeed, as I discuss in the last section of this chapter, questions of responsibility are likely to provide a better perspective to evaluate current practices, and more insights for reform, than are questions of justification.

Before turning directly to a theory of responsibility, I want to make one more methodological observation: any political theory of criminal law will be quite complex, much more complex than many familiar theories that focus only on the justification of punishment. Theorizing, again, is an effort to understand some observed phenomenon, but in this area there is much to see, and perhaps much of what matters goes on behind the scenes. It is daunting—overwhelming, even—to think that to explain and evaluate the criminal law, one must be able to explain and evaluate the behemoth that is the modern state. Small wonder that so many theorists have narrowed their field of vision, choosing to take both the state and the substantive criminal law for granted, and devoting their energies to the moral relationship between a single individual's criminal act and that same individual's subsequent hard treatment. Theories drawn within these narrow parameters have the virtue of simplicity, but it is a simplicity born of myopia. It will soon be evident how greatly an inquiry into responsibility must complicate matters.

2 CRIMINAL RESPONSIBILITY: INDIVIDUAL, COLLECTIVE, OR BOTH?

To frame 'criminal responsibility' or 'responsibility for crime' as a characteristic of the accused wrongdoer, and the wrongdoer alone, is to neglect important questions. The individualist approach to responsibility separates questions of criminalization, or the appropriate scope of the substantive criminal law, from questions of criminal responsibility, and thus gives insufficient attention to the distinction between responsibility for an *act* and responsibility for a *crime*.[17] A general theory of action

---

[17] As discussed below, many scholars who address criminal responsibility also address the appropriate scope of the criminal law. The charge here (also discussed in greater detail below) is that they treat the issue of criminalization as independent of the issue of criminal responsibility, when in fact these issues are intertwined.

or agency is invoked to analyse the specific acts proscribed by the criminal law, but the designation of acts as crimes is not scrutinized as itself an action for which persons or communities are responsible. In this and other ways, individualist theories of criminal responsibility often fail to attend to the political dimensions of responsibility. On the alternative account I defend here, responsibility is a matter of human relationships, of attitudes and practices. One may act alone, but one is responsible in relation to others.[18] When we keep in view both the relational, political dimensions of responsibility and the distinctively political characteristics of crime, it becomes clear that some of the most important questions of criminal responsibility are questions of collective responsibility.

The action theory approach to criminal responsibility is exemplified by Michael Moore's influential work.[19] On this account, criminal responsibility requires an act, and an act is understood as a willed bodily movement. Of course, Moore's account is far more complex, but the nuances of his claims are not essential to my argument here. It is worth emphasizing, as Moore himself does, that his claimed relationship between action and criminal responsibility must be understood in the context of broader philosophical commitments to moral realism and a retributive theory of punishment.[20] Moore argues that responsibility is an objective fact about a person, not simply an attitude that a person or persons might take toward someone else.[21] And he has also defended punishment as the imposition of retributive desert on a deserving offender.[22] These commitments to moral realism and retribution produce an account in which one dimension of responsibility is the commission of an act. It is an individualist account, or an account of personal responsibility, in that the relevant considerations are considerations about the specific individual. To decide whether an individual is responsible, we must ask whether she has acted, and whether her actions are the result of practical reasoning.[23]

Other criminal law theorists reject Moore's specific account of the link between action and responsibility. Various scholars have connected criminal responsibility

---

[18] On some theoretical accounts, even action, properly understood, is dependent on other people. '[A]ction...is never possible in isolation; to be isolated is to be deprived of the capacity to act.' H Arendt, *The Human Condition* (Chicago: University of Chicago Press, 1958), 188. But Arendt's normative theory of action is so different from the accounts of action in criminal law theory that I think it fair to say that she is addressing a different concept altogether.

[19] MS Moore, *Act and Crime: The Philosophy of Action and Its Implications for Criminal Law* (Oxford: Oxford University Press, 1993); MS Moore, *Law and Psychiatry: Rethinking the Relationship* (Cambridge: Cambridge University Press, 1984).

[20] MS Moore, 'More on Act and Crime' (1994) 149 *University of Pennsylvania Law Review* 1749, 1753.

[21] Ibid; see also MS Moore, 'Moral Reality Revisited' (1992) 90 *Michigan Law Review* 2424.

[22] MS Moore, 'The Moral Worth of Retribution', in F Schoeman (ed), *Responsibility, Character, and the Emotions* (Cambridge: Cambridge University Press, 1987).

[23] MS Moore, *Law and Psychiatry*, 51–2.

to the individual's ability to control a specified state of affairs,[24] to the individual's character,[25] or to some combination of capacities and character.[26] On any of these accounts, criminal responsibility is a question to be asked about the individual accused—about what the individual has done. We might put the inquiry in terms of agency rather than action, and say that to be responsible is to be an autonomous agent.[27] As mentioned above, Arthur Ripstein has described these approaches under the umbrella phrase 'the agency conception of responsibility'.

Notice: these questions of agency and action could be raised with respect to any human action, whatever its legal status. We could apply action theory to analyse my responsibility for the outfits I select, for the ways I entertain or mistreat my friends, or for the articles I write. But criminal law theory is concerned with the narrower class of actions that are proscribed by the law, a class of actions usually thought to carry greater social significance than my sartorial choices or (even) my intellectual labours. If we are to focus on responsibility for crime rather than responsibility for acts to which the law is indifferent, then we must pay attention to the designation of actions as crimes.[28] Such designation is itself an action—not of the individual wrongdoer, of course, but of the political or legal institutions that generate and enforce the criminal law.

My claim is that we should think of 'criminal responsibility' as necessarily involving agents other than the individual accused. This is not to deny that characteristics of the individual accused are important to assessing responsibility, but these characteristics are not alone sufficient to explain responsibility. The act requirement, the control requirement, or some other variation may be an important limitation on the ascription of criminal responsibility. But when we speak of responsibility, we should be clear that it is always ascribed, and someone is doing the ascribing.

This last emphasis on the ascription of responsibility is at odds with the moral realist claim that responsibility just exists, independent of any person's decision to

---

[24] D Husak, *The Philosophy of Criminal Law* (Rowman & Littlefield, 1987); D Husak, 'Does Criminal Liability Require An Act?', in his *The Philosophy of Criminal Law: Selected Essays* (New York: Oxford University Press, 2010) 77–82. An alternative way of framing a control-based understanding of criminal responsibility is to ask whether the individual had both the capacity for control and a 'fair opportunity' to exercise it. HLA Hart, *Punishment and Responsibility* (Oxford: Clarendon Press, 1968), 152.

[25] N Lacey, *State Punishment*.

[26] V Tadros, *Criminal Responsibility* (Oxford: Oxford University Press, 2005).

[27] 'In general, though obviously not in all cases, I am responsible for my actions and you are responsible for yours. And that is because my actions can be attributed to me as an agent and yours to you.' V Tadros, 'The Scope and Grounds of Responsibility' (2008) 11 *New Criminal Law Review* 91.

[28] Tadros does distinguish between killing and murder, and between taking and theft. But on his account, the distinctive wrongfulness of those killings we call murder (and those takings we call thefts) appears to dictate, rather than follow from, criminalization choices. V Tadros, *Criminal Responsibility*, 2. The political responsibility of those who make and enforce the criminal law is not a focus of Tadros's account in *Criminal Responsibility*. However, Tadros does take up questions of political, collective responsibility for crime in a subsequent article, 'Poverty and Criminal Responsibility', discussed in more detail below.

hold another responsible. As it happens, I have my doubts about moral realism. But notice that even on the moral realist account, someone other than the individual accused bears a degree of responsibility for crime, insofar as someone bears responsibility for the criminal law. The individual wrongdoer may be responsible for the wrongful act that is a crime, but some other agent is responsible for the fact that it is a crime.

Many scholars would probably agree that the community or the government bears some responsibility for the creation and enforcement of the criminal law, but would suggest that this particular kind of responsibility is simply not the meaning of the phrase 'criminal responsibility'.[29] This intellectual bifurcation is both conceptually misleading and politically costly. It is conceptually misleading because even when we focus on the individual wrongdoer and his capacities, choices, or character, we can affix the label 'criminally responsible' to him only if certain political and legal constructions are in place. When we leave those constructions out of an account of criminal responsibility, we engender a way of thinking and talking about the criminal law that allows those constructions to go unscrutinized. In a kind of simplistic retributivism, the offender's individual responsibility becomes viewed as a sufficient condition for punishment; put colloquially, punishment is a manner of holding the offender responsible.[30] The political cost of this way of thinking is high. (I mean that the cost to the overall polity is high; to public officials, in contrast, the rhetoric of individual responsibility may prove a useful way to avoid accountability.) In several nations, especially the United States, increasingly severe punishments and climbing rates of incarceration have been justified as necessary efforts to hold offenders responsible, and there is little if any effort to address the enormous social costs of mass incarceration.

To develop the argument for a more comprehensive approach, it may help to examine the concept of responsibility directly, setting aside for the moment the baggage of responsibility claims made in the specific context of criminal law. Responsibility appears to mean, literally, answerability—the ability to respond. A number of scholars have taken the concept of capacity (or obligation) to answer as a departure point for theorizing responsibility.[31] This approach usually leads to an emphasis on the

---

[29] Moore (eg) is attentive to questions about the appropriate scope of the substantive criminal law, but he separates those questions from the issue of criminal responsibility. See eg *Placing Blame* (Oxford: Clarendon Press, 1997), 36–45 (on the concept of criminal responsibility) and 75–8 (on the scope of the criminal law).

[30] Eg Stephen Morse, 'Immaturity and Responsibility' (1997) 88 *Journal of Criminal Law & Criminology* 15, 50.

[31] RA Duff, *Answering for Crime: Responsibility and Liability in the Criminal Law* (Oxford: Hart Publishing, 2007); CM Korsgaard, *Creating the Kingdom of Ends* (Cambridge: Cambridge University Press, 1996), 188; JR Pennock, *Democratic Political Theory* (Princeton, NJ: Princeton University Press, 1979), 267; G Watson, *Agency and Answerability* (Oxford: Clarendon Press, 2004); M Stone, 'The Significance of Doing and Suffering', in G Postema (ed), *Philosophy and the Law of Torts* (Cambridge: Cambridge University Press, 2001), 159.

relational nature of responsibility, for if we think of answering we think of one agent answering to another. But answerability within relationships is only the beginning of a concept of responsibility. We use the language of responsibility to express normative judgments about human relationships and the actions humans take within those relationships. In those normative judgments, we use a number of different verbs: we might say that Adam *bears* responsibility, that Betty *takes* responsibility, or that Charlie *should be held* responsible. Bearing and taking responsibility, as well as holding oneself or someone else responsible, are human practices, and a theory of responsibility should focus on this practical dimension of it. Simply put, responsibility is a matter of human relationships and practices within those relationships.

A practical, relational conception of responsibility might begin with the individual, but it will not end there. 'Responsibility is in the first instance something taken rather than something assigned.'[32] With this claim, Christine Korsgaard distinguishes a Kantian theory of moral responsibility from the view that responsibility is primarily a matter of praising or blaming others. One need not adopt a specifically Kantian moral theory to share Korsgaard's view that responsibility is closely associated with individual autonomy, and that one must first be responsible in order to make judgments of others' responsibility. But though Korsgaard begins with taking responsibility, she moves quickly to holding one another responsible: 'holding one another responsible is the distinctive element in the relation of adult human beings. To hold someone responsible is to regard her as a person—that is to say, as a free and equal person, capable of acting both rationally and morally.'[33] On this account, responsibility is connected to reciprocity; to hold another responsible (after, of course, taking responsibility oneself) is to enter into a relationship of reciprocal respect.[34] 'Abandoning the state of nature and so relinquishing force and guile, you are ready to share, to trust, and generally speaking to risk your happiness or success on the hope that she will turn out to be human.'[35]

It is clear that to hold someone responsible in this threshold sense need not entail blame, criticism, or any other negative evaluation. Korsgaard's work may thus offer a useful departure point for a theory of responsibility disentangled from retributive impulses. (That is not to say that Korsgaard's account of responsibility is inconsistent with retributivism, but only that it does not equate a judgment of responsibility with an assessment of retributive desert.) Still, though, we need to be somewhat more specific about what it is to hold one responsible. We should all want to be held responsible, insofar as we want to be regarded as autonomous humans. It may be true that in a very general sense, we hold others responsible whenever we view them

---

[32] Korsgaard, ibid 189.

[33] Ibid.

[34] Though Korsgaard also emphasizes that respecting and holding responsible are not identical. 'Respect for someone's humanity is not always best expressed by holding him responsible for each and every action. It may be better to admit that even the best of us can just slip.' Ibid 211.

[35] Ibid 189.

as rational agents and enter into reciprocal relationships with them. But there is a narrower sense in which we hold someone responsible *for* a particular act or characteristic. This sense of holding responsible will often, though not always, involve blaming or criticizing. This sense of holding responsible seems the one most relevant to criminal law theory.

Even in the narrow context of blaming, Korsgaard's account offers key insights that criminal law theorists have too often overlooked.[36] Korsgaard distinguishes between what she calls the theoretical and practical conceptions of responsibility. Under the theoretical conception, 'responsibility is a characteristic of persons'— akin, perhaps, to the moral realist view I described earlier: a person just is or is not responsible, independent of the judgments her fellow citizens may make of her.[37] Under the practical conception, 'holding one another responsible is something that we do, the more or less deliberate adoption of an attitude'.[38] Under this conception, 'it may be perfectly reasonable for me to hold someone responsible for an attitude or an action, while at the same time acknowledging that it is just as reasonable for someone else not to hold the same person responsible for the very same attitude or action'.[39] Holding another responsible is something we do in the context of particular relationships, and those with other relationships may make different responsibility judgments. Furthermore, and of great importance for a political theory of responsibility, 'if deciding whether to hold someone responsible is something that we do, it is something that we may in turn be held responsible for'.[40] This claim has clear implications for a theory of criminal responsibility: those who hold offenders responsible are themselves responsible for that decision.

Notice that on this account, holding someone responsible doesn't itself dictate any particular action toward that person. If my neighbour promises to water my houseplants while I am away, I may hold him responsible if he forgets and the plants are dead when I return. But whether I then rely on my neighbour again the next time I travel, or make alternative arrangements for plant care, or poison my neighbour's shrubs in retaliation, is still a further question. This insight also has important

[36] There are important exceptions. Notably, some recent work in criminal law theory has emphasized the practical dimension of responsibility—the fact that it is a matter of human practices. RA Duff, 'Who Is Responsible, for What, to Whom' (2005) 2 *Ohio State Journal of Criminal Law* 441; V Tadros, 'The Scope and Grounds of Responsibility' (2008) *New Criminal Law Review* 1933–4192.

[37] CM Korsgaard, *Creating the Kingdom of Ends*, 197.

[38] Ibid. Blaming actually involves both conceptions of responsibility; it requires us to 'make a moral assessment of someone's action, on the basis of a theoretical explanation of what she did.' Ibid 205.

[39] Ibid 199. Korsgaard cites Bernard Williams's discussion of Gauguin in *Moral Luck* (B Williams, *Moral Luck* (Cambridge: Cambridge University Press, 1979)) and suggests that it might be reasonable for Gauguin's Danish wife to hold him responsible for deserting her, and yet not reasonable for others to hold him responsible for this action. For other suggestions that the reasonableness of holding responsible depends on particular relationships, see the discussions of Ripstein's reciprocity conception of responsibility and Tadros on poverty below.

[40] Korsgaard, ibid 199.

consequences for the criminal law: holding a criminal responsible need not entail holding him in custody, or even necessarily imposing any punishment at all.[41]

Also inspired by Kant, Arthur Ripstein develops an account of responsibility that similarly emphasizes the relationships in which responsibility practices take place. Rejecting the agency conception of responsibility as 'a two-term relation between agent and outcome', Ripstein advocates an alternative 'reciprocity conception' in which responsibility is understood 'as a relationship between persons with respect to consequences of a morally relevant kind'.[42] On Ripstein's account, agency and responsibility are separate issues. Even when a person has acted as an agent, it may be inappropriate to hold that person responsible, depending on the particular relational context.[43]

With these insights from Korsgaard and Ripstein—that responsibility involves multiple persons, that agency and responsibility are distinct concepts, that holding someone responsible is itself an action for which one is responsible, and that holding someone responsible doesn't yet tell us how to act toward that person—we might return our attention to the criminal law. Clearly, the personal responsibility of the accused is not the only relevant responsibility inquiry. We must also evaluate those who hold the accused responsible. Those who impose judgment and punishment are responsible for their actions, but more broadly, those who criminalize and those who demand criminalization and enforcement bear responsibility for those decisions and demands. Thus various public officials, and members of the general community, may be rightly held responsible for the criminal justice system. To say all these persons may be held responsible is not, of course, to say that they should be blamed or condemned—again, holding responsible is not equivalent to a negative appraisal. But holding a community and its officials responsible for its criminal law does entail a careful scrutiny of the various decisions that go into the criminal law, and it implies that the officials or community are answerable for the consequences, good and bad, of the criminal justice system.[44]

---

[41] This point has been recognized by scholars who see responsibility as a necessary but not sufficient condition for punishment. Eg Lacey, *State Punishment*, 69. Along similar lines, Thomas Scanlon argues that even if we privately hold an actor responsible, it is a further question whether we should express that judgment to him or to others. TM Scanlon, *What We Owe to Each Other* (Cambridge, MA: Harvard University Press, 1998), 269, 276.

[42] Ripstein, 'Justice and Responsibility' (2004) 17 *Canadian Journal of Law & Jurisprudence* 361, 366; see also RA Duff, 'Who Is Responsible, for What, to Whom?' (2005) 2 *Ohio State Journal of Criminal Law* 441, 442.

[43] Ripstein, ibid 363, 365. In this article, Ripstein is concerned primarily with private law and not with criminal responsibility. He offers as an example an individual who as, under conditions of full agency, made 'a terrible choice' such as 'default[ing] on a loan worth more than his assets'. It may be appropriate not to hold this person responsible—for reasons intrinsic to the concept of responsibility. Ibid 383–5.

[44] As they are answerable for its failures and omissions: for decisions not to criminalize certain harmful acts, or not to enforce particular laws, or not to protect certain victims. Recognizing responsibility for the criminal law need not imply an affirmative duty to punish, since a recognition of

Of course, public officials and a political community may bear responsibility for many political acts, not only those pertaining to criminal justice. And, as a number of scholars have emphasized, public responsibility for these acts may have implications for the individual responsibility of a given defendant. In a recent account of criminal responsibility as answerability, Antony Duff argues that to be responsible, the accused must be answerable to his fellow citizens, which requires that the fellow citizens have 'standing' to demand an answer from the accused.[45] If an individual has been 'systematically excluded from full participation in the polity', the polity arguably 'lacks standing to call him to account' for his violation of the laws.[46] Duff distinguishes this argument from the 'Rotten Social Background' defence once advanced by Richard Delgado and others, which would excuse a defendant for criminal conduct produced by severe social injustice.[47] Duff's standing claim is still more radical; it proposes that 'serious, systemic injustice' may actually serve as 'a moral bar to trial'.[48] On this account, the defendant is not responsible to the polity (though he may be responsible to others, including the direct victim of his crime) because the polity has failed in its obligations. Ideally, the polity would itself take responsibility for its own failures. '[W]e must ourselves be collectively ready to be called to account, and indeed show that we hold ourselves to account, for the injustices such defendants have suffered at our collective—and typically passive—hands.'[49]

Victor Tadros has developed a similar argument, beginning with the premises that poverty is criminogenic and that the state has a responsibility to reduce criminogenic social conditions.[50] These two conditions are sufficient to establish that 'the state [is] complicit in the crimes of the poor' and thus the poor have a moral claim 'for the state to refrain from holding them responsible for their crimes, even if they are in fact responsible for them'.[51] (Note that for Tadros, being responsible and being held responsible are distinct. His argument also seems to presume that a wrongdoer should be held responsible only once.[52]) Finally, Alan Norrie has offered a broad critique of the individualist understanding of criminal responsibility, arguing that

responsibility does not yet tell us what to do. But in emphasizing that a community bears responsibility for its criminal law, I do not mean to obscure the fact that it also will bear responsibility if it fails to respond to harm and violence among its members.

[45] Duff, *Answering for Crime*, 53, 191–3; see also RA Duff, *Punishment, Communication, and Community* (New York: Oxford University Press, 2001), 185–8.

[46] Duff, *Answering for Crime*, 191.

[47] R Delgado, 'Rotten Social Background: Should the Law Recognize a Defense of Severe Environmental Deprivation?' (1985) 3 *Law & Inequality* 9.

[48] Duff, *Answering for Crime*, 192.

[49] Ibid 193.

[50] V Tadros, 'Poverty and Criminal Responsibility' (2009) 43 *Journal of Value Inquiry* 391, 391.

[51] Ibid 393.

[52] Tadros makes this claim to explain why the state, if complicit in crime, should not hold the criminal responsible. '[I]n holding another responsible for what he has done through a defective practice of responsibility, the accuser might block practices of responsibility that are closer to the ideal.' Ibid 403.

it is based on a 'false separation' of personal agency and social conditions.[53] If, as Norrie argues, the individual is 'always-already social', then criminal responsibility is always already social as well.[54] Not only poverty but other social conditions help constitute the individual and his actions, and an account of criminal responsibility must acknowledge that.

In various ways, Duff, Tadros, and Norrie each include questions of collective responsibility in the assessment of criminal responsibility. Notice that the collective responsibility under examination on these accounts involves the community's actions prior to the instant offence, and it often concerns actions largely independent of the criminal process. For example, collective responsibility may involve responsibility for grossly unequal distributions of wealth, or for denial of educational opportunity, or for systemic racism. I have little doubt that these actions or conditions are ones for which a polity might rightly be held responsible. But I want to emphasize that even if the accused has been treated fairly in matters of economic, educational, and racial justice, the community's decisions to punish (and decisions to criminalize) will themselves still incur responsibility. Duff asks whether a community has 'suitably clean collective hands' such that it may legitimately bring an accused to court and demand that he answer for his crimes.[55] I want to suggest that the criminal process may itself dirty or at least smudge the community's hands—and whether or not it dirties them, the criminal process inevitably entails collective action and collective responsibility.

To develop this point, it is helpful to consider a recent discussion of the 'moral burdens' of punishment. Alon Harel argues that a state should not ask private citizens to impose punishment—shaming penalties, for example—because to do so imposes impermissible moral burdens on the individuals charged with punishing.[56] Harel assumes, for purposes of his argument, that the state will continue to determine who is to be punished and how much. He also assumes that the private citizens are cooperative, willing punishers who can be trusted to impose punishment on the right people in the right amounts.[57] Even under these conditions, the private individuals run the risk that they may be asked to impose sanctions that they, as individuals, believe to be inappropriate—Harel calls this risk 'the conscience-based

---

[53] Norrie, *Punishment, Responsibility, and Justice*. Norrie attributes the dominant approach to criminal responsibility, with its emphasis on individual agency and relative inattention to social conditions or collective responsibility, to Kantian theory. But as indicated by the discussions of Korsgaard and Ripstein above, Kantianism does not preclude a relational, contextualized approach to responsibility.

[54] Norrie, 'The Limits of Justice: Finding Fault in the Criminal Law' (1996) 59 *Modern Law Review* 540, 551.

[55] Ibid 192. As noted above, Tadros expresses a similar inquiry in the language of complicity. V Tadros, 'Poverty and Criminal Responsibility' (2009) 43 *Journal of Value Inquiry* 391, 404–5.

[56] A Harel, 'Why Only the State May Inflict Criminal Sanctions: The Argument from Moral Burdens' (2007) 28 *Cardozo Law Review* 2629.

[57] Ibid 2638.

moral burden'.[58] Further, the private punisher following public instructions may inflict a punishment that is in fact inappropriate; the defendant may turn out to be innocent, or to deserve much more punishment than she receives. This latter burden, the risk of imposing 'erroneous' punishment, Harel calls 'the moral responsibility burden'.[59]

But is it only 'erroneous' punishment that generates moral responsibility? And do private citizens avoid moral responsibility if they avoid direct involvement in punishing, delegating that task to public officials? With respect to the second question, Harel distinguishes between collective and individual responsibility. 'The moral burden argument does not claim that individuals are not responsible in any way for the justness of the state-inflicted sanctions in a democratic polity, but merely that they are not individually responsible.'[60] Collective responsibility, according to Harel, is 'a special mitigated type of responsibility'.[61] Harel does not explain the sense in which collective responsibility is 'mitigated'; I consider this issue in the concluding section of this chapter. For now, note that this collective responsibility seems to exist even if the punishments imposed are fair and legitimate. Those who punish, including the citizens of a democratic polity whose involvement is quite indirect, are responsible for what they do. They are responsible for wrongly imposed sanctions, but they are responsible for rightly imposed sanctions, too.

Put differently, responsibility and justification are not quite the same issue. In the first place, one may be both responsible for an act and justified in taking it. Some commentators have recognized this point with respect to individual defendants and justification defences: the defendant who has a valid justification defence is nonetheless (maybe, all the more) a responsible agent, even though he is not subject to punishment.[62] Additionally, justification does not necessarily relieve a responsible agent of all prospective obligations. Indeed, in some cases justification is conditioned on fulfillment of prospective obligations, as when courts recognize a necessity defence for prison escape, but only for those escapees who promptly report to authorities after escaping a dangerous institution.[63]

Some readers may complain not that I have distinguished between responsibility and justification, but that I have confused the issues. Many of the political issues that I portray as bearing on collective responsibility for the criminal law—such as questions of criminalization or sentence severity—are more typically characterized as issues related to the justification of punishment. No doubt the concepts and

---

[58] Ibid.

[59] Ibid 2639–40.

[60] Ibid 2643.

[61] Ibid.

[62] Eg Kyron Huigens, 'The Continuity of Justification Defenses' (2009) 2009 *University of Illinois Law Review* 627, 693–4; Thorburn, 'Justification, Powers, and Authority' (2008) 117 *Yale Law Journal* 1070.

[63] Eg *People v Lovercamp* (1974) 43 Cal App 3d 823.

questions could be shuffled in myriad ways, but there are good reasons to think of the normative status of the criminal law in terms of responsibility rather than justification. I examine those reasons in the next section.

3 Justification, Responsibility, and Bureaucratic Violence

Incarceration is a type of bureaucratic violence.[64] It involves the use of force against persons, and this use of force takes place in a complex institutional context. There are other forms of bureaucratic violence, including military force, police force, state torture, and civil detention. Philosophical scrutiny of such actions has almost universally focused on questions of justification: what are the circumstances in which the use of force is justified? Having answered that question, the theorist views his work as complete; he can only hope those who control the use of force will adhere to the guidelines he has pronounced.

But justifying force is not the only relevant question, and it may not even be the most important one. It is possible, as I have suggested, that punishment (at least in its physically injurious or custodial forms) cannot be satisfactorily justified in a liberal democracy. It is possible that punishment always indicates a failure of consensual self-government and a resort to rule by violence. Indeed, though criminal law theorists almost invariably find some principle to justify punishment (disagreeing, of course, on what that justification is), in the political theory literature on 'dirty hands,' punishment is sometimes cited as an illustration of the claim that political rule inevitably entails corrupt or immoral acts.[65] 'I have dirty hands. Right up to the elbows. I've plunged them in filth and blood', says Sartre's Colonel Hoederer. 'Do you think you can govern innocently?'[66] And perhaps it is foolish to think one can *punish* innocently.[67]

---

[64] To be clear, even ordinary incarceration, in the absence of physical attacks by prison officials or fellow prisoners, is violent in the sense that it involves the use of superior physical force against an embodied, and thus vulnerable, human being. A private individual who confined captives in cages would almost certainly be classified as a violent offender. Nevertheless, some observers resist the language of violence in the context of official, state-sanctioned, and thus arguably legitimate uses of force. I begin with no assumptions about the legitimacy of punishment (or the necessary illegitimacy of violence), and find the term violence to be the best description of the use of physical force against human bodies.

[65] M Walzer, 'Political Action: The Problem of Dirty Hands' (1973) 2 *Philosophy & Public Affairs* 160.

[66] JP Sartre, 'Dirty Hands', in *No Exit and Three Other Plays* (New York: Vintage International, 1989), 218.

[67] A Ristroph, 'Games Punishers Play', in P Robinson, S Garvey, and K Ferzan (eds), *Criminal Law Conversations* (Oxford: Oxford University Press, 2009); A Ristroph, 'Respect and Resistance in

Even for those—for the many—who would reject this sceptical account and insist that punishment can be morally justified, responsibility for the criminal law is an independent question in need of attention. We acknowledge that the criminal justice system sometimes goes awry—it sometimes convicts and punishes the innocent, or produces inhumane conditions of confinement, or needlessly painful executions. When things go awry, we need a way to assess responsibility. And if the state, or its agents, or the people it represents, bear responsibility when things go wrong, they are also responsible when things go right. Of course, the consequences of public responsibility may vary depending on whether we think a particular punishment was justified. As we have seen, a judgment of responsibility is not a mandate on what to do next. It may, however, lead us to conclude that something must be done.

Sometimes, the ancient principle of habeas corpus is described in terms that evoke this concern with responsibility for state violence. In theory if not always in practice, habeas relief is available to anyone physically held by the state, whether his detention is labelled criminal or civil. A petition for a writ of habeas corpus is a demand that the state be called to answer for its ongoing violence; it is a way 'to call the jailer to account'.[68] Of course, modern habeas law is riddled with limitations on judicial authority, and it does not presently function as a source of the sort of responsibility assessment I am urging here. But in the principles that underlie habeas corpus, one can see one dimension of responsibility for state violence.

Responsibility has both backward-looking and forward-looking dimensions. Both aspects are important questions to ask of the criminal justice system, and of other uses of state force. When we look back, we are trying to figure out the origins of an act of violence. Admittedly, this can be much more difficult in the political realm than it is with an individual defendant. 'The state' is a complex and mysterious entity. It is not always easy to identify which actions or events are properly attributed to it, or to know whether attributions of responsibility to 'the state' should implicate or exonerate the flesh-and-blood humans who act as state officials. Somebody has to pull the trigger, to inject the condemned, to close the handcuffs, to lock the cell door. Somebody has to write the legal memos, too. Since a complex bureaucracy authorizes and orders these actions, it is not always clear how to allocate responsibility among the various members of that bureaucracy.

And in the case of a liberal democracy, citizens are involved too; they may be demanding that these cell doors be locked, or at least allowing this violence to be done in their name. Collective responsibility is surely a different kind of responsibility than sole individual responsibility, but it is responsibility nonetheless. One

Punishment Theory'(2009) 97 *California Law Review* 601. I have argued elsewhere that punishment is at best incompletely or imperfectly legitimate. Ibid. This claim is not equivalent to penal abolitionism. Instead, it is a claim that crime often presents a liberal democratic state with a tragic dilemma. To leave crimes unpunished may produce intolerable consequences, but to impose punishment will violate various liberal principles.

[68] *Boumediene v Bush* (2008) 128 S Ct 2229, 2247.

danger of bureaucratic violence is that the bureaucratic complexity will render responsibility invisible or obsolete. No single actor seems individually responsible, and so (it may be argued) no one is responsible. These dangers shadow Harel's account of responsibility for punishment. Harel claims that a public official who punishes on behalf of the state—a judge, prison guard, or executioner—'is often entitled or obliged to execute faithfully the state's sentencing decisions'.[69] This obligation relieves the official of the moral responsibility for punishment that a private citizen would bear were she to inflict punishment. But as we have seen, Harel also argues that state-inflicted punishment involves at most a 'mitigated responsibility' of democratic citizens. Responsibility does not lie with state officials (not even the judge or executioner), and it does not lie (fully) with private citizens. The danger, again, is that responsibility will lie nowhere, that the structure of the bureaucracy will enable violence to be done with no one to answer for it.[70]

And answering for state violence is a requirement of a legitimate political entity. This brings us, finally, to the forward-looking dimension of responsibility, and the reason that we should speak of responsibility rather than merely of justification. A claim of justification tends to close a conversation, whereas a claim of responsibility only raises new questions. Imagine a polity that did not merely hold others responsible for crime, but that *took* responsibility for crime. This polity might scrutinize the accusations it makes and the acts it criminalizes. Even if the polity were satisfied that the bounds of its substantive criminal law were properly drawn, it would then examine the extent to which social and political conditions within its control contributed to the commission of (properly defined) crimes. And even if the polity were satisfied that it had defined the criminal law fairly and secured a just social order, it would also have to consider the political and social consequences of its responses to criminal acts. If its penal policies caused significant harm to individuals and communities, a responsible polity would not dismiss such harms as collateral consequences to justified violence. It would seek to address those harms, to mitigate them, perhaps to compensate for them. Such scrutiny and remedial action would be difficult, but that is what it means to take responsibility.

---

[69] A Harel, 'Why Only the State May Inflict Criminal Sanctions: The Case Against Privately Inflicted Sanctions' (2008) 14 *Legal Theory* 113, 130.

[70] This danger was the theme of much of Hannah Arendt's work. See eg HA Arendt, *Responsibility and Judgment* (J Kohn ed, New York: Schocken Books, 2003); HA Arendt, *Eichmann in Jerusalem: A Report on the Banality of Evil* (New York: Viking Press, 1963).

7

RESPONSIBILITY, CITIZENSHIP, AND CRIMINAL LAW

RA DUFF[*]

IT would be rash to posit a single, determinate purpose or function as *the* purpose or function of criminal law. That would be misguided as an interpretive claim about existing systems of criminal law: we cannot understand a set of institutional practices with as long and complex a history as those that constitute the criminal law of any developed polity in terms of any single purpose or function. It might seem more tempting to posit some unitary purpose as a matter of normative theory: to argue, for instance, that the purpose of criminal law is to maximize dominion,[1] or to achieve retributive justice by securing the punishment of moral wrongdoers.[2] I cannot argue the point here, but believe that such normative claims are also untenable: any plausible normative theory of criminal law will be complex and messy,[3] positing

---

[*] Thanks to participants in the Rutgers workshop at which an earlier version of this chapter was discussed, and especially to Stuart Green.
[1] See J Braithwaite and P Pettit, *Not Just Deserts: A Republican Theory of Criminal Justice* (Oxford: Oxford University Press, 1990).
[2] See MS Moore, *Placing Blame* (Oxford: Oxford University Press, 1997), ch 1.
[3] See the comments on complexity and messiness in the Introduction, at nn 17–27.

a collection of purposes that cannot fit together into a tidy whole. This chapter starts with a less ambitious claim: not about *the* purpose, but about *a* central, distinctive purpose of criminal law—one that helps distinguish criminal law from other modes of legal regulation.

My claim is modest in another way. To posit either the or a purpose of 'criminal law' might be taken to make a claim about all systems of criminal law, at all times in all places; but I make no such claim here. My starting point is more local, with our systems of criminal law, rather than with 'criminal law' as such. That identifying description ('our systems') is deliberately vague: I leave open the question of how wide its extension might be, of how large a 'we' can join in the discussion of the purposes of 'our' criminal law. I begin with an imagined (though I hope not imaginary) group of potential interlocutors: of theorists who work within the broad traditions of Western liberalism, and citizens (including theorists) who live in polities that aspire to be liberal democracies. It would be a substantial achievement to engage, and to secure either agreement or fruitful disagreement, with a 'we' of that scope. We must also hope that the conversation can expand— and one task for legal theorists is to see how far it can expand, and which other conversations they can join. But my present concern is with the earlier stages of that process—with what a relatively limited 'we' can say about our systems of criminal law.

A distinctive and proper purpose of our criminal law has to do, I will argue in section 1, with accountability and the attribution of responsibility. The criminal law provides the institutional framework within which, and procedures through which, perpetrators of public wrongs can be called to account (held responsible) for those wrongs. Such a practice of calling to account is possible, however, only within a normative community to which both called and callers can be said to belong. In section 2 I will discuss the kind of community that our criminal law, criminal law of a kind apt for a liberal republic, requires, and argue that in the context of the domestic criminal law of nation states (still the salient paradigm of criminal law) it is the community of citizens. Anyone who gives citizenship this central significance faces a range of objections, to the effect that such a conception of criminal law cannot do justice to transnational criminal law, to the status of non-citizens who are either permanent residents of or temporary visitors, or to the status of citizens who may find themselves excluded from full membership of the polity; that it fosters a dangerous distinction between an exclusive group of 'citizens', who are full members of the polity and receive all the protections that the criminal law offers both victims and offenders, and a wider group of outsiders, of actual or potential 'enemies', to whom such membership and protection are denied. I will face such objections in section 3, and will argue that although the concept of citizenship can be given this unacceptably exclusionary significance, we need not do so: we can and should retrieve a more inclusionary conception of liberal citizenship that can structure a normatively plausible picture of criminal law.

1 ANSWERING FOR CRIME[4]

The criminal law, in its substantive dimension, defines certain types of conduct as criminal (and defines certain defences for those who commit such criminal conduct). In so doing, it defines and condemns such conduct as wrong: not merely, and trivially, as legally wrong, as a breach of the rules of this particular game, but as morally wrong in a way that should concern those to whom it speaks, and that warrants the further consequences (trial, conviction, and punishment) that it attaches to such conduct. To say that it defines such conduct as wrong is not, however, to say that it creates that wrongfulness: although it is trivially true that criminal conduct is criminally wrongful only because the criminal law so defines it, it is substantively false to say that such conduct is morally wrongful only because the criminal law defines it as wrong. The criminal law does not (cannot) turn conduct that was not already wrongful into a moral wrong: it does not determine, but presupposes, the moral wrongfulness of the conduct that it defines as criminal; it determines which pre-criminal wrongs should count as 'public' wrongs whose perpetrators are to be called to public account. Its adjectival dimension then specifies the procedures through which those accused of perpetrating such wrongs are called to account: the criminal trial, as the formal culmination of the criminal process, summons a defendant to answer to a charge of public wrongdoing, and to answer for that wrongdoing if it is proved; if he cannot offer an exculpatory answer, he is convicted and thus condemned as a wrongdoer. Finally, in its penal dimension, the criminal law provides for the determination and administration of punishments for those convicted of such public wrongdoing.

   To spell out this conception of criminal law in a little more detail, we can begin with the familiar range of so-called *mala in se*—crimes consisting in conduct whose (supposed) moral wrongfulness is largely independent of the law. We do not need the criminal law to tell us that rape, murder, and other attacks on the person are wrong. It rather takes for granted our pre-criminal understanding of these as wrongs from which we already have good reason to refrain, and identifies them as wrongs that are 'public' in the sense that they are the business of the whole polity and require a public response from the polity.[5] The salient purpose of criminal law, on this view, is not directly to guide conduct (although the prospect of criminal liability might have that effect, and securing that effect might be a proper purpose for criminal law); it

---

[4] For more detailed discussion, see my *Answering for Crime* (Oxford: Hart Publishing, 2007), chs 4, 6.

[5] Note first, however, that the criminal law may provide distinctive definitions of the public wrongs that it identifies, especially when the pre-criminal understanding of those wrongs is conflicted or uncertain. Second, my claim is not that only morally wrongful conduct is actually criminalized, but that to criminalize conduct must be to portray it as morally wrong (see V Tadros and S Tierney, 'The Presumption of Innocence and the Human Rights Act' (2004) 67 *Modern Law Review* 402).

is to provide for an appropriate formal, public response to the pre-legally wrongful conduct that it defines as criminal. That response includes police action, preventive and investigative; prosecutorial action in deciding whether and how to pursue alleged offenders; court action in trying alleged offenders and sentencing convicted offenders; and punitive action in punishing sentenced offenders. What is central to it, however, is holding alleged public wrongdoers to public account. (By 'public' wrongs, and holding to 'public' account, I do not refer only to wrongs committed 'in public' or having a direct impact on 'the public', or only to callings to account conducted in public, like criminal trials in open court. A domestic assault committed in the home is as much a public wrong as an assault committed in a public street, since it is as much a wrong that properly concerns all members of the polity: to call a wrong public in this sense is not to give a reason for the public to take an interest in it, but to express the judgment that it is their business.[6] An offender who receives a formal caution, or a prosecutor's fine,[7] without going to court is still called to public account, by an authorized public official, whose actions are subject to public scrutiny, acting on behalf and in the name of the polity.)

It might seem that even if this account of criminal law can deal with *mala in se*, it cannot cope with so-called *mala prohibita*, which are orthodoxly understood as offences consisting in conduct that is not wrongful prior to its legal proscription.[8] But it can make room for *mala prohibita* (though we should not expect it to justify the vast range of such offences found in our existing laws) once we distinguish the question of regulation from that of criminalization. There are two routes to criminalization—more precisely, two routes to the determination that we have good reason in principle to criminalize a particular type of conduct (the question of whether we should, all things considered, criminalize that conduct raises further very complex issues). One begins with wrongfulness: we ask of some kind of pre-legally wrongful conduct whether it involves a type of wrong that is in principle the polity's business, and that merits public condemnation as a wrong; we thus identify a category of potential *mala in se*.[9] The other route starts with a decision that we have

---

[6] See SE Marshall and RA Duff, 'Criminalization and Sharing Wrongs' (1998) 11 *Canadian Journal of Law and Jurisprudence* 7; also MM Dempsey, *Prosecuting Domestic Violence: A Philosophical Analysis* (Oxford: Oxford University Press, 2009), especially chs 8–9.

[7] See P Duff, 'The Prosecutor Fine' (1994) 14 *Oxford Journal of Legal Studies* 565.

[8] See D Husak, '*Malum Prohibitum* and Retributivism', in RA Duff and SP Green (eds), *Defining Crimes* (Oxford: Oxford University Press, 2005), 65; *Overcriminalization: The Limits of the Criminal Law* (Oxford: Oxford University Press, 2007), 103–19. The distinction between *mala in se* and *mala prohibita* is of course neither clear nor undisputed: see eg RL Gray, 'Eliminating the (Absurd) Distinction between Malum in Se and Malum Prohibitum Crimes' (1995) 73 *Washington University Law Quarterly* 1369.

[9] I leave aside the complicating, but not now crucial, point that our understanding of some *mala in se* may be structured by the law, as our understanding of theft is structured by the law of property; see AM Honoré, 'The Dependence of Morality on Law' (1993) 13 *Oxford Journal of Legal Studies* 1.

reason to regulate a particular type of conduct, a reason that does not depend on the wrongfulness of such conduct. We have good reason, for instance, to regulate driving; and while some of the regulations that we may introduce will be grounded in pre-legal moral demands (as speed limits are grounded in the demand to drive safely), others (such as regulations concerning driving licences or vehicle registration) cannot be seen as formalized versions of such moral demands—indeed, it is, often impossible to engage in the conduct prohibited by the regulation prior to the regulation's existence. Now such regulations must of course be justified by showing, as with any legal regulation, that they serve an aspect of the common good. But that justification need not be grounded in the supposed pre-legal wrongfulness of the conduct in question; nor have we yet asked how the regulations should be enforced, or how we should respond to breaches of them. The question of criminalization comes up only when we ask that latter question; and we have good reason to criminalize such breaches if and only if, given the regulation and its justification, a breach of it constitutes a moral wrong for which the perpetrator should be called to public account.[10]

That is why it is misleading to say (as it is often said) that the substantive criminal law consists in 'prohibitions': for that implies that the criminal law seeks to make wrong what was not wrong before, or to offer us new reasons (reasons grounded in its authority or power) to refrain from the conduct that it criminalizes. What is distinctive about criminal law, what marks it out from other modes of legal regulation, is that rather than prohibiting or requiring conduct, it defines certain types of conduct that are already supposedly wrongful as wrongs of a kind that call for a particular kind of response—a response that formally condemns that conduct, and that seeks to call its perpetrator to public account: criminal law is focused on the polity's formal response to the conduct with which it deals.

It is thus significant from this perspective that criminal codes are not typically cast in the language of prohibitions: they rather tell us that a 'person is guilty of' a specified offence if... (Model Penal Code); or 'commits an offence if...' (a standard formula in English statutes); or that '[w]hoever' acts in a specified way 'shall be liable to' a specified punishment (German *Strafgesetzbuch*); or that certain kinds of act 'constitute' a specified offence, or 'are punished' by a specified kind and degree of sentence (French *Code Pénal*).

It might seem that what is most distinctive of the criminal law's response to crime is that it involves punishment: this is explicit in the formulations of French and German law, and is perhaps implicit in the formulations of English and American law. It is true that punishment is a significant aspect of our formal responses to

[10] See further Duff, *Answering for Crime*, chs 4.4, 7.3. The conduct constituting a *malum prohibitum* is thus not necessarily wrongful prior to its legal regulation, but must be wrongful prior to its criminalization.

crime: any adequate theory of criminal law must either explain the legitimizing rationale of punishment or show how criminal law can do without it. But the criminal process that connects crime to punishment is an independently significant dimension of the formal response for which the criminal law provides. A criminal trial (the most publicly visible manifestation of the criminal process) is not just a procedure through which punishments are allocated to those who supposedly deserve them. It is best understood as a process through which alleged offenders are called to answer or to account: to answer to the charge of wrongdoing (initially by pleading 'Guilty' or 'Not Guilty'); and then, if the prosecution proves that they committed the offence charged, to answer for that commission—either by offering an exculpatory defence, or by accepting the condemnation that a conviction expresses.[11]

The criminal process is not the only legal process through which people may be called to answer. Some civil cases have this character, at least in the eyes and intention of those who bring them: their aim is not so much to secure the compensation that provides their suit's formal focus, as to bring to account those whom they hold responsible for the loss they have suffered. First, however, a civil case is formally focused on providing remedies rather than on calling anyone to account: the question is who should bear the cost of the harm that must be repaired or averted. Second, the formal focus is on harms rather than wrongs: even if fault, and thus wrongdoing, is a condition of civil liability, the focus is on paying for the harm for which the defendant is culpably responsible rather than on the wrongfulness of his conduct.[12] Third, the case is brought by the allegedly injured claimant: although the law enables her to pursue the complaint, it is her case; it is to her that the defendant (if liable) owes explanation, apology, and compensation. In many criminal cases there is also a direct victim to whom the defendant owes something,[13] and there is much to be said about the role of victims in the criminal process: but the case is brought by the state or the polity, not by the direct victim; the defendant is called to answer by and to, not (just) the direct victim, but the whole polity. That is the force of calling crimes public wrongs: they are wrongs in which the whole polity takes a proper interest, not simply by providing the institutions through which victims can pursue 'their' offenders, as the civil law does, but by calling the offender to answer for a wrong that is public rather than private.

If this is right, however, it raises a further important question about the criminal law: who calls the alleged wrongdoers to account; to whom must they answer?

---

[11] See further RA Duff, L Farmer, SE Marshall, and V Tadros, *The Trial on Trial III: Towards a Normative Theory of the Criminal Trial* (Oxford: Hart Publishing, 2007).

[12] Punitive damages, which precisely focus on fault and wrongdoing, are inconsistent with this account, but are arguably inconsistent with the proper purposes of civil law.

[13] Though what he owes, what (if anything) could count as reparation for wrongdoing, is another question that we cannot pursue here.

2 CRIMINAL LAW AND CIVIC COMMUNITY

A central purpose of criminal law which distinguishes it from other modes of legal regulation is to provide for those who commit public wrongs to be called to public account for what they have done. Now any account of criminal law raises questions about who has the authority to do what to whom: whether we see criminal law as, for instance, a technique for preventing harm by deterring or incapacitating potential harm causers, or as a method of ensuring that wrongdoers suffer the punishments they deserve, we must ask not only who should be subject to the criminal law's coercive attention, but who is authorized to coerce them, in whose name. An account focused on calling to account raises such questions very directly. We must ask, of course, who is called to account; and the obvious first answer—'those who commit public wrongs'— cannot be a full answer, since any plausible criminal process must also summon some innocents to answer to criminal charges. So we need an account of the conditions given which people who might well be (and must be presumed to be) innocent may be subjected to investigation and prosecution; of the procedures through which people may be called to answer; and the conditions given which they may be convicted. But we must also ask by, and to whom, they are called to account. For accounting is a two-way relationship: A is called to answer by and to B, who claims the right thus to hold A to account. When A is the defendant in a criminal trial, who or what is B?

Furthermore, a practice of calling to account presupposes a community to which caller and called belong, within which this process makes sense. More precisely, it must presuppose a linguistic and normative commonality; and a substantial community, though not necessarily one to which caller and called both fully belong.

It must presuppose some linguistic and normative commonality because when B calls A to answer, the legitimacy (indeed, the intelligibility) of that calling depends on A being able to understand and respond: it makes no sense to call someone to answer if that person cannot do so.[14] But the calling (and answering) must then be conducted in a language that, even if it is not A's (or B's) own language, is accessible to him either directly or, failing that, through an interpreter. It also requires that the values by reference to which A is called to account, the values that he is accused of violating, are accessible to him as values that he could make his own. We call A to account for doing something that he should not, we claim, have done, ie for acting as he had good reason not to act; but we can say that A ought to Φ, or has good reason to Φ, only if that reason to Φ is within A's conceptual and motivational grasp.[15]

---

[14] Which is why it matters that the defendant in a criminal trial is fit to plead—able to understand and answer to the charge.

[15] There is much more to be said about the sense in which the reasons that we take A to have must be within his reach: for useful surveys see J Lenman, 'Reasons for Action: Justification vs. Explanation', *Stanford Encyclopedia of Philosophy (Spring 2010)*, at <http://plato.stanford.edu/archives/spr2010/

Furthermore, in calling A to account we seek a response from him—an answer that might involve a denial that he acted as we allege; or a denial that he violated the values to which we appeal; or a reasoned denial of those values; or an explanation of his action which, whilst admitting that he acted against the reasons that we cite, seeks to justify or excuse his action; or an admission that he acted wrongly, and an apologetic explanation of his conduct which does not seek to exculpate him. But whatever kind of answer he is to give, he will be able to give it only if he can understand the charge to which it is to be an answer: only if he can understand, that is, not merely whatever factual claims we make about what he did, but the values to which our accusation appeals, and recognize those values as imaginable sources of reasons for action.

I won't spend longer on the need for this kind of linguistic and normative commonality between caller and called here, because our concern is with a more substantial requirement of community as a framework within which people can be called to account.

Calling to account involves a relationship between caller and called: a relationship which, though it might be transformed by the calling (and answering), cannot be created *ex nihilo* by this interaction. There must be some relationship between B who calls and A who is called that gives B the right or the standing thus to call A: some relationship that makes A's alleged wrongdoing B's business, and that entitles B to make this demand. This is a central aspect of our dealings with each other— that not everything is everyone's business. If you see me in a cafe, eating a large hamburger with double chips, you might think that I am being imprudent with my health; but if you take it on yourself to approach me and call me to account for my behaviour, I might reasonably respond, not by answering to you for my conduct (explaining, justifying, excusing my behaviour, or admitting its imprudence), but by saying that it is none of your business. I answer to some people for my dietary misconduct—my family, my doctor, perhaps my friends; but I am not answerable to you, a passing stranger.[16] To show that A is being legitimately called to account, we must show not just that there is something for which he should have to answer, but that those who call him have the standing to do so—that it is their business. We must therefore understand just who is calling the defendant to account in a criminal trial; only then can we ask whether they have the appropriate standing.

It might seem that I am exaggerating the problem here. I have argued that criminal law is concerned with moral wrongdoing (of certain kinds); but whilst my dietary or other species of imprudence might not be a stranger's the business, surely moral

---

entries/reasons-just-vs-expl/>; S Finlay and M Schroeder, 'Reasons for Action: Internal vs. External', *Stanford Encyclopedia of Philosophy* (Fall 2008), at <http://plato.stanford.edu/archives/fall2008/entries/ reasons-internal-external/>.

[16] Matters might be different if your reason for challenging me had to do not with my health but (eg) with the immorality of eating meat; I turn to this kind of case shortly.

wrongdoing is the business of every moral agent.[17] So what gives us standing to call criminal offenders to account is the fact that we are all members of the broad, indeed universal, community of moral agents. Such a view is implied by Moore's account of the function of criminal law—to punish 'all and only those who are morally culpable in the doing of some morally wrongful act':[18] if an action is made eligible for the criminal law's attention by its culpable immorality, it is the business of all moral agents. One question that this suggestion provokes is whether moral wrongdoing is always the business of all moral agents. That seems true of the most egregious moral wrongs: if I see or become aware of a murder, a rape, a violent assault, a serious fraud, I cannot say that it is none of my moral business and literally or metaphorically pass on by; I have reason to intervene, or to take steps to secure intervention by others.[19] But there are many wrongs in relation to which both wrongdoer and victim can reasonably rebuff an intervener with some version of 'It's not your business': the wrongdoer can argue that he is not answerable to this stranger; nor can we plausibly explain this by saying that whilst any other moral agent has reason to intervene, countervailing reasons often make intervention on balance inadvisable. If I regularly fail to buy my round for the friends with whom I drink, that is their business; but it is not even in principle the business of the passing stranger who happens to hear about it.

However, even if all moral wrongdoing is in principle the business of all moral agents, this does not provide a plausible account of whose business crime is: of who has the standing to call criminal wrongdoers to account. For, first, the criminal law is not properly concerned with every kind of moral wrongdoing: of some matters it is appropriate to say, in a liberal polity, that they are, 'in brief and crude terms, not the law's business'.[20] It could be argued that although all moral wrongs are in principle the criminal law's business (there is good reason to criminalize them so that their perpetrators can be called to account), for many kinds of moral wrong there are persuasive countervailing reasons against criminalization:[21] but it seems as implausible to say that there is reason to criminalize my failure to buy a round as to say that it is anyone's moral business except my friends.

[17] Compare TM Scanlon, *Moral Dimensions: Permissibility, Meaning, Blame* (Cambridge, Mass: Harvard University Press, 2008), 139–40: 'the moral relationship' that grounds the legitimacy of moral blame is a matter of the 'mutual concern that, ideally, we all have toward other rational beings'.

[18] Moore, *Placing Blame*, 33–5.

[19] I have moral reason to intervene, even if I have no legal duty to do so.

[20] As the Wolfenden Committee famously put it, in relation to consensual homosexual activity between adults: J Wolfenden, *Report of the Committee on Homosexual Offences and Prostitution* (London: HMSO, 1957), para 61. Even those who believe, misguidedly, that such conduct is morally wrong should also agree that this is not a moral issue on which the criminal law should take a view—that it is in that sense private.

[21] Compare Moore, *Placing Blame*, ch 16; 'A Tale of Two Theories' (2009) 28 *Criminal Justice Ethics* 27, 31–3.

Second, domestic criminal law is limited not merely in the kinds of wrong over which it claims jurisdiction, but in the jurisdiction it claims even over the kinds of wrong with which it deals. If a Polish citizen attacks a French citizen in Germany, that is not a crime for which he could be tried or convicted in an English court, even if he happened to come to England, and sufficient evidence for a conviction was available in England. He might be arrested, and extradited to face trial in Germany:[22] but to extradite someone is not to call him to answer in the jurisdiction from which he is extradited; it is to assist another jurisdiction in holding him to account under its laws.

It might be argued that this is a matter of pragmatic convenience (and of international politics). What ultimately matters is that wrongdoers be brought to account, but it is sensible that those who are best placed to discharge this task should take charge of it; when properly functioning nation states are able and willing to deal with wrongs committed within their territory, they should be allowed sovereignty over these as over other matters, and neither other states nor international bodies should have the right to intervene.[23] This provides one rationale for the Territoriality Principle, which largely determines the issue of jurisdiction in many legal systems:[24] a state's courts have jurisdiction over all crimes committed within its territory. One way to put this point would be to say that the offences defined by the criminal law can be committed anywhere, so that the Polish assailant commits the crime of wounding under English law; but that English courts have no jurisdiction over that token of the crime. That would, however, be misleading: criminal statutes passed by the UK legislature do not extend to other parts of the world (they might not extend to all parts of the United Kingdom). The better way to put the point is that an assault in Germany is not a crime under English criminal law: not because English law permits such conduct, but because it has no authority over it and is therefore rightly silent about it. If we ask why that should be, an obvious answer is that this promotes the efficient enforcement of the demands of criminal justice, whilst respecting state sovereignty: so long as a state deals efficiently with the kinds of wrong committed within its territory that require some formal response, it should be left free to do so; other states should not intrude by trying to deal with such wrongs themselves. English law and courts should be allowed exclusive local jurisdiction over crimes committed in England, if and because this is an efficient way to satisfy the (universal, non-local) demands of justice. Should a state utterly fail to satisfy those demands of justice, however, other states or international bodies might be entitled to intervene. They

---

[22]   On whether he could be tried in France or in Poland, and on the 'universal jurisdiction' that some systems of domestic criminal law claim over some crimes, see at nn 29, 31 below.

[23]   Compare the account of international law offered in A Altman and CH Wellman, *A Liberal Theory of International Justice* (Oxford: Oxford University Press, 2009), esp ch 4; and see Wellman in this volume.

[24]   See M Hirst, *Jurisdiction and the Ambit of the Criminal Law* (Oxford: Oxford University Press, 2003), ch 1; also eg German Criminal Code, s 3.

hold back from claiming jurisdiction (a jurisdiction which they could in principle have claimed) over crimes committed within another state's borders out of respect for that state's sovereignty and a recognition that it is better placed to deal with such crimes; but in principle that claim can be revived if that condition is not satisfied.

That answer, however, seems unsatisfying, rather as comparably impersonal accounts of morality are unsatisfying. Moral philosophers sometimes struggle to make moral sense of a range of partial, particular attachments that are central to our lives, but that do not fit easily into the structure of impartialist moral theories, in particular consequentialist theories whose grounding principle is some version of the Utilitarian maxim that our single moral duty is to promote the greatest good of the greatest number. From the perspective of that impersonal maxim, our particular attachments to our friends, families, colleagues, countries seem hard to justify: surely we could often achieve more good by benefiting strangers than by benefiting our own friends, family, colleagues, or fellow citizens. On the other hand, and though most of us should certainly do much more than we do for distant strangers, it is very hard to imagine a satisfactory human life without such partial attachments: can we really accept that we act wrongly in showing preference for friends, families, and others who are in various ways close to us?[25] I cannot discuss this question here, save to notice one kind of attempt to reconcile the demands of an impersonalist morality with our partial attachments by arguing that we usually serve those impersonal demands most efficiently by fostering suitable partial attachments: I may pay special attention to my friends, my family, and so on, so long as by doing so (and by maintaining those dispositions that lead me to do so) I am actually doing as much as could be reasonably expected of me to advance the general good. However, apart from doubts about the large empirical claims on which such arguments depend, they do not do justice to the role that such attachments play in our lives: the worth, including the moral worth, of my love for my friends or family does not depend on the contribution that such love, or the disposition it manifests, makes to some larger, universal, general good; we find its value within, rather than beyond, the relationships that it structures.[26]

Somewhat similarly, such a pragmatic or instrumentalist explanation of the jurisdiction of domestic criminal law should be unsatisfying for members of any properly functioning polity. One reason for this emerges when we ask why it seemed important for Saddam Hussein to be tried in Iraq for crimes he committed against Iraqis; or why people might object when 'crimes against humanity' committed within a particular nation (as happened in former Yugoslavia, for instance) are taken over by the International Criminal Court (ICC); or why it would have been better for

---

[25] Some would say firmly that we do, because mere distance (whether physical or psychological) cannot be a relevant modifier of the basic demands of morality—a position associated particularly with Peter Singer.

[26] L Blum, *Friendship, Altruism and Morality* (London: Routledge, 1980); J Cottingham, 'Partiality and the Virtues', in R Crisp (ed), *How Should One Live?* (Oxford: Oxford University Press, 1996), 57.

Augusto Pinochet to be tried in Chile for his crimes against Chilean victims, rather than in a European state's courts under a claim of universal jurisdiction; or why the victim of a serious attack (and those close to him) might not be content to see his attacker convicted in a foreign court, even if he was able to attend. The thought is in each case that 'we' should try 'our' wrongs and their perpetrators, and that trial by some foreign or international court, even if it produces a warranted conviction and sentence, can be at best an inadequate substitute.[27] 'We' should try the case not because we are contingently best placed to do so, but because it is our business in a way that it is not so especially the business of other states or bodies. Who then is this 'we'? It is not a 'we' as large as humanity, or the realm of moral agents—for that would not explain these more local feelings. Nor is it a 'we' as limited as the direct victims of the crimes in question, or their families and friends: it is, I suggest, a 'we' consisting in all members of the political community within which the crimes were committed, who recognize the victims as fellow members whose wrongs they should share.

It is worth noting too that while the pragmatic account can say something both about the authority of international criminal tribunals, and about claims to universal jurisdiction over some crimes made by some legal systems, it cannot explain why the principles of nationality and of passive personality should seem plausible. As to international or universal jurisdiction, the founding statute of the ICC affirms 'that the most serious crimes of concern to the international community as a whole must not go unpunished',[28] and claims to universal jurisdiction typically focus on crimes of which something similar could be said:[29] a pragmatic theorist could explain such provisions by arguing that international or universal jurisdiction is appropriate for crimes in relation to which, given their seriousness, the demand that their perpetrators be brought to justice is so insistent that it is worth making international provision for their punishment if the local courts cannot (or will not) carry out that task.[30] As to the principles of nationality and of passive personality, the former gives the national courts jurisdiction over crimes committed abroad by the state's citizens, whilst the latter gives them jurisdiction over crimes committed abroad against the state's citizens:[31] neither of these can be readily

---

[27] There are of course other reasons bearing on these examples: eg arguments against trying Saddam Hussein in Iraq that have to do with his chances of a fair trial; reasons for mistrusting the ICC having to do with its perceived political character. The Eichmann case is also worth considering in this context: should he ideally have been tried in Israel, or in Germany, or by an international court?

[28] Rome Statute of the International Criminal Court, Preamble.

[29] Eg Criminal Justice Act 1988, s 134: torture committed or sanctioned by public officials is a crime triable in English courts, wherever and against whomever it is committed; applied in *R v Bow Street Metropolitan Stipendiary Magistrate ex p Pinochet Ugarte* [2000] 1 AC 147.

[30] Such a theorist might also find support in the ICC's principle of complementarity—that it can try only cases that have not been properly investigated by a state with jurisdiction (Rome Statute, art 17).

[31] See eg French *Code Pénal*, art 113.6–7; German *Strafgesetzbuch*, s 7.1–2, Sex Offenders Act 1997, s 7. See generally Hirst, *Jurisdiction and the Ambit of the Criminal Law*, ch 5.

rationalized in terms of the efficient satisfaction of the demands of an impersonal and universal justice.

Other explanations of a Territoriality Principle might be offered which do not appeal to any rich notion of political community. It might be argued, for instance, that everyone living, permanently or temporarily, in a geographical area has an interest in the enforcement within that area of a legal system which criminalizes certain kinds of harmful wrongdoing, and that this grounds the jurisdiction of that system's courts over crimes committed within that area. The interests of everyone within that area are served by a criminal law that binds and protects them all; this gives the state in whose territory that area falls the authority to maintain such a system of law.[32] It is certainly true that we each have an interest in being protected against the kinds of wrong that a decent system of criminal law criminalizes; it is also true that, for many such wrongs, we have that interest whether we are living in a state of which we are members, or are temporary residents in or visitors to a foreign land.[33] But is this enough to make sense of a state's peculiar jurisdiction over crimes committed within its territory?

Such an account separates the state, as the source and enforcer of criminal law, from the political community whose law (one might think) it should be, and of which the state should be the formal manifestation: the state has, apparently, just the same relationship to all those living within its territory. However, if we are to understand the criminal law not simply as a set of prohibitions, but as a practice through which wrongdoers are called to public account, we must be able to ground it in some kind of community—a 'we' who call them to account. This 'we' requires not merely an aggregate of individual interests in such matters as security, but a collective interest that is 'our' interest.[34] A collective interest, however, requires more than a collection of people who happen to find themselves in the same geographical territory; it requires people who can see themselves as being engaged in a common enterprise of living not just alongside each other, but together. People who happen to be thrown together might form some such common enterprise (as they do, with greater or lesser success, in films about castaways), and the criminal law can strengthen such an enterprise: but it must presuppose an already existing 'we', an already existing (even if partly aspirational) community whose law it is. Nor can that community be simply a moral community to which all rational agents, or all human beings, belong.[35] The intelligibility of such an all-embracing community is crucial to the

---

[32] See A Chehtman, 'The Extraterritorial Scope of the Right to Punish' (2010) 29 *Law and Philosophy* 127 (he argues against universal jurisdiction, and against the principles of nationality and passive personality).

[33] Only 'for many such wrongs' because some criminal wrongs, notably those that threaten the longer term operations of the state, can plausibly be said to affect only members.

[34] As Chehtman realizes in 'The Extraterritorial Scope of the Right to Punish', eg at 134.

[35] Compare Scanlon, *Moral Dimensions*; on the difference between talk of rational agents and talk of human beings, see R Gaita, *Good and Evil: An Absolute Conception* (2nd edn; London: Routledge, 2004), ch 3.

prospects of a cosmopolitan political theory,[36] and perhaps to the ambitions of the ICC, if we take the Preamble to the Rome Statute seriously.[37] But systems of domestic criminal law are the laws of smaller communities than that; and since the criminal law is part of the apparatus of the state, they belong to political rather than to purely moral communities: the criminal law's community must be a polity.

That is why I have argued previously that we should appeal to citizenship as the basis of the community on which criminal law depends.[38] There are two stages to this argument. The first claim is that any system of criminal law requires a political community whose law it is: a 'we' whose business the criminal law declares certain kinds of wrong to be, to whom those who commit such wrongs must answer. That is the 'we' over whom the law primarily claims authority; and since the criminal law is an aspect of the state, the 'we' must be the members of the polity whose state it is. Furthermore, criminal law is an ongoing, not just a momentary, enterprise: it involves laws, not mere orders; institutions and procedures, not merely ad hoc arrangements. It is possible only within the framework of a larger political community, which embodies the constitutional structures that make law possible (and that are themselves made possible by law), and structures the form of life within which criminal law can operate.[39]

This is not yet to say, however, that criminal law requires the kind of democratic polity that talk of citizens might connote: non-egalitarian political communities have criminal laws. A conception of criminal law as a law for citizens depends on a democratic political theory, to argue that a legitimate criminal law requires a political community whose members share the status of citizen; citizenship being understood roughly as equal, mutually respectful participation in the civic enterprise.[40] The nature of that civic enterprise, and the character and extent of its claims on citizens' lives, is a matter for political deliberation. At one extreme lie ambitiously demanding kinds of communitarianism that make what liberals see as oppressively intrusive demands on citizens, and leave too small a 'private' realm in which individuals can pursue their own conceptions of the good, in the company of those with whom they choose to associate: religious communities that claim the bodies and souls of their members are extreme examples of this communitarian vision, or

---

[36] See eg S Caney, *Justice Beyond Borders: A Global Political Theory* (Oxford: Oxford University Press, 2005); D Held, *Cosmopolitanism: A Defence* (Cambridge: Polity Press, 2003).

[37] See at n 28 above; RA Duff, 'Authority and Responsibility in International Criminal Law', in S Besson and J Tasioulas (eds), *Philosophy of International Law* (Oxford: Oxford University Press, 2010).

[38] See Duff, *Answering for Crime*, ch 2.2.

[39] On the importance of setting criminal law in its constitutional context, see Thorburn in this volume.

[40] Such a theory is best articulated in republicanism: see eg R Dagger, *Civic Virtues: Rights, Citizenship and Republican Liberalism* (Oxford: Oxford University Press, 1997), and in this volume; also RM Dworkin, *A Matter of Principle* (Cambridge, MA: Harvard University Press, 1985), ch 8, on the equal concern and respect that citizens owe each other.

nightmare. At another extreme lies the kind of radical individualist liberalism that communitarian critics fear, which insists upon an extensive realm of 'private' life, and a minimal 'public' sphere. We need not engage in this debate here, however. All we need to note is that however minimal the public sphere of matters that concern all citizens is taken to be, any polity must have a public sphere, structured by its self-defining values. Those values include norms about how citizens should treat each other, which gives us the basis for an idea of public wrongs—of wrongdoing that violates the polity's defining values; and this then gives us a basis for an idea of criminal law as a formal way of identifying and responding to such wrongs.[41]

Public wrongs are our wrongs as citizens—wrongs in which we take a proper interest, to which we should collectively respond, for which we claim the right (and perhaps the duty) to call the perpetrator to answer to us. Some such wrongs are public in their material impact: if we ask who is wronged the answer is 'the public'; this is true of, for instance, some wrongs of general endangerment and environmental damage; of wrongs that threaten public institutions; of frauds committed against the public purse. Others take individuals as their direct victims, but count as 'our' wrongs because they violate our public values, and because we share them with the victim: our concern for the victim as our fellow citizen makes them our business. So does our recognition of the wrongdoer as a fellow citizen: what is done by one of us, when it impinges on our shared values, is our business.[42] If a wrong is our business, we may, perhaps should, respond to it, and seek to call its perpetrator to account.

To avoid misunderstanding, I should make clear that the wrongfulness of a public wrong does not depend on its being public: public wrongs are, in this context, wrongs that concern us all as citizens. Sometimes, as I noted above, conduct is wrongful because of its impact on the public—because it attacks or threatens a public good, or an institution that is crucial to our civic life. Sometimes the wrongfulness of a public wrong lies partly in its civic character: the wrong consists, for instance, in failing to show a fellow citizen the respect or concern due to her as a fellow citizen. Often, however, what makes the conduct wrong is independent of its impact on a wider public, and it is wrong because that is not how one should treat anyone, fellow citizen or not. This is obviously true of familiar *mala in se*: what makes murder or rape wrong has to do with what is done to the direct victim; nor is it plausible to argue that what makes them criminalizable is some further feature to do with their effect on 'the public'.[43] To say that such wrongs are 'public'

[41] But only a basis: see further RA Duff, 'Responsibility, Restoration and Retribution', in M Tonry (ed), *Retributivism Has a Past: Has it a Future?* (Oxford: Oxford University Press, forthcoming).

[42] That is what grounds the principles of nationality and passive personality (see at n 31 above).

[43] See further Marshall and Duff, 'Criminalization and Sharing Wrongs'; Duff, *Answering for Crime*, ch 6.5. Contrast J Gardner and S Shute, 'The Wrongness of Rape', in J Horder (ed), *Oxford Essays in Jurisprudence*, 4th Series (Oxford: Oxford University Press, 2000), 193, arguing that although the moral wrongness of rape does not lie in its harmful effects, our reasons for criminalizing it do depend on the wider effects of failing to criminalize it; for an incisive critique, see J Stanton-Ife, 'Horrific

wrongs is, rather, to say that they are wrongs that concern all citizens, in virtue of their civic fellowship with the victim (and the offender). To identify a wrong as a public wrong in the context of a particular polity's criminal law thus does not imply that it is not a wrong, or not so serious a wrong, when committed elsewhere or against someone who is not a citizen of the polity. In saying that a rape committed in England is a crime in English law for which the rapist must answer in an English court, whilst a rape committed in Poland is not a wrong in English law or a matter for the English courts,[44] we do not imply that the rape in Poland is not wrong, or less wrong, or wrong on different grounds. Nor do we imply that it is not a wrong that matters to us as human beings, or as moral agents: it is, we can say, our moral or human business (though that raises the question of what we can do about it simply as human beings or moral agents), as a serious wrong committed against a fellow human being. What is at issue here, however, is what concerns us as citizens, and what concerns the criminal law of this particular polity; we cannot see a rape committed in Poland as a wrong committed within our civic enterprise as a polity or, therefore, as a wrong that concerns our criminal law.

We can put the core point here in the language of associative obligations.[45] The criminal law gives institutional form to a particular subset of what we might call secondary associative obligations: associative because they are obligations we owe to our fellow citizens in virtue of our shared membership of the polity; secondary because they concern our civic responses to breaches of the primary obligations that the criminal law presupposes—to commissions of the kinds of wrong with which the criminal law is concerned. As citizens, we have a special duty to attend to public wrongs committed within the polity: a duty to respond to such wrongs by calling the wrongdoer to public account, which we owe to both victim and wrongdoer; a duty to answer to our fellows for our own commissions of such wrongs, and to answer to any accusations of such wrongdoing that are reasonably brought against us.

I cannot develop this account of the relationship between citizenship and the criminal law here, though much more clearly needs to be said about citizenship, about the civic enterprise, and about how we can determine which kinds of wrong are to count as public, criminalizable wrongs—the central issue of criminalization. Instead, I want to consider a set of objections to giving citizenship so central a role in our understanding of criminal law: objections that focus on the exclusionary potential of the idea of citizenship.

Crime', in RA Duff, L Farmer, SE Marshall, M Renzo, and V Tadros (eds), *The Boundaries of the Criminal Law* (Oxford: Oxford University Press, 2010).

[44] Unless we accept a principle of nationality or of passive personality (see at n 31 above), and count it as our business if it is committed by or against an English citizen: but the view offered here, while it shows how we can make sense of those principles, does not commit us to adopting them.

[45] See RM Dworkin, *Law's Empire* (London: Fontana, 1986), ch 6; J Horton 'In Defense of Associative Political Obligations' (2006) 54 *Political Studies* 427 and (2007) 55 *Political Studies* 19.

3 CITIZENS AND NON-CITIZENS

One question about the ideas of citizenship and political community as I have used them here is whether we can see the societies in which most of us live as genuine political communities, whose citizens share a commitment to a substantial set of values that define a civic enterprise in which they see themselves as mutually engaged. All I can say on that question here is that if we do not live in what can count as political communities, the legitimacy of criminal law is radically undermined, as is the legitimacy of much else about the state. However, if we bear in mind that the reality of a political community can be a matter of aspiration as much as of achieved fact; and that a political community can still be a relatively thin one, structured by a range of liberal values that leave extensive room for other kinds of community free from the demands of the polity and its civic enterprise, we might be less pessimistic. The questions I want to focus on, however, concern the limits of citizenship.[46]

Citizenship has both inclusionary and exclusionary dimensions. In a generously minded polity, citizenship is inclusive: all those born within the polity are citizens; incomers can gain citizenship relatively easily. Even then citizenship is also exclusionary: absent a cosmopolitan world order, when there are citizens there are also non-citizens, who are excluded from such rights and benefits as citizenship brings. Such exclusion is not always disturbing. It is no cause for concern that state *A* does not grant the benefits of citizenship to people living in stable and prosperous states elsewhere; nor that it does not grant *citizenship* to those living elsewhere, under more adverse conditions, who do not seek entry to it—though there is much else that it should do to assist. Nor is it cause for concern that those who visit *A* as tourists, or to do business, are not eligible for full citizenship, though we must ask about their status. But focusing on citizenship raises at least two worries about the treatment of non-citizens.

One worry concerns those who are not, and do not seek to become, citizens, but who visit the state for shorter or longer periods. How will a criminal law for citizens treat such visitors? This worry is not a deep one. Polities can be hostile, disrespectful, uncaring towards foreign visitors, denying them the protections that citizens enjoy; but that is not an implication of a focus on citizenship. Many social groups or institutions operate with a conception of guests or visitors: the group (a family; a village; a group of cohabiting friends; a university) consists, at its core, in its members; but it welcomes visitors, whom it treats with respect and concern. They do not play the role that members play in determining the group's activities (they do not take decision-making roles in political deliberation or its analogue); but decent groups accord visitors the kinds of support and protection that their members enjoy. There

---

[46] I am especially grateful to Lucia Zedner for forcing me to think more seriously about these issues.

is much more to say about the status of guest or visitor, and what it can involve; but the crucial point is that in any decent polity, guests and visitors are protected by its criminal law in the same way as its citizens.

More precisely, they are protected and bound by the criminal law. As to protection, the key issue is not whether conduct towards them that the local law defines as criminal when done to a citizen counts as wrong. There might be some wrongs that can only be committed against fellow citizens: electoral misconduct, for instance, or failing to pay one's taxes. Most criminal wrongs, however, are wrongs whether committed by, or against, citizens or non-citizens: the criminal law, as we saw, presupposes wrongfulness rather than creating it. The more important point concerns responses to wrongdoing: a decent polity will count and treat wrongs committed within its borders against visitors as no less public, no less wrongful, than wrongs committed against citizens. Not only should we not wrong guests: if a guest in our home is wronged, that is our business; and whilst there are dangers that citizens will not take wrongs against visitors as seriously as they take wrongs against citizens ('She was only a tourist'), members of a civilized polity will not discriminate in this way.[47]

That is true whether the guest is attacked by a citizen or by another visitor, which brings us to other side of the coin: that guests are both protected and bound. The fact that the person I attack is a visitor, rather than a citizen, does not exempt me from criminal prosecution; nor does the fact that I am myself a visitor who attacks another visitor. There are two versions of this point, relevant to different types of crime. On one version, visitors are expected to abide by the local rules ('When in Rome...'), and may be called to account by their hosts if they do not: whatever kinds of conduct might be permissible at home (as to which the local law is properly silent), when they are here they should obey 'our' rules. This version is appropriate in some contexts. The point is not merely that local conventions often differ—for instance, that here we drive on the left: in such cases the wrong itself, whether committed by a guest or by a citizen, consists in failure to respect a justified convention. Rather, it is that sometimes we must recognize the fact of reasonable disagreement (especially given different cultural backgrounds that may alter the meanings of actions) about values that inform our criminal law—for instance, about what counts as offensive conduct, or as dishonesty. In such cases we say to visitors that they should eschew such conduct while they are here, not (just) because it is wrong, but out of respect for the local values and attitudes.[48] In other cases, however, our claim should be more

---

[47] Suppose the guest is uninvited—an illegal immigrant? One question that I cannot pursue here concerns the conditions under which a polity should admit would-be entrants either to residence or to citizenship (how open its doors should be); but for so long as they are in the polity they must be treated with respect.

[48] Another question that I cannot pursue here is whether we should sometimes say something analogous to a citizen who reasonably dissents from the values expressed in the law: should we (eg) say to one who believes that certain kinds of euthanasia should be legally permissible, not that she

robust: such conduct is wrong, wherever it is committed, although it becomes our business as a polity (the business of our criminal law) only when it is committed in our territory. We should not say to a wife-beater, for instance, that he ought to refrain from beating his wife whilst he is here out of respect for local laws; we should say that wife-beating is a wrong that he ought not to commit anywhere, and for which we will call him to answer if he commits it here. Sometimes we criticize guests for failing to respect local rules or sensibilities; sometimes we criticize them for committing wrongs in our home, when the significance of the location is not that it makes wrongful what might not have been wrong elsewhere, but that it makes our business a wrong that would not have been our business had it been committed elsewhere.

An account that emphasizes citizenship faces deeper worries in other kinds of case, which we can approach via Jakobs' notorious distinction between *Bürgerstrafrecht* (citizen criminal law) and *Feindstrafrecht* (enemy criminal law).[49] *Bürgerstrafrecht* is for citizens. It respects the presumption of innocence, not only as a principle governing the allocation of burdens of proof in the trial, but as a broader principle of trust: we should presume each other to be 'free of harmful intentions',[50] and trust each other to refrain from future crimes. It treats offenders as members of the polity, whose trials and punishments must respect that status. By contrast, *Feindstrafrecht* abandons criminal law as I have characterized it: it treats those on whom it is imposed not as citizens, but as actual or potential enemies; it seeks to control them for the sake of security, rather than to address them as members of the normative community.

Such a distinction is certainly drawn in contemporary penal theory, rhetoric, and practice. In penal theory, some argue that those who commit crimes lose their standing as citizens, so that we can treat them in ways in which we could not treat citizens, and deny them the respect and concern that we owe to citizens;[51] such a view finds formal legal expression in the loss of the right to vote (a central aspect of citizenship) suffered during their incarceration by those serving prison terms in Britain,[52] and for life by convicted felons in some American states.[53] In penal rhetoric, we are all too familiar with talk of a 'war on' drugs, or crime, or terrorism, which portrays the

---

ought to accept the law's declaration that they are wrong, but that though her view is reasonable, she should respect the public view as expressed in the law? (In both cases we must of course ask whether we could so revise the law that reasonable dissenters could act as they think right without facing criminal liability.)

[49] See eg G Jakobs: 'Bürgerstrafrecht und Feindstrafrecht' (2004) HRRS 88 at <http://www.hrr-strafrecht.de/hrr/archiv/04-03/hrrs-3-04.pdf>. For critical discussion, see C G-J Díez, 'Enemy Combatants Versus Enemy Criminal Law' (2008) 11 *New Criminal Law Review* 529; also L Zedner, 'Security, the State, and the Citizen: the Changing Architecture of Crime Control' (2010) 13 *New Criminal Law Review* 379.

[50] See J Floud and W Young, *Dangerousness and Criminal Justice* (London: Heinemann, 1981), 44.

[51] Eg AI Goldman, 'Toward a New Theory of Punishment' (1982) 1 *Law and Philosophy* 57; CW Morris, 'Punishment and Loss of Moral Standing' (1991) 21 *Canadian Journal of Philosophy* 53.

[52] Despite the (very qualified) ECtHR ruling in *Hirst v UK* (2006) 42 EHRR 41.

[53] See L Wacquant, 'Deadly Symbiosis' (2001) 3 *Punishment & Society* 95.

disfavoured group of (actual or potential) offenders as outsiders—a 'them' against whom the law-abiding 'we' must be protected. In penal practice the distinction is seen in, for instance, the provisions for 'imprisonment for public protection' in England,[54] and the 'three strikes' provisions in the United States;[55] in provisions for those suspected of being involved in terrorist activities, in particular provisions for detention, or other kinds of restriction, without a conviction;[56] and in a wide range of other restrictive measures that are more concerned with preventing future crime than with responding appropriately to past crimes.[57] So is it a sound objection to a citizenship-based account of criminal law that it allows, or even encourages, such discrimination between 'citizens' and 'enemies'?

The answer is a firm but qualified 'No'. The answer is firm, because the criminal law can and should be a criminal law for all citizens—including actual and suspected offenders: as I argued in section 2, the criminal law must address us all, including the many of us who are actual or potential offenders, as members of the normative community whose law it is. It must take our public wrongdoing seriously, holding us to account for it, and thus also aiming to repair our civic relationships with our fellow citizens: but it holds us to account precisely as citizens whose full membership of the polity is not in doubt—which is why the right to vote in prison is symbolically important. Such a conception of those who commit crimes is challenging: it is tempting for self-defined 'law-abiding citizens' to regard offenders as less than (full) citizens. But that is to say only, and unsurprisingly, that political community is challenging. Nor is the communitarian approach that I have taken peculiarly vulnerable here: the aspiration to secure respect for the rights (human, moral, political, legal) of offenders, or to treat them still as full parties to the social contract, is no less challenging. The problem of exclusion, whether from citizenship, from the realm of rights, or from the social contract, need not be a problem for normative theory; it is a moral problem for our attitudes and practices.[58]

---

[54] See Criminal Justice Act 2003, ss 224–36; Criminal Justice and Immigration Act 208, ss 13–20; P Ramsay, 'A Political Theory of Imprisonment for Public Protection', in Tonry (ed), *Retributivism Has a Past*.

[55] See eg California Penal Code, §§ 667, 1170.12; F Zimring, G Hawkins, and S Kamin, *Punishment and Democracy: Three Strikes and You're Out in California* (Oxford: Oxford University Press, 2001).

[56] L Zedner, 'Securing Liberty in the Face of Terror: Reflections from Criminal Justice' (2005) 32 *Journal of Law and Society* 507; V Tadros, 'Justice and Terrorism' (2007) 10 *New Criminal Law Review* 658.

[57] See generally Ashworth and Zedner in this volume, and 'Defending the Criminal Law: Reflections on the Changing Character of Crime, Procedure, and Sanctions' (2008) 2 *Criminal Law and Philosophy* 21.

[58] For an argument to similar conclusions from contractualist premises, see C Brettschneider, 'The Rights of the Guilty: Punishment and Political Legitimacy' (2007) 35 *Political Theory* 175; see also RA Duff, 'A Criminal Law for Citizens' (2010) 14 *Theoretical Criminology* 293. A citizenship-based approach can also explain why we should worry about punishing those who have suffered seriously unjust disadvantages (see Green in this volume): our collective failure to treat them as fellow citizens undermines our standing to call them to account (see V Tadros, 'Poverty and Criminal Responsibility'

The firm 'No' offered in the previous paragraph must also, however, be qualified, since two kinds of case put it under pressure: but such cases must be problematic for any normative theory of criminal law, and therefore do not cast doubt on the account offered here.

The first kind of case concerns those who engage persistently in crimes of a character and seriousness that deny the basic values on which the civic enterprise depends (or, others might say, deny the most basic terms of the social contract); crimes so persistent that they constitute a criminal career, rather than a series of individual wrongs. Should we insist that such people must still be recognized and treated as full members of the normative community—that such membership is wholly unconditional? Or does there come a point at which we may, or must, say that whilst we still owe them the respect and concern due to any human being, the chance to restore themselves to full citizenship by showing that they can again be trusted, and help in achieving this, we cannot now treat them as full members? But we cannot tackle the question in such abstract terms: we must ask what is at stake in retaining or losing 'full citizenship' in this context—and bear in mind that what is at stake need not be 'citizenship' as a unitary or seamless status, but more particular aspects of membership of the polity.

Some of those aspects, we should surely say, are not alienable or conditional, for instance, the rights to such benefits of citizenship as education, health care, and social security. Others might be argued over—for instance, the right to vote or otherwise participate in the political process: just because the right to vote is so important a symbol of citizenship, should we say to the serious career criminal 'Given your persistent and flagrant violation of the bonds of the polity, you can now claim no right to help determine the direction of its civic life'; or should we insist that we must still give this symbolic expression to the hope that he will rehabilitate himself? The most obviously problematic aspects, however, concern the kinds of liberty and privacy that citizens normally have a right to expect, and the associated right to be restored to full liberty, and to be free from intrusive supervision, once one has served an appropriate and determinate punishment for one's crimes. An essential feature of a liberal penal system is that punishment is finite and limited: what the offender is to undergo is determined in advance by a sentencing process structured by the question of what constitutes an appropriate response to his crime. His sentence might involve restrictions on his liberty, including imprisonment, and forms of supervision that would normally be illegitimate;[59] but once it is over, he is free from those restrictions and from such supervision, without having to prove that he will refrain from future

---

(2009) 43 *Journal of Value Inquiry* 391; RA Duff, 'Blame, Moral Standing and the Legitimacy of the Criminal Trial' (2010) 23 *Ratio* 1).

[59] On the role of different modes of punishment in a penal system that takes citizenship seriously, see RA Duff, *Punishment, Communication and Community* (New York: Oxford University Press, 2001), ch 4.2.

crimes; having served his sentence, he is once again entitled to the broad presumption of innocence.[60] Provisions for 'dangerous' persistent offenders that allow for their indefinite or life-long detention abandon this aspect of liberal criminal law,[61] and imply that a persistent offender can lose his right to that presumption—not just for a limited time, but indefinitely or for life. Those provisions are certainly far too broad: they deprive far too many offenders of their civic standing. But should we recognize that there may be what we must hope is a very small class of determined, persistent, and dangerous offenders whose criminal careers do disqualify them from that presumption: offenders whom, given their history of unrepentantly flagrant criminality, we can no longer be expected to trust as fellow citizens?

Were we to go down this route, much more work would of course need to be done on the conditions given which, and the procedures through which, such exceptional measures could be imposed; on the form that such measures could properly take; on the procedures through which they could be lifted. That last point is crucial: even if a sufficiently persistent career of sufficiently serious criminality could justify us in turning the presumption of innocence into a presumption of criminality, that presumption would have to be rebuttable; we might place on the offender the onus of offering sufficient evidence that he has changed his ways, but it must be an onus that he could discharge. We might then find that we cannot specify procedures for such measures that would be adequately safe and reliable, but the question here is whether we should even consider them in principle. I remain uncertain about how to answer that question: about whether the civic presumption that those who have undergone their punishment can be trusted, as any citizen is trusted, to refrain from future crime (a presumption that is central to a liberal republican criminal law) should be irrebuttable:[62] but it is one that faces any penal theory, and any polity that takes citizenship seriously.

The second kind of problem case concerns those involved in terrorist activities—or, more precisely, given the difficulty of defining 'terrorism', those involved in violence that aims to destabilize the polity.[63] Might we have to say that such terrorists deny their membership of the polity that they attack: whether or not they are, formally, citizens of that community, they make themselves in substance enemies engaged in a war against it? This would not exclude them from the polity on the basis of our own view of their activities: it would accept at face the value the denial of membership that their actions express; they act and should be seen as enemy soldiers engaged in covert military operations. If we are fighting a war, the criminal law withdraws somewhat: we do not charge enemy soldiers who kill in action with

---

[60] See at n 50 above.

[61] See at nn 54–5 above.

[62] See Duff, *Punishment, Communication and Community*, ch 4.4.

[63] Compare S Scheffler, 'Is Terrorism Morally Distinctive?' (2006) 14 *Journal of Political Philosophy* 1, 5.

murder in a criminal court. We try to thwart them, if necessary using fatal military force against them; if we capture them, we detain them as prisoners of war, while the war lasts. But such detention is not punishment: it does not depend on criminal conviction, or express condemnation, or aim to bring the detainee to recognize his wrongdoing; it is a preventive measure justified by the detainee's status as an enemy soldier.[64]

Enemy soldiers are not outside the law. They are both protected and bound by the laws of war: our conduct towards them, as soldiers or as prisoners of war, is governed by the laws of war; their conduct is subject to the demands of those laws, both *ad bellum* and *in bello*; they can be charged with war crimes if they violate them. This creates an obvious problem for this perspective on terrorist activities: they do not fit into the orthodox framework of the laws of warfare. There is no formal declaration of war between states; fighters do not wear uniforms that mark them as combatants (and activate the protections that combatants can claim); and if they attack civilian targets, they violate the rules of *jus in bello*. Furthermore, whatever can be said about terrorists who attack from outside the polity, those who attack from within, at least if they are formally citizens, cannot be so readily portrayed as enemy soldiers: they look more like traitors, who under the laws of war are not entitled to be treated as enemy soldiers. However, it could be argued that the phenomena of modern terrorism require us to rethink our existing categories: neither the framework of 'normal' criminal law, nor that of warfare as classically conceived, can accommodate modern terrorism; we must either articulate a new normative category, or develop our existing categories.[65]

If we should see those engaged in terrorism within the normative framework of warfare rather than of criminal law, we should not expect a liberal criminal law to deal with them. But there are two reasons for not going down this route. One is that insofar as terrorism involves attacks on civilian targets that must count as innocent, those who commit such attacks should have to answer for them as wrongs, and such answering is properly done in a criminal court (although there is a case for looking to international rather than domestic criminal courts to try serious terrorist cases). The other reason is that, absent proof of terrorist activity of a kind that could ground a criminal conviction, our question must concern the measures that we may use not against terrorists, but against *suspected* terrorists. Enemy soldiers in classical warfare wear their status visibly as a uniform: although under the conditions of modern

---

[64] On the issues raised by such detention, see A Walen, 'A Unified Theory of Detention, with Application to Preventive Detention for Suspected Terrorists', forthcoming in (2011) 70 *Maryland Law Review*.

[65] See P Gilbert, *New Terror, New Wars* (Edinburgh: Edinburgh University Press, 2003). Others might argue that the terrorist is neither criminal nor soldier, but an outlaw, *hostis humani generis* (see Blackstone, *Commentaries on the Laws of England* (Oxford: Clarendon Press, 1765–9), iv.5); against this view, we should insist that terrorists are fellow human beings who must be protected as well as bound by law.

warfare it is often difficult to distinguish combatants from non-combatants,[66] we know how to recognize an enemy soldier. In terrorism-related cases that come before our courts, however, in which special preventive measures might be imposed,[67] those who are liable to these modes of legal coercion appear not as proven terrorists, but as people suspected of involvement in terrorism who might be innocent citizens. They are therefore entitled to the presumption of innocence, and to a proper criminal process; any question of special, preventive measures can arise only after they have been duly convicted of an offence that can properly be said to amount to a determined attack on the polity itself. This is not to deny that criminal law can come under pressure in times of emergency, or that measures which subvert or bypass the requirements of liberal criminal law might then be qualifiedly justified. I cannot discuss this possibility now;[68] the point to note here is that it does not reveal a weakness in a citizenship-based account of criminal law, since it is not that account of law that invites or encourages us to exclude some people from the law's protection.

4 CONCLUSION

I have argued that we can best understand the authority and claims of criminal law in a liberal polity by understanding it as a law for citizens: a law to which citizens subject each other and themselves, under which they call public wrongdoers to account for what they have done, and are themselves ready to answer to their fellows. I have also argued that such an account need not have the kinds of exclusionary effect that worry some critics—but that it does highlight two problematic kinds of case in which it is not clear that a citizens' criminal law remains viable.

---

[66] Which is why there are serious grounds to doubt whether many kinds of warfare can be compatible with the classical *jus in bello* protections for non-combatants.

[67] See at n 56 above. The key point here is that the procedures through which such measures are imposed do not involve proof of involvement in terrorism of a kind that a criminal conviction would require.

[68] See Zedner, 'Securing Liberty in the face of Terror: Reflections from Criminal Justice'; Tadros, 'Justice and Terrorism'; J Waldron, 'Security and Liberty: The Image of Balance' (2003) 11 *Journal of Political Philosophy* 191; F Tanguay-Renaud, 'Individual Emergencies and the Rule of Criminal Law' CLPE Research Paper No. 37/2008, <http://ssrn.com/abstract=1292805>.

PART II

THE SUBSTANCE
OF CRIMINAL LAW

8

THE RESURGENCE OF CHARACTER: RESPONSIBILITY IN THE CONTEXT OF CRIMINALIZATION

NICOLA LACEY[*]

[C]riminal law does not drive criminal punishment. It would be closer to the truth to say that criminal punishment drives criminal law.[1]

(WJ Stuntz)

When guilt or innocence turns on an unmanifested intent [ie, in the subjective pattern of liability], the proof of guilt is likely to turn on an inference from the type of person the defendant is to a probabilistic conclusion about his having the prohibited intent at the relevant moment in time.[2]

(GP Fletcher)

  [*] I am grateful to David Soskice for discussion of the argument of this chapter, and to Antony Duff, Stuart Green, Kyron Huigens, Peter Ramsay, Mike Redmayne, Paul Roberts, Victor Tadros, and Lucia Zedner for comments and advice. The chapter was written during tenure of a Leverhulme Major Research Fellowship: my thanks go to the Trust for its support.
  [1] WJ Stuntz, 'The Pathological Politics of Criminal Law' (2001) 100 *Michigan Law Review* 505–600, 506.
  [2] GP Fletcher, *Rethinking Criminal Law* (Boston: Little, Brown, 1978), 131.

IN criminal law theory today, it is generally accepted that the gradual moderniza-
tion of English law has followed an uneven but clear trajectory towards the refinement of a 'general part' encompassing legal doctrines of responsibility-attribution
trained on an assessment of individual culpability. While it is conceded that some
parts of criminal law hold defendants responsible simply for causing harmful or
otherwise undesirable outcomes, the paradigm of culpability is grounded in the
idea that individual responsibility is justly attributed only when certain cognitive
and volitional capacities are engaged in the relevant conduct. Accordingly, there is
scepticism about whether assumptions about, and indeed evaluations of, character, central to pre-modern attributions of criminal responsibility, continue to play
any role in the application of the substantive law. Such assumptions are generally
regarded as having been displaced onto the pre- and post-trial stages of criminalization, where they undoubtedly structure factors such as policing and prosecution
decision making in what are often covert and other morally questionable ways.[3] And
as the most persuasive recent normative theory of character as a component of criminal responsibility argues,[4] doctrinal arrangements which ostensibly resonate with
a character principle can often be rationalized within a 'fair opportunity' account
of capacity-responsibility: criminal conduct may justly be condemned as expressing
vicious character, but only when capacity-responsibility is engaged in relation to the
relevant disposition.

In a number of recent papers,[5] I have suggested that this account is in need of
revision in at least two respects. First, there is reason to doubt whether assumptions
about character were ever entirely evacuated from criminal law in its path towards

[3] B Harcourt, 'From the Ne'er-Do-Well to the Criminal History Category: The Refinement of the
Actuarial Model in Criminal Law' (2003) 66 *Law and Contemporary Problems* 99.

[4] V Tadros, *Criminal Responsibility* (Oxford: Oxford University Press, 2005). The normative literature on character responsibility—both for and against—is vast: for key examples, see M Bayles,
'Character, Purpose and Criminal Responsibility' (1982) 1 *Law and Philosophy* 5 (drawing on Hume's
philosophy); J Gardner, 'The Gist of Excuses' (1998) 1 *Buffalo Criminal Law Review* 575; DM Kahan and
MC Nussbaum, 'Two Conceptions of Emotion in Criminal Law' (1996) 96 *Columbia Law Review* 269;
essays by K Huigens ('Homicide in Aretaic Terms'), KW Simons ('Does Punishment for "Culpable
Indifference" Simply Punish for Bad Character?'), and VF Nourse ('Hearts and Minds'), in G Binder
(ed), *The New Culpability: Motive, Character and Emotion in Criminal Law* (2002) 6 *Buffalo Criminal
Law Review Special Issue*, pp 97, 219, 361; K Huigens, 'Virtue and Inculpation' (1995) 108 *Harvard Law
Review* 1423; AC Michaels, 'Acceptance: The Missing Mental State' (1998) 71 S Cal L Rev 953; RA Duff,
'Choice, Character and Criminal Liability' (1993) 12 *Law and Philosophy* 345; RA Duff, 'Virtue, Vice
and Criminal Liability: Do We Want an Aristotelian Criminal Law?' (2002) 6 *Buffalo Criminal Law
Review* 147; E Yankah, 'Good Guys and Bad Guys: Punishing Character, Equality and the Irrelevance
of Moral Character to Criminal Punishment' (2004) 25 *Cardozo Law Review* 1019; see also John Rawls,
A Theory of Justice (Cambridge, MA: Harvard University Press, 1971), 314–15.

[5] N Lacey, 'Character, Capacity, Outcome: Toward a Framework for Assessing the Shifting Pattern
of Criminal Responsibliity in Modern English Law', in MD Dubber and L Farmer (eds), *Modern
Histories of Crime and Punishment* (Stanford: Stanford University Press, 2007), 14–41; N Lacey, 'Space,
Time and Function: Intersecting Principles of Responsibility across the Terrain of Criminal Justice'
(2007) 1 *Criminal Law and Philosophy* 233–50; N Lacey, 'Psychologising Jekyll, Demonising Hyde: The
Strange Case of Criminal Responsibility' (2010) 4 *Criminal Law and Philosophy* 109–33.

the refinement of a notion of individual capacity-responsibility. Second, there is reason to think that in substance if not always in form, character-based patterns of attribution are enjoying a revival in contemporary English (and American) criminal responsibility-attribution. Emerging from their subterranean position in prosecution and sentencing practice, they are enjoying an explicit revival not only in mandatory sentencing laws applying to particular categories of 'dangerous' offender, and in phenomena such as sex offender notification requirements, but also in the substantive law, particularly that dealing with terrorism, and in the operation of evidential presumptions, detention rules, practices of offender profiling, and the renewed admissibility of evidence of bad character.[6]

In this chapter, I further develop the diagnosis of a revival of character in contemporary criminal law. First, I offer a more differentiated conceptual framework for identifying the waxing and waning influence of character in criminal law. In doing so I set out, deliberately, from a broad definition of character as a pattern or practice of responsibility-attribution which is premised in whole or in part on an evaluation or estimation of the quality of the defendant's (manifested or assumed) disposition as distinct from his or her conduct. Second, drawing on this broad model of character, I aim to demonstrate in greater detail the variety of ways in which contemporary criminal law is marked by a resurgence of character. The broad model of character serves to illuminate family relationships between a range of ostensibly varied phenomena. In particular, by including within my purview the notions of not only bad character as *constitutive* of guilt but also bad character as *probative* of guilt, I am able to explore the ways in which, in the practical context of criminal justice, the recognition of the latter may shade into a practice closer to the former. In other words, I argue that criminal conviction, understood within prevailing conventions of communication, is coming more frequently to imply a judgment of criminal character.

The upshot of this analysis is that the doctrinal arrangements of substantive criminal law, though not without importance, are in themselves rarely determinative of whether a character- or a capacity-approach to criminal responsibility prevails. Hence, third, I sketch an extra-doctrinal explanation of why we have seen a

---

[6] See eg V Tadros, 'Justice and Terrorism' (2007) 10 *New Criminal Law Review* 658–89; L Zedner, 'Fixing the Future: the Pre-emptive Turn in Criminal Justice', in B McSherry et al (eds), *Regulating Deviance: The Redirection of Criminalization and the Futures of Criminal Law* (Oxford: Hart Publishing, 2008); M Redmayne, 'The Relevance of Bad Character' (2002) 61 *Cambridge Law Journal* 684–714; M Redmayne, 'The Ethics of Character Evidence' (2008) 61 *Current Legal Problems* 371–99. In criminal justice more generally, many of the developments canvassed in D Garland, *The Culture of Control* (Chicago: University of Chicago Press, 2001) and J Simon, *Governing Through Crime* (New York: Oxford University Press, 2007), as well as the rise of actuarialism charted in M Feeley and J Simon, 'The New Penology: Notes on the Emerging Strategy of Corrections and its Implications' (1992) 39 *Criminology* 449–74 and B Harcourt, *Against Prediction: Profiling, Policing and Punishing in an Actuarial Age* (Chicago: University of Chicago Press, 2007), form part of the broad development to which I want to draw attention here. On reverse burdens of proof, see in particular A Ashworth and M Blake, 'The Presumption of Innocence in English Criminal Law' (1996) *Criminal Law Review* 306.

resurgence of interest in and reliance on ideas of character responsibility: one which finds the roots of the ideology of responsibility which shapes the criminal law in broad practices of criminalization, themselves influenced by a political, economic, and social context. Finally, I draw some conclusions from this analysis for methodology in criminal law theory, and in particular for the appropriateness of a framework which locates its interpretation of criminal responsibility primarily within a conceptual analysis of legal doctrine in isolation from its context.

1 CHANGING INFLECTIONS OF CHARACTER

Before proceeding with the argument, it will be important to clarify the precise senses in which character may be implicated in practices of criminal responsibility-attribution, and to locate them within a broad account of the role of responsibility in modern criminal law. Key to this account is the view that criminal justice systems confront two broad tasks in which ideas of responsibility have come to play a central role: the task of specifying and coordinating the evidential base from which conviction and punishment proceed; and the task of legitimating their power over social actors.[7]

I take it as given that conceptions of criminal and other forms of responsibility take their colour from the institutions in which they are mobilized. Those institutions, and the broader social context in which they operate, have undergone decisive changes since the middle of the eighteenth century. Changes since the eighteenth century have affected both the legitimation needs and capacities of the criminal process, and its requirements and capacities for garnering evidence and turning it into legal knowledge or truth.[8] To name but the most important: the form of the modern adversarial criminal trial was shaped over the last decades of the eighteenth and the early decades of the nineteenth century; the law of evidence developed slowly and over a yet longer period, but was already becoming the object of some formalization during this period; the gradual systematization of matters such as law reporting, a framework for the regular testing of points of law via criminal appeals, and legal education fostered the decisive formalization and professionalization of criminal law. All of these developments spoke to changing legitimation needs, and changed

---

[7] N Lacey, 'In Search of the Responsible Subject: History, Philosophy and Criminal Law Theory' (2001) 64 *Modern Law Review* 350–71; N Lacey, 'Responsibility and Modernity in Criminal Law' (2001) 9 *Journal of Political Philosophy* 249–77.

[8] See further N Lacey, *Women, Crime and Character: From Moll Flanders to Tess of the d'Urbervilles* (Oxford: Oxford University Press, 2008), 23–40.

coordinating capacities. Most obviously, the gradual extension of democracy fundamentally changed the legitimation conditions for criminal law. The development of the police, and the emergence of medical science and other forms of specialist knowledge and technology posed further challenges—and possibilities—for legitimation, as well as transforming the criminal justice system's powers of coordinating the evidential base from which its judgments could be made. And the inexorable move to urbanization and towards a more mobile and anonymous society deprived the criminal justice system of reliable sources of local knowledge on which the early eighteenth century criminal process—decentralized and far less professionalized—had been able to rely in the prosecution of 'insiders', while also undermining the long-standing English practice of judging 'outsiders' in terms of their appearance.[9]

Given these decisive historical developments and changes in the nature of the criminal process, it would be extremely surprising if conceptions of criminal responsibility had remained unchanged. Certainly, practices of criminal responsibility-attribution have continued to draw upon some relatively stable funds of legitimation; but the inflection of the resulting conceptions has changed over time, as has the relationship between them. So while, at an abstract level, the conceptual resources out of which particular legitimating and coordinating notions of criminal responsibility are constructed have remained relatively constant over the last three centuries, the particular notions which those resources have allowed to be constructed have been shaped by the contingent form of legal, political, and social institutions, by the changing history of ideas, and by changing technologies and accepted bodies of knowledge in the natural and social sciences. Thus practices of criminal responsibility-attribution have long exhibited a concern with some combination of character, capacity, and outcome: with 'character' standing in for a particular conception of how criminal evaluation attaches to persons and relates to identity; 'capacity' standing in for the concern with agency, choice, and personal autonomy; and outcome standing in for the concern with the social harms produced by crime. Yet the precise configuration of these elements, and the shape which each of them takes, has changed markedly over time.

For this reason among others, it is worth unpacking a number of different senses in which criminal responsibility-attribution draws upon ideas of character. There are at least three different senses in which assumptions about, or evaluations of, character have informed attributions of responsibility in English criminal law. First, we have the most fundamental sense of 'character responsibility'—what we might call 'character responsibility proper': in other words, the idea that an attribution of criminal responsibility *is* in some sense a judgment of bad or vicious character.

---

[9] Eg in the 14th century, local parishes were enjoined to exclude 'sturdy beggars' and vagabonds, refusing them alms and requiring them to return to their own villages: G Harriss, *Shaping the Nation: England 1360–1461* (Oxford: Oxford University Press, 2005), 244. On the long-standing tendency to project criminality onto outsider status in English history, see N Lacey, C Wells, and D Meure, *Reconstructing Criminal Law* (1st edn; London: Weidenfeld and Nicolson, 1990), ch 2.1.

Note that this sense of character responsibility itself consists in two distinct components: first, there is the component of strong evaluation—of criminal responsibility-
attribution as a moral or quasi-moral judgment; second, there is the projection of
that moral judgment onto the quality of individual character.

Even though it invites us to condemn not merely the sin but also, and fundamentally, the sinner, character responsibility proper itself occupies a rather wide spectrum. At its most extreme, it exhibits what we might call 'character essentialism' and
'character determinism'. In other words, it proceeds from a view of human character
or identity as fixed,[10] or at least as relatively stable; and it regards character as determining conduct. At the other end of the spectrum, we have character responsibility
in the sense of a view of criminal conviction as grounded in the manifestation of
a vicious characteristic or character trait, or a disposition hostile to the norms of
criminal law—a disposition which might be, as it were, 'out of character', and which
does not necessarily mark out a stable propensity to express such characteristics.
Between these ends of the spectrum, we have intermediate positions in which criminal conduct expressing vicious characteristics gives rise to a (stronger or weaker)
presumption of bad character in the sense of propensity.

Analytically, the distinction between evaluation of an act and evaluation of the
character of the actor is clear. But the dynamics which shape the practice of criminal
law and criminal justice, and the socially received meaning of criminal conviction,
are no respecters of philosophical integrity. The impulse to move from evaluation
of conduct to the sort of evaluation of character which marks the more extreme versions of character responsibility—an impulse which, as I shall try to show, surfaces
at key points in the history of English criminal justice—is in my view a hugely significant phenomenon. It has large implications for the extent to which criminal law
exhibits an inclusionary versus an exclusionary temper, and for how far it is seen as
addressing free and equal subjects as opposed to managing a threat posed by particular categories of subject. Yet it is one which has received relatively little attention
from criminal law theorists (as distinct from criminologists, for whom the question
of 'criminal character' has long been central, as well as deeply contested).

The idea of character responsibility, then, encompasses a spectrum of practices of
responsibility-attribution. In charting its form and its varying influence in criminal
law, the main focus has been on the forms of mens rea and the structure of defences.
But to get a full picture, we need to focus on two further mechanisms which occupy
a particularly important place in practices of responsibility-attribution based on
character: character evidence, and the criminalization of status. For as legal arrangements structuring the admissibility of evidence of bad character become more expansive, the practical line between character responsibility proper and bad character as

---

[10] The underlying account of just what fixes character ranges from theological conceptions of evil
through to scientific theories of pathology: see my 'Psychologising Jekyll, Demonising Hyde', 109–33.

probative becomes blurred. In this context, the creation and enforcement of status offences assumes a particular significance.

The rationale for allowing evidence of bad character is obvious enough: it is that past manifestations of bad or vicious character are relevant to the *proof* of responsibility. In the attributive practice of character responsibility proper, criminal conviction is, as it were, irrebuttable evidence of bad character; it is a judgment of bad character, based on the premise that criminal conduct amounts to the expression of vicious characteristics. The evidential character mechanism, rather, addresses the process leading to conviction: bad character as manifested in previous offending behaviour or, perhaps, undesirable behaviour more generally, is seen either as indicative of a propensity towards such behaviour, and hence as tending towards proof of guilt, or as tending to undermine the credibility of a defence or a plea of not guilty, with the same result. A commitment to the more extreme forms of character responsibility would seem to imply a wide embrace of the relevance—indeed the centrality—of character evidence; conversely, a responsibility principle strongly trained on proof of engaged capacity at the time of the offence would be likely to take a more modest view of the relevance of character evidence.[11]

Character evidence needs in turn to be distinguished from a second mechanism which has been influential in facilitating the character-based attribution of responsibility. This is the idea that being a certain kind of person—or bearing a certain sort of status—itself grounds criminal responsibility. In this sense, criminality might be seen as inhering in a type or group rather than in an individual. Within the logic of status offences, a group membership or a given status is, presumptively or absolutely, criminal: we know criminals from the company they keep, or from the kind of person that they are. Like character evidence, status offences expand the time frame in relation to which a putatively criminal act is interpreted, attaching the offender to some part of his or her history. In some forms, status offences further impose a form of guilt by association. These mechanisms of history and association—what we might call the 'bad apple' mechanism and the 'knowing an offender by the company he keeps' mechanism—reinforce one another: a judgment of guilt by association becomes a part of the history in relation to which a person is judged in the future, while a history of bad character may be indicative of the likelihood of guilty association. These mechanisms are, I shall suggest, of great importance in interpreting the varying fortunes of character responsibility in criminal law.

From at least the second half of the nineteenth century, through to the latter part of the twentieth century, character responsibility in its more extreme forms was on the wane. Certainly, traces of older notions of character responsibility could be found in judicial condemnations of offenders' evildoing, particularly at the sentencing stage; in the survival of pre-modern mens rea terms such as 'malice'

---

[11] On the relevance of character evidence under modern conceptions of responsibility, see Redmayne, 'The Relevance of Bad Character', 684–714; 'The Ethics of Character Evidence', 371–99.

and 'wickedness'; and in the persisting relevance of motive to responsibility-attribution.[12] The notion of the offender as wrongdoer remained central to the practice of criminal condemnation, albeit mediated through increasingly elaborated legal doctrines. We could also cite the nature of certain stigmatizing penalties as reflecting the view of criminal conviction as expressing a judgment of bad character. But the development of doctrinal conceptions of mens rea was markedly psychological: the question of wrongdoing was, accordingly, increasingly separated from attribution of responsibility, which was premised on the finding of 'intention', knowledge, or foresight. Such an attribution was, certainly, regarded as a sine qua non for culpability and hence—absent any defence—wrongdoing. But the finding of responsibility itself—or at least the view of the paradigm states of responsibility such as intention, knowledge or foresight—was increasingly elaborated in factual, psychological terms.

Other things being equal, it seems clear that this would have made legal doctrine less hospitable to character responsibility: whereas it is natural to think in terms of a 'malicious' or 'wicked' person, to think in terms of an 'intentional' person makes no sense whatsoever. So once intentionality becomes the key marker of agency and responsibility, an inference from responsibility to character becomes less straightforward. Moreover, the move to a psychological paradigm of intentionality engendered a dualistic approach in legal doctrine: did the defendant commit the alleged criminal conduct? Was he or she responsible for doing so?[13] The evaluative weight of criminal judgment was projected, in other words, onto the definition of criminal conduct—a tendency which, given the (until recently[14]) dearth of normative scholarship on criminalization, left a gap at the heart of criminal law theory. Hence it was not only a question of evaluation no longer being projected onto character as opposed to conduct: the discipline of criminal law scholarship—perhaps even the practice of criminal law—evinced something akin to a discomfort with the evaluative aspect of criminal law more generally. As older ideas of crime as public wrong were undermined by a more extensive criminal law and a more heterogeneous society, the burden of legitimating criminal culpability was borne to an ever greater extent by the general part, of which increasingly elaborate psychological doctrines

[12] On the persisting importance of motive, see AW Norrie, *Crime, Reason and History* (2nd edn; Cambridge: Cambridge University Press, 2001), 226 ff; on motive and character, see further text at n 31 below.

[13] RA Duff, 'Codifying Criminal Fault', in IH Dennis (ed), *Criminal Law and Criminal Justice* (London: Sweet and Maxwell, 1987).

[14] J Feinberg, *The Moral Limits of Criminal Law: Harm to Others; Offense to Others; Harm to Self; Harmless Wrongdoing* (New York: Oxford University Press, 1984–8); D Husak, *Overcriminalization* (New York: Oxford University Press, 2007); J Schonsheck, *On Criminalization* (New York: Springer Verlag, 1994); L Katz, 'Villainy and Felony' (2002) 6 *Buffalo Criminal Law Review* 451–482; RA Duff, L Farmer, SE Marshall, M Renzo, and V Tadros (eds), *The Boundaries of the Criminal Law (Criminalization)* (Oxford: Oxford University Press, 2010).

of mens rea and defence came to occupy a significantly larger proportion during the course of the late nineteenth and the twentieth centuries.[15]

Past bad character as evidence tending to the proof of criminal responsibility had also experienced a decisive change in fortunes. Throughout the eighteenth century, trials were dominated by evidence about the accused's (and witnesses') standing and reputation. But as rules of evidence began to be formalized, doubts arose about the reliability and legitimacy of evidence of bad character, and those doubts themselves added to the impetus for reform. The relatively static, predictable world in which reputation or known qualities of status were regarded as reliable indicators of cred-ibility—either of witness testimony, or of a not guilty plea—was being displaced by an increasingly individualistic world, and one in which, particularly in the cities, the old distinctions between insiders and outsiders, on which English mechanisms of social control had long relied, made little sense. Moreover a freely choosing, respon-sible citizen stood centre stage, posing new legitimation problems as well as new challenges of coordination. In terms of legitimation, the proposition that the proof of a subject's guilt should be facilitated by mechanisms based on the assumption that his or her previous behaviour manifested a criminal character suggestive of a propensity to commit a crime was at odds with the vision of freedom implicit in the emerging social imaginary, and might moreover be seen as introducing informa-tion which was irrelevant to the charge at issue. The seeds, in other words, of what we today think of as objections to character evidence based on moral autonomy and double jeopardy were sown.[16] The emerging conception of individual agency was reflected in the provisions of the Criminal Evidence Act 1898, which re-established the accused's right to give testimony in their own defence, thus producing in the late nineteenth century context a new form of knowledge available to courts. This in turn provided resources for putting into operation a notion of criminal responsibil-ity as residing in psychological states of mind—an evidentiary matter on which the emerging forensic sciences and sciences of mind and brain were also able to make a contribution. In the wake of these developments, from the early nineteenth century, character evidence was rendered inadmissible other than in some special cases.[17]

[15] See L Farmer, *Criminal Law, Tradition and Legal Order* (Cambridge: Cambridge University Press, 1996), ch 1; N Lacey, 'Contingency and Conceptualism: Reflections on an Encounter between Critique and Philosophical Analysis of Criminal Law', in RA Duff (ed), *Philosophy and the Criminal Law* (Cambridge: Cambridge University Press, 1998)

[16] See P Roberts and A Zuckerman, *Criminal Evidence* (2nd edn; New York: Oxford University Press, 2010), ch 14.

[17] There is some doubt about the timing and causes of the demise of character evidence. John Langbein attests to doubts about its reliability from the mid-17th century: JH Langbein, *The Origins of Adversary Criminal Trial* (Oxford: Oxford University Press, 2003), 190–202, in particular 191, citing JW Strong (ed), *McCormick on Evidence* (5th edn; West Group, 1999), 649, para 186. David Leonard, who traces a rule of limited admissibility subject to (inadequately rationalised) exceptions to the early 19th century, explores doubts about character evidence's relevance and its fairness, given its capacity to surprise (often unrepresented) defendants and present problems of rebuttal. D Leonard, *The New Wigmore: A Treatise on Evidence: Evidence of Other Misconduct and Similar Events* (Austin: Wolters

Given the case which can undoubtedly be made for the relevance and legitimacy of reliance on character evidence,[18] this policy of exclusion is of real significance. The reasons appear to have been anxiety about the reliability of such evidence; about surprising the defendant with a very difficult task of rebuttal; and about its capacity to have undue sway with juries, with the result that its prejudicial effect outweighs its probative force. But it is important to see that this anxiety (never, it should be remembered, decisive in the civilian systems, where official scrutiny of evidence in the inquisitorial process is regarded as a sufficient safeguard, and the contextualization of a defendant's actions within a broader narrative of his or her life as normal[19]) was itself shaped, and its intensity increased, by broader social changes. These changes disrupted the dense networks of local knowledge which, centuries after the demise of the self-informing jury, continued to allow evaluation of character to play a robust and central role in the criminal trial. Amid an ever more individualistic society, confidence about evaluations of character—or jurors' ability to 'read' character from conduct, reputation, or appearance—declined sharply, and long-standing doubts about the unduly prejudicial effect of airing the defendant's 'dirty linen' prevailed.[20] Just as doctrinal standards of responsibility shifted from external, evaluative to internal, psychological modes, so favoured forms of evidence shifted from a concern with external appearances or status to a focus on direct reports of experience, opinion, and observation.[21]

What, finally, of character as status? It is, of course, a truism of contemporary scholarship that modern criminal law eschews the criminalization of status: defendants are punished not for who or what they are, but simply for what they have done (or for what they have attempted, encouraged others, or conspired with others to do). Survivals of status offences or semi-status offences such as the famous example of prostitution[22] are, of course, noted and regretted. But it is assumed that it is a fundamental of criminal law in a liberal democracy that criminal responsibility pertains

Kluwer, Aspen Publishers, 2009), chs 1–3. See further TP Gallanis, 'The Rise of Modern Evidence Law' (1999) 84 *Iowa Law Review* 499; CJW Allen, *The Law of Evidence in Victorian England* (Cambridge: Cambridge University Press, 1997); and references at n 21 below. I have also benefited from draft chapters of Mike Redmayne's *Character Evidence in the Criminal Trial* (forthcoming).

    [18] See Redmayne, 'The Relevance of Bad Character', 684–714; 'The Ethics of Character Evidence', 371–99.

    [19] S Field, 'State, Citizen and Character in French Criminal Process' (2006) 33 *Journal of Legal Studies* 522–46; cf M Damaska's distinction between systems of 'coordinate' and 'hierarchical' authority: *The Faces of Justice and State Authority* (Conneticut: Yale University Press, 1991).

    [20] See J Stone, 'The Rule of Exclusion of Similar Fact Evidence: England' (1932–3) 46 *Harvard Law Review* 954–85, at 983–4; D Leonard, 'Character and Motive in Evidence Law' (2001) 34 *Loyola of Los Angeles Law Review* 439–537, at 450; Lacey, *Women, Crime and Character*, 34–40.

    [21] On changing conceptions of what counted as the most persuasive form of evidence in the process of modernization, see Gallanis, 'The Rise of Modern Evidence Law', 499; A Welsh, *Strong Representations: Narrative and Circumstantial Evidence in England* (Baltimore: The John Hopkins University Press, 1992).

    [22] N Lacey, C Wells, and O Quick, *Reconstructing Criminal Law* (3rd edn; Cambridge: Cambridge University Press, 2003), ch 5.III.b.

only to voluntary acts (or, more rarely, omissions), and that this is inconsistent with the criminalization of status.

Notwithstanding this theoretical consensus, the history of status criminalization in the English system cannot be told simply as a story of decline. Examples such as vagrancy and prostitution, as well as regular recreations of 'dangerousness' categories, show that the impulse to organize responsibility-attribution along status lines is a pervasive one in the history of criminal law. Moreover, status categories have often marked the administration of criminal justice: the most spectacular example being the group of late Victorian statutes instituting particular criminalizing regimes for groups such as inebriates and the feeble-minded.[23] The persistence of status offences may be regarded as a distinct manifestation of the character dimension of criminal responsibility-attribution. Moving beyond the notion of bad character as evidence of individual criminal propensity, the criminalization of status engages directly with the assumed criminality of a type or a group—and hence imposes, in its pure form, a rather extreme form of character responsibility proper. And while such pure forms are, happily, rare, I shall argue below that hybrids which bear in practice a family resemblance to character-based status liability—what we might call de facto instances of status criminalization, particularly in relation to terrorist suspects, migrants, and asylum-seekers—appear to be on the increase.

2 THE RESURGENCE OF 'CHARACTER'?

Bearing in mind the variety of ways in which character shapes patterns of responsibility-attribution—through the substantive law; through rules of evidence; through pre-trial discretionary decision making—it is now time to review the evidence for the proposition that the idea of a criminal conviction as expressing a judgment of bad character is enjoying a revival.

2.1 Character responsibility in substantive criminal law

Even amid the supposed triumph of subjective, capacity-based criminal responsibility, we see a somewhat mixed picture in terms of patterns of responsibility-attribution. Though reliable evidence is hard to find,[24] it seems likely that, for

---

[23] L Zedner, *Women, Crime and Custody in Victorian England* (Oxford: Oxford University Press, 1991); L Radzinowicz and R Hood, *The Emergence of Penal Policy in Victorian and Edwardian England* (Oxford: Clarendon Press, 1999).

[24] See N Lacey, 'Historicising Criminalisation' (2009) 72 *Modern Law Review* 936–61.

162   NICOLA LACEY

example, offences of strict liability are increasing in number.[25] Human rights or other constitutional standards—fast becoming the standard resort of criminal law theorists in search of something hopeful to say about how rampant criminalization might be restrained[26]—hold out no cause for optimism here, at least in England and Wales, given that strict liability has been held to be compatible with the European Convention on Human Rights (ECHR).[27] Moreover, notwithstanding the House of Lords' resounding defence of subjectivism in *B v DPP*,[28] and the demise of 'objective recklessness' in *R v Graham*,[29] the terrain over which subjectivism holds sway consists in a relatively restricted range of criminal offences. Admittedly many of them, such as murder, assaults, and theft, lie at what is perceived as the core of criminal law; but, even leaving aside the impact of plea bargaining, they hardly constitute the overwhelming majority of criminal laws actually enforced. As Victor Tadros has emphasized,[30] the widespread operation of reasonableness standards—not only in offences of negligence, including manslaughter and, in effect, rape and sexual penetration, but also in defences such as self-defence and duress—may assume the meaning of an imposition of character liability through an *inference* from conduct to character. For there is nothing in the doctrinal standard itself which militates one way or another on the question of whether, in effect, such standards imply that *the person* who behaved in a particular way was unreasonable, or that they have *done* what was unreasonable. (Note that this ambiguity exists whether or not they allow for investigation of the individual defendant's capacity to reach the reasonable standard of conduct or care.) It is contextual factors, external to legal doctrine, which shape this aspect of the social meaning of the standard.

Perhaps more surprisingly, a similar story can be told when we move from objective to subjective mens rea mechanisms. Motive, though technically irrelevant to psychological notions of mens rea such as intention, has always entered into the 'interpretive construction' of mens rea, through mechanisms such as shifts in time frame,[31] and is arguably enjoying a new prominence, notably in the form of

[25] A Ashworth and L Zedner, 'Defending the Criminal Law: Reflections on the Changing Character of Crime, Procedure and Sanctions' (2008) 2 *Criminal Law and Philosophy* 21–51, 32, quoting an unpublished paper by Ashworth, 'Criminalization: what do 2005's new crimes tell us about the law?' at n 39.

[26] Eg Ashworth and Zedner (ibid); Husak, *Overcriminalization*. For a provocative argument that formalization via constitutional challenges can have counter-productive effects, see WJ Stuntz, 'The Political Constitution of Criminal Justice' (2005–6) 119 *Harvard Law Review* 781–851.

[27] *R v G* [2008] UKHL 37: as Paul Roberts has noted, Article 6(2) of the ECHR was not designed, and is ill-adapted, to deliver a constitutionalization of the mens rea principle: 'Strict Liability and the Presumption of Innocence: An Exposé of Functionalist Assumptions', in A Simester (ed), *Appraising Strict Liability* (Oxford: Oxford University Press, 2005), 151–94, at 193.

[28] *B v DPP* [2000] 2 AC 428; cf *R v G* [2008] UKHL 37.

[29] *R v G and R* [2003] UKHL 50.

[30] Tadros, *Criminal Responsibility*.

[31] See Norrie, *Crime, Reason and History*, 226 ff; M Kelman, 'Interpretive Construction in the Substantive Criminal Law' (1981) 33 *Stanford Law Review* 591.

aggravated liability attendant on racial or religious motivation.[32] Where liability turns on motive, assumptions about good and bad character are invited into jury deliberations. And at the very heart of the doctrinal marker of criminal law's modern formalization of mens rea, subjective mens rea concepts such as intention or knowledge are susceptible of interpretation as bearing on character as much as—or rather than—conduct. As George Fletcher has noted in relation to the American Law Institute's Modern Penal Code, even subjective liability for unsuccessful (including impossible) attempts—the prime terrain of the modern liberal doctrine of autonomy-respecting principles of criminal responsibility—is susceptible of capture as a mechanism for criminalizing bad character:

> The contemporary justification for focusing on the internal attitude of the actor is that acting on the intention to cause harm to others represents a rejection of the legal order ... The frame of mind that underlies expansive attempt liability resembles, therefore, the us-against-them social policy that has led to the use of life sentences against third-time offenders ...
>
> [T]wo anti-liberal principles convince many jurists that they should punish innocuous attempts ... The first is the principle of gearing the criminal law to an attitude of hostility toward the norms of the legal system. The second is changing the focus of the criminal law from acts to actors. These two are linked by the inference: people who display an attitude of hostility toward the norms of the system show themselves to be dangerous and therefore should be subject to imprisonment to protect the interests of others.[33]

Doctrinal mechanisms in modern criminal law are not, in short, decisive as between capacity- and character-based approaches to responsibility attribution, which are driven rather by extra-doctrinal factors to which we shall turn below. However, this is not to say that recent criminal legislation includes no developments which actually invite—rather than merely respond to—a more expansive practice of criminalization on the basis of assumptions about character. The area in which we see the clearest evidence of a revival of something akin to a character principle of responsibility is that of terrorism. For many years, criminal provisions directed specifically at terrorism in England and Wales were crafted with the specific case of Northern Ireland in mind. They were, formally, emergency powers. Accordingly, the Prevention of Terrorism Act had to be renewed by Parliament each year. Over the last decade, we have seen a vivid case of the 'normalization of special powers',[34] with no fewer than five substantial pieces of legislation specifically directed to the criminalization of terrorism, even leaving aside provisions within other pieces of legislation which were drafted with an eye to terrorism or are susceptible of being used in terrorist

---

[32] Crime and Disorder Act 1998, ss 28–32 (amended to include religion by Anti-Terrorism, Crime and Security Act 2001).

[33] GP Fletcher, *Basic Concepts of Criminal Law* (New York: Oxford University Press, 1998), 179–80 (with thanks to Peter Ramsay).

[34] P Hillyard, 'The Normalization of Special Powers', in P Scraton (ed), *Law, Order and the Authoritarian State* (Milton Keynes: Open University Press, 1987).

cases.[35] The extraordinary events of September 2001 are, of course, an important part of the genesis of this new legislative concern with the criminalization of terrorism. But many of the powers and regulations which have been enacted in the wake of public anxiety about global terrorism may be deployed against suspected offenders who have no link with terrorism whatsoever. The anti-terror reaction has created a wave of criminalization—particularly of what we might call preliminary or pre-inchoate activities—which significantly expands the boundaries of criminal law.[36] In doing so, it adds to police and prosecutorial power, weakens defence lawyers, curtails the scope of judicial discretion, and, in some of its more radical 'adjustments' to normal standards of procedure, arguably deploys some of the methods of terror itself.

Why should we regard anti-terrorism criminalization as a form of character responsibility? The offences require, after all, proof of dangerous or harmful conduct, or at least the planning of or preparation for such conduct. Are terrorist offences not, therefore, perfectly standard cases of criminalized conduct? This is, up to a point, a valid view. But only up to a point. To see why, consider the fact that the 'acts of terrorism' which form the ostensible object of public concern—and, hence, one assumes, of criminalization—are acts which are already proscribed. Leaving aside the expansion of liability into pre-inchoate areas such as holding information or being a member of a proscribed group, most of what is encompassed by anti-terror legislation could be prosecuted independent of its existence. When we seek the rationale for the criminalization of terrorism specifically, we see, certainly, governments seeking to bolster their electoral credibility by 'doing something' about terrorism. But in the meaning of what they create, we see something akin to character responsibility: the idea that, on top of committing or planning acts of violence, there is something additionally and intrinsically wrong about being a certain kind of person, engaged in a certain kind of activity—an aggravation of blameworthiness which justifies a special criminalization regime.

Notwithstanding the House of Lords' finding that one of the most egregious aspects of the legislation (the application of indefinite detention exclusively to foreign nationals) contravened the Human Rights Act 1998, much of the counter-terrorism legislation—notably, as discussed below, the control order, implemented as a result of the House of Lords' decision—is redolent of the criminalization of status.[37] Note, for example, the assertion of Lord Phillips, the Lord Chief Justice, in a

---

[35] Terrorism Acts 2000 and 2006; Anti-Terrorism, Crime and Security Act 2001; Prevention of Terrorism Act 2005; Counter-Terrorism Act 2008; see also Criminal Justice Act 2003. Of the terrorism-specific statutes, only the PTA 2005 is subject to the renewal requirement which characterized the earlier legislation. For discussion, see Tadros, 'Justice and Terrorism', 658–89; L Zedner, *Security* (London: Routledge, 2009), 116–42; Tom Bingham, *The Rule of Law* (London: Allen Lane, Penguin Books, 2010), ch 11; P Hillyard, 'The normalisation of Special Powers', in Scraton (ed), *Law, Order and the Authoritarian State*.

[36] Tadros, 'Justice and Terrorism', 658–89, at 670–5; 'Crimes and Security' (2008) 71 *Modern Law Review* 940.

[37] *A v Secretary of State for the Home Department* [2004] UKHL 56.

key case examining the ECHR-compatibility of control orders under section 3 of the Prevention of Terrorism Act 2005, that: 'The PTA seeks to achieve this object [of preventing or restricting a person's further involvement in terrorism-related activity] by empowering the Secretary of State to impose control orders on those suspected of *being terrorists*.'[38]

Another way of putting this would be in terms of motive: normalized terrorism legislation introduces a motive-based differentiating principle to the heart of an allegedly universal criminal law, and does so in terms of an inference about criminality drawn from that particular motivation. A natural (though not a necessary) implication of such an inference is a judgment of bad character. As Tadros puts it, these are 'individualized' offences, targeting members of a particular group.[39] A further whiff of character responsibility lies in the legislation's extended conception of accomplice liability via membership offences which enact 'the fallacy of "guilt by association"'.[40] Moreover the articulated rationale both of the legislation and of aspects of foreign policy in relation to international terrorism (notably cooperation with 'extraordinary renditions' and counter-terrorism operations in Iraq and Afghanistan) participates in a strong form of character essentialism and character determinism: the assumption is that there is a finite number of 'bad people' who are 'terrorists', and if we can simply detain or 'take out' enough of them, the world will be a safer place for those of 'good character', who alone deserve the full protections of the rule of law.

2.2 Character as evidence

Part 11 of the Criminal Justice Act 2003 fundamentally changes the rules on admissibility of evidence of bad character. Departing from a long-established principle of restricted admissibility of such evidence, section 101(1) of the Act allows evidence of bad character, in the sense not only of previous convictions, but also of previous misconduct or reprehensible behaviour, to be admitted so long as its probative value is not outweighed by its prejudicial effect; and so long as it passes one of seven tests or 'gateways'. These include not only circumstances where the defendant has put their own character in question by questioning that of another witness, or where all parties agree to the evidence's being admitted, but also—most importantly for our purposes—where it is important explanatory evidence; where it is relevant to an important matter in issue between the defendant and the prosecution; or where it

---

[38] *Secretary of State for the Home Department* [2006] EWCA 1140 (emphasis added): the case subsequently went to the House of Lords, where Lord Bingham's analysis was more careful in preserving the fragile line between conduct- and character-based liability: [2007] UKHL 46.

[39] Tadros, 'Justice and Terrorism', 658–89, at 683–5.

[40] Zedner, *Security*, 130.

has substantial probative value in relation to an important matter in issue between the defendant and a co-defendant.

A recent study of the operation of the new provisions conducted for the Ministry of Justice suggested that by far the most common use of the provision was through the gateway of 'relevant to an important matter in issue', with 'important explanatory evidence' as the next most cited but far rarer justification, and assault and theft cases the most common context.[41] Among the cases in which character evidence was admitted in relation to a matter at issue, the main use of the evidence was to establish propensity. A vivid sense of the sort of argument enabled by the legislation is given in the report, which cites the Crown Prosecution in one case as stating that 'the defendant is of bad character as he has previous reprehensible behaviour' which was relevant, as it relates to 'an important matter in issue' between the prosecution and defence. 'He has several times been physically and verbally abusive to [the complainant] throughout the course of their sexual relationship when [the complainant] was only 14 or 15 at the time. These matters demonstrate a propensity to commit offences of child abuse. He has admitted the sexual relationship commenced when [the complainant] was 14 years old. She became pregnant with his child when she was 15 years old.'[42] It is hard to think that the prejudicial force of such a sketch would be other than significant.

It is important not to exaggerate the practical significance or broader ramifications of section 101. The research study suggests that the provision is being used primarily to introduce evidence of previous convictions, particularly in relation to similar crimes. Among contested cases, half concerned similar offences, with 29 per cent concerning offences featuring a similar modus operandi, and only 13 per cent featuring a claim about propensity to commit crime founded more generally on past reprehensible behaviour.[43] Furthermore, evidence of bad character-based propensity did already find its way into the courts. For example, in *R v Kingston*,[44] the House of Lords upheld a defendant's conviction for indecent assault on a young boy notwithstanding the defendant's involuntary intoxication, on the basis that the finding of child pornography at his home supported an inference that he had the relevant mens rea notwithstanding his intoxication. Nonetheless, the fact that, with the 2003 Act, a political/legislative decision was made explicitly to enlarge the admissibility of evidence of bad character tells us something important about both the politics of criminal justice and the contemporary conception of criminality and

[41] Morgan Harris Burrows LLP, Ministry of Justice Research Series 5/09, Office for Criminal Justice Reform, March 2009, at 14–23; for a considered review of the operation of the new law, see Roberts and Zuckerman, *Criminal Evidence*, ch 14; and for cases illustrating the potential breadth of the new provisions see *R v McMinn* [2007] EWCA 3024, and with specific reference to the relevance of previous reprehensible but non-criminal conduct, *R v Manister* [2006] 1 WLR 1885.

[42] Morgan Harris Burrows, ibid 20.

[43] Morgan Harris Burrows, ibid 15, 17, 23.

[44] *R v Kingston* [1994] 3 WLR 519.

the legitimation of punishment. For the legislative change appears to proceed from a view of criminality as importantly located in stable features of character or personality which underpin the claim of propensity.[45]

But do these and other possible examples really amount to a belief in criminal character: to what I have called 'character essentialism' and 'character determinism'? Or do they rather amount to a sorting for convenience into types, on an actuarial basis?[46] Might the persistence of such short cuts to proof in the English system proceed from an anxiety about the power to coordinate information adequate to satisfying what criminal law scholars take to be 'normal' standards of proof? And might this anxiety itself proceed from concern about the incentives for law-abiding behaviour among those not fully included in society, polity, or economy? In tracing the gradual erosion, in practice, of the distinction between bad character as tending to proof of guilt and character as constitutive of guilt, the causation is hard to trace, and seems likely to run in more than one direction. In this context, it is worth noting that another evidential mechanism geared to easing the path to conviction—the reversal of burdens of proof—has itself tended to be deployed in areas, notably that of drug regulation and terrorism, in which the object of criminalization is what is regarded as a dangerous lifestyle, group membership, or set of beliefs as much as an individual criminal act.

2.3 Character as status

This leads to our final object of analysis: the phenomenon of criminal responsibility-attribution based on status. This, one might have thought, belongs firmly to pre-modern criminal law systems. As Lucia Zedner reminds us, this is unfortunately not the case:

The recasting of citizenship as a status that has to be earned ... is also discernible in domestic criminal law. Policies directed first against immigrants and asylum seekers, as well as foreign nationals suspected of involvement in terrorism, have come to be applied equally to those who are cast as 'irregular citizens' within society. These include but are not limited to anti-social youth, persistent offenders, sexual offenders, and suspected terrorists: all of whom occupy liminal spaces at the margins of civil society and are consigned to a probationary or provisional status akin to that imposed upon immigrants and asylum seekers.[47]

---

[45] As anti-terrorism legislation suggests, the intensity of the character inference in current evidence law is context-dependent: while the case law tends to give weight to how recent a previous conviction is, this criterion will be regarded as of lesser importance in areas such as very serious or sexual crimes: *R v M* [2006] EWCA Crim 3408; *R v Cox* [2007] EWCA Crim 3365.

[46] Harcourt, 'From the Ne'er-Do-Well to the Criminal History Category', 99.

[47] L Zedner, 'Security, the State, and the Citizen: The Changing Architecture of Crime Control' (2010) 13 *New Criminal Law Review* 379–403, 389.

The proliferation of such arrangements, which forms the core of my diagnosis of a spike in this form of what we might call doctrinally explicit character short cuts to responsibility, has come to be associated with so-called 'enemy criminal law'.[48] Preventive in temper; disproportionate in reaction; indifferent to normal procedural protections, 'enemy criminal law' is essentially a police power which treats its objects as dangers to be managed, as distinct from citizen criminal law, which responds to subjects invested with rights.[49] Arguably the most important source of offences which amount to or come uncomfortably close to the criminalization of status is the movement towards ever greater preventive criminalization. Preventive criminalization is, of course, not a new phenomenon: inchoate offences; offences of possession; and the binding over power attendant on an anticipated breach of the peace are long-standing examples of the preventive impulse in English criminal law.[50] But this preventive turn appears to have taken on a new intensity in the last two decades. In a recent paper, Ashworth and Zedner have identified no fewer than nine families of preventive measures,[51] many of them combining civil and criminal modes of enforcement in what have been widely regarded as troubling ways.[52]

It has been less widely noted that several of these new forms of preventive order impose what is in effect a form of (highly targeted) status liability. Take, for example, civil preventive hybrid orders aimed at preventing risk or at preventing harm (Anti-social behaviour orders (ASBOs),[53] travel restriction orders, football spectator banning orders, drinking banning orders, risk of sexual harm or violent crime orders); civil preventive orders such as anti-social behaviour injunctions; pre-trial orders such as remands in custody; licence conditions on release from a sentence of imprisonment; or criminal court orders aimed at preventing harm or risk of harm, such as disqualification from driving or from being a company director. A criminal

---

[48] For a general discussion of the notion of enemy criminal law, originated by German scholar Gunther Jakobs, see C Gomez-Jara Diez, 'Enemy Combatants versus Enemy Criminal Law' (2008) 11 *New Criminal Law Review* 529, at 531, 556; cf Tadros's notion of 'individualised offences', Tadros, 'Justice and Terrorism', 658–89, at 683–5.

[49] Gomez-Jara Diez, ibid 542: on the distinction between police and legal power, see MD Dubber, *The Police Power* (New York: Columbia University Press, 2005).

[50] On the long English history of preventive justice, see Zedner, *Security*, 30–1.

[51] Zedner and Ashworth, 'Preventive Orders: A Case of Under-criminalization?', in Duff et al (eds), *The Boundaries of the Criminal Law*. See also Ashworth and Zedner, 'Defending the Criminal Law', 21–51; L Zedner, 'Security, the State, and the Citizen: The Changing Architecture of Crime Control' (2010) 13 *New Criminal Law Review* 379–403.

[52] P Ramsay, 'What is Anti-social Behaviour?' (2004) *Criminal Law Review* 908; P Ramsay, 'The Theory of Vulnerable Autonomy and the Legitimacy of the Civil Preventative Order', in B McSherry et al (eds), *Regulating Deviance: The Redirection of Criminalization and the Futures of Criminal Law* (Oxford: Hart Publishing, 2008); A Ashworth, 'Social Control and "Anti-social behaviour": The Subversion of Human Rights?' (2004) 120 *Law Quarterly Review* 263–91; A Simester and A von Hirsch, 'Regulating Offensive Conduct through Two-step Prohibitions', in Simester and von Hirsch (eds), *Incivilities: Regulating Offensive Behaviour* (Oxford: Hart Publishing, 2006), 173–94.

[53] On the ASBO as a form of character responsibility, see P Ramsay, *The Insecurity State: Criminal Law after the ASBO* (Oxford: Oxford University Press, forthcoming), ch 2.

conviction resulting from the breach of any of these orders is a form of criminalization which applies specifically to a group identified in terms of its subjection to the
relevant order. As Ashworth and Zedner note, the implications are considerable:
they include stigma, the imposition of (often long-lasting) restrictive conditions,
and, on breach, possible imprisonment.[54] Hence severe measures associated with
the quasi-moral terrain of 'real crime' are finding their way, insidiously, into the terrain of regulatory or police offences. Moreover in the area of serious crime, the new
indefinite sentence of 'imprisonment for public protection' (IPP)—a variant of the
intermittent attempt to identify 'dangerous' offenders—is more draconian and far-
reaching than any previous such provision. Indeed, Ashworth has estimated that the
introduction of the IPP may result in as many as one-third of the prison population
serving indefinite sentences by 2012.[55]

Perhaps the most spectacular examples of the latest generation of preventive
measures are the control orders applying to those suspected of terrorism[56]—worthy of an article in their own right—and the notification orders which replaced sex
offender registration under the Sexual Offences Act 2003. Under these latter provisions, certain sex offenders must render themselves visible to the police by providing details such as address, virtually ensuring that they will be investigated should
any sexual (or perhaps other) offence be committed in the area. This amounts to a
quasi-criminal status—indeed to a prima facie judgment of criminal propensity.[57]
Reminiscent of ancient sanctions such as maiming and branding, it sits unhappily
with the idea of punishment as commensurate to crime. It must be set alongside other
contemporary initiatives—such as the effort to extend the legal period of detention
without trial—in assessing how far the criminal law is moving towards a system of
de facto status criminalization on the basis of inferences about criminal character.

3 Explaining the Resurgence of Character

I hope to have done enough to convince the reader that certain significant recent
developments in criminal law and procedure may justly be described as a 'resurgence
of character'—as an underlying mechanism facilitating proof of guilt, certainly; but

---

[54] Ashworth and Zedner, 'Defending the Criminal Law', 21–51, 36.

[55] A Ashworth, *Sentencing and Criminal Justice* (Cambridge: Cambridge University Press, 2005),
36, 210–18.

[56] Zedner, *Security*, 132–4; Tadros, 'Justice and Terrorism', 658–89, at 666–70.

[57] Zedner, *Women, Crime and Custody in Victorian England*, 74.

also, to some extent, as an organizing principle of, and a message emanating from, responsibility-attribution. This is not, of course, to say that recent developments amount to a reversion to eighteenth-century-type arrangements; nor to claim that the relevant developments are evenly distributed across the three forms of character which I have distinguished. I have already noted that the criminalization of status, albeit in shifting forms, has enjoyed prominence in English criminal law at various points since the eighteenth century. A concern with the prevention of harm most certainly dates back at least to the creation of an expansive administrative state in the first half of the nineteenth century. The specific form taken by today's move to 'preventive justice' is shaped by the particular capacities, dynamics, and aspirations of nation states in a world of advanced technologies of communication, physical mobility, and interdependence.[58] Moreover, particularly in the liberal market countries, criminal policy is formed by governments accountable to an electorate within an adversarial system which fosters the politicization of criminal justice, creating a volatile policy-making environment.[59] In stark contrast to the mid-nineteenth century, that electorate is broadly drawn; it is informed by a scientific culture which has made it optimistic about the power to control risk; and it is, hence, rather intolerant of risk, and rather insistent on government efforts to control it—particularly in the wake of insecurity attendant on economic restructuring and cultural disembedding.[60]

The political context in which decisions about criminalization are taken—a context in which legitimation and coordination problems have to be resolved by accountable actors—provides a good place to start in any attempt to unravel the puzzle of character's rise and fall as an organizing principle and symbol in criminal law. Consider the following, over-simplified but suggestive, model. In a stable, relatively homogeneous, and non-democratic world based on status hierarchy, and a world in which the state had limited ambitions and capacities, yet was able to draw on considerable local resources of knowledge, norm-enforcement, and regulation, a pattern of responsibility-attribution based on character made practical and cultural sense. Local knowledge provided evidence of character in relation to insiders: the wandering mobility of the poor was long regarded as a significant social problem to be curtailed by the town watch, by the structure of the poor law, and, not least, by the fact of 'outsider' status carrying with it its own stigma of presumptive criminality. Character evidence was key to the conduct of the trial; criminality was readily associated with status (an association also reflected in stigmatizing punishments which left marks on the body); criminal prosecution was based on an assumption of bad character; and criminal conviction gave official imprimatur to that assumption.

[58] Harcourt, 'From the Ne'er-Do-Well to the Criminal History Category', 99.

[59] N Lacey, *The Prisoners' Dilemma: Political Economy and Punishment in Contemporary Democracies* (New York: Cambridge University Press, 2008), 62–77.

[60] Zedner, *Security*, 91–100.

With a move to a more individualized, mobile, anonymous, and democratic world, the shape of both legitimation and coordination problems changed. The subject of criminal law gradually became a rights-bearing agent, entitled to be judged in terms of his or her own capacities, intentions, and knowledge. At the same time, the local resources of knowledge coordination diminished, and a formalized system of policing and criminal trial had gradually to be constructed so as to garner the evidence necessary for trial. The resulting domination of the trial by lawyers allowed in turn for the refinement of technical doctrines of culpability. Moreover the prevailing legal and political culture attached—via both enlightenment conceptions of agency and utilitarian theories of human psychology[61]—special importance to individual mental states. This psychological and essentially factual view of responsibility in turn served to divert attention from contested issues of value in a world which urbanization, social mobility, and democratization were already rendering less morally homogeneous.

This trajectory—at least across the terrain of 'serious' criminal law—towards an advertence-based standard of responsibility proceeded relatively smoothly thanks to two things: first, the creation of many 'regulatory' offences of strict liability, which allowed the emerging state to pursue its instrumental goals cheaply and efficiently; second, the extraordinary success of the early Victorian state's creation of a modern criminal justice system featuring, in particular, a regular police force and an extensive prison system. Crime, especially in the rapidly expanding cities, became a serious social concern: but this in itself became a spur to further institutional innovation. In a fascinating amalgam of character and capacity cosmologies, the penal system of the first two-thirds of the nineteenth century organized itself to shape convicts' own capacities to work on their characters: declining crime rates then further helped to legitimate the gradually modernizing system.[62]

But this move towards the investigation of individual capacity responsibility was never complete. This was, not least, because the costs of a system fully realizing the ideal of capacity responsibility proven beyond reasonable doubt would have been prohibitive, even had the newly created criminal justice infrastructure been extensive enough to deliver it. Short cuts to proof—the burgeoning category of strict liability offences, and mechanisms such as the presumption of intended consequences—remained, even in relatively peaceful and optimistic times, important. And in more difficult periods—those when the costs of determining individual capacity-based responsibility were particularly high, for example, because of the scale of perceived crime problems—not only those short cuts, but findings of mens rea, have been liable to become nested, explicitly or implicitly, within a legitimating

---

[61] KJM Smith, *Lawyers, Legislators and Theorists* (New York: Oxford University Press, 1998).

[62] M Wiener, *Reconstructing the Criminal: Culture, Law and Policy in England, 1830–1914* (Cambridge: Cambridge University Press, 1991); M Foucault, *Discipline and Punish: The Birth of the Prison* (trans A Sheridan; London: Allen Lane, 1977).

framework of 'criminal character', itself shaped, variously, by scientific or religious doctrines. Hence the historical trajectory towards proof of individualized responsibility premised on engaged capacity or choice was neither an unbroken one, nor a guarantee in itself of the abandonment of character-based responsibility-attribution in practice.

For example, the social and economic disruption of the 1870s to the 1890s saw a significant reversal: in the wake of widespread economic insecurity in an extended recession, and of cultural anxieties attendant on the first hints of the collapse of empire and the Fenian challenge in Ireland, British governments reverted to a concern with the idea of criminal types who might be targeted and identified, with consequent improvements to public safety. In a frightening world, the quasi-Darwinist, eugenicist view of crime as pathology gave birth to a new conception of criminal character—a scientific character essentialism—and issued in legislative arrangements identifying particular criminal classifications geared to separating off and managing a distinct criminal class.[63] The epitome of this moment is, of course, Lombroso's criminology, with its fantasy of not only the existence of stable types of criminal character but, crucially, of being able to identify those types in terms of physiognomy; and Francis Galton's equally fantastic ambition to identify, visually, the essence of criminal personality by superimposing multiple photographs of offenders.[64]

With the resolution of the economic and social crisis in the 1890s, the more extreme versions of positivist criminology were, at least in England, gradually consigned to the academy rather than the prison or reformatory; criminal types legislation gradually fell into desuetude; and, as David Garland has charted in a remarkable book,[65] the years around the turn of the century saw the gradual assembly—in politics, the criminal process and institutional infrastructure—of the basis for the eclectic 'penal welfarist' settlement which, sustained by a relatively stable social culture itself fostered by the two great national struggles represented by the First and Second World Wars, endured until the 1970s. And just as the penal system was being reconstructed on more inclusionary lines—lines which implied a certain focus on human character as shapeable by reformist interventions—so, during this major part of the twentieth century, capacity-based and subjective principles of responsibility were continuing their steady progress in the courts. They found their intellectual acme in Glanville Williams' *Criminal Law: The General Part* (1953);[66] and their fullest legislative support in section 8 of the Criminal Justice Act 1967 which, by in effect reversing

---

[63] See Zedner, *Women, Crime and Custody in Victorian England*.

[64] See in greater detail, Lacey, 'Psychologising Jekyll, Demonising Hyde', 109–33.

[65] D Garland, *Punishment and Welfare* (Brookfield, Vermont: Gower Publishing Company, 1985).

[66] G Williams, *Criminal Law: The General Part* (2nd edn; London: Steven and Sons, 1961); at the turn of the century, one of the most influential texts was still conflating objective and subjective mens rea standards: CS Kenny, *Outlines of Criminal Law* (1st edn; Cambridge: Cambridge University Press, 1902), 40.

DPP v Smith,[67] finally abandoned the presumption that natural consequences are intended.

As many commentators have shown,[68] this penal welfarist settlement began to break down in the early 1970s, under pressure from rising crime and a welter of economic, demographic, and cultural changes which fundamentally altered the structure of criminal justice politics in Britain and in several other countries, notably the United States. This is not the place to rehearse the familiar story of how 'penal welfarism' gave way to 'penal populism' amid a 'culture of control', creating a 'prisoners' dilemma' for politicians and a tendency to 'govern through crime'.[69] The power of the narrative is, sadly, all too clearly attested in the soaring imprisonment rates in the liberal market economies which have seen this trend. My aim here is to suggest that the factors charted by criminologists in relation to criminal justice arrangements, such as policing and punishment, also explain the resurgence of character, and the declining practical significance of individual responsibility as proof of engaged capacity, in criminal law. The example of the late Victorian 'criminal types' legislation—the feeble-minded, the inebriate, the vagrant, the fallen woman—is hence a real clue to the explanation for waxing and waning patterns of character responsibility. Amid a crisis of security analogous to that experienced at the end of the nineteenth century, legislators today are reaching for definitions and mechanisms which can reassure an anxious public that their concerns are being taken seriously—and that 'the criminal threat' can be contained. The construction of criminal classifications is a tempting mechanism here. And just as the late nineteenth-century classifications reflected prevailing anxieties and contemporary scientific theories and technologies, so today's categories—the anti-social youth, the sex offender, the migrant, and, above all, the terrorist—are appropriate symbols of 'otherness' relative to contemporary anxieties and technologies.

Both these anxieties, and the technologies available to meet them, are developing all the time. Amid an economic crisis which seems likely to add a further intensity to the concerns about insecurity which have underpinned the readmissibility of character evidence and the invention of what amounts to a new generation of criminal status offences, we have reason to fear that those who form easily identifiable objects of anger, fear, or resentment will find themselves increasingly the target for what we might call character-facilitated criminal responsibility-attribution. Non-citizens in general, and recent immigrants and asylum-seekers more specifically, are an obvious potential target, particularly where their origins may be associated in

---

[67] *Smith* [1961] AC 290.

[68] Garland, *Punishment and Welfare*; J Pratt, *Penal Populism* (Oxford: Hart Publishing, 2006); R Reiner, *Law and Order: An Honest Citizen's Guide to Crime and Control* (Cambridge/Malden, MA: Polity Press, 2007); J Young, *The Exclusive Society* (London: Sage Publications, 1999).

[69] J Pratt, ibid; D Garland, ibid; Lacey, *The Prisoners' Dilemma*; Simon, *Governing Through Crime*.

popular or police consciousness with either terrorism or drug production.[70] More speculatively—and yet more nightmarishly—new technologies such as DNA profiling[71] and computer programmes formalizing offender profiling or identifying crime 'hot spots' which might be taken to indicate 'postcode presumptive criminality'[72] offer, or perhaps threaten, yet more sophisticated mechanisms of responsibility-attribution based on notions of character essentialism to come, just as the emerging sciences of mind and brain, and of statistics, did in the late nineteenth century.[73] Note moreover that several of these new scientific classifications exhibit more extreme forms of character essentialism than did their nineteenth-century forebears.

4 IMPLICATIONS FOR CRIMINAL LAW THEORY

It might reasonably be objected that the diagnosis of a resurgence of 'character' in criminal law is a storm in a teacup. Surely, a sceptical reader might say, most of the recent developments outlined in this paper have to do more with the criminal process, with evidence, and with sentencing than with criminal law proper. They tell us something, and perhaps something worrying, about the failures of criminal enforcement and of patterns of criminalization to respect the values enshrined in the legal doctrines of individual responsibility which are the jewel in the crown of the 'general part'. But they do not touch the integrity of those principles, nor do they undermine the claim about a triumph of capacity-responsibility set out at the start of this chapter.

[70] Zedner, 'Security, the State, and the Citizen', 379–403; see also A De Giorgi, *Rethinking the Political Economy of Punishment: Perspectives on Post-Fordism and Penal Politics* (Aldershot: Ashgate, 2006); L Wacquant, 'Suitable Enemies: Foreigners and Immigrants in the Prisons of Europe' (1999) 1 *Punishment and Society* 215

[71] The Brown government's consultation and commissioned research, geared to reframing current policy so as to be compatible with the ECHR, can be found at <http://www.homeoffice.gov.uk/documents/cons-2009-dna-database/>. The (then) Home Secretary's commentary disclosed an approach based on a judgment of risk founded in assumed propensity.

[72] Since drafting this chapter, the human rights organization Liberty has exposed 'Project Champion'—an intensive CCTV surveillance scheme targeted at areas of Birmingham with a high proportion of Muslim residents: significantly, the project is funded by the anti-terrorism division of the police: <http://www.guardian.co.uk/commentisfree/libertycentral/2010/jul/06/birmingham-cctv-unlawful-liberty>.

[73] For a few examples drawn from a vast pool of empirical research on the salience of race in offender profiling, see Ian Ayres, *Racial Profiling and the LAPD* (2008), <http://www.aclu-sc.org/lapdracialprofiling>; Civil Rights Bureau, Office of the Attorney General, *The New York City Police Department's 'Stop and Frisk' Practice: A Report from the Office of the Attorney General* (December 1999).

This argument has a tempting conceptual neatness, and it has long been deployed by criminal law theorists. Its effect has been to direct attention away from aspects of criminal law which sit uncomfortably with prevailing normative theories: notably the widespread existence of strict liability; of reverse burdens of proof; or of reasonableness requirements applied without investigation of individual capacity.[74] The result is that criminal law theorists are writing about a small proportion of criminal law. This self-imposed limitation enables many of them to retain an attachment to the idea(l) of a unitary theory of criminal law—an aesthetically pleasing idea, but one which is seriously at odds with the legal and social reality of both the substance and the source of criminal law—the supposed object of analysis. In a world in which the proliferation of overlapping criminal offences has given increasing power to prosecutors through plea-bargaining, William Stuntz has suggested that, in the United States, prosecutors have become not merely the real lawmakers but even the effective adjudicators in the vast majority of cases in which the judge in effect rubber stamps a plea deal and a jury is never empanelled. It is worth quoting his argument, which is almost equally relevant to England, at length:

The cumulation of criminal prohibitions that we have seen over the past half-century has made it ever easier for prosecutors to generate guilty pleas in street crime cases, making prosecutors the system's prime adjudicators in such cases. When it comes to vice—today, drugs—prosecutors are the system's real lawmakers. When it comes to a range of ordinary street crimes, prosecutors often function as judge and jury; they are the system's real adjudicators. That is how enforcement discretion changed criminal law...Legislative crime definition has a natural tendency to become, in practice, prosecutorial crime definition, as legislatures define broad nominal liability rules, leaving prosecutors to determine what behaviour actually leads to conviction and punishment.[75]

My analogous suggestion is that a change in patterns of prosecution and criminalization amounts, in substance, to a change in the contours of criminal responsibility; that we cannot, in other words, separate the moment of responsibility-attribution from the moments of selection and case-processing which precede (and in most instances supplant) it, or indeed from the moments of penal execution which conclude the criminal process. I therefore conclude, with Stuntz, that:

One unfortunate consequence of the sheer mass of current law and literature on [policing, adjudication and crime definition, punishment...] is that lawyers, judges, and scholars

[74] For honourable exception, in relation to strict liability, see RA Duff, *Answering for Crime* (Oxford: Hart Publishing, 2008); A Simester (ed), *Appraising Strict Liability* (Oxford: Oxford University Press, 2005).

[75] Stuntz, 'The Pathological Politics of Criminal Law', 505–600, at 578. In the English context, the discretionary powers of the police are probably of equal if not greater importance than those of prosecutors. Stuntz further suggests that the judicial development of constitutional devices such as the vagueness doctrine have, perversely, led to a greater incentive for lawmakers, in an attempt to avoid nullification, to enact a welter of very specific crimes whose overlapping nature has further increased the bargaining power of prosecutors and hence further marginalized the criminal trial—an unconscious judicial *auto da fé*.

rarely talk about any two of them ... in tandem. These are separate subjects, each with its own body of rules and theoretical underpinnings and policy debates. But the subjects interact. Changes in one area tend to produce changes in others ... Seeing the system whole, considering change in all its parts together, may be the key to wise reform.[76]

It may be objected in turn that an orientation to reform is not the priority of scholarship concerned with the philosophical foundations of criminal law. But scholars concerned to explore and refine the normative basis for criminal liability must, surely, be concerned with the conditions under which those principles and values will be most likely to survive. In a world in which the criminal trial is increasingly regarded an 'expensive luxury'[77]—let alone the American context in which 'criminal law is becoming a sideshow'[78]—we had better try to understand the nature of the environment which confronts the principles to which we are committed.

Normative criminal law theory purports, after all, to have some grounding in the reality of criminal law: to offer an account of the implicit normative structure of an actually existing social practice. My contention is simply that these principles can only be understood in the contexts of both the institutions in which they are mobilized, and the environment in which those institutions exist. To the extent that the refinement of capacity-based principles of responsibility is today juxtaposed with a diminishing practical significance of capacity-responsibility as a principle of attribution, this raises questions for criminal law theory. Developments in the criminal process, in the penal system, and in the political and economic world, in short, affect the *meaning* as well as the *normative significance* of criminal responsibility; and that meaning, produced within an influential system of social signalling, should be a core concern of criminal law theory.

5 CONCLUSION

For over six hundred years,[79] the English political system has been grappling with how to marshall existing institutional resources in the pursuit of social control and the identification and punishment of crime. Not surprisingly, the problems of disorder, and the mechanisms mobilized to respond to them, have been far from static. In our increasingly heterogeneous and mobile world, both the objects and the mechanisms of social control have changed. Yet while the forms of conduct addressed by

---

[76] Stuntz, ibid 831.
[77] Ashworth and Zedner, 'Defending the Criminal Law', 21–51, 38.
[78] Stuntz, 'The Pathological Politics of Criminal Law', 505–600, 509.
[79] See Harriss, *Shaping the Nation*, 244.

English criminalization have long been varied and extensive, the impulse to deploy 'outsider' status as a mechanism of labelling and of social control has a very long history.

As we confront the extensive, confusing, and heterogeneous terrain of criminal law and criminal justice today—the regulatory offences and the offences of serious violence; the retributive 'acting out' of vengeful penal populism and the 'actuarialism' of the 'criminology of everyday life'—it is helpful, I would argue, to reflect on our history. The revival of 'character' is not the only show in the sprawling city of contemporary criminal law. To take just one example, we might argue that the efflorescence of superficially contractual precursors to criminal liability such as the non-molestation order or the ASBO in fact serve a rather different purpose: to pre-empt the criminal trial's evaluative role by specifying the content of the relevant duties or values, leaving the trial merely to determine whether a contractual term has been breached.[80] Yet there is reason to think nonetheless that the balance between the quasi-moral and the regulatory aspects of criminal law has shifted over the last 30 years, with an increasing moralization of the regulatory (or police) sphere, and a converse importation of techniques (notably of prevention) developed in the police sphere into the rest of criminal law. Along with the 'acting out' typical of criminal and penal policy in relation to serious crime and terrorism, this underpins in my view the resurgence of short cuts to proof reminiscent of the extreme form of character responsibility which we might have hoped to have been laid to rest along with the *ancien régime* in English criminal justice.

Developments in criminal law and criminal procedure are being driven by political pressures which we see manifested most clearly in the rise in the prison population and the salience of criminal policy to national politics. These political pressures are the product of broader economic and cultural dynamics, themselves refracted through the frame of existing institutional arrangements. The days of excluding 'sturdy beggars', or relying on dense networks of 'local knowledge', are gone. But new political pressures, new social preoccupations, and new technologies are changing how our institutions 'think' about criminal responsibility,[81] creating new mechanisms for its attribution, and affecting how such attributions are interpreted in social discourse. Some of these recent developments, I have argued, verge upon forms of character essentialism and character determinism which sit uncomfortably with the liberal values which twenty-first-century English criminal justice purports to protect. More radically, I have suggested that, while the resurgence of character is made most manifest in these new developments, the seeds of that revival have long lain dormant in doctrinal arrangements ostensibly favourable to the triumph of capacity-responsibility. The balance, in short, between character and capacity in

---

[80] Zedner, 'Security, the State, and the Citizen', 379–403, at 14–15; see also L Zedner, 'Preventive Justice or Pre-Punishment? The Case of Control Orders' (2007) 59 *Current Legal Problems* 174.

[81] M Douglas, *How Institutions Think* (London: Routledge and Kegan Paul, 1987).

the attribution of criminal responsibility has relatively little to do with doctrinal arrangements in the criminal law, and a great deal to do with the context in which the criminal process operates. While this context may present itself as a suitable object of social scientific rather than of philosophical investigation, it nonetheless shapes the social practices with which a scholarship committed to an analysis of the philosophical foundations of law must engage. The resurgence of short cuts to proof relying on mechanisms fostering guilt by association or the identification of 'bad apples' may not figure in a normatively polished conception of criminal responsibility as based on character. But to the extent that it exists, we must try to assess its implications not only for the implicit structure of criminal responsibility, but also for the feasibility of our normative vision of criminal law.

9

INTENTION AS A MARKER OF MORAL CULPABILITY AND LEGAL PUNISHABILITY

MICHAEL S MOORE*

1 THE ROLES OF INTENTION IN ASSESSING RESPONSIBILITY IN LAW AND MORALS

THE concept of an intention serves four important functions in the attribution of both moral responsibility and legal liability in the law of torts and of crimes. The first of these is as a marker (arguably *the* marker) of serious culpability in the doing

* This chapter was written under the aegis of the MacArthur Foundation's Project in Law and Neuroscience, the support of which is gratefully acknowledged. Various parts of the chapter were given to various meetings of the Law and Neuroscience Research Group, held at the University of California-Santa Barbara, and at Vanderbilt University.

of wrongful actions. As the laws of both crimes and of torts recognize, doing some wrongful action because one intended to do it merits greater blame and more severe sanctions than does doing that same wrongful action recklessly or negligently. This implication of intention for responsibility is learned early on by children, who frame serious accusations of others in terms of their doing things 'on purpose'. As Justice Holmes famously put it, 'even a dog knows the difference between being stumbled over and being kicked'.[1] Criminal law shares with dogs and children this emphasis on intention as essential to serious blame. As the US Supreme Court once put it: 'The contention that an injury can amount to a crime only when inflicted by intention is no provincial or transient notion. It is...universal and persistent in mature systems of law...[and] is almost as instinctive as the child's familiar exculpatory, "But I didn't mean to"...'[2]

The second of these functions deals with wrongdoing, not culpability. More specifically, intention plays a role in justification of otherwise wrongful behaviour. It thus deals with permissibility in this role, not culpability. Intention is commonly thought to mark the border of permissible consequentialist justification for otherwise categorically forbidden actions. This is the well known 'Doctrine of Double Effect', according to which good consequences may be used to justify the doing of some wrong such as killing of the innocent so long as such killings were a side effect or by-product of the actor's chain of reasons; but if the killing was intended, either as an end or as a means, those same good consequences are ineligible to be used to justify such actions.[3]

Third, intention is commonly thought to be at the root of human agency. This is the idea that the very possibility of persons doing *actions* depends on persons having intentions. The old way of putting this was to say that 'every action must be intentional under some description of it'. A more modern rendition is to say that every action begins with an intention, in the sense that intentions must be the immediate cause of those bodily movements through which persons act, for those movements to be actions at all.[4]

Fourth, intentions are crucially involved in the exercise of normative powers by persons. A normative power is an ability to change the content of our rights and responsibilities.[5] When I promise to do some action A, for example, it is commonly

---

[1] Oliver Wendell Holmes, Jr, *The Common Law* (Boston: Little, Brown, 1881), 7.

[2] *Morissette v United States*, 342 US 246 (1952).

[3] I explore the doctrine of double effect in MS Moore, 'Patrolling the Borders of Consequentialist Justifications: The Scope of Agent-Relative Restrictions' (2008) 27 *Law and Philosophy* 35–96, reprinted as ch 3 of MS Moore, *Causation and Responsibility* (Oxford: Oxford University Press, 2009); see also L Alexander and MS Moore, 'Deontological Ethics' (2007) *Stanford Encyclopedia of Philosophy*, <http://plato.stanford.edu>.

[4] I explore this thesis at length in MS Moore, *Act and Crime: The Philosophy of Action and its Implications for Criminal Law* (Oxford: Clarendon, 1993), ch 6.

[5] On the general idea of a normative power, see J Raz, *Practical Reason* (Oxford: Oxford University Press, 1976).

thought that I have changed my obligations: now I am obligated to do A, whereas before my promise I was free not to do A. I have voluntarily created something that was not there before, and my ability to do this is a power. Intention is bound up with normative powers because the valid exercise of a normative power depends, at least in part, on the intention of the holder of the power. To continue the example of promising, utterances that accidentally have the form of a promise do not have the force of a promise: the utterer must intend to promise.[6] As the contract lawyers say, 'there is no binding promise if there is an intent not to be bound'.[7] In the context of responsibility assessments for non-promissory obligations, this powers-marking role of intentions appears in the guise of consent. When a victim consents to be touched by another, the wrongness of touching evaporates. As Heidi Hurd colourfully puts it, this is the 'moral magic of consent': it changes rape into love-making, battery into sport, trespass into licence, and slavery into marriage.[8] But consent does this, as Hurd also shows,[9] only by virtue of the intent of the one who consents.

Interesting as are all four of these roles of intention vis-à-vis responsibility, I shall focus in this chapter only on the first, the use of intention to mark serious culpability. To assess intention's role here more precisely requires first that we step back to some more general considerations about the relations of responsibility to culpability, which I shall pursue in the next section.

2 RESPONSIBILITY, CULPABILITY, AND INTENTIONS

When we say that 'intention marks most serious culpability', what exactly are we saying? We could be saying that doing an action intentionally rather than negligently increases overall blameworthiness. While this is true, it doesn't capture where intention fits in to the criteria by which we parcel out praise and blame. To isolate more precisely the role of intention here requires that we distinguish culpability from responsibility, which I now propose to do, starting first with the more general notion, that of responsibility.

To get started with responsibility, consider the cartoon below.[10]

---

[6] See C Fried, *Contract as Promise* (Cambridge, MA: Harvard University Press, 1982).

[7] Eg E Allan Farnsworth, *Contracts* (3rd edn; New York: Aspen, 1999), 120. This matter is complicated by the 'objective theory' of contracts and by doctrines of promissory estoppel, where an unreasonably created appearance of a promise may create a promise-like obligation.

[8] Hurd's examples, in her 'The Moral Magic of Consent', (1996) *Legal Theory* 2, 121–46.

[9] Ibid.

[10] With the written permission of the author, Tom Batiuk.

As the cartoon illustrates, 'responsibility' has several usages in idiomatic English. One can *have* certain responsibilities, in the sense that one has certain obligations; one can *be* responsible in the sense that one generally takes care of his obligations; one can be a responsible adult, in the sense that one has the capacities (rationality and autonomy) to be held responsible for failure in doing what one is obligated to do.[11] The sense pertinent here is none of these, however. The relevant sense is that of being responsible *for* some harm or some other unhappy state of affairs.

Even restricted to responsibility for some harm, there are some further distinctions to be drawn. We might say, 'the storm was responsible for the loss of life', and we might say, 'the ship owner was held responsible in tort damages for the loss of life'.[12] Putting aside primitive animism, storms are not morally responsible for anything; all that is meant here is that the storm was a cause (or the cause) of the loss of life. Likewise, the ship owner's responsibility is better phrased as legal liability. A liability is (in Hohfeld's well-known logic) the absence of any immunity.[13] We need a sense of 'responsibility for harm' that is different from either of these. What we want to isolate is a sense of 'responsibility' that in a just legal system grounds (justifies) legal liability in criminal law and perhaps in torts; and a sense that is in turn partly grounded, but not constituted by, causal responsibility. Responsibility in the sense relevant here is a kind of liability, but the liability is to a moral, not a legal, sanction: to be responsible for a harm is to be morally blameworthy for that harm. The harm,

---

[11] These senses are fruitfully distinguished in HLA Hart, 'Postscript: Responsibility and Retribution', in his *Punishment and Responsibility* (Oxford: Oxford University Press, 1968), 211–12.

[12] Ibid.

[13] W Hohfield, *Fundamental Legal Conceptions* (New Haven, Conn: Yale University Press, 1919).

in other words, goes on one's moral ledger; in a good novel, or in St Peter's reckoning at the Gates, it shows up as a demerit.

Notice that to say this does not tell us anything about *when* someone is responsible for some harm; it only gives a logical consequence of their being so responsible, viz they are blameworthy for it. To say when someone is blameworthy is to have a theory of responsibility. The dominant theory underlying Anglo-American criminal law is this one. A person P is responsible for some harm H if and only if:[14]

A. P is a moral agent, meaning that he has the capacities (of rationality, autonomy, emotionality) that animals, the insane, the very young, and the very intoxicated lack; and

B. P is guilty of wrongdoing, meaning that:

  1. P performed some voluntary action A; and
  2. A (in fact and proximately) caused H; and
  3. Causing H is prima facie prohibited by one of morality's stringent prohibitions; and
  4. There are no features of A causing H that distinguish it from run-of-the mill cases of A causing H and that could justify the causing of H on this occasion (ie P had no agent-relative permission or consequentialist justification for violating his prima facie obligation); and

C. P was culpable in his wrongdoing, meaning that:

  1. P was motivated by an intention to cause H (alternatively: P believed A would cause H with some degree of likelihood, or P should have so believed); and
  2. P's intention or predictive belief in (1) was formed in circumstances where he had both adequate capacity and a fair opportunity to use his capacities, not to do A (ie P had no excuse).

When legal theorists speak of the 'relationship between punishment and responsibility', it is this sense of 'responsibility' that they have in mind. Turning now to 'culpability', the word is often used as a synonym for responsibility in the sense just articulated, viz moral blameworthiness. To be culpable, in this sense, just is to be blameworthy. More useful for our purposes is to distinguish two less inclusive senses, senses that correspond to the criminal law theorists' distinctions between *special* and *general* mens rea (guilty mind).[15]

A person P is culpable (in the special sense of the word) with respect to having wrongly caused some particular harm h when:

1. P either intends some type of harm H to be caused by P's action A, or P believes that H will be so caused, or P would believe this if he were reasonable; and

---

[14] Explored in much greater detail by me in MS Moore, *Law and Psychiatry: Rethinking the Relationship* (Cambridge: Cambridge University Press, 1984), ch 2; MS Moore, *Placing Blame: A General Theory of the Criminal Law* (Oxford: Oxford University Press, 1997), 35–45, 191–3.

[15] Special and general mens rea are distinguished in S Kadish, 'The Decline of Innocence' (1968) 26 *Cambridge Law Journal* 273.

2. the particular harm h that P has caused is an instance of the type of harm H that P intended; or h is an instance of the type of harm H that P foresaw; or h is an instance of the type of harm H the risk of which made P negligent on this occasion.[16]

It is in this sense of 'culpability' that criminal lawyers intend when they speak of 'the culpability requirements of the criminal law,' or when they say, 'P did the wrong thing but he has no culpability'.[17]

One is culpable in the general sense when conditions of possible excuse are taken into account. Diminished capacity to exercise sound judgment (by an agent generally possessing such capacities—no idiots, stones, mentally ill, or infants allowed) can arise by virtue of human threats, natural necessities, overwhelming emotions of fear, anger, or hatred, the cravings of addiction, and the like. Even when the proverbial 'cool hand' has no diminished capacities, circumstances may be such that he has no fair opportunity to exercise his undiminished capacities.[18] In an old Jack Benny skit, the hold-up man threatens Benny with 'your money, or your life'. Benny, playing on his famous cheapness, hesitates, saying, 'I'm thinking'. When Benny hands over the money his capacities are fine, only he did not have the opportunity that the rest of us have to keep both his money and his life. One is culpable in this general sense where one is culpable in the special sense (articulated earlier) in circumstances of fair opportunity and adequate capacity to have chosen otherwise.

The role of intention in all of this should be plain. Intention is a marker of culpability in the special sense just distinguished. Moreover, intention is at the top of the scale of culpability in the special sense: intending to cause some harm H is more culpable than merely foreseeing that some act A will cause H, or being willing to risk that A will cause H.[19] It is in this sense that the first role of intention is to be more precisely defined. It is in this way that intention is the marker of most serious culpability, and it is in this way that intention increases overall blameworthiness (or 'responsibility', in the sense defined).

Intention is of course not alone in its capacity to affect overall blameworthiness. Degrees of causal contribution, degrees of counterfactual dependence, degrees of objective risk, degrees of justification, degrees of excuse, degrees of moral agency, also have this capacity.[20] But intention is alone in the way in which it affects overall

[16] This second requirement of culpability in the special sense is codified in the American Law Institute's Model Penal Code, § 2.03 (2) and § 2.03 (3) (Philadelphia: ALI, 1962). As applied to negligence, the requirement is very problematic. See H Hurd and MS Moore, 'Negligence in the Air' (2002) 3 *Theoretical Inquiries in Law* 333–411, reprinted in Moore, *Causation and Responsibility*, chs 7–9.

[17] The distinction of culpability from wrongdoing is a watershed issue in responsibility theory, bound up with the distinction between justification and excuse. See generally Moore, *Placing Blame: A General Theory of the Criminal Law*, 191–93.

[18] On the capacity/opportunity theory of excuse, see ibid ch 13.

[19] A sometimes disputed print. For its defence, see ibid 408–10.

[20] As I argue in *Causation and Responsibility*, chs 3 and 18.

blameworthiness: intention affects culpability in the special sense just defined and none of these other items do.

3 ORDINARY AND LEGAL CONCEPTS OF INTENTION

What *are* intentions? An older style of philosophy of mind translated such questions from 'the material mode' to what was called 'the linguistic mode'. The question then became, 'what do we mean by our usages of the word, "intention"?'. Despite the refusal of contemporary philosophy to equate these two 'modes', asking after the common concept of an intention will be a useful place to start.[21] Finding the criminal law to be as instructive as ordinary speech, I shall in this section briefly mine both bodies of discourse for their meaning(s) of 'intent' and like terms.

Giving the meaning of a term used in a discrete body of discourse (such as ordinary speech or the criminal law) is not usually a matter of locating some authoritative definition. As empirical linguistics and ordinary language philosophy are equally fond of pointing out, giving such meanings is rather a matter of teasing out the implicit contours of some concept from that concept's usage in the whole body of discourse. Definitions (including those provided in otherwise authoritative sources such as dictionaries or penal codes) are only someone's fallible, contestable theory as to the shape of those implicit contours. What follows is thus my own reconstruction of the meaning of 'intention', from both ordinary and legal usages, noting the difference between the two where relevant.

It is common to distinguish using 'intend' and 'intention' as a verb or noun, on the one hand, from using 'intentional' and 'intentionally' as an adjective or adverb.[22] Notice the difference it makes in scenarios like this one:[23] you and I are in some grade B American Western movie (probably starring Ronald Reagan); we are crouched behind some rocks so as to avoid detection by the savages, who are all around us; a rattlesnake is next to us, coiled to strike, and I (knowing that the sound will reveal our location) shoot the snake dead so that it does not strike us. I did not, in ordinary

---

[21] As JL Austin presciently said, ordinary language will not be the last word in metaphysics but sometimes it will be the first word. JL Austin, 'A Plea for Excuses' (1956) 57 *Proceedings of the Aristotelian Society* 1–30. As Austin also saw, the law is often a fertile ground from which to mine the insights of common sense. Ibid.

[22] As in, eg, GEM Anscombe, *Intention* (2nd edn; Ithaca, NY: Cornell University Press, 1963); and HLA Hart, 'Intention and Punishment', in his *Punishment and Responsibility*.

[23] From H Morris (ed), *Freedom and Responsibility* (Stanford: Stanford University Press, 1961), 160.

speech, intend (verb) to alert the Indians; nor was the intention (noun) with which I shot to alert the Indians. Still, I did alert the Indians with my shot, as I knew I would: did I alert the Indians *intentionally* (adverb), or *unintentionally*, or neither? Was my act of alerting the Indians *intentional* (adjective), *unintentional*, or neither?

Ordinary usage is determinate about the verb/noun meaning: to have a predictive belief is not to have an intention and to so believe is not to so intend. Ordinary usage is indeterminate about the adverb/adjective meaning: foreseen consequences are not comfortably regarded as intentional or unintentional.[24]

Sometimes the question of intentionality arises, not with respect to the consequences of our actions (such as alerting the Indians), but with respect to circumstances.[25] Suppose I shoot and kill Bill, as I intended; if Bill is a police officer, did I intend to kill a police officer? Does the answer change if I knew Bill was a police officer? Or must I be motivated by that fact, as I would be if I were in a cop-killing contest, for example? Ordinary language here is also indeterminate, even with respect to noun/verb usages of 'intend'. In one sense (often called the 'de re' sense) of 'intend', if Bill is a cop and I intended to kill him, I intended to kill a cop; in another sense (often called the 'de dicto' sense), even believing that Bill is a cop is not enough—I have to represent the state of affairs I intend to bring about as the killing of a cop.[26]

Anglo-American criminal law (both common law and Model Penal Code) (1) recognizes the ambiguity of the two usages as to consequences; (2) resolves the vagueness of the adverb/adjective usage as to consequences in favor of intentionality; and (3) resolves (sort of) the de re/de dicto ambiguity regarding circumstances. Taking each in order.

1. The criminal law recognizes the ambiguity of the two usages by distinguishing 'specific intent' from 'general intent'. The dominant meaning (there are unfortunately others) of 'specific intent' is that of a further intention, further in the sense that it is an intention having as its object some state of affairs beyond the action done.[27] The further ('specific') intention with which I shot the snake was to prevent us getting bitten. Correspondingly, a general intention is just to do the act the criminal law prohibits; in the example, let that be, alerting the savages. Most crimes having some form of intentions as mens rea are general intent crimes, such as rape, arson, and murder; specific intent crimes tend to be inchoate crimes (where the evil the law ultimately seeks to prevent need not have occurred). Assault with intent to kill, breaking and entering with intent to steal, taking the

---

[24] See Hart, 'Intention and Punishment', 122; A Mele and P Moser, 'Intentional Action' (1994) 28 *Nous* 39–68, at 45.

[25] The consequence/circumstance distinction is explored in Moore, *Act and Crime*, 197–213.

[26] The *locus classicus* of the *de re / de dicto* distinction (although not put in these terms, and not applied to intentions specifically) is WVO Quine, *Word and Object* (Cambridge, MA: MIT Press, 1960).

[27] *People v Hood*, 1 Cal 3d 444, 462 P 2d 370 (1969).

property of another with intent to deprive permanently, are well-worn examples of specific intent crimes.

2. The criminal law stipulates that, on the facts given, I alerted the Indians intentionally, ie I had the requisite general intention. In a nutshell, predictive belief (a cognitive state) is sufficient for general intention; for specific intent it is not enough, because what is needed is a motivational state (with regard to either ends or means).[28]

3. With regard to the circumstance elements of various crimes—such as the lack of the woman's consent in rape/attempted rape cases—the criminal law is complicated. The one simple truth is that the law nowhere requires true purpose with regard to such circumstances. This is certainly true of general intent crimes such as rape: the actor need only know that the woman is consenting, he need not be motivated by that fact (wanting only forced sex, for example). But this is even true for specific intent crimes such as assault with intent to rape: the actor who assaults intending penetration is guilty if he merely believes there is no consent, no less than if he is motivated by that fact.[29]

There is less agreement about what mental state *is* required regarding circumstances. The common law generally indulges the fiction (through its unreasonable mistake doctrines) that an unreasonable belief that there *is* consent constitutes a general intention that there be *no* consent;[30] although this fiction is not indulged for specific intent crimes, which require knowledge of circumstance elements such as the lack of consent.[31] The Model Penal Code requires belief as to such circumstances for both crimes requiring knowledge as well as purpose, what the common law would call general and specific intent crimes, respectively.[32] Even the Code, however, waffles awkwardly for certain specific intent crimes like attempt and complicity (arguably requiring only the mens rea required for the underlying crime to be held to have these specific intents).[33]

Criminal codes typically prohibit thousands of act types, from killing to transporting corrosive liquids without proper labels. The English language and the criminal law are rich in words with which to describe the mens rea requirements attached to these thousands of prohibitions: we may be forbidden to do some action A if we: intend A; do A intentionally; do A knowingly, or wilfully, or consciously, or

---

[28] J Dressler, *Understanding Criminal Law* (2nd edn; New York: Mathew Bender, 1995), 105–07. I am given to understand that English law is less uniform on this point.

[29] The Model Penal Code accomplishes this result by defining its term for specific intent, 'purpose', as mere knowledge with respect to circumstances (whereas for consequences, 'purpose' is defined motivationally as 'conscious object'). Model Penal Code, § 2.02 (2)(a).

[30] Dressler, *Understanding Criminal Law*, 138–9. The House of the Lords sought to change the English common law on this point, in *R v Morgan* [1976] AC 182.

[31] Ibid 137.

[32] Model Penal Code, § 2.04 (1).

[33] Model Penal Code, § 2.06, 5.01 (1).

being aware or believing that it is A we are doing. In addition, some verbs of action also contain within them not only action prohibitions but implicit mens rea provisions as well. To lie, for example, is not only to tell an untruth; in addition, one must know that what one is saying is false. As another example, some verbs of action are 'intention-drenched'[34] in the sense that one cannot do such an act except with a certain intention, such as 'motioning a pedestrian across the street' (one's arm must move with an intention to so signal)[35] or 'endeavoring to obstruct justice' (one's act must be done with an intention to obstruct justice),[36] etc.

The general part of the criminal law is supposed to bring order to this otherwise riotous prolixity by reducing all of these sorts of mens rea requirements to either general or specific intent requirements.[37] Other *mens rea* terms, however, are not supposed to be so reduced, and they form an informative contrast to 'intention/intentional'.

1. *Deliberate and premeditated intentionality.* This phrase, taken from the dominant form of homicide statute in the United States (where it is a prerequisite for first degree murder), has two different meanings in criminal law, depending on which state one is in. Consider this well-known inference: 'If defendant D killed intending to kill, then his killing was deliberate; if his killing was deliberate, then he deliberated about it; if he deliberated about it, then his killing was premeditated. Therefore all intended killings are also deliberate and premeditated killings.'[38] States like Pennsylvania regard this as a true conclusion;[39] states like California (the majority) do not.[40] In the latter states, 'deliberate and premeditated' requires that the killing be deliberate—they require more than that the killing be deliberated about in a sense not synonymous with the killing being deliberate. Such deliberation requires conscious weighing of reasons and/or consideration of means—datable mental process—to either precede or succeed the forming of an intention to kill.

2. *Malice aforethought—the absence of passionate intentionality.* The phrase, 'malice aforethought', also taken from the dominant form of homicide statute in the United States (where it is used to distinguish murder from mere manslaughter), includes as part of its meaning that the intent to kill not be formed because of

---

[34]   Moore, *Act and Crime*, 198–9.

[35]   *Smith v Bocklitz*, 344 SW 2d 97 (Mo 1961).

[36]   18 US Code, § 1503.

[37]   Other popular terms, such as 'heedlessly', 'maliciously', 'carelessly', etc, are to be regimented to the legal categories of recklessness or negligence.

[38]   B Cardozo, *Law and Literature: And Other Essays and Addresses* (New York: Harcourt, Brace, and World, 1931), 97–101. Cardozo's actual chain of inference was: 'There can be no intent without choice, yet... the choice without more is enough to justify the inference that the intent was deliberate and premeditated... If intent is deliberate and premeditated whenever there is choice, then in truth it is always deliberate and premeditated, since choice is involved in the hypothesis of the intent.'

[39]   *Commonwealth v Carroll*, 194 A 2d 911, 917 (Pa 1963).

[40]   *People v Anderson*, 447 P 2d 942 (Cal 1968).

'an understandable passion arising out of a reasonable provocation' (one common law formulation)[41] or because of 'extreme mental or emotional disturbance for which there is a reasonable explanation or excuse' (the broader Model Penal Code version).[42] Here again a different mental state distinction is presupposed, distinct from the distinctions between intended/unintended and intentional/unintentional. This different distinction is between intentions formed because of passion and intentions formed out of either dispassionate impulse or cool deliberation.

3. *Involuntary intentions.* Both ordinary speech and the criminal law recognize the psychological truth that decisions made under duress—whether due to human threats or natural necessity—are still decisions, ie intentions, and that the actions done yielding to such threats, while in a popular sense 'involuntary',[43] are nonetheless intentional actions. Such actions may or may not be excused by the defense of duress, but irrespective these are intentional actions. 'Involuntary' in this sense does not negative intention.

4. *Intentions as willing/volition/voluntary action.* These terms require a very particular kind of intention: the defendant must intend the basic act (usually a bodily movement) by which he brings about the complex act the criminal law forbids.[44] Where defendant kills another by shooting him, for example, the defendant must intend (*will*, have as the object of his *volition*, be *voluntary* with respect to) the bodily movements that cause the trigger to move. Note that a defendant can have such intent (to move his finger) and *not* have either a general or a specific intent to kill. Note also that a defendant's act can be voluntary in this technical, criminal law sense and yet involuntary or non-voluntary in the popular sense of being under duress.

My own interest in this chapter is not on deliberate, impassioned, compelled, or volitional intentions; these are add-ons to the more basic notion of an intention. Moreover, my focus will be on intention in the sense that criminal lawyers call 'specific intent' and that ordinary language philosophers call 'intention with which' or 'further intention'. It is not that doing some action *intentionally* lacks interest for responsibility theorists. Yet intentionality in this sense is not a natural kind as are the psychological states of intention and belief; indeed, it is only a construction out of intention in my sense, so I shall focus on the more basic item.

There are two questions to explore about intentions so limited. One is the question of their *nature*: to what sort of mental state does 'intention' refer? The second is a question of *content*: how do we fix (and what sort of thing is it that we are fixing when we fix) the object or content of an intention? To use intention as the marker of most serious culpability supposes that we have some answer to both of these questions.

[41] Dressler, *Understanding Criminal Law*, 490–8.
[42] Model Penal Code, § 210(1)(b).
[43] Or at least not voluntary. See G Ryle, *The Concept of Mind* (London: Hutchinson, 1949), 69–74.
[44] Moore, *Act and Crime*, ch 6.

4 Suppositions about the Nature of Intention in Responsibility Assessments

At the most general level uses of intention in responsibility assessments presuppose a realism about intentions. As one common law court put it, the law supposes that 'the state of a man's mind is as much a fact as the state of his digestion'.[45] We suppose this in law and in ethics because any naturalist view of legal and moral qualities is committed to there being some natural property on which moral and legal properties supervene.[46] There have to be intentions for responsibility to depend on intentionality in the way that it does.

Less generally, our assessment of responsibility also supposes that the folk psychology of intention is at least roughly correct. Intention, in other words, not only exists as a distinct kind of mental state, but it is the kind of mental state that folk psychology posits it to be. One sees this supposition plainly in the way that the mens rea doctrines of the criminal law are built entirely on the back of that folk psychology.

The folk psychology in question is that relating to practical rationality. On the standard view of this psychology there are three sorts of representational states that cause the behaviour of rational agents: there are states of desire, where we represent the world as we want it to be; states of belief, where we represent the world as we believe it is; and there are states of intention, where we represent the world as we intend to make it.[47] For rational action, these states need to be related in their contents according to the following schema:

1. Δ Desires (q)   (Motivational premise)
2. Δ Believes (if p, then q)[48]   (Cognitive premise)
3. Δ Intends (p)   (Conational premise)
4. Δ Does the action described in p.

The grading of culpability (between most culpable states of purpose or specific intent, less culpable states of knowledge or general intent, still less culpable states of recklessness and negligence) done by the criminal law is built entirely on the back

---

[45] *Edington v Fitzmaurice*, LR 29 Ch Div 459, 483 (1882).

[46] Defended in MS Moore, *Objectivity in Law and Ethics* (Aldershot, UK: Ashgate Press, 2004), ch 6.

[47] I have adopted Michael Bratman's version of practical rationality in separating intention from desire. See M Bratman, *Intention, Plans and Practical Reason* (Cambridge, MA: Harvard University Press, 1987). The older view is to lump intentions in with desires as a general 'pro attitude'. See eg D Davidson, 'Intention', in his *Essays on Actions and Events* (Oxford: Oxford University Press, 1980).

[48] The sufficiency of p for q is too strong. Intention/belief consistency (a strand of practical rationality) only requires that it not be the case one believes it impossible that the action described by p will bring about the state of affairs desired (q).

of this folk psychology. One can see this clearly if one charts the mens rea concepts of the criminal law against the folk psychology of desires, intentions, and beliefs. Consider first the grading of culpability regarding the result elements of crimes. This is depicted in Figure 9.1.

As Figure 9.1 shows, the law uses the three representational states of desire, intention, and belief as the base in terms of which it defines the states that grade culpability. The law does not distinguish offenders who desire some prohibited result for its own sake, from those who intend that state only as a means to achieving something else desired for its own sake. Thus, 'specific intent' or 'purpose' is defined so as to include either state. The law does distinguish predictive belief from desire/intention; thus, 'general intent' or 'knowledge' is defined so that belief (that a legally prohibited result will be caused by one's action) will suffice, whereas it will not for specific intent or purpose. Furthermore, the reckless/knowledge and the reckless/negligence lines are drawn in terms of beliefs. For the first line, belief to a practical certainty ('knowledge') is distinguished from belief of a substantial risk ('recklessness'); for the second line, belief that there is a substantial risk ('recklessness') is distinguished from absence of such a belief when it would have been reasonable to have formed such a belief ('negligence').

The law's use of the folk psychology is just as evident in its definition of the states that grade culpability with respect to the circumstance elements of crimes. The law itself, however, is a bit more complicated, as is shown in Figure 9.2.

As Figure 9.2 shows, for circumstance elements the law allows any of the three representational states to suffice for the state of highest culpability, specific intent or purpose. That is, one is guilty of assault with intent to kill a policeman (a specific intent crime) if: (1) one wanted to kill a cop as an end in itself; or (2) one was competing in a cop-killing contest and one intended that the person killed be a cop so that his killing counted in the contest; or (3) one was indifferent to whether the victim killed was or was not a cop, although one believed with certainty that he was a cop. Although the law allows any of these states to suffice for most serious culpability, even here it defines that most serious culpability in terms of these three states. Even here the law's mens rea requirements are thus built on the concepts of the folk psychology.

This is also true with regard to the distinctions in belief the law draws with respect to circumstance elements. Notice the common law allows mistaken belief or absence of belief (when it would have been reasonable to have had a certain belief) to suffice for general intent[49] and malice, as well as for negligence. The common law thus has a simple grading scheme regarding circumstances: belief to a practical certainty constitutes specific intent, and not having such a belief when one should have suffices for all other grades of culpability. This distinction, while simple, is still wholly in terms of the folk psychological concept of belief.

---

[49] On this, see the qualification for later English common law in n 30 above.

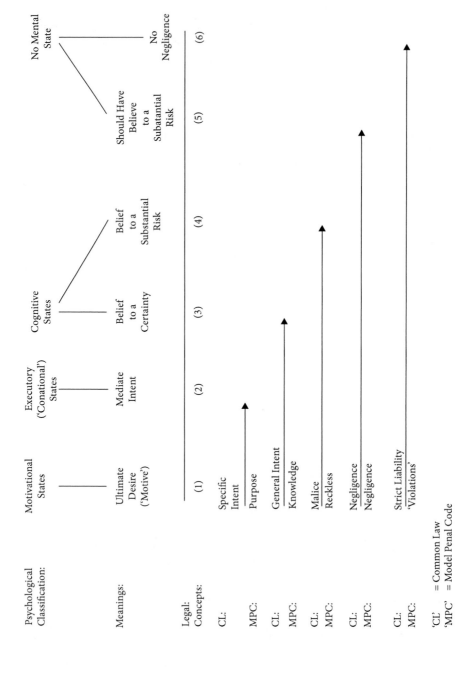

Figure 9.1 *Mens rea* concepts re consequences.

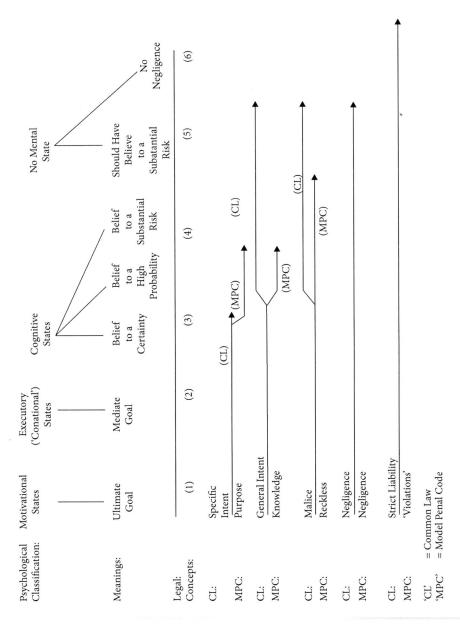

Figure 9.2 Mens rea concepts re circumstances.

The Model Penal Code's use of belief to grade culpability with regard to circumstance elements is more complicated than the common law. With its notion of wilful blindness, the Code introduces a belief 'to a high probability' between belief to a practical certainty ('knowledge') and belief of a substantial risk ('reckless'), and then allows the intermediate belief to suffice for knowledge.[50] The Code also distinguishes unreasonable absence of belief ('negligence') from the having of a belief that there is a substantial risk that some circumstance is present ('recklessness'). But the only point here is that these distinctions are wholly drawn in terms of the folk psychological notion of belief.

There are a number of other suppositions (about intentions) that responsibility assessments are commonly thought to make, in addition to supposing the basic belief/desire/intention ('BDI') psychology of rational action just sketched. I shall consider three of them. The first is that intentions are causally efficacious. More specifically, the idea is that intentions (sometimes, at least) cause the acts that are their object. When I go downtown *because* I intended to go downtown, the 'because' is meant causally.

It is often urged that something more than causation is required here. This is thought to be shown by 'deviant causal chains' kinds of case.[51] Suppose I intend to run you down with my car; yet this intention causes such excitement in me, such conflict, etc, that I tremble, my foot slips off the brake, hits the accelerator, and my car does indeed run you down. You are run down *because* of my intention, but my running you down was still an accident. So we must amend the supposition here: the intention must cause the act 'in the right way',[52] or better, the action must be done in execution of the intention. In any case, however this is put, *at least* the intention must cause the action for one to be regarded as seriously culpable because one intended the wrong done.

In criminal law this supposition is sometimes put as a temporal supposition, a 'simultaneity requirement'.[53] On this construal the requirement is that the act and the intent be simultaneous with one another. Yet this temporal criterion is only doing proxy work; what is really required is the kind of causal connection we get when an act is done in execution of an intention. Given the temporal proximity of intentions with the acts that execute them, such acts and intentions will be close to simultaneous. Yet the converse is not true: I can intend to run you down, and start the action of running you down at the same time, yet *not* do that act in execution of that intention. For example, I also intend to escape the large truck bearing down behind me, and accelerate for that reason.

[50] Model Penal Code, § 2.02(5) defines wilful blindness as belief to a high probability that some fact exists, so long as one does not believe that it does not exist.

[51] See eg A Goldman, *A Theory of Human Action* (Englewood Cliffs, NJ: Prentice Hall, 1970), 55–63.

[52] Ibid 61.

[53] As in Dressler, *Understanding Criminal Law*, 177–9.

However put, at a minimum intentions need to cause the actions that are their objects in order for intention to be a marker of serious culpability. There is a lively debate in contemporary neuroscience about whether such causal connection can exist,[54] those denying this defending the alternative conclusion that intentions are merely epiphenomenal with the behaviour they putatively cause. But our responsibility assessments plainly suppose otherwise.

The second additional supposition that responsibility assessments are said to make has to do with the causes of intentions rather that what intentions can cause. The supposition is that intentions are free in the sense of uncaused. The idea is that intentions are a species of choice, decision, and willing, and that all of these processes must be free, else they would not be what they are. This is of course nothing less than the supposition of free will.

This would be an extraordinary supposition for our use of intention in our blaming practices to make. Think of it: something that can cause things like actions to occur, but that is itself uncaused. The Big Bang is supposed to be like that, on some cosmologies; God is supposed to be like that, on some theologies. But it is ludicrous to think that each human choice is like that. Fortunately nothing in the use of intention to mark serious culpability in law or morality demands this extraordinary postulate.[55]

The third additional supposition has to do with consciousness. Many think that one can have an intention only if one is conscious of what the content of that intention is.[56] (Alternatively, one might think that although one can have unconscious intentions, the only intentions that affect one's culpability are conscious intentions.[57]) This

---

[54] One important strand of the argument here is based on the finding that action-initiators in the brain are formed before the subject is aware of his intention to move; if one identifies intentions only with awareness, one gets the epiphenomenal conclusion quickly. The debate begins with the work of the late Benjamin Libet and his associates. See eg B Libet, CA Gleason, EW Wright, and DK Pearl, 'Time of Conscious Intention to Act in Relation to Onset of Cerebral Activity (Readiness Potential). The Unconscious Initiation of a Freely Voluntary Act' (1983) 106 *Brain* 623–642. Related is the work of D Wegner (*The Illusion of Conscious Will* (Cambridge, MA: MIT Press, 2002)) and Haggard (P Haggard and M Elmer, 'On the Relations Between Brain Potentials and the Awareness of Voluntary Movements' (1999) 126 *Experimental Brain Research* 128–33). The most recent entry is the work of John-Dylan Haynes (J-D Haynes et al, 'Reading Hidden Intentions in the Human Brain' (2007) 17 *Current Biology* 323–8; 'Unconscious Determinants of Free Decisions in the Human Brain' (2008) 11 *Nature Neuroscience* 543–5). This work in neuroscience is subject to vastly different appraisals in terms of the efficacy of intentions in causing behaviour. See the discussions in: the symposium on Libet, in (1985) 8 *Behavioral and Brain Sciences*; S Pockett, WP Banks, and S Gallagher (eds), *Does Consciousness Cause Behavior?* (Cambridge: MA: MIT Press, 2006). My own entry in the fray is 'Libet's Challenge(s) to Responsible Agency', in L Nadel and W Sinnott-Armstrong (eds), *Conscious Will and Responsibility: A Tribute to Benjamin Libet* (Oxford: Oxford University Press, 2010).

[55] Or so we compatibilists have long argued. See Moore, *Placing Blame*, ch 12.

[56] See eg F Siegler, 'Unconscious Intentions' (1967) 10 *Inquiry* 51–67.

[57] I defend a version of this thesis in MS Moore, 'Responsibility and the Unconscious' (1980) 53 *Southern California Law Review* 1563–675, rewritten as chs 7, 9, 10 of *Law and Psychiatry*. The essential idea is that we need mental states of persons to have some connection to consciousness in some sense

is a much more nuanced supposition about intentions and responsibility than were the previous two; for with them it was a black and white 'yes' or 'no' as to whether such a supposition is made. Here there are nuanced shades of grey.

It helps to be clear what one means by 'consciousness'. If one means the phenomenological, experiential notion—the stream of consciousness of Joycean fiction—then pretty plainly the use of intention to mark culpability does not require it. Many of the actions that we do, intending to do them, and being rightly blamed for doing them, are done while we literally 'have our minds on something else'. The exercise of well-honed skills, all forms of habitual behaviour, and the like, are intended but do not require conscious attention to perform them competently.[58] This is why the overlay of 'premeditated and deliberate' required for first degree murder (as above discussed) is a true addition to the requirement of intentionality for murder itself; for intention itself does not require that such datable processes in consciousness occur.

However, it is preferable to understand 'conscious' here to refer to an ability, a disposition. This is the ability to turn one's attention to the intended action if the need arises, and the ability to state *what* was intended if that need arises.[59] Such abilities do not depend on there being silent soliloquies going on earlier in the heads of those who have intentions. It is much more plausible to think either that intentions without consciousness in this sense are impossible, or at least that there is no responsibility for intentions that do not meet this consciousness condition.

5 SUPPOSITIONS ABOUT THE CONTENT OF INTENTION IN RESPONSIBILITY ASSESSMENTS

Like all representational mental states, intentions take objects. One doesn't just intend, full stop, any more than one just desires or believes, full stop. Necessarily, we intend *that* something be the case. The 'something' is what I have been calling the content of

if we are to distinguish such states from the sub-personal states of brain functioning that are not at all accessible to consciousness.

[58] In part because habitual and skilled routines use a different upper motor pathway than do consciously planned routines, many neuroscientists classify such routines as unintended. Morality, common sense psychology, and the criminal law built on both classify such routines as intended. Model Penal Code, § 2.01(2)(d).

[59] In *Law and Psychiatry*, ch 7, I distinguish weaker from stronger senses of privileged access to our own mental states; all forms are cashed out in terms of verbal dispositions, however. I also allow that one might have 'deferred privileged access' to unconscious mental states.

an intention. Because intentions have content, it is never enough to know that someone had an intention (as opposed to some other kind of mental state); we also need to know *what* she intended. I thus move from the nature of intention to questions of content.

In using intention to mark serious prima facie culpability we have to ask and answer two questions related to the content of intentions. The first is a question of comparing what the defendant intended on a particular occasion, the 'intention-token', with the *type* of intention legal or moral norms require for conviction or blame. The question is whether the defendant's intention-token is an instance of the type of intention legally or morally required. The second is a question of comparing what the defendant intended on a particular occasion with the act the defendant actually did on that occasion. The question is whether the defendant's action is an instance of the type of action that he intended to do or not.[60]

These are both questions regarding the representational content of intentions. They both require that we fix *what* the defendant intended on some occasion as a matter of psychological fact, and then compare that content with: either the type of content the law or morality requires, for the first question; or the action done by the defendant in execution of that intention, for the second question.

The need to ask the first of these questions is probably obvious. After all, to apply legal or moral norms to particular facts always requires us to ask questions about particular facts instantiating general norms. The need for asking the second question may be less obvious, however. Yet asking such a question is also indispensable in using intention to mark most serious prima facie culpability. Suppose defendant D shoots and hits his victim V. If we wish to know whether the hitting of V was intended, we need to know the object of D's intention in shooting on this occasion: if it was to hit V, or to wound V, or to kill V, then the battery on V was intended; if it was to scare V, or to hit the apple on V's head, or to hit a target, then the hitting of V was unintended. In the latter case, the hitting of V may have been foreseen, or consciously risked, in which case D is somewhat culpable for the wrong of shooting V. But to be most seriously culpable for the intended hitting of V, the content of the intention of D's (that caused him to shoot) must have been one of the former representations. Using intentions to grade culpability thus requires that we ask both of these matching questions about *what* the defendant intended.

Both of these questions may seem to be not much different than the omnipresent classification questions lawyers and moralists always face in applying general norms to particular facts. To decide whether a defendant violated some rule against driving

---

[60] Notice that although the intention the defendant had on a particular occasion is a particular, its object is a representation of a *type* of action. This is on the Quinean supposition that intentions and predictive beliefs never refer to particular act-tokens that will occur in the future, only to there being in the future some instance of an act type. This admittedly flies in the face of ordinary speech ('he intended the killing', 'he predicted the fire') but is a necessary regimentation to avoid heavy duty use of possible worlds and trans-world identity claims. See MS Moore, 'Intentions and *Mens Rea*', in *Placing Blame*, 461, n 27.

a vehicle through the city park, for example, we have to decide whether what the defendant did amounted to driving, whether what he drove constituted a vehicle, and whether the land on which he drove was city park land. While there are problems here, they are the familiar problems of fixing the extension of the predicates used in the relevant rules: problems of vagueness, ambiguity, core cases, the penumbra, 'letter' versus 'spirit', and the like.[61]

Our two match questions about intentions raise different, and harder, problems of classification. For with these intention-related questions we are bereft of the usual resources (of identity and instantiation) on which we rely for normal classificatory questions. We can see this via two old examples of Edwin Keedy's.[62] Keedy was applying the common law rule for 'legally impossible attempts': if the defendant did all he intended to do and yet what the defendant did would still not have been criminal, then his attempt was 'legally impossible' and not punishable. Keedy gave two examples in application of this common law rule:

1. Defendant intended to take the umbrella in his hand; he believed that that umbrella was the property of another; in fact that umbrella was his own. Therefore, Keedy concluded, since the umbrella in his hand was his own umbrella, the defendant did not intend to take the property of another (and is not guilty of attempted theft).
2. Defendant intended to shoot at what he thought was a person; in fact the thing shot at was a stump; therefore, defendant did not intend to shoot at a person, and is not guilty of attempted murder.

These are pretty obviously daffy inferences. But notice they would not be so silly if we were not classifying intentions, but were classifying actions; for then we could use the true identities (the umbrella in his hand *is* the taker's own umbrella, this target *is* a stump) to make analogous inferences (if the defendant took the umbrella in his hand, then he took his own umbrella; if the defendant shot that person-looking object, then he shot a stump.)

When classifying intentions by their representational content, we cannot rely on true identities, extensional equivalences, or normal instantiations. Rather, we have to rely on how the defendant represented what he was trying to achieve in his mind. Put simply, here the descriptions matter, not just the underlying identities of the real world things those descriptions seemingly describe.

This long-noticed fact about intentions (and other representational mental states) is often called their Intentionality.[63] Notice how hard the Intentionality of intentions

[61] I explore these problems in legal interpretation in MS Moore, 'The Semantics of Judging' (1981) 54 *Southern California Law Review* 151–294, and 'The Natural Law Theory of Interpretation' (1985) 58 *Southern California Law Review* 277–398.

[62] E Keedy, 'Criminal Attempts at Common Law' (1954) 102 *University of Pennsylvania Law Review* 464–7.

[63] 'Intentionality' (with a capital 'I') is a term of art. It was rediscovered (from its early use by the Scholastics in the Middle Ages) by Franz Brentano, who mystified it with his notions of 'Intentional inexistence'. For some history, see D Dennett, *Content and Consciousness* (London: Routledge, 1969),

makes our classificatory questions. Take the first of them. Suppose the defendant drives a city bus through the park, and suppose it is clear that buses are vehicles for purposes of this ordinance (as well as in normal English); then defendant drove a vehicle through the city park. But did he intend to drive a vehicle through the park? Suppose we know he intended to drive a bus through the park—the fact that buses are vehicles in reality does not mean that they are such in his own mind, so we cannot easily infer he intended to drive a vehicle. After all, he might regard buses (both in normal English and in the law) as non-vehicles, in which event he would say that what he intended was *not* to drive a vehicle in the park (and, given consistency of intentions), therefore it is not the case that he intended to drive a vehicle through the park.[64]

Or consider Intentionality's effect on the second question. Suppose we know that the defendant did represent what he intended as, 'killing a human being' (one intention sufficient for conviction of murder is to intend to kill a human being). We also know that what he did was shoot and kill a member of another race, a race that defendant regards as non-human or 'sub-human'. He was, we may suppose, shooting at a member of his own race but missed, hitting instead the different-race victim. If we fix the extension of his representation of human being as we fix the extension of the words, 'human being', this is an easy case. Yet is this so clear for defendant's representation? By his own lights, he failed to achieve what he set out to achieve, which was to kill an instance of what he regarded as a human being.

In morality but even more in the law we have some detailed generalizations to help with these otherwise intractable classification questions about intentions. Let me consider each question separately, beginning with the first. The first question, as we have seen, requires a comparison of two things: the type of intention required by law or morality; and the intention-token had by some defendant on some occasion.

As a start, consider this old injunction of Phillippa Foot's in ethics: 'ask whether an action is intentional under that description of its content that makes it bad'.[65] In my own language: 'we are prima facie culpable when we act under a representation of the world that would make our action wrongful if the representation were true'.[66] This requires that we first discover the types of actions that are wrongful (because violative of the norms of negative obligation); and then ask if the defendant had such type of action as the content of his intention. Culpable intentions are in this way conceptually parasitic on the deontic norms of wrongdoing.

The criminal law, here as elsewhere, sharpens this moral point. Given the statutory nature of contemporary Anglo-American criminal law, finding out what is

ch 2. For an update, see J Perry, 'Intentionality', in S Guttenplan (ed), *Blackwell's Companion to the Philosophy of Mind* (Oxford: Blackwells, 1994), 386–95.

[64] We infer, that is, ~ I (p) from I(~ p) via a premise of consistent intentions, namely, ~ (I(p) and I(~ p)).

[65] From my memory of the late Phillippa Foote's Ethics class at UC-Berkeley many years ago.

[66] MS Moore, 'Prima Facie Moral Culpability', in *Placing Blame*, 405.

wrong is easy: we but open up Bentham's 'great book of laws'[67] to see what actions and what further intentions are prohibited by statute. Call this our first maxim in construing what type of intention is required for conviction: the intention must have as its object the actus reus of some statutory offence, or, in the case of specific intent crimes, some other legally prohibited state of affairs.

Our second maxim makes the first more precise. It is that the actus reus we must look to in construing the type of intention required for conviction must be the actus reus of the crime charged. One doesn't get to 'mix and match', any more here than with a pair of socks. If the defendant is charged with arson—say, burning down a ship—it will not do to find that he intended the actus reus of some other offence, such as theft.[68] Prima facie, the object of the prohibited intention must match the actus reus of the type of offence charged, not any other offence.

The third maxim is a qualification of the second. Many statutory actus reus prohibitions have elements within them that are irrelevant to the moral wrong that underlies the statutory actus reus.[69] As an example, the California Privacy Act prohibits one from 'intentionally recording a confidential communication without the consent of all participants by means of any electronic amplifying or recording device, excluding a radio'.[70] What if one mistakenly believes he is recording via a radio—is that relevant? Does the statutory mens rea require that one intentionally recorded *with a non-radio device*? There is nothing morally worse about recording without a radio than with one; the 'not a radio' requirement is in the statute for jurisdictional reasons, namely, to avoid pre-emption of a state statute by federal communications law. So we should eliminate any representation of radio-hood from the object of the intention required to be convicted under this statute. This will be to apply the third maxim.

The fourth maxim has to do with the tricky problem of conditional intentions. A conditional intention is not present when it is only true of some defendant that, if money were found on the pavement, he would form the intention to take it.[71] There the condition is external to his intention, and is a condition precedent to his having any intention to steal. A true conditional intention is where the condition is within the object of some present intention of the defendant. For example: the defendant now intends that, if the money is still on the pavement where he saw it an hour ago, he will take it.

The issue with conditional intentions is whether they carry with them the same degree of culpability as do unconditional intentions to do the same thing. The law

---

[67]   J Bentham, *The Limits of Jurisprudence Defined* (New York: Columbia University Press, 1945), 343.

[68]   *R v Faulkner*, 13 Cox Crim Cas 550, 555, 557 (1877).

[69]   I shall here ignore whatever differences may exist between the common law's 'moral wrong' doctrine (*R v Prince*, 2 Crown Cases Reserved 154 (1875)) and the Model Penal Code's 'material elements' doctrine (where an element is material if and only if it affects the 'evil sought to be prevented by the law defining the offense': Model Penal Code, § 1.13(10)). For whatever the nuanced differences here, both doctrines eliminate elements of offences from *mens rea* consideration on moral grounds.

[70]   California Penal Code, § 632.

[71]   G Yaffe, 'Conditional Intent and *Mens Rea*' (2007) 10 *Legal Theory* 277.

purports to give more help here than it actually can deliver. The common law maxim was that if the condition (when communicated to the victim as a demand, as is common) was one the defendant was not entitled to make, then a conditional intention is to be treated as an instance of the type of intention required for conviction.[72] The Model Penal Code version of this maxim is even broader, equating conditional with unconditional intentions across the board.[73] As Justice Scalia observed, this cannot be right: 'the doctrine of conditional intent cannot reasonably be applied across-the-board to the criminal code.'[74] The most we should conclude is that presumptively, that an intention is conditional in its content makes no culpability difference, recognizing that this will not always be true.

The fifth maxim is actually a collection of *ad hoc* substitution rules. I view these as ad hoc exceptions to the second maxim above. Here are some examples.

a. The 'legal wrong' doctrine: the defendant need not intend the actus reus of the crime he did so long as he did intend the actus reus of *some other grade* of that crime (as in doing a first degree, night-time burglary, thinking it was a second or third degree, day-time burglary).[75]

b. The felony/murder rule: the defendant needn't intend to kill to be convicted of murder, even though killing is the actus reus of murder, so long as the defendant intended to do some other felony and during that felony the victim died.[76]

c. The grievous bodily harm murder doctrine: the defendant needn't intend to kill for murder, even though killing is the actus reus of murder, so long as he intended the victim grievous bodily harm, and the victim died as a result of that harm.[77]

d. The battery-assault interchange: the defendant needn't intend to hit (cause contact with) the victim, even though hitting is the actus reus of battery, so long as the defendant did intend to frighten (cause apprehension of contact by) the victim; conversely, the defendant needn't intend to scare the victim, even though causing apprehension is the actus reus for assault, so long as defendant did intend to hit the victim.[78]

---

[72] The US Supreme Court adopted this version of the maxim in the car-jacker case, where the intent was assault with a deadly weapon if the victim did not give up her car. *Holloway v United States*, 526 US 1 (1999).

[73] Model Penal Code, § 2.02(6) simply provides that: 'When a particular purpose is an element of an offense, that element is established although such purpose is conditional, unless the condition negatives the harm or evil sought to be prevented by the law defining the offense.'

[74] *Holloway v United States*, 526 US 1 (1999) (Scalia J dissenting).

[75] See generally Dressler, *Understanding Criminal Law*, 141-2. The common law holds the offender to the greater degree of the crime he in fact did; the Model Penal Code (s 2.04(2)) holds the offender to the lesser degree of the crime he thought he was doing.

[76] See generally Dressler, *Understanding Criminal Law*, 479-89.

[77] *Director of Public Prosecutions v Smith* [1960-3] All ER 161.

[78] The assault/battery interchange is most forthrightly acknowledged by the *Restatement of Torts (Second)*, §§ 13, 18, 21.

e.   The mayhem substitution rule: the defendant needn't intend to disfigure the victim even though disfigurement is the actus reus of mayhem, so long as the defendant did intend to hit the victim and that hit did cause disfigurement.[79]

These and other rules substitute one type of intention for that which would normally be required by the second maxim above (the one requiring that the object of the intention required for conviction be the actus reus of the crime charged and not the actus reus of some other crime), apparently on the rationale that to intend the substituted thing is close enough in culpability to be treated as if it were to intend the actual wrongdoing of the offence.[80]

The sixth maxim is intended to deal directly with the problems raised by the Intentionality of intentions. The maxim is usually put as a short and snappy aphorism, 'ignorance of the law is no excuse'.[81] What is really being said, however (in the terms relevant here), is that the defendant need not represent what he intends to do or achieve in the literal language of the law describing the actus reus of the offence.[82] To revert to the earlier example of the no vehicles in the park ordinance, the defendant need not represent what he intends to drive as a *vehicle*; he may be ignorant that buses are vehicles, or even mistaken in a belief that buses are not vehicles, and still have the intention required for conviction.[83]

The doctrine is based on the reasonable enough assumption that few offenders formulate the objects of their intentions in the legal terminology used by statutes. Even lawyers don't intend, for example, to 'cause asportation of property of another' (the old common law actus reus of theft) when they steal. We have to allow many other representations to qualify as prohibited intentions, in addition to the occasional *in haec verba* representation that we may encounter. The unresolved problem, however, is how we are to classify particular representations under this more sensibly relaxed requirement. Because of the Intentionality of intentions, we cannot confidently rely on the ordinary extensions of the terms used in the content of the prohibited intentions. But without this, what should be our guide?

Lawyers commonly think they can answer this with a seventh maxim: representations of a defendant that are not *in haec verba* of the relevant statute will be sufficient for conviction if based on some erroneous *legal* belief by the defendant, not if based on some erroneous *factual* belief by the defendant. The earlier hypothesized defendant who erroneously believes buses are not vehicles would get off if he believed buses to lack motors (when motors are a necessary condition of legal

---

[79]   *State v Hatley*, 72 NM 377, 384 P. 2d 252 (1963).

[80]   I ignore the utilitarian rationalizations sometimes produced in defence of these doctrines.

[81]   *United States v International Minerals and Chemical Corp*, 402 US 558, 563 (1971).

[82]   The Model Penal Code sees with admirable clarity this fact: the doctrine that ignorance of the law does not excuse is not really about excuses at all; it is about what mental states are required for guilt. The Code also sees that for guilt the accused need hold the correct interpretation of the laws no more than he need have knowledge of such laws' existence. Model Penal Code, § 2.02(7).

[83]   *People v Marrero*, 69 NY 2d 382, 507 NE 3d 1068 (1987).

vehicle-hood), a factual error; not if he believed (erroneously) that the law exempted modes of public transport from its prohibition on vehicles. Yet how does such a distinction handle the racist killer who intends to kill a member of another race, believing that members of such race lack some essential criterion of legal person-hood (such as membership in the species, *homo sapiens*)? Seemingly such a rac-ist killer cannot be convicted of intending to kill a human being, yet I doubt any court has or would so hold. More broadly, the maxim's distinction invites all of the problems of distinguishing analytic from synthetic judgments so much the focus of post-World War II philosophy.[84]

Despite all of these problems, in both law and morality we do seem to muddle along in formulating the type of intention that can mark serious culpability. Yet notice that only gives us half of what we need to answer the first match question distinguished earlier. We also need to know as a matter of psychological fact what a defendant intended on a given occasion. We need, moreover, a rather precise formu-lation of the content of the intention with which he did some prohibited action. We need this in order to match it up to the precisely detailed type of intention required by our seven earlier maxims. Both law and morality plainly suppose that psychology can deliver up some truths here that make the comparison in question possible.

Whether psychology is up to this is of course a hotly contested matter.[85] Both law and morality suppose that the optimistic side of this debate is right, and think the sceptical side is wrong. They suppose that there is a 'language of thought' in the brain,[86] an incorrigible and transparent accuracy in the verbal behavior of self-reporting,[87] an infallible stream of consciousness, a complex array of counterfactu-als about hypothetical behaviour, or some other basis for formulating with precision what a person intends on a given occasion. Whether this is a well-founded supposi-tion of law and morality remains to be seen.

The second match question asked about the content of intentions was, how well does the action the defendant did in execution of some intention match the type of action that was the object of that intention? Here also lawyers and moralists receive some help from the criminal law. The best known of these criminal law aids is the 'transferred intent' rule.[88] While sometimes construed to be a rule helping with the first match question,[89] this is in actuality a rule aimed at helping with the second.

---

[84] Larry Alexander has a go at disentangling some of these issues in his 'Inculpatory and Exclupatory Mistakes and the Fact/Law Distinction' (1993) 12 *Law and Philosophy* 33–70.

[85] For the neuroscientific challenges to the folk psychology, see S Morse, 'Determinism and the Death of Folk Psychology: Two Challenges to Responsibility from Neuroscience' (2008) 9 *Minnesota Journal of Law, Science, and Technology* 1–35. For the challenges from within philosophy, see J Greenwood (ed), *The Future of Folk Psychology* (Cambridge: Cambridge University Press, 1991).

[86] J Fodor, *The Language of Thought* (Cambridge, MA: MIT Press, 1975); Fodor, *Psychosemantics: The Problem of Meaning in the Philosophy of Mind* (Cambridge, MA: MIT Press, 1987).

[87] See the citations in Moore, *Law and Psychiatry*, 252–65.

[88] See generally W Prosser, 'Transferred Intent' (1967) 45 *Texas Law Review* 650–62.

[89] See eg Dressler, *Understanding Criminal Law*, 109.

What the rule says is that differences in the identity of the victim don't count when assessing whether what the defendant did matches the type of act he intended to do closely enough to be graded an intended wrongdoer.

Suppose (a real if unreported case, as it turns out) that some skier at a ski resort restaurant makes an off-colour comment to the waitress. She is so incensed that she hurls a heavy glass ashtray at the offending skier's head. With quick reflexes, however, he ducks in time and the ashtray hits another skier sitting behind the first. The transferred intent rules say that the waitress is guilty of the intentional tort (and crime) of battery. True, she did not in fact do what she intended to do: she intended to hit the offending skier, and she in fact hit another skier. But the transferred intent rule holds this to be 'good enough for government work', ie adequate for conviction. She otherwise did what she intended to do, and the difference in the identity of the victim is put aside as immaterial.

Such a rule at most creates a safe harbour where we know certain differences don't matter. Left unaided by such rules are all other differences. For example, the defendant intends to hit victim with a stick, but does not intend to injure the victim with such a light blow (the victim is, unbeknownst to defendant, peculiarly susceptible to injury),[90] or the defendant intends to put out the victim's left eye with a blow from a stick, but instead puts out the victim's right eye;[91] or the defendant intends to scare a victim into thinking that the defendant wants to kill her by doing an act with some risk of killing her, but that act actually does kill the intended target of scaring.[92] In cases such as these, whether the act done in execution of some intention comes close enough to the type of act intended is left open by the transferred intent rule.

Indeed, this rule does not even create the safe harbour it purports to create. Suppose a defendant intends to hit his girlfriend, who happens to be holding their baby; she turns to avoid the blow, which lands on the baby instead.[93] Normally the transferred intent rule would say that the type of act the defendant intended differed only in the identity of the victim from the act done, and this is good enough to be adjudged culpable for intended hitting of the child. Yet this may well not be true where battery on an adult is regarded lightly (a misdemeanour), whereas battery on a child is regarded much more seriously (a felony). If the difference in the moral wrongness of these two act types is as great as such statutory grading schemes assume, then one should be reluctant to 'transfer the intent' in the manner contemplated by the transferred intent doctrine.[94] The defendant only negligently or perhaps recklessly hit the child, even if he also attempted to hit the girlfriend.

---

[90] The facts of *Vosburg v Putney*, 78 Wis 84, 47 NW 99 (1890); 80 Wis 523, 50 NW 403 (1891).

[91] Discussed in Moore, 'Intentions and *Mens Rea*', 475–6, n 50.

[92] See the amazing facts of *Hyam v Director of Public Prosecutions* [1974] 2 All ER 41, particularly as construed in the opinion of Lord Hailsham.

[93] The facts of *State v Cantua-Ramirez*, 718 P 2d 1030 (Ariz, 1986).

[94] As were the three dissenting members of the Arizona Supreme Court in *Cantua-Ramirez*, ibid.

Notice that this second match question again supposes that psychology can deliver up rather precise formulations of what it is that some defendant intended on a particular occasion. Even with such precisely formulated objects of intentions we have the classificatory difficulties adverted to, but without such formulations the comparison is hopeless to begin with.

6 Conclusion

The law of torts and of crimes, together with the morality of blaming behind both, thus makes a lot of assumptions about what is true in psychology. They assume that persons act because of representational states that really exist and that exhibit Intentionality, that those states are of three distinct kinds, that those kinds are related to one another in the distinctive pattern of practical rationality charted earlier, that intentions are a part of that schema, that there is a difference in kind between intentions (or intentions cum desires) and beliefs, that intentions can be causally efficacious, that some form of privileged access exists with respect to an intention by its holder, that there is a fact of the matter about *what* someone intends on a particular occasion, and that this can be formulated with sufficient precision to allow the two comparisons responsibility assessments require in order to grade culpability by intentions. A tall order, to be sure, but a lot we care about besides using intentions to mark most serious culpability goes by the board if psychology/neuroscience cannot deliver on such an order.

10

WRONGDOING
AND MOTIVATION

VICTOR TADROS*

HOW should we understand the relationship between a person's motivations and whether they have done what it was wrong for them to do? On one view, motivation is irrelevant to wrongdoing. A person's wrongdoing is determined by motive-free facts about the situation, such as the fact that her action will harm another person. These facts give rise to reasons that a person has for and against action. The reasons that I have ought to guide me in my motivations. But the motive with which I act does not make the act wrong.

If a person's motivations are irrelevant to wrongdoing, intentions are also irrelevant to wrongdoing. Criminal lawyers are sometimes wont sharply to distinguish intentions and motives. There is a sense in which this is right. Motives such as jealousy or greed do not relate in any simple way to a person's intentions. But in another sense of motive, the sense that I am concerned with here, the idea is false. In standard cases, if a person intends to v in order to w and she wants to w for its own sake, she intends both v and w. She is also motivated by both v and w. She is motivated to v for the instrumental value she believes it to have and she is motivated to w for the intrinsic value she believes it to have.

Many moral philosophers reject the significance of motivation to permissibility. The disagreement was once one between consequentialists and non-consequentialists. The latter group typically thought that the wrongfulness of an action could be affected

* Thanks to participants at a research seminar at the Centre for Ethics, Law and Public Affairs, University of Warwick and the conference at Rutgers for discussion of an ancestor of this chapter. Thanks in particular to Matthew Clayton, Antony Duff, Gerald Dworkin, Lindsay Farmer, Sandra Marshall, Jeff McMahan, Massimo Renzo, Prince Saprai, and Andrew Williams for their thoughts.

by the attitudes of the person performing it, and pointed to the fact that, with respect to the same magnitude of harm, it may be wrong to harm a person intentionally but permissible to harm a person with mere foresight. That was denied by many consequentialists. Ordinary morality may invite that view, they claimed, but we should revise ordinary morality on a more rational basis. It is the consequences that matter. I have no good reason to care whether I am harmed intentionally or with foresight. What matters is how much I am harmed, or so they claimed.

The significance of motivations now also divides non-consequentialists. For example, Judith Jarvis Thomson,[1] Frances Kamm,[2] and TM Scanlon[3] are non-consequentialists who argue motive is irrelevant to permissibility. They think that we should distinguish blameworthiness from permissibility. Motives are relevant to blameworthiness but not to permissibility. And some draw a similar conclusion about the criminal law. We separate out the question of permissibility from the question of fault. The first question has priority over the second. Motivations matter only insofar as the person has done something wrong. Whether something is permissible or not is to be determined by the harm that it causes. Hence, the harm principle is still commonly regarded as the standard principle that must be satisfied to warrant criminalization. If and only if principles of criminalization are satisfied do we turn to the fault requirements that must be satisfied to render the defendant liable to a criminal conviction for his conduct.

In this chapter I defend the view that motivation plays a more direct role in determining what is wrong than this view suggests. This idea helps us to clarify the structure of wrongdoing and also to understand one way in which morality and criminal law come apart. An act can be wrong in virtue of the motivation with which it was done. But, for various reasons, we have good reason not to criminalize all action that is wrong. Sometimes we will wish to tolerate wrongful action because of its desirable consequences.

1 THE PRIORITY OF FACTS?

Let's begin by outlining in some more depth the view that wrongdoing is determined by motive-independent facts. This provides us with one way to understand the structure of wrongdoing. We begin by identifying certain facts that have moral

---

[1] JJ Thomson, 'Self-Defense' (1991) 20 *Philosophy and Public Affairs* 283; JJ Thomson 'Physician-Assisted Suicide: Two Moral Arguments' (1999) 109 *Ethics* 497.

[2] FM Kamm, *Intricate Ethics: Rights, Responsibility, and Permissible Harm* (Oxford: Oxford University Press, 2007), ch 5.

[3] TM Scanlon, *Moral Dimensions: Meaning, Permissibility, Blame* (Cambridge, MA: Harvard University Press, 2008).

salience. Those facts provide us with reasons for and against actions and omissions. We must respond to those reasons. Sometimes a fact will give rise to a decisive reason against performing an action. If that is so, we ought to be guided by that reason and not perform the action. Sometimes a fact will give rise to a decisive reason to perform an action. If that is so, we ought to be guided by that reason and perform that action. Whether the action or omission is wrong is determined by whether there was a decisive reason for or against the action.

Motivation, on this view, does no work in determining whether the person's action is wrongful. Whether the action is wrongful is determined by the facts which give rise to reasons for action or omission. If a person *has* decisive reasons for action or omission, she ought to be motivated by those reasons. But the question of whether a person *has* such reasons is prior to the question of whether she is appropriately motivated by them. Another way of putting this is to say that culpability is parasitic on wrongdoing. Whether a person is culpable depends on the motives that the person has. Whether those motives are culpable depends on whether they appropriately track the motive-independent facts that ought to govern the person's practical reasoning.

For example, it is morally salient that a person will suffer a certain injury, or that a person will be prevented from completing a worthwhile project that they have, or that a person will be assisted in a worthwhile project, or will avoid suffering a certain injury. When a person is faced with a decision about what to do, he must take into consideration these morally salient facts. The morally salient facts provide the person with reasons for and against doing certain acts, and in that way morally salient facts provide people with reasons for action. Some of these reasons will, in some circumstances, be decisive. For example, there may be some reasons in favour of a certain action, but in the absence of very compelling reasons in favour of doing it the fact that my act will cause another person to suffer a serious injury is a decisive reason against that action.

We might doubt whether a fact can provide a reason in the absence of evidence of this fact. A fact can give rise to a reason for a person against doing an action, we might think, only if that person has evidence on which to form a belief that the fact obtains. For example, the fact that my action will cause serious injury to another person, we might think, does not provide me with a decisive reason against doing that action if I do not have any evidence that the fact obtains.[4]

---

[4] Whether facts can ground normative reasons where there is no evidence for those facts is a subject of disagreement amongst those who think that motives are irrelevant to permissibility. JJ Thomson is an advocate of the view that they can. See *The Realm of Rights* (Cambridge, MA: Harvard University Press, 1990). TM Scanlon thinks that they can't. See *Moral Dimensions*, 47–52. In the context of the criminal law, John Gardner is an advocate of Thomson's view. See *Offences and Defences: Selected Essays in the Philosophy of the Criminal Law* (Oxford: Oxford University Press, 2007), especially chs 5 and 12.

In order for a fact to give rise to a normative reason for an agent to act, some argue, that fact must be capable of having some purchase on the practical reasoning of the agent. If I lack evidence of a fact, that fact can have no purchase on my practical reasoning, and so it cannot give rise to a reason for action. Others disagree. They may point to the idea that I can have a reason to do something based on a fact that I have no evidence for if others could have informed me of that fact. For example, some may think that I have a reason not to drink a colourless liquid that is poisonous even if I have no reason to believe that it is anything but water. The person who knows that it is poisonous ought to inform me that the liquid is poisonous, they may claim, in order to prevent me from doing what I have reason not to do: to drink the liquid.

We might also think that evidence for a fact provides a reason to act even if that fact does not obtain. If I have evidence that my action will cause some undesirable outcome that evidence does have purchase on my practical reasoning. If I act contrary to the evidence I do what I have reason not to do. For example, if I have evidence that I have meningitis, say because I have the symptoms, I have reason to call emergency services. That is true even if it turns out that I only have flu. I have reason to believe that I may have meningitis and that provides me with a reason to call emergency services.

Whether facts themselves, or evidence of facts, or both can provide normative reasons for action is controversial. I think, at least, that evidence of a fact can provide us with reasons for action even if that evidence leads us to form false beliefs.[5] Whether facts can provide us with reasons for action if there is no evidence of those facts is a more difficult question. But whatever view we take on these matters, we can still hold the view that wrongdoing is independent of motivation. Even if evidence of a fact can give rise to a reason for action independently of that fact obtaining, nothing follows about the significance of motivation for wrongdoing. A person may or may not be motivated by the evidence that he has.

For example, if a person has sufficient evidence to believe that he will kill someone if he pulls the trigger of a gun, we might think it wrong for him to pull the trigger even if the gun is unloaded. That is true because of the evidence that the person has, evidence that he ought to act in the light of, and not because he would be badly motivated in pulling the trigger. The question of what our normative reasons for action are, and hence of what constitutes a wrong, may still be exhausted before we come to the question of a person's motivations.

Everyone agrees that a person's motivations *do* make a difference to whether that person deserves moral criticism. We can see this from the fact that people can sometimes deserve moral criticism with respect to a morally permissible action if that person is not motivated in the right way. If I save a drowning baby only for personal glory and not because I care about the child, I deserve criticism for the way in which I was motivated. But that does not make my action of saving the child *wrong*. We

---

[5] See V Tadros, *Criminal Responsibility* (Oxford: Oxford University Press, 2005), ch 10.

might question, as Immanuel Kant did, whether the action has *moral value*. But whether an act has moral value does not, or at least does not always, determine the permissibility of that act. The fact that an act lacks moral value does not make the act wrong. Hence, on this view, we must be careful to separate the question of whether a person did something wrong from the question of whether he was blameworthy. A person's motivations may be irrelevant in considering the former question, but significant in considering the latter.[6]

This view about morality corresponds to one version of a familiar view about the criminal law. According to some criminal lawyers, we ought to distinguish between the rules that are to be used to guide the conduct of citizens (conduct rules) and the rules that are to be used in guiding the decisions of judges (decision rules).[7] In determining what to do we need rules of conduct. However, the fact that a person has breached rules of conduct is only one thing amongst others that is of significance in guiding judges in making decisions about imposing criminal liability on a defendant.

For example, we ought not to hold a person criminally responsible for her conduct if her responsibility has been undermined by involuntary intoxication. But the fact that a person is involuntarily intoxicated does not normally make a difference about what she is required to do. If I attack you whilst involuntarily intoxicated to the relevant degree a judge ought to acquit me of assault. But that is not (normally at least) because my involuntary intoxication is something that I can take into consideration in deciding to attack you.

On one version of this view mens rea terms ought to be excluded from the set of conduct rules except in special cases, such as attempts, where the intention is necessary to specify the conduct.[8] It is enough for me to know that harming you is prohibited. I need not know whether intent, knowledge, subjective recklessness, or objective recklessness determines the limits of criminal liability for harm. If I know that I am prohibited from harming you I also know that I ought to avoid harming you. It follows that I ought not to intend to harm you or to create serious risks of harming you. I ought also to find out whether my conduct is likely to harm you. What we need, then, is a list of harms, which provide reasons for action, and which can then guide me in deciding how to act, and how to form the beliefs in the light of which I decide to act.[9]

---

[6]   See especially Scanlon, *Moral Dimensions*.

[7]   See M Dan-Cohen, 'Decision Rules and Conduct Rules: On Acoustic Separation in Criminal Law', in *Harmful Thoughts: Essays on Law, Self, and Morality* (Princeton: Princeton University Press, 2002) and P Robinson, *Structure and Function in the Criminal Law* (Oxford: Oxford University Press, 1997).

[8]   See eg Robinson, ibid.

[9]   A view like this is also outlined in L Alexander and K Ferzan, *Crime and Culpability* (Cambridge: Cambridge University Press, 2009), though it is legally protected interests rather than harms that they focus on.

I doubt that things are as simple as this. We do not have the same epistemic obligations in relation to every morally salient fact. In some cases, we ought not to act unless we have taken steps to discover whether some morally salient fact obtains. In other cases, we are entitled to act unless we know that the relevant morally salient fact obtains. The law might provide me with guidance about whether I need to gather evidence about some fact before acting, and that may be determined by imposing different mens rea requirements on different offences.

For example, suppose (as is true of the law of England and Wales) that I can be convicted of handling stolen goods only if I know or believe that the goods are stolen. In imposing knowledge rather than recklessness as the mens rea requirement for the offence the law indicates to me that I am not prohibited from handling goods unless I know or believe that they are stolen. I do not have an obligation to discover whether they are stolen even if I think that the goods look suspicious. And there might be good reason for the law to be set up that way. A rule that required people to investigate whether suspicious looking goods were stolen might be a significant setback to economic efficiency.[10]

We might contrast handling with rape. I am not permitted to have intercourse with a person unless I have taken sufficient steps to ensure that the person I am having intercourse with is consenting. The law can make this explicit, setting out not only my duties in action (don't have intercourse with a non-consenting person) but also my duties of investigation (don't have intercourse with a person without taking steps to ensure that the person is consenting).[11]

Even if I am right in thinking that mens rea rules are not best thought of as purely decision rules, the significance of motivation to wrongdoing has not been established. We must be guided by the facts, and evidence of those facts. And sometimes we must gather evidence before acting. But that does not establish that the motives of the agent make a difference to permissibility.

2 MEANS AND MOTIVATIONS

What arguments might be given in defence of the view that motives are irrelevant to wrongdoing? One argument can be dismissed quite quickly. Scanlon suggests that whilst people can choose what to do, they cannot choose the reasons for which they act. Hence, in order to ensure that permissibility is appropriately choice-sensitive we must focus on actions rather than intentions.

---

[10]   See, further, Tadros, *Criminal Responsibility*, ch 9.
[11]   See Sexual Offences Act 2003, s 1.

It might be doubted that there is an important relationship between permissibility and choice of this kind.[12] But even if there is, Scanlon is not very clear in his explanation of *why* people can't choose the reasons for which they act. He argues as follows: 'one can adopt an end only if one sees some consideration as counting in favour of it, and it is at this most basic level that I do not think that we can *choose* what to see as reasons'.[13] The idea might be as follows. There are things that a person values or doesn't value.[14] Those things lie at the heart of what a person intends. But we do not choose to value something. Valuing something is a matter of perception and judgment rather than choice. As permissibility ought to be grounded in choice, and not just in perception and judgment, intentions ought not to affect permissibility.

This conclusion would follow only if lack of choice over what to intend followed from lack of choice over what to value. But it does not. Suppose that intentions are relevant to permissibility. In that case it is wrong to form an intention to harm another person. But that does not require that one values that other person. One can refrain from forming the intention to harm another for all sorts of reasons.

Settling on an intention to do something is importantly similar to deciding to do that thing. To see this, consider picking out which shirt to wear. I look in my closet at all of the neatly ironed shirts, and think that the blue one would look nicest. I select the blue one. Now imagine that I am lying in bed thinking about which shirt I will wear. I think about the ones in my closet and think that the blue one would look best. I decide on that one. These processes are really the same. I have as much control over the second decision as over the first. But in the first case I select the blue shirt and in the second case I intend to select the blue shirt. We should conclude that I have the same kind of control over which intentions to form as I have over my actions.

A more significant argument is that when we determine what to do, we ought primarily to be focused outwards, on the people whose interests will be affected by our actions, rather than inwards, on our own motivations. The idea that motives are significant to wrongdoing makes practical reasoning into a form of self-investigation. But our actions are wrong not because of what they reveal about ourselves, but rather because of the way in which they interfere with the interests of others.

For example, suppose that I refrain from harming you, even though I feel an urge to do so. I refrain from harming you not because of the suffering that it will cause you, but rather because were I to see my urge as a reason to harm you I would be a corrupt person. What makes me resist my urge is the fact that I want to avoid corrupting myself: recognition of your moral value, if I recognize it at all, plays only

---

[12] See J McMahan, 'Intention, Permissibility, Terrorism, and War' (2009) 23 *Philosophical Perspectives* 345.

[13] See Scanlon, *Moral Dimensions*, 59–60.

[14] For more discussion of the role of valuing in grounding free action, see eg G Watson, 'Free Action and Free Will', in *Agency and Answerability* (Oxford: Oxford University Press, 2004) and M Bratman, 'Three Theories of Self-Governance', in *Structures of Agency* (Oxford: Oxford University Press, 2007).

a subordinate role to my self-regarding ambition. When I explain this to you, you might complain at me that I am wrongly focused on myself and my own moral purity when it is *your* interest in not being harmed that is crucial in this case.

To flesh this concern out further, it will be helpful to focus on the principle that it is impermissible to harm a person as a means for the greater good of others (the *means principle*). We are less often justified in harming a person as a means than we are in harming a person as a side effect, or so ordinary morality tells us.

The (very familiar) trolley problem will sharpen our focus on the problem.[15] The trolley problem invites a comparison between two cases.

> *Trolley Driver.* The driver of a trolley is hurtling down a track and he realizes that the brakes have failed. Five people are on the track in front of him, and if he does nothing the trolley will run into them and kill them. However, he can turn the trolley onto another track. If he does so, the trolley will run into one person and kill them.
>
> *Bridge.* The driver of a trolley is hurtling down a track and the brakes have failed. Five people are on the track in front of the trolley. However, there are two people on the bridge between the trolley and the five. One of those is a large person, large enough to stop the trolley if he falls in front of it. The other is a very strong small person. The only way for the small strong person to prevent the trolley hitting the five is by knocking the large person off the bridge in front of it.

In both cases, if one person dies five are saved. The problem is that we tend to judge it permissible for the driver to turn the trolley in *Trolley Driver*, but to judge it wrong for the strong small person to push the large person off the bridge in *Bridge*.

As we shall see, the most promising way to preserve our intuitions about the difference between these two cases is to focus on the way in which the one person is harmed. In *Bridge* the large person on the bridge would be harmed as a means to save the five. In *Trolley Driver* the one person would be harmed as a side effect of the action which saves the five. If this is the right way to preserve our intuitions, it suggests that the fact that we harm a person as a means makes a significant difference in our judgments about the wrongness of our actions. We can call this the *means principle.*

The means principle is highly intuitive but it is difficult both to specify it further and to justify it. One familiar approach distinguishes between what a person intends and what they know will come about as a consequence of their actions. It is worse to intend harm than it is to know that one will harm as a side effect of one's actions. Whether a person acts permissibly on this view depends on the person's motivations in acting. That this is so is clear from what I said about intentions and motivations in the introduction. A person acts with an intention insofar as he acts for a reason. The reason for which he acts is his motivation in acting. To know what a person intended we need to know what motivated that person.

---

[15] I've cleaned this up a bit from the original problem developed by Philippa Foot in 'The Problem of Abortion and the Doctrine of Double Effect', in *Virtue and Vices* (Oxford: Oxford University Press, 2002).

Now let us return to the claim that motivation is not relevant to permissibility. Those defending that claim will resist focusing on the intentions of the person turning the trolley. The argument under consideration suggests that focusing on intentions requires the person about to turn the trolley to focus inwards, on their attitude towards the people saved and the people harmed, rather than outwards at the people who they will otherwise harm.

We can illuminate this concern by imagining that the driver in *Trolley Driver* is badly motivated. Suppose that the trolley driver has no inclination to save the five people. However, he has intense hatred for the one person. He turns the trolley towards the one only in order to crush the one. In that case, in turning the trolley, he has done just what a good trolley driver might permissibly have done. But he has done it for nasty motives. Has he acted wrongly? We might be tempted to say that the trolley driver has acted permissibly but for the wrong reasons. He knows all the relevant facts, and those facts do not give rise to a morally decisive reason against turning the trolley. If he does just what the well-motivated person might have done, we might conclude that he has not acted wrongly.

This judgment might be reinforced in the following way. Imagine that an ambivalent trolley driver is heading down the track and asks for advice about what he should do. He asks you whether it would be wrong for him to turn the trolley. What would your advice be? Some people think it odd to say to him: 'well, that depends on what your motivations will be. If you act in order to save the five you would be acting permissibly, but if you would be intending to kill the one, you would not be acting permissibly.'

Or, imagine that I, a well-motivated person, am on the trolley with a badly motivated trolley driver. He tries to turn the trolley. It would be odd for me to prevent him from turning the trolley so that I, with my better motivations, could turn it in exactly the same way. And surely I would not do that if he is more skilful at trolley turning than I am. Suppose I did interfere with the bad trolley driver so that I, with good intentions but poorer trolley turning skills, could try to turn it. Many people will conclude that I was overly concerned with motivations and insufficiently concerned with saving the five. These judgments have considerable intuitive appeal, and provide a significant challenge to the idea that motivations have significance with respect to permissibility.

A view which focuses on intentions can provide an intuitive explanation of the trolley problem presented at the beginning of the previous section. But we have seen some reason to doubt that it is the right explanation. Defending a motivation-based view against this challenge has two parts. The first part, outlined in section 3, casts doubt on other explanations that have been given for the trolley problem. We will wish to explain the powerful intuition that there is an important difference in the permissibility of harming the one person in *Trolley Driver* and *Bridge*. But theories that exclude motivation have their own difficulties. The second part, outlined in section 4, provides an explanation for the judgments that we tend to make in cases where the trolley driver is not properly motivated, an explanation that is consistent with the idea that motivations are relevant to permissibility. This will also allow us to consider some cases where it is intuitively implausible to *reject* the significance of motives to permissibility. This will provide us with a better platform for understanding the structure of wrongdoing, which will help us to clarify the way in which we should understand criminal wrongdoing.

3 ARE THERE BETTER EXPLANATIONS?

Abandoning the significance of motivation to permissibility may lead some to doubt that there is a significant difference between *Trolley Driver* and *Bridge*. But few will want to accept either that it is wrong for the trolley driver to turn the trolley, or that it is permissible for the small strong person to throw the large person off the bridge. Judgments like these are intuitively appealing in pairs of cases across a range of circumstances.

For example, many people will think that it is permissible to bomb a munitions factory to make a significant advance in a just war even if it will kill some civilians as a side effect. Many people will think that it is wrong to kill the same number of civilians in order to induce terror in the population to make a similarly significant advance in the just war. Many people will think that it is permissible to divert medical resources away from a needy person to save five other needy people. Many people will think that it is wrong to kill one healthy person to distribute his organs to five other people who will otherwise die.

Rather than abandoning the judgments that we tend to make in the trolley problem, we might look for explanations of these cases that don't focus on motivations. Furthermore, although Scanlon doubts it, we should expect a single principle, or a reasonably modest set of principles, to explain these judgments. Scanlon thinks that different principles will explain different cases depending on their context. But it would be very surprising if this were so. One of the reasons for the enduring appeal of the doctrine of double effect and related ideas is that very many of our intuitions about pairs of cases across contexts are explained by the doctrine. The rare exceptions are not intuitively powerful enough to erode our expectation that a general principle of some kind is at work here.

One supposed counter-example is the infamous *Loop* case. *Loop* is a variation on *Trolley Driver* devised by Thomson. The difference from *Trolley Driver* is that the track with one person on it loops round so that if the trolley did not hit that person the trolley would return to the track on which the five people are standing and kill them. In that case, it appears that the presence of the one person on the line motivates us to turn the trolley, and so we intend to kill the one. Thomson thinks that intuition tells us that it is permissible to turn the trolley in *Loop*. I lack strong intuitions about the case. If a theory tells us that it is wrong to turn the trolley in loop we should not regard that as a strong reason to reject the theory.

We will do best, then, to focus on general principles that purport to explain our judgments in the trolley problem, and in related cases, that do not rest on motivations. There are two main possibilities. The first, which can be dismissed quite quickly, is based on the distinction between acts and omissions. Many people think that it is worse to bring about some harm than it is to fail to prevent an equivalent harm. In *Trolley Driver* the driver of the trolley has a choice either to kill the five or to kill the one whereas in *Bridge* the person on the bridge has a choice between killing one or failing to save five. For as he is the driver of the trolley, it might be argued, if the driver does not turn the trolley he will nevertheless kill the one.[16]

But it is difficult to believe that this explains the trolley problem. The distinction between acts and omissions, when considered alone, has both under-inclusive and over-inclusive implications with respect to permissibility. It is under-inclusive in that it is sometimes permissible to act to save five people, killing one, even if the alternative would have been a failure to save five. We can see this from the fact that just as it is permissible for the driver to turn the trolley, so it would be permissible for a bystander to turn the trolley in *Trolley Driver*. But the bystander, if he did not turn the trolley, would be allowing the five to die. If that is right, we should conclude that it is sometimes permissible to kill one person rather than allowing five people to die.

It is over-inclusive in that it is often wrong to fail to rescue someone where it would be easy to do so even if that failure would avert a greater harm. For example, just as it is wrong for me to kill you to distribute your organs to five other people, it is wrong for me to fail to rescue you even if through that failure your organs might become available to be distributed to five other people who would otherwise die. Or, if you were about to fall in front of a trolley which will crush you to death it would be wrong for me not to give you a hand to prevent that happening. That is so even if failing to give you a hand would lead you to fall in front of the trolley preventing five people from being crushed to death.

A second alternative is that it is the causal and non-causal relationships between a harmful event and a good event that distinguish between these cases.[17] In *Trolley Driver*, in contrast with *Bridge*, the harm to the one is 'causally downstream'[18] from the act that produces the greater good of saving the five. In *Bridge* the benefit to the five is brought about through the event which is a harming of the one. The harming of the one is not caused by the event which saves the five. It *is itself* the act which saves

---

[16] For a recent defence of this view, see JJ Thomson, 'Turning the Trolley' (2008) 36 *Philosophy and Public Affairs* 359. I discuss this view in more depth in *The Moral Foundations of Criminal Law* (forthcoming).

[17] See Kamm, *Intricate Ethics*, ch 5.

[18] Kamm describes her own view as 'downstreamish'. The reasons why need not trouble us here.

the five. In *Trolley Driver* that is not so. Turning the trolley *causes* harm to the one in *Trolley* but it is not *itself* a harming of the one. Harming a person as a constituent of an action that gives rise to a greater good is wrong, we might think. Acting in a way that gives rise to the greater good may be permissible, however, even if that act also causes a lesser harm. If that view is right, it is the objective features of wrongdoing that are at the heart of wrongdoing.

An attractive feature of this view is that its implications are relatively close to the traditional motivational account of the trolley problem. When we intend to do something in order to achieve some further end, we see the thing that we do as a cause of the further end. If we intend to harm someone as a means to the good, that good will be causally downstream from the harm. In contrast, if we harm someone as a side effect, the harmful act will not cause the good consequence. The harmful act will rather be a bad consequence that is caused by the good act. In consequence, an account based on the causal and non-causal relationships between the harm and the good can explain why accounts based on motivation have a range of intuitive implications.

Some may attempt to bolster this view by pointing to the familiar difficulty of 'closeness'.[19] Return to *Bridge*. We might think that the small strong person, if he throws the large person off the bridge, does *not* intend to harm the large person. He intends to stop the trolley, and the trolley can, in principle at least, be stopped without the large person being harmed. The small strong person's plan to stop the trolley would not be thwarted if the large person suddenly developed an impervious shell. He would then stop the trolley and remain unharmed. It is not harm to the large person that is intended, we might conclude.

The problem of closeness does not pose difficulties for the view that motivation is relevant to permissibility. If we think that our powerful intuitions about *Bridge* (and a range of similar cases) ought to be preserved by the best moral theory, we will conclude that we must solve the problem of closeness. For it is not harm to the large person per se that saves the five. But any solution that is available to a non-motivational explanation will be available to the motivational explanation.

For example, we might agree with Frances Kamm that what matters here is the difference between harms that are causally related to the good-producing act and harms that have a closer, non-causal, relationship to the good-producing act.[20] If the small strong person throws the large person in front of the trolley perhaps we would

---

[19] Both moral and legal philosophers have attempted solutions to the problem. See, eg, W Quinn, 'Actions, Intentions, and Consequences: The Doctrine of Double Effect', in *Morality and Action* (Cambridge: Cambridge University Press, 1993); J Bennett, *The Act Itself* (Oxford: Oxford University Press, 1995), 208–13; WJ Fitzpatrick, 'The Intend/Foresee Distinction and the Problem of Closeness' (2006) 128 *Philosophical Studies* 585; AP Simester, 'Moral Certainty and the Boundaries of Intention' (1996) 16 OJLS 445; KK Ferzan, 'Beyond Intention' (2006) 29 *Cardozo Law Review* 1147.

[20] Kamm distinguishes between harms caused by the act that produces the good result and harms which are the 'non-causal flip-side' of those acts. See *Intricate Ethics*, ch 5.

not say that the harm was caused by his being thrown in front of the trolley. Perhaps we would say that throwing him in front of the trolley *is* harming him. If that is the right view, we can incorporate it into the motivational view I defend here: a person who intends *v* also intends *w*, as far as the *means principle* is concerned, if *w* has the appropriate non-causal relationship to *v* and the person knows this to be the case. The problem of closeness is interesting, but it is not a special problem for a motivational explanation of the trolley problem.

Now let's investigate the causation-based alternative more directly. It is difficult to believe that causal and non-causal relationships between the harm and the good can explain the trolley problem in an adequate way. The reason for this is that the *means principle* is underpinned by the relationships between people that would be implied by permitting some to be harmed as a means for the good of others. Treating a person as a means involves a failure to respond appropriately to the special moral status that human beings have. Causation-based accounts lack an obvious connection to this idea.

We can see very clearly that relationships between persons underpin the *means principle* by substituting objects for the people down the track in trolley problems. When we do this, we find that our intuitions alter significantly. It *is* permissible to damage valuable things in order to preserve more valuable things. If I can save five giant redwoods from being felled by a trolley only by felling one giant redwood, which will fall in the path of the trolley, I am permitted to do that even though I harm one redwood as a means to preserving the five. And the same thing is true of non-human sentient beings. I am permitted to throw one deer in front of an oncoming trolley, causing it severe pain, in order to prevent the trolley running into five deer, causing them each to suffer the same degree of pain.

We should expect the means principle to be underpinned by the moral status of the person harmed. But moral status is not something to be protected and promoted. It is rather something to be respected. A person who harms another as a means fails to respect the status of that person.[21] The central reason to endorse the *means principle*, then, is that the principle provides us with a proper way of governing our relationships with each other. And it is natural to conclude that when a person violates the principle she does so by virtue of the attitude that she shows towards others. It seems plausible that this attitude is made manifest in her motivations in acting.

It is admittedly difficult convincingly to vindicate the *means principle*. Here is a suggestion: we are each entitled to choose between a range of ends for the sake of which we will use our lives. That is one way of understanding right to autonomy: the right to set one's ends for oneself. It is wrong to expend a person's life for the sake of an end that that person need not have taken as an end for herself. In doing so we would fail to respect that person's autonomy. When a person is harmed as a means

---

[21] See FM Kamm, *Morality, Mortality vol 2* (Oxford: Oxford University Press, 1996), ch 10 and T Nagel, 'The Value of Inviolability', in P Bloomfield (ed), *Morality and Self-Interest* (Oxford: Oxford University Press, 2008).

to a greater good, the greater good is imposed on her as an end. That is not so when a person is harmed as a side effect. Although what I have said here is quite vague, it at least points to, or hints at, some deeper account of the means principle, grounded in our moral autonomy.

It also suggests that we ought not to seek accounts of the *means principle* that are independent of the attitudes that would be implicit in accepting or rejecting that principle or in acting in accordance with it. What is wrong with harming a person as a means to a greater good is that pursuit of the good is imposed on the person who is harmed. And imposing an end on a person that the person is entitled not to take as their end is something that we do intentionally. To harm the one for the sake of saving the five in *Bridge* is wrongfully to impose the saving of the five as an end on the large person at the cost of his life. As he need not expend his life for the sake of that end it is wrong to harm him as a means to that end.

It is very difficult to understand how to motivate us to endorse principles based on causal and non-causal relationships between the good and the harm. Those relationships do provide answers to trolley problem cases that are no less intuitive than accounts based on motivation. But it is difficult to see why causal and non-causal relationships between the harm and the good are morally significant to morally autonomous agents.[22] They do not have the right kind of connection to the ideas that underpin the *means principle*.

To reinforce this argument, consider variations on our cases where we substitute the *trolley driver* with an object, thus removing any attitudes that people might have towards each other. Think about the causal and non-causal relationships between the harm and the good without the involvement of agents by comparing the following cases:

> *Asteroid I.* A trolley is hurtling down a track and the brakes have failed. Five people are on the track in front of it. No one can do anything to alter the situation. However, an asteroid falls on the trolley diverting it onto another track where it kills one person.

> *Asteroid II.* A trolley is hurtling down a track and the brakes have failed. Five people are on the track in front of it. No one can do anything to alter the situation. A large person is on a bridge between the trolley and the five. An asteroid falls on the large person causing him to fall in front of the trolley, killing him. This prevents the trolley from killing the five.

If it were true that there were motivation-free facts that our motivations ought to track, we should expect our judgment about this pair of cases to be similar to the judgment that we have about *Trolley Driver* and *Bridge*.

You might wonder what kind of judgment we can make about this pair of cases. One kind of moral judgment that we often make about the world, when people aren't involved, concerns how bad it is *that something happened*. If it is worse that something happens, it is normally also worse to bring that thing about. For example, we say that it is worse that more people than expected were killed in a flood, even if there was nothing

---

[22] Despite exhaustive analysis of difficult cases, Kamm's own attempt to explain her objectivist view is, by her own admission, hardly compelling. See *Intricate Ethics*, 165–7.

that anyone could have done about it. And that is reflected in the judgment that it is worse for me to kill more people by flooding them than to kill fewer people. From these judgments, we make judgments about luck. When it is better that something happened, we say that the event was lucky, and when they go badly that it was unlucky.

If the causal and non-causal relationships between the good and the harm were important, we might expect our judgments about the luckiness of the events in this pair of cases to track our judgments about the badness of the conduct in the trolley problem. But I doubt many will think it lucky that an asteroid fell from the sky in *Asteroid I*, but that it was unlucky in *Asteroid II*. In *Asteroid II* there is no difference between the asteroid causing the person to fall in front of the trolley and him simply already being there preventing the five from being killed. Just as it would have been lucky if the one person was on the track preventing the five from being killed, so it is lucky that the asteroid causes the one person to fall in front of the trolley saving the five. Where agency is not involved the causal relations between harms and goods are not morally significant.

It might be suggested that what matters is not that *there is* a causal relationship of a particular kind between the harm and the good. Defenders of the causal relationship view might indicate that a person cannot justify harming a person by pointing to the fact that harming them caused a good result. In *Asteroid II* there is no agency at all, and hence there is no question of justifying harming another. But if causal relationships themselves do not matter morally, and we can see from the pair of asteroid cases that they don't, what can be said to support the idea that it is wrong to harm a person as a cause of a greater good? Friends of the causal view need to show that it is wrong to harm one where five will be saved because the one would be the cause of the five being saved even though it would be lucky, all things considered, that harm to one person is the cause of five being saved. It is not obvious to me what more can be said to support that view.

If that is right we have a strong general reason to doubt the idea that motivations are irrelevant to permissibility. There is no motivation-free value, such as that 'it is better if the good is not causally downstream from the harm', which we ought to track with our motivations. This suggests that the motivations with which we act have direct moral significance to permissibility. Rather than being parasitic on motivation free-facts, motivations are central to the best account of wrongdoing.

4 How Intentions are Relevant to Permissibility

The difference between intentionally harming and knowingly harming provides an intuitively satisfactory explanation of the trolley problem. It explains a range of cases across contexts in an appealing way. It is also easier to motivate than objective theories such as theories based on the causal and non-causal relationships between harms and goods. If this view is right, it implies that motivations are relevant both to blameworthiness and to permissibility.

However, in section 2 we encountered some apparently compelling difficulties with a motivational account of permissibility. I will consider one objection here and one in the next section. Here is the first. A person who is deliberating about what to do should not normally focus on her motivations, it was claimed. She should focus outwardly, on the effects that her action would have on herself and on others, not inwardly on her attitudes. To explore this issue further, let us return to *Trolley Driver*. It is intuitively permissible for the trolley driver to turn the trolley away from the track with five people, killing one. But when we ask whether it is permissible for the driver to turn the trolley, it *does* seem odd to ask what intentions he would do this with. Why might that be?

We can make some progress by focusing on what it means to say that it is permissible to turn the trolley. What it means is that turning the trolley is an option for a properly motivated person. That will be so if there is no decisive reason against turning the trolley. From this we can see why, when asking the question whether it is permissible to turn the trolley, it is odd to focus on the intentions that the person would have in turning it *even if* intentions are relevant to permissibility. If intentions are relevant to permissibility it is not permissible to turn the trolley *with the intention of harming the one person*. But that does not imply that it is not permissible for him to turn the trolley at all. There *is* no decisive normative reason against turning the trolley; no decisive reason for *anyone*. *Anyone* has the option to turn the trolley. That is so because the trolley can be turned without intending to kill the one person.[23] If a motivation-based account of wrongdoing is right, when we ask whether it is permissible for the driver to turn the trolley, we ask whether the trolley could be turned without intending to kill the one person. As it is possible to turn the trolley without intending to kill the one person, it is permissible to turn the trolley. Turning the trolley is an option for a well-motivated person. There is no morally decisive reason against doing so. Anyone could turn the trolley because anyone could do so with the intention of saving the five, knowing that the one will be killed.

What of the bad trolley driver, then? Should we say that *he* acted permissibly when he turned the trolley with the intention of killing the one? No. *His* turning of the trolley has a wrong-making feature: it was done with the intention of killing the one. Turning the trolley was permissible but not when done with the intention of killing the one.

---

[23] This view is also defended in WJ Fitzpatrick, 'Acts, Intentions, and Moral Permissibility: In Defence of the Doctrine of Double Effect' (2003) 63 *Analysis* 317. It is hastily rejected in Kamm, *Intricate Ethics*, 134–6.

We see this structure of the evaluation of actions clearly in more straightforward contexts, where intentions are not the focus. Suppose that I ask whether it is permissible for me to go to the shops. You say that it is: there is no morally decisive reason against doing that. It is an option for those who respond appropriately to the normative reasons that apply to them. Now suppose that, following your advice, I go to the shops, but in doing so I walk all over your flowerbed. Going to the shops *that way* is wrong. For going that way has a wrong-making feature. To make it permissible for me to go to the shops it must be true that there is one way for me to go to the shops that lacks a decisive wrong-making feature. But if there is such a way that does not imply that it is permissible for me to go to the shops in *any* way. Similarly, in *Trolley Driver* the fact that I could turn the trolley with the intention of saving the five renders turning the trolley permissible. But this does not imply that turning the trolley in order to kill the one is permissible.

Another way of seeing this is to distinguish less and more complete action descriptions. When we focus on the less complete action description 'going to the shops' we conclude that it is permissible for me to do that. When we focus on the more complete action description 'going to the shops trampling all over your flowerbed' we conclude that *that* is wrong. When we focus on a person's action ex post we ask whether *the most complete* description of this person's action has a wrong-making feature. And where the person tramples on the flowerbed, it does.

A similar thing can be said about the trolley driver. If the driver asks: 'is it permissible for me to turn the trolley?', we focus on the less complete action description contained in his question. And when we do that we conclude that it *is* permissible for him to turn the trolley. We need not investigate the intentions with which the trolley driver will act to conclude that this is so. For turning the trolley *can* be done without intending to kill the one person. In other words, the incomplete action description can be completed without incorporating an intention to kill. But if the trolley driver asks 'is it permissible for me to turn the trolley *intending to kill the one*?' we ought to conclude that it is wrong for him to do *that*.

To make this even more intuitive, we can follow Antony Duff in describing an intentional harm as an *attack*.[24] Imagine that the trolley driver asks you whether it is permissible for him to attack the one person given that he knows that attacking that person will result in the five being saved. You will say that it is impermissible for him to do that. The permissibility of turning the trolley does not imply the permissibility of attacking the one person.

Now that we have an account of the way in which intentions are, and are not, relevant to the question of permissibility, we can bolster the view by considering the significance of motivation to permissibility and wrongdoing in another context, that of duress. Consider the range of German citizens who participated in Nazi activities.

[24] For Duff's latest account of the importance of attacks in criminal law, see *Answering for Crime* (Oxford: Hart, 2007), ch 7.

Some people only participated to a modest degree. Suppose, as was probably true, that failure to participate to some modest degree carried very grave risks for some German citizens and their families. Some citizens participated because they wished to avoid those risks. Others participated because they were fully committed to the Nazi cause.

I take it that if the degree of participation was very modest and the threat was very great, it was permissible for a citizen to participate.[25] For example, suppose that the only way of avoiding a grave risk of having a family member being sent to the concentration camp was to help to distribute Nazi propaganda. Assuming that distributing the propaganda only made a trivial difference to the Nazi cause, it would be permissible for a person to distribute the propaganda to avoid that risk being realized. But are we to say that *all* citizens who distributed the propaganda did so permissibly, even those who were fully committed to the Nazi cause, and who were not at all motivated by the threat they faced?

To see that this cannot be right, consider the situation where members of a group threaten each other in order to motivate the group to commit some wrongful act. We will not conclude that *all* act permissibly when they perpetrate that wrong. Imagine a gang with three members who wish to rob the post office. The gang is ruthless. Any member who pulled out of the plan would suffer a very serious fate, say having members of their family executed. All of the members are fully committed to robbing the post office and the threats make no difference to their conduct. We must surely conclude that all members of the gang act *impermissibly*, not that they all act permissibly, in robbing the post office in order to get rich. However, if one gang member does not wish to go ahead with the robbery and does so only in order to avert the credible threat that her family member faces, we will conclude that she has acted permissibly in robbing the post office. The fact that she was motivated to avert the threat and not by the takings makes a difference to whether we regard her action of robbing of the bank to be permissible. Perhaps we might doubt these judgments if she was at fault in joining the gang. If you do, imagine that she was innocent in joining the gang, say because it was not obviously a criminal gang, or because she was a child when she joined.

Those who think that motivation is irrelevant to permissibility, and who focus on objective features of these situations, must conclude either that *all* of the people acting in the Nazi cause, or *all* of the gang members, act permissibly, or that *none* of them do. That conflicts powerfully with our intuitions. Responding to these threats, we typically conclude, may be permissible, but one's action is permissible only if one acts with the intention of averting the harm.

---

[25] Many people seem to think that duress is only *ever* an excuse. But that is not very plausible. If a credible threat to one of my family members is very great I may be morally justified, and perhaps even morally required, to commit a minor wrong to avert that threat. See, further, Tadros, *Criminal Responsibility*, ch 4.

These cases are importantly different from those we were concerned with in the trolley problem, of course. They involve a person who *intends* to do a lesser harm in a way that will avert a greater harm. It is only permissible to intend to do a lesser harm to avert a greater harm if the lesser harm is *much* lesser than the greater harm.[26] It would be impermissible intentionally to shoot one person to save five from being shot. But whether the person doing the much lesser harm acts permissibly depends on the motivation with which the lesser harm is done. If motivations are relevant to permissibility in this context they ought to be relevant in other contexts as well.

5 Conclusions: Motivation and Criminal Wrongdoing

We must now face a further challenge. It might be asked how we are to *limit* the role of motivation in assessing permissibility. Suppose that the trolley driver acts with the intention to save the five, foreseeing harm to the one. However, he wants to save the five not because he values their lives, but rather because he wants personal glory. Were other people not to care what he did, he would quite happily have let the trolley run into the five. But he knows that people will congratulate him for his justified act if he turns the trolley. In that case, we can also say, in a way, that the driver treats the *five* as a means. He answers the question about whether they will live or die by reflecting on the extent to which he will benefit.

Or imagine that the trolley driver saves the five because he values their lives, but he values their lives not because of their moral autonomy but rather because he sees them as God's most beautiful works of art. God is like a sculptor, he thinks, and to allow more people to die is like allowing more beautiful paintings by a great artist to be destroyed. We might think that he has a mistaken view about what makes a human life valuable. He acts not to save the lives of these individuals because they are valuable in themselves, but rather because as objects crafted by God. Do these motives also matter in wrongdoing? Is it not wrong to kill one person *for personal glory* or to kill one person *in order to save God's most beautiful works of art*?

Some will resist the conclusion that *these* motivations are relevant to wrongdoing. We may want to say that they are relevant in determining the extent to which we think that the driver would deserve moral credit for what he has done. But they do not affect permissibility. And even those who believe that these motivations

---

[26] Some people believe that there is an absolute rule against harming a person intentionally for the greater good. But that is not, I think, the best view. See also Nagel, 'The Value of Inviolability'.

can affect permissibility will want to resist the idea that they can make the person's conduct criminal. Investigating this issue will help us to see one way in which morality and the criminal law come apart: in our moral investigations we can go deeper into a person's motivations in assessing their actions than we do in the criminal law.

First let us focus on the moral question. In the cases under consideration the driver has made a moral mistake about the value of the five. In having the wrong motive concerning the five people, the trolley driver treats the five in some way or other as objects. But that also impacts on the attitude that he has towards the one person. He harms the one person without adequately respecting him as a human being. Certainly, if the driver had made a *factual* mistake, we would have said, in a sense at least, that he had acted impermissibly. For example, suppose that the driver had turned the trolley toward the one person thinking that, in doing so, he was saving five rare flowers, rather than the five people who, unbeknownst to him, were further down the track. We would then say that he acted wrongly, at least relative to the belief that he had.

In the cases that we are considering here, the driver makes a different kind of mistake. He kills one person to save five people. But he is mistaken about the special value of the people who he saves. He regards them as having the kind of value that the five rare flowers have. And perhaps, though I am unsure about it, we might conclude that there *is* a sense in which he has acted wrongly. Just like the driver who turns the trolley to save five rare flowers, the driver in this case has treated the life of the one person as though it has a value equivalent to or less than an object.

It is true that the driver has not *aimed* at harming the one person. But that is not all that matters to permissibility. A person is harmed permissibly only if, in harming them, we treat them with the respect that they are due as an autonomous agent. The driver who is motivated by personal glory or by the idea that humans are God's most beautiful works of art does not treat the person harmed with the respect that they are due. Harming a person in the pursuit of personal glory, or in order to preserve the greatest works of art that God has created, we might conclude, is wrong.

Even if this is the right view to have about the relationship between a person's deeper motivations and wrongdoing, and I am not confident that it is, a person's deeper motivations are not significant in the criminal law. We do not focus on these kinds of motivation in the criminal law for many reasons. Here are three. First, there are limits to the kind of investigation that we wish to conduct in a court of law. Suppose that a person has diverted a trolley away from five people onto a track with one person on it. We may ask her, in court, about her intentions in doing this. If she responds that she did it in order to save the five it would be unwarranted to investigate her further moral views about why she thought that the five were worth saving. There is a limit to what we can expect people to divulge about their moral convictions in court. An investigation into a person's deeper moral views would often wrongly invade their privacy.

Secondly, liberal societies may wish to remain neutral in the face of disagreements about the value of human beings. It may be that there are deep conflicts about the reasons that different people have for valuing other human beings. We may think that it is undesirable to take a public stance about the way in which human beings ought to be valued unless it is really necessary to do so. When answering questions about abortion or euthanasia it may be difficult to avoid these deeper questions. In the kinds of case that we have been considering, it may be that our law can be rendered satisfactory without having to take such a stance. Limiting the depth of our investigations in the criminal law, even in cases involving life and death, seems important to maintain stability in the law where there are deep and unresolved disagreements between us.

And thirdly, we may not always want to deter people from acting wrongly when we object to the motivations with which they have acted. Earlier I asked whether I have good reason to prevent the bad trolley driver from turning the trolley, and attempt to turn it myself, for the right reasons. Would I do this even if it would jeopardize to some extent the trolley being turned? That seems a strange thing to do. If I am motivated by saving the five I will want to give them the best chance of being saved. And they may reasonably prefer having a better chance of being saved by a wrongful action rather than having a lesser chance of being saved by a permissible action. Sometimes, we should conclude, we may tolerate, if not encourage, impermissible actions for the sake of achieving our morally valid goals.

Return to *Trolley Driver*. We not only think it permissible for the driver to turn the trolley, we wish him to do so. Whilst it may not be wrong for him to refrain from turning the trolley, he has good reason to turn it. Now imagine that he would be inclined to turn the trolley, but only for bad reasons. We may not wish to deter him from doing so even though what he would do would be wrong. If we threaten him with punishment for turning the trolley for bad reasons he will be less likely to turn it and hence the five will be more likely to be killed.

Cases like this, I think, pose a dilemma for the criminal law. They bring into conflict different functions that it has. Where the bad trolley driver turns the trolley in order to kill the one person, we wish to see the person condemned. I also believe that the person is liable to be punished. Were we to punish him for his wrongful action he could have no complaints. And yet we have good reason to refrain from condemning and punishing him. For were we to do so we would discourage other bad trolley drivers from acting in a way that saves the five. The reasons against punishing the bad trolley driver are not grounded in *his* interests in not being punished, but rather in the interests of other people who will not be saved by bad trolley drivers (and the like) if we do punish him.

People may disagree about the strength of the considerations in conflicts such as this. Some people will see strong reason to condemn and punish the bad trolley driver even if this is likely to result in fewer people being saved in conflict cases in the future. I tend to think that reasons of this kind are fairly weak: where condemning and punishing the bad trolley driver will do more harm than good we ought to refrain from doing so. If we fail to deter bad trolley drivers less people will be killed, but more people will be killed wrongfully. The question, then, is whether we have much stronger reasons to rescue people from wrongful killing than from non-wrongful death. My suspicion is that whilst there is more reason to save a person from being wrongfully killed than from being killed non-wrongfully, the difference between the two is modest. If I could save two people from natural disaster or one person from being wrongfully killed, other things being equal, I ought to save the two.[27]

This judgment, I think, is even stronger in the case of the glory hunter and the case of the person who rescues the five in order to preserve God's greatest works of art. In these cases we have many reasons not to condemn and punish the person for what they have done even if we believe that what they have done is wrong. Whilst a person who kills one person as a side effect of saving five for personal glory does deserve to be condemned for what she has done, we have every reason not to do this through our public institutions. For we do not wish to deter glory hunters from seeking glory where they will save lives in the process.

This investigation, if it is along the right lines, suggests that one of the main questions for criminal law theorists to ask, in exploring the structure of criminal wrong-doing, is which motivations are relevant in determining whether a person is liable for criminal conviction and punishment. If a defendant has harmed another, in determining whether that defendant was criminally responsible for what he did, is it appropriate to investigate the reasons for which he acted? Or is it enough that a properly motivated person might also have harmed a person in the circumstances in which the defendant acted? And if his reasons are relevant, just where do we stop in our investigation into the motives with which the defendant acted?

I have done no more than to sketch some of the considerations that may be important in making judgments about that issue. What is clear, though, is that the criminal law and moral judgment must come sharply apart. Many people who have acted wrongly in harming others nevertheless ought to be acquitted of a criminal offence. The criminal law is not in the business of investigating the full motivational structure that guided the defendant's decision in deciding to do what he did. Morality is, in this way, much more stringent than the criminal law. Only a person who properly recognizes the value of those he harms and those he saves has acted in a morally permissible way in harming others. The law cannot afford to be as deep, in this respect at least, as morality.

[27] See, also, J McMahan, 'Humanitarian Intervention, Consent, and Proportionality', in N Ann Davis, R Keshen, and J McMahan, *Ethics and Humanity: Themes from the Philosophy of Jonathan Glover* (New York: Oxford University Press, 2010).

UNDERSTANDING THE TOPOGRAPHY OF MORAL AND CRIMINAL LAW NORMS

KENNETH W SIMONS[*]

1 INTRODUCTION

WHEN we survey the space of criminal law norms, different maps are available. One standard type of map differentiates actus reus (conduct, circumstance, and result elements of an offence) from mens rea (fault or state of mind elements). On the usual account, we first must identify the 'objective' actus reus elements that the defendant must satisfy, and then must determine what mens rea, if any, corresponds to each element. More abstractly, actus reus elements are said to represent social harms while mens rea elements represent different degrees of blameworthiness with respect to those harms. And, on one common understanding, we determine an actor's just deserts by a straightforward formula: first, rank social harms according

* I thank Antony Duff, Stuart Green, Alon Harel, and Peter Westen for their very helpful comments and Andrew Keutmann for valuable research assistance.

to seriousness; next, rank mens rea terms according to relative blameworthiness; then, simply combine these two operators.[1]

A second, more detailed map distinguishes culpability from wrongfulness. An act can be wrongful but not culpable, as when D kills an innocent person in the reasonable but mistaken belief that the person was unjustifiably threatening to kill D; or culpable but not wrongful, as when D attempts to kill an innocent person without justification but his gun misfires.[2]

How are the two maps related? Actus reus is relevant to, but alone does not determine, wrongfulness; rather, an act is wrongful only if it both falls within the actus reus and also falls outside the scope of a legal *justification*. By the same token, mens rea is relevant to, but alone does not determine, culpability; rather, an act is culpable only if the actor's state of mind or fault both falls within the mens rea and also falls outside the scope of a legal *excuse*.[3] This second map suggests a straightforward formula quite similar to the first: first, rank the seriousness of different wrongs along a single scale; next, rank the degree of culpability along a second single scale; then, once again, combine the two operators to produce a net value that measures the actor's just deserts.

The simplicity of these two formulas is alluring. But they do not accurately depict the subtlety of criminal law doctrine. And they represent a flawed ideal. For they provide a deficient account of the proper level of generality or specificity of criminal law norms; they falsely suggest that all such norms must be commensurable; and they conceal the complexity of both the relationship between criminal law norms and underlying moral norms, and the relationship between criminal law norms and the demands of political morality.

---

[1] Consider the retributive formulation of R Nozick, *Philosophical Explanations* (Cambridge, MA: Harvard University Press, 1981), 363:

The punishment deserved depends on the magnitude H of the wrongness of the act, and the person's degree of responsibility r for the act, and is equal in magnitude to their product, r x H. The degree of responsibility r varies between one (full responsibility) and zero (no responsibility)...

Nozick also suggests that r can encompass 'the degree to which the person *flouts* correct values', including consideration of 'what we intend or attempt' and of whether the actor knowingly or merely negligently ignores the right. Ibid at 388, 390. Thus, r appears to encompass more and less blameworthy mental states. For a critique of this picture as oversimplified, see KW Simons, 'When is Strict Criminal Liability Just?' (1997) 87 *Journal of Criminal Law and Criminology* 1075, 1095–103.

[2] See eg G Fletcher, *Rethinking Criminal Law* (Boston: Little, Brown 1978), 454–91; A Dillof, 'Punishing Bias: An Examination of the Theoretical Foundations of Bias Crimes Statutes' (1997) 91 *Northwestern University Law Review* 1015, 1024–31; A Harel and G Parchomovsky, 'On Hate and Equality' (1999) 109 *Yale LJ* 507; H Hurd, 'What in the World is Wrong?' (1994) 5 *Journal of Contemporary Legal Issues* 157; M Moore, 'Prima Facie Culpability', in his *Placing Blame: A General Theory of the Criminal Law* (Oxford: Oxford University Press, 1997), ch 9; Simons, ibid 1095–103.

[3] See Dillof, ibid 1030–1; M Moore, 'Actus Reus', in J Dressler (ed), *Encyclopedia of Crime & Justice* (2nd edn; New York: Macmillan, 2002); H Hurd, 'The Deontology of Negligence' (1997) 76 *Boston University Law Review* 249.

This chapter explores the following questions. Should criminal law norms be relatively general? Or instead relatively specific? Recent codification movements tend to simplify offence definitions by limiting the number of harms or wrongs that the criminal law addresses, and also by restricting the number of mens rea categories that are employed for purposes of grading the seriousness of a crime.[4] Does that simplification come at too great a price? At the same time, a more particularist approach increases the chance that criminal law norms will be incommensurable. Is this outcome regrettable, or instead desirable? Finally, what is at stake in the decision whether to have the legal fact-finder employ descriptive or instead explicitly evaluative criteria, as criteria either of mens rea or of actus reus? Are evaluative criteria preferable, simply because criminal law norms depend, to some extent, on moral norms?

The perspective I take is non-consequentialist, for the most part, and concentrates on the justification for punishing *malum in se* rather than *malum prohibitum* crimes. The focus will not be on the narrower (but important) questions of how to distinguish mens rea from actus reus, or culpability from wrongfulness.

2 GENERALITY, PARTICULARITY, AND INCOMMENSURABILITY

2.1 The generality/particularity problem

When we formulate mens rea/actus reus or culpability/wrongfulness norms, how specific, or how general, should we expect those norms to be? The ideal degree of particularity depends on the role that both moral norms and political principles play in justifying criminal law norms.

Let us begin by examining more and less specific criteria of culpability. Suppose a state is interested in punishing actors who unjustifiably cause death and also actors who unjustifiably cause serious bodily injury (SBI). On the standard modern account, if we wanted to articulate differences in culpability, we would do so by articulating varying levels of mens rea for homicide and for serious battery. Thus, we could punish purposely or knowingly causing death as murder, recklessly causing death as manslaughter, and negligently causing death as negligent homicide. (This is essentially the Model Penal Code's approach.) And we could punish purposely or knowingly causing SBI as aggravated battery, and recklessly causing SBI as simple battery.

---

[4] The Model Penal Code exemplifies this approach, as does Paul Robinson's proposed Code of Conduct. P Robinson, *Structure and Function in Criminal Law* (Oxford: Clarendon Press, 1997), app A.

But even this simple example immediately runs into a problem: the culpability criterion seems to be under-inclusive. We might well judge that one who intends to wound seriously though not to kill another, and whose acts cause the other's death, is at least as culpable as one who knowingly (but not purposely) kills another. (Compare A, who deliberately stabs V1 in the stomach in order to steal his watch and thereby causes his death, with B, who deliberately pushes V2 off a cliff in order to grab the watch that V2 has dropped, knowing that V2 will probably not survive the fall.) If this judgment is persuasive, then we have reason to expand murder to include this category—as many American jurisdictions indeed do. Or suppose that some-one intends to seriously endanger the life of another. (For example, C plays Russian Roulette with an involuntary victim: he spins the cylinder of a six chamber gun and pulls the trigger only once, and thus intentionally creates a 1/6 chance of killing the victim.) We might plausibly conclude that this actor, too, should be treated as a mur-derer if his act causes the victim's death.

In short, we might decide that 'purposely or knowingly causing death' is too nar-row a criterion for murder. And we might remedy this deficiency by supplementing that criterion with a variety of *particular* additional subcategories, such as causing death by acts that are intended to cause SBI or that are intended to create a substan-tial risk of death.

However, another way to remedy the under-inclusiveness of the original criterion is to articulate a different and broader *general* culpability criterion. In American law, it is common to impose murder liability for acts displaying a 'depraved heart' (the common law term) or 'extreme indifference to the value of human life' (the Model Penal Code); and German law's '*dolus eventualis*' recognizes a similarly broad cate-gory of murder. The two subcategories I just mentioned would almost always qualify as 'depraved heart' or 'extreme indifference' murder.[5]

How should we decide between these two methods of addressing the under-inclusiveness of the 'purpose or knowledge' definition of the culpability for murder, the particularist method of specifying different possible criteria, or instead the gen-eral criterion? One important consideration is rule of law values. The particularist approach to mens rea will tend to develop criteria that, on the spectrum from rules to standards, are more rule-like. These criteria will therefore be somewhat easier for fact-finders to apply accurately and consistently;[6] and, perhaps, easier for potential

---

[5] However, in a small subset of cases, one who intends to seriously wound might demonstrate less culpability than a purposeful or even knowing killer—eg when the actor 'inflicts serious injury while taking express precautions not to kill his victim'. L Weinrib, 'Homicide: Legal Aspects', in S Kadish (ed), 2 *Encyclopedia of Crime & Justice* (New York: Free Press, 1983), 855, 859.

[6] The most obvious examples here are bright-line rules, such as minimum age requirements for lawful sexual contact, specific weight requirements for grading drug possession, or minimum value requirements for elevating petty larceny to grand larceny. Such rules do not perfectly correspond to the underlying wrong or the culpability with which a wrong is committed, but their clarity serves other social purposes, including fair notice and more consistent application. At the same time, even more rule-like criteria sometimes have vague contours. In my examples, the fact-finder must determine

offenders to understand and follow. The generalist method is more apt to employ criteria that are closer to the 'standard' end of the spectrum, and thus more problematic with respect to fair application and comprehensibility. But these are only tendencies, not inexorable implications. Sometimes, a criminal prohibition expressed as a standard—for example, 'display a reasonable degree of concern for whether your sexual partner consents before you initiate sexual contact'—is a perspicuous reminder of the underlying rationale for the criminal prohibition. In this circumstance, a standard is both comprehensible and capable of guiding action.[7]

However, another consideration in deciding between the approaches turns on a more fundamental question: how we understand the nature of criminal law norms. An advocate of the particularist approach might believe that those norms are instrinsically particularistic and pluralistic. With respect to minimum culpability for punishment, on this view an actor is sufficiently culpable to deserve punishment if he commits any of a wide range of distinct, specified types of acts with a specified intention, belief, or other relevant mental state. With respect to the proper grading of punishment, this view acknowledges incommensurability: not all acts that we properly punish at a particular level can be directly compared with respect to culpability, for there is no general criterion of culpability that explains and justifies their equivalent treatment. Thus, a particularist might believe that knowingly killing a person as a side effect of another activity is highly culpable, and properly punished as murder, but also believe that playing Russian Roulette and causing someone's death by intentionally exposing him to a 1/6 (or even 1/6,000) risk of death is also properly punished as murder.

By contrast, a generalist believes that criminal culpability, properly understood, reduces to a small number of general principles. 'Extreme indifference to human life' might, on this view, be the general criterion for murder, encompassing purposeful and knowing killing as well as the other examples.

Unfortunately, when scholars or legal decision makers argue in favour of understanding culpability in terms such as 'insufficient concern' or 'indifference to the value of human life', a serious ambiguity arises: they might not be advocating a generalist approach in the sense I just described, for they are not necessarily arguing that the terms should serve as actual criteria of culpability.[8] To be sure, that is sometimes just

whether A intended to cause 'serious' bodily injury, and whether C intended to create a 'substantial' risk of death.

[7] See J Gardner, 'Rationality and the Rule of Law in Offences', in his *Offences and Defences: Selected Essays in the Philosophy of Criminal Law* (Oxford: Oxford University Press, 2007), 33, 44–5, distinguishing textual clarity (useful to judges, prosecutors police, and other legal actors) from moral clarity (achieved by reference to extralegal moral norms, often more useful to ordinary citizens); J Horder, 'Rethinking Non-Fatal Offences Against the Person' (1994) 14 OJLS 335 (more particularized crime definitions are preferable in affording fair notice or fair labelling).

[8] In prior writing, I have identified three different approaches to 'extreme indifference': one employing a general cognitive counterfactual criterion (eg would the agent have caused the harm if he had known that it was likely to occur?); a second employing a general idealized criterion (of falling well short of the weight that a person ideally should give to the interests of others); and a third

what they intend: the term is supposed to function as a genuine criterion of culpability, one that will apply to new fact patterns and will differentiate instances in which criminal punishment is warranted from those in which it is not, or instances in which greater rather than lesser punishment is warranted. The many courts that confront enormous difficulty when trying to clarify the meaning of the 'extreme indifference' and 'depraved heart' murder criteria struggle precisely because they see these standards as genuine criteria.[9] But such terms sometimes carry a distinct, second meaning, as a label, an umbrella term, for a level of culpability that is actually determined by other, more specific, and perhaps pluralistic, criteria. When Larry Alexander and Kim Ferzan argue for 'insufficient concern' as their sole conception of criminal culpability,[10] they do not actually mean that the legal decision maker should determine, case by case, whether the defendant, given the choices he made and the attitudes those choices expressed, displayed 'concern', insufficient or otherwise, for his victims. Rather, they intend to signal that 'insufficient concern' is a term of art for other, more specific criteria, including the actor's beliefs about the risks he is running, his reasons for running those risks, and the quality of his decision making; it is those other criteria that actually determine whether and to what extent the actor is criminally culpable.[11]

The question of whether to employ general or instead particularist criteria has also arisen in the debate about whether to reduce the plethora of distinct mens rea terms that were recognized at common law to a handful (as the Model Penal Code does and all recent criminal law codifications seem to do). A few dissenters argue that the criminal law should not be afraid to employ more varied and plentiful *mentes reae*.[12] And, indeed, much contemporary criminal law continues to employ mental state

amounting to an umbrella category embracing distinct criteria (eg acting from especially inculpatory motives or with especially culpable desires, participating in an immoral or illegal activity, or creating multiple risks). See K Simons, 'Does Punishment for "Culpable Indifference" Simply Punish for "Bad Character"? Examining the Requisite Connection between Mens Rea and Actus Reus' (2003) 6 *Buffalo Criminal Law Review* 219, 259–67 and 296–313.

[9] Consider the struggles of the highest court in New York. A Abramovsky and J Edelstein, 'People v Suarez and Depraved Indifference Murder' (2006) 56 *Syracuse Law Review* 701.

[10] L Alexander and KK Ferzan, *Crime and Culpability: A Theory of the Criminal Law* (Cambridge: Cambridge University Press, 2009).

[11] Ibid 44, 102. On this 'mere label' interpretation, it remains unclear what relationship the more specific criteria bear to the general 'insufficient concern' label.

However, some passages in their book are amenable to the 'genuine criterion' interpretation. For further discussion, see K Simons, 'Book Review: Retributivism Refined—Or Run Amok?' (2010) 77 *University of Chicago Law Review* 551, 566–8.

Similarly, Peter Westen, in arguing for an attitudinal theory of excuses, supposes that excuses negate blame, and that 'a person is normative blameworthy for engaging in conduct that a statute prohibits if he was motivated by an attitude of disrespect for the interests that the statute seeks to protect, whether the attitude consists of malice, contempt, indifference, callousness, or inadvertence toward those interests'. P Westen, 'An Attitudinal Theory of Excuse' (2006) 25 *Law and Philosophy* 289, 374–5. Westen appears to be employing 'disrespect' as an umbrella term for other criteria of culpability.

[12] John Gardner (eg) endorses the use of terms such as 'dishonesty' and 'malice' in particular, 'localized' contexts: J Gardner, 'On the General Part of the Criminal Law', in RA Duff (ed), *Philosophy and the Criminal Law: Principle and Critique* (Cambridge University Press, 1998), 205–55, at 231. See also J Gardner, 'The Wrongness of Rape', in his *Offences and Defences*, 1, 27.

terms that are not found among the Model Penal Code's fundamental four (purpose or intention, knowledge, recklessness, and negligence).[13]

Thus far we have examined mens rea categories and criteria. But analogous issues of generality and particularity arise with respect to actus reus doctrine. Even if we were to hold constant the mens rea—assume, for example, that a jurisdiction always requires proof that the defendant has knowledge of all of the legally relevant features of the prohibited conduct—we would still need to determine how many actus reus categories to employ. For example, should arson be a distinct crime, or should it be absorbed into offences of destruction of property and of reckless endangerment (or attempted murder)?[14] Or consider the question whether to 'consolidate' the crime of theft into a single crime,[15] or instead to retain traditional distinctions between larceny, false pretences, embezzlement, and extortion. George Fletcher and Stuart Green, among others, have challenged the modern consolidation approach, and have found some value in the traditional particularist classification scheme.[16]

So we arrive at the central question: in creating categories of mens rea or actus reus, should we be particularists or generalists? The answer depends on two further inquiries: first, the relationship between moral norms and criminal law norms; and second, the relationship between political morality and criminal law norms.

2.2 Moral norms, criminal law norms, and incommensurability

First, insofar as conceptions of criminal culpability and wrongfulness depend on, or to some degree incorporate, conceptions of *moral* culpability and wrongfulness, we must ask whether the latter are best understood as particularist or generalist. When

---

[13] Other recognized mental states include not only 'depraved heart' or 'extreme indifference', already discussed, but also 'wilful blindness', 'dishonestly', 'fraudulently', 'wilfully', and 'maliciously'. A Ashworth, *Principles of Criminal Law* (5th edn; Oxford: Oxford University Press, 2006), 196–7; AP Simester and GR Sullivan, *Criminal Law: Theory and Doctrine* (3rd edn; Oxford: Hart, 2007), §§ 5.6, 13.8, 15.2 (iii); J Dressler, *Understanding Criminal Law* (5th edn; LexisNexis, 2009), 128–30.

[14] See M Cahill, 'Grading Arson' (2009) 3 *Criminal Law and Philosophy* 79–95.

[15] For a breathtakingly concise consolidated definition, see P Robinson, *Structure and Function in Criminal Law*, 215, Draft Code of Conduct, § 24: 'You may not damage, take, use, dispose of, or transfer another's property without the other's consent.'

[16] S Green, 'Consent and the Grammar of Theft Law' (2007) 6 *Cardozo Law Review* 2505, 2517; Fletcher, *Rethinking Criminal Law*, 30–57. Green has also emphasized moral wrongfulness, in addition to harm and mens rea, as a differentiating feature of different white-collar crimes. S Green, *Lying, Cheating, and Stealing: A Moral Theory of White-Collar Crime* (Oxford: Oxford University Press, 2006), especially 39–47. See also M Berman, 'On the Moral Structure of White Collar Crime' (2007) 5 *Ohio State Journal of Criminal Law* 301, 315 ('Whereas most theorists think about moral wrongfulness in terms of very abstract considerations like the violation of victims' rights, Green views wrongfulness, in a broadly Rossian spirit, as the violation of fairly concrete norms that might not be reducible to more fundamental moral principles').

we categorize conduct as morally impermissible or morally required, and when we 'grade' or judge some morally impermissible acts as worse than others, which perspective should we take? To answer this question, we need to remember the context: justifying criminal law norms that in some manner incorporate moral norms.

Consider some examples of principles characterizing morally wrongful conduct. 'Acts displaying disrespect for the autonomy of another' (P1) is highly abstract. 'Acts displaying disrespect for the sexual autonomy of another' (P2) is more specific. 'Use of violence to coerce another to submit to sex' (P3) and 'Use of deception to trick another into submitting to sex' (P4) are more specific still. What is the most defensible level of generality? The answer, alas, is not straightforward, for it depends on the moral theory being invoked, and on the type of principle that does justificatory work in that theory.

Thus, a Kantian principle might simply enjoin agents to obey the categorical imperative. Specific principles such as P3 and P4, and even more abstract principles such as P1 and P2, are the justificatory offspring of that simple injunction. A Scanlonian might simply enjoin agents not to perform an act 'if its performance under the circumstances would be disallowed by any set of principles for the general regulation of behaviour that no one could reasonably reject as a basis for informed, unforced, general agreement'.[17] Again, principles of varying levels of generality might be implied by this general injunction. Of course, a utilitarian will also begin with a straightforward and extremely general principle, of maximizing utility (however that is defined by the theory in question).

To be sure, even theories of this sort must, if they are to guide individuals faced with choice situations, be reformulated into useful rules and standards for action. But the issue before us is the justificatory force of principles. We are *not* asking what form these principles should take in order to be action-guiding in the most literal sense, ie in order to serve as effective decision-procedures for ordinary human beings with epistemic and psychological constraints. Kantians and Scanlonians need not endorse the idea that the moral rules that we try to self-consciously follow should be as abstract as the Categorical Imperative or the 'reasonable rejection' principle. The issue before us is not the optimal level of specificity or generality of moral rules and standards if they are to operate as effective decision procedures. Rather, the question is the appropriate level of specificity of those moral principles and judgments that we must invoke in order to justify criminal law norms (at least on a non-consequentialist perspective).

Returning to the main argument, are all forms of moral justification as 'top-down' as Kantian, Scanlonian, or utilitarian theories? They are not. Consider three plausible alternative forms that recognize the justificatory force of much more concrete principles and judgments. Let us call all of these forms of justification 'particularist', albeit in different ways.

---

[17] TM Scanlon, *What We Owe to Each Other* (Cambridge, MA: Harvard University Press 1998), 153.

(1) The first is foundational pluralism,[18] or 'the view that there are plural values at the most basic level— that is to say, there is no one value that subsumes all other values, no one property of goodness, and no overarching principle of action'.[19] The best known example is the 'intuitionism' of WD Ross, which offers a complex but more concrete set of injunctions: give prima facie weight to a variety of specific prima facie duties, such as the duty not to injure others, to keep promises, to make reparations for one's wrongful acts, or to benefit others. Notice, however, that these duties are still rather general, on the order of P1 rather than P2, P3, or P4. Accordingly, only an unusually specific version of Rossian intuitionism will provide anything analogous to the quite detailed, distinct norms of wrongful conduct that we see in modern criminal codes.

Another moral perspective that could be viewed as a form of foundational pluralism, and that at least moves in the direction of concrete moral norms, is the view that we should make use of 'thick ethical concepts' in determining what actions to perform. Bernard Williams emphasized this approach.[20] In his view, morality is richer and more nuanced than the standard ethical theories would suggest, for it employs not just 'thin' concepts such as 'good', 'right', and 'obligation', but also 'thick' concepts such as 'courage', 'treachery', and 'brutality'. The latter concepts have both descriptive and evaluative dimensions, and understanding their meaning requires an appreciation of both dimensions, as well as practical judgment.

I agree with Williams that thick ethical concepts play a significant role in our actual moral practices, especially our practices of blaming others for their misdeeds; and these are of course the moral practices most relevant to our present inquiry. A multiplicity of factors bear on blame and desert, in subtle, complex ways, ways that depend on social context.[21] Again, however, one need not descend very far from the abstraction of 'thin' general concepts before one finds 'thick' concepts such as 'brutality'. So again, it is not clear that principles as specific as P3 or P4, or even P2, will be generated by the effort to differentiate thick from thin.

---

[18] The pluralism at issue here must be distinguished from the pluralism of beliefs and cultures within a given political community that is the concern of political philosophy (such as Rawls in his later work). 'Foundational pluralism' concerns the multiplicity of values contained within a single moral perspective, not the multiplicity of values generated by the need to accommodate different moral perspectives.

[19] E Mason 'Value Pluralism', in EN Zalta (ed), *The Stanford Encyclopedia of Philosophy* (Fall 2008 edn; <http://plato.stanford.edu/archives/fall2008/entries/value-pluralism/>), section 1.1. Mason characterizes the views of Judith Jarvis Thompson (defending distinct types of goodness) and perhaps John Stuart Mill (defining distinct types of pleasures) as falling within this category.

[20] B Williams, *Ethics and the Limits of Philosophy* (Cambridge, MA: Harvard University Press, 1986), 140–55.

[21] The most prominent analysis along these lines is Peter Strawson's 'Freedom and Resentment' (1962) 48 *Proceedings of the British Academy* 1–25, which can be understood as a sophisticated account of the thick ethical concept of blame itself.

(2) The second particularist alternative is an approach that combines concrete moral intuitions with abstract principles, and that recognizes the justificatory force of both. John Rawls' reflective equilibrium is the most famous exemplar of this approach.[22] Moreover, the view that one must use practical judgment in the individual case, and that such judgment is not reducible to the deductive implications of more abstract principles, also falls within this second general category.[23] The traditional role of judges in sentencing, which permits them to equitably assess a broad range of aggravating and mitigating factors, is one possible (though controversial) implication of this perspective.

These methods of justification are especially promising accounts of our concrete blaming judgments about the wrongness of acts that are the concern of the criminal law, such as acts intended to injure or kill, or to dominate another, or to harm distinct types of property or economic interests; or known to violate the sexual autonomy of others in very specific ways; or serious acts of deceit or disloyalty of particular kinds. Perhaps abstract moral theories offer persuasive justifications of highly general principles such as P1 and P2. But when we are analysing what acts are wrong, and how wrong they are, it seems inescapable, and indeed consistent with many such moral theories, to take into account not just the general principles of permissibility, justification, and desert offered by the theory, but also our concrete, considered moral intuitions. And if we do take cognizance of such intuitions, by a method such as Rawls' reflective equilibrium, or Frances Kamm's 'intricate ethics' methodology,[24] we are much more likely to arrive at more specific, localized moral judgments, such as P3 or P4.

(3) A third alternative is a distinctive form of particularism, 'variable relevance (VR) particularism', an approach vigorously defended in recent years by Jonathan Dancy.[25] This approach might be less familiar to the reader, so I will provide a more extended discussion. In the end, however, I believe that this form of the generalist/particularist distinction is only occasionally relevant in justifying the contours of the criminal law.

The claim here is that a principled explanation of what morality requires is not always possible—or, even more strongly, that only 'particularized',

---

[22] J Rawls, *A Theory of Justice* (Cambridge, MA: Harvard University Press, 1971); J Rawls *Justice as Fairness: A Restatement* (E Kelly ed; Cambridge, MA: Harvard University Press, 2001). Of course, Rawls' concern was to justify principles of political justice. Whether his method is persuasive as a justification of interpersonal moral duties is another question.

[23] McNaughton and Rawling call this pragmatist perspective 'moral verdict' particularism. DA McNaughton and P Rawling, 'Unprincipled Ethics', in BW Hooker and M Little (eds), *Moral Particularism* (Oxford: Oxford University Press, 2000), 256–75.

[24] FM Kamm, *Intricate Ethics: Rights, Responsibilities, and Permissible Harm* (Oxford: Oxford University Press, 2007), 14–15.

[25] J Dancy, *Ethics Without Principles* (Oxford: Clarendon Press, 2004); *Moral Reasons* (Oxford: Blackwell, 1995). See also GE Moore, *Principia Ethica* (Cambridge: Cambridge University Press, 1903), 35 (on organic unities); S Berker, 'Particular Reasons' (2007) 118 *Ethics* 109 (offering a comparative analysis of particularism with foundational pluralism).

non-principled moral judgments can be made. The VR particularism view is not, however, simply the view that principles are complex, or are based on plural values, or require judgment and wisdom to apply to concrete situations. Rather, the view is about the valence of moral considerations. The claim is that the morally relevant properties that operate in concrete moral judgments do not have the same significance or even valence in all other moral contexts. Although a minority view, this particularist approach has gained adherents in recent years. Here is a representative statement by Dancy:

> The core of particularism is its insistence on variability. Essentially the generalist demands sameness in the way in which one and the same consideration functions case by case, while the particularist sees no need for any such thing. A feature can make one moral difference in one case, and a different difference in another. Features have, as we might put it, *variable relevance*. Whether a feature is relevant or not in a new case, and if so what exact role it is playing there (the 'form' that its relevance takes there) will be sensitive to other features of the case. This claim emerges as the consequence of the core particularist doctrine, which we can call the holism of reasons. This is the doctrine that what is a reason in one case may be no reason at all in another, or even a reason on the other side. In ethics, a feature that makes one action better can make another one worse, and make no difference at all to a third.[26]

For example, suppose Kara drives home at a very high rate of speed because she enjoys the sheer sensation of acceleration and high velocity; Sarah drives home at the same high speed because she enjoys endangering others; and Tara drives home at the same high speed but derives no pleasure of any sort from her speeding. Otherwise, the morally relevant characteristics of the conduct are the same; each actor poses the same risks to bystanders, is equally aware of the risks, and so forth. A particularist can say that even if Kara's act is somewhat more justifiable than Tara's (because Kara at least derives pleasure from her conduct), Sarah's act is not more justifiable than Tara's, even though Sarah's act gives her pleasure while Tara's does not. The explanation? Obtaining pleasure does *not* count morally in favour of Sarah's action at all, because in this context, the pleasure is malicious. Thus, for the particularist, the same moral feature can sometimes count in favour of an action but sometimes count against. By contrast, a generalist might conclude that the driver's pleasure must count in favour of her conduct in both contexts; thus, in order to condemn Sarah as especially culpable, the generalist would have to find some other feature of Sarah's act that counts against it morally (such as the fact that potential victims would feel offended if they discovered why she drove as she did) and that outweighs or overrides the pleasure she obtains.[27]

---

[26] J Dancy 'Moral Particularism', in EN Zalta, *The Stanford Encyclopedia of Philosophy* (Spring 2009 edn; <http://plato.stanford.edu/archives/spr2009/entries/moral-particularism/>), section 3.

[27] One way that generalists might respond to examples such as this is to argue that the particularist is simply ignoring the full scope of the reason that differentiates the examples. In my examples, they

For another example, consider the question whether the act/omission distinction, or the distinction between doing and allowing harm, affects the moral permissibility of an act. A particularist might conclude that no general answer to the question is forthcoming. Suppose Smith intentionally drowns a young child in the bathtub. Jones plans to drown a young child, but someone else has already unintentionally left the water on while the child is in the bathtub, the child is now certain to drown, and Jones refrains from saving him.[28] If both Smith and Jones are a parent of the victim, the distinction probably makes no moral difference. If each is a malicious neighbour, the distinction might matter. In this case, perhaps Smith's act is impermissible while Jones's omission is permissible; or, we might at least conclude that Jones's omission is less morally reprehensible.[29]

Although this third ('variable relevance') interpretation of 'particularist' is plausible in certain cases, such as those just described, I am less persuaded that it is central to explaining moral permissibility in most contexts. And in any event, it is very unlikely to play a crucial role in justifying criminal law norms. *In*variable relevance accounts of the moral concepts, norms, and judgments that underlie the criminal law are quite plausible, in part because the criminal law addresses such a small and extreme subset of human behaviour. With more commonplace moral decisions, by contrast, such as how to treat family members or friends in our daily lives, the decisions are more complex and fact-sensitive; thus it is much more plausible that in some of these cases, our judgments are 'VR particularistic'.

For example, recall actor C, who plays Russian Roulette with an involuntary victim, subjecting him to a 1/6 chance of death just for fun, thereby causing death. It is not difficult to identify moral principles and judgments (at least non-consequentialist ones) that would support blaming C as harshly as a knowing or purposeful killer. A Kantian would place little weight on whether the actor sees the probability of death as 1/6 or instead 99 per cent, or whether the actor commits himself (for manifestly unjustifiable reasons) to creating a very significant

---

might argue, it is not the consequential or accompanying pleasure *simpliciter* that always counts in favour of an action, but only *non-malicious* pleasure. But particularists need not be satisfied by this response. Why, they ask, do only non-malicious pleasures invariably count in favour of an action? One still needs an account of why such exceptions and qualifications are properly included in an explanation of the operative moral reasons. (Dancy offers such an account, distinguishing between 'enabling' and 'favouring' reasons, and insists that he can thereby preserve the point that not all moral considerations have invariant relevance.)

[28] The example is from J Rachels, 'Active and Passive Euthanasia' (1975) *NEJ of Medicine* 292. In Rachels' two examples, the malevolent person intends to kill his young cousin.

[29] To be sure, one could also explain this pattern by invoking an apparently 'generalist' principle—that the act/omission distinction is morally relevant only when the agent has no independent moral duty to act. The subtle question here is whether the differential relevance of the distinction shows: (1) that its actual weight or valence changes in different contexts; or instead (2) that its weight, although invariant, happens to make a difference in some contexts but not others. A generalist can endorse the second position but not the first.

risk of death or instead to causing death itself. And our concrete moral intuitions about such cases undoubtedly entail the same conclusions. But in this type of example, a moral factor's varying relevance does not seem to play any role.

I have identified three different senses in which the moral norms that help justify criminal law norms might properly be understood as relatively concrete and particularistic. But all of these particularist perspectives share one very important feature: all increase the risk of (or perhaps we should say 'opportunity for'!) incommensurability. Thus, insofar as we rely on specific considered moral intuitions that each of several specific acts is wrong, or is especially wrongful, we might have no principled way of comparing those judgments with each other. Suppose, in addition to P3 and P4, we reach the judgment that this act is wrongful: 'Use of deception to trick another into submitting to a medical operation' (P5). How wrongful is this act? More or less wrongful than using deception to induce sex, as in P4? If the moral judgments supporting the wrongfulness of both P4 and of P5 are each largely based on intuition, then we might lack a principled way to commensurate those judgments: we cannot say that one is clearly more wrong than the other, or that they are both clearly the same or similar in their wrongfulness.[30] With the third type of particularism, we face incommensurability even more often: for we cannot even say that deceiving another is always a wrong-making property. (Perhaps it is a neutral or even right-making property if the deception is what the victim desires or deserves.)

Is such incommensurability a problem? Not necessarily. Critics of retributive accounts of criminal law often complain that those accounts offer no principled explanation of how to rank radically dissimilar offences (white collar v violent crime; political corruption v sexual offences, and so forth). But the criticism ignores the possibility that the underlying moral wrongs that these crimes instantiate are themselves at least partially incommensurable. In our concrete judgments, most of us acknowledge some degree of incommensurability when we try to compare criminal law wrongs or the moral wrongs that the law expresses. Perhaps *causing harm* is a category over which we can more readily generalize: death is worse than serious personal injury, which is worse than mild personal injury; theft of $1 million dollars is worse than theft of $10,000 or $1. (Of course, even here, determining the degree of harm caused requires evaluation of distinct qualitative dimensions that are difficult to compare: pain is distinct from loss of function, emotional harm differs from physical harm, and so forth.) But most people have much greater difficulty arriving at confident conclusions about the relative seriousness of distinct wrongs.[31] Causing harm through deceit is a distinct

---

[30] Moreover, the generalist's comparative advantage in this respect might be overstated. For even if P4 and P5 are entailed by more general principles such as P1 and P2, it is not clear that those principles alone specify the degree of wrongfulness expressed by P4 relative to P5. I thank Antony Duff for this observation.

[31] For discussion of the distinction between harms and wrongs, see RA Duff and SP Green, 'Introduction: The Special Part and its Problems', in RA Duff and SP Green (eds), *Defining Crimes: Essays on the Special Part of the Criminal Law* (Oxford: Oxford University Press, 2005), 1, 15–16; Hurd,

wrong from causing the same harm through violence or threat; causing harm by an action is distinct from causing (or permitting) the same harm through an omission; breaking someone's leg by use of justified defensive force that is excessive in degree is distinct from breaking their leg by force not justified at all.[32] It is very difficult to identify any single moral principle, or any small set of principles, that permits the simple ranking of wrongfulness across all types of wrongs and harms.

Incommensurability should not terrify us. The following picture is quite plausible: our moral topography contains distinct domains, within which a comparison of wrongfulness or culpability is meaningful and feasible, but across which it is not. Local comparisons of minor assault, aggravated assault, and murder are meaningful, but 'cross-border' comparisons between those crimes and crimes of deceit, or appropriation of property, or public corruption, or tax evasion, or treason, arguably are not.[33]

If this is right, then the ambition of the simple view, noted in the introduction, is unattainable. We cannot simply rank all harms and wrongs in one scale of significance, then rank all mens rea or culpability criteria in a second scale, then multiply the values to arrive at a composite measure of the actor's just deserts. Comparisons across the first scale are sometimes impossible. Moreover, certain mental state distinctions in the second scale might matter more, or less, for certain first-scale interests. Intentionally causing emotional distress is arguably a much more serious wrong than knowingly causing the same level of emotional distress, whereas intentionally causing a particular level of physical harm is often roughly comparable in seriousness to knowingly causing that level of physical harm. Finally, even if it were possible to intelligibly rank items within each of the two scales, considered separately, it might not be possible to rank the composite seriousness of acts that vary in *both* dimensions, wrongfulness and culpability. Compare two acts:

(1) wrong W_2 accompanied by culpability C_2; and

(2) more serious wrong W_1 accompanied by less serious culpability C_3.[34]

'What in the World is Wrong?', 157, 209–14 (pointing out that there are harmless wrongs, such as rights violations that do not make the victim worse off; and wrongless harms, such as justified harms).

[32] Consider this passage from John Gardner:

In morality, as in law, it matters how one brings things about. It matters, first and foremost, in deciding which wrong one committed. You have not been mugged, although you have been conned, if I trick you into handing over your money by spinning some yarn. You have not been coerced, although you have been manipulated, if I get you to do something by making you think you wanted to do it all along. You have not been killed, although you have been left to die, if a doctor fails to prescribe life-saving drugs.

Gardner, 'Rationality and the Rule of Law in Offences', 33, at 36.

[33] Or more precisely, many of these wrongs are incommensurable within a significant range: perhaps treason is neither more nor less wrongful than murder, and public corruption is neither more nor less wrongful than tax evasion, but each of the first two wrongs is more wrongful than each of the second.

[34] Nozick notices (though he does not resolve) a similar problem. What if two acts are equal in composite seriousness, but differ in their wrongfulness/culpability inputs? Should the acts be punished (or otherwise treated) differently? See Nozick, *Philosophical Explanations*, 390 fn.

For example, suppose A intentionally causes a serious physical injury (exemplifying (1)), while B recklessly causes a death (exemplifying (2)). Even if we are confident that intention is more culpable than recklessness, it is by no means clear which act is more deserving of moral sanction or of punishment.[35]

Incommensurability is inescapable, and indeed may well be a valuable feature of moral judgments in appropriate domains, such as blaming judgments of the sort we have been discussing. At the same time, it poses a danger, given the practical politics of crime legislation. Scholars need to provide a better account of how much incommensurability is consistent with a defensible moral theory, and of where we should, and should not, expect to find such incommensurability. Otherwise, it would be too easy for drafters of criminal codes to excuse any hodgepodge of rules and doctrines as reflecting inevitable incommensurability. 'This is a distinct problem', they could say, without making any effort to reconcile the new criminal prohibition with the existing framework of criminal and moral wrongdoing. (The problem of incommensurability, it should be noted, is not limited to *non*-consequentialist theories; so, when critics of incommensurability target only retributivists, their complaint is unfairly one-sided.[36])

2.3 Political morality and criminal law norms

We also need to examine the relationship between *political* morality and criminal law norms. Principles of political morality might support a more particularist (or, less often, a more generalist) articulation of criminal law doctrine than moral principles alone would demand. Thus, even if *moral* principles of wrongdoing and culpability are best understood as generalist, principles of political morality might support a particularist expression of those principles in the criminal law. For example, political legitimacy plausibly demands that criminal law norms be articulated with sufficient specificity that citizens understand what acts count as salient instances. (Recall the discussion earlier of the advantages of rules over standards.) A sparely described prohibition, for example, 'Do not unjustifiably and culpably cause the death of another', would run afoul of that demand.[37]

---

[35] See Simons, 'When is Strict Criminal Liability Just?', 1075, 1093–4.

[36] It is no simple matter to specify the degree of harm, or the quantity of welfare losses, that different kinds of crimes bring about. Even a consequentialist needs to explain whether and why, say, burglary or a simple assault causes more harm than, say, theft or public corruption.

[37] In their recent book, Larry Alexander and Kim Ferzan claim that criminal law norms can be reduced to a simple injunction of this sort. '[T]here is really only one injunction that is relevant to criminal culpability: choose only those acts for which the risks to others' interests—as you estimate those risks—are sufficiently low to be outweighed by the interests...that you are attempting to advance (discounted by the probability of advancing those interests).' Alexander and Ferzan, *Crime and Culpability*, 263. However, once they elaborate on this idea, it becomes clear that they do recognize a number of specific categories of mens rea and actus reus. See Simons, 'Book Review', 551, 563–6.

Conversely, however, we might conclude that some or all of the moral principles expressed in the criminal law are relatively specific, but that political principles demand that their articulation in criminal law be generalist. For example, we might endorse a political principle favouring decentralized, ad hoc legal decision making in the face of democratic disagreement about what counts as a moral and legal wrong. Thus, suppose that citizens cannot agree on whether to permit the use of marijuana to alleviate some or any medical conditions. We might consider it appropriate to permit the issue to be evaluated under the broad terms of a lesser evils defence, whereby individual judges and juries can decide the issue case by case. More broadly, political principles of accountability and legitimacy obviously are crucial to the question of how to allocate decision-making authority among the legislature, prosecutor, judge, and jury. At the same time, such allocation principles substantially affect how retributive principles are realized.[38]

It is worth noting one practical reality that intrudes on this analysis of political principles. Suppose that, at a given point in time (for example, just after a comprehensive codification effort), an ideal criminal code is in place, one that classifies and grades different offences in a way that reflects the relevant moral and political principles and judgments as faithfully as is humanly possible. The legislature then begins to add new crimes. Often this is perfectly justifiable. Some of the new crimes might reflect moral wrongs that were inadequately appreciated before (consider, for example, the recent expansion of sexual assault to encompass non-consensual sexual encounters not accompanied by threats of violence). Or some subcategory of previously regulated behaviour might have become more common or more dangerous and thus in greater need of deterrence. But, very often, a new criminal prohibition is not really a newly recognized wrong or harm, and is not more important to deter. Legislators are under enormous media and constituent pressure to respond to the problem of crime, especially when a dramatic, horrific crime occurs that the current system seems to have inadequately addressed. Consequently, even when criminal codes are comprehensively rethought and rationalized, a series of new ad hoc prohibitions often accumulate like 'barnacles collecting on the hull of a ship'.[39] Those barnacles could express a genuine new species of moral and criminal wrongdoing. But they also could simply express a salient instance of a wrong already addressed by the criminal law; and all too

---

[38] In sentencing (eg) permitting judges broad discretion to give a defendant his just deserts undermines the power of legislatures and juries to define and implement their own conceptions of just deserts.

[39] See P Robinson and M Cahill, 'Can a Model Penal Code Second Save the States from Themselves?' (2003) 1 *Ohio State Journal of Criminal Law* 169, 172. As the authors explain: 'The cumulative effect is a distortion of the original hull shape such that it can no longer perform its function. At this point, one might justifiably say that the barnacles have dwarfed the ship.' Ibid. See also S Green, 'Prototype Theory and the Classification of Offenses in a Revised Model Penal Code: A General Approach to the Special Part' (2000) 4 *Buffalo Criminal Law Review* 301, 326–34 (analysing how to bridge gaps in criminal law coverage); Duff and Green, 'Introduction: The Special Part and its Problems', 16.

often, the punishment for the resulting new crime is disproportionately severe relative to the punishment for the extant crime.[40] In short, we must be extremely cautious before concluding that the extraordinary heterogeneity and complexity of criminal offences in most extant American criminal codes is justifiable, notwithstanding the theoretical point that that degree of heterogeneity and complexity might, in a more perfect world, be justifiable.

2.4 Implications for the drafting of criminal codes

At this point, the reader might be wondering: all this discussion of generality, particularity, and commensurability is interesting enough, but what does it have to do with how criminal codes are actually drafted? Quite a bit, as it turns out. For the generalist strategy is to reduce sharply the number of actus reus and mens rea elements in a criminal code. The particularist alternative creates much more diversity and complexity. Among other things, by employing more fine-grained notions of legal and moral wrongdoing, the particularist is likely to create more crimes, and crimes with more elements. For example, she will differentiate numerous different crimes of theft, depending on the method of appropriation, the type and degree of nonconsent, whether deception or violence was used, and so forth. A radical generalist could create a single theft crime: unjustifiably depriving a person of their property rights without their consent.

One type of generalist strategy is superficially attractive: focus on whether the actor has brought about a harm, and on the severity of that harm, and then couple this harm-based actus reus with differentiation by a small number of mental states.[41] But this approach, as we have seen, is problematic. It tends to flatten the moral topography, reducing all moral and legal wrongs to the question whether one has unjustifiably caused (or unjustifiably risked) harm. This harm-focused approach is most congenial to a consequentialist view of the point of moral and legal constraints. Retributivists should be far more sceptical.

To be sure, we must be wary of the opposite danger—that a particularist approach could be a mere rationalization of ad hoc legislative 'barnacles', or an excuse not to think systematically about the interests, harms, and wrongs that criminal prohibitions properly address. Legislative codification is an extremely worthwhile endeavour. The

[40] Robinson and Cahill give a number of examples—eg a new Illinois crime of breaking into a house while armed, which is punished about as harshly as intentionally stabbing someone to death. Ibid 172. See also P Robinson, T Gaeta, M Majarian, M Schultz, and D Weck, 'The Modern Irrationalities of American Criminal Codes: An Empirical Study of Offense Grading', U of Penn Law School, Public Law Research Paper No 10–04, for numerous illustrations of irrationality in offence grading.

[41] This is essentially the strategy followed by criminal law scholar Paul Robinson. Robinson, *Structure and Function in Criminal Law*, Appendix A, Draft Criminal Code of Conduct and Appendix B, Draft Code of Adjudication. See also Alexander and Ferzan, *Crime and Culpability*.

question, rather, is whether the outcome of such a process should be a highly simplified code, or instead should include some particularized mens rea and actus reus criteria.

Even if one's map of wrongdoing and culpability exhibits a more irregular and diverse terrain, critical questions linger: in articulating wrongfulness, should criminal law doctrine rely more on actus reus? More on mens rea? More on defences of justification and excuse? These questions are to some extent independent of how fine- or coarse-grained the doctrines are—but not entirely independent. Suppose unjustifiably depriving a person of her property without her consent were the only actus reus for theft. Then, in order to grade different levels of wrongfulness in theft, we would have to turn to other doctrinal elements such as mens rea (distinguishing knowledge from recklessness, for example). Unjustifiably causing death is the essential actus reus for homicide; thus, further differentiation of degrees of homicide depends on mens rea and on partial excuse.

The example of homicide is both important and misleading. A significant, and perhaps under-appreciated, reason for the modern aspiration towards generalism is the assumption that what works for homicide should work for other crimes. In homicide, the actus reus is quite straightforward. Mens rea does virtually all[42] of the work of differentiating degree of wrongdoing (murder, manslaughter, and negligent homicide). And homicide is perhaps the most important criminal offence, judged by its social significance. So it is tempting to treat homicide as the paradigm crime, and then to seek similar simplicity in the structuring of other offences: causing harm X simpliciter should be the actus reus, and then different categories of mens rea should differentiate different degrees of each offence. Yet a moment's reflection discloses that homicide is not the only relevant paradigm. Most offences do not require proof that the actor brought about a resulting harm. And, in order to differentiate degrees of many offences, mens rea gradations are sometimes insufficient or even irrelevant. The hypothetical 'general' theft actus reus, described in the prior paragraph, is obviously an awkward, useless method of articulating the wrong, even if it were divided into degrees according to different types of mens rea. An especially telling illustration of the point is American law's treatment of another significant category of crime, sexual offences. These offences are increasingly divided into numerous grades, but the gradation is accomplished almost entirely by distinguishing categories of actus reus, not mens rea.[43] Why is homicide not a useful paradigm here? Because the different actus reus categories and distinctions in other crimes often reflect different underlying wrongs.

---

[42] Virtually all, but not all. In death penalty doctrine, an aggravating factor supporting the death penalty is the causation of distinctive, additional harm, eg causing multiple deaths, or causing the death of a police officer or prison guard. And first-degree murder is sometimes defined in part by actus reus, eg lying in wait or use of poison.

[43] Grading distinctions often turn on whether the victim was asleep or unconscious, or underage; the actor inflicted injury on the victim, or used a weapon; or the actor was in a specified professional relationship to the victim (eg teacher, therapist, prison guard, or probation officer).

3 DESCRIPTIVE OR EVALUATIVE CRITERIA

Modern criminal law codes not only tend to employ simpler and more general criteria, they also tend to make greater use of purely 'descriptive' criteria, relative to 'evaluative' criteria.[44] Is this a welcome or unwelcome development? Insofar as descriptive criteria appear to suppress the moral norms underlying criminal law norms, it would seem to be unwelcome. But the story is more complicated than this.

On one view, the ideal criminal code is entirely descriptive. That is to say, the legislature (perhaps with the interpretive aid of the judiciary) announces in advance certain criteria that the jury can apply simply by making factual determinations. With respect to mens rea, for example, the jury would determine whether D acted with purpose, knowledge, or recklessness, in the purely cognitive sense (ie subjective awareness that he was posing a risk of harm or that some circumstance exists). And with respect to actus reus, again, the jury would apply purely descriptive criteria: Did D strike the victim? Did D have illegal drugs in his possession? Did D's vehicle exceed the speed limit? Was D's act a but-for cause of the death?[45]

On another view, the ideal code permits or even requires the jury to make some explicit evaluative judgments of one or both sorts. Negligence, for example, is clearly an evaluative judgment: the question is whether D should have been aware of a risk, or whether D should have taken more care in conducting an activity. Indeed, recklessness, in American law, usually is not simply a cognitive state of mind (in the sense noted above). Rather, it is a compound concept, encompassing both descriptive and evaluative elements. The jury must find, not just that D was aware of a risk, but that the risk was unjustifiable, and that taking the risk was a gross deviation from reasonable behaviour.[46] Similarly, some actus reus concepts also are evaluative. What kinds of misrepresentations are 'material' to a judicial proceeding, and thus perjurious? If a statute forbids the dissemination of 'obscene' media to children, what falls within the category?

RA Duff and Stuart Green offer an illuminating perspective on this issue. One argument for a descriptive code, they note, is the concern that explicitly evaluative criteria presuppose a moral consensus about criminal law norms that simply does

---

[44] See generally RA Duff and SP Green, 'Introduction: The Special Part and its Problems', in Duff and Green (eds), *Defining Crimes*, 10–16 (distinguishing the 'descriptivist' from the 'moralist' approach); A Michaels, '"Rationales" of Criminal Law Then and Now: For a Judgmental Descriptivism' (2000) 100 *Columbia Law Review* 54.

[45] Determining even but-for cause might, however, require some evaluative judgment. Determining proximate cause clearly so requires.

[46] Similarly, recklessness in English law (though defined differently than under the Model Penal Code) is also a partially evaluative concept. In English law, even the more subjective Cunningham form of recklessness requires a finding that it was unreasonable for D to take the risk. See Simester and Sullivan, *Criminal Law*, §5.2.

not exist.[47] But they also identify a counter-argument favouring evaluative criteria: the criminal law needs to use 'thick' concepts, corresponding to the 'thick' ethical concepts that we analysed above. These concepts 'seem to express a union of fact and value...On this view, we should...look for an ethically rich criminal law, which speaks to the citizens not of descriptively specified types of conduct that they must or must not engage in, but of wrongs that they must not commit'.[48]

This counter-argument has considerable merit. When jurors make 'thick' moral judgments of unreasonableness, or culpable indifference, or obscenity, those determinations will, in theory and sometimes in practice, achieve a snug fit between the underlying moral deficiency or wrong and the law's judgment of criminal guilt. In judging the defendant negligent, for example, a jury appears to be directly translating the moral wrong into a legal conclusion.

Nevertheless, we should hesitate before endorsing the evaluative approach as the general, preferred style of specifying criminal law norms, for three reasons. First, granting broad discretion to the fact-finder in this manner is problematic in familiar ways: too many norms will lack sufficient clarity, will fail to afford fair notice, or will be inconsistently applied. Although these difficulties can beset descriptive criteria, evaluative criteria are likely to pose them more acutely.[49] Second, we need to examine realistically how juries actually apply legal criteria. As implemented, descriptive criteria often will capture the underlying moral norm better than evaluative criteria will. Suppose, for example, we simply ask the jury to directly employ an evaluative criterion of murder: did the actor who caused another's death displayed 'extreme indifference to the value of human life'? So instructed, some juries will convict an absent-minded, mildly negligent driver who, after inadvertently killing a pedestrian, drives off with selfish indifference to the death he has already caused. If instead we define 'extreme indifference' much more carefully, in part by employing descriptive criteria such as awareness of a risk of death, intention to impose a risk of death, or failure to attempt to minimize the risk of death, the jury is more likely to effectuate the relevant moral norm.[50] And third, sometimes the moral norms underlying criminal law norms are themselves best expressed by descriptive criteria. Specifically, the moral norm against causing unjustified, serious harm to others might be an example. Although criminal law addresses wrongs as well as harms, and violations of duty as well as setbacks to welfare interests, it nevertheless does address the latter categories.

---

[47] See Duff and Green, 'Introduction: The Special Part and its Problems', 14 (reciting, though not endorsing, this concern).

[48] Ibid 14, quoting Williams, *Ethics and the Limits of Philosophy*, 129.

[49] These problems are especially serious when they affect the prima facie elements of the offence rather than the definition of a defence.

[50] For discussion, see Simons, 'Does Punishment for "Culpable Indifference" Simply Punish for "Bad Character"?', 219.

Now, we should not misunderstand the significance of a criterion being 'descriptive' rather than 'evaluative'. Even if an ideal code uses wholly descriptive criteria, the legislature or appellate court is of course employing those criteria for an avowedly normative purpose: to punish D for his criminal behaviour. So we should not be suspicious of a descriptive approach on the ground that it requires a mysterious alchemy from fact to value, from the natural to the normative. When a legislature says 'If you purposely cause death, you are guilty of murder', and then a jury finds that D satisfies the descriptive criterion, purposely causing death, the jury is simply playing its proper role in determining facts that, as a matter of law, constitute murder. The descriptive approach differs from a more evaluative approach not in being more mysterious or more magical, but in how it allocates explicitly evaluative decision-making authority. The descriptive approach gives the jury much less official authority to apply their own moral judgment to the case. (Juries do, of course, sometimes exercise such independent judgment, rejecting the legal outcome that the jury would concede is best supported by the facts and the governing law.)

The extent to which juries are encouraged to render their own judgments of wrongfulness and culpability depends, therefore, on what type of actus reus and mens rea criteria the crime employs. Interestingly enough, the pattern here, at least in American law, is murky at best. Very few crimes contain explicitly evaluative actus reus elements. Evaluative criteria are more commonly elements of a mens rea requirement; the most frequent instances are negligence and compound recklessness (and also 'extreme indifference', 'depraved heart', and 'wilful blindness'). But these criteria play a significant role only in certain crimes, such as involuntary manslaughter and depraved heart murder.[51]

Nevertheless, the question remains: *should* we ask the trier of fact to render an overtly evaluative judgment in a wider range of cases? Consider three arguments potentially supporting an affirmative answer. First, recall the argument of Duff and Green that when criminal law uses 'thick' evaluative concepts, it often (though not always) directly and effectively expresses the underlying moral norms. Two additional arguments are: (a) a fear that purely descriptive criteria will be

---

[51] The fact that many crimes contain a mens rea of negligence or compound recklessness has caused Larry Alexander and Kim Ferzan to assert baldly that most of American criminal law is governed by standards, not rules. Alexander and Ferzan, *Crime and Culpability*, 292. But this greatly overstates the extent to which evaluative judgments by juries actually affect criminal liability. Many crimes contain mens rea requirements of knowledge or purpose. And even when the formal legal requirement is recklessness or negligence, the evaluative dimension of the standard is very often not at serious issue in the case. Suppose D is charged with recklessly injuring a person in a bar after he punches the victim in the head without provocation. It is true that the jury's liability determination formally requires a finding, not only that D was aware that his punch might injure the victim, but also that the risk D posed was unjustifiable, and that D's punch was a gross deviation from reasonable behaviour. But these latter findings are quite straightforward given the facts. Here and in many other scenarios, the technical requirement of proof that D satisfied an open-ended, evaluative mens rea standard makes no real difference to the jury's decision making. The jury's role is still almost entirely descriptive in most cases.

under-inclusive; and (b) the opposing fear that descriptive criteria will be over-inclusive and thus will punish blameless behaviour.

The under-inclusiveness worry is exemplified by the mens rea categories of murder, discussed earlier. Punishing only purposeful and knowing killings as murders fails to include Russian Roulette and other seemingly equally culpable killings. The broader depraved heart murder category is a possible solution, yet jurisdictions that employ it frankly acknowledge that they really don't know how to define this category. At what point do the disadvantages of empowering juries with vaguer liability standards outweigh the advantages of correcting the under-inclusiveness of a merely descriptive criminal prohibition? It is difficult to say in the abstract, but we should certainly require the use of more specific criteria in applying standards such as 'depraved heart'—for example, require that the actor was aware of a non-trivial risk of death; that he acted for an especially heinous, antisocial, or clearly unjustifiable reason; and that he made no effort to ameliorate the harm.

The over-inclusiveness worry is as follows. As a formal matter, the legislature ordinarily imposes a mens rea requirement for each offence element. But that requirement might be only formal, not substantive, in which case the defendant will be punished despite lack of substantive culpability.[52] Moreover, this danger is much greater when the mens rea requirement is descriptive, not evaluative.

Consider a simple illustration.[53] To reduce the risk of forest fires, a state contemplates punishing any person who causes a forest fire. This obviously imposes strict liability, both formally (given the lack of a mens rea requirement) and substantively (given the real possibility that blameless individuals who accidentally cause forest fires will be punished). Now suppose the state instead punishes knowingly carrying a match in or near a forest, but only if that conduct causes a forest fire. The statute has a formal mens rea requirement of knowledge, but it imposes substantive strict liability, because an actor might well handle a match carefully and yet contribute to a forest fire.[54]

This over-inclusiveness problem is even greater if the formal mens rea is descriptive. For then the trier of fact, if it stays within its assigned role, will not ask the more fundamental question: even if D satisfied the descriptive criterion (for example, purpose or knowledge), is he really culpable enough to deserve criminal punishment? By contrast, if the fact-finder is asked to consider whether D was 'negligent' or 'reckless' (in the composite sense), then it should also consider whether D's act

[52] I suggested the distinction between formal strict liability and substantive strict liability in my 'When is Strict Criminal Liability Just?', 1075, 1085–93. For further discussion of the distinction, see RA Duff, *Answering for Crime: Responsibility and Liability in the Criminal Law* (Oxford: Hart Publishing, 2007), 232–5, 252–61, 233, n 14; S Green, 'Six Senses of Strict Liability: A Plea for Formalism', in AP Simester (ed), *Appraising Strict Liability* (Oxford: Oxford University Press, 2005), 1–20 (arguing for a formal rather than substantive conception of strict liability).

[53] The illustration is from my 'When is Strict Criminal Liability Just?', 1075, 1085–87.

[54] If the reader has difficulty conceiving of such an actor, here is a more extreme version of the example: homicide liability for causing the death of another as a result of knowingly moving one's limbs.

was unjustifiable, and whether D's conduct was a 'gross deviation' from reasonable care.[55] These broader inquiries make it significantly easier[56] for the fact-finder to address the fundamental question whether, apart from whether the defendant otherwise satisfies the formal actus reus and mens rea requirements of the crime, the defendant deserves punishment.

However, whether the fact-finder will actually take advantage of the explicitly evaluative criterion to engage in this more radical inquiry into all-things-considered culpability is an open empirical question. After all, in the United States the defendant's attorney cannot directly argue for jury nullification, nor may the judge instruct the jury that they have that power. And if a jury determines that D is not 'negligent' or 'reckless' because punishment would be unjust, this will often amount to nullification of the law. Suppose, for example, D is prosecuted for knowing possession of marijuana, reckless as to whether the amount possessed exceeds a particular weight (thus triggering a higher sentence). The composite recklessness principle permits the jury to determine that although D knew he probably possessed more than the prescribed amount of the drug, he did not thereby disregard an 'unjustifiable' risk and did not grossly deviate from the standard of reasonable behaviour. The availability of these inquiries might conceivably encourage the jury to conclude that the marijuana laws themselves are unjust and thus to acquit. But it is plain that permitting this conclusion was not the aim of the legislature in employing a mens rea category of recklessness. Rather, the intention was simply to permit the jury to exercise some judgment in evaluating why the defendant, despite some awareness of the risk, nevertheless chose to possess the drugs.[57]

If we wish to give the fact-finder more discretion to question the justice of a criminal prosecution, there are other options. In theory, we might recognize an 'insufficient culpability' defence, analogous to the lesser evils defence, that the fact-finder would apply on a case-by-case basis. To a limited extent, German criminal law incorporates a version of this idea: the state must prove not only a Tatbestand (roughly, actus reus and mens rea[58]) and a lack of Rechtfertigung (a justification), but also Schuld (guilt or blameworthiness). The last category incorporates what Anglo-American law would consider excuses and also (to a limited extent) lack of mens rea—for example, subjective incapacity to conform to a negligence standard,

---

[55] These are the Model Penal Code's specific criteria; but other evaluative criteria will be similarly open-ended.

[56] Only 'significantly' easier because D can still assert a defence of lack of justification to a crime requiring knowledge or purpose.

[57] Imagine a case where D was justified in thinking that the package of marijuana he purchased only contained a small amount because the seller only charged a price consistent with the smaller amount.

[58] German criminal law does recognize the correspondence principle, requiring proof of mens rea for each element as part of the first stage. See J Spencer and A Pedain, 'Approaches to Strict and Constructive Liability in Continental Criminal Law', in Simester (ed), Appraising Strict Liability, 237, 249–52.

'unavoidable' (reasonable) mistake of law and, possibly, mistakes about justifying facts.[59] On this approach, the jury would have the power to reject a criminal prosecution because, considering all of the relevant factors, the defendant is insufficiently culpable to deserve punishment.

Granting this form of extremely broad, untethered discretion to a fact-finder is very powerful medicine, however. A much less arbitrary, more predictable type of cure for over-criminalization and over-charging would be reform of the criminal laws themselves so that both wrongfulness and culpability criteria conform to defensible principles of just deserts.

In short, both descriptive and evaluative criteria play a valuable role in a legitimate system of criminal law. It is neither realistic nor just to employ one type of criterion to the exclusion of the other.

4 Conclusion

....

The world is not flat. Neither is the topography of criminal wrongdoing and culpability, or of actus reus and mens rea. This complex terrain should not surprise or frighten us. It is a complexity built upon the varied, and in some instances incommensurable, moral norms that lie beneath criminal law doctrine.

This chapter suggests the following conclusions. Criminal law norms can be more general or more particular. How particular should they be? The answer depends, in significant part, on the underlying landscape of the moral norms that criminal law instantiates, and on the political principles through which those moral norms are refracted. On three plausible accounts of moral justification—foundational pluralism, reliance on concrete moral intuitions, and variable relevance particularism— moral norms are relatively particularistic. At the same time, such accounts entail that the moral map contains localized areas of incommensurability. Finally, criminal law norms can be purely descriptive, or instead partially evaluative. But the difference that this distinction makes should not be overstated. A partially evaluative criterion does empower the fact-finder to play a more significant role in appraising

[59] See M Bohlander, *Principles of German Criminal Law* (Oxford: Hart Publishing, 2009), 16–17, 115–21; see also Duff, *Answering for Crime*, 204–206. Indeed, George Fletcher has recently argued that under this structure, descriptive mens rea judgments are made at stage one, but normative mens rea judgments are made at stage three. G Fletcher, *The Grammar of Criminal Law* (Oxford: Oxford University Press, 2007), § 1.4.3 (discussing the tripartite German system and its influence). The accuracy of his interpretation has been forcefully disputed, however. R Christopher, 'Tripartite Structures of Criminal Law in Germany and Other Civil Law Jurisdictions' (2007) 28 *Cardozo Law Review* 2675, 2677–8.

the moral wrongfulness and the moral culpability of the defendant's actions than does a purely descriptive criterion, but either type of criterion ultimately serves a normative function.

Modern criminal law scholars and reformers have made enormous progress in simplifying and rationalizing criminal statutes. But we should not assume that if a set of criminal law norms are complex and messy, then those norms cannot be cogently justified. In the moral domain, Bernard Williams noted that 'thick' ethical concepts tend to give way to 'thinner' concepts as the Enlightenment belief in rational progress becomes more widely shared. Yet he cautioned against wholesale rejection of thick concepts.[60] In the related domain of legal punishment, we should heed his caution.

---

[60] B Williams, 'Reply to Simon Blackburn' (1986) 27 *Philosophical Books* 203, 205.

BEYOND THE SPECIAL PART

LARRY ALEXANDER AND KIMBERLY KESSLER FERZAN*

1 THE SOLE CRITERION FOR DESERT: ACTING WITH INSUFFICIENT CONCERN

WE have some rather definite and no doubt controversial views about the criminal law. We believe that punishment must be *deserved*. We believe that what people deserve is based upon their culpability, which is in turn based upon the risks they choose to take to others' legally protected interests and their reasons for imposing those risks. And we believe that a liberal criminal law cannot punish an actor until the point at which he unleashes that risk of harm, but that unleashing that risk—and not the harm that eventually results—is what determines the actor's blameworthiness. In this section, we briefly elaborate on these views.

In *Crime and Culpability*,[1] we analyse what it would mean for the criminal law to take retributive justice seriously. How would we formulate crimes if they were

* We thank Michelle Madden Dempsey, Mitchell Berman, Stuart Green, and Antony Duff for their written comments. We also benefited from the Rutgers Conference on Philosophical Foundations of Criminal Law, the Boston University School of Law faculty workshop, and the Florida State University School of Law faculty workshop.

[1] L Alexander and KK Ferzan, with SJ Morse, *Crime and Culpability: A Theory of Criminal Law* (Cambridge: Cambridge University Press, 2009).

designed to give individuals what they deserve? In our view, individuals deserve punishment when they act culpably, and an actor is culpable when he exhibits insufficient concern for others.[2] (Culpability as insufficient concern for others is a view not only of criminal culpability but also of moral culpability more generally; for us, culpability is a univocal notion.) Actors demonstrate insufficient concern for others when they (irrevocably) decide to harm or risk harming other people (or their legally protected interests) for insufficient reasons—that is, when they act in a way that they believe will increase others' risk of harm without and regardless of any further action on their part, and their reasons for unleashing this risk fail to justify doing so. If Alex decides to drive 100 miles an hour on the highway, whether we deem Alex culpable and deserving of blame and punishment will depend upon whether he has chosen to impose this risk to impress his friends with how fast his car can drive or, alternatively, to transport a critically injured friend to the hospital.

As criteria for insufficient concern, the criminal law need not employ the Model Penal Code's four mental states—purpose, knowledge, recklessness, and negligence.[3] The same type of assessment is involved whether we are judging purpose, knowledge, or recklessness—a weighing of the risks the actor believes he is imposing and his reasons for doing so. When an actor purposefully aims to injure another—injuring is his conscious object for acting—his reasons are presumptively culpable. When an actor knowingly harms another—believes to a practical certainty that his act will harm—the degree of risk is presumptively culpable. But, in instances of both purpose and knowledge, these presumptions may be rebutted by showing that the actor was justified in imposing the risk that he did. In contrast, as formulated, recklessness requires the risk to be unjustified, thus building lack of justification into the mental state itself. In all of these cases, however, for a defendant ultimately to be deserving of punishment, the risks he takes must be unjustified. The current approach of separating this single criterion for culpability into three discrete mental states creates doctrinal difficulties as well as the false impression that these three mental states neatly line up in a culpability hierarchy.

Negligence, on the other hand, is not culpable.[4] There is no principled and rationally defensible way to construct the 'reasonable person' against whom we judge the actor and who we are to presume would have adverted to the risk to which the actor failed to advert. Infinite possible constructs exist between full omniscience and the actor's own subjective beliefs, but there is no reason to privilege any of these constructs as the appropriate normative standard against which to judge the actor. Moreover, even if we could construct such a perspective, the negligent actor lacks

[2] See generally ibid ch 2.
[3] Ibid.
[4] See generally ibid ch 3.

the requisite control over this 'risk'. Risk is a matter of epistemic perspective, and a 'negligent' actor who assesses a risk as lower than others would is not culpable for his epistemic shortcomings. It is the risk that the actor estimates—not the risk an actor possessed of more information, a better perspective, or superior inferential ability would have estimated—that determines culpability.

Beyond our focus on the risks the actor perceives and his reasons for imposing them, we have sought to refine our understanding of what types of acts are blame-worthy. Notably, we would jettison incomplete attempts from the criminal law.[5] When we punish an actor for taking a step toward his goal, we are punishing him for intending harm and perhaps for a prediction that he will try to commit the crime if we do not intercede. But until the actor unleashes a risk of harm over which he no longer has complete control, he may revoke his intention and decide not to commit the crime at all. The actor who is lying in wait may suddenly change his mind and decide to go home. To punish him for lying in wait, then, is to punish him for some perceived future risk, a risk that may actually turn out to be zero, and a risk that the actor correctly perceives to be entirely within his control until the very moment when he either unleashes the risk of harm or changes his mind and decides not to harm his potential victim.

On the other hand, once an actor has unleashed this risk of harm, we believe that whether he causes the harm is immaterial to his culpabilty.[6] The actor has decided to risk harming others, and the unleashing of the risk itself manifests the actor's insufficient concern: the result does not tell us any more about the choice the actor has made or how little he values the victim, and thus, the result does not increase (or decrease) his desert.

To us, then, there is really only one injunction that is relevant to criminal culpa-bility: choose only those acts for which the risks to others' interests—as you estimate those risks —are sufficiently low to be outweighed by the interests, yours and others', that you are attempting to advance (discounted by the probability, as you perceive it, of advancing those interests). In Model Penal Code parlance, we have done away with the special part of the criminal code. We have a general rule that encompasses all crimes, not specific rules of conduct.

Notably, our criminal code would still be complex. It would not consist of only one rule. Rather, a legislature would need to specify those interests worthy of legal protection.[7] Moreover, we envision a system akin to the United States Sentencing Guidelines (though far more principled!) that would assist the jury in calculating an actor's culpability and would ensure proportional punishment. Nevertheless, it is quite clear that this system would radically alter the criminal law terrain.

---

[5] See generally ibid ch 6.
[6] Ibid ch 5.
[7] For discussion of these issues, see ibid ch 8.

2 A Normative Defence of Unpacking Crimes

One might object that something is missing from a criminal code that does not list *wrongs*—those specific act-types that harm or cause harm to specific legally protected interests. We commonly speak of rape, murder, and robbery, not of unjustifiable risks. Is there not something missing from an account of the criminal law that does not mirror our ordinary understanding of wrongful conduct? Although we defend this manner of unpacking crimes in *Crime and Culpability*, in this section, we address two recent arguments espousing contrary points of view: the moral wrongfulness view advanced by Antony Duff and the view asserting the relevance of intentions advocated by Doug Husak. We then turn to the concern that it is conceptually problematic to place culpability prior to wrongdoing.

2.1 Duff

In *Answering for Crime*, Antony Duff argues that we punish *wrongs*, not harm causings.[8] He argues that for crimes such as burglary and murder, the harm principle is insufficient, as we 'cannot appeal to a non-moralised or pre-moral notion of harm to pick out the kinds of wrong that properly concern the criminal law'.[9] Murder requires recognizing 'the distinct harm of being wrongfully killed', and burglary is about the '*invasion*' of one's home.[10]

Duff then distinguishes between two kinds of wrongs that provide the basis for criminal offences: attacks and endangerments.[11] Attacks are purposeful and display the practical attitude of hostility. Endangerments are risk creations, and endangerments in the criminal law will typically require recklessness, thus displaying practical indifference. To Duff, crimes of knowledge are endangerments.

Duff claims that attacks and endangerments are two distinct types of wrongs. Attacks are guided by the wrong reason, whereas endangerments are not guided by the right reasons.[12] Although Duff is not claiming that attacks are more culpable than endangerments, he is claiming that they are different moral kinds.[13] The

[8] RA Duff, *Answering for Crime: Responsibility and Liability in the Criminal Law* (Oxford: Hart Publishing, 2007).
[9] Ibid 128.
[10] Ibid.
[11] Ibid 149–53.
[12] Ibid 151.
[13] Ibid 152.

significance of the distinction is 'only clear when we focus on the intentional structure of the agent's actions and the practical attitudes displayed in and partly constituted by those actions'.[14]

Duff's views lead to a structure radically different than the one we propose. He
argues that for *mala in se* attacks, the law 'serves to exclude the conduct from consideration as an option'.[15] The qualification of 'normal' consideration opens the
door to justification in 'exceptional circumstances'.[16] Because endangerments are
unjustified risk creations, their criminalization differs. With endangerments, one
can still offer an excuse, but justifications are subsumed within the recklessness
analysis. Thus, in these instances, as Duff recognizes, the offence/defence distinction 'collapses'.[17]

Our view, in contrast, collapses everything into endangerments. At the outset,
we believe hostility should be collapsed into indifference. Culpability is a function of the risks that the actor perceives and his reasons for acting. If one thinks
of recklessness as the paradigm (unjustifiably imposing risks for the attainment
of some possible end), then knowledge and purpose are simply limiting cases on
the spectrum, with knowledge (belief to a practical certainty) representing the
upper level of perceived risk and purpose representing an extremely bad reason
for imposing a risk. That is, Duff is certainly correct that cases of knowledge that
harm will result are a species of endangerment, but so, too, are purpose cases. In
purpose cases, the actor creates a risk of harm for a presumptively unjustifiable
reason (the harm or risk of harm itself). True, with attacks the reasons for acting are presumptively evil, but they are still only presumptively so. Joe can steal
a candy bar if doing so will save ten lives. This 'attack' is justified by necessity.
The practical attitude of an attack ultimately requires one to look not just to the
fact of attack, but also to the reason the attack is executed. With attacks, as with
endangerments, one must look at all risks and reasons before 'hostility' can be
assessed. Ultimately, what attacks and endangerments both evince is insufficient
concern. The actor has chosen to impose risks for insufficient reasons. All culpability assessments are of this nature, and their evaluation proceeds along the same
continua of risks and reasons.

Indeed, recognizing the relationship between recklessness and intention may
resolve current confusions. For example, New York courts have struggled with the
question of whether a depraved indifference murder conviction is appropriate where
an actor shoots his victim at point blank range but the jury acquits on an intentional murder charge. Current New York cases maintain that depraved indifference

[14] Ibid 154.
[15] Ibid 222.
[16] Ibid 223.
[17] Ibid 225.

is inappropriate because intentional killings cannot be depraved heart killings.[18] But this conclusion is certainly incorrect. A person who shoots at point blank range with no good reason has surely manifested extreme indifference to human life. Intentional killings are just one (typical) species of such indifference.

Not only do we reject Duff's attack/endangerment distinction, but we also reject his view that there is something special about certain kinds of wrongs. To explicate our objections, let us consider two prototypical special part crimes—murder and arson.

Duff claims that murder is a distinct attack. But murder, as the criminal law currently understands it, includes purpose, knowledge, and extreme indifference; yet Duff considers attacks to be just purpose crimes (and some recklessness offences). However, it seems hard to believe that Duff's distinction represents the structure of 'murder' as a particular moral kind. Knowledge cases, after all, are endangerments, not attacks, as are extreme indifference killings. The distinction between the two is a difference of degree of recklessness, not a difference of kind.

We believe the criminal law would function more seamlessly if it recognized that all culpable risks to life are blameworthy, rather than assuming that the special part distinction between 'murder' and 'manslaughter' marks a true distinction in kind. Thus, even though it appears that we have clear conceptual categories of homicide—murder and manslaughter—the reality is somewhat different. Both protect the same interest, and the culpability that supposedly distinguishes them is a line on a culpability continuum.

Additionally, consider arson. Arson seems to be a paradigmatic special part offence, but it is riddled with questions and problems. Setting fire to another's property creates a risk to property, but also a risk to persons, both physically and emotionally. If a house fire set intentionally burns down the house but also part of the house next door and a car in the neighbor's driveway, is it one crime of arson or three? If it kills one person sleeping in the house, physically injures another, and emotionally scars another, how many crimes were committed? Our approach asks which of these risks and with what magnitude did the actor believe he was imposing when he set the match to the kerosene. The actor's total culpability is based on the sum of those various risks of harm and their estimated magnitudes—what we call the holistic approach to risk[19]—and on his reasons for taking those risks. We believe that only this approach accurately captures the actor's culpability for his act of setting the fire. Nor do we care which of these risks actually materialize (had a probability of one) and which do not (had a probability of zero). There is only one crime per act, and its culpability is fully determined by the actor's perception of its risks and his reasons for imposing them.

---

[18] See eg *People v Payne*, 3 NY 3d 266, 786 NYS 2d 116, 819 NE 2d 634 (2004); *People v Suarez*, 6 NY 3d 202, 811 NYS 2d 267, 844 NE 2d 721 (2005).

[19] See Alexander and Ferzan, with Morse, *Crime and Culpability*, ch 2.

2.2 Husak

In a recent article, Douglas Husak discusses, as the title reveals, 'The Costs to Criminal Theory of Supposing that Intentions are Irrelevant to Permissibility'.[20] In our view, the title is misleading, as it seems to indicate that Husak's only concern is with those who reject the Doctrine of Double Effect (DDE), that is, the view that some *actions* are permissible so long as they are not performed with a specific intention. Husak's target, though, is much broader. He is aiming not only at those who reject the DDE but also at those who believe that intentions are irrelevant to culpability. To Husak, the relevance of intention to punishability bears on '*whether* defendants have committed acts'; '*what* criminal wrongs they have perpetrated'; and 'the *degree* of wrongfulness of a given act'.

Husak throws down the gauntlet, stating: 'Intentions matter to the criminal law in countless ways I can barely mention.'[21] He claims: 'Intentions are relevant both to *whether* a defendant commits an offense as well as to *what* offense he commits. These offenses are an entrenched staple of criminal codes we can scarcely imagine doing without.'[22]

As a descriptive matter, we do not dispute that many crimes use the concept of intention. But, as Husak knows, recklessness is the most significant mental state in the criminal law as a whole. It is the default culpable mental state under the Model Penal Code. In state codes, recklessness is a sufficient mens rea for offences that range from the mundane, such as arson[23] and deceptive business practices,[24] to the bizarre, such as aggravated unpermitted use of indoor pyrotechnics,[25] defacing traffic signs and signals,[26] and interference with police service animals.[27] Moreover, many states have also followed the Model Penal Code's lead and enacted a blanket misdemeanour for reckless endangerment.[28]

More importantly, we recognize that our view radically recasts the legal terrain. We are getting rid of rape, murder, and arson, after all. We think that the critical question is the normative one—how does criminal law best punish only those who deserve it and only as much as they deserve? We doubt Husak would disagree.

Let us turn then to the crimes that Husak cites as evidencing the *normative* importance of intentions. Husak begins with crimes of *ulterior intent*, such as

---

[20] D Husak, 'The Costs to Criminal Theory of Supposing that Intentions are Irrelevant to Permissibility' (2009) 3 *Criminal Law & Philosophy* 51.

[21] Ibid 57.

[22] Ibid 58.

[23] Alabama Code, s 13A-7-43 (1975) (arson in the third degree).

[24] Hawaii Revised Statutes, s 708–870 (2006).

[25] NY Penal Law, s 405.18 (2003).

[26] NJ Stat Ann, s 2C:17-3.1 (2007).

[27] Tex Penal Code Ann, s 38.151 (2007).

[28] See eg Ala Code, s 13A-6-24 (1975); Conn Gen Stat Ann, s 53a-63 (2007); Md Code Ann, Crim Law, s 3-204 (2007); NY Penal Law, s 120.20 (2007); 18 Pa Cons Stat Ann, s 2705 (2007).

burglary or kidnapping.[29] The ulterior intention makes the defendant guilty of a 'different and more serious offence'. But we do not need intentions here. First, the reason why someone breaks and enters clearly matters and can matter under our system as well as any other. When one imposes a risk by, say, breaking a window, what matters are both the risks of harm the defendant is aware that he is impos- ing and his reasons for acting as he does. Indeed, our view would distinguish (as morally we ought to) between the person who breaks and enters in order to steal a television and a person who breaks and enters in order to rape or murder. Under current law, these are both a single type of burglary. On our view, the harm imposed or risked—breaking and entering—is more or less culpable depending on the actor's reasons for imposing it, with rape and murder being worse reasons than theft. Our perspective also avoids the problems of punishing someone based solely on a prediction of what they might do, which is how ulterior intention cases are currently framed. That is, as currently conceptualized, breaking and entering is not the central wrong; rather, the central wrong is the further intention—an intention that the defendant may or may not choose to follow through on. But our view allows us to focus on *the actual act committed and the reason this act was committed.*

Husak also points to cases in which 'intentions are partly constitutive of the crim- inal act itself'.[30] We call these intention-drenched wrongs. One cannot 'lie' without the intention to deceive. One cannot 'torture' without the intention to cause pain. One cannot 'attempt' to kill without intending to do so.[31] These crimes are unrav- elled by our approach not only because we focus on risks to interests and not act- types, but because we deny the significance of intention as its own separate culpable mental state.

We believe that nothing is lost by our approach, however. These offences can and should be analysed by their discrete elements. If the perceived risk is not a risk of 'harm' in the absence of an intent to harm, then we would deny that the act in ques- tion is culpable.

Moreover, although these crimes entail intention,[32] there is no reason we need to rely on these particular crimes as currently understood. First, as we have argued, conceptually, intention (or purpose) is but a particular species of recklessness so there is no conceptual reason why we cannot speak of recklessness instead of inten- tions. Even if consciously imposing a high risk that another will be misled is not

---

[29] Husak, 'The Costs to Criminal Theory of Supposing that Intentions are Irrelevant to Permissibility', 58.

[30] Ibid 58.

[31] This is a case where even those theorists who believe that crimes can be understood without mental elements, like Paul Robinson, create an exception. PH Robinson, *Structure and Function in Criminal Law* (Oxford: Oxford University Press, 1997), 133.

[32] But see Model Penal Code, s 5.01(6) (making knowledge as well as purpose a sufficient mens rea for an attempted result crime).

'lying', it still may be—or may not be, depending upon the actor's reasons—a culpable, reckless act with respect to the interest in not being misled.

Husak's central case is that of criminal attempts.[33] With respect to attempts, normatively, there is no reason to restrict punishment to instances of risking with the intent to bring about the harm risked. If the actor consciously disregards an unjustifiable risk of harm, her action is culpable even if she does not want that harm to occur. Indeed, given an actor's reasons for acting, her 'reckless attempt' (currently called 'reckless endangerment'[34]) may be more culpable than another actor's 'intentional attempt'.

Or consider complicity, which has traditionally been limited to the mens rea of purpose. But why? When Iago taunts Othello, he may not wish for Desdemona to die. Instead, Iago may believe it sufficient to torture Othello mentally. But when Othello kills Desdemona, Iago is surely largely to blame for this. His conduct—lying about Desdemona's infidelity—created an unjustifiable risk that Othello would kill his wife. We see no reason why Iago should escape liability because Desdemona's death was not within the scope of Iago's intention if Iago was aware that his conduct increased the risk of such a result and for no good reason.

Indeed, although ordinary language and lay intuitions may be useful, they cannot be the last word on drafting criminal codes. Even if as a matter of semantics, an actor cannot 'attempt' a reckless homicide because one cannot intentionally commit an unintentional act, we may alternatively label the reckless actor's conduct 'endangerment'; but labels aside, the only distinction, then, between the 'attempt' and the 'endangerment' is the actor's reason for imposing the risk. We see no reason not to focus on the interest risked and the actor's culpability regarding that risk rather than on the actor's intention.

To put the point another way, consider the following claim by Husak:

After all, most of us concur that acts of attempted arson, for example, are wrongful. If asked: 'Is it permissible to try to burn your neighbor's haystack?' Almost anyone would answer: 'Of course not.' If I am correct, however, we cannot specify what is wrongful about such attempts unless we stress the centrality of intention.[35]

Importantly, though, Husak simultaneously footnotes that he is leaving out justifications which complicate his account.[36]

Let us recast this question. Should you *try* to burn down your neighbour's haystack? Of course not. Should you *risk* burning down your neighbour's haystack? Not unless you have a good reason (ie justification). Is wanting to harm your neighbour a bad reason to risk burning the haystack down? Yes. What are we missing?

---

[33] See Husak, 'The Costs to Criminal Theory of Supposing that Intentions are Irrelevant to Permissibility', 60.

[34] See Model Penal Code, s 211.2.

[35] See Husak, 'The Costs to Criminal Theory of Supposing that Intentions are Irrelevant to Permissibility', 63.

[36] Ibid n 50.

Finally, Husak contends that we must keep intentions for purposes of fair labelling.[37] But this presupposes that the labels are meaningful ones. We have our doubts. Frequently, the labels obscure, rather than clarify, the very blameworthiness at issue.

2.3 Do we get morality exactly backwards?[38]

The typical understanding of culpability and wrongdoing is that wrongdoing is prior to culpability. One must know what is wrong (killing) before one can know not to intend to do it. Culpability is thus parasitic on wrongdoing. A worry about our approach, then, would be that it seems to flip this understanding. If one acts wrongfully only when the risks one adverts to are justified by one's reasons, then culpability appears to be prior to wrongdoing.

But appearances are deceiving and we need to separate out some questions. First, consider the question of whether we are subjectivists or objectivists about justifications. Our view is somewhat complex. Insofar as culpability is concerned, if one does not believe justifying facts exist, then one is culpable even if those facts *do* exist; and one is non-culpable if one believes they exist even if they do not. In that sense, we are subjectivists. On the other hand, if justifying facts do exist, third parties aware of those facts may aid those who are unaware and culpable. That is, we would say that even if Alex is unaware that by burning down Betty's farm he is saving the city, the act *is justified*, and others, aware of the justifying circumstances, can aid and encourage Alex to burn down Betty's farm. We thus endorse the objectivist view that 'one may burn a barn to save a town' irrespective of any individual's beliefs. In this way, the priority of wrongdoing to culpability holds.

There is also a second related question here, and that is whether morality consists of simply one meta-principle, or whether morality itself has action-guiding narrow rules. Action-guiding rules (thou shalt not kill) are merely instantiations of the more general standard about risks versus reasons. As we have seen above, there is no clear boundary to murder—at some point risking becomes so reckless as to meet the depraved indifference standard. Moreover, the action-guiding rule (do not kill) admits to exceptions. Ultimately, you *may* kill in self-defence, and you *may* even kill when you choose to impose a justifiable risk (like driving) and someone dies. We may spell out the rules, and the exceptions to those rules, but these rules are ultimately instantiations of a more general principle. These rules provide the same benefits and problems that other rules do (issues we attend to directly below), but morality may have some advantages when it comes to granting exceptions that would be difficult for the criminal law.

---

[37] Ibid 64.
[38] We thank Mitch Berman for pressing us to examine this issue.

3 From an Idealized Code to a Practical One—Implementing our Theory in 'The Real World'

No doubt, our idealized code will seem bizarre to many people. Gone are references to rape, murder, and intention. In their place are risk impositions and legally protected interests. One might object that although our 'Golden Rule culpability formulation' works in theory, it can never work practically.

This section looks at how one might implement our idealized code in the current legal system. We first argue that our current criminal codes, although they appear to be rule-based, ultimately rely on standards. Thus, it is no argument in favour of the status quo and against our code that ours is standards-based. We then note the tangles the current law gets into when it tries to count offences. The criminal law currently does not take a holistic approach to risk. Hence, it constantly struggles with the determination of how many crimes an actor has committed and how much punishment an actor deserves.

After surveying the current state of criminal law, we turn to the question of whether a rule or standards-based system is preferable. Here, we discuss the value of having rules, and how values that law is meant to serve are better served by rules than by standards. However, we then discuss a significant problem with rules—the existence of an ineliminable gap between the reasons for promulgating a rule and the reasons that a citizen has to obey it. For a retributivist, this problem is particularly worrisome because any actor who falls within this gap is an innocent (non-culpable) actor who does not deserve punishment—even if he has violated the rule.

Because this gap exists and cannot be eliminated, we argue that in almost all cases, the criminal law should opt for standards. However, we note that in some cases, the pressure for rules may be overwhelming. We thus discuss the form in which these rules should be enacted and how violations should be punished. We also argue that even when rules—what we call proxy crimes—are not enacted, our standards-based system is consistent with the principle of legality.

3.1 Do our current criminal codes contain rules?

Does our criminal law consist of rules? We should note at the outset that we are not making a normative claim here as to whether rules or standards are preferable. We shall address that question shortly when discussing how to implement our theory. For now, the question is an empirical one—what sort of criminal code do we have?

Although our criminal code may have many specific criminal statutes, ultimately, standards are abundant. Indeed, crimes are standards-based whenever they require a mens rea of either recklessness or negligence.[39] Both mental states require that the jury determine whether the risk taken was 'unjustifiable', an open-ended normative assessment.

Consider first the number of standards embedded within the Model Penal Code. Attempts require the actor take a 'substantial step'.[40] Some attempts are entitled to mitigation (or even dismissal) if they are 'so inherently unlikely to result... in the commission of a crime'.[41] An actor is guilty of gross sexual imposition if he compels his victim to have sex by 'any threat that would prevent resistance by a woman of ordinary resolution'.[42] One may commit a crime by 'loitering' or 'prowling'.[43] Mistake of law is a defence if the actor 'acts in reasonable reliance upon an official statement of law'.[44] An actor has a duress defence if he succumbs to a threat 'which a person of reasonable firmness would have been unable to resist'.[45] An actor is held to consent to 'reasonably foreseeable hazards of joint participation in an athletic contest'.[46] An actor is justified if, among other things, 'the harm or evil sought to be avoided is greater than that sought to be prevented by the law defining the offense charged'.[47] Law enforcement may not use deadly force if it creates a 'substantial risk of injury to innocent persons'.[48] Parents may not use force on their children if such force is 'known to create a substantial risk' of death, serious bodily harm, or 'extreme pain', or 'gross degradation'.[49]

State statutes likewise embed standards. One can be guilty of murder if one commits a crime recklessly under circumstances manifesting *extreme indifference* to human life,[50] or guilty of manslaughter for acting recklessly as to death.[51] In Montana, drivers even managed for years with a 'careful and prudent manner' standard rather than a speed limit.[52]

Juries determine when an act goes beyond 'mere preparation' to 'dangerous proximity' such that the actor has committed an attempt.[53] A jurisdiction that extends

[39] See above nn 23–8.

[40] Model Penal Code, s 5.01(1)(c).

[41] Ibid s 5.05(2).

[42] Ibid s 213.1(2)(a).

[43] Ibid s 250.6.

[44] Ibid s 2.04(3)(b).

[45] Ibid s 2.09(1).

[46] Ibid s 2.11(2)(b).

[47] Ibid s 3.02(1)(a).

[48] Ibid s 3.07(2)(b)(iii).

[49] Ibid s 3.08(1)(b).

[50] Ala Code, s 13A-6-2 (1975).

[51] Ibid s 13A-6-3; Conn Gen Sta Ann, s 53a-56 (2007).

[52] See RE King and CR Sunstein, 'Doing Without Speed Limits' (1999) 79 *Boston University Law Review* 155.

[53] See MT Cahill, 'Punishment Decisions at Conviction: Recognizing the Jury as Fault-Finder' (2005) *University of Chicago Legal Forum* 91, 101.

complicity to crimes that 'naturally and probably' follow from the encouraged act also requires a jury determination about that linkage.[54] These examples are just the tip of the iceberg.

3.2 Conceptual concerns with 'repacking' crimes

Despite the prevalence of standards within the criminal law, some might think we take this too far. The criminal law's standards operate within 'hard edged' rules. We separate assault from rape, and cocaine possession from contempt of court. That is, the criminal law carves up crimes by the interests it wishes to protect. Why not keep the current state of the law but just use recklessness as a default mental state?

The problem is that when an actor chooses to impose a risk for insufficient reasons, she does not choose to impose just one risk. Rather, she is reckless because her act imposes risks to a whole host of legally protected interests (life, bodily integrity, property) for insufficient reasons. It is all the risks the actor foresees weighed against all of her reasons that leads to the determination that she is reckless.

For this reason, when the criminal law delineates crimes based upon discrete risks, it artificially carves up a criminal act. Indeed, criminal law's current attempt to carve up crimes leads to crime counting problems—problems that come to light when considering the application of the double jeopardy clause. Consider *Kansas v Neal*.[55] The victim drove the defendant home from a bar, and upon arrival at the defendant's apartment building, the defendant pretextually requested a 'hug'. When the victim got out of the car, the defendant carried her to a secluded patch of grass and raped her. In accomplishing this rape, the defendant punched the victim in the face and choked the victim to the point at which she twice lost consciousness. The defendant challenged his convictions for both rape and aggravated assault, claiming that the charges were multiplicitious. According to him, there was just one crime—a rape—accomplished by the use of force.

Despite the state's claim that the defendant went beyond the force necessary to accomplish a rape, the appellate court reversed. Because no distinction was made in the indictment, in the presentation of evidence, or in the jury instructions, the jury might have relied on the same acts of force that constituted the aggravated assault charge to determine that force was used to accomplish the rape. The court went on to say that:

an additional problem with the State's argument that the battery went 'far beyond the force used to accomplish rape' is its imprecision. How much force is necessary to rape someone? By what gauge do we measure violence? Is not each victim unique? This was a horrible crime

---

[54]   Eg *People v Luparello*, 87 Cal App 3d 410, 231 Cal Rptr 832 (1987). Of course, this view is antithetical to ours.

[55]   34 Kan App 2d 45, 120 P 3d 366 (2006).

committed with great continuous violence during its entire course; therefore, the application of single act of violence paradigm is appropriate here.[56]

But why should we assume that all instances of forcible rape are equal? An actor who suffocates his victim risks her life more than an actor who punches his victim and more than an actor who uses force only to hold down his victim. Let us be clear—all of these defendants are exceedingly culpable. But if Neal used excessive amounts of force to accomplish his forcible rape, he should be differentiated from an actor who uses lesser force. He is more culpable and deserving of more punishment.

Under our approach, there are no act types. The question is whether the actor, by way of a willed bodily movement, believed that he risked unjustifiable harm to a legally protected interest. For every willed bodily movement, we must ask about *all* the reasons the actor was aware of in support of so acting (discounted by the probabilities of their being realized), and *all* the risks that the actor believed he was imposing. Indeed, without an evaluation of all the risks and reasons, the jury cannot assess whether the conduct was justified and, accordingly, whether the defendant was culpable for imposing the risks. Our approach allows us to focus on the discrete interests that are risked (sexual autonomy, bodily injury) and the different degrees of the risks imposed (as the actor perceives them). Not all rapes are created equal.

But to see the true clarity that a focus on legally protected interests brings, consider the Supreme Court's divided opinion in *United States v Dixon*.[57] Although *Dixon* involved a pair of appeals, let us focus on the *Dixon* case itself. Dixon was arrested for second-degree murder and released on bond, subject to the condition that he not commit any additional criminal offence. After his release, Dixon was arrested for possession of cocaine with intent to distribute. The court held him guilty of contempt and sentenced him to 180 days in jail. Dixon later moved to dismiss his indictment for the drug possession on double jeopardy grounds. The trial court granted the motion, and a majority of the Supreme Court concurred that the drug prosecution would violate the double jeopardy clause.

Though the Court was deeply fractured in reaching this decision, we wish to spend a moment on Justice Scalia's opinion, in which Justice Kennedy joined, because Scalia rejected the very analysis that we advance here. Scalia reasoned that because the contempt order incorporated the drug offence, the underlying substantive drug offence was a 'species of a lesser-included offense'.[58] Scalia explicitly rejected the view that because the interests that the offences protect are different, the offences are not the same for double jeopardy purpose.[59] To Scalia, the test turns on legislative definitions—the text of the double jeopardy clause speaks to whether the *offences* are the same, not whether the *interests* they protect are identical.[60]

---

[56] Ibid 492–93.
[57] 509 US 688, 113 S Ct 2849 (1993).
[58] Ibid 698 (citations omitted).
[59] Ibid 699.
[60] Ibid.

But to apply the double jeopardy clause in this manner strikes us as very odd. One of the primary purposes of the double jeopardy clause is to prevent double punishment. If the legislature prohibits burglary, the legislature should not have to consider the possible combinations of crimes with which the defendant could be charged in crafting the punishment for burglary. So, if burglary warrants a maximum of five years in jail, we would not think that the defendant should also be punished for criminal trespass and breaking and entering if both of these crimes are lesser-included offences within burglary.

Not only does this make sense with respect to how a rational legislature might behave, but it also makes sense with respect to the legally protected interests at stake. A trespass, a breaking and entering, and a burglary all risk harm to the same sorts of legally protected property rights, but they risk that harm to different extents. Thus, the burglary is a greater risk to a property right than a simple trespass; and if one is being punished for the full extent of the risk to the property right, then it would be double punishment also to punish the defendant for the simple trespass.

However, once we begin to think of crimes as risks to legally protected interests, we see why it is that the contempt charge did not fully exhaust the punishment that Dixon deserved for drug offence. Although we find the underlying drug possession charge potentially problematic, the legally protected interests at stake go beyond the interests at stake in the criminal contempt charge. Dixon's violation of his release condition revealed that he might be either dangerous or a flight risk. *Any* criminal offence would have shown this to be true. On the other hand, if possession of cocaine with intent to distribute risks harm to life,[61] the offence is deserving of far more punishment than a mere 180 days. It is hard to conceive of how this offence constitutes a lesser-included offence within the contempt charge.

In summary, viewing crimes as instances of risk imposition does not obfuscate the underlying blameworthiness of the conduct. To the contrary, a direct focus on risks and reasons allows us to make fine-grained distinctions between criminal defendants who would otherwise be deemed to have committed the same offence. In addition, by tying crime directly to risks to legally protected interests, we avoid the problems of overlapping offences that present multiple description problems under the double jeopardy clause.

3.3 Retributivism's problem with rules

Thus far, we have argued that any attempt to repackage insufficient concern into discrete offences will require artificially analysing one act as multiple offences. Having discrete crimes fails to recognize the holism of risk assessment. But there is another

---

[61] For the difficulties of articulating the harms at stake with drug offences, see D Husak, *Legalize This! The Case for Decriminalizing Drugs* (London: Verso, 2002).

problem with the adoption of bright line rules to define crimes. Most of the values that underlie having *rules* are consequentialist. However, there is an ineliminable gap between when a legislator should create rules and when a citizen should follow them. A citizen can thus violate a justified rule justifiably. Such a citizen should not be punished because he is not culpable and therefore does not deserve punishment. A criminal law that truly cares about an actor's culpability cannot punish a non-culpable actor simply to preserve the (consequentialist) value of rules.

3.3.1 *The argument for rules over standards*

The value of rules is that they authoritatively settle moral disagreements.[62] That is, even when individuals are ethically well-disposed actors, they need the assistance of posited, determinate rules. Authoritative settlement by determinate rules resolves problems of coordination, expertise, and efficiency.

Rules solve coordination problems.[63] In some cases, there are several incompatible ways to act and no reason to prefer one solution to another.[64] Which side of the street to drive on is one example. In other instances, rules solve social coordination problems: in a world of imperfect information, and in which the morally right thing to do turns at least in part on what others are likely to do, rules provide actors with a basis for such a prediction.[65]

In other instances, the rules reflect the expertise of their promulgators. We may believe that a particular authoritative decision-maker has greater moral and factual expertise than the typical rule subject. Although there may be reason to doubt this superior expertise in any given case, in general, legal rules can resolve questions about how to act that most individuals on their own may not be capable of resolving as well because they lack the rule promulgator's information or expertise.[66] Rules also avert errors. When, due to complexity, actors must look at a multitude of factors in order to determine what to do, they may simply get the calculations wrong.[67]

Finally, rules reduce decision-making costs. It is simply more efficient for us to have a traffic law that tells us how fast to go than for us to calculate a safe speed each moment that we are driving.[68] A rule that dispenses with the necessity of complex calculations can also be said to promote predictability because everyone will arrive

---

[62] For further discussion of this argument, see L Alexander and E Sherwin, *The Rule of Rules: Morality, Rules, and the Dilemmas of Law* (Durham: Duke University Press, 2001), ch 1.

[63] Ibid 56; F Schauer, *Playing by the Rules: A Philosophical Examination of Rule-Based Decision-Making in Law and in Life* (Oxford: Oxford University Press, 1991), s 7.7.

[64] Alexander and Sherwin, *The Rule of Rules*, 56.

[65] Ibid 57–8.

[66] Ibid 55.

[67] Schauer, *Playing by the Rules*, 150.

[68] Ibid s 7.3.

at the same result—what the rule prescribes—rather than different results through different calculations.[69]

All of these benefits of rules stem from both rule addressees and rule enforcers having the same understanding of the rule.[70] In other words, it is rules' determinacy that produces these consequential and hence moral benefits.

All of these reasons for having legal rules are thus reasons for having legal *rules*, not standards. Enacting a legal rule settles normative disputes. In this respect, standards are unhelpful. For example, laws that tell individuals to 'drive safely'—a standard—leave (ethically well-disposed) individuals with no better idea about what to do than if there were no laws at all.[71]

As one of us has argued:

> The quality that identifies a rule and distinguishes it from a standard is the quality of deter-
> minateness. A norm becomes a rule when most people understand it in a similar way. When
> this is so, the rule will give the same answer to unsettled moral questions to every affected
> individual and so bring about coordination. Although a standard is transparent to back-
> ground moral principles and requires particularistic decision-making, rules can be applied
> without regard to questions of background morality. They are opaque to the moral princi-
> ples they are supposed to effectuate. Thus, a rule is a posited norm that fulfills the function of
> posited norms, that is, that settles the question of what ought to be done.[72]

3.3.2 *Problems with rules*

Despite the benefits of having legal rules, there are also problems with having them. Rules may be over-inclusive.[73] Because rules rely on act-type generalizations, and not on particulars, there is always a possibility that a particular instance of the act-type would not be prohibited if one relied solely upon the underlying justification for the rule.[74] Fred Schauer enumerates three possible ways that a rule might be ill-fitting—the probabilistic generalization may be incorrect on this occasion; the universal generalization turns out not to be universal; or a property suppressed by the rule is germane.[75]

Given that rules can be over-inclusive, it is a bit surprising that rules are followed as often as they are. In our view, the reason why rules generally work is through a form of (benign) deception.[76] People mistakenly believe that rules dictate the morally

---

[69] Ibid 137.

[70] Ibid 138.

[71] Alexander and Sherwin, *The Rule of Rules*, 29.

[72] Ibid 30.

[73] Rules may also be under-inclusive. That is, the reason that justifies prohibiting conduct *a* may also extend to conduct type *b*, but the rule may apply only to conduct type *a*. Schauer, *Playing by the Rules*, 32–3.

[74] Ibid 32; Alexander and Sherwin, *The Rule of Rules*, 35.

[75] Schauer, *Playing by the Rules*, 39.

[76] See generally L Alexander and E Sherwin, 'The Deceptive Nature of Rules' (1994) 142 *University of Pennsylvania Law Review* 1191.

preferable course of action in the cases that they cover, and because of that belief they comply. The use of a rules-based law ultimately entails deceiving the citizenry, leading them to believe that rules dictate correct results when they do not.

Although the over-inclusive nature of rules—the fact that they apply even when their underlying justifications do not—is generally troubling, it is far more troubling in the context of the criminal law. In the criminal law context, an over-inclusive rule is a rule that creates the potential for punishing an innocent actor. There will be cases where it is rational for a lawmaker to create a specific rule, and at the same time, there will be cases where it is irrational for a citizen to obey it. For it is neither rational nor morally preferable for a citizen to obey a rule the underlying justification for which does not apply in the case at hand.

This gap—between what a legislator should proscribe and what a citizen should do—cannot be closed.[77] There are different approaches to confronting this gap, but none of these approaches will eliminate it. Thus, a retributivist will have to face the reality that a rule that promotes authoritative settlement may do so at the expense of punishing an 'innocent' person.

Consider the imminence requirement in self-defence. One reason for the requirement (though not the only one) is that it is a proxy for the underlying justification of necessity. It is a proxy because it is more determinate—more rule-like—than the standard of necessity. In most instances, defensive force is not necessary if the threat is not imminent. However, a battered woman may need to defend herself before the threat becomes imminent. In such a case, she is prejudiced by an over-inclusive rule.[78] Should the criminal law punish her?

The retributivist faces a dilemma. She must decide whether to announce broad standards—standards that ultimately rely on the pre-existing moral knowledge of citizens—or narrow rules that may ultimately mandate the punishment of non-culpable actors.

This problem is acute for retributivists because all retributivists reject the infliction of punishment greater than deserved in order to achieve better consequences. Elsewhere we have defined deontological side-constraints in terms of using others' bodies, talents, and labours without their consent to achieve good consequences.[79] The question then is whether *knowingly* punishing someone more than he deserves to preserve the consequentialist benefits of rules violates this side-constraint. Although this issue is not free from doubt,[80] there is a respectable argument that such punishment does violate the side-constraint.

For those who construe the deontological side-constraint differently than we do, say, by claiming that one cannot *intend* to punish the innocent, the problem is more

---

[77] Alexander and Sherwin, *The Rule of Rules*, 54.
[78] KK Ferzan, 'The Values and Costs of Imminence', in PH Robinson, S Garvey, and KK Ferzan (eds), *Criminal Law Conversations* (Oxford: Oxford University Press, 2009), 419–20.
[79] Alexander and Ferzan, with Morse, *Crime and Culpability*, ch 2.
[80] Ibid ch 8.

significant. If intending to kill someone whom one knows to be black is intending to kill a black man, or if intending to have sex with someone whom one knows is not consenting is intending to rape, then intending to punish someone whom one knows to be innocent is intending to punish the innocent. The problem here is that at the time of adjudication and punishment, we will know that the person is in fact innocent of the offence.

Doug Husak argues that over-inclusive legislation is permissible so long as it is no more extensive than necessary.[81] In justifying a blanket rule prohibiting crossing a median line on a curved highway, Husak argues that, although some actors will be epistemically privileged (and know that crossing is safe), others will be epistemically arrogant (and therefore culpable). According to Husak, because there is no reliable method to distinguish these two types of actors, we may justly punish them both.

The problem, however, is that even if we cannot distinguish these two actors ex ante, there may be ways to distinguish them *ex post*. We must justify, not only a rule that may be over-inclusive, but also *punishing* an actor for violating the rule in situations in which, had we perfect information (or simply the information available ex post), we never would have criminalized his conduct to begin with.

To justify the imposition of punishment based on over-inclusive legislation, then, requires a justification for the knowing (and perhaps intended) punishment of the innocent. If we use a 'beyond a reasonable doubt standard' to prevent the *risk* of punishing the innocent, how much consequential good must we achieve in order to justify the knowing infliction of punishment on innocent individuals? The trade-off here, at the time of the imposition of punishment, seems almost insurmountable.

Our argument for standards over rules, then, stems from our commitment to retributivism, and a deep concern about the punishment of the innocent. It is also the natural implementation of our view that for any willed bodily movement we must look to all the risks and all the reasons to assess the actor's culpability. Breaking the conduct into separate crimes creates artificial distinctions, distinctions that must then be 'undone' at the back end. And, this unpacking is essential—it too is required to prevent over-punishment.

What we have not argued is that standards are simply 'preferable' to rules.[82] We are compelled to our conclusions by the force of the arguments. Although we have defended this view, and argued it gives fair notice,[83] it is not our notice argument that compels the conclusion. Thus, Stuart Green's recent review of our book strikes wide of the mark when he claims that our discussion 'of the Golden Rule is brief and uncharacteristically casual'[84] and then takes issue with our statement that the

---

[81] D Husak, *Overcriminalization: The Limits of the Criminal Law* (Oxford: Oxford University Press, 2008), 155–6.

[82] SP Green, 'Review Essay: Golden Rule Ethics and the Death of Criminal Law's Special Part' (forthcoming *Criminal Justice Ethics*) (manuscript on file with authors).

[83] Alexander and Ferzan, with Morse, *Crime and Culpability*, ch 8.

[84] Green, 'Review Essay'.

Golden Rule is 'clear, concise, and easy to memorize'[85] and therefore is a 'good model for criminal law rulemaking'.[86] Green instead claims that the Golden Rule is too vague to serve as *the* criminal law standard—although he does not disagree with us that crimes such as rape and murder are overly broad and the terms need to be 'more precise and meaningful'.

Green's argument fails to draw blood. Our argument is neither intended as an explicit adoption of the Golden Rule *itself* nor a defence of the use of the standards ubiquitously. Moreover, our arguments against the labels of rape and murder are not themselves arguments for standards; rather, they are an argument that we do not lose anything by moving to standards, because the labels do not mark out distinct wrongs. Green essentially concedes this point.

Our defence of a standards-based criminal law has been and remains grounded in retributive theory; thus, to challenge our approach, one must take on the arguments that compel it, specifically, our arguments about double jeopardy and over-inclusive rules. After devoting numerous paragraphs to critiquing a position with respect to *the* Golden Rule that we never adopt, Green gives scant attention to these arguments. With respect to crime counting, Green gestures at the ability to specify crimes more precisely, thus ignoring our overarching theory about the holism of risk assessment. With respect to over-inclusive rules, Green believes the solution is to give various actors within the criminal justice system 'appropriate discretion'. This is not sufficient. Green ignores the problems we detail in our book. First, citizens must believe the rules do tell them what to do if we want to get the value of rules; Green's approach therefore requires that we deceive the citizens about whether the rules are definitive of what to do in individual circumstances. Second, Green ignores the fact that if we hide this discretion, then we are deceiving citizens a second time, by deceiving them about the consequences of violating a rule. If avoiding punishing the innocent requires us to abandon the special part, so be it. It is a price we have to pay, even if it 'scares [you] silly'.[87]

3.4 Inevitable proxy crimes

Despite our defence of standards over rules, we recognize that there may be cases in which a legislature chooses to reject our arguments. Rather than dismissing these enactments of proxy crimes as possibly immoral, we believe that it may be better to 'get real' and give some guidance to legislatures about how and when proxy crimes should be enacted.

---

[85] Alexander and Ferzan, with Morse, *Crime and Culpability*, 314.
[86] Green, 'Review Essay'.
[87] Ibid.

3.4.1 *Recognizing the alternatives*

The first question is whether there is some sort of halfway house between a broad standard and an over-inclusive rule. We wish to introduce four methods for getting a large portion of the benefits of rules in a standards-based system.

The first method for achieving rule-like precision in a standards-based world is to move beyond the criminal law. The government has a tremendous array of resources that stop short of the criminal sanction. To the extent the war against drunk driving has been successful, it has not been so solely because of enforcement; it has also achieved success by changing the social norms. It is simply no longer acceptable to the degree that it once was to drink and to drive. Indeed, the government's ability to create and to reinforce social norms will also indirectly achieve the benefits sought by the criminal law. If public service announcements make clear the risks inherent in any given activity, any given actor will be (1) less likely to underestimate the risk and (2) less able to justify the risk he recognizes.

A second method is to allow a legislature to place 'commentaries' within the criminal code.[88] This would allow the legislature to elaborate on when a harm is 'serious', or to specify when a particular reason for acting is 'evil' as opposed to 'anti-social'. The commentaries could also inform citizens that certain 'personal considerations' may be valued, such as the liberty interests we all enjoy by driving instead of using public transportation, biking, or walking. These commentaries, when applicable, could also be read to juries. A significant benefit of these commentaries is that they can serve to counteract the possibility of over-deterrence. The commentaries can inform both actors and juries that certain conduct is presumptively acceptable, thus giving actors guidance that, for example, driving at 55 miles an hour is generally safe driving in the absence of extenuating conditions.

Another key advantage of the use of commentaries is that they require the legislature to 'fit' its commentaries within our framework. This prevents any given legislature from disrupting an entire statutory scheme by introducing new terminology or providing a punishment for one type of conduct that is too harsh relative to the rest of the statutory scheme. It allows legislatures to achieve some degree of specificity without creating the gap inherent in rules—the norm is still a standard, not a rule—but the commentary provides *guidance* and *structure* for decision making.

A third method also seeks to strike a balance between providing the determinacy of clear rules and the justice of standards. Legislatures could specify legally protected interests, but insist upon a mental state of recklessness as to those interests. A crime that specifies a legally protected interest and requires the mental state of recklessness (as we have refined it) will simply be an instance of the insufficient concern that our

---

[88] PH Robinson and MT Cahill, 'The Accelerating Degradation of Criminal Codes' (2005) 56 *Hastings Law Journal* 633, 654–5.

Golden Rule omnibus standard prohibits. It will not be an imperfect approximation. That is, if the law states that it is criminal to 'recklessly create a risk of death', this crime is merely a specific instance of the more global prohibition on consciously and unjustifiably risking harm to legally protested interests, an instance where the type of legally protected interest is specified.

The enactment of these types of crimes, which are delineated simply by the type of legally protected interest, does not produce over-inclusive rules. However, these types of crimes are problematic to the extent that they raise the possibility that multiple crimes may be charged for the same conduct. They also raise the possibility that no crime will be charged for conduct that does not recklessly risk any specific harm but that recklessly risks a basketful of such harms. That is, they have the potential to resurrect the problems inherent in our current system of individuating offences. But what these 'proxies' do *not* do is create over-inclusive crimes.

Finally, the legislature could consider using presumptions. For instance, in defining murder as 'extreme indifference to human life', the Model Penal Code further clarifies that this indifference is presumed when the actor is taking part in one of several enumerated felonies.[89] If the use of a presumption is only permissive—for example, one that allows the jury to infer extreme indifference from participation in what is now a discrete felony—then such a presumption would function in the same way that code commentaries would.

Could a jurisdiction go beyond permissive presumptions and employ a mandatory rebuttable presumption, and would such a presumption be constitutional? A mandatory rebuttable presumption would state a *rule*, but would permit the actor to show, by some burden of proof, that the underlying justification for the rule did not apply. Given that an actor who then violates the rule would have to have good reason—that is, show that she was epistemically privileged or the like—there is some merit in such a rebuttable rule. Such an approach is also better than just enacting an irrebuttable rule, one that would completely bar the actor from showing that she does not fall within the rule's justification.[90]

One substantial hurdle to such a burden-shifting approach is the current state of constitutional law. Because the presumption would undoubtedly apply to an element of our offence (we have no defences per se), such a presumption violates the requirement that the government prove every element beyond a reasonable doubt. Ironically, although such an approach would create greater fairness, it is currently considered unconstitutional. In contrast, a rule that is simply over-inclusive—without any ability to rebut its applicability—would undoubtedly pass constitutional muster.[91]

---

[89]   Model Penal Code, s 210.2 (1985).

[90]   PH Robinson and MT Cahill, *Law Without Justice: Why Criminal Law Doesn't Give People What They Deserve* (Oxford: Oxford University Press, 2009), 205–09.

[91]   Ibid 208–9 (noting this difficulty).

3.4.2 *Enacting proxy crimes*

In translating our idealized code into a practical one, we recognize that a legislature might wish to enact 'proxy crimes'. A proxy crime is a particular instance of conduct, commission of which frequently (but not always) risks unjustifiably harming a legally protected interest. But because any given instance of the conduct proscribed by proxy crimes may or may not impose an unjustifiable risk of harm on legally protected interests, proxy crimes will ordinarily be over-inclusive. That is, they will sweep in the non-culpable actors along with the culpable.[92]

We believe the proxy crimes that a legislature is justified in enacting are precisely those crimes that give actors significant epistemic guidance. In particular, these rules may be justified in circumstances where agents are particularly prone to rationality errors.[93]

One area in which we may find 'proxies' to be necessary is where there are questions of maturity and capacity. For instance, at some point, a teenage girl becomes sufficiently rational to consent to sexual intercourse. But this point varies from girl to girl. Here, miscalculations may occur on both sides of the equation—some 15-year-olds are sufficiently mature that they should be able to determine for themselves whether to consent to intercourse, but many may not be. The putative defendant, who has every incentive to *want* to believe that his future partner is competent, may not adequately take opposing information into account. Because we know that these mistakes are bound to happen, a nice clear cut-off point—a set age restriction—gives epistemic guidance to actors who may greatly need it.

Clearly, under these conditions, the criminal law should require recklessness as to this new material element. Indeed, since age is a mere proxy for consent, and we only wish to punish those actors who risk having unconsented-to intercourse, it would make no sense whatsoever to punish the actor who honestly believes the victim was at the appropriate age (and also consenting).

Of course, allowing for any proxy crimes returns us to where we began. What should we do with a person who does not culpably risk the harm, but who does violate the proxy crime?[94]

---

[92] Our usage of 'proxy crime' for these purposes does not cover those cases in which the crime is enacted for the benefit of law enforcement and no (or nearly no) instance of the offence risks a legally protected interest—eg possession of burglar's tools. See MS Moore, *Placing Blame* (Oxford: Oxford University Press, 1997), 784 ('The problem with ... "wrongs by proxy" is that [they] give liberty a strong kick in the teeth right at the start. Such an argument does not even pretend that there is any culpability or wrongdoing for which it would urge punishment; rather, punishment of a non-wrongful, non-culpable action is used for purely preventive ends.').

[93] Husak, *Overcriminalization*, 38–9.

[94] Antony Duff favours punishing these individuals because they manifest 'civic arrogance', or, one might also say, 'epistemic arrogance'. RA Duff, 'Crime, Prohibition, and Punishment' (2002) 19 *Journal of Applied Philosophy* 97. But Duff's view—that we should punish actors because they do not *know* the rule does not apply—simply ignores the fact that in some cases actors know exactly this fact. Moreover, Duff cannot explain why this arrogance leads to punishment for the underlying offence

We advocate a modified rule-sensitive particularist view. If the actor does not risk harm to a legally protected interest, the question is whether he has still shown sufficient respect for the 'rule of law'. Here, the jury could be asked whether the actor, knowing that he was violating the law (the proxy crime), gave sufficient weight to (1) the chance that he might be wrong about the girl's capacity to consent, and thus, enough weight to the risk of epistemic error, and (2) gave sufficient weight to the value of having rules decide these cases for all citizens (that is, to the risk that he is undermining the moral message of the law). (The first condition, that the actor give sufficient weight to the possibility of error, is really tantamount to requiring an actor, aware of the proxy crime, to treat what he believes is a slight risk that the girl is underage as if it were a greater risk when he weighs risks of harm against his reasons for acting.) If taking these values into account, his action was still justified—for example, in this particular case, he had excellent reasons to believe the girl had the capacity to consent—then he is not culpable for violating the proxy crime. On the other hand, if he is epistemically arrogant without good reason—she was very mature and gave valid consent, but he had no good reason to believe this and gave no weight to the proxy crime's existence—then he may be punished for his failure to show sufficient respect to rule of law values.

Of course, this does not completely resolve the problem. The actor may honestly believe that the woman (girl?) with whom he is about to have intercourse is sufficiently mature to consent, no matter what the statutory required age. And the actor may be wrong. He may be wrong because he is weak-willed, foolish, or simply aroused and not thinking straight. Whatever the case may be, these errors that cause him to miscalculate may not be culpable in themselves, and he may not then be culpable for taking the risk of miscalculation. The actor may not be culpable for the underlying rape—his estimate of the risk of non-consent was sufficiently low—and he may not be culpable for disrespecting the law. He may simply be a fool. But it is not the criminal law's purpose to punish rationality errors or character flaws per se.

Because we advocate 'undermining the rule of law' as its own legally protected interest, there are two related questions we should address here. These are the questions of how to deal with exculpatory and inculpatory mistakes of law.

First, imagine that Alex intends to have sexual intercourse with Betty, and he accurately assesses that she is sufficiently mature to consent. As it turns out, a proxy crime has been enacted that prohibits females under 17 from consenting to

---

instead of punishment for the actors' arrogance itself. See also Husak (ibid) 107–12 (critiquing Duff's approach). We do not believe that Duff's (2007) response meets the objection, as he continues to claim that an individual 'must be sentenced on the basis of what is proved against him'. See Duff, *Answering for Crime*, 171, n 94. We believe the approach set forth below speaks to the root of the actor's blameworthiness—his dismissal of rule of law values. This is probably not that different from Duff's view that individuals should respect laws in the name of 'mutual civic assurance and recognition', except that we would not punish those individuals who are correct that their conduct does not violate the underlying justification for the offence and who have shown sufficient respect for the rule of law.

intercourse. Betty is 16. Alex, however, does not know about the existence of the proxy crime.

In our view, if the actor does not know about the proxy crime's existence, then he should be entitled to a mistake of law excuse. Indeed, this 'excuse' is built into the nature of the legally protected interest. Because Alex does not culpably risk undermining 'the rule of law', he *should* not be punished for refusing to follow the guidance of a proxy crime of which he was unaware.

On the other side of the coin, allowing the value of the rule of law itself to be a legally protected interest may allow us to punish actors who until this point have been beyond the law's reach—those who commit legally impossible attempts. A legally impossible attempt is an action that the actor believes violates the law, but does not do so because there is no law of the sort that he believes he is violating. Under our idealized regime, a legally impossible attempter would be someone who believes that he is risking harm to a legally protected interest (for an insufficient reason), but the interest is not a legally protected one (dancing on Sundays, perhaps?). With the addition of proxy crimes, one can imagine an actor who believes that it is an offence to have intercourse with a 16-year-old, only to find that (1) she is sufficiently mature to consent, and (2) the proxy age is set at 15. If the actor chooses—indeed perhaps desires—to break the law (but to have consensual sexual intercourse), should anything be done with such an actor?

We believe that once we deem 'undermining the rule of law' to be a legally recognized harm, then such an actor is culpable. Moreover, because the seriousness of the offence is not tied to the imagined harm but to the specific value of the rule of law, the same weight will apply to all potential scofflaws. Likewise, our 'epistemically arrogant' actor, who ignores the proxy crime's bright line of 16 because he believes he can ascertain valid consent in a 15-year-old girl, if he is not reckless as to non-consent, will be guilty, not at the level of one who is so reckless, but at the uniform level set for all scofflaws.

4 CONCLUSION

No doubt, we have provided you with more questions than answers. At the implementation level, the task is daunting. The current criminal law is an agglomeration of retributive punishment, preventive detention, rules for guidance, rules to constrain abuse of power, accommodations to the limits of criminal procedure, and pure politics.

Perhaps no ideal theory is possible in the real world. However, we believe that ideal theory is the place to start. We at least ought to begin with the question, what would the criminal law look like if we were to give defendants as much and no more than what they deserve.

From this perspective, we should then figure out which concessions are truly necessary to make. Although we may be wary of legality concerns, when these concerns are held up to the light, the worries appear to be misplaced. As Peter Westen has shown, we do not need rules (as opposed to broad standards) to serve the purposes of predictability or equal treatment.[95] As Westen persuasively argues, a vague term is potentially quite broad, so an actor can hardly claim that he did not have *notice* that the term applied. Rather, the concern is the concern that underlies the 'rule of lenity'—the concern that actors not be punished unless 'it can confidently be said the political community believes [the actor] is deserving of it'.[96] And according to Westen, arbitrary and discriminatory enforcement raise equal protection or liberty concerns—not due process (fair notice) ones.[97] The point is that before we contort our criminal law principles to serve other values, we ought to be sure that we have to do so.

The special part may be inevitable when one makes concessions to the real world. But we ought not to start with the special part. We ought to look beyond it to where criminal law could be if it held true to the values that underlie it.

---

[95] P Westen, 'Two Rules of Legality in Criminal Law' (2007) 26 *Law and Philosophy* 293.
[96] Ibid 293.
[97] Ibid.

13

JUST PREVENTION: PREVENTIVE RATIONALES AND THE LIMITS OF THE CRIMINAL LAW

ANDREW ASHWORTH AND
LUCIA ZEDNER[*]

WE start from the assumption that one of the roles of the state is to take measures to prevent, or at least significantly to reduce, the incidence of harm. We also assume that the prevention of harm is one of the rationales of the criminal law. In this chapter

[*] The authors are grateful to the editors and to participants at the Rutgers Conference on the Philosophical Foundations of the Criminal Law (especially Adil Haque and Paul Roberts) for their comments on a previous draft, and to the AHRC for the award of a grant for a three-year study of 'Preventive Justice' (ID: AH/H015655/1).

we raise a number of questions about these assumptions and their implications. To what extent should harm prevention be one of the criminal law's functions? If it should, in what ways may the criminal law properly carry out this function? What limiting principles to the pursuit of prevention through the criminal law should be recognized? In particular, how far may the criminal law properly go in the direction of criminalizing the creation of a risk of harm, as distinct from the causing of harm? If and insofar as the limiting principles are found too restrictive by governments pursuing preventive goals, to what extent is it proper to invoke other coercive mechanisms closely related to the criminal law? In considering these questions, we will touch on principles of criminalization, on issues relating to the definition of criminal offences, on the significance of the criminal process and criminal procedure, and on the relevance of principles of punishment. First, however, let us examine some general assumptions about the preventive role of the state.

1 THE STATE'S ROLE IN THE PREVENTION OF HARM

What are the grounds for and extent of the state obligation to take steps to prevent harm and to protect citizens from it? A full answer to this question would require a lengthy disquisition on political theory. Much has been written on the grounds for, and limits of, the political obligations of individual citizens; rather less has been written on the state's duties to individuals. One argument is that voters consent, actually or tacitly, to the powers of the state by virtue of their involvement in the democratic process. Another well-established account posits a hypothetical contract as the basis of political obligation, inasmuch as citizens are deemed to have agreed to the authority of the state in exchange for the state assuring various benefits to citizens. This leads towards a further argument that the citizen's obligations to the state stem from the acceptance, or at least from the positive seeking, of benefits provided by the state.[1] Other accounts suggest that political obligations are grounded in arguments of gratitude, fair play to others, or respect for authority. All these are in-principle arguments, leaving it to be determined how much liberty should be sacrificed for what degree of increased security—for one of the state's central undertakings is to prevent people from mistreating others, and to safeguard good order and the basic means by which citizens can live good lives. We look to the state for

---

[1] These are brief summaries of sophisticated arguments, elaborated and assessed eg by D Knowles, *Political Obligation: a Critical Introduction* (Abingdon: Routledge, 2010), chs 7, 8, and 9.

this kind of protection, not least because the alternative would be for individuals (victims, their families, protection groups) to 'deal with' those who harm others and disturb the peace, and that might tend towards anarchy. Thus one of the criminal justice system's distinctive roles is to perform a kind of 'displacement function', taking measures to deal with these disruptions as a way of pre-empting vigilantism and private vengeance.[2] Accepting this rationale does not, however, indicate the limits to which the state can legitimately go in the exercise of its preventive function.

Given the problems of identifying limits, let us focus first on what may fairly be taken to be the core. Any account of the state's obligations towards citizens ought surely to include the obligation to take all reasonable measures to protect people from death or serious physical harm.[3] This suggests the provision of public health services to identify and treat serious medical conditions; regulation of activities such as driving on the roads to ensure maximum coordination as well as safety; and the prevention of physical harm through a mixture of regulation (health and safety, for example), private law (a system of tort law), and criminal law. Much more could be said on all these issues, but the important point is that in pursuing this preventive aim the state has a wide range of techniques from which to choose; and that, if law is the chosen technique, there are at least three main possibilities—private law, regulatory law, and criminal law. Resort to the criminal law, rather than another possible approach, is a decision that therefore needs to be justified independently.

Let us move to a central case, in an endeavour to clarify the analysis. When the law criminalizes culpable homicide (assuming this to be an incontestable category, though that is for discussion), it does so partly because these are egregious wrongs that call for censure and punishment of those responsible, and partly to prevent or reduce their occurrence. These preventive and punitive rationales are intertwined. It makes no sense to suggest that the criminal law's purpose is simply to declare the most serious wrongs and to provide for the conviction and punishment of those who commit them, as if the prevention of such wrongs is not also part of the rationale. Surely it is because these wrongs are so serious that it is important to reduce the frequency of their occurrence: the 'backward-looking' justification for making these wrongs punishable must imply a 'forward-looking' concern that fewer such wrongs should occur in the future. Thus, even the purest retributivists must recognize that a concomitant of the decision to declare certain conduct to be a serious wrong and therefore criminal is a commitment to reduce the frequency of that conduct. What of those consequentialists who regard the prevention of serious harm as the primary

---

[2] J Gardner, 'Crime: In Proportion and in Perspective', in A Ashworth and M Wasik (eds), *The Fundamentals of Sentencing Theory* (Oxford: Oxford University Press, 1998), 31–52; N MacCormick and D Garland, 'Sovereign States and Vengeful Victims: The Problem of the Right to Punish', in Ashworth and Wasik (eds), *The Fundamentals of Sentencing Theory*, 11–29.

[3] L Lazarus, 'Mapping the Right to Security', in B Goold and L Lazarus (eds), *Security and Human Rights* (Oxford: Hart Publishing, 2007), 325–46; RA Duff, *Answering for Crime: Responsibility and Liability in the Criminal Law* (Oxford: Hart Publishing, 2007), 87.

rationale of the criminal law? In principle, as most systems of criminal law recognize, pursuit of that rationale should be limited by doctrines that demonstrate respect for individuals as moral agents. Thus the preventive purpose should only be pursued subject to the importance of defining the wrong clearly (so that people know what they should avoid) and of making provision for a fault element in liability and for proportionality of punishment. In this way, for the most serious offences, it may be claimed that the preventive and punitive rationales of the criminal law go hand in hand—although the emphasis can differ, as we shall see below.[4]

The position is somewhat different for other parts of the criminal law, where it is not the seriousness of the wrongdoing that bolsters the case for criminalization but rather that of coordination and regulation of activities, whether they be in the spheres of finance, industry, commerce, road traffic, transportation, or whatever. The coordination function ensures a common approach—for example, driving on a particular side of the road, or stopping at a red traffic light. The regulatory function is more about arranging the activity so as to minimize danger, to ensure fair practices, and so forth. The criminal law tends to play a reinforcement role in this sphere, with a number of offences created to ensure that significant departures from the regulatory regime can result in conviction and sentence. The arguments for and against criminalization are rather different here, and are sometimes intermixed with arguments about having a lower level of sanctions and dispensing with the need for proof of fault (strict liability). In the context of this chapter, however, the point is that the punitive and preventive rationales may both have a role here too. The preventive rationale is clear, since one purpose of creating criminal offences in this field is to add a further preventive thrust to the regulatory regime. The punitive rationale for the regulatory use of the criminal law is much more controversial, at least unless proof of fault is required and the sanction is not disproportionate; but we will say no more about those controversies,[5] and instead direct our attention to the contours of the criminal law in its preventive function. In what follows, we are concerned not with the justifications for criminalizing a particular form of wrongdoing or the causing of a particular kind of harm, but rather with the justifications for and proper limitations on going beyond the criminal law paradigm for preventive purposes.

---

[4] The term 'prevention' may be regarded as too uncompromising, inasmuch as it suggests the total elimination of the wrongdoing or risk involved. Reductivism, an uglier and less conventional term used by Nigel Walker in his many writings (eg N Walker, *Sentencing in a Rational Society* (Harmondsworth: Allen Lane, 1972), 18), is a more accurate rendition of the realistic objective of preventive policies. We persist here with 'prevention', but in the more attenuated sense of 'reductivism'. What remains unresolved, of course, is the degree to which preventive policies should be pursued: can one say more than 'reduction to a tolerable level'?

[5] For recent examination of the issues, see AP Simester (ed), *Appraising Strict Liability* (Oxford: Oxford University Press, 2005).

2 Examining the Preventive Function of the Criminal Law

2.1 The criminal law paradigm

We begin by identifying the paradigmatic or ideal form of a criminal offence—an offence that penalizes the causing of a certain type or degree of harm with a particular level of culpability, usually intention or recklessness. This is not to assume that most offences in most criminal law systems conform to this paradigm: indeed, that would certainly be untrue of English law, where a majority of criminal offences impose strict liability. But even in the English system, the harm plus culpability model predominates for serious offences. We adopt this as our paradigm, in order to demonstrate how pursuit of the preventive function leads to different instances of divergence from it.

2.2 Inchoate offences

Where a wrong is so egregious as to justify criminalization, does it follow that there is an equally strong case for creating inchoate offences around the substantive crime? Most legal systems seem to operate on this premise, insofar as they have general inchoate offences that attach automatically to every new crime. Thus the Model Penal Code treats inchoate offences as being of general applicability, so that offences of attempt, conspiracy, and solicitation attach to every substantive crime. Similarly, English law has operated for many years on a presumption that the inchoate offences of attempt, conspiracy, and incitement apply to all substantive crimes, although the offence of incitement has recently been replaced.[6] Thus it appears that in common law systems the inchoate offences belong to the general part of the criminal law, and consequently there is a presumption that the relevant inchoate offences attach to every substantive crime. The strength of this presumption must derive from the strength of the justifications for inchoate offences—typically attempts and conspiracy, but in some legal systems including other offences. One argument is that the punitive rationale should apply to people who have sufficiently committed themselves to the wrong, even though they have not yet caused it: they are equally or substantially or sufficiently culpable and therefore deserve censure and punishment. This argument assumes that the conduct requirement and the fault requirement for conspiracy and for an attempt (actus reus and mens rea) are satisfactorily defined, issues that will

---

[6] Incitement was abolished in favour of three new (and wide-ranging) offences of encouraging or assisting crime, introduced by Part 2 of the Serious Crime Act 2007. For a brief assessment, see A Ashworth, *Principles of Criminal Law* (6th edn; Oxford: Oxford University Press, 2009), 458–63.

not be examined here.[7] Another argument is that the inchoate offences are a justified extension of the preventive principle: if the substantive offence is there partly to prevent such wrongs, the inchoate offences strengthen that preventive function by enabling the police and others to intervene in situations where a person is on the way to perpetrating the wrong itself. Just as the punitive rationale makes little sense without a commitment to prevention, so it also makes little sense for the criminal law to wait until the wrong has been done before defining the conduct as an offence. A further argument is that the rationale lies in the dangerousness manifested by a person who demonstrates an intention and willingness to commit the substantive wrong: this danger justifies early intervention. Our interest here lies not in examining the strengths and weaknesses of those rationales, but simply in indicating the underlying reasons for the presumption of inchoate liability that appears to operate throughout the common law world.

2.3 Substantive offences defined in the inchoate mode

Thus far we have assumed that the structure of substantive crimes is in the paradigmatic form—harm plus culpability. This paradigm is challenged by a growing group of substantive crimes defined in the inchoate mode. The US federal bribery statute makes it criminal to 'give, offer or promise' or to 'demand, seek, receive or accept' a benefit in given circumstances.[8] A recent English example is the Fraud Act 2006, section 2 of which criminalizes the dishonest making of a false representation with intent to make a gain or cause a loss. This replaced the traditional result-crime of obtaining property by deception, and the distinguishing feature of the new offence is that there is no need for the prosecutor to prove any 'obtaining': no gain or loss needs to be made, no result achieved.[9] Simply the dishonest making of a false representation, with the intention to cause loss or gain, is sufficient. Such a formulation may have advantages for the prosecution (less has to be proved),[10] and may be perfectly consistent with the preventive rationale. But the style of drafting, in the inchoate mode, means that the substantive offence already occupies the space that the offence of attempt would have occupied in relation to the former offence of obtaining property by deception. Yet in accordance with the general presumption,

---

[7] See the masterly treatment by RA Duff, *Criminal Attempts* (Oxford: Oxford University Press, 1996).

[8] See 18 USC, para 201, discussed by SP Green, *Lying, Cheating and Stealing: a Moral Theory of White-Collar Crime* (Oxford: Oxford University Press, 2006), ch 16. See also the bribery offence in American Law Institute, Model Penal Code, s 224.8.

[9] This form of definition was used as long ago as 1872 in the US federal statute on mail fraud: Green, ibid 158–9.

[10] See Duff, *Criminal Attempts*, 56; also A Ashworth, 'Defining Criminal Offences without Harm', in P Smith (ed), *Criminal Law: Essays in Honour of JC Smith* (London: Butterworths, 1987).

the law of inchoate offences applies automatically to offences defined in this mode, as in other modes. The effect is that, just as the law of inchoate offences casts a preventive circle around all result crimes, here the law of inchoate offences casts a preventive circle around offences that have already been defined in the inchoate mode, thereby producing a much broader and more extensive preventive domain.

Thus, by operation of the general presumption, the criminal law expands beyond its normal boundary so as to extend to some fairly remote conduct, penalizing an early preparatory act such as attempting to make a false representation (for example, by composing a false email and trying unsuccessfully to send it to a mail-list). Yet the rationale for the general presumption of inchoate liability does not apply where the substantive offence is already defined in the inchoate mode, since an offence so defined has already expanded the preventive circle. This obvious counter-argument has not been adopted, and seems to have little purchase with law reform bodies or legislatures, perhaps because there are hardly any prosecutions for such offences. But it appears that the presumption of (further) inchoate liability applies to every substantive offence, thereby producing some doubly inchoate and doubly preventive extensions of the criminal law. No separate justification has been offered for these over-extensions of the criminal law, and we would argue that they are unprincipled.

2.4 Preparatory crimes

Rather more deliberate extensions of the normal reach of the criminal law take place when legislatures enact what may be termed preparatory crimes, those which are created in the special part of the criminal law, outside and beyond the boundaries of inchoate offences. Thus, whereas the offence of attempt penalizes a person who takes a substantial step towards the substantive crime or does a more than merely preparatory act, preparatory offences are much more remote from the harm of the substantive offence. An example is section 5 of the Terrorism Act 2006 (UK), which makes it an offence for a person, with intent to commit an act of terrorism or to assist another to do so, to engage in 'any conduct in preparation for giving effect to' that intention. The conduct may therefore be perfectly normal and non-dangerous of itself—buying a map, a railway timetable or a computer manual may fulfil the actus reus[11]—and well short of the minimum required for a criminal attempt ('substantial step' or 'more than merely preparatory act'). The outcome is a kind of pre-inchoate liability that depends either on a subjectivist rationale that a person who does preparatory acts with the intention of committing a substantive crime is sufficiently culpable to be held criminally liable at that stage, on account of the level of culpability, or on a claim that that such a person has manifested sufficient social danger to justify the

---

[11] Examples cited by V Tadros, 'Justice and Terrorism' (2007) 10 *New Criminal Law Review* 658, 672, discussing a similar offence in s 58 of the Terrorism Act 2000 (UK).

intervention of the criminal law.[12] There are major objections to this further extension of criminal liability. It denies people the opportunity to change their mind (even
if that change stems only from a lack of courage) and it gives undue power to the
police, since the conduct itself may be entirely neutral, so that questioning the person about intentions (in England, with a limited right of silence) becomes central to
the investigation. These objections must be convincingly rebutted if this extension
of the criminal law beyond the normal ambit of inchoate offences is to be justified.

If, contrary to our argument, the criminalization of preparatory conduct of this
kind is justifiable, what is the proper basis for sentencing? Should the sentence be
limited by the conduct proved, or should it rather take account of the offender's
intended goals? The purpose of the offence is surely preventive, allowing the criminal justice system to intervene before harm has been done. The offender's intent is
therefore of the essence. The sentence for a criminal attempt ought to be determined
chiefly by the seriousness of the crime attempted, and then discounted by reference to the distance between the offender's conduct and the substantive offence.[13]
Similarly, the sentence for a preparatory offence ought to be determined by reference to the crime intended by the offender, but then significantly discounted by
reference to the fact that only an early stage of preparation has been reached. This
discount acknowledges the autonomy of the individual by recognizing the possibility of a change of mind.

2.5 Crimes of possession

Objections based on undue police power and on allowing time for the defendant
to change his mind may be raised against another species of preparatory crime:
offences of possession. Two particular types of possession offence pose further problems. First, there are offences of possessing articles which are regarded as dangerous
in themselves, perhaps because they indicate the possessor's intention to put them to
a criminal use (counterfeiting articles, burglary tools, and unlicensed guns), or perhaps because they create the risk of deliberate, or indeed careless, use by others that
might result in harm (unlicensed guns not properly secured). Because the articles
are regarded as giving rise to a risk of harm in one of these ways, possession is typically criminalized without the need for the prosecutor to prove an intention to carry
out that criminal use. This is a major difference from the inchoate and preparatory

---

[12] B McSherry, 'Expanding the Boundaries of Inchoate Crimes: the Growing Reliance on
Preparatory Offences', in B McSherry, A Norrie, and S Bronitt (eds), *Regulating Deviance* (Oxford:
Hart, 2008).

[13] A Ashworth, 'Criminal Attempts and the Role of Resulting Harm under the Code, and in the
Common Law' (1988) 19 *Rutgers Law Journal* 725, introducing the distinction between 'complete' and
'incomplete' attempts; and Duff, *Criminal Attempts*, ch 4.

offences discussed so far, for which intention must usually be proved, and it raises deep questions of principle of two kinds. Insofar as the danger is that the possessor may use the prohibited article(s) to cause harm, there are significant concerns about the presumption of innocence if the prosecution is not required to prove intent and/ or the burden of proving 'reasonable excuse' is cast on the defendant. Even more troublesome is criminalizing the possessor on the basis of the risk that someone else may misuse the prohibited article. In principle this is an unsatisfactory basis on which to criminalize anyone, unless the possessor can be regarded as having a sufficient 'normative involvement' in the other person's misuse of the article—for example, by way of encouragement or assistance of that other.[14] Duff observes that the question of 'how far a polity can justifiably demand that its citizens constrain their own otherwise lawful conduct because of a risk that others might take advantage of it, or be encouraged or enabled by it, to commit crimes' is not susceptible of an easy or general answer.[15] The law of complicity deals with some of those 'normatively involved' in the conduct of others. Beyond that the question is whether the criminal law should penalize a failure to take care of articles so as to prevent other people from taking them and misusing them, as it does when penalizing the unlawful possession of firearms. The argument is presumably that a firearm has such a high potential to inflict serious harm that this justifies negligence liability for failure to register guns and to keep them under appropriate guard. Whether this can justify strict liability, with significant prison sentences as the result, is open to grave doubt.[16]

Second, there are offences of possessing ordinary (usually innocent) articles with a further intention of committing a wrong, such as a crime or terrorist act. An example is provided by section 16(2) of the Terrorism Act 2000 (UK), which makes it an offence for a person to possess money or other property where the person 'intends that it be used . . . for the purposes of terrorism'. The property possessed may be innocent (for example, money), and so, as with the preparatory offences discussed above,[17] the focus of the offence is upon the required fault. The further intention (the intention to use the money for the purposes of terrorism) is part of the definition of the offence—unlike possession offences of the first kind identified above. However, it is not the only fault element specified: section 16(2) also penalizes a person who 'has reasonable cause to suspect' that the money may (ultimately) be used for terrorist purposes, presumably by someone else. Given that the article possessed may be innocent this is a significant departure from the normal approach and raises deep questions of principle. Dubber argues that possession offences defy 'traditional categories and principles of criminal law, they are paradigmatic of the

---

[14] AP Simester and A von Hirsch, 'Remote Harms and Non-Constitutive Crimes' (2009) 28 *Criminal Justice Ethics* 89, 98–102.

[15] RA Duff, 'Criminalizing Endangerment', in RA Duff and SP Green (eds), *Defining Crimes: Essays on the Special Part of the Criminal Law* (Oxford: Oxford University Press, 2005), 64.

[16] Criminal Justice Act 2003 (UK), s 287.

[17] See the offence contrary to s 5 of the Terrorism Act 2006 (above, n 11).

Police Model of the criminal process, which regards criminal law not as an institution for the regulation of interpersonal conflict but as an administrative mechanism for the enforcement of state authority'.[18] Although Dubber may well be right that possession offences are not readily integrated within the established parameters of the criminal law, it remains to be considered whether such offences are no more than the exercise of the state's police power, or whether any principled basis can found for these offences within the parameters of preventive justice. Here we have identified two objections of principle: first, that offences of possession *tout court* seem inconsistent with normal principles of imputation in the criminal law; second, that offences of possession that require proof of intention are open to objection as mere preparatory offences, particularly if extended to those who merely have 'reasonable cause to suspect' the further use of the article by another person.

2.6 Offences of risk creation

In sketching preventive forms of criminal law, we have thus far considered two forms of substantive criminal offence (result-crimes and crimes defined in an inchoate mode) and two forms of preparatory offence (the inchoate offences and pre-inchoate offences including crimes of possession). Some of these offences could be interpreted as seeking to prevent harm by penalizing risk creation: the attempter creates a risk of the harm prohibited by the substantive offence, as does the fraudster who makes a false representation in order to cause gain (a substantive offence defined in the inchoate mode), the person who does a preparatory act with a terrorist intent, and the person who possesses an offensive weapon in public. What has traditionally characterized inchoate offences is the general insistence on proof of intent. In common law theory a high level of culpability is thought appropriate for both inchoate offences and complicity (usually intent or actual knowledge). The foundations of this position appear to lie in a mixture of 'ordinary language', common intuitions, and a belief that the culpability requirement should be higher as the offences become more remote from the actual wrongdoing and infliction of harm,[19] although Duff argues that attempts should require intention since they are a form of 'attack.'[20]

As noted in the foregoing paragraphs, the requirement of intent is being diluted in various ways and contexts, so that many crimes of possession require no further intent, or at least only 'reasonable cause to suspect' the use of the article, for example, for terrorist purposes. These tendencies suggest a transition from inchoate liability

---

[18] MD Dubber, 'The Possession Paradigm: The Special Part and the Police Model of the Criminal Process', in Duff and Green (eds), *Defining Crimes*. Available at SSRN: <http://ssrn.com/abstract=529882>, at 1.

[19] Duff, *Criminal Attempts*, 30–1; he rightly criticizes the 'ordinary language' argument.

[20] Duff, ibid ch 13.

to risk-based liability. In the present context, we will include within the term 'risk-based liability' any offence that penalizes conduct on the ground of the risk it creates, typically requiring a fault element of recklessness or negligence but sometimes imposing strict liability. Included within this category would be speeding and drunk driving (both of which are penalized because of the risk they create or might create, and which are essentially offences of strict liability), careless driving and dangerous driving (which have a fault element), endangerment of rail passengers, criminal damage to property endangering the life of another, and so forth. The Model Penal Code contains a general offence of 'recklessly engag[ing] in conduct which places or may place another person in danger of death or serious bodily injury',[21] but English law has no such generic offence.

Risk-based liability is chiefly rationalized on grounds of harm prevention. This sometimes appears to be an irresistible goal: but in this section we raise a number of questions about the pursuit of prevention through risk-based crimes. First, since risk is all around us, what special justification exists for invoking the criminal law? Can risk of harm be seen as a form of harm in itself? Second, if the criminal law is to be concerned in penalizing risk creation, on what principles should it do so? Third, what restraining principles ought to be relevant to this enterprise?

In relation to the first question, one possibility is to argue, as Finkelstein does, that 'risk of harm is itself a harm' regardless of outcome, on the grounds that 'imposing a risk of harm on a person may itself be to harm him'.[22] This position diverges from that which argues that 'two individuals who impose precisely the same unjustified risk of harm are in equivalent moral positions, even if one ends up causing a person's death and the other does not', on the ground that whatever the moral foundations of this argument, its legal significance is dubious because 'law is more concerned with harm infliction than with blameworthiness'.[23] The basis for Finkelstein's argument is that individuals have 'a legitimate interest in avoiding unwanted risks' and that 'a person who inflicts a risk of harm on another damages that interest'.[24] An individual exposed to risk of harm is worse off than he would have been if he had not been so exposed, and the reduction in welfare resulting from exposure persists even if the risk does not materialize. Oberdiek also argues in favour of what he terms a 'right against risking', arguing that a person who subjects another to unwanted risks is diminishing that other's autonomy, and that the right against risking is distinct from the right not to be harmed.[25] Both Finkelstein and Oberdiek would therefore

---

[21] American Law Institute, Model Penal Code, s 211.2.

[22] C Finkelstein, 'Is Risk a Harm?' (2003) *University of Pennsylvania Law Review* 151, 963–1001, at 1000 and 998.

[23] Ibid at 988. This claim will not be examined further here, but it is manifestly contestable: compare RA Duff, 'Acting, Trying and Criminal Liability' with A Ashworth, 'Taking the Consequences', both in S Shute, J Gardner and J Horder (eds), *Action and Value in Criminal Law* (Oxford: Oxford University Press, 1993).

[24] Finkelstein, 'Is Risk a Harm?', 966.

[25] J Oberdiek, 'Towards a Right against Risking' (2009) *Law and Philosophy* 28, 367.

support a general offence of reckless endangerment, and indeed offences creating the risk of any harm, the direct causing of which has already passed whatever criminalization test we have. But one might reach the same conclusion on most versions of the harm principle, by arguing that it supplies good reasons for offences not only of causing harm but also of creating the (unjustifiable) risk of harm.

There are, however, difficulties with these approaches to criminalizing risk. One is the danger of double counting, namely that the offender will be held liable both for creating the risk of harm *and* for the eventual outcome harm, which might lead to the offender suffering double punishment.[26] Finkelstein suggests that this difficulty can be overcome by the 'Absorption Thesis' whereby the risk of harm is absorbed into the resulting harm, thus avoiding the danger of double counting.[27] Yet another difficulty is that of infinite regress: if creating the risk of harm is a sufficient ground for imposing criminal liability, why is not creating the risk of a risk of harm, and so on? This suggests the need for a remoteness limitation. Indeed, it leads to a further difficulty that is inherent in discussions of risk: unless the magnitude, probability, and social justifications or reasonableness of the risk are tightly specified, the discussions are likely to remain at a general and unhelpful level.

We therefore turn to the second question identified earlier: if the criminal law is to penalize risk creation, on what principles should it do so? We may assume that the criminal law is the strongest form of official censure of an individual for conduct. It might also be argued that the further we travel from the paradigm of the harm-plus-culpability model of criminal offences the stronger should be the justifications for invoking the criminal law, with its censure and punishment. Three factors should be relevant to the criminalization of risk creation: the magnitude of the harm, the probability of its occurring, and any social justification for, or reasonableness of, the risk-creating conduct. On the first issue, the magnitude of the harm, Husak has argued for a restrictive approach: applying his 'substantial risk' requirement, he argues that 'because the prevention of trivial harms cannot justify state infringements of the right not to be punished, it is apparent that the prevention of trivial risks provides even less of a rationale'.[28] This emphasis on the trivial is perhaps rather tentative, and Duff takes a seemingly stronger approach by arguing: 'only the more serious kinds of endangerment' should be criminalized, including within that category those that create risks of serious harm.[29] He advances two arguments for this restrictive position—first, that 'a luckily harmless act of endangerment is further removed from the harm that it might have caused, but did not cause', and 'is only potentially harmful',

---

[26] Cf the argument in L Alexander and KK Ferzan, *Crime and Culpability* (New York: Cambridge University Press, 2009), that 'purpose and knowledge are simply species of recklessness. Culpability, at bottom, is just about risks and reasons', 41.

[27] Finkelstein, 'Is Risk a Harm?', 993.

[28] D Husak, *Overcriminalization: the Limits of the Criminal Law* (Oxford: Oxford University Press, 2008), 61.

[29] Duff, 'Criminalizing Endangerment', 58.

whereas a failed attack is 'still intrinsically or essentially harmful'; and secondly, that the endangerment must be 'serious enough to merit the coercive attentions of the criminal law, and the various costs that criminalization involves'.[30] This is an appropriately restrictive approach to the question of when to criminalize. It points in the direction of offences of risk creation limited, for example, to 'death or serious injury' (as in the Model Penal Code). It calls into question the definition of dangerous driving in English law, which refers to danger of 'injury to any person or serious damage to property',[31] since the latter is potentially wide.

Turning to the second issue, the probability of the harm occurring, this should interact with the magnitude of the harm. In principle, where the harm risked is a serious one, a relatively low probability of its occurrence might be thought sufficient—especially since, in practice, fine distinctions between levels of actual (and believed) probability may be difficult to assess; on the other hand, where the harm risked is not a serious one, if for some reason it is thought justifiable to criminalize such risk creation,[32] the level of probability required should be high. These stipulations flow from the two arguments advanced by Duff, and accepted in the previous paragraph. The result is to require the creation of a significant risk of serious harm.

The third issue concerns the reasonableness of the conduct, or any social justifications for it. Once again, we turn to Duff for elaboration:

If we act, without justification, in a way that we realise might harm others, when that prospective harm provides a conclusive reason against acting thus, we do wrong; we do wrong *to* those whom we thus endanger. The wrong consists not merely in creating a risk of harm, but in creating an unreasonable or unjustified risk of harm—a risk whose unexcused creation manifests our lack of proper concern for the interests of those we endanger.[33]

There will not be many occasions on which the creation of a significant risk of serious harm can be regarded as reasonable or socially justified. Among the possibilities might be a person who drives dangerously in order to reach hospital more quickly with a dying passenger, or a person who opens a dyke in order to avert a major flood that is expected to cause many fatalities, knowing that there is a risk that one or two people may be drowned as a result of the action. These are justifications that can be accommodated either through defences or through the concept of recklessness; very few such arguments would affect the drafting of an offence of risk creation.

Finally, we examine what restraining principles might be appropriate here, and suggest that two such principles may be put forward for consideration. The first would be that offences of risk creation should require a fault element, which should

---

[30] Ibid 58.

[31] Road Traffic Act 1988 (UK), s 2(3).

[32] Contrary to the submission here that risk creation should only be criminalized if the prospective harm is serious. Cf the lesser (summary) English offence of careless driving, rarely prosecuted in the absence of the actual causing of harm.

[33] Duff, 'Criminalizing Endangerment', 53.

normally be subjective recklessness. In other words, it is argued that the criminal sanction should generally not be applied to risk creation unless the defendant is proved to have known that he or she was creating a significant risk of the particular form of serious harm. Whether, and in what circumstances (risk of death?), the fault element should drop down to gross negligence or even negligence is for discussion: Husak leaves this question open, framing his culpability requirement as 'withhold[ing] liability from persons who create a risk of harm unless they have some degree of culpability for the ultimate harm risked'.[34] There is also the question of various strict liability offences that penalize conduct that presents what Duff calls 'implicit risk', such as speeding and drunk driving. What constitutes an unreasonable risk taken by one person may not do so in other, more competent, hands (speeding would be an obvious example). The law adopts a strongly protective stance here, maintaining that those who exceed speed limits or drive while over the alcohol limit are irrebuttably presumed to create an unacceptable level of risk of serious injury; and, certainly in the case of drunk driving, that there can be no countervailing social value in the conduct. Duff recognizes that not all offences of implicit risk are justifiable: much depends on the nature of the link between the conduct penalized and the harm or wrong that is risked. It is certainly right that individuals should not be able to determine for themselves whether they are safe to drive above the speed limit or after having consumed alcohol above the limit.[35] Accepting that some offences of implicit risk are justified by a sufficient link between the prohibited conduct and the harm risked, the penalty must still be discounted from that applicable to the direct causing of that harm. Thus speeding is treated as a relatively minor matter, whereas driving with excess alcohol can attract a moderate prison sentence because it is thought more likely to cause harm.

This brings us to a further restraining principle, concerning remoteness. In principle the more remote the prohibited conduct is from the causation of the harm, the weaker the argument for criminalization. Also, as argued earlier,[36] it is contrary to principle to justify criminalization by reference to acts that might be performed in the future by the individual concerned or by another person. As for future acts by the individual, the limiting arguments set out in relation to criminal attempts (in section 2.2 above) apply with added force to preparatory offences and to crimes of possession (sections 2.4 and 2.5 above). As for future acts by another person, we adopted the argument of Simester and von Hirsch that criminalization can only be justified in instances where the individual defendant can be said to be 'normatively involved' in the other person's conduct,[37] in line with general principles of agency and individual

---

[34] Husak, *Overcriminalization*, 174.

[35] Duff argues that this is because such a claim would set its maker above fellow citizens: it is 'a denial of civic fellowship' in its failure to 'accept this modest burden as an implication and expression of citizenship'. Duff, *Answering for Crime*, 171.

[36] See text at nn 14–15.

[37] Simester and von Hirsch, 'Remote Harms and Non-Constitutive Crimes'.

autonomy and normal principles of causation to hold that it is not fair to impute the other's action to this defendant. We noted that this would not criminalize those who fail to take precautions against the misuse of articles (such as firearms) by others, and raised the possibility of negligence liability in such situations.

3 THE CRIMINAL LAW AND CIVIL PREVENTIVE ORDERS

The first two sections of this chapter have established that central parts of the criminal law have a preventive as well as a punitive rationale. The criminal law has a distinctive technique, two elements of which are particularly important—first, the element of public censure backed by a sanction that is inherent in conviction; and second, recognition that the process of criminal trial and conviction requires respect for certain fundamental rights. Little needs to be said here about the first element: convicting a person of a crime is an act of public censure of that person for that wrongdoing (no other legal proceeding carries such a strong flavour of public condemnation), and it normally leads to the imposition of a sentence which should be proportionate to the degree of wrongdoing exhibited by the offending behaviour. The justifications for imposing state punishment on persons convicted of crime have been discussed extensively elsewhere, and will not be taken further here.[38]

More significant for the argument of this chapter is the insistence that, before a person can be convicted of a crime, that person is entitled to a fair trial with a range of procedural safeguards. In some countries, such as the United States, Canada, Germany, and South Africa, those safeguards have the status of constitutional guarantees. In other countries, such as the United Kingdom and several other European jurisdictions, the rights are reinforced by protection from the European Convention on Human Rights (ECHR). What is significant about these rights is that they are additional to those declared for civil trials. Thus defendants in civil and criminal trials are entitled to 'a fair and public hearing within a reasonable time by an independent and impartial tribunal'.[39] Defendants in criminal trials have additional rights that typically range from the presumption of innocence, through the right

---

[38] For selected readings, see A von Hirsch, A Ashworth, and J Roberts (eds), *Principled Sentencing: Readings in Theory and Policy* (3rd edn; Oxford: Hart Publishing, 2009). For censure-based theories, see eg RA Duff, *Punishment, Communication and Community* (New York: Oxford University Press, 2001); A von Hirsch and A Ashworth, *Proportionate Sentencing* (Oxford: Oxford University Press, 2005).

[39] These words form part of art 6(1) of the ECHR.

to legal assistance and the right to confront witnesses, to the privilege against self-incrimination, and the principle of equality of arms. As we have argued elsewhere, 'these doctrines are intended to provide fundamental guarantees against arbitrary state conduct and potential misuse of its authority',[40] an authority that is considerable when the public censure of conviction and state punishment are at stake. Similarly, as Duff, Farmer, Marshall, and Tadros argue, the criminal trial is a process of considerable social importance, required to determine accountability and to determine whether the accused should be held criminally liable for certain conduct; but the state must also establish the legitimacy of its own claim to hold the defendant to account, by observing 'norms that require defendants to be treated as citizens of a liberal polity, not as mere subjects of power'.[41]

This discussion of the criminal trial and of safeguards for defendants indicates an important concomitant of the decision to criminalize: if the state decides to create a crime of X-ing, all those persons accused of X-ing are entitled to a criminal trial that observes those additional safeguards, in view of the public censure and liability to punishment that follow conviction in such a trial. All those types of offence that were criticized above as questionable extensions of the criminal law also attract those rights, although the significance of the rights is diminished in jurisdictions that allow elements of strict liability into offence definitions, allow reverse burdens of proof, curtail the right of silence, and so forth. In principle, however, the decision to criminalize is also a decision to recognize that persons accused of that conduct have extra procedural rights that have to be respected. This brings us on to the question of alternative techniques. If a particular government wants to pursue its preventive obligations by seeking to reduce X-ing but concludes that the approach of criminalization–trial–conviction–punishment is unlikely to be effective, what other options exist?

One important corollary of the pursuit of preventive justice is its effect on the boundaries between criminal and civil law. One such boundary is that between criminal sentences and civil commitment of mentally disordered persons. This boundary has been challenged by the increased provision for the detention of so-called 'dangerous' offenders beyond a proportionate sentence, for example by sexual psychopath laws in the United States and by 'imprisonment for public protection' in England.[42] Another important boundary is that between public wrongs, attracting the twin consequences of public censure and state sanction, and wrongs that are deemed only private matters between parties to be remedied by civil suit. In practice

---

[40] A Ashworth and L Zedner 'Preventive Orders: a problem of under-criminalization?', in R A Duff, L Farmer, S Marshall, M Renzo, and V Tadros (eds), *The Boundaries of the Criminal Law* (Oxford: Oxford University Press, 2010).

[41] A Duff, L Farmer, S Marshall, and V Tadros, *The Trial on Trial, volume 3: Towards a Normative Theory of the Criminal Trial* (Oxford: Hart, 2007), 288.

[42] Introduced under the Criminal Justice Act 2003 and as amended by the Criminal Justice and Immigration Act 2008, s 13. L Zedner 'Erring on the side of safety: Risk assessment, expert knowledge, and the criminal court' in I Dennis & GR Sullivan (eds), *Seeking Security* (Oxford: Hart Publishing, 2011).

this boundary has been subject to exceptions and incursions on both sides—strict liability offences and punitive damages being two obvious examples of measures that do not fully accord with criminal or civil law principles. The philosophical and practical challenges of drawing a line between criminal and civil have been the subject of vigorous debate. As preventive measures proliferate, determining an appropriate response to these challenges becomes all the more urgent. To permit coercive preventive measures to be pursued in different legal channels (be they civil, administrative, or contractual) is liable to result in the application of inappropriate or improper standards, principles, and values.[43] Placing a measure in a particular legal form or procedural channel should not be determinative without considering the normatively prior question of whether the choice of form is itself defensible.[44]

One response is to argue that the criminal–civil boundary is so fundamental to the proper allocation of appropriate procedural protections that it must be preserved at all costs. If that is to occur, an immediate task is to determine how or according to what criteria measures should be judged to fall either side of the line. One simple, but not unproblematic, solution would be simply to defer to the framers of the legislation and to ask on which side they intended a measure should be placed.[45] The advantage is that a measure legislatively designated criminal is so treated, and a measure labelled as civil is likewise accepted as such without need for further inquiry or critical reflection. The obvious disadvantage is that such an approach constitutes an open invitation to legislators to opt for the least costly (in terms of both time and resources) procedural path—which will nearly always be to place a measure in the civil channel, even where to do so would be to deny those subject to it the appropriate procedural protections. Uncritical acceptance of legislative labelling would be likely to increase the number of measures that seek punitive purposes or implement coercive conditions under the guise of civil orders, without regard for fundamental rights. Examples from the United States include draconian practices of lifelong imprisonment for those deemed mentally abnormal and dangerous; confiscation of personal property; and permanent deprivation of livelihood.[46] In effect, deference to labels would give governments free rein to impose punishment through the civil channel in the name of prevention.

A second, related but qualified response is to allow the legislative label to stand, other than a case where a court determines that a measure is in fact so punitive as to negative the legislature's intention that it be classed as civil. This second approach

[43] C Steiker, 'Civil and Criminal Divide', in J Dressler (ed), *Encyclopedia of Crime and Justice* (New York: Macmillan Reference, 2002), 165.

[44] L Zedner, 'Seeking Security by Eroding Rights: The Side-Stepping of Due Process', in Goold and Lazarus (eds), *Security and Human Rights* (Oxford: Hart Publishing, 2007).

[45] See *Helvering v Mitchell* (1938) 202 US 391, *Addington v Texas* (1979) 441 US 418, and other cases discussed by SR Klein, 'Redrawing the Criminal–Civil Boundary' (1999) *Buffalo Criminal Law Review* 2, 681–723, at 683.

[46] Ibid 685.

has the merit of avoiding passive acceptance of labels and may deter governments from seeking to subvert the constitutional and human rights protections that adhere to criminal measures by labelling them as civil.[47] For it to be effective, however, requires careful consideration and articulation of what amounts to punitiveness, and it should be acknowledged that the very definition of punishment is open to redefinition by the courts in ways that might render this a less robust safeguard than might at first appear. American case law, for example, has held that deterrence is a legitimate goal of the civil law.[48] As Klein observes: 'If the Court truly means that the government's attempt to deter people from violating criminal prohibitions is a remedial purpose justifying a civil action, then there are few government initiated actions that would be inappropriate candidates for a civil appellation.'[49] In the United States the high-water mark was reached in the case of *Kansas v Hendricks*[50] in which it was concluded that preventive detention for life did not constitute a penalty because the commitment was not intended to punish for past deeds but rather to prevent future risk. As Klein observes: 'If life imprisonment for a crime actually committed requires criminal procedure, life imprisonment for a crime anticipated but not committed surely does as well.'[51]

In Europe, the Strasbourg Court has developed two anti-subversion doctrines in order to prevent precisely this kind of manipulation of the preventive/punitive distinction. It has done this by giving an 'autonomous meaning' to two key terms in the ECHR. It has insisted that the term 'criminal charge' is given an autonomous meaning (that is, its interpretation is within the preserve of the Court, and not domestic laws) with the result that the additional safeguards applicable to criminal proceedings may apply even though the domestic legislation classifies the case as civil, regulatory, or disciplinary.[52] It has also insisted that the term 'penalty' has an autonomous meaning that transcends national labels: a measure may be punitive in effect even if preventive in purpose and is therefore a penalty to which the non-retroactivity rule applies.[53] The logic of this approach is that if resort to civil procedure is no more than a pretext under which to circumvent the strictures of the criminal law, then mere reliance upon the legal form must not be permitted to suffice. Instead it is necessary to interrogate the motives lying behind categorization of a preventive measure as criminal or civil, to challenge the formal ascription of labels, and to develop criteria by which to judge which legal form is appropriate.

[47] Ibid; *United States v Ursery* (1996) 518 US 267.

[48] *Bennis v Michigan* (1996) 516 US 442; Klein, 'Redrawing the Criminal–Civil Boundary', 681–723, at 701.

[49] Ibid 701.

[50] (1997) 521 US 346.

[51] Klein, 'Redrawing the Criminal–Civil Boundary', 708–9.

[52] The leading judgment is *Engel v Netherlands* (1979) 1 EHRR 647, holding that a court must examine whether the process is criminal in substance (eg whether it involves fault, or a significant punishment).

[53] *Welch v UK* (1995) 20 EHRR 247, para 27.

Only then is it safe to invoke the accepted jurisprudential principles that pertain to that legal form.

A third possible approach is to permit coercive preventive measures designated civil to continue to reside on the civil side of the boundary but to import such criminal procedural protections as appear apposite or necessary to those civil measures that have a significantly coercive aspect to them. In such a case the proceedings remain civil but selected criminal procedural rights or evidential standards are applied.[54] This approach has the advantage of pragmatism in that it accepts that, in an increasingly complex regulatory environment, administrative agencies will inevitably have resort to cheaper, quicker, and less demanding civil proceedings and that it may be a hopeless task to seek to withstand this trend. In England the House of Lords, in one leading case, has sought to resolve the conflicting considerations raised by the question of whether a preventive measure falls on the civil or criminal side by reaching the compromise solution of imposing a high (quasi-criminal) standard of proof upon a preventive measure while reaffirming that in other respects civil procedures apply.[55]

This leads towards a fourth[56] and increasingly discussed view—that the attempt to maintain a bright line between criminal and civil spheres is simply a failure to acknowledge the overwhelming erosion that has taken and is continuing to take place. On this view a better and more honest strategy is to acknowledge the development of a 'jurisprudential middle-ground' which either absorbs and combines features of both criminal and civil domains (which might vary according to how close any given measure lies to the criminal or civil margins of that middle ground) or, more ambitiously, calls for the articulation of a new set of principles and procedures apposite to the emerging terrain.[57] This approach might also be said to reflect more closely what is already happening in practice—namely the development of hybrid civil–criminal measures that typically employ civil procedures backed up by punitive sanctions for breach.

---

[54] Eg *United States v Halper* (1989) 490 US 425; *Austin v US* (1993) 509 US602; and *US v Kurth Ranch* (1994) 511 US 767, all discussed in Klein, 'Redrawing the Criminal–Civil Boundary'.

[55] *Clingham v Royal Borough of Kensington and Chelsea; R (on behalf of McCann) v Crown Court of Manchester* [2003] 1 AC 787, on which see the notes by S Macdonald (2003) 66 MLR 630 and by C Bakalis [2003] Camb LJ 583.

[56] We recognize that there are other, more radical views which are not discussed in detail here; eg the argument of C Slobogin, 'The Civilization of the Criminal Law' (2005) *Vanderbilt Law Review* 58, 121–168, that 'individual prevention' should be embraced as the primary goal in criminal and civil spheres that are not sharply differentiated.

[57] K Mann, 'Punitive Civil Sanctions: The Middleground between Criminal and Civil Law' (1992) *Yale Law Journal* 101/8, 1795–873. See also responses by Goldstein, Coffee, and Zimring: AS Goldstein, 'White-Collar Crime and Civil Sanctions' (1992) *The Yale Law Journal* 101/8, 1895–9; JC Coffee, 'Paradigms Lost: The Blurring of the Criminal and Civil Law Models. And What Can Be Done About It' (1992) *The Yale Law Journal* 101/8, 1875–93; FE Zimring, 'The Multiple Middlegrounds between Civil and Criminal Law' (1992) *The Yale Law Journal* 101/8, 1901–8.

The best-known hybrid in UK law is the civil preventive order. The order is civil in the sense that it may be made by a civil court, according to civil rules of evidence.[58] The model of a civil preventive order has been much used and there are now more than a dozen different types, running from football banning orders through travel restriction orders to control orders and serious crime prevention orders.[59] Its attraction to the British government was that it appears to avoid criminal procedure and the additional safeguards for defendants that accompany it. Let us take the anti-social behaviour order (ASBO)[60] as the model: an order may be made where the court finds that the defendant has acted in an anti-social manner, ie 'in a manner that caused or was likely to cause harassment, alarm or distress', and that an order is necessary to protect persons from further such behaviour. The court may then make an order 'which prohibits the defendant from doing anything described in the order' for at least two years. Breach of this civil order is a criminal offence, with a maximum punishment of five years. Now there were good social reasons for introducing some such preventive measure: genuine problems of neighbourhood disturbances, such as noisy neighbours or groups of youths perceived as threatening, that adversely affected the quality of life for residents; reluctance of people to give evidence in court against the persons responsible; and a belief that a criminal trial, focused on a single charge, could not respond appropriately to the totality of the conduct or convey the sense of an ongoing menace.[61] But in the form in which it was introduced, the ASBO has long been open to several objections.

First, the court is able to impose broad prohibitions on the defendant, going well beyond the scope of the anti-social behaviour proved. This delegates considerable rule-making discretion to the courts to determine what prohibitions to place upon the defendant. Second, the requirement that the prohibitions be 'necessary' for the protection of others from anti-social behaviour has not been enforced rigorously; some prohibitions are framed broadly in order to prevent the defendant from having an opportunity to engage in the anti-social behaviour (for example, banning a person from the whole Tyneside metro system, in order to prevent the spraying of graffiti),[62] and thus by trying to eliminate the risk that the person will commit certain

---

[58] Except the standard of proof, which is equivalent to the criminal standard (beyond reasonable doubt): this was the compromise crafted by the House of Lords in *Clingham v Royal Borough of Kensington and Chelsea: R (on behalf of McCann) v Crown Court at Manchester* (above, n 55).

[59] For detailed analysis and discussion, see Ashworth and Zedner 'Preventive Orders'.

[60] Introduced under the Crime and Disorder Act 1998, and as amended.

[61] See further E Burney, *Making People Behave: Anti-Social Behaviour, Politics and Policy* (2nd edn; Cullompton: Willan Publishing, 2009); S Macdonald, 'A Suicidal Woman, Roaming Pigs and a Noisy Trampolinist: Refining the ASBO's Definition of Anti-Social Behaviour' (2006) 69 *Modern Law Review* 183; A Ashworth, 'Social Control and Anti-Social Behaviour: The Subversion of Human Rights?' (2004) 120 *Law Quarterly Review* 263; AP Simester and A von Hirsch, 'Regulating Offensive Conduct through Two-Step Prohibitions', in A von Hirsch and AP Simester (eds), *Incivilities: Regulating Offensive Behaviour* (Oxford: Hart Publishing, 2006).

[62] *R v Lamb* [2006] 2 Cr App R (S) 11.

anti-social acts the court may spread the net of prohibition so wide as to impinge on ordinary social movement. Third, the maximum penalty for the criminal offence of breaking the conditions of an ASBO is five years, higher than the maximum for many other offences (including assault, affray, assaulting a police officer, etc); and yet the substance of this offence is breach of a prohibition in a civil order. Around half of all ASBOs are breached, and around half of those convicted of breach are sent into custody.[63] Fourth, this high maximum penalty seems disproportionate not only when the prohibitions concern otherwise non-criminal conduct, but also when the prohibitions concern conduct that is criminal but non-imprisonable. When in 1982 Parliament abolished imprisonment for the offences of begging and of soliciting for prostitution, it was clearly conscious of the fact that some people commit these offences repeatedly; evidently it took the decision that, no matter how often the offences are repeated, the offender should not be liable to imprisonment.[64] Yet this democratic decision can now be undermined by a court if it decides to insert into an ASBO a prohibition on begging or on soliciting, breach of which prohibition may result in imprisonment for up to five years. This shows the tremendous power—and the subversive power—of the ASBO as currently constituted. One can concede that the ASBO was designed to deal with a genuine and significant social problem, while criticizing the sacrifice of values resulting from its particular legal form.

It should be recalled that it was the alleged ineffectiveness of criminal law as a response to anti-social behaviour that led to the call for this new legal form—the civil preventive order—to be created in order to remedy these alleged shortcomings, and to open the way to a more effective response to the unwanted behaviour. A large part of the attraction to the British government of using the hybrid, two-step approach of civil preventive orders for prohibiting certain forms of behaviour is that it circumvents the additional safeguards that apply to criminal proceedings. Yet the coercive power of the ASBO is considerable, especially in view of the substantial maximum penalty available when the subject of an order breaks its terms.

Another variety of the civil preventive order in use in Britain is the control order. If ASBOs are the best known of these measures, control orders are arguably the most pernicious and, as a result, have been the subject of extensive appellate review. Introduced under the Prevention of Terrorism Act 2005, control orders place severe restrictions upon those subject to them. These can include prescription as to place of abode and of work, lengthy curfews, restrictions and bans on visitors, and restrictions upon association outside the home. Other commonly imposed terms include surrender of passports, bans on internet access, restrictions on freedom of movement, daily reporting to the police or daily monitoring by phone, electronic tagging,

---

[63] S Hoffman and S Macdonald 'Should ASBOs be Civilized?' (2010) *Criminal Law Review* 6, 457–73, at 457.

[64] Criminal Justice Act 1982, ss 70 and 71; see E Burney, ' "No Spitting": Regulation of Offensive Behaviour in England and Wales', in von Hirsch and Simester (eds), *Incivilities*.

and extensive surveillance of 'controllees'. Notwithstanding their invasive and coercive nature, control orders are civil orders that can be imposed in cases where, on the balance of probabilities, the Home Secretary: '(a) has reasonable grounds for suspecting that the individual is or has been involved in terrorism-related activity; and (b) considers that it is necessary, for purposes connected with protecting members of the public from a risk of terrorism, to make a control order imposing obligations on that individual.'[65] It follows that the extensive restrictions of liberty imposed by control orders are supported by reference to the prevention of harms or risks of harm that may be too barely specified, remote, or indirect to satisfy the requirements of criminalization. Yet, following the two-step or hybrid format of the civil preventive order established by the ASBO, breach of their expansive restrictions may result in a prison sentence of up to five years' imprisonment. Given that control orders find their justification in the prevention of the potentially catastrophic harms posed by the risk of terrorist attack, the pressure to impose extensive restrictions is even greater than in the case of ASBOs. However, even if their coercive power may be justified in times of exceptional risk or 'emergency', it is not surprising that, as normality returns, a long run of appeal cases has shown the courts to be highly critical of the deprivations imposed and denial of ordinary procedural protections entailed.[66]

What implications does the technique of the civil preventive order have for the criminal law? Two stand out. One is the difficulty of applying standard justifications for criminalization to the offence of 'doing anything which he is prohibited from doing by an anti-social behaviour order',[67] which is the type of offence that accompanies all civil preventive orders and which usually carries a maximum sentence of five years' imprisonment. The ambit of the offence is entirely constructed by the civil court that heard the initial application in the particular case. As already noted, the legislation does not limit the prohibitions to circumstances that have been proved by the applicant, and the requirement that the prohibitions be 'necessary' to protect others from anti-social behaviour has not been the subject of strict scrutiny. So the question is whether any respectable theory of criminalization can support such an indeterminate and under-specified offence, particularly when the various restraining principles support objections to such an offence. Thus, even if we were to accept the initial thrust of the government's argument that a person who contravenes an order of the court may fairly be criminalized, it can be countered that the prohibitions that constitute the order (and therefore the offence) are not subject to a requirement that the risk be substantial, in terms of the harm to be avoided and the probability of it occurring; and that they are not subject to any culpability requirement.[68] Those

---

[65] Prevention of Terrorism Act 2005, s 2(1); L Zedner 'Preventive justice or pre-punishment? The case of control orders' (2007) 60 *Current Legal Problems* 174–203.

[66] See eg, *Re MB* [2007] UKHL 46; *JJ and others v SSHD* [2007] UKHL 45; *AF v SSHD* [2008] EWCA Civ 1148; and *SSHD v AF* [2009] UKHL 28.

[67] The wording is taken from s 1(10) of the Crime and Disorder Act 1998 (UK).

[68] See Husak, *Overcriminalization*, 159 and 166.

two restraining considerations should be all the more powerful when the offence is not only imprisonable but carries a maximum of five years' imprisonment.

A second implication is a constitutional one—that the content of criminal offences is normally a matter for the legislature, sometimes delegated to government departments, but never delegated in such an open-ended way to courts. Thus von Hirsch and Simester argue that the preventive order 'is a form of criminalization: an *ex ante* criminal prohibition, not an *ex post facto* criminal verdict'.[69] In conferring such wide powers on courts in relation to ASBOs in the Crime and Disorder Act 1998, Parliament has effectively delegated to courts the power to put together a list of specific prohibitions for this defendant (a personal criminal law), with a formidably severe maximum penalty attached to any breach of the order. There appears to be no other example of this in the criminal law, and it is objectionable for many reasons. The prohibitions may relate to non-criminal conduct; or they may relate to conduct that is non-imprisonable, such as begging on the street or soliciting by sex workers; or they may relate to serious offences (such as burglary), which are penalized anyway. In all cases, the potential penalty is the same.

What are the implications for defendants' rights? A core element in the British government's purpose, when introducing civil preventive orders, was to ensure that the making of the orders is not subjected to the regime of criminal procedure. The government evidently regarded the additional procedural rights applicable in criminal cases as curtailing the effectiveness of the criminal law in dealing with these forms of behaviour. The civil preventive order has been devised in order to separate the two steps, the first being the making of the order (which is regarded as purely civil) and the second being the criminal offence (which is committed simply by breaching a prohibition in the order). The English courts have upheld this separation,[70] whereas critics have argued that the potential criminal sanction and substantial maximum penalty are such a prominent part of the context of the making of the order that the initial (civil) proceedings should be treated as criminal for the purposes of European human rights law.[71]

Of particular concern is that, if the technique of the civil preventive order is not regarded as subject to criminal procedure, then it is unclear what rights a defendant has in this hybrid procedure. Measures such as the civil preventive order fall into a 'jurisprudential black hole',[72] in which there is no presumption of innocence, no prohibition on retrospectivity, and no prospect of the additional rights that are available in criminal cases. There is some support in European human rights law for three restraining principles—the principle of necessity, that it must be clear that the restrictions are necessary to prevent the harm; the principle of subsidiary, that

---

[69] Simester and von Hirsch, 'Regulating Offensive Conduct through Two-Step Prohibitions', 178.

[70] See n 59 above for references.

[71] Eg Ashworth and Zedner, 'Preventative Orders'.

[72] A Ashworth, 'Criminal Law, Human Rights and Preventative Justice', in McSherry et al (eds), *Regulating Deviance*, 100.

less intrusive measures must have been considered and adjudged to be insufficient; and the principle of proportionality, that the measures taken must not be out of proportion to the danger apprehended.[73] But it is not certain how restrictively those principles would be applied. The fact is that the British government, spurred on by the courts,[74] seized on the civil preventive order as a model for increasing social control without the need to abide by the protections accorded to defendants in criminal cases. This becomes a major field of prevention in which the criminal law is clearly implicated and involved—since it is the criminal offence of 'doing anything he is prohibited from doing by an anti-social behaviour order' with a substantial maximum penalty, that gives the preventive teeth to this kind of measure.

4 Preventive Rationales and the Limits of the Criminal Law

In this chapter we have raised several questions about the assumption that the criminal law ought to serve a preventive purpose. While the assumption has deep foundations, accepted even by many whose primary rationale for the criminal law is retributive or declaratory, we have doubted that prevention is a satisfactory or sufficient justification for many significant features of contemporary criminal law. These have tended to grow in an unprincipled manner, propelled by the apparent irresistibility of preventive purposes, whether they are grounded in the protection of the public, the promotion of public safety, the prevention of harm, or the assurance of security. Our examination of the philosophical foundations of criminal law in its preventive aspect has encountered many difficulties with the rationales offered.

The inchoate offences, which cast a kind of preventive circle round each substantive offence, have long given rise to controversy. The prevailing doctrine is that the inchoate offences should be restricted by requiring proof of intention (rather than a lesser form of culpability) and by requiring a significant step towards completion. However, we have shown that this doctrine is stretched by the growth of preparatory or pre-inchoate offences, some of which do not require proof of a further intention,

---

[73] For the details, see Ashworth and Zedner 'Preventive Orders'.

[74] The apotheosis of judicial obtuseness is the decision in *R v Field and Young* [2003] 2 Cr App R (S) 175, where the Court of Appeal held that, because a particular order could be made in respect of persons found not guilty by reason of insanity, it was therefore a civil order (not being confined to convicted persons), and thus the prohibition on retrospectivity did not apply. This judicial focus on form over substance suggests that legislators need only make an order applicable to the insane in order to ensure that it is not regarded as criminal penalty.

and most of which penalize conduct remote from the harm they are supposed to prevent. Applying to them the objections rightly raised towards inchoate offences, we have argued that there are substantial problems with these preparatory and pre-inchoate offences: they deny an individual the opportunity for a change of mind; they convict an individual on the basis of what others may do (even where the individual is not normatively involved in the other's conduct); and they provide incentives to law enforcement agents to press people to confess, especially if the right to silence is qualified to the extent that it is in English law. Possession offences are the most problematic group, since there is sometimes no requirement of further intent and sometimes a reverse burden of proof.

We have also argued that offences of risk creation have tended to accumulate in an unprincipled way. Averting a 'risk of harm' may appear to be an incontrovertible instantiation of the state's preventive obligation, but the problems of principle are parallel to those presented by the pre-inchoate and preparatory offences. Thus we have argued in favour of a principle of criminalization that restricts such offences to the causing of a significant risk of a serious harm, and in favour of limiting principles that insist on a culpability requirement of subjective recklessness and on a remoteness bar that prevents liability where the nature of the risk is that a person may decide to cause the prohibited harm. This might be regarded as a 'moral agency' limitation.

Our concern has been not only that the criminal law has been driven by preventive rationales to expand in an unprincipled manner, but also that legal techniques situated on the edge of the criminal law have been designed in order to pursue prevention while avoiding the procedural safeguards that are recognized as a proper concomitant of criminal liability. We have set out many objections to civil preventive orders, such as ASBOs and control orders, and have argued that their growth constitutes a challenge to the values of the criminal law which cannot be met merely by re-asserting the criminal law's preventive rationale or the state's preventive obligations. Our criticisms indicate how far the criminal law has travelled from its principled paradigm and how important it is to formulate and to re-assert those principles,[75] particularly where they do most work—at the very limits of criminal liability.

[75] One of the central aims of our 2010–2013 AHRC-funded project on 'Preventive Justice' is the development and articulation of principles and values that should guide and limit the state's use of preventive techniques that involve coercion.

THE ONTOLOGICAL PROBLEM OF 'RISK' AND 'ENDANGERMENT' IN CRIMINAL LAW

PETER WESTEN[*]

1 INTRODUCTION

PENAL codes are rife with what Antony Duff calls 'crimes of explicit endangerment',[1] that is, offences that are explicitly framed as the conduct of 'endangering', 'jeopardizing',

[*] I wish to thank my former students, Shawn Bayern, Christa Cottrell, and Matthew Turnell, for helping me think through these issues and to express my deep debts to Mitch Berman, Antony Duff, Eric Johnson, Kimberly Ferzan, Jim Krier, Ken Simons, and Victor Tadros for thorough and helpful comments on an earlier draft.

[1] RA Duff, *Answering For Crime* (Oxford: Hart, 2008), 166. Doug Husak adopts the same terminology but defines 'explicit' risk creation slightly differently. D Husak, *Overcriminalization* (Oxford: Oxford University Press, 2008), 163.

and creating a 'risk', 'danger', and/or 'likelihood' of harm.[2] Risks and dangers, in turn, are conventionally understood to be probabilistic in nature, consisting of factual likelihood of harm. This conventional understanding is compatible with some such crimes of endangerment. However, it cannot account for most, including most that arise under provisions modeled upon Model Penal Code (MPC), section 211.12.[3] Specifically, it cannot account for commonplace offences that punish persons for creating what I call 'agent-independent' risks or dangers—that is, risks that exist 'objectively' apart from the mental states of those who bring them about[4]—regarding events that by their nature must either materialize in harm or not by the time of trial but do *not* thus materialize in harm. The ontological problem of risk is that the law regularly punishes actors for creating risks and dangers that conventional wisdom deems not to exist.

I shall argue that this problem of risk can be resolved, but only by replacing conventional, probabilistic understandings of risks and dangers with an alternative understanding. I shall proceed by (1) locating offences like MPC, § 211.2 within the larger taxonomy of crimes of risk creation; (2) summarizing conventional understandings of risk as probability; (3) explaining why probability fails to account for most crimes of explicit endangerment; (4) proposing an alternative, non-probabilistic understanding derived from the defence of impossibility; and (5) suggesting that the alternative understanding may also resolve a nagging problem regarding what Duff calls crimes of 'implicit endangerment',[5] that is, offences that, rather than making explicit reference to 'risks' or 'dangers', consist of conduct that legislatures regard as sufficiently risky to justify categorical prohibition (for example, failing to come to a full stop at a stop sign). Before I do, however, I will say something about the terms 'risk' and 'danger' and how I shall be using them.

2 THE TERMS 'RISK' AND 'DANGER'

The nouns 'risk' and 'danger' are often synonyms in ordinary language, at least when used non-idiomatically. Thus, the dictionary defines 'risk' as 'danger',[6] and

---

[2] Eg Wisconsin Statutes, s 941.30(2) (2007) ('endangering'); 18 USC Appendix C, amend 647 (2008) ('jeopardiz[ing]'); Arkansas Compiled Acts, s 5–13–205(a)(1) (2008) ('risk'); Hawaii Revised Statutes ss 707–714(1)(a) (2008) ('danger'); 18 USCS Appendix s 2Q1.3 (2008)('likelihood').

[3] MPC, § 211.2 is a generic reckless endangerment statute that two states—Pennsylvania and Vermont—have adopted verbatim. At least 22 other states also possess generic reckless endangerment statutes framed in various ways. See M Cahill, 'Attempt, Reckless Homicide and the Design of Criminal Law' (2007) 78 *University of Colorado Law Review* 924, n 132. In addition, many states possess specific reckless endangerment statutes. See ibid 934–5.

[4] I prefer the term 'agent-independent' risks to 'objective' risks because 'agent-independent' risks contrast nicely with 'agent-relative' risks and because 'objective risk' has a meaning of its own in probability theory.

[5] Duff, *Answering For Crime*, 166.

[6] *Oxford English Dictionary* (2nd edn; 1989) vol 4, 240–1.

'danger' as 'risk'.[7] And both terms are defined as meaning a 'possibility' or 'chance' of 'loss or injury'.[8]

'Danger' and 'risk' can also be used interchangeably in criminal law. Consider, for example, the relationship between 'reckless burning' under MPC, section 221.1(2) and 'felonious restraint' under MPC, section 212.2. The former makes it an offence to 'purposely star[t] a fire...[and] thereby recklessly place another person in *danger* of... bodily injury'. The latter makes it an offence to 'knowingly restrain another unlawfully in circumstances exposing him to *risk* of serious bodily injury'. The former speaks of 'danger' of bodily injury, while the latter speaks of 'risk' of serious bodily injury, but each would retain the same meaning if the words were interchanged.[9]

The same interchangeability sometimes also exists between 'danger' and 'substantial risk'. Thus, some states make it an offence to 'recklessly engage in conduct that places another person in *danger* of death or serious bodily injury',[10] while others make it an offence to 'recklessly engage in conduct that creates a *substantial risk* of death or serious physical injury to another person'.[11] The former statutes speak of 'danger' of death or serious bodily injury, while the latter speak of a 'substantial risk' of the same. But nothing in the case law suggests that outcomes depend upon which term is used.

Nevertheless, although 'danger' and 'risk' can be synonymous when used as nouns, 'risk' has additional connotations that are useful in law. The nouns 'danger' and 'risk' typically refer to probabilities of harm that are agent-independent. However, the verb 'risk' can be used idiomatically to refer to something that is also legally significant, namely, an assessment of the probability of harm from an actor's perspective. Thus, to say that an actor 'risked it', or 'ran a risk', can mean that he subjectively believed that a probability of harm existed, even if the risk did not exist. Accordingly, because 'risk' has the broader and more useful range, I shall typically use 'risk' in lieu of 'danger'. And when the context does not reveal how I am using 'risk', I shall distinguish between 'agent-relative risks' and 'agent-independent risks', depending upon whether or not risks exist solely by reference to the minds of actors who bring them about.

3 A TAXONOMY OF CRIMES OF RISK

Penal codes abound with references to 'risk' and 'danger' and to concepts that presuppose them, namely, 'recklessness' and 'negligence'. For our purposes,

---

[7] Ibid, vol 13, 987–8.
[8] *Webster's Ninth New Collegiate Dictionary* (1991) 324, 1018.
[9] Compare also MPC, § 221.1(2)(a)('risk') with MPC, § 220.2(2) ('danger').
[10] Eg Hawaii Revised Statutes, ss 707–714(1)(a) (2008).
[11] Eg Wyoming Statutes, s 6-2-504(a) (2008).

however, these references fall into two distinct categories: (a) the prohibited *conduct* of creating agent-independent risks; and (b) *states of mind* regarding such prohibited conduct, whether the latter consists of actual harms or risks of such harms.

3.1 The conduct of creating agent-independent risks

The conduct of creating wrongful, agent-independent *risks* is best understood by reference to what it is not—namely, the conduct of wrongful *harming*.[12] To wrongfully harm an individual or institution is to bring about prohibited injuries that the state mourns for their own sake, all things considered—apart from those which consist solely of attitudinal injuries that actors inflict upon persons by manifesting malice, disrespect, or lack of respect toward them. Thus, offences of murder, rape, and placing others in fear of battery are crimes of wrongful harm because they are defined by reference to injuries, including psychic traumas, that the state mourns for their own sake. In contrast, attempted murder is not a crime of harm because is not defined by reference to injury, apart from the attitudinal injury that an actor inflicts by intending his putative victim's death and acting upon his intent. Drunken driving and reckless endangerment are not crimes of harm because, rather than being predicated upon injuries or losses that the state mourns for their own sake, all things considered, drunken driving is predicated upon conduct that the state prohibits for fear that it will *lead* to losses of life, limb, and property that are mourned for their own sake, and reckless endangerment is predicated upon the mere *potential* for such losses.

Philosophers differ regarding the ultimate nature of injuries and losses that are mourned for their own sake, all things considered. Some argue that they consist of setbacks to a victim's interest that can be identified without reference to the victim's rights. Others argue that they consist in whole or in part of abridgements of a victim's rights.[13] Whichever view may prevail, it suffices for our purposes that wrongful harms consist of prohibited injuries (other than attitudinal injuries) that the state mourns for their own sake, all things considered.

---

[12] S Perry, 'Risk, Harm and Responsibility', in D Owen (ed), *Philosophical Foundations of Tort Law*, (Oxford: Clarendon Press, 1995), 321–46, 330–9 (arguing, contrary to C Finkelstein, 'Is Risk a Harm?' (2003) 151 *University of Pennsylvania Law Review* 963–1001, that risk creation is not an infliction of harm). Accord M Adler, 'Risk, Death and Harm: The Normative Foundations of Risk Regulation' (2003) 87 *Minnesota Law Review* 1444; M Moore, *Causation and Responsibility* (Oxford: Oxford University Press, 2009) 309–10.

[13] Husak, *Overcriminalization*, 126–35.

All other wrongful conduct that is punished at its respective level consists of wrongful risk creation.[14] Wrongful risk creation falls into three categories, which are sometimes conjoined in single statutes:[15]

(1) *Implicit risk creation.* Some unlawful risk creation consists of non-harmful conduct that tends to be so unjustifiably risky that, rather than prohibit it in the vague language of 'risk', legislatures prohibit it categorically, regardless of any ulterior intent on an actor's part to produce harm and regardless of whether it presents risks in every instance.[16] Drunk driving,[17] discharging a firearm in a populated area,[18] distributing harmful drugs,[19] and fleeing a police officer[20] are common examples. None of the actions is defined by reference to a wrongful harm. Yet all of them tend so strongly to involve unjustifiable risks that they are prohibited in themselves.

(2) *Criminal attempts and other crimes of ulterior intent.* Other unlawful risk creation consists of conduct that, regardless of whether it is predicated in part upon wrongful harm, is punished at its respective level only because is performed with risk-creating ulterior intent. 'Possession of drugs with intent to sell', 'breaking and entering with intent with intent to commit a felony', and 'attempted rape' are examples. Some of the conduct is defined by reference to wrongful harm (for example, 'breaking and entering with intent to commit a felony'); other is not (for example, possession of drugs with intent to sell'). All of it, however, is defined by reference to conduct that, though not regarded as sufficiently risky to be prohibited categorically without reference to ulterior intent, is regarded as sufficiently risky when combined with wrongful ulterior intent such as an 'intent sell drugs' or 'intent to kill'.

(3) *Explicit 'risk' creation.* The final category of unlawful risk creation consists of what Antony Duff calls 'crimes of explicit endangerment', namely, offences that are explicitly framed in terms of agent-independent 'risks' and/or 'dangers'.[21]

---

[14] Doug Husak draws a distinction within what I call crimes of risk prevention between crimes of 'risk prevention;' and 'ancillary crimes'. Husak, *Overcriminalization*, 40–4. But see Duff, *Answering For Crime*, 158 (including what Husak calls ancillary crimes among 'crimes of endangerment').

[15] For a statute that conjoins risk creation 1 and 3, see Wyoming Statutes, s 6-2-504 (2008) ('Reckless endangering. (a) A person is guilty of reckless endangering if he recklessly engages in conduct which places another person in danger of death or serious bodily injury. (b) Any person who knowingly points a firearm at or in the direction of another, whether or not the person believes the firearm is loaded, is guilty of reckless endangering unless reasonably necessary in defense of his person, property or abode or to prevent serious bodily injury to another...')

[16] Duff refers to these offences as crimes of 'implicit' endangerment. See Duff, *Answering For Crime*, 166.

[17] Eg Texas Penal Code, s 49.04 (2008)

[18] Eg Hawaii Revised Statutes, s 707–714(b) (2008).

[19] Eg New Jersey Statutes, s 2C:12–2 (2008).

[20] Eg Texas Transportation Code, s 545.421(a) (2007).

[21] Duff, *Answering For Crime*, 163, 166.

MPC, section 211.2, which punishes an actor who 'recklessly places...another person in danger of death or serious bodily injury', is an example. So is the Maine aggravated reckless conduct statute which punishes an actor who, with terroristic intent, 'engages in conduct that in fact creates a substantial risk of serious bodily injury to another person'.[22]

Paul Robinson agrees that MPC, section 211.2 punishes the culpable creation of agent-independent risks. He denies, however, that MPC, section 211.2 *confines* itself to punishing such risks. Instead, he argues that MPC, section 211.2 combines two alternative offences within a single statute: (1) an offence of *conduct*, ie the offence of recklessly creating agent-independent risks of death or serious bodily injury; and (2) a crime of *attempt*, ie the offence of acting in the *belief* that such agent-independent risks exist even if they do not.[23]

Robinson bases his argument upon a three-word phrase in MPC, section 211.2 that distinguishes it from most state endangerment statutes. Unlike most state endangerment statutes (which either require that an actor recklessly 'place' another in substantial risk or require that he recklessly 'create' a danger), MPC, section 211.1 and the two states that have adopted it verbatim[24] punish an actor who 'recklessly engages in conduct which places *or may place* another person in danger of death or serious bodily injury'. Robinson interprets the three italicized words to mean that an actor who does not place another in danger is, nevertheless, guilty, if he acts with a state of mind of doing so, even if the risk is entirely imaginary.[25]

I do not believe that the phrase 'or may place' is designed to punish actors for imagined and imaginary risks, and I do not believe it does so within states that have adopted it.[26] Indeed, the MPC Commentary implicitly warns against placing very much weight on the phrase. After noting that several states adopt the phrase 'place or may place' verbatim, the Commentary describes other statutes that conspicuously *omit* the phrase as using 'generally comparable phrasing'.[27]

To be sure, the Commentary also makes a statement that might be understood (mistakenly, I believe) to support Robinson's view that section 211.2 punishes imagined and imaginary risks. It states:

Section 211.2 requires that the actor engage in conduct 'which places or may place another person in danger of death or serious bodily injury'. This formulation applies to risk creation

---

[22] Maine Revised Statutes tit 17-A, s 211, 213 (2006).

[23] See P Robinson, 'Prohibited Risks and Culpable Disregard or Inattentiveness' (2003) 4 *Theoretical Inquiries In Law* 390, 392–3.

[24] See n 3 above.

[25] See n 20 above.

[26] Tennessee, which is one of five states that have adopted the phrase (the other being New Hampshire, New Jersey, Pennsylvania, and Vermont), instructs juries that to convict, they must find that the defendant actually placed another person or class of persons in a 'zone of danger'. *Tennessee Pattern Jury Instructions—Criminal*, s 6.03.

[27] Model Penal Code and Commentaries (1980) pt 1, vol 1, § 211.2, p 197.

regardless...of whether anyone is actually endangered by the actor's conduct. Thus, for example, firing a gun at an occupied building may suffice for liability, even if none of the inhabitants is at home at the time.[28]

In reality, however, the statement is ambivalent. It admittedly states that section 211.2 applies, regardless of whether anyone is 'actually endangered'. However, it also states that the actor must actually have 'creat[ed]' a 'risk'. And it merely states that recklessly firing into an 'occupied' dwelling *may suffice* for liability if none of the inhabitants happens to be home, thus refraining from saying (as Robinson says) that mistakenly believing one is discharging a loaded weapon into what one mistakenly believes is an occupied dwelling *does* suffice for liability. The Commentary's statement is entirely consistent with the position that *if* recklessly firing into an occupied building from which occupants happen to be absent violates section 211.2, it is because, and only because, liability for the shooting is consistent with a tenable notion of agent-independent risks.[29]

What, then, does the MPC Commentary mean in saying that liability requires that an agent-independent 'risk' exist even where no one is actually 'endangered?' And what is the difference between a wholly imagined and imaginary risk and an agent-independent one? Why does the MPC resort to the phrase 'places or may place in danger' where other statutory authors believe 'places in danger' suffices?

These are important and difficult questions that go to the heart of the ontological problem of risk. Because they do, however, we must postpone addressing them until we have resolved the problem.

3.2 Risk taking as a culpable state of mind

Criminal law references to 'risk' and 'danger' are not confined to the prohibited conduct of creating agent-independent risks. They also include purely *mental states* of risk taking regarding prohibited conduct, whether prohibited conduct consists of (i) harms, (ii) implicit risk creation, (iii) the actus reus of crimes of ulterior intent, or (iv) agent-independent 'risks'.

'Recklessness' under MPC, section 2.02(2)(c) is an example. Recklessness is the mental state of consciously disregarding what one perceives to be a substantial and unjustified 'risk' that a prohibited event (or 'material element') exists or will result under circumstances in which such disregard is a gross deviation from the conduct of a law-abiding person in the actor's situation.[30] 'Negligence' under MPC,

---

[28]   Ibid 203.

[29]   cf North Dakota Code, s 12.1–17–03 (2009) (providing that although its reckless endangerment statute does not require that a 'particular person' actually be 'jeopardized', it does require that 'a potential for harm exist').

[30]   MPC, § 2.02(2)(c) ('A person acts recklessly with respect to a material element of an offense when he consciously disregards a substantial and unjustified risk that the material element exists or will

section 2.02(2)(d) is the mental state of being unaware of what, were one a reasonable person, one would perceive as a substantial and unjustified 'risk' that a prohibited event ('material element') exists or will result, the disregard of which would be a gross deviation from the conduct of a reasonable person in the actor's situation.[31]

Now it might be thought that, because MPC, section 2.02(2)(c) speaks of 'disregarding... *a* risk' and MPC, section 2.02(2)(d) speaks of being 'aware of *a* risk', each requires two things: (1) a mental state of risk taking, whether of advertence or inadvertence, and (2) an agent-independent risk of which the actor is advertent or inadvertent, respectively. However, the text of MPC, section 2.02(2)(c–d) and accompanying Commentary indicate the opposite. They both make it clear that 'risks' for purposes of recklessness and negligence are not agent-independent but rather are defined by reference to 'circumstances known to [the actor]'.[32]

Robinson agrees that recklessness and negligence under MPC, section 2.02(2)(c–d) define mental states of risk taking that are entirely agent-relative.[33] However, he believes they are wrong to do so. He believes that all definitions of recklessness and negligence should be supplemented to require the additional existence of agent-independent risks, something along the following lines:

Robinson's Riskcreation Statute

An actor may not be held liable for recklessness or negligence without proof that he created a prohibited risk. Nothing in this Section bars liability for an inchoate offense.[34]

Robinson takes this position for two reasons. First, given his interpretation of MPC 211.2, Robinson believes his 'Risk Creation' statute is necessary to prevent section 211.2 from being used to punish imagined and imaginary risks as severely as agent-independent risks.[35] I agree with Robinson that it is appropriate to distinguish imaginary risks from agent-independent risks for purposes of punishment.[36] However, as

---

result from his conduct. The risk must be of such a nature and degree that, considering the nature and purpose of the actor's conduct and the circumstances known to him, its disregard involves a gross deviation from the standard of conduct that a law-abiding person would observe in the actor's situation').

[31] MPC, § 2.02(2)(d) ('A person acts negligently with respect to a material element of an offense when he should be aware of a substantial and unjustifiable risk that the material element exists or will result from his conduct. The risk must be of such a nature and degree that the actor's failure to perceive it, considering the nature and purpose of his conduct and the circumstances known to him, involves a gross deviation from the standard of care that a reasonable person would observe in the actor's situation.').

[32] MPC, § 2.02(2)(c-d). Cf *MPC and Commentaries* pt 1, vol 1, § 2.02(2)(c), p 238 ('[The jury] is to examine the risk and the factors that are relevant to how substantial it was and to the justification for taking it. In each instance, the question is asked from the point of view of the actor's perception...').

[33] Robinson, 'Prohibited Risks and Culpable Disregard or Inattentiveness', 373–4, 377, 385–8.

[34] Ibid 386.

[35] Ibid 385–90.

[36] P Westen, 'Resulting Harms and Objective Risks As Constraints on Punishment' (2010) *Law and Philosophy* (forthcoming) (arguing that it is inappropriate to punish objective risks at the same level as imaginary risks). Cf Maine Revised Statutes tit 17-A, s 211, 213 (2006) (punishing an actor who 'in

I have previously argued, MPC, section 211.2 presents no danger of conflating them because it eschews punishing imagined and imaginary risk altogether. Robinson's Risk Creation statute is redundant upon MPC, section 211.2 because the latter itself requires that agent-independent risks exist.

Second, Robinson fears that, without his Risk Creation statute, all actors whose risk taking causes harm will be punished identically, regardless of whether the resulting harms are within the *scope* of the risks they took. To illustrate, consider the following variations upon a Robinson hypothetical:

> **Friday Driver**: A city posts a sign at a school-zone, stating: 'Reduce Speed on School Days—Children Crossing'. A Friday Driver refuses to reduce his speed on Friday and, as a result, kills a child who dashes into the street to get to school. Friday Driver is charged with involuntary manslaughter for 'recklessly' causing the child's death.
>
> **Saturday Driver**: The same as above, except that a Saturday Driver, mistakenly thinking it is Friday, refrains from reducing speed on Saturday and, as a result, kills a child who *also* mistakenly thinks it is Friday and dashes into the street mistakenly trying to get to school on time. Saturday Driver, too, is charged with involuntary manslaughter.

Robinson is right that, because recklessness is purely a mental state of risk taking, Friday and Saturday Drivers are equally reckless in that respect. And he is right that, absent a further provision like his Risk Creation statute, Friday and Saturday Drivers will be punished identically—a result that seems counterintuitive. Nevertheless, his Risk Creation statute is not needed to prevent the drivers from being punished identically because existing rules already prevent it. MPC, section 2.03(3) already provides that, despite their recklessness or negligence, actors like Saturday Driver avoid liability when the harms they actually cause, for example, killing a child on a *non-school* day, are 'not within the risk of which [they are] ... or ... should be aware', eg killing a child on a *school* day.

Commentators differ regarding the nature of defences like MPC, section 2.03(3). Although commentators originally regarded the defence as causal in nature, HLA Hart and Tony Honore[37] persuaded many students of criminal law, including the authors of the MPC, to conceptualize the defence, not as a lack of causation, but as a lack of 'culpability'.[38] I believe the pre-Hart/Honore view is the preferable one. In terms of culpability, Friday and Saturday Drivers are equally blameworthy because they both possessed the same guilty mind and were both willing to act upon it. Friday and Saturday are also identical in terms of but-for cause because, but-for the failure of each driver to reduce what each perceived to be excessive speed, each victim would have safely crossed the street before the fateful car arrived. What distinguishes

---

fact creates a substantial risk' more severely than one creates a substantial risk that does not 'in fact' exist).

[37]   HLA Hart and T Honore, *Causation in the Law* (2nd edn; Oxford: Clarendon Press, 1985), 394–403.
[38]   *MPC and Commentaries* (1980) pt 1, vol 1, § 2.03(3), pp 257–8. See also P Robinson, *Structure and Function in Criminal Law* (Oxford: Clarendon Press, 1997), 27–31.

Saturday Driver is the same thing that explains all lack of proximate cause: despite Saturday Driver's equal culpability, public sentiment does not attribute the harm to him, probably in this case because the public senses that if Saturday Driver had been cautious and had *accurately* observed the sign's warning, he would still have killed the child at the same time and place. And because public sentiment does not attribute the harm to him, the rationale for punishing harm-based offences more severely than impossibility attempts is not served by punishing him at the higher level, despite his equal culpability.[39]

The distinction I have drawn in this section between risk as the *conduct* of agent-independent risk creation and risk as a *mental state* is significant because, as we shall see in the two following sections, the crimes of risk that raise ontological problems are solely a subset of the former.[40]

4 CONVENTIONAL WISDOM REGARDING RISK

Risks are commonly understood to be a function of probabilities, that is, factual likelihood of harm.[41] Probability, in turn, has both mathematical and philosophical aspects. The mathematics consists of certain, well-accepted formulas, known as the 'calculus of probability'[42] or 'standard mathematical axioms of probability',[43] that seventeenth- and eighteenth-century mathematicians devised to account for popular games of chance. The theory of probability, or its 'philosophy', consists of contested efforts to interpret the calculus by expounding what it is a calculus *of*—that is, what the calculus manifests about real or possible events and/or the knowledge or beliefs of people regarding them.[44]

---

[39] P Westen, 'Why Criminal Harms Matter: Plato's Abiding Insight In *The Laws*' (2007) 1 *Criminal Law and Philosophy* 15–24.

[40] I have argued that the criminal law does not present punish imaginary risks. But we shall see that doing so would not present ontological problems about the nature of such risks.

[41] D Gardner, *The Science of Fear* (New York: Dutton, 2008), 127–8; G Gigerenzer, *Calculated Risks* (New York: Simon and Schuster, 2002), 26; T Lewens, 'Introduction: Risk and Philosophy', in T Lewens (ed), *Risk: Philosophical Perspectives* (London: Routledge, 2007), 1, 17; D Mellor, 'Acting Under Risk', in Lewens (ed), *Risk*, 113, 118–19; Perry, 'Risk, Harm and Responsibility', 321.

[42] R Weatherford, *Philosophical Foundations of Probability Theory* (London: Routledge, 1982), 5.

[43] D Gillies, *Philosophical Theories of Probability* (London: Routledge, 2000), 69.

[44] D Mellor, *Probability: A Philosophical Introduction* (London: Routledge, 2005), 18–19; M Galavotti, *Philosophical Introduction To Probability* (Stanford: CSLIP, 2005), 39–55; Gillies, *Philosophical Theories of Probability*, 69; Weatherford, *Philosophical Foundations of Probability Theory*, 5, 48, 142, 229, 243–4.

For our purposes, probability theories are characterized by two sets of often over-lapping distinctions. One is the distinction between theories that regard probabilities as epistemic in nature and those that regard them as realistic in nature.

Epistemic Theories. Some theorists, including Pierre Simon de Laplace and John Maynard Keynes, regard probabilities as likelihood of events as perceived by observers who possess knowledge of some or all of the factors that causally determine the events.[45] For persons who believe that all events (or, at least, certain classes of events) are causally determined,[46] the probability of such events for omniscient observers is always equal to 0 or 1, from which it follows that probabilities that are *greater* than 0 and *less* than 1 are necessarily a function of epistemic deficiency or lack of omniscience regarding the factors that together determine the events.[47] Thus, when a person who believes that physical factors and laws wholly determine whether rolls of dice are odd or even declares that the probability that a particular roll of the dice will be odd is 0.5, he is assuming that such probability is a function of his lack of ex ante omniscience of those determining factors.

Realism Theories. In contrast, other theories regard probabilities as likelihood of events that are greater than 0 and less than 1 even when all causal factors, if any, are taken into account. Thus, when quantum-mechanics theorists who believe that the decay of uranium isotopes is inherently stochastic rather than causal in nature declare that the probability that a given isotope will decay within a year is 0.5, they take such probability to be an ontological feature of atomic particles themselves, not a function of lack of knowledge regarding causal factors.

A second distinction obtains, regardless of whether events are assumed to be deterministic or indeterministic in nature. The second distinction, which in practice can overlap with the first,[48] is between theories that regard probabilities as objective and those that regard them as essentially subjective.

Objective Theories. Some theorists, including Richard von Mises and Karl Popper, regard probabilities as objective facts about the world, or 'chances', that obtain regardless of individual perceptions.[49] Thus, to say that, regardless of any wagers that individuals may make about it, a probability of approaching 0.05 exists that North American men who are unmarried at age 30 will be married by the time they turn 31 is to assume that such probability obtains independently of subjective assessments of it.

---

[45] Galavotti, *Philosophical Introduction To Probability*, 57–69, 144–53; Weatherford, *Philosophical Foundations of Probability Theory*, 18–143.

[46] For the argument that determinism and free will are both incomprehensible, see P Westen, 'Getting the Fly Out of the Bottle: The False Problem of Free Will and Determinism' (2004) 8 *Buffalo Criminal Law Review* 101–54.

[47] Gillies, *Philosophical Theories of Probability*, 17 ('In a completely deterministic system, probabilities cannot be inherent in objective nature but must be relative to human ignorance'). See also J Schaffer, 'Deterministic Chance?' (2007) 58 *British Journal of Philosophy Science* 113–40.

[48] Thus a theory can be both epistemic and objective, see Gillies, *Philosophical Theories of Probability*, 20, 33 (describing John Maynard Keynes's theory); Galavotti, *Philosophical Introduction To Probability*, 3–4, 147 (same). And a theory can be both epistemic and subjective, see ibid 191–93; S Perry, 'Risk, Harm, and Rights', in Lewens (ed), *Risk*, 190, 192.

[49] Gillies, ibid 89; Galavotti, ibid 71–134; Mellor, *Probability*, 3 ('chances'); Weatherford, *Philosophical Foundations of Probability Theory*, 9, 67, 79, 144–5, 178, 216, 246.

Subjective Theories. In contrast, other theorists, including Frank Ramsey and Bruno de Finetti, regard probabilities as inherently individual and subjective in nature, consisting of degrees of belief, or 'credences', by specific individuals at specific times based upon evidence that propositions are true, as measured by wagers they are willing to make.[50] Thus, when theorists say, as some do, that differing wagers by professional gamblers all constitute equally genuine probabilities,[51] they are declaring probabilities to be irreducibly subjective in nature.

This does not mean that all probability theories are exclusive. Although some commentators advocate single theories to the exclusion of others,[52] others adopt the 'pluralist' view that the appropriateness of probability theories is context-dependent.[53]

I will argue in the next section that none of these theories of probability—and, hence, nothing in conventional wisdom regarding risk—can account for significant ways in which the criminal law predicates liability upon 'risks'. Before I do so, however, I would like to identify three areas in which conventional wisdom is compatible with criminal law references to 'risk'.

First, conventional wisdom can explain risk taking as a *state of mind* of recklessness or negligence. Conventional wisdom, after all, regards risk as a matter of probability, and some commonplace theories of probability are epistemic and/or subjective in nature. Subjective theories are consistent with recklessness because, in accord with such theories, recklessness consists of an actor's state of mind—or subjective wager—regarding the probability of harm. Subjective theories are also consistent with negligence because, like recklessness, negligence is an assessment of probability from the viewpoint of the actor himself, qualified only by the requirement that he possess appropriate normative concern for the interests of others.[54] Epistemic theories, too, are consistent with states of mind of recklessness and negligence—at least regarding the mental states of actors regarding events that are regarded as causally determined—because such mental states consist of less-than-omniscience regarding the causal factors that determine the outcome.

[50] Galavotti, ibid 189–233; Mellor, ibid 3 ('credences'); Weatherford, ibid 9–10, 219–32, 236.

[51] H Kyburg and H Smokler (eds), *Studies In Subjective Probability* (New York: Wiley, 1964), 7. Compare S Blackburn, 'Opinions and Chances', in D Mellor (ed), *Prospects for Pragmatism* (Cambridge: Cambridge University Press, 1980), 175–96 (arguing that their being equally genuine is nevertheless consistent with some being better than others); Gillies, *Philosophical Theories of Probability*, 120–3.

[52] Weatherford, *Philosophical Foundations of Probability Theory*, 220 (describing certain subjective theories like Bruno de Finetti's).

[53] Gillies, *Philosophical Theories of Probability*, 3–4, 186–205 (arguing that epistemic and subjective theories are appropriate in economics, while realist and objective theories are appropriate in science).

[54] Recklessness and negligence are often characterized as 'objective' standards of culpability because they are not solely a function of what actors subjectively perceive. With reference to probability theory, however, they are 'subjective' judgments of probability because they begin with what actors perceive or would perceive facts to be.

Second, conventional wisdom can account for *some* conduct that falls under statutes like MPC § 211.2 that punish persons for creating agent-independent 'risks'—namely, risk-creating conduct that does not result in harm by the time of trial but may do so thereafter. To illustrate, consider the following hypothetical case:

Poisonous Scorpion: Teenager-1 releases a poisonous scorpion into a rival's attic bedroom. The scorpion scurries into a crack in the floor beneath the rival's bed and disappears. State A charges Teenager-1 under its equivalent of MPC, section 211.2 with recklessly creating an agent-independent risk of death or serious bodily injury. The scorpion is seen from time to time but does not sting anyone by the time of trial.

Such risks are consistent with subjective theories of probability because they can be understood to consist of subjective wagers on the part of scientists or others regarding the likelihood that the scorpion will eventually sting Teenager-1's rival. And the latter risks are also consistent with epistemic theories of probability because they can be understood to consist of less-than-omniscience regarding all the causal factors that will eventually suffice to render it certain that the scorpion will or will not sting an occupant of the attic room.

Third, and finally, conventional wisdom is consistent with risk-creating conduct that *does* materialize in harm by the time of trial. To illustrate, consider the following hypothetical case:

Unlucky Roulette: Teenager-2 goads a friend into submitting to a single round of Russian Roulette in which Teenager-2 spins the cylinder of a six-chamber revolver that contains a single bullet, points it at the palm of his friend's hand and pulls the trigger, believing that there is a 1/6 chance that the bullet is in the chamber and a high probability that, if it is, the gun will fire and maim his friend. Indeed, the single bullet does end up in the fateful chamber, the guns fires, and his friend's hand is maimed. State B does not possess a statute prohibiting reckless assault and, therefore, charges Teenager-2 under a statute equivalent to MPC, section 211.2 with recklessly creating an agent-independent 'risk' of death or serious bodily injury.

Conventional wisdom can account for Unlucky Roulette because the latter is consistent with epistemic theories of probability. The distinguishing feature of Unlucky Roulette, after all, is that the risked harm actually materializes by the time of trial and jurors know it materialized. Accordingly, jurors are omniscient in that they know that when Teenager-2 pulled the trigger, the bullet *was* in the gun, the gun *was* functioning, and Teenager-2's friend would *not* withdraw his hand—thus enabling them to conclude that (i) there was a genuine probability that the friend would suffer serious bodily injury, and (ii) the probability consisted of a certainty of 1.[55]

---

[55] Weatherford, *Philosophical Foundations of Probability Theory*, 41. But see Mellor, *Probability*, 11 (arguing that, under epistemological theories, probability is never fully 1 because there is always an uncertainty about whether one is mistaken in thinking one knows something, eg that (1) Teenager's friend's hand was maimed, and (2) Teenager 2's conduct is responsible for the maiming).

5 THE FAILURE OF CONVENTIONAL WISDOM REGARDING MOST EXPLICIT CRIMES OF ENDANGERMENT

Conventional wisdom, as I have said, regards risk as a matter of probability. Yet one class of explicit crimes of endangerment exists that conventional wisdom cannot explain. The class consists of risks that, by their nature, must either materialize in harm or not by the time of trial, but do *not* thus materialize in harm. Consider, for example, the following variation on an earlier hypothetical situation:

Lucky Roulette: Teenager-3 also goads his friend into engaging in a round of Russian Roulette that is identical to Unlucky Roulette, except that, luckily, the bullet is not in the fateful chamber, and the friend thus escapes injury. State C charges Teenager-3 under a statute equivalent to MPC, section 211.2 with recklessly creating an agent-independent risk of death or serious bodily injury.

Lucky Roulette differs from each of the prior hypothetical cases. It differs from Unlucky Roulette because, although both involve risks that must either materialize in harm or not by the time of trial, Lucky Roulette involves a risk that *fails* to materialize in harm. It also differs from Poisonous Scorpion because, although neither of the risky acts materializes in harm by the time of trial, the risky act in Poisonous Scorpion may nevertheless result in harm in the future, while the risky act in Lucky Roulette, by virtue of not materializing in harm by the time of trial, will never do so.

The class of cases represented by Lucky Roulette is significant. Indeed, if appellate decisions are any measure, they constitute the great majority of litigated cases regarding explicit crimes of endangerment.[56] They do so for at least three reasons. First, the acts of explicit endangerment for which prosecutors seek convictions tend to consist of acts creating imminent risks; and imminent risks tend to be risks that will either materialize in harm or not by the time of trial. Second, while harm-based offences like involuntary manslaughter and assault exist to prosecute risks that *do* materialize in harm by the time of trial, they cannot be used to prosecute risks that do not materialize in harm, while offences of explicit endangerment can. Finally, because the offence of attempt is typically confined to intentional conduct, it cannot be used to prosecute crimes of reckless or negligent risk creation that do not materialize in harm by the time of trial, while crimes of explicit endangerment can.

The significance of Lucky Roulette is that, although such cases are regularly prosecuted, conventional wisdom regarding probability cannot account for them. Let us

---

[56] See eg the hundreds of case annotations under Texas Penal Code, s 22.05 and New York Penal Code, ss 120.20 and 120.25.

start with 'objective' theories of probability, whether realist or epistemic in nature—
that is, theories that understand probabilities to be actual features of the world
rather than individual beliefs about them. The most venerable objective theory is
Richard von Mises's 'relative frequency' theory. Von Mises extrapolates probabilities from statistical samples regarding the frequency with which certain 'attributes'
occur within a 'reference class' of persons or things. Assume, for example, that a
statistically reliable survey finds that, within a reference class of 'all human males in
America', 22 per cent of those who were surveyed between 1990 and 2000 exhibited
the attribute of 'dying before the age of 41'. The figure of 0.22 is not *itself* the actual
probability that human males in America will die before the age of 41 but rather the
relative frequency with which such deaths occurred within a limited, time-bound
sample. The actual probability of men in America dying before the age of 41, von
Mises would say, is the numerical limit toward which the relative frequency of that
attribute (ie dying before the age of 41) *tends* within an infinite series of empirical
events that exhibit the frequency within the reference class.

Frequency theory is useful in predicting patterns in the physical and social sciences. Nevertheless, frequency theory presents several theoretical problems, including that it defines 'probability' in such a way that, rather than being something that
can be known, is something that can only be approached, and that frequency theory
excludes events that are finite in number.[57] For our purposes, however, the principal
problem is that frequency theory does not even *purport* to determine the probability
of particular events, whether it is the probability that a particular coin toss will come
up heads or the probability that a particular teenager will kill his friend by pulling
a particular trigger.[58] Frequency theory is a theory about the likelihood within a
reference class of *sets* of events, for example, male deaths in America before the age
of 41.[59] It does not govern criminal cases like Lucky Roulette involving the probability of particular events because it possesses no non-arbitrary way of selecting one
reference class as opposed to another with respect to a particular event that consists
of countless individual features—other than a reference class that takes account of
all its features and, hence, yields probabilities of either 1 or 0.[60] As von Mises puts it:
'We can say nothing about the probability of death of an individual even if we know
his condition of life and health in detail. The phrase, "probability of death", when it
refers to a single person, has no meaning at all for us.'[61]

Admittedly, some objective theorists , starting with Karl Popper, have modified
frequency theory under the rubric of 'propensity' theory that, they claim, redresses
the inability of frequency theory to produce probabilities for individual events

---

[57] Weatherford, *Philosophical Foundations of Probability Theory*, 170, 202–5.
[58] Weatherford, ibid 161–7, 174; Gillies, *Philosophical Theories of Probability*, 97, 115–16, 182–3.
[59] Mellor, *Probability*, 32.
[60] Gillies, *Philosophical Theories of Probability*, 119–25; Perry, 'Risk, Harm, and Rights', 193–7.
[61] Weatherford, *Philosophical Foundations of Probability Theory*, 161 (quoting Richard von Mises).

such as those upon which quantum physics is premised.[62] Propensity theorists conceptualize probabilities as limiting relative frequencies in infinite sequences of repeatable experiments based upon the same generating conditions—whether such experiments are virtual or actual—thus revealing, they say, a 'disposition' or 'propensity' of the conditions to generate their own characteristic limiting relative frequencies. It is doubtful, however, that propensity theories apply outside indeterministic realms of microphysics.[63] And even if they do, it is doubtful that they fare any better than frequency theories in being able to predict the probability of individual events, because it is doubtful that individual events fall into unique reference classes that can instantiate repeatable experiments.[64]

Now let us consider epistemic theories of probability, whether they are subjective or objective in nature. Epistemic theories understand probabilities to consist of the likelihood of events, including the likelihood that an individual coin toss will come up heads, when some (or, in the case of ex post omniscience, all) of the factors that altogether are assumed to causally determine the events are taken into account. These theories are highly useful, particularly in understanding the probability of individual events and the probability of sets of events for which statistical information is lacking.

Nevertheless, epistemic theories cannot produce probabilities regarding an event like the one at issue in Lucky Roulette because they presuppose something that such cases lack. Epistemic theories presuppose the existence of specified observers, whether they are real or hypothetical, who possess either limited knowledge or omniscience regarding the totality of factors that determine whether events will occur. Yet cases like Lucky Roulette involve risks that, not having materialized in harm by the time of trial, never will. No real or hypothetical observer exists in such cases whose epistemic viewpoint can serve as a measure of probability.

To support the foregoing assertion, let us address several possible candidates for such epistemic viewpoints. First, it might be thought that the real or hypothetical observers, which epistemic theory requires, consist of the actors themselves (for example, Teenager-3), possessed of their personal ex ante viewpoints. However, that will not do, for we have previously seen that reckless endangerment offences are not predicated solely upon the ex ante mental states of the actors themselves.[65] Rather, they require that actors produce agent-independent risks or dangers.

[62] C Howson, 'Theories of Probability' (1995) 46 *British Journal of Philosophy Science* 1, 21–3; Mellor, *Probability*, 4, 49–55.

[63] Gillies, *Philosophical Theories of Probability*, 189.

[64] C Howson, 'Theories of Probability' (1995) 46 *British Journal of Philosophy Science* 1, 21; Gillies, *Philosophical Theories of Probability*, 118–25,184–6, 188; Galavotti, *Philosophical Introduction To Probability*, 236.

[65] See nn 3, 22 above. Only two states follow the MPC in punishing an actor who 'places or may place another person in danger of death or serious bodily injury', see n 3. And I have argued that even those states should not be understood to punish actors for imagined or imaginary risks. See nn 20–28.

Agent-independent risks, in turn, cannot be established by measuring probabilities from the viewpoint of actors like Teenager-3. They must be established by reference to real or hypothetical agents *other* than the actors themselves.

Second, it might be thought that, just as epistemic theory invokes the ex post omniscience of trial jurors to find probabilities of harm in cases like *Unlucky Roulette*, epistemic theory can also invoke the *ex post* omniscience of trial observers—whether they are real or hypothetical—to find probabilities in cases like *Lucky Roulette*. Again, however, that is not so. The two sets are not parallel. An omniscient viewpoint produces acceptable results in cases like Unlucky Roulette because the risked harms have materialized by the time of trial. Given the harms that have materialized and our knowledge of the factors that entered into them, we possess *ex post* certainty that a substantial probability of harm existed ex ante—thus rendering the actor's culpability a function of whether he possessed the mens rea of recklessness or negligence regarding that substantial probability. In contrast, an omniscient viewpoint produces unacceptable results in cases like Lucky Roulette. For it produces ex post certainty that *no* substantial probability of harm ever existed in such cases. And that would mean that no actor could *ever* be punished for conduct that constitutes the bulk of crimes of explicit endangerment—namely the conduct of creating agent-independent risks that by their nature must either materialize in harm or not by the time of trial but do not thus materialize in harm.

Third, the viewpoint that epistemic theory requires might be argued to consist of one that, though a species of omniscience, is nevertheless consistent with criminalizing some agent-independent risks that must either materialize in harm or not by the time of trial but do not thus materialize. Specifically, it might be argued to be the viewpoint of hypothetical, *ex ante* observers who know everything about the facts that human beings are *capable* of knowing *ex ante*, being ignorant only of things that are incapable of being known until after the fact. To illustrate, contrast Lucky Roulette with the following hypothetical case:

Flash Racer: Flash is a skilled race car driver who drives at leisure on a two-lane mountain road where he attempts at high speed to pass a slow vehicle on a blind curve, not knowing whether a vehicle is approaching in the oncoming lane. In fact, an oncoming car is approaching at high speed. Although a serious collision seems nearly inevitable ex ante to everyone involved, thanks to fortunate swerves by the other two drivers and thanks to Flash's skilled reflexes, the three cars manage to emerge with nothing more than body damage to the three cars. Flash is charged with reckless endangerment under a statute equivalent to MPC, section 211.2.

Flash Racer and Lucky Roulette both involve risked harms that must either materialize or not by the time of trial but do not materialize. Yet the two cases also differ. Although the actor in Lucky Roulette does not know which chamber contained the bullet, the location of the bullet—and, hence, the harmlessness of Teenager-3's act—was humanly knowable ex ante. In contrast, once Flash moved into the incoming lane, it was humanly impossible to know until after the fact whether the three drivers would escape serious injury. Accordingly, it might be argued an actor is guilty of creating a risk if, and only if, as in Flash Racer, it is humanly impossible to know until after the fact that harm is *not* going to materialize.

The foregoing test has some virtues: it is definite and manageable; and it captures one sense of what renders risks frightening, ie, the unknowable. The problem is that it fails to punish risks that legislatures appear to have in mind in enacting statutes like MPC, section 211.2. It would punish actors like Flash Racer. But it would acquit Teenager-3, as well as paradigmatic culprits who engage in drive-by shootings, only to discover afterwards that putative victims were in positions in which they could not be struck.

Fourth, the viewpoint that epistemic theory requires might be argued to consist of a *reasonable* observer in the actor's position at the time he acts. The term 'reasonable' is commonplace in criminal law. Significantly, however, 'reasonable' is commonplace only in *not* being employed in the way that is proposed here. 'Reasonable' is typically used as a *normative* criterion—that is, a standard of either normatively acceptable conduct or normatively acceptable thinking.[66] It is not used, as proposed here, as a non-normative criterion of empirical cognition. And for good reason. There is no non-arbitrary way of determining the amount of cognition that an actor should possess other than a normative measure of acceptable thinking on his part.[67] Yet a normative measure cannot be the viewpoint we are seeking. A normative measure of acceptable thinking on an actor's part is agent-relative—that is, a normative measure of events entirely as perceived by the actor himself. What is needed, and what does not exist, is a non-arbitrary, agent-independent measure of acceptable cognition.

Finally, another possibility might exist regarding rare risks, like Russian Roulette, that lend themselves to the mathematics of games of chance—namely, that, despite their possessing ex post omniscience, jurors may imagine themselves knowing nothing ex ante but commonplace mathematics of chance. Thus, with respect to 'Lucky Roulette' in which jurors know ex post that the fateful bullet failed to land in a firing position, the jurors might reason as follows:

We now know—given the particular chamber in which the defendant chose to place the bullet, the mass of the cylinder, the revolver's degree of friction, and the degree of force the defendant brought to bear in spinning the cylinder—that the revolver could not have fired. Nonetheless, we can easily imagine knowing nothing ex ante except that the six-chambered cylinder contained a single bullet when the defendant spun it—thus yielding a probability of 1 out of 6 (0.167) that pulling the trigger would result in death or serious bodily injury.

It is doubtless true that jurors may resort to such reasoning if judges allow them to do so. Nevertheless, there are at least two reasons why doing so is not a probabilistic solution to non-materialized risks generally.

---

[66] P Westen, 'Individualizing the Reasonable Person In Criminal Law' (2008) 2 *Criminal Law and Philosophy* 137, 138 (arguing that the law should treat all such risks as agent-relative).

[67] L Alexander, 'Inculpatory and Exculpatory Mistakes and the Fact/Law Distinction' (1993) 12 *Law and Philosophy* 33–70, 65–7; Perry, 'Risk, Harm, and Rights', 190–209, 197.

First of all, insofar as jurors think that the one-time chance of injury from a particular person placing a particular bullet in a particular chamber and spinning it in a particular way is 0.167, they are simply mistaken and may be instructed accordingly. The purpose of all probability theories, as we have seen, is to relate the mathematics of probability to the actual world of infinitely particularized events. Frequency theories, for example, endeavour to relate the mathematics of probability (for example, the relation of 1 chance out of 6) to statistical data regarding the frequency within generic references classes (for example, class of 'games of Russian Roulette with a single round in a six-chamber revolver') of target sets of events (for example, 'a grievous injury'), a frequency that in the case of Russian Roulette approaches but never reaches 0.167. However, frequency theories do not even purport to speak to the probabilities of one-time, particularized events that are the focus of criminal trials. Thus, if a juror in Lucky Roulette reasons, 'There was a 0.167 probability that the defendant's game of Russian Roulette would be injurious because statistics show that between 195 and 205 of 1,200 sample games of Russian Roulette result in injury', the juror is guilty of mixing apples (ie probability of grievous injury regarding a particularized event) with oranges (ie frequency within a reference class of a *set* of grievous injuries).

Second, and more importantly, the risks that come before criminal courts, for example, drive-by motorists shooting into occupied building or motorists passing on blind curves, tend to be highly particularized events that do not lend themselves to the mathematics associated with games of chance. While Russian Roulette might leave jurors mistakenly thinking that they can precisely calculate chances, the vast bulk of risks that are criminally prosecuted do not.

6 AN ALTERNATIVE UNDERSTANDING OF RISK

The failure of conventional wisdom to account for criminal-law references to risk leads some commentators to claim that the law's only option is to acknowledge that no such agent-independent risks exist.[68] Happily, an alternative exists in the form of an alternative conception of agent-independent risks—and one that is similar to the notion of danger and threat that underlies the defence of impossibility.

Commentators have famously struggled to explain widely shared intuitions regarding when impossibility attempts should and should not be punished.

---

[68] L Alexander, 'A Unified Conception of Criminal Culpability' (2000) 88 *California Law Review* 931, 935–6.

Numerous commentators take the view that the deciding consideration is how *dangerous* or *risky* or *threatening* the actor has revealed himself to be.[69] Some of them argue that defences of impossibility should be explicitly framed as an absence of such threats.[70] Others argue in favour of objective rules regarding absences of threat, for example, rules that actors ought not be punished for attempting to kill persons by means that are inherently defective or persons who, unbeknownst to them, were already dead or physically absent at the time.[71] In either event, however, they agree that an actor should not be punished for an impossibility attempt unless, in the language of the MPC, he reveals himself to have 'threatened the harm or evil sought to be prevented by the law defining the offense'.[72]

The challenge for those who hold the foregoing view is to explain how ostensibly failed endeavours can nevertheless constitute 'threats'. What are 'threats' for purposes of impossibility attempts, ie, attempts that given actors' mistakes of law and/or fact appear ex post to have been destined to fail?

Some possibilities can be dismissed out of hand. Such threats cannot consist of harms that actors threaten *to bring about in the future*; for if they did, actors whose failed attempts in the past render them harmless in the future could not be rightly condemned for attempt (for example, an assassin who, in the course of missing his target and being shot in response, is rendered a paraplegic).[73] Nor can threats consist, as George Fletcher argues, of the harms that actors would inflict if they were *disabused of their mistakes before acting*; for if they did, a husband who puts poison in his seemingly sleeping wife's water glass in order to be rid of her, only to discover the next morning that she had died of a heart attack shortly before he acted, could not rightly be punished for attempted murder. Nor can threats consist, as Paul Robinson argues,[74] of the harms that actors will produce if they *repeatedly do the same thing*; for if 'the same' is defined by the entirety of what such actors do, no actor can be punished for an impossibility attempt, while if 'the same' is defined by what actors mistakenly believe they are doing, all actors must be punished for impossibility attempts.

Rather, as I have argued elsewhere, when the law refers to an impossibility attempt as a threat or a danger, it is using 'threat' and 'danger' to refer not to *factual*

---

[69] Eg I Dennis, 'Preliminary Crimes and Impossibility' (1979) 31 *Current Legal Problems* 31, 45; RA Duff, *Criminal Attempts* (Oxford: Oxford University Press, 1996), 380–3; G Fletcher, 'Constructing a Theory of Impossible Attempts' (1986) 5 *Crim J Ethics* 53, 63–7; H Gross, *A Theory of Criminal Justice* (New York: Oxford University Press, 1979), 194–6, 209, 215–16; J Hasnas, 'Once More unto the Breach' (2004) 54 *Hastings Law Journal* 1, 73–4; T Weigend, 'Why Lady Eldon Should Be Acquitted' (1977) 27 *DePaul Law Review*, 231–73, 263–4, 268–9.

[70] G Fletcher, *Rethinking Criminal Law* (Oxford: Oxford University Press, 1978), 57–9, 64; Weigend, 'Why Lady Eldon Should Be Acquitted', 231–73, 263–4, 268–9; P Westen, 'Impossibility Attempts: A Speculative Thesis' (2008) 5 *Ohio State Journal of Criminal Law* 523, 546–9.

[71] Eg Duff, *Criminal Attempts*, 380–3; L Crocker, 'Justice in Criminal Liability: Decriminalizing Harmless Attempts' (1992) 53 *Ohio State Law Journal* 1057, 1103–7.

[72] MPC, § 2.12(2). See also MPC, § 5.05(2).

[73] Duff, *Criminal Attempts*, 381.

[74] See Robinson, 'Prohibited Risks and Culpable Disregard or Inattentiveness', 367, 389–90.

probabilities of harm but to fears of *counterfactual* events of a certain kind—counterfactual events that judges and/or juries fear could have occurred and that, had they occurred, would have produced the very harms that the offence being attempted is designed to prevent.[75] Thus, under this view, an attempted assassin who shoots and barely misses his target is a homicidal threat because the assassin would, indeed, have succeeded under slightly differently counterfactual conditions that judges and juries are likely to fear could easily have occurred, for example, 'if he had happened to use a slightly different line of fire'. In contrast, a vengeful but fearful octogenarian who attempts to kill a target by sticking pins in a voodoo doll is not a homicidal threat because he would have succeeded only under fundamentally different counterfactual conditions that judges and juries are likely to believe could never have occurred, ie 'if pin-sticking were actually lethal'.

Traditional rules of impossibility are implicitly designed to capture these counterfactual judgments, but, being rules of thumb, they roughly approximate them. Thus, common law courts exculpate actors when their criminal attempts fail because their intended victims or their intended objects are 'missing'.[76] 'Missing-victim' and 'missing-object' rules can produce results that square with counterfactual intuitions in individual cases, for example, when they exculpate actors for trying to kill persons who never existed or who died years beforehand. However, because the rules are rigid, they can also exculpate actors for attempts that counterfactual judgments regard as threatening, for example, shooting a person who, unbeknownst to the actor, died moments earlier, or attempting to pick a pocket that is empty.[77] It would be better to leave it directly to triers of fact to make the counterfactual judgments themselves.[78]

In short, I believe that 'risk' and 'danger' within the law of explicit risk creation have the same meaning as 'threat' within the law of impossibility, with one modification. The modification concerns the degree to which fact-finders must fear that counterfactual conditions could have occurred in light of the gravity of the possible harm. Attempt and other crimes of ulterior intent are defined by reference to wrongful acts that actors reveal themselves to have been willing to commit and, hence, by reference to the essential elements of criminal desert. Because the defence of impossibility is invoked by actors who have revealed themselves to be deserving of punishment, the defence does not apply so long as judges and/or juries even *slightly* fear that harmful counterfactual conditions could have occurred. In contrast, because crimes of explicit risk creation require that actors produce 'significant' risks, liability requires that judges and/or juries possess a *significant fear* that harmful counterfactual conditions could have occurred.

---

[75] See Westen, 'Impossibility Attempts', 523–65.

[76] Duff, *Criminal Attempts*, 85–92.

[77] For an endeavour to preserve missing-victim rules that, I fear, only codifies the author's personal counterfactual judgments, see Duff, *Criminal Attempts*, 222–36, 380–4.

[78] Westen, 'Impossibility Attempts', 523, 563–5 (proposing such a rule).

7 A Problem Regarding Implicit Risks

I have thus far discussed two classes of risk-creation offences: (1) crimes of attempt and other crimes of ulterior intent to which impossibility is a defence;[79] and (2) crimes of explicit risk creation, which are predicated on assessments of risk. And I have argued that to a greater or lesser degree, both classes of offences require the presence of agent-independent threats measured often, if not always, by fears that with slight changes in fortune, harm would have occurred.

A third class of risk-prevention offences remains, however—crimes of implicit risk creation. The latter consist of conduct that legislatures regard as sufficiently risky to justify categorical prohibition, for example, failing to come to a full stop at a stop sign even on a deserted road where visibility reveals no approaching vehicles or pedestrians. Such offences abound in penal codes because, by virtue of not requiring proof of ulterior intent and not requiring proof of significant risks, they are relatively easy to detect and easy to prosecute. Nevertheless, they raise a problem of justice: what is the justification for punishing a person for engaging in conduct that is conclusively presumed to be risky but in reality is innocuous?[80]

Doug Husak argues that it is unjust to punish such actors in the event that they non-negligently believe their conduct to be safe. And he proposes two legislative solutions: (1) amending statutes regarding implicit risks to require proof of actual 'risks' or 'dangers', thereby transforming them into crimes of explicit risk creation; and (2) amending statutes regarding categorically wrongful risks to require that actors possess mens rea, such as knowledge, recklessness, or negligence, regarding the harms that such statutes seek to prevent.[81]

Husak's proposals merit serious attention. However, they also raise problems of their own. The first proposal remedies the injustice that concerns Husak but at the cost of requiring individualized showings of dangerousness, thereby eliminating the features that cause legislators and prosecutors to prefer crimes of implicit risk-creation to crimes of explicit risk-creation. The second proposal protects those who are blameless, but it fails to address the problem of punishing actors for imaginary and non-existent risks, for example, momentarily crossing a painted median in violation of a per se rule against doing so, mistakenly thinking that one cannot tell whether vehicles may be approaching in the oncoming lane when, in fact, one can.

---

[79] There is scant authority, either one way or another, that the impossibility defence extends to crimes of ulterior intent other than attempt, but there is some and, I believe, ought to be more. See A Simester and G Sullivan, *Criminal Law: Theory and Practice* (2nd edn; Oxford: Hart, 2003), 268–9 (impossibility is a defence to the crime of incitement).

[80] See Duff, *Answering For Crime*, 166–74.

[81] Husak, *Overcriminalization*, 173–4.

There is, however, a solution that courts can invoke without having to await legislative change. Just as courts impose court-created impossibility defences on statutory crimes of attempt, they can also impose court-created impossibility defences on crimes of implicit risk creation.[82] And they can do so for the same reason, namely that no one should be punished for a crime of risk creation—whether a crime of ulterior intent, a crime of explicit risk creation, or a crime of implicit risk creation—unless judges and/or juries fear that harmful, counterfactual conditions could have occurred.

Now it might be thought that, like Husak's first proposal, my proposal transmutes crimes of implicit risk creation into crimes of explicit risk creation. But that is not so. Crimes of explicit risk creation require proof of a *significant* risk of harm. My proposal provides a defence when there is *no* risk at all. Though both notions of risk are a function of counterfactual conditions that fact-finders fear could have occurred, they consist of different degrees of fear.

8 CONCLUSION

What, then, does the criminal law mean by 'risks' and 'dangers' regarding events that appear ex post to have been harmless? What is the difference between real dangers and imaginary ones? Why does the MPC prohibit conduct that 'places or may place' others in danger, while most states are content to prohibit 'placing' others in danger?

Antony Duff implicitly addresses these concerns by distinguishing between '*actually*' endangering others (for example, 'driv[ing] around a blind corner on the wrong side of the road' when other drivers are approaching) and '*not*' endangering others (for example, when 'no one is in fact coming').[83] However, Duff provides no test to distinguish actual from non-existent dangers, and none is manifest in his examples. If driving in the wrong lane does not endanger anyone when a birds-eye view would show that no one is approaching, then pulling the trigger in a game of Russian Roulette does not endanger anyone when a birds-eye view would show the operative chamber to be empty. Yet if pulling the trigger in a game of Russian Roulette does not endanger anyone, what conduct that fact-finders know ex post to have been harmless *would*?

The answer to these questions does not lie in factual assessments, that is, in trying to identify facts that manifest dangerousness regarding events that are known ex post

---

[82] Simester and Sullivan, *Criminal Law*, 315–17 (impossibility is a defence to common law conspiracy, a crime of implicit risk creation).

[83] Duff, *Criminal Attempts*, 163 (emphasis added).

to have been harmless. The answer lies in counterfactual judgments of a kind that cannot be verified—which may explain why the MPC waffles between conduct that 'places' and 'may place' others in danger. The resolution of Russian Roulette cases and Duff's driving cases turn on how fearful the events seem in retrospect to fact-finders who know ex post that threatened harms did not, and now will never, occur. Such fears are a function of how easily fact-finders can imagine the occurrence of counterfactual conditions under which the fateful harms would have occurred.

The thesis, if correct, has consequences in criminal law theory and practice: in theory, because it argues for commonality between the law of endangerment and the defence of impossibility; and in practice, because it affects the way juries are instructed.[84]

---

[84] For an instruction that would have to be changed, see *Tennessee Pattern Jury Instructions—Criminal*, s 6.03 (instructing juries to convict of reckless endangerment only if they find that 'a reasonable probability exist[ed]' at the time the defendant acted that his conduct would place others in imminent danger of death or serious bodily injury).

15

THE DE MINIMIS 'DEFENCE' TO CRIMINAL LIABILITY

DOUGLAS HUSAK*

1 INTRODUCTION

OF the many defences sufficiently important to be included in the influential Model Penal Code, surely the de minimis defence has attracted the least scholarly attention and generated the fewest judicial opinions.[1] Despite its potential availability in a broad range of circumstances, treatises often neglect this defence altogether. Entire

* Ken Levy, Peter Westen, and Jae Lee provided very helpful and detailed comments. Special thanks to Stuart Green, whose parallel research on the topic of de minimis theft has been extraordinarily valuable.

[1] The text of the statute is:

Model Penal Code §2.12. De Minimis Infractions

The Court shall dismiss a prosecution if, having regard to the nature of the conduct charged to constitute an offense and the nature of the attendant circumstances, it finds that the defendant's conduct:

(1) was within a customary license or tolerance, neither expressly negated by the person whose interest was infringed nor inconsistent with the purpose of the law defining the offense; or

(2) did not actually cause or threaten the harm or evil sought to be prevented by the law defining the offense or did so only to an extent too trivial to warrant the condemnation of conviction; or

monographs are written about self-defence, insanity, entrapment, and the like. But a search of legal periodicals reveals only a small handful of articles that focus on this mysterious plea.[2] Most of these articles presuppose a utilitarian, cost-benefit perspective on liability and punishment, and thus are only marginally relevant to the desert-based approach I invoke here. My aim is to correct this oversight by critically examining the de minimis defence from the standpoint of desert—if, indeed, it *has* a desert base and is properly categorized as a defence at all. Despite reaching few firm conclusions, my work is pioneering almost by default. But my objective is not merely to fill a lacuna among criminal law commentators by examining a neglected topic. I hope to demonstrate that de minimis is significant in its own right, but my inquiry is valuable largely because of what it reveals about other doctrines and principles in criminal theory that have attracted far more scrutiny from philosophers of law. I aim to establish that careful thought about de minimis helps to shed light on such central and fundamental topics as criminalization, the rule of law and the parameters of discretion, the relationship between morality and law, the structure of wrongdoing, the contrast between offences and defences, the concepts of justification and excuse, and even the nature of retributive justice itself.

2 PRELIMINARY MATTERS

Before turning to these broader topics, some preliminary matters must be addressed. In what follows, my discussion focuses on what I take to be (and what I will subsequently call) true de minimis rather than on the particular text of section 2.12 of the Model Penal Code. My reasons are simple. By its own terms, section 2.12 creates a defence, and de minimis may not always function as a defence. Moreover, section 2.12 contains what I take to be *four* separate but loosely related defences that are misleadingly assimilated in a single statute titled 'De Minimis Infractions'. Perhaps only one and at most two of these distinct defences can plausibly be construed as a formulation of de minimis. Section 2.12(1) applies when the defendant's conduct is 'within a customary license or tolerance', and section 2.12(3) bars liability when the defendant's conduct 'presents such other extenuations that it cannot reasonably be regarded as envisaged by the legislature in forbidding the offence'.[3] Fascinating

---

(3) presents such other extenuations that it cannot reasonably be regarded as envisaged by the legislature in forbidding the offense.

[2] Perhaps the most conceptually sophisticated piece is S Pomorski, 'On Multiculturalism, Concepts of Crime, and the De Minimis Defense' (1997) 51 *Bringham Young University Law Review* 51.

[3] Model Penal Code, § 2.12.

though these (equally neglected) provisions may be, there need be nothing *minimal* about the extent of the harm or evil caused when either section 2.12(1) or section 2.12(3) is invoked. Thus I will confine almost all of my remarks to section 2.12(2)—which is the sole part of the statute that could be said to create a true de minimis defence.[4]

Section 2.12(2) provides that 'the court shall dismiss a prosecution if, having regard to the nature of the conduct charged to constitute an offence and the nature of the attendant circumstances, it finds that the defendant's conduct . . . did not actually cause or threaten the harm or evil sought to be prevented by the law defining the offence or did so only to an extent too trivial to warrant the condemnation of conviction'.[5] Each clause in this disjunctive provision creates a separate defence, only the second of which is clearly described as de minimis. It is one thing to deny that the defendant's conduct caused or threatened *any* of the harm or evil sought to be prevented by the law defining the offence, and quite another to admit that her conduct *did* cause or threaten that very harm or evil, but did so only to an extent too trivial to permit a conviction. Why would anyone describe the former phenomenon as de minimis? In a true de minimis situation, the harm or evil is caused, albeit to a minor degree. To avoid possible confusion, I will refer only to cases that arise under the second clause of section 2.12(2) as instances of *true* de minimis.

When the first clause of section 2.12(2) is invoked, the defendant alleges that the harm or evil to be avoided by the offence is not caused or threatened at all. De minimis or not, such circumstances create a powerful case for exculpation—even more powerful than true de minimis. The example provided by the draftsmen involves an 'unconsented-to contact' that 'might constitute a technical assault in some jurisdictions, even though the harm that was threatened and that in fact occurred was too trivial for the law to take into account'.[6] Although a case in which the harm or evil to be prevented by the statute did not occur to any degree provides an even more powerful basis for exculpation, an intuitive basis for acquittal is also compelling in a true de minimis situation. Liability in this situation would be unjust, even though persons may disagree about exactly what is unjust about it. In section 6 of this chapter I will attempt to support this intuition and suggest why a de minimis principle is needed. As we will see, the rationale I will provide—although not especially original—has important but easily overlooked implications for a large body of criminal law doctrine. Before turning to this issue, however, several additional observations about the Code's de minimis provision are helpful.

First, I subsequently omit the '. . . or evil' part of section 2.12(2) when referring to the statutory codification of a true de minimis defence. Part of my reason is simplicity. It is not entirely clear what the 'evil' disjunct is designed to add to the 'harm'

---

[4] The Comments to the Code acknowledge that the considerations contained in § 2.12(2) lie 'more literally within the de minimis label'. Comments to § 2.12, p 403.

[5] Model Penal Code, § 2.12(2).

[6] Model Penal Code, Comments to § 2.12, pp 403–04. Presumably, this problem could be rectified by better draftsmanship; an assault statute should ban only non-trivial unconsented touchings.

disjunct. Perhaps they are redundant. A second reason for deleting reference to evil is my contention that conduct is best construed as de minimis when its degree of wrongfulness is too minimal to justify a criminal conviction.[7] This contention may seem peculiar in an argument for retaining that part of the statute that refers to *harm*. After all, wrongfulness and harm are distinct. Many and perhaps most types of acts, however, owe much of their wrongfulness to their tendency to cause harm; their wrongfulness consists solely or partly in their harmfulness. A true de minimis defence is most easily granted when the wrongfulness of the offence is too trivial to warrant a conviction because the amount of harm caused (or risked) is too small to justify the imposition of criminal liability.[8] Thus I will continue to refer to harm in my examination of de minimis.

Notice also that no one can hope to decide whether a given crime is de minimis unless he is able to identify the particular harm a given statute is designed to prevent. How do we know what objective given statutes are intended to achieve? Often the answer is apparent. Statutes proscribing core offences such as murder and rape are designed to prevent the obvious harms caused by these crimes. In many cases, however, the harm a statute is designed to prevent is much less clear. Unfortunately, legislators have no duty to inform citizens of the harms they intend their penal laws to proscribe. Courts are generally unwilling to attribute a purpose to a piece of legislation, and thus are reluctant to find that the application of a given statute to a particular situation will not facilitate its objective. Judgments about whether a crime is de minimis may remain contested in the absence of agreement about the nature of the harm a statute is designed to prevent.

Although the two clauses of section 2.12(2) are easy to distinguish analytically, the difficulty of identifying the harm a statute is designed to prevent may contribute to uncertainty about *which* clause is invoked in a particular case in which the defence is potentially available. In some contexts, the defendant *cannot* cause the harm or evil the statute seeks to prevent precisely because of the sense in which his offence is too trivial to produce it. The offence of drug possession illustrates this phenomenon. Consider a defendant who is arrested and prosecuted after non-usable traces of drugs are vacuumed from the carpet of his house or car. If the point of a statute proscribing drug possession is to prevent persons from using a drug for a given purpose—say, to produce intoxication—the defence should be applicable when the

---

[7] Commentators who have addressed this topic concur in formulating de minimis in terms of wrongfulness, eg A Ashworth, *Principles of Criminal Law* (5th edn; Oxford: Oxford University Press, 2006), 47. Still, one might find it useful to contrast de minimis *wrongs* from de minimis *harms*.

[8] Admittedly, my interpretation makes it difficult to decide whether and under what conditions given violations of (so-called) regulatory offences are de minimis. Suppose (eg) that a defendant breaches a law requiring him to certify that he has complied with a rule. Since the wrongfulness of a breach is not easily construed as a function of the harm caused or risked, it is hard to know how a de minimis principle would apply. For similar worries see ibid 47.

amount possessed is too miniscule to cause that psychological effect.[9] Admittedly, this defence seldom succeeds,[10] and some statutes contain language that seems to disallow it. Some offences attach liability to the intention of the defendant rather than to a result he causes. These offences may render immaterial the fact that the amount of a drug is too small to produce an effect.

Next, it is noteworthy that codifications of de minimis are fairly uncommon throughout the Anglo-American world. Despite the remarkable success of the Model Penal Code in stimulating statutory reform among the 50 states, only four— New Jersey, Maine, Hawaii, and Pennsylvania—have actually adopted a true de minimis defence.[11] The absence of comparable language in the vast majority of state penal codes is peculiar. After all, de minimis is hardly a strange idea with ties to a controversial political ideology. Nor is it of recent vintage.[12] Even a child knows something is amiss when she is punished for a trivial violation of a rule. The absence of a de minimis defence would seem to increase the probability of injustice. As commentators recognized over 50 years ago, if criminal statutes were enforced as 'precisely and narrowly laid down, the penal law would be ordered but intolerable'.[13] The potential for mischief is even greater today than when the Model Penal Code was drafted. The recent trend has been to enact exceedingly broad and open-ended statutes that legislators do not expect to be enforced as written. Greater numbers of crimes reaching a broader range of conduct magnify the opportunities for unjust convictions.[14] Under these circumstances, the absence of something resembling a de minimis defence seems unthinkable. We know that few employees who commit petty theft against their employers are actually punished. How do we achieve results we take for granted when no explicit provision of law requires exculpation? In other words, how do states manage to avoid injustice without a de minimis defence?

Presumably, states circumvent the need for a true de minimis defence largely through exercises of official discretion. Police and prosecutors inevitably enjoy vast discretionary powers as a result of the extraordinary breadth of penal laws. These officials can hardly proceed in every case in which a person is thought to have violated the literal terms of a law, and thus have little choice but to use their judgment

---

[9] See Comment, 'Criminal Liability for Possession of Nonusable Amounts of Controlled Substances' (1977) 77 *Columbia Law Review* 596.

[10] But see *State v Vance,* 602 P 2d 933 (Haw 1979), and cases cited therein.

[11] Each of these states has tinkered with the language of § 2.12. See *NJ Stat Ann* 2C:11; *Me Rev Stat Ann* 17A, 12; *Haw Rev Stat* 702–236; and 18 *Pa Cons Stat Ann* 312. Guam also includes a de minimis provision.

[12] Indeed, it is dignified with a Latin formulation: *de minimis non curat lex.* This maxim typically is translated as 'the law does not concern itself with trifling matters'. The classic piece is ML Veech and CR Moon, 'De Minimis Non Curat Lex' (1947) 45 *Michigan Law Review* 537.

[13] CD Breitel, 'Controls in Criminal Law Enforcement' (1960) 27 *University of Chicago Law Review* 427, 427.

[14] D Husak, *Overcriminalization* (New York: Oxford University Press, 2008).

about which conduct is worth arresting and prosecuting. Although the principles they employ in exercising their discretion are not always clear, it seems obvious that police and prosecutors fail to arrest or to bring charges in circumstances they assess to be de minimis. Thus injustice is more readily avoided than in a system in which little or no discretion is entrusted to these officials.

If few jurisdictions expressly contain statutory language modelled after section 2.12(2), what actually happens to defendants in those rare and regrettable circumstances in which they are arrested and prosecuted for causing a minor harm? Are such persons more likely to be convicted and punished than in jurisdictions that contain a true de minimis defence? Reliable data on this important question are unavailable. But one reason to be sceptical that the outcomes in these two kinds of jurisdictions differ is that few defendants actually succeed on a de minimis plea even where the defence exists. No one should doubt, however, that many prosecutions that involve de minimis infractions are resolved through less visible means—whether or not an explicit defence is recognized.[15]

3 THE ROLE OF DE MINIMIS

Few would deny that de minimis does and should affect sentences. *Ceteris paribus*, offences that cause minor harms should be punished less severely. But it is crucial to appreciate that de minimis may play at least three distinct but related roles in a theory of criminal liability prior to the sentencing stage. Each of these three roles admits of subtle variations and occasionally blur into one another. First and perhaps most obviously, de minimis may function as a constraint on criminalization. Second, de minimis—or, more precisely, the contrary of de minimis—may appear as an element of a criminal offence. Third, de minimis may serve as a true defence from liability. Criminal theorists have reason to carefully distinguish each of these three roles. Among the ultimate objectives of a theory of de minimis is to specify when this exculpatory consideration should play one role rather than another. Unfortunately, my own efforts will fall short of this aspiration. My more modest goal is to identify some of the factors that should be brought to bear in deciding which of these roles de minimis should play in given situations. One reason I will be unable to reach the more ambitious objective is that theorists are bound to disagree about some of

---

[15] Impressive evidence that jurors invoke de minimis concerns in reaching verdicts is presented in the path-breaking study by H Kalven, Jr, and H Zeisel, *The American Jury* (Chicago: University of Chicago Press, 1965), ch 18.

the moral intuitions I will invoke in particular cases.[16] Although I will eventually attempt to support some of these intuitions, I am aware that the entire topic of de minimis is riddled with intractable controversy. No starting point in a theory of de minimis is secure and capable of supporting a foundation. Some theorists are likely to reject its exculpatory force altogether.

I will briefly describe each of the three roles de minimis might play in a theory of criminal liability. First, de minimis is among the cornerstones of a theory of criminalization, serving to limit the kinds of penal offences legislatures should enact. As we will see, de minimis concerns often arise when a particular instance of criminal conduct is trivial, even though most other acts of that type are not. Some acts of theft are petty, for example, even though theft in general is relatively serious. When a statute proscribes conduct that is *always* innocuous, however, de minimis is applicable in its first and most fundamental sense. If a problem is trivial, the heavy hand of a punitive sanction is not an appropriate mechanism to address it. A social concern may be small and thus not require a penal solution for at least two reasons, only the second of which involves a genuine de minimis rationale. In the relevant sense, a problem is small not because few persons engage in the activity that causes it, but regardless of the number of such persons. If the problem is insufficiently serious to justify subjecting persons to punishment, a genuine de minimis rationale entails that a penal statute should not be created. Statutes that proscribe types of minor harms should not have been enacted in the first place.

Clearly, perceptions of the seriousness of given harms may evolve over time. When an existing law is designed to prevent a type of harm that comes to be regarded as trivial, one would expect de minimis concerns to bring about de facto if not de jure change. One of the main reasons that offences fall into desuetude is because the community has ceased to believe they are sufficiently serious. I suspect that the non-enforcement of such crimes as adultery and fornication (in jurisdictions where they still exist) is explained partly by applications of a de minimis principle. The law in action is bound to reflect judgments about de minimis, even when the law on the books does not.

It is hard to offer examples of de minimis offences that should not have been enacted, since many acts that should not be punished are tokens of types that are legitimately criminalized. Consider a law proscribing the defacing of library books. Most citizens would differentiate between a borrower who uses a pencil to place a faint dot next to a memorable passage in a paperback and a patron who rips whole pages from valuable hardcover books. In light of this phenomenon, can any examples of de minimis statutes be identified? The best candidates would be laws utilizing

---

[16] One source of intuitive complexity is that judgments about de minimis are likely to be relative to the status of victims. Eg it may be less culpable to steal a dollar from a wealthy merchant than from someone who is impoverished. The former act is a better candidate for de minimis than the latter.

verbs that necessarily describe relatively trivial behaviour. A statute prohibiting conduct that causes annoyance, irritation, or inconvenience, for example, would fail a de minimis test; serious harms simply do not satisfy these descriptions—although they might be useful to prosecutors in plea-bargaining. In any event, I am unsure whether any existing law proscribes a type of activity for which no token is serious.

De minimis plays a second role in the criminal law: its contrary may be an element of a criminal offence. This function might be performed implicitly. Absent language to the contrary, it is arguable that all offences should be construed to include clauses that exculpate de minimis offenders. This contention might be defended by a principle of statutory interpretation that forbids laws to be applied to reach absurd results.[17] But are de minimis convictions really *absurd*? This second function is performed with less controversy when such clauses are explicit. A given offence might expressly provide that violations must exceed a given threshold of harm. At least two distinct means are available to ensure that statutes cannot be construed to punish minimal harms. First, a statute might specify exactly what quantum of harm is needed before a violation occurs. This result is achieved most readily when harms are easily quantifiable. Consider, for example, a noise (or pollution) ordinance. Obviously, activities that cause some amount of noise are necessary and beneficial. Ideally, then, legislators should provide guidance by specifying exactly how *much* noise—in decibels—persons are permitted to make.

When levels of harm resist simple quantification, however, it is nearly impossible to describe what amount of harm is needed before an offence occurs. In these situations, a second device can be used to ensure that statutory infractions exceed a given threshold. The offence itself might explicitly require violations not to be de minimis, without specifying exactly which actions do or do not qualify. A statute might include a vague standard by stipulating that an infraction must be serious, severe, substantial, or the like. A probable example is the Federal Copyright Law. The complex scheme governing copyright infringements creates an exception for 'fair use', defined in part by reference to 'the amount and substantiality of the portion used'.[18] Although this exception does not literally employ the term 'de minimis', it seems reasonable to construe it to permit infringements deemed to be trivial.[19] Much of the recent commentary about de minimis addresses this second role.[20] Theorists have struggled to draw the line beyond which a copyright infringement becomes substantial.[21] The fact that the bulk of legal commentary on de minimis seeks to answer

---

[17] I owe this suggestion to Alessandro Spena.

[18] 17 USC §107.

[19] Eg *Sony Corp of America v Universal City Studios*, 464 US 407 (1984).

[20] Eg A Inesi, 'A Theory of De Minimis and a Proposal for Its Application in Copyright' (2006) 21 *Berkeley Technology Law Journal* 945.

[21] Eg DS Blessing, 'Note, Who Speaks Latin Anymore?: Translating De Minimis Use for Application to Music Copyright Infringement and Sampling' (2004) 45 *William and Mary Law Review* 2399.

such questions demonstrates the remarkable extent to which a true de minimis *defence*—the third role I will eventually discuss—is invoked so infrequently.

On some occasions, statutes are construed to contain language said to require the conviction of the de minimis offender. As we have seen, for example, courts have wrestled with the question of whether to punish persons for possessing quantities of drugs too small for the body to detect.[22] Some judges have purported to resolve this issue through statutory interpretation. Laws prohibiting the possession of 'any controlled substance' or a controlled substance 'in any amount' have been construed to bar the de minimis plea.[23] I suspect, however, that statutory interpretation does not wholly explain the result in these cases. When a drug offender alleges de minimis, courts sometimes respond that: 'narcotics are contraband and dangerous, causing untold harm to users and to the public by illegal use. A more liberal interpretation favorable to drug addicts cannot reasonably be given.'[24] Such remarks raise the question of whether the commission of some types of crime *cannot* be de minimis. If so, what properties must a crime possess before de minimis pleas are ruled out? One would think that the most serious crimes—murder and rape, for example—might qualify. Drug possession, however, does not seem especially serious.[25] Moreover, I have pointed out that even though a *type* of offence is serious, it hardly follows that each *instance* of that type must be serious as well. In principle, it is hard to see why *any* crime (that does not explicitly allow minor infractions) should be construed to forbid an acquittal on de minimis grounds. I suspect that cases of de minimis rapes and murders are possible, although examples are bound to generate controversy.

De minimis plays yet a third conceptually distinct role in the criminal law. Suppose a given statute prohibits a type of harm that is normally serious and does not contain language governing the trivial offender (one way or the other). Still, no defendant should be convicted if his particular conduct causes only a trivial amount of the harm the law is designed to prevent. Most of my subsequent comments will focus on this third and final role—which alone is properly described as a true de minimis defence.

It is important to notice that de minimis cannot play this third role—as a true defence—when it plays its second role, and its contrary is included as an explicit element of a criminal offence. Suppose, for example, that a statute forbids lenders to charge a rate of interest greater than 18 per cent. Defendants will have an uphill struggle in contending that their lending is de minimis when it exceeds, however trivially, the specified threshold. In addition, a de minimis defence is unavailable

---

[22] One-half grain (32 millilitres) was possessed in *People v Leal,* 413 P2d 665 (Cal 1966).

[23] See *State v Forrester,* 564 P2d 289 (Ore 1977).

[24] *State v Dodd,* 137 NW 2d 465, 473 (Wisc 1965).

[25] See D Husak, 'Desert, Proportionality, and the Seriousness of Drug Offences', in A Ashworth and M Wasik (eds), *Fundamentals of Sentencing Theory* (Oxford: Clarendon Press, 1998), 187.

when statutes are graded. Suppose a law specifies that a defendant commits grand larceny when he steals property worth $100,000 or more, and otherwise commits petty larceny. If a defendant steals property worth exactly $100,000, has he committed de minimis grand larceny so that his charge should be reduced to petty larceny? Obviously not. Once a clear numerical threshold has been established, no crimes beyond that level can be de minimis.

The fact that de minimis is hard to plead when statutes create a precise numerical threshold may help to explain the dearth of cases in which the defence is invoked for violations of speed limits. Intuitively, speed limits may seem to be among the very best examples of laws that should allow a de minimis defence. We all know that persons who drive faster than the speed limit by a single mph are almost never arrested or prosecuted. But if a statute expressly specifies that drivers may not exceed 35 mph, for example, it is problematic to argue that a speed of 36 is de minimis. Legislatures would have had no difficulty exempting persons who drive at this speed from liability. The fact that they stipulated 35 as the exact threshold is powerful evidence that they did not regard drivers who travel at 36 mph as qualifying for this defence.[26] If drivers should not be liable under these circumstances—as I am inclined to believe—the basis of their acquittal is probably not de minimis. Perhaps the 'customary license or tolerance' provision of section 2.12(1) provides a better rationale for acquittal than the true de minimis defence of section 2.12(2).

The defence of de minimis is unavailable even when statutes include a vague standard rather than a bright quantifiable line. Suppose that an offence imposes liability only when an act of littering, for example, is 'substantial', 'serious', or the like. Defendants are ineligible for sanctions when they produce insubstantial amounts of litter; those below that level would simply not be in violation of the statute and therefore would have no need for a defence. This point is important, since the contrary of de minimis is implicitly incorporated into statutory definitions of recklessness and negligence.[27] Both culpability terms require that defendants create a *substantial* risk of harm before liability may be imposed. Substantial risks, I assume, cannot be de minimis.[28] If a defendant who is otherwise reckless or negligent creates a risk that is not substantial, he has no need for a de minimis *defence*, as

---

[26] The 'plain meaning' of such laws is hard to reconcile with a tolerance for de minimis violations. See eg *US v Locke*, 471 US 84 (1985).

[27] Analogues to § 2.12(2) can be found in other statutory language as well. A prosecution for attempt, solicitation, or conspiracy (eg) can be dismissed if the conduct charged is 'so inherently unlikely to result or culminate in the commission of a crime that neither such conduct nor the actor presents a public danger'. See Model Penal Code, § 5.05(2).

[28] Admittedly, a substantial risk of harm is different from a risk of substantial harm. The former refers to the probability that harm would occur while the latter refers to the seriousness of the harm. Although it is hard to be sure, I assume that the requirement that a risk be substantial in the definitions of both recklessness and negligence is designed to preclude both a trivial risk of a serious harm as well as a large risk of a trivial harm.

he has not breached the statute itself. Since the contrary of de minimis is implicitly incorporated into statutory definitions of recklessness and negligence, a true de minimis defence should be available only for crimes requiring the culpability of knowledge or purpose.

In describing de minimis as a true *defence*, I mean to ignore the most familiar rationale in its favour. Frequently, judicial proceedings involving a de minimis infraction are denounced as an inefficient use of judicial resources.[29] Clearly, the social costs of applying a legal rule to a particular infraction may outweigh their benefits, and a de minimis provision allows a criminal justice system to allocate its resources wisely. But even though this rationale for de minimis is sensible and important, I will not explore it further here. As I have indicated, I am interested in arguments of principle, that is, in the issue of whether defendants *deserve* to be acquitted for de minimis infractions. Although a defendant may complain if a court is using its resources inefficiently, his complaint cannot be couched in terms of desert. In what follows, I will investigate whether de minimis might be construed as a *substantive* defence—a defence to which persons are entitled as a matter of justice.[30] I continue to put utilitarian arguments aside.[31]

If the foregoing distinctions between the three possible roles played by de minimis are tolerably clear, we should inquire whether and under what conditions these distinctions are important. In what circumstances should the contrary of de minimis be an element of the offence and when should de minimis function as a true defence? What difference does it make which of these roles de minimis plays? Procedurally, of course, these distinctions can be crucial for the assignment of burdens of proof. But do these contrasts matter substantively? Unless the answer is affirmative, it is unclear *why* these distinctions should have any procedural significance. As I have indicated, I will not hazard a general answer to these difficult questions. The best way to make progress toward their resolution is by deciding whether and why the contrast between offences and defences is important. Thus this inquiry about de minimis plunges us directly to the heart of some of the most central topics in criminal law theory. To these issues I now turn.

---

[29] This rationale pertains to civil litigation as well. When a man sued a company for tricking him into opening an envelope, a California appellate court called the suit 'an absurd waste of the resources of this court, the superior court, the public interest law firm handling the case and the citizens of California whose taxes fund our judicial system'. *Harris v Time, Inc* 191 Cal App 3d 449, 458 (Ct App, 1987).

[30] D Husak, *Philosophy of Criminal Law* (Totowa, NJ: Rowman & Littlefield, 1987), ch 7.

[31] Although many of the considerations he invokes would seem to support the conclusion that defendants deserve to be acquitted for de minimis infractions, the rationale Paul Robinson eventually cites is more clearly consequentialist in nature. He indicates: 'By excluding [from the criminal justice process those harms and evils that are too trivial to merit the special condemnation of criminal conviction] the condemnation value of conviction is maintained and is more likely to be effective in serious cases, where it is most useful.' P Robinson, *Criminal Law Defenses* (St Paul: West Pub Co, 1984), 324.

4 OFFENCES AND DEFENCES

Assume that a statute does not violate principles of criminalization by proscribing a trivial *type* of harm. De minimis might still play the second or third of the foregoing roles I have distinguished. Either its contrary may appear as an element of a criminal offence, or de minimis may serve as a true defence from liability. Which of these remaining roles should it play? Various proposals for distinguishing offences from defences appear to have very different implications for understanding the exculpatory significance of de minimis. To be sure, a few distinguished theorists have contended that this contrast is wholly irrelevant for substantive purposes.[32] Nearly all commentators, however, concur that the distinction between offences and defences is normatively important. They disagree, however, about *what* is substantively significant about it, and thus about how this distinction should be drawn. I assume that all issues that are substantively material to liability must be relevant either to whether the defendant has committed an offence or to whether he has a defence for committing it. Careful thought about how to understand the significance of de minimis—whether it should be treated as a defence or whether its contrary should somehow be included in an offence—may help us to gain insight not only about this plea, but also about the contrast itself.

Some of the most distinguished criminal theorists have sought to show how the distinction between offences and defences should be drawn and why this contrast matters substantively. In what follows, I will briefly examine how thoughts about de minimis reflect on the merits of three such proposals. Unfortunately, the implications of these views for the categorization of de minimis are far from clear, and my attempts to apply their positions to questions about this plea involve enormous conjecture and speculation. Thus I say that each of these proposals to distinguish offences from defences *appears* to have very different implications for how de minimis might be understood.

It may be instructive to try to assess the implications of these three proposals for *theft*—a crime for which it seems intuitively plausible to suppose that a defendant should not be punished when his conduct is de minimis. If a theft involves property of exceptionally low value, a de minimis defence seems applicable.[33] In *State v Smith*, for example, a defendant was acquitted despite stealing three pieces of bubble-gum.[34] In *State v Nevens*, a defendant escaped liability when he took home a few items of

---

[32] G Williams, 'Offences and Defences' (1982) 2 *Legal Studies* 233.

[33] Somewhat surprisingly, acquittals for de minimis thefts are infrequent. Eg in *Commonwealth v Campbell*, 417 A2d 712 (1980), the defence failed when the defendant shoplifted goods valued at $1.59.

[34] 480 A2d 236 (1984).

fruit from an all-you-can-eat restaurant buffet.[35] Although I will try to support this intuition later, for the moment I will tentatively suppose that the above decisions are correct. I will use this supposition to assess scholarly attempts to contrast offences from defences. If the defendants in the above cases deserve to be exculpated, should the basis of their acquittal be located in the offence or in a defence? Admittedly, we need not reach the same answer for each and every situation involving de minimis in which we believe that exculpation is warranted. Still, a single example of a crime may be helpful both to understand and to evaluate the following three proposals to distinguish offences from defences.

George Fletcher was perhaps the first theorist to propose that the distinction between offences and defences matters for normative purposes. According to Fletcher, offence definitions should describe conduct that: 'incriminates the actor in a given society at a given time ... The minimal demand on the definition of an offense is that it reflects a morally coherent norm.'[36] These sketchy remarks are insightful, but are difficult both to interpret as well as to apply. Fletcher admits that 'we find it hard' to specify the precise 'questions of degree' that inevitably arise in deciding whether there exists a 'coherent moral imperative' against particular modes of conduct.[37]

As I construe it, Fletcher's methodology for distinguishing offences from defences yields no single answer to whether de minimis should be treated as a defence or whether its contrary should be included in the definition of an offence. Uncertainty of application is not surprising here. The contrast between acts that are trivially wrongful and acts that are not wrongful at all is hard to draw. Thus I regard this uncertainty as an advantage of his view. In some contexts, like copyright, my own interpretation of 'moral imperative' is that we do not regard behaviour as incriminating *at all* when persons commit given de minimis infringements. As one court has noted:

most honest citizens in the modern world frequently engage, without hesitation, in trivial copying that, but for the de minimis doctrine, would technically constitute a violation of law. We do not hesitate to make a photocopy of a letter from a friend to show another friend, or of a favorite cartoon to post on the refrigerator ... Waiters at a restaurant sing 'Happy Birthday' at a patron's table. When we do such things, it is not that we are breaking the law but unlikely to be sued given the high cost of litigation. Because of the de minimis doctrine, in trivial instances of copying, we are in fact not breaking the law.[38]

If this judgment is correct, as I believe it to be, Fletcher's view entails that the contrary of de minimis should be included in the definition of the behaviour that

---

[35]   485 A2d 345 (1984).

[36]   G Fletcher, *Rethinking Criminal Law* (Boston: Little, Brown and Co, 1978), 562 and 567.

[37]   Ibid 568.

[38]   *Davis v Gap, Inc*, 246 F3d 152, 173 (2d Cir 2001). Presumably, Fletcher's proposal to distinguish offences from defences would apply just as well to *civil* norms designed to prevent faulty behaviour.

constitutes a violation of copyright law. As I have indicated, existing copyright (apparently) does just that.

In other contexts, however, our judgments about the exculpatory significance of de minimis almost certainly differ. Consider my example of the theft of a small amount of merchandise. The act of stealing a piece of bubble-gum from a store unquestionably violates a coherent moral imperative, even though its *degree* of wrongfulness is minimal.[39] If so, the exculpatory significance of de minimis must be conceptualized as a true defence to this act of theft. Although there may be good reason *not* to recognize such a defence—a reason to which I will return—my attempt to apply Fletcher's proposal for contrasting offences from defences would not allow the contrary of de minimis to function as an element of the crime of theft.

Still other examples are hard to categorize either way. The parameters of what employees are permitted to take from their employers for personal use are vague.[40] Is it a 'coherent moral imperative' to forbid office managers, for example, from taking pens and pencils from their workplace to the home? Or do our norms permit such behaviour? As Fletcher anticipated, judgments about coherent moral norms may be ambivalent and unclear. If so, reasonable minds will differ about whether the contrary of de minimis should be treated as an element of the offence that prohibits such conduct or whether de minimis should be treated as a true defence.

Next, consider Antony Duff's novel proposal for distinguishing offences from defences. According to Duff, the contrast between offences and defences mirrors the contrast between responsibility and liability. Persons are responsible for that for which they may be made to answer, and it is fair to require them to answer in criminal court for a presumptive (or prima facie) wrong. Persons are liable when they lack a defence for a presumptive wrong for which they are responsible. A presumptive wrong, in turn, consists in conduct that individuals normally have categorical and conclusive reasons not to consider as options. Thus presumptive wrongs must be defined as wrongs for which persons will be convicted unless they can offer an exculpatory defence.[41] Is conduct a presumptive wrong even when it is de minimis? In other words, should a defendant be required to answer in criminal court for his de minimis wrongs? If so, the exculpatory significance of de minimis must be treated as a true defence. If not, the contrary of de minimis must be included among the set of elements that comprise an offence.

Although the above *question* is tolerably clear, its *answer* is not. Superficially, at least, it seems that persons should never be made to appear in criminal court for a de minimis infraction. If someone engages in conduct that causes a trivial harm, it seems unjust to deem him responsible (in Duff's sense) and to require him to

---

[39] *State v Smith*, 480 A2d 236 (1984).

[40] S Green, 'De Minimis Thefts' (forthcoming). Green provides data suggesting that as many as 60% of all American employees admit to having taken office supplies from work for personal use.

[41] RA Duff, *Answering for Crime: Responsibility and Liability in the Criminal Law* (Oxford: Hart, 2007), esp at 220–4.

respond by pleading a defence on pain of liability. Unless I have misunderstood it, Duff's theory makes it hard to see why de minimis should *ever* be a true defence. To return to my example, suppose our bubble-gum thief is arrested and prosecuted. If his conduct should not be punished, as I have tentatively claimed is intuitively correct, it must be because he should not be required to answer for it in criminal court. What could this defendant possibly say to a judge that was not already known? If I am correct, legislators who implement Duff's methodology for contrasting offences from defences are well advised to include the contrary of de minimis in any offence for which it has exculpatory significance. In other words, all statutes for which de minimis is exculpatory should be defined analogous to copyright law. A defendant whose conduct causes a trivial harm should not be treated as having committed a crime in the first place.

Finally, consider John Gardner's view that the contrast between offences and defences should be drawn by deciding what we have reasons *against* and what we have reasons *for*.[42] According to this conception, offences consist in what the law gives us reason *not* to do, whereas defences consist in what the law gives us reason *to* do. Applications of this test, like those of its rivals, generate borderline cases in which reasonable minds differ. Inasmuch as we have difficulty deciding whether to treat a given factor as material to performing an action or as material to abstaining from it, we will be unsure whether that factor belongs in an offence or should be treated as a defence. Still, this test does not seem unclear in its categorization of de minimis. In the vast majority of contexts, it would be bizarre to say that persons had reasons to commit a de minimis crime. Surely the law does not give our petty thief reason a reason in favour of stealing bubble-gum. If defences consist solely of conduct we have reason to perform, and the contrast between offences and defences is drawn pursuant to Gardner's proposal, it is difficult to comprehend why de minimis should *ever* function as a true defence.

So far, Gardner's methodology yields the same results as Duff's. But applications of Gardner's proposal appear to produce a more radical conclusion. If he is correct, it is not clear why the contrary of de minimis should ever function as an element of a crime. Although there may be a handful of exceptions to this generalization—the 'Happy Birthday' example might qualify—in most contexts persons have reason not to commit even those crimes that are de minimis. Their reasons not to commit a de minimis offence are weaker than their reasons not to cause substantial harm, but they still *have* reason not to commit either one. If offences consist solely of conduct we have reason not to perform, the contrary of de minimis should no more be included in an offence than de minimis should be treated as a defence. On Gardner's

---

[42] J Gardner, 'Fletcher on Offences and Defences' (2004) 39 *Tulsa Law Review* 817. He attributes this suggestion to K Campbell, 'Offence and Defence', in I Dennis (ed), *Criminal Law and Justice* (London: Sweet & Maxwell, 1987), 73.

proposal, it is hard to see why de minimis should have *any* exculpatory significance in a theory of penal liability.

As we have seen, these three scholarly attempts to contrast offences from defences *appear* to have very different implications for the treatment of de minimis in penal codes. Of course, my own efforts to apply these abstract proposals to the plea of de minimis—a plea that none of these theorists had in mind when drawing the distinction—may be misguided. As I have said, my interpretations involve enormous conjecture and speculation. But where does this brief exercise leave us if my efforts are on the right track? My very tentative conclusions are as follows. We have reason to prefer Fletcher's proposal for distinguishing offences from defences if we hold that de minimis should sometimes function as a true defence and sometimes should function as the contrary of an element of an offence. But we have a basis to prefer Duff's device for drawing this contrast if we think that de minimis should function as the contrary of an element of an offence but never as a true defence. And we have reason to prefer Gardner's idea for distinguishing offences from defences if we believe that de minimis should play no role in a theory of criminal liability at all, but only in sentencing. Once again, however, I repeat the highly speculative nature of these conclusions.

I have further suggested that we might begin with an example in which we are inclined to believe that a defendant should be acquitted because his conduct is de minimis—such as the theft of a piece of bubble-gum. If we are relatively certain either that the contrary of de minimis should be part of an offence or that de minimis should be a defence from liability, we can use our confidence to assess the foregoing proposals about how the contrast between offences and defences should be drawn. Unfortunately, with the possible exception of a handful of cases, I suspect that criminal theorists will lack firm intuitions about such matters. Reflective equilibrium is not a methodology that can generate clear conclusions when intuitions about matters both abstract and specific are so frail and uncertain. At the end of the day, I draw no straightforward and unambiguous lessons about de minimis by reflecting on the distinction between offences and defences. Nonetheless, I hope to have moved the inquiry a small way forward by hazarding a few tentative observations.

5 WHAT KIND OF DEFENCE?

Assuming that de minimis sometimes has exculpatory significance, criminal theorists should be uncertain when it should serve as a true defence or when its contrary should be included in the definition of an offence. Part of the explanation for this uncertainty is that we are unclear about how to contrast offences from defences and how various proposals for drawing this distinction apply to our fuzzy intuitions about de minimis. In this section I will suppose that we somehow overcome these obstacles and decide in a given case to treat de minimis as a true defence—as it is portrayed in the Model Penal Code. I then ask: What *kind* of defence could it be? As we will see, enormous confusion surrounds the question of how to conceptualize and understand this plea within conventional defence categories. De minimis cannot qualify as (what might be called) a denial that the offence occurred, since this allegation does not amount to a defence. Among true defences, there are only three possible ways to construe de minimis unless we jettison a great deal of orthodox wisdom in criminal theory. First, de minimis might function as a justification. Second, it could be an excuse. Finally, the existence of a true de minimis defence might show that not all substantive defences can be conceptualized either as justifications or excuses, thus demonstrating the need for additional categories. In my judgment, none of these three possibilities should be dismissed out of hand. If each proves to be untenable, however, we have reason to re-examine our initial decision to treat de minimis as a true defence. The exculpatory significance of this curious plea must be located in offences—or rejected entirely.

Paul Robinson endorses the third of these alternatives. He claims: 'the de minimis infraction defence . . . does not exculpate a defendant because of a justifying or excusing condition, but rather serves to refine the offence definition . . . [The defendant] is outside the harm or evil sought to be prevented and punished by the offence.'[43] Some theorists believe that justification and excuse exhaust the terrain of substantive defences so that no third type is possible. Still, Robinson *may* be correct to suppose that not all defences can be pigeon-holed into our pre-existing categories of justification and excuse.[44] If he is right, however, one wonders why conduct that is 'outside the harm or evil sought to be prevented by the offence' is properly proscribed by the offence in the first place. Robinson's position seems more apt with respect to the first rather than the second disjunct of section 2.12(2). As I have indicated, de minimis offences are not literally *outside* the harm the statute is designed to prevent.[45] Statutes that are vulnerable to the problem Robinson recognizes are overinclusive; if possible, they should be redrafted more narrowly.[46] Despite some sympathy with Robinson's remarks, I do not believe we should be quick to concede that de minimis cannot be assimilated into more familiar defence categories. Although I think we

---

[43] Robinson, *Criminal Law Defenses*, 79.

[44] Duff (eg) believes that the category of justification should be subdivided into permissible and warranted. Duff, *Answering for Crime*, 275.

[45] Moreover, Robinson himself seems to attach no significance to the distinction between the second and third functions I have assigned to de minimis. He writes: 'Whether the negative of the defense is written into the definition of an offense . . . or stated as an independent defense applicable to that particular defense . . . may be merely a matter of drafting ease or efficiency.' Robinson, *Criminal Law Defenses*, 82.

[46] But see SW Buell, 'The Upside of Overbreadth' (2008) 83 *New York University Law Review* 1491.

should allow the possibility that it should be regarded as an excuse, I will argue that the preferable option is to treat a true de minimis defence as a justification.

Despite major differences, the accounts of Fletcher, Robinson, and Gardner are all incompatible with efforts to construe true de minimis as an instance of this type of defence. According to Fletcher, 'grounds of justification represent licenses or permissions to violate the prohibitory norm'.[47] He goes on to construe justifications as Hohfeldian privileges or liberties: 'one has a duty to obey a prohibitory norm and a privilege to violate it when justificatory circumstances are present.'[48] It would be misguided, of course, to conceptualize de minimis as a *permission* or *privilege* to violate a prohibitory norm—as though persons have no duty *not* to violate a norm when their wrongdoing is trivial. To express the matter bluntly, no one is permitted to steal bubble-gum. Even more obviously, de minimis cannot be understood as a justification by those who share Robinson's more general views about this type of defence. All justifications, according to Robinson, describe circumstances in which defendants infringe norms to avoid a greater societal harm or to gain a greater societal benefit.[49] Clearly, no greater good is achieved when defendants commit de minimis offences. In addition, it would be ludicrous to believe that de minimis has the implications for third-party assistance and interference that Robinson assigns to justifications. If de minimis were a justification that operated pursuant to Robinson's principles, the state should encourage persons to commit de minimis infractions and forbid them to interfere when others perpetrate them.[50] Needless to say, each of these implications is patently false. Finally, suppose that Gardner is right to think that a justification does not cancel but rather 'defeats the reasons against an action'.[51] No one believes that the fact that a particular crime is de minimis serves to wholly defeat the reasons against committing it. If any of these theorists were correct about the nature of justification, a true de minimis defence could not possibly qualify as an instance of this kind of defence.

If de minimis *can* be a justification, each of the above theorists must be mistaken about the nature of this type of defence. How should our understanding of justification be altered to allow the possibility that de minimis might justify criminal conduct? Details aside, conduct is generally regarded as justified when it is permissible, that is, when it is not wrongful all-things-considered. Suppose we say, however, that a person is justified not only when his conduct is not wrongful, but also when his conduct is *not wrongful enough*—in other words, not *sufficiently* wrongful—to merit criminal condemnation. De minimis does not cancel, negate, or override the presumptive wrongfulness of a criminal offence altogether, but precludes a sufficient

---

[47] Fletcher, *Rethinking Criminal Law*, 563.
[48] Ibid 564.
[49] Robinson, *Criminal Law Defenses*, 90.
[50] Ibid 9.
[51] J Gardner, 'Justifications and Reasons', in AP Simester and ATH Smith (eds), *Harm and Culpability* (Oxford: Clarendon Press, 1996), 103, 109.

degree of its presumptive wrongfulness to render the defendant ineligible for punishment. In section 6, I will address the issue of why we should withhold criminal liability from defendants whose conduct is not literally permissible, but is relatively close to being permissible. For now, the crucial point is that this conception of the nature of justification would allow a de minimis plea to function as a justification (or what might be called a quasi-justification) from criminal liability.

Whether or not we accept my proposal to revise our understanding of the nature of justification, we should also inquire whether de minimis could function as an excuse from criminal liability. Although the nature of excuse has probably created even more controversy than the analogous debate about justification, scholarly thought about this topic is equally unreceptive to the possibility that this plea could be an instance of this type of defence. Typically, excuses are thought to cancel or eliminate altogether the blame deserved by a defendant who commits a criminal act without justification.[52] If de minimis were to qualify as an excuse, however, this characterization must be too narrow. De minimis offenders are not totally blameless. How would theorists have to characterize excusing conditions in order for de minimis to be an instance of this defence type? My answer is not unlike that provided in the context of justification. Perhaps an excuse should not be understood to preclude blame for unjustified conduct altogether, but merely to reduce it to an amount too small to merit punishment. Again, we may be dubious that excuses *should* be construed in this way. But this interpretation allows de minimis to be conceptualized as an excuse (or a quasi-excuse) from liability.

Although I do not believe that it is obviously mistaken to conceptualize de minimis as an excuse, my own slight preference is to regard it as a justification—if we amend the nature of justification in the way I have described. I tend to believe that excuses pertain to persons, and justifications pertain to conduct. Even though distinguishing properties of agents from properties of their actions is often difficult, this general problem is not especially troublesome in the case of de minimis. Clearly, the claim that a crime is de minimis describes the action rather than the agent who performed it. If so, de minimis is better regarded as a justification than as an excuse—assuming, of course, that we accept my device for contrasting these two types of defence.

Alas, matters are not so simple. An additional consideration might be thought to militate in the opposite direction, indicating that a true de minimis defence is better construed as an excuse than as a justification. A number of theorists have contended that justifications are part of the 'conduct rules' of law so that persons are entitled to rely ex ante on their content.[53] Defendants should be placed on notice of what behaviour is justified, and may employ this information when deliberating what to do. By

---

[52] For further clarification, see D Husak, 'On the Supposed Priority of Justification to Excuse' (2005) 24 *Law and Philosophy* 557.

[53] See eg M Dan-Cohen, 'Decision Rules and Conduct Rules: On Acoustic Separation in Criminal Law' (1984) 97 *Harvard Law Review* 625.

contrast, excuses are 'rules of adjudication', addressed *ex post* to courts rather than to persons. Thus defendants should not be entitled to rely on the availability of an excuse in planning their behaviour. For example, a defendant is not treated unjustly simply because the state alters the legal test of insanity to his detriment. So much the worse for him if he would not have committed the crime but for his expectation of an excuse. If indeed justification and excuse differ in this respect, it should be apparent that a true de minimis defence should not be categorized as a justification. No one should rely on the availability of a de minimis defence in planning his behaviour. Shoppers in retail stores, for example, should not be encouraged to calculate the threshold at which their theft exceeds de minimis in order to insulate themselves from criminal liability.

Clearly, the supposition that persons are entitled to rely on the availability of a justification must be mistaken if de minimis is to count as an instance of this defence type. Fortunately, the foregoing revision in the nature of justification gives us good reason to reject this supposition. Justified conduct need *not* be all-things-considered permissible; it may still be wrongful. If justified conduct is wrongful, although not wrongful enough to merit criminal liability, the law has less reason to allow defendants to use their knowledge about justification when making plans. Thus this argument, at least, does not show why a true de minimis defence cannot be regarded as a justification.

What *should* we say about notice? Even though I have argued that the recognition of a de minimis justification need not be construed to entail that the theft of a miniscule amount is literally permissible, I am sure that the inclusion of a specific dollar amount that could be stolen before a defendant would become liable for theft would be misconstrued to authorize takings under that amount. In the words of Stuart Green, this information would be misinterpreted to confer a 'license to steal' on petty shoplifters.[54] This fear would arise whether de minimis were a true defence or its contrary were included in an offence. On either alternative, the law should avoid precise language about what counts as de minimis. This result is yet another surprising implication of the claim that de minimis should be afforded exculpatory significance. Ordinarily, we tend to value precision and specificity in statutory language—whether that language is included in an offence or in a defence of justification. Vagueness is typically regarded as antithetical to the rule of law. But the threshold for de minimis should remain uncertain. Since the state wants to discourage *all* thefts, a true defence of de minimis should probably say that defendants are not liable for causing minimal harms—without specifying which harms qualify.[55] Unfortunately, this strategy guarantees that different officials will make different

---

[54] Thus Green is lukewarm about recognizing explicit numerical thresholds in a theft statute. Green, 'De Minimis Thefts'.

[55] Even so, some defendants are bound to calculate that they will not incur liability when they commit infractions that officials will deem to be trivial. Should such persons lose the de minimis defence? Although arguments can be constructed to show that they *should* lose the defence, I am inclined to prefer the view that it should be retained even in the case of calculating defendants. A different unresolved question is whether repeat de minimis offenders should lose the defence.

judgments about which particular cases are eligible for exculpation under a de minimis rationale. But the price paid for uniformity is too great.

Suppose I am correct to conclude that the law should sometimes, somehow, acquit defendants for de minimis crimes. Even in the context of petty shoplifting, where it seems that persons should not be punished for trivial infractions, it is tempting to punish them anyway—to prevent others from incorrectly believing that such behaviour is permissible. But justice requires us to reject this argument. No one should be punished in the absence of desert, and I have assumed that defendants who commit de minimis offences do not deserve to be punished.[56] Thus they do not deserve to be punished even to serve the broader goals of crime prevention. What, then, *should* be done to such persons? If de minimis shoplifters should not be punished, but cannot be allowed to steal with impunity, it follows that mechanisms to discourage de minimis shoplifting must be found outside the parameters of the criminal law. According to Green, such mechanisms are already in place.[57] Criminal theorists should applaud these developments.

I emphasize yet again that often it is appropriate for the contrary of de minimis to appear in an offence. Sometimes, however, I assume that de minimis should function as a true defence. When this is so, I am not altogether confident that it should be regarded as a justification, an excuse, or as some third category of defence—although I have a slight preference for the former alternative. The important point, however, is that we would need to reconceptualize the nature of justification and excuse in order to categorize de minimis as an instance of either of these types of defence. The necessary reformulations seem plausible to me, and no competing conceptualization of the de minimis defence is less problematic. However this issue is ultimately resolved, I hope it is clear that careful thought about the exculpatory force of de minimis has broader significance, helping to shed light on the nature of justification and excuse more generally.

6 NORMATIVE CONSIDERATIONS

Thus far I have relied almost solely on intuitions in supposing that some defendants who commit de minimis crimes should somehow escape liability and punishment. I

---

[56] On the other hand, de minimis offenders are not entirely blameless, so familiar worries about sacrificing wholly innocent persons for the common good are not as forceful here.

[57] See Green, 'De Minimis Thefts'. Presumably, these devices vary enormously with the circumstances of the offender. Eg shoplifters might be shamed, barred from shopping at that store, have their credit revoked, warned that the police will be contacted if another incident occurs, have their parents notified, or the like.

admit that these intuitions are frail and unlikely to be universally shared. Perhaps the formidable difficulties in conceptualizing de minimis within orthodox criminal law theory provide reason to be sceptical that this plea has exculpatory significance. Why should de minimis *ever* be relevant to liability as opposed to sentencing? A response to this question must begin by taking a few points for granted. Unquestionably, de minimis crimes are less serious, *ceteris paribus*, than crimes that are not. The seriousness of crime is a function of its culpability, wrongfulness, and harm.[58] A particular offence is de minimis when it is much less wrongful because it causes much less harm than a typical offence of that type, and therefore is far less serious. The controversial claim is that the imposition of liability and punishment are unjust when the seriousness of a given criminal act meets this description. In the remainder of this chapter I try to offer some inconclusive support for this claim.

Why should the degree of wrongfulness of criminal conduct have to exceed a given threshold before punishment is warranted? Of course, consequentialists have a powerful reply. Criminal law is expensive, error-prone, and subject to abuse, and should not be invoked when its costs exceed its benefits.[59] Resort to penal sanctions is likely to do more bad than good when an offence is trivial. Little more needs to be said to explain why de minimis should have exculpatory significance in criminal law. But this reply, as I have indicated, does not purport to show why defendants do not *deserve* to be punished for their minor misdeeds. A conception of retributive justice is required to find a desert-based rationale to preclude liability for de minimis offenders. Retribution should not be exacted through the penal law when defendants engage in trivial wrongdoing. Why not?

I contend that the very meaning of retributive guilt entails that the censure and blame that attends a criminal conviction *cannot* be trivial. A penal conviction is and ought to be stigmatizing. Labelling a person as a criminal expresses not only that he acted wrongfully, but also that his wrongful act rises (or sinks) to a level of seriousness that makes the application of that label appropriate.[60] A principle of fair labelling governs not only particular crimes, but also the criminal category as a whole. The criminal law is and ought to be *different* from other devices to convey censure.[61] A principle of retributive justice should be construed not to allow the punishment of all culpable wrongdoing, but only of culpable wrongdoing that is wrongful enough to merit the powerful stigma of a criminal conviction. After all, criminal blame is not simply a judgment of censure. It is a judgment that is publicly and formally expressed, and used for countless practical purposes that disadvantage those to whom it is applied. A given offence must be relatively serious if a conviction

---

[58] See A Hirsch and N Jareborg, 'Gauging Criminal Harm: A Living-Standard Analysis' (1991) 11 *Oxford Journal of Legal Studies* 1.

[59] For the implications of these facts for a retributive theory of punishment, see D Husak, 'Why Punish the Deserving?' (1992) 26 *Nous* 447.

[60] Ashworth, *Principles of Criminal Law*, 47.

[61] Husak, *Overcriminalization*.

should automatically trigger a wide variety of collateral consequences.[62] As long as we want a criminal record to retain its expressive meaning and real-world significance, we should not impose penal liability on a trivial breach.

Applications of the principle of proportionality suggest a similar result. I construe this principle to require the severity of the punishment to be a function of the seriousness of the offence.[63] As I have said, the seriousness of the offence, in turn, is partly a function of its wrongfulness. When wrongdoing is utterly trivial, *no* criminal sanction—not even a suspended sentence—can be proportionate to it. Any amount of state punishment, no matter how lenient, imposes greater stigma on defendants than they deserve and is disproportionate to the seriousness of their offence.[64] If so, a theory of criminal law that takes proportionality seriously has reason to afford exculpatory significance to de minimis.

If the foregoing considerations are cogent, some of the most fundamental concepts in criminal law function somewhat differently than their moral counterparts. Although I generally believe that the criminal law should track moral philosophy closely,[65] the exculpatory significance of de minimis indicates an important respect in which they appear to diverge. Unlike moral blame—which arguably exists notwithstanding its triviality—the blame that attends a criminal conviction *cannot* be trivial.[66] To be sure, wrongdoing and blame admit of degrees, both in morality and in law. In morality, however, infinitesimal amounts of blame are cognizable. In criminal law, by contrast, quanta of blame beneath a given threshold cease to qualify as criminal blame at all.

I admit that the foregoing considerations are sketchy and provide almost no guidance in deciding when de minimis should be afforded exculpatory significance—either as the contrary of an element of an offence or as a true defence. *How* wrongful must conduct be before it is not wrongful enough to merit penal liability? Although I doubt that this question is possible to answer generally,[67] we might turn to our reactive emotions for clues. Under what conditions do victims of crime feel resentment or indignation, and when do offenders feel guilt or remorse? De minimis offenders should be exculpated when persons with normal sensibilities in a given community

---

[62] Eg M Pinard, 'An Integrated Perspective on the Collateral Consequences of Criminal Convictions and Reentry Issues Faced by Formerly Incarcerated Individuals' (2006) 86 *Boston University Law Review* 623.

[63] See A von Hirsch and A Ashworth, *Proportionate Sentencing: Exploring the Principles* (Oxford: Oxford University Press, 2005).

[64] Kalven and Zeisel speculate that juries sometimes acquit on de minimis concerns when the lack of seriousness of the crime combines with the sentiment that the defendant has already been punished enough by extrinsic circumstances. See Kalven Jr and Zeisel, *The American Jury*, at 262. For a general discussion, see D Husak, 'Already Punished Enough' (1990) 18 *Philosophical Topics* 79.

[65] See D Husak, 'The Costs to Criminal Theory of Supposing that Intentions are Irrelevant to Permissibility' (2009) 3 *Criminal Law and Philosophy* 51.

[66] I assume, however, that there must be a point below which judgments of moral blame should not be *expressed* because of the triviality of the wrongdoing.

[67] See J Nemerofsky, 'What is a "Trifle" Anyway?' (2001/2002) 37 *Gonzaga Law Review* 315.

do not exhibit a sufficient degree of these reactive attitudes to warrant imposing the stigma that attends a criminal conviction. This approach introduces an empirical dimension into our inquiry. We may find that many crimes—such as petty acts of shoplifting or employee theft—attract little stigma. Moreover, large numbers of persons commit these offences,[68] and it is hard to see how a response to wrongdoing can stigmatize if a great many individuals in similar circumstances engage in the same behaviour.[69] Particular crimes are de minimis when the demand for retributive punishment recedes to the vanishing point. Admittedly, precise lines about this matter are exceedingly hard to draw. But no one should conclude that the de minimis plea lacks exculpatory significance because of the difficulty in drawing precise lines. In this respect, controversies about de minimis resemble those about almost every topic in moral and criminal theory. My primary ambition has not been to resolve these debates, but to respond to the scholarly neglect about de minimis by demonstrating how careful reflection about this exculpatory consideration relates directly to several of the most basic issues in the philosophy of criminal law.

---

[68] Green provides data suggesting that as many as 60% of all American consumers have committed shoplifting at some time in their lives. Green, 'De Minimis Thefts'.

[69] See D Husak, 'The "But Everybody Does That!" Defense' (1996) 10 *Public Affairs Quarterly* 307.

JUST DESERTS IN UNJUST SOCIETIES

A CASE-SPECIFIC APPROACH

STUART P GREEN[*]

SHOULD the fact that a criminal offender lives in a society that fails to give him what he 'deserves' in terms of economic or political or social rights affect the determination of what he 'deserves' from that society in terms of punishment? More generally, to what extent is the fairness of a given system of retributive justice dependent on the fairness of the system of distributive or socio-economic justice within which it is situated? Are questions of distributive or socio-economic justice conceptually prior to questions of retributive justice?

Most writing on these issues has tended to assume that there is one set of principles that will explain the proper relationship between retributive and socio-economic justice. The fact that an offender has been denied the basic entitlements of a just

* Helpful comments and questions were received from fellow symposiasts at the University of Chicago Law School, the University of Warsaw Faculty of Law, and Rutgers School of Law, Newark. Special thanks to Antony Duff, Kim Ferzan, and Jae Lee for their insights.

society, however defined, is taken to have implications for criminal liability across the board, regardless of the offence charged and the circumstances of the victim harmed.[1] Under such an approach, if an offender is deemed to be subject to unjust economic impoverishment, or deprived of the right to participate in the political process, or denied the basic protections owed him by the state, the argument is made that it would be unjust, or at least problematic, to impose criminal liability on him for a whole range of offences, whether murder or rape, theft or assault, welfare fraud or obstruction of justice.

An analogous tendency informs much criminal law theory scholarship more generally. We often assume that there is one proper understanding of various issues in the general part (concerning, say, acts and omissions, justifications and excuses, or principals and accomplices), and that, if we can just get that understanding straight, it should apply across the board to all offences within the special part. Under such an approach, either one need not go to the trouble of considering how a given theory would apply with respect to specific offences; or, if one does, and discovers that the theory works for some offences but not others, one should conclude that the theory is incomplete or defective.

I aim to take a different approach here. The argument to be developed suggests that a proper analysis of the relationship between retributive and socio-economic justice should proceed on a case-by-case basis. Such an analysis would take account of three distinct factors. First, it would look to the specific offence with which the offender is charged. The fact that an offender is deeply and unjustly disadvantaged might be relevant to determining his blameworthiness for committing one kind of criminal offence (say, an offence against the person) but not another (say, an offence against property or against the administration of justice). Under this approach, we would need to consider what makes an offender blameworthy for committing a particular kind of offence in the first place, and then ask whether and how his disadvantage affects such blameworthiness. Second, we would need to look at the precise form that the offender's disadvantage takes. The fact that an offender has been denied any reasonable opportunity to obtain property, for example, might be relevant to determining his blameworthiness for committing a particular kind of offence in a way that his being denied the opportunity to participate in the political process or the right to certain kinds of basic police protections by the state might not. Third, we would need to consider the economic and social circumstances of the crime victim (assuming there is an identifiable victim). For example, other things being equal, a criminal act directed by a disadvantaged offender at a similarly disadvantaged

---

[1] See eg SR Perry, 'The Relationship Between Corrective and Distributive Justice', in J Horder (ed), *Oxford Essays in Jurisprudence: Fourth Series* (Oxford: Oxford University Press, 2000); W Sadurski, 'Distributive Justice and the Theory of Punishment' (1985) 5 OJLS 47, 58–9; S Smilansky, 'Control, Desert and the Difference Between Distributive and Retributive Justice' (2006) 131 *Philosophical Studies* 511.

victim might be blameworthy in a way that the same crime directed at a privileged member of the political or economic elite would not.

The analysis developed here is also intended to reflect another goal of criminal law theory. Philosophical theorizing about the criminal law should, I believe, aspire to universality, both descriptively, in the sense of providing an analysis of what the criminal law *is* in a wide range of systems around the world, and prescriptively, in the sense of providing a normative vision, across many systems, of what criminal law *ought* to be. It should seek to provide an understanding of the criminal law that is relevant not just in our own society, but also in societies whose values and practices are very different from our own.[2] Consideration of how a system of retributive justice would apply in a society with a profoundly unjust economic or political order provides an opportunity to develop such an understanding.

1 Socio-Economic Deprivation, Crime, and Injustice

Why should criminal law theorists be concerned with the problem of poverty and other forms of disadvantage, whatever their source? One reason is that the poor and disadvantaged account for a disproportionately high percentage of crime victims. According to US Department of Justice figures, during 2006 the annual rate of victimization for all crimes, both violent and non-violent, per 1,000 persons with incomes of less than $7,500 was 64.6, compared with 14.6 for persons with incomes over $75,000.[3] During the same period, the burglary rate for those with a household annual income of less than $7,500 was 55.7 per 1,000 households, while the rate for those with a household annual income of $75,000 or more was 22.4 per 1,000.[4] Thus, the higher the rate of poverty, the greater the number of people, at least at the low end of the scale, likely to be victims of crime and the more harmful such crime is likely to be.

A second reason is that the poor and disadvantaged account for a disproportionately high percentage of criminal offenders. While the Department of Justice does

---

[2] I have addressed this aspiration in SP Green, 'The Universal Grammar of Criminal Law' (2000) 98 *Michigan Law Review* 2104.

[3] US Census Bureau, *Statistical Abstract of the United States 2009*, table 305, online at <http://www.census.gov/prod/2008pubs/09statab/law.pdf>. The rates were 45.9 per thousand for persons with incomes between $7,500 and $14,999, 31.4 for persons with incomes between $15,000 and $24,999, 34.5 for persons with incomes between $25,000 and $34,999, 22.5 for persons with incomes between $35,000 and $49,999, and 24.5 for persons with incomes between $50,000 and $74,999.

[4] Ibid at table 309.

not tabulate arrest or conviction rates by class or income (instead, it does so for interrelated factors such as race, sex, age, and geographic area), there are a number of scholarly studies which suggest that the lower one's income, the more likely one is to engage in criminal activity, whether violent or non-violent.[5] (This is hardly to imply, of course, that all or even a particularly significant percentage of impoverished people commit crime, or that well-to-do people do not also commit crimes.)

A third reason why criminal law scholars should be concerned with the problem of poverty and disadvantage is the one with which we shall mainly be concerned here—namely the possibility that an offender's impoverishment or other form of disadvantage might bear on his blameworthiness in committing his offence. Whether this is the case would seem to turn, in the first instance, on whether the offender's disadvantage is itself unjust. A person might be impoverished or otherwise disadvantaged for any number of reasons other than systematic injustice: for example, she might be indolent, reckless, or merely unlucky. When we talk about desert in the context of distributive justice, we refer to the fair distribution of burdens and benefits among the members of a given society.[6] In order to say whether a person's impoverishment is truly unfair or unjust, we need an underlying theory that explains what people are entitled to in terms of wealth and opportunity, and exactly how such entitlements arise. Such a theory would consider, for example, whether society is obligated to:

(1) provide for the basic public safety of all its members (whether citizens or mere residents),[7] including basic police protections;
(2) create conditions which make it possible for its members to have an opportunity for a decent life, including conditions that make it possible for members to earn a living, and to obtain healthy food, medical care, adequate shelter, and an education;
(3) provide members with the opportunity to participate in the political process, enjoy certain basic human rights, such as freedoms of speech, conscience, assembly, privacy, and the like, and to resolve disputes, and obtain legal process; and

---

[5] See eg B Western, *Punishment and Inequality in America* (New York: Russell Sage, 2006), 34–51; J Hagan and RD Peterson, 'Criminal Inequality in America: Patterns and Consequences', in J Hagan and RD Peterson (eds), *Crime and Inequality* (Stanford, CA: Stanford University Press, 1995), 19–22; RM Howsen and SB Jarrell, 'Some Determinants of Property Crime: Economic Factors Influence Criminal Behavior but Cannot Completely Explain the Syndrome' (1987) 46 *American Journal of Economics & Society* 445, 454; E Kühlhorn, 'Victims and Offenders of Criminal Violence' (1990) 6 *Journal of Qualitative Criminology* 51, 55.

[6] WC Heffernan, 'Social Justice/Criminal Justice', in WC Heffernan and J Kleinig (eds), *From Social Justice to Criminal Justice* (New York: Oxford University Press, 2000), 47, 49.

[7] There is an interesting question, though not one that I shall pursue here, concerning the extent to which societies have an obligation to extend to non-citizen residents and to aliens the rights that they extend to their citizens. See generally S Benhabib, *The Rights of Others: Aliens, Residents, and Citizens* (Cambridge: Cambridge University Press, 2004).

(4) impose demands on members, such as the obligation to pay taxes and serve in
the military, according to some principle of fair distribution.[8]

To what extent society has an obligation to provide in these ways for its members, and
where such obligation comes from, are obviously among the most complex and contested questions in all of normative political theory.[9] Indeed, the nature of such obligation involves some of the most contested issues in our political discourse as well.
To try to resolve these issues here would lead us well beyond the scope of this chapter.
Moreover, even if we could agree about what constitutes distributive injustice in the
abstract, we would face additional problems in trying to decide if and when a given
society qualifies as unjust, or, more precisely, exactly who in a given society should be
regarded as unjustly deprived of the basic opportunities that they deserve.

Later on, I will offer a means of sidestepping these problems. Rather than try to
develop a theory of what constitutes social injustice, I will simply stipulate a set of
scenarios that almost everyone, I assume, would regard as unjust. Beginning with
these scenarios, we will then trace the implications of distributive injustice for the
assignment of retributive blame.

2 SOCIO-ECONOMIC INJUSTICE AND BLAMEWORTHINESS

In this section, we consider four approaches previously developed for addressing
the possible normative effect of an offender's poverty or other form of disadvantage on her blameworthiness and liability for criminal conduct. I shall refer to these
approaches, respectively, as: (1) necessity, (2) excuse, (3) broken social contract, and
(4) non-justiciability.

2.1 Necessity

Under current Anglo-American law, the most plausible argument a disadvantaged
defendant could make for avoiding liability for at least some crimes is one based on

---

[8] Here, I loosely follow an approach suggested in Heffernan, 'Social Justice/Criminal Justice', 50–1.
[9] For helpful surveys, see S-C Kolm, 'Distributive Justice', in RE Goodin and P Pettit (eds), *A
Companion to Contemporary Political Philosophy* (Oxford: Blackwell, 1993); J Lamont and C Favor,
'Distributive Justice', in *Stanford Encyclopedia of Philosophy*, online at <http://plato.stanford.edu/
entries/justice-distributive/>.

the idea of necessity. Under the standard common law formulation, the defendant must show that:

(1) she was faced with a clear and imminent danger of harm or serious bodily injury;
(2) she reasonably believed her action would be effective in abating the danger that she sought to avoid;
(3) there was no effective legal way to avert the harm;
(4) the harm caused by her criminal act was less serious than that sought to be avoided; and
(5) she was not to blame for creating the emergency conditions in which she found herself.[10]

A defendant who asserts a necessity defence argues that even though she did in fact commit all of the requisite acts, she nonetheless did nothing morally wrong. This is so because the crime's definition of prohibited conduct is, in a sense, incomplete.[11] Contemporary law permits what the crime as-defined otherwise prohibits where circumstances make her action the right (or at least not the wrong) thing to do.

The applicability of the necessity defence depends entirely on the nature of the offence committed and the circumstances that occasioned its commission. One who committed trespass or theft because she otherwise would have suffered the effects of hunger or exposure can argue, at least in theory, that her conduct was justified under the defence of necessity.[12] By contrast, one who committed rape or murder or assault as a result of her impoverishment would almost never be able to establish a defence of necessity, because her action: (1) would not be effective in abating the danger she sought to avoid; and (2) even if it was (say, if she killed V to get the loaf of bread he was holding), the harm caused by the criminal act would be no less serious than that sought to be avoided.

In practice, even a starving or homeless person charged with theft or trespass will have a hard time establishing a necessity defence if the prosecution can show that: (1) she would not have suffered any serious injury if she had not committed the crime; (2) there were legal alternatives available to her, such as attending a soup kitchen or homeless shelter; or (3) she somehow bore responsibility for the impoverished situation in which she found herself. Presumably as a result of these stringent

---

[10] J Dressler, *Understanding Criminal Law* (5th edn; Newark: LexisNexis, 2009), 291–3.

[11] The idea of 'incompleteness' in this context is suggested by SH Kadish, 'Excusing Crime' (1987) 75 *California Law Review* 257, 258.

[12] See Model Penal Code and Commentaries, § 3.02 at 9–10 ('A speed limit may be violated in pursuing a suspected criminal. An ambulance may pass a traffic light...A druggist may dispense a drug without the requisite prescription to alleviate grave distress in an emergency.'). Cf BA Hudson, 'Beyond Proportionate Punishment: Difficult Cases and the 1991 Criminal Justice Act' (1995) 22 *Crime, Law & Social Change* 59, 61–3.

requirements, reported cases in which a defendant, charged with theft or trespass, was acquitted by virtue of the necessity defence are virtually non-existent, at least in modern times.[13]

Still, the defence exists in theory and it is worth saying how it differs from the problem with which this chapter is specifically concerned. The first point is simply that the necessity defence is only loosely correlated with poverty and other forms of chronic disadvantage. Poverty, in the systematic sense described above, is neither a sufficient nor a necessary condition for the application of the necessity defence. No matter how impoverished a person might be, she will not be eligible for the defence unless it can be shown that at the moment of her crime her death or injury was imminent and unavoidable.[14] If she could find temporary sustenance by, say, attending a soup kitchen, then she is unlikely to be able to claim the defence. By the same token, a hiker stranded in the wilderness in a snow storm has the privilege to commit trespass and theft if doing so will prevent death or serious bodily injury. The fact that she has millions in the bank back home is irrelevant; the only thing that counts is her immediate circumstances at the moment she commits her offence. Second, there is no requirement that the defendant's disadvantage, if there is one, be unjust (though one can perhaps imagine that in some cases the fact that the offender's disadvantage was unjust would increase the harm she was seeking to avoid). More generally, the defence of necessity functions (though at times uneasily[15]) within the settled confines of the criminal law. It does not question the basic justice of how property rights are distributed. Nor does it question the basic integrity of theft law. Indeed, to the extent that lawmakers have anticipated a given choice of evils and 'determined the balance to be struck between ... competing values' in a manner that conflicts with the defendant's choice, the defence would be unavailable.[16]

---

[13] The history of the necessity defence is a particularly convoluted one. In the famous lifeboat case of *Dudley & Stephens* (1884) 14 QBC 273, 283, the court accepted as a given Matthew Hale's statement that it was not the law of England that a starving man could be justified in stealing a loaf of bread. Prior to Hale's time (1609–76), however, English law was apparently more receptive to economic necessity as a defence to theft. See generally DY Rabin, *Identity, Crime, and Legal Responsibility in Eighteenth-Century England* (New York: Palgrave 2004), 86–9. For an account of how medieval European law dealt with the question of poverty, see B Tierney, *Medieval Poor Law: A Sketch of Canonical Theory and Its Application in England* (Berkeley: University of California, 1959). Rabbinic law also permits one to commit property crimes such as theft in order to preserve life. See *The Babylonian Talmud: Seder Mo'ed: Yoma* 83b (Rabbi Dr Leo Jung trans; Brooklyn: Soncino Press, 1938).

[14] Of course, it could be argued that the law of necessity is too limited in this sense and that it should be expanded to apply to cases of 'cumulative' necessity, in something like the way that the law of provocation has been expanded, under the Model Penal Code's defence of extreme mental or emotional disturbance, to apply to cumulative provocation. See Model Penal Code, § 210.3(1)(b).

[15] See JT Parry, 'The Virtue of Necessity: Reshaping Culpability and the Rule of Law' (1999) 36 *Houston Law Review* 397, 403–4 (noting 'anxiety' regularly felt by courts applying the necessity defence).

[16] *State v Tate*, 505 A2d 941, 946 (NJ 1986). See also Model Penal Code, § 3.02(1)(c).

2.2 Excuse of 'rotten social background'

A second way in which the criminal law might respond to the problem of the impoverished or otherwise disadvantaged offender is that such deprivation might constitute, or provide the basis for, an excuse defence. Whereas justification defences consist of arguments that the defendant's conduct was not harmful or wrongful, excuse defences focus on the culpability of the actor himself. Thus, to say that a given criminal act is excused is not to say that the offender's act was not wrong (in the sense that a justified act is not wrong), but rather that the offender should not be held fully responsible for his conduct and should either be exempt from punishment entirely or have his punishment mitigated.[17]

Judge David Bazelon, who had previously crafted a significant expansion of the insanity defence,[18] was one of the first to write about the possibility that a background of extreme poverty might serve to relieve a criminal defendant of liability. In *United States v Alexander*, one of the defendants had shot and killed a victim who had called him a 'black bastard'.[19] The defendant, who was not mentally ill according to the recognized diagnostic categories, nevertheless wanted to present evidence that his conduct was the result of an 'emotional illness', which in turn was the product of a socially and economically deprived childhood growing up in the Watts section of Los Angeles. The trial judge instructed the jury to disregard the evidence regarding the defendant's so-called 'rotten social background' (RSB), and the court of appeals affirmed the conviction. Judge Bazelon wrote separately, laying out his views on the possibility of an RSB defence: 'Because of his early conditioning', Bazelon suggested, the defendant may well have been 'denied any meaningful choice when the racial insult triggered' his reaction.[20] It was possible, he wrote, that the defendant's underprivileged childhood had impaired his 'mental or emotional processes and behavior controls, rul[ing] his violent reaction in the same manner that the behavior of a paranoid schizophrenic may be ruled by his "mental condition"'.[21]

The idea that an RSB might provide a criminal law defence was subsequently developed by Richard Delgado.[22] Relying on empirical data establishing a correlation between criminal behaviour, on the one hand, and poverty, unemployment, substandard living conditions, inadequate schools, a climate of violence,

---

[17] See generally J Horder, *Excusing Crime* (Oxford: Oxford University Press, 2004).

[18] Most famously in *Durham v United States*, 214 F2d 862, 874–76 (DC Cir 1954).

[19] 471 F2d 923, 957 (DC Cir 1973) (Bazelon concurring in part, dissenting in part).

[20] Ibid at 960.

[21] Ibid. Bazelon subsequently elaborated on his views in an exchange with Stephen Morse. See DL Bazelon, 'The Morality of the Criminal Law' (1976) 49 *Southern California Law Review* 385, 387–98; SJ Morse, 'The Twilight of Welfare Criminology: A Reply to Judge Bazelon' (1976) 49 *Southern California Law Review* 1247; DL Bazelon, 'The Morality of the Criminal Law: A Rejoinder to Professor Morse' (1976) 49 *Southern California Law Review* 1269.

[22] R Delgado, '"Rotten Social Background": Should the Criminal Law Recognize a Defense of Severe Environmental Deprivation?' (1985) 3 *Law and Inequality* 9.

inadequate family structure, and racism, on the other, Delgado argued that courts should recognize a novel excuse defence based on extreme poverty and social deprivation. In particular, Delgado offered the possibility that a person's RSB might cause various behavioural disabilities which in turn might constitute various excusing conditions such as that the actor's conduct was not the product of his voluntary effort, that he did not accurately perceive the nature or consequences of his act, that he did not see his conduct as wrongful, or that he did not have the ability to control his conduct. The defence envisioned by Delgado is one that is closely analogous to defences such as automatism and battered woman syndrome. According to Delgado:

a review of medical and social science literature show[s] that life in a violent, overcrowded, stress-filled neighborhood can induce a state in which a resident reacts to certain stimuli with automatic aggression. Some defendants should be able to prove that they lived under such conditions and that these conditions were causally connected to the crimes charged.[23]

There are a few points to note about the RSB approach. First, as in the case of the necessity defence, Bazelon and Delgado's defence is developed from within the existing structure of criminal law. It does not challenge the basic framework of the law or the legitimacy of our institutions of punishment. Instead, Bazelon and Delgado argue for an expansion of available excuse defences. Second, as in the case of the necessity defence, there is no requirement that the offender's RSB necessarily be unjust, though perhaps one could argue that the defence takes on a distinctive character when it is. Third, in contrast to the necessity approach, the RSB approach makes no distinction based on the nature of the crime committed; it would apply not only to theft and other property crimes but also to a wide range of violent crimes (indeed, given the facts of *Alexander*, it seems to have been conceived expressly with violent crimes in mind). Fourth, the RSB defence would recognize no distinction based on the circumstances of the victim of the crime; it would presumably be available even when the victim came from the same deprived background as the defendant.

2.3 Broken social contract

A third approach to the problem of the disadvantaged defendant looks at criminal punishment from the perspective of social contract theory.[24] The argument consists of three basic steps. The first is to assert, or intuit, that our legal system exists within a social contract. Under such a contract, citizens agree (or would agree in a

---

[23] Ibid at 85–6.
[24] A leading example is JG Murphy, 'Marxism and Retribution' (1973) 2 *Philosophy & Public Affairs* 217, 224–31.

hypothetical original position)[25] to abide by the rules of the system in return for the security and predictability that such rules bring. Since war and disorder threaten to make everyone's life nasty, brutish, and short (in Hobbes' memorable phrase), it is reasonable from each person's self-interested standpoint to accept the authority of a governmental authority that will enforce rules, protect property, and make life generally safe. As Jeffrie Murphy has put it: 'since he [the citizen] derives and voluntarily accepts benefits from [the] operation [of rules that it is a crime to violate], he owes his own obedience as a debt to his fellow-citizens for their sacrifices in maintaining them.'[26]

Second, when people fail to abide by the rules of the system and accept the benefits that the system brings without reciprocating, they gain an unfair advantage. Criminal punishment is said to be a means of restoring the equilibrium of benefits and burdens by taking from the individual what he owes.[27] If a citizen 'chooses not to sacrifice by exercising self-restraint and obedience, this is', again in Murphy's language, 'tantamount to his choosing to sacrifice in another way—namely, by paying the prescribed penalty'.[28] In other words, part of the social contract consists of citizens' agreeing to be punished if they break the rules.

The third step of the argument requires us to consider what it would mean to live in a society that is unjust. Under the social contract theory, we judge the justness of laws by asking whether it would be reasonable for people to agree to them in light of their self-interest. But if the social arrangement is not one that would be reached behind a hypothetical veil of ignorance, the obligation to abide by the rules of the system cannot exist. If the state and its citizenry fail to uphold their end of the bargain, then the law ceases to be binding; it loses its moral authority. Citizens emerge, in Murphy's neo-Marxist term, 'alienated' from their fellow citizens and the government.

And what are the implications of such breach in the context of criminal justice? Criminal justice can be thought of as a 'two-way street'. Where society has breached its obligation to its citizens, say, by distributing property in an unjust manner, those citizens no longer have a duty to comply with the law. And where citizens no longer have a duty to comply, society no longer has a right to punish for lack of compliance. Indeed, if there is no moral obligation to obey the law, it would be unjust to use the power of the state to impose criminal penalties on those who fail to obey the law.

That, in any event, is the theory. There are, however, a number of potential problems that should be noted.[29] First, the theory rests on what Okeoghene Odudu has

[25] J Rawls, *A Theory of Justice* (Cambridge, MA: Harvard University Press, 1971), 17–22.

[26] Murphy, 'Marxism and Retribution', 228.

[27] For a well-known formulation of the punishment-as-equilibrium-restorer argument, see H Morris, 'Persons and Punishment' (1968) 52 *The Monist* 475.

[28] Murphy, 'Marxism and Retribution', 228.

[29] For a helpful summary of criticisms, and attempted refutation, see R Dagger, 'Playing Fair with Punishment' (1993) 103 *Ethics* 473.

called a 'grotesque conception of crime'.[30] The social contractarians seem to assume that while we all desire to engage in various forms of criminal activity, we voluntarily refrain from doing so in order to reap the benefits of others forgoing such conduct as well. While this may be true with respect to paying one's taxes and refraining from price-fixing, however, it hardly explains why we abstain from committing murder and rape. It seems very odd indeed to suggest that the wrongfulness of rape or murder consists in taking an 'unfair advantage' over those who comply with the law.[31] In fact, as I shall suggest below, such offences are based on a different kind of moral imperative entirely. Second, the theory seems more suited to explaining why a tort system requires the defendant to compensate the injured party. It is harder to see how it can explain the obligation of one convicted of crime to serve hard time in prison. In cases where the injury is done to some individual victim, it is not at all clear how criminal punishment is an appropriate means for restoring the equilibrium.[32] Third, to the extent that the social contract theory relies on a monolithic conception of the social contract, it seems overly broad in its reach. Society is deemed to be either just in the main, or it is not. If it is not, then the contract is void, and the citizen owes no duty to obey the law. Under this approach, it would seem not to matter what offence was being violated or who the victim was. The offender will be no more obliged to comply with the laws against murder and assault than with those against theft and obstruction of justice. Indeed, in explaining how the broken contract theory applies, Murphy himself offers the example of an impoverished and discriminated-against African-American man who commits armed robbery.[33]

2.4 Non-justiciability

Antony Duff has offered yet another approach to the problem of imposing criminal sanctions on the severely impoverished and politically excluded.[34] Duff is interested in what he calls the 'preconditions' of punishment, the conditions that must be satisfied before a defendant can be tried at all (as opposed to the conditions that must be satisfied before he can be justly convicted). He argues that one precondition of criminal punishment is that the agent be bound by the laws under which she is to

---

[30] O Odudu, 'Retributivist Justice in an Unjust Society' (2003) 16 *Ratio Juris* 416, 419.

[31] See J Hampton, 'Correcting Harms Versus Righting Wrongs: The Goal of Retribution' (1992) 39 UCLA L Rev 1659, 1660. Murphy himself recognized this and other problems with the theory in his later writing. See JG Murphy, 'Does Kant Have a Theory of Punishment?', in JG Murphy (ed), *Retribution Reconsidered: More Essays in the Philosophy of Law* (Alphen aan den Rijn: Kluwer, 1992), 31.

[32] Odudu makes a similar point, 'Retributivist Justice in an Unjust Society' 419.

[33] Murphy, 'Marxism and Retribution' (1973) 242.

[34] RA Duff, *Punishment, Communication, and Community* (Oxford: Oxford University Press, 2001), 181–201.

be tried and punished. Under this approach, people are bound by the law only when they are treated as a responsible part of the community.

Duff then considers the case of an offender who has been excluded from the community whose law she has violated. There are three ways in which this exclusion might take place: first, she is 'excluded from participation in the political life of the community, having no real chance to make [her voice] heard in those fora in which the laws and policies under which' she must live are decided. Second, she has been 'excluded from a fair share in, or a fair opportunity to acquire, the economic and material benefits that others enjoy'. And, third, she has been denied by the state and her fellow citizens the 'respect and concern due' to her as a citizen.[35]

In each such case, he says, 'there is reason to doubt whether [the precondition of being bound by law] is adequately satisfied'.[36] He is careful to explain that those who have been systematically excluded or unjustly disadvantaged are not necessarily justified or excused in their criminal acts. Rather, his argument is that the polity itself has no standing to 'call' the disadvantaged person 'to account'.[37] In effect, he is arguing that such a case is non-justiciable.

Duff's approach differs markedly from the first three considered. Unlike the necessity approach, there is no claim that the impoverished offender's act is justified. Unlike the RSB approach, there is no claim that the defendant's act should be excused. And, unlike the broken social contract approach, there is no claim that a citizen is relieved of his obligation to obey the law. Indeed, what is striking about Duff's account is his lack of concern, one way or the other, with the moral status of the offender. Rather, his focus is on the moral status of *society* in judging the offender.

So, exactly what are the implications of Duff's argument? It is noteworthy that most of the 'exclusion' scenarios he describes involve impoverished defendants committing relatively minor, economically driven offences against relatively wealthy victims: for example, he describes the case of an impoverished single parent stealing clothes from a supermarket for her children.[38] But at the same time, Duff properly recognizes that 'if the law lacks the standing to call the unjustly excluded to account, it lacks that standing in relation to *all* crimes, including the most serious *mala in se*'.[39] Indeed, he considers the hypothetical case of a black South African brought to trial in the apartheid era for 'committing a serious assault against a neighbor', and concludes that, 'given his systematic exclusion from citizenship in the polity in whose name the courts act, he is not responsible for his conduct before this court,

---

[35] Ibid 183.

[36] Ibid 183–4.

[37] Ibid 184–88. For a similar argument, see V Tadros, 'Poverty and Criminal Responsibility' (2009) 43 *Journal of Value Inquiry* 391, 393–4 (even if an unjustly impoverished offender is responsible for her actions, society might not be entitled to hold her responsible).

[38] Duff, *Punishment, Communication, and Community*, 182.

[39] Ibid 184 (emphasis in original).

or to this polity'.[40] In other words, under Duff's approach, society would have no more right to prosecute and punish an impoverished and excluded defendant who committed a serious *malum in se* crime than it would to prosecute an impoverished defendant who committed a *de minimis malum prohibitum* offence. Moreover, it would seem to make no difference, in terms of society's right to punish, whether the victim of *D*'s crime was a wealthy member of the ruling class, or was no less impoverished than *D* herself.

At one level, Duff's argument seems unassailable: if one accepts the premise that a society in which some are profoundly disadvantaged lacks the moral authority ever to judge its citizens, then it follows that such authority will be lacking regardless of what kind of crime a given citizen has been accused of. But is the premise valid? It seems to me that a society might well have the moral status to make judgments in some cases but not others. For example, even if a society with a profoundly unjust division of property lacks the moral authority to make moral judgments regarding certain property crimes, it might still retain the moral authority to make moral judgments with respect to crimes like murder and rape. Moreover, even if society did lack the moral authority to pass judgment on one or more of its citizens with respect to all offences, it would still be worth asking if such citizens deserved blame, in some abstract or free-floating sense, to begin with.[41] Indeed, if we assume (as retributivists do) that moral blameworthiness is a prerequisite for just criminal punishment, the question of society's standing to judge would not even arise where the offender was determined to be blameless. It is to the issue of blameworthiness that we therefore now turn.

3 A Case-Specific Approach to Assessing Blameworthiness

My main criticism of the previously described attempts to assess the culpability of severely disadvantaged offenders has been that they are painted with too broad a

---

[40] RA Duff, *Answering for Crime: Responsibility and Liability in the Criminal Law* (Oxford: Hart Publishing, 2007), 191–3.

[41] Duff would presumably dispute the idea that blame can be deserved in some free-floating or abstract sense, insisting that: '[b]lame requires a suitable relationship between blamer and blamed, as fellow members of a normative community whose business the wrong is: it is an attempt at moral communication, appealing to values by which blamer and blamed are, supposedly, mutually bound.' RA Duff, 'Blame, Moral Standing and the Legitimacy of the Criminal Trial' (2010) 23 *Ratio* 123, 125. At the same time, Duff acknowledges that even if society as a whole lacks standing to blame the offender, there might still be individuals within society, such as the offender's victims, who have the standing to do so. Duff, *Answering for Crime*, 193.

brush. As an alternative to the four approaches just discussed, I now propose an approach that looks more narrowly at the specifics of the offender's case.

3.1 Kinds of deprivation, victim, and offence

The approach developed here takes account of three variables in considering the crime committed:

(1) the kind of unjust deprivation, if any, to which the offender has been subjected;
(2) the kind of unfair advantage or disadvantage to which the victim, if any, has been subjected; and
(3) the particular offence committed.

Let us consider, first, the character of the offender's deprivation. So far in this chapter we have focused primarily on the offender's poverty and economic disadvantage. But, as Duff recognizes, there are also other forms of disadvantage that may be relevant, such as systematic exclusion from social and political involvement, and failing to receive the 'respect and concern' to which one is presumably entitled.[42]

What does it mean to live in a society in which one is unjustly denied basic social, political, or economic rights? Earlier, we noted the difficulty of resolving such a contested question. I promised to sidestep the issue and instead simply stipulate what I assume to be clear and uncontroversial examples of disadvantage. I now offer three such cases:

Denial of property rights. D lives in a society which, as a result of the social caste into which he has been born, entirely denies him and others in his class (but not others outside his class) the right to own property.[43] The fact that *D* is not merely without property, but is legally barred from owning it allows us to avoid the possibility that *D* is in some way to blame for his impoverishment. Nor do we need to worry about cases in which *D* voluntarily decides to forgo property ownership, as in a commune. I take it that a legal order that denied *D* property rights in this way would qualify as unjust even if *D*'s basic day-to-day needs were provided for.

Denial of political rights. The society in which *D* lives denies him and others similarly situated, again as a result of social caste, the basic rights of citizenship, such as the right to vote, petition, express one's views, assemble, and receive due process in court proceedings. Once again, by assuming that such disentitlements are imposed on *D* owing to his caste, we avoid

---

[42] Duff, *Punishment, Communication, and Community*, 183.

[43] This is a situation that more or less appears to have been true of slaves in the ante-bellum South (though for present purposes, we need not add the additional condition that *D* is himself treated as another's property). See DC Penningroth, *The Claims of Kinfolk: African American Property and Community in the Nineteenth-Century South* (Chapel Hill: University of North Carolina, 2003), 45. Though, as Penningroth explains, slaves were often able to participate in a substantial informal economy and thereby gradually accumulate property. Ibid 46.

the possibility that *D* is somehow arguably to blame for his circumstances, as is the case, say, where a felon is deprived of the right to vote as part of his punishment.

Denial of right to basic state protections. *D*'s society offers him and others in his class few of the basic public safety protections that it offers others. For example, the police rarely respond to emergency calls emanating from *D*'s neighbourhood, and they routinely fail to investigate crimes occurring there; prosecutors regularly fail to initiate prosecutions for crimes that occur in *D*'s part of town; and emergency medical services and fire crews are slow to respond to emergencies that occur there. (*D* presumably does still benefit from 'public good' protections that necessarily apply to society as a whole, such as military defence, clean air and water regulations, and food and drug safety measures.)

Beginning with these hypothetical 'worst cases' will allow us to consider the means by which an offender's economic or social deprivation might bear on judgments of blameworthiness without directly addressing the difficult normative and empirical issues of what it means to live in a society that fails to give people what they deserve, and which, if any, societies in the world today would qualify as economically or socially unjust.

It should be clear that these kinds of deprivation are by no means mutually exclusive; indeed, they are mutually reinforcing and closely interrelated. Those who are economically impoverished are often the same people who are politically marginalized and deprived of basic state protections. Race plays a significant role here. In the United States, members of minority groups often suffer the highest rates of unemployment and poverty, are the most common targets of police harassment, experience the most acute sense of political alienation, and are subject to the highest rates of arrest and incarceration.[44] There is also a deeper conceptual link between categories: the right to participate in the political process, own property, receive basic police and emergency protection, and have access to court processes can each be meaningless, standing alone, unaccompanied by the other rights. For example, the right to own property may be of little value unless it is backed up by due process rights in court. And the right to speech may be essentially meaningless unless one has access to basic means of communication necessary to express oneself in the modern world.

The second variable concerns the economic, political, and social circumstances of the crime's victim (where the crime has an identifiable victim). Here we will want to ask whether the victim himself: (1) suffered unjust disadvantage; (2) benefited from unjust advantage; or (3) experienced neither unjust advantage nor unjust disadvantage.

The final variable is the type of offence committed. For present purposes, I shall focus on three offence types: offences against the person (such as rape and murder); offences against the administration of justice (such as perjury and obstruction of justice); and offences against property (such as theft and criminal trespass). These

---

[44] See generally Western, *Punishment and Inequality in America.*

categories are by no means meant to encompass all of the criminal law's Special Part. There are numerous offences that do not fall clearly into any of these categories.

3.2 The offender's blameworthiness

The goal here is to determine the extent to which an offender's unjust social, economic, or political disadvantage affects his blameworthiness for committing various kinds of offence. Before we proceed, however, it is appropriate to say something briefly about why we should care whether an offender's act is judged blameworthy in the first place. For present purposes, I shall assume that it is intrinsically wrong for society to punish criminal offenders who are blameless (and also wrong to punish blameworthy offenders more harshly than they deserve). To talk this way is to appeal to a familiar 'negative' version of retributivism. The claim, for present purposes, is not that we should punish the blameworthy because they deserve it, but simply that we should not punish those who are not blameworthy. In short, I intend to rely on moral desert as a 'side constraint' on whatever other rationale we have for imposing criminal sanctions (such as some version of consequentialism).[45]

To say that a criminal offender is at fault for violating a given law presupposes, at some level, that the law itself is just. Determining exactly what it means for a law to be just, however, is another matter. We often ask what requirements must be satisfied in order for conduct to be properly criminalized.[46] But a law that fails to satisfy such requirements is not necessarily unjust; it may merely be unwise or imprudent. There may also be laws that are just on their face but which are applied in an unjustly selective or discriminatory manner.

For present purposes, we need not resolve these issues. Instead, let us consider laws that almost everyone would agree *are* unjust: one is a law that made it a crime for blacks to sit at a white-only lunch counter; another is a law that made it a crime for a Jew to marry or have sexual relations with a gentile. Such laws are unjust, I take it, because they further no legitimate interest of the state and because they discriminate on the basis of morally impermissible criteria, such as race, religion, and ethnic identity. It is hard to imagine any circumstance in which the application of such laws would be considered just. One who violated such laws would have done nothing morally wrong and could not properly be said to be at fault. The argument is not that the offender would be justified or excused in breaking the law, or that society would be morally unjustified in bringing a prosecution (though each of these claims is surely true), but rather that the offender did not do an act that was blameworthy

---

[45] In so doing, I follow Duff and others. See Duff, *Punishment, Communication, and Community*, 11–14.

[46] See generally D Husak, *Overcriminalization: The Limits of the Criminal Law* (New York: Oxford University Press, 2008).

to begin with. And because the offender was not at fault, it would be unjust, from a retributive standpoint, to impose criminal penalties on him.

The question that needs to be addressed is whether a 'lack of blameworthiness' would also occur in other contexts involving laws that are not unjust on their face, but which might be unjust as applied in the context of certain kinds of political, social, and economic circumstances. For reasons that will become clearer as we proceed, I think it is reasonable to say that, in a liberal social democracy which provided basic political and economic rights to all of its citizens, a person who committed each kind of offence identified—that is, offences against the person, against public order and the administration of justice, and against property—and had no excuse or justification for doing so, would have done an act that was morally wrong, and would deserve to be punished. The question is whether, with respect to each type of offence, we would reach the same conclusion in cases where the offender lived in a society in which he was denied basic social, political, or economic rights.

3.3 Offences against the person

Imagine that *D* commits a violent, non-defensive act of murder or rape or assault against a fellow citizen. Should the fact that he has failed to receive what he deserves from society in terms of economic, political, or social opportunities affect our judgment about whether he deserves to be punished for his act?

Assuming that *D*'s impoverishment and disenfranchisement have not caused his criminal act to be excused or justified by means of insanity, mistake, duress, or necessity, his impoverishment and disenfranchisement should not affect our judgment of his culpability. The reason is that the moral underpinnings of offences such as murder and rape do not depend on background considerations of social justice. Such offences arise out of what Rawls called 'natural duties' (which are to be contrasted, as we'll see in a moment, to crimes like perjury and obstruction of justice, which arise out of what he called 'political obligation'). In Rawls's words:

[I]n contrast with obligations [like those derived in the original position, natural duties] have no necessary connection with institutions or social practices; their content is not, in general, defined by the rules of these arrangements. Thus we have a natural duty not to be cruel, and a duty to help another, whether or not we have committed ourselves to these actions. It is no defense or excuse to say that we have made no promise not to be cruel or vindictive.... Indeed, a promise not to kill, for example, is normally ludicrously redundant, and the suggestion that it establishes a moral requirement where none already existed is mistaken.... A further feature of natural duties is that they hold between persons irrespective of their institutional relationships; they obtain between all as equal moral persons.[47]

---

[47] Rawls, *A Theory of Justice*, 114–15.

In short, the moral obligations that D breaches when he commits a violent offence against another person are obligations owed to his fellow human beings, as individuals, rather than to the government or to society generally. We can recognize the special sanctity of life and physical and sexual integrity, and therefore the wrongfulness of murder, assault, and rape, without presupposing any developed institutional structure.[48]

Should it matter which class the victim of D's crime is a member of? Perhaps if V was also disadvantaged, we might think that D would be guilty of exploiting V's vulnerability and that D's act would therefore be more wrongful than it otherwise would be.[49] On the other hand, if V was a member of the ruling class that was responsible for D's unjust impoverishment or social disadvantage, it is hard to see why D's act should be regarded as any less wrongful than in a case in which V was neither disadvantaged nor specially advantaged. There is nothing about unjustly advantaged V's complicity in D's impoverishment or disenfranchisement, wrongful as it is, that would invalidate V's claim to life or bodily integrity. Even in those cases in which V could have, but failed to, protect D from acts of violence directed against him by others, D would not be justified in using violence against V unless V himself posed a direct threat to D's physical well being.

3.4 Offences against public order and the administration of justice

Imagine now that the offence committed by D is a non-violent offence against public order or the administration of justice, such as obstruction of justice, bribery, or perjury. How would we judge his blameworthiness with respect to these offences, assuming again that D has failed to get what he deserves from society in terms of economic, political, or social opportunities?

The moral content of such offences is complex; I have dealt with them at length elsewhere.[50] At one level, such offences seem directed primarily at the government, or at the polity on whose behalf the government claims to act; at another level, they are directed at individual victims. An offender who commits perjury or obstruction, for example, not only undermines the integrity of the judicial process but might

---

[48] Regarding this point, Antony Duff has asked me what we should say about a legal system that defined rape as intercourse with a woman without her husband's or parent's consent. I would respond that such a crime would be so different from our modern understanding of rape that we should regard it as a distinct offence, one lacking the 'natural duty' background of rape defined as intercourse without the *victim's* consent.

[49] I have previously considered the exploitative character of crimes against the vulnerable in SP Green, 'Looting, Law, and Lawlessness' (2007) 81 *Tulane Law Review* 1129, 1147.

[50] SP Green, *Lying, Cheating, and Stealing: A Moral Theory of White-Collar Crime* (Oxford: Oxford University Press, 2006).

also cause significant harm to a litigant whose cause is damaged by false testimony or destruction of documents. As for bribery, it typically harms the integrity of the governmental process as well as the constituents of the official who, in accepting the bribe, acted in his own self-interest rather than in the public interest.

The fact that *D* has been denied the right to participate fully in the political life of his community, or denied the police protections that are afforded other citizens, might, depending on its precise context and purpose, mitigate, or even negate, the wrongfulness of his offence against the administration of justice. For example, a bribe paid by a disenfranchised citizen to a corrupt dictator in order to avoid the implementation of an ecologically damaging and unwarranted agricultural policy might lack culpability in a way that a bribe paid by the same citizen to the same dictator for the purpose of avoiding conscription in what was otherwise a just war might not. Unlike murder, assault, and rape, which involve a violation of natural duties, bribery, obstruction of justice, and perjury are precisely the sorts of offence that involve a violation of political obligations. Their moral content is rooted in complex institutional practices involving a dense network of reciprocal duties. A defendant who commits such a crime has done a blameworthy act only when he has an obligation to obey such laws.

Our judgment of *D*'s blameworthiness may also be affected by the circumstances of his victim. If *D* committed perjury or obstruction of justice in litigation against a member of the ruling elite who was in part responsible for creating a process that systematically favoured people of his own class, we might think that *D* would do nothing wrong in trying to 'level the playing field' through his unlawful acts. Our judgment would be likely to differ, however, if *D* committed perjury or obstruction in litigation against a similarly disempowered fellow citizen. Even though neither *D* nor his disadvantaged victim would be part of the web of political obligations that, I have argued, underlies the crime of perjury and obstruction, *D* would nevertheless have derived some benefit from that web, if only temporarily, and he would have done so at the expense of a victim who was even more disempowered than he. As such, we should regard his act as a wrongful one.

The fact that *D* has been denied the right to *own property*, by contrast, seems to bear less directly on his culpability for such offences than his being denied the right to participate in the political process or receive basic protections from the state. Normally, there is no necessary connection between economic and political rights. One can easily imagine cases in which *D* was unjustly impoverished without being unjustly disenfranchised, and unjustly disenfranchised without being unjustly impoverished. (Though one can also imagine circumstances in which *D*, whose state-imposed poverty makes it impossible for him to hire a lawyer, and who is not otherwise provided with indigent counsel, uses perjury or obstruction as a means of levelling the playing field. Perhaps in such cases his impoverishment could be said to mitigate the blameworthiness of his act.)

3.5 Offences against property

Finally, let us imagine that the crime D commits is not a violent offence against another's physical well-being, or an offence against public order or the administration of justice, but is instead an offence against another's rights in property, such as theft or fraud or criminal trespass.[51] How should we judge his blameworthiness for these offences, assuming again that D has been denied the right to own property, to participate in the political life of his community, or to enjoy the basic public safety protections had by other citizens?

Here we need to examine the moral content that underlies crimes against property.[52] The essence of property offences is that they involve an offender's (wrongfully) causing harm to another's interests in, and rights to, property.[53] Property, in turn, is best thought of not as a physical thing but as the bundle of rights organized around the idea of securing, for the right of the holder, exclusive use or access to, or control of, a thing.[54] Control may take various forms, including the right to exclude others, the privilege to use the property, the power to transfer it, and immunity from having it taken from the owner, or harmed without the owner's consent.[55]

Crimes against property therefore involve harms to persons in the sense that they involve harms to persons' interests in property; and property, properly understood, concerns legal relations among people regarding the control and disposition of valued resources. While the term 'crimes against property' may provide a convenient shorthand, it is nonetheless more accurate to speak of 'crimes affecting persons' rights and interests in property'.[56] Such conduct is harmful because it undermines the very reasons we have a system of property in the first place—namely to facilitate

---

[51] My concern here is with property crimes of general application. I leave to the side property crimes that are said to be aimed specifically at the poor. See generally K Gustafson, 'The Criminalization of Poverty' (2009) 99 *J Criminal Law & Criminology* 643.

[52] This topic is dealt with in far more detail in my forthcoming book, tentatively titled *Thirteen Ways to Steal a Bicycle: Theft Law in the Information Age*.

[53] Historically, this has not always been the case. As George Fletcher has argued, at early common law, the law of larceny was intended primarily to protect society from manifest breaches of the peace, rather than to protect owners' property rights per se. See GP Fletcher, *Rethinking Criminal Law* (Boston: Little, Brown 1978), 31–9.

[54] For a useful discussion, see JW Singer, *Introduction to Property* (2nd edn; New York: Aspen, 2005), 2–3.

[55] Tony Honoré divides what he calls the 'liberal concept of ownership' into a list of components: the right to possess, use, and manage a thing; the right to income from its use by others; the right to sell, give away, consume, modify, or destroy it; the power to transmit it to the beneficiaries of one's estate; and the right to security from expropriation. AM Honoré, 'Ownership', in AG Guest (ed), *Oxford Essays in Jurisprudence* (Oxford: Oxford University Press, 1961), 107, 112–24.

[56] With the possible, and interesting, exception of morals, offences such as prostitution and consensual bigamy, and perhaps a few other unusual offences such as animal cruelty, and possibly certain crimes against the environment, *all* crimes are crimes affecting persons' rights and interests—whether in their property or physical safety, in public order, in the family, or elsewhere.

the creation and preservation of wealth that makes many forms of human endeavour possible.

On the continuum of offences described by Rawls, ranging from pure or nearly
pure 'natural duty' offences like murder and rape, at one end, to pure or nearly pure
'political obligation' offences like obstruction of justice and perjury, on the other,
theft lies somewhere in the middle, having attributes of both. While we may recognize in some natural or pre-legal sense that it is morally wrong to appropriate what
'belongs' to another without her permission, it is often impossible to make anything
like a fully informed moral judgment about the blameworthiness of such conduct
until we know a good deal about what is meant by highly legalized concepts such as
property, ownership, possession, custody, title, contract, appropriation, fiduciary
duty, and the like.

Claims of property make sense only in a social context in which there is some level
of cooperative behaviour.[57] Whether it is wrong to violate a given law against theft,
and whether it is therefore just to be subjected to criminal penalties for doing so,
depends on whether the property regime within which such law functions is itself
just. This is very different from the violent-crimes-against-the-person paradigm we
considered earlier because the set of norms on which the two kinds of offence are
based are different. As Jim Harris put it:

The background right [to property] is historically situated. It does not have the same ahistorical status as do rights not to be subjected to unprovoked violence to the person. There are
no natural rights to full-blooded ownership of the world's resources.

Good faith implementation of the moral background right may or may not achieve a
threshold of justice for a property institution. If it does, the trespassory rules of the institution are, *prima facie*, morally binding. Murder, assault and rape are always moral wrongs.
Theft is morally wrong only when this justice threshold is attained.[58]

And when does a given property institution achieve a threshold of justice? That, of
course, is an immensely complex and controversial question, one that lies beyond
the scope of this chapter. For the moment, however, we can safely assume that the
threshold would not be met by a regime under which a whole class of citizens was
legally forbidden from owning property. In such a society, we should be able to say
that D was not morally blameworthy for stealing property from V, where D was
unjustly barred from owning property, and V helped create or perpetuate the conditions that caused D's unjust impoverishment.[59]

The harder question arises in cases in which an unjustly impoverished offender
steals from one who has not unjustly benefited from the system, including victims

---

[57] For a useful discussion, see CM Rose, 'The Moral Sense of Property' (2007) 48 *William & Mary
L Rev* 1897, 1899.

[58] JW Harris, *Property and Justice* (Oxford: Oxford University Press, 1996), 14.

[59] Compare with Tadros, 'Poverty and Criminal Responsibility', 392 (suggesting that a justification
rationale applies only 'to people who have less than their fair share of wealth who take goods from
people who have more than their fair share of wealth').

who are themselves unjustly impoverished.[60] (This supposes, for purposes of discussion, that otherwise impoverished citizens were permitted to own certain limited types of property, or property of very low monetary value.) An argument could be made that, unless a given law of theft was enacted against a background of property laws that treated D fairly, the law would simply not be binding on D, and his stealing would not be wrong. This approach seems inconsistent, however, with our intuition that the impoverished victim would have had what few rights he possessed violated, and that it would be D who was responsible for the violation. For this reason, I am inclined to say that D should be viewed as non-culpable only when he steals from those who are in some way complicit in causing his unjust impoverishment.

Finally, what about a thief who was denied not the right to own property, but rather the right to participate in the political process or the right to protection by the police? Here, there should be no impediment to finding that D had done a blameworthy act. Such theftuous conduct would still undermine the system of property of which D was in some sense a beneficiary.

4 Conclusion

We end where we began, with the question whether the fact that a criminal offender lives in a society that denies him what he deserves in terms of economic, social, or political rights should affect the determination of what he deserves in terms of punishment, a question that is all the more urgent given the ever-widening gap in our society between the haves and have-nots. The answer offered here has been a qualified 'yes', depending on the type of crime the offender has committed, the type of deprivation to which he has been subjected, and the circumstances of the crime victim. It should be clear, however, that my analysis is intended as nothing more than a 'first cut'. With so many variables, one can imagine an almost infinite number of hypothetical situations. My goal has been not to resolve, or even spell out, all of these hypothetical cases, but rather to suggest the complexity of the problem and the error of thinking that there is a one-size-fits-all solution.

---

[60] In fact, as noted above, a disproportionate percentage of the victims of property crimes in the United States are impoverished. Criminologists have offered various explanations for the peculiar fact that the very people with the least amount of property worth stealing are the same people who are most likely to be the victims of theft. See eg D Larsson, 'Exposure to Property Crime as a Consequence of Poverty' (2006) 7 J Scandinavian Studies in Criminology and Crime Prevention 45 (two reasons why poor people are more exposed to property crime than those who are not poor are that they live in neighbourhoods with more crime and that they have fewer opportunities to keep their property safe from crime).

By stipulating what would constitute serious cases of distributive and political injustice, we have been able to avoid some deeply contested issues in political theory. Still, the question remains whether, in the real world, we are in danger of imposing retributive penalties on offenders who, by virtue of their social circumstances, should be regarded as blameless. The concern, I believe, is a legitimate one. Vast segments of the world's population are habitually denied basic opportunities to obtain property, participate in the political life of their communities, and enjoy the protection of the state; and while we certainly cannot assume that every such deprivation is the result of injustice, it seems likely that many are.

Few societies in history have distributed wealth equitably, but the current disparity between rich and poor within the United States and elsewhere seems particularly gross. The gap between the haves and have-nots is now greater than at any time since 1929, and it continues to grow.[61] In 1980, the poorest 20 per cent of families in the United States earned 4.2 per cent of aggregate income, while the richest fifth received 44.1 per cent; by 2008, the share of the poorest 20 per cent had dropped to 3.4 per cent, while the richest fifth's share had risen to 50 per cent.[62] The sheer breadth of poverty is staggering. According to Census Bureau statistics, there were 43.6 million people living in poverty in the United States during 2009, up from 39.8 million the year before.[63] This represents a poverty rate of 14.3 per cent in 2009, up from 13.2 per cent in 2008 and the highest rate since 1997.[64] According to US Department of Agriculture figures, the number of Americans who lived in households that lacked consistent access to adequate food during 2008 was at the highest level since the government began tracking what it calls 'food insecurity' in 1995.[65]

---

[61] EN Wolff, *Top Heavy: A Study of the Increasing Inequality of Wealth in America and What Can Be Done About It* (2nd edn; New York: New Press, 2002), 2.

[62] See C DeNavas-Walt, BD Proctor, and JC Smith, *Income, Poverty, and Health Insurance Coverage* (Washington: US Government Printing Office, 2009), Table A3 at 45–6, online at < http://www.census .gov/prod/2010pubs/p60-238.pdf>. See also T Piketty and E Saez, 'Income Inequality in the United States, 1913–1998' (2003) 118 *Q J Economics* 1.

[63] DeNavas-Walt, ibid 13. Social scientists have traditionally distinguished between two different senses of poverty—'absolute' and 'relative'. See eg A Sen, 'Poor, Relatively Speaking' (1983) 35 *Oxford Economic Papers* 153. Absolute poverty measures the number of people living below a certain income threshold (the 'poverty line'), who thereby lack the resources to meet the basic needs for healthy living. See European Anti-Poverty Network, *Poverty and Inequality in the European Union*, online at <http:// www.poverty.org.uk/summary/eapn.shtml>. Relative poverty, by contrast, has been defined as the inability of citizens to participate fully in economic terms in the society in which they live. It measures the extent to which a household's financial resources fall below an average income threshold for the relevant economy. Under this approach, people are said to be living in poverty if 'their income and resources are so inadequate as to preclude them from having a standard of living considered acceptable in the society in which they live'. Council of the European Union, *Joint Report by the Commission and the Council on Social Inclusion* 8 (2004), online at <http://ec.europa.eu/employment_social/ soc-prot/soc-incl/final_joint_inclusion_report_2003_en.pdf>.

[64] DeNavas-Walt, Proctor, and Smith, *Income, Poverty, and Health Insurance Coverage*, 13.

[65] See M Nord, M Andrews, and S Carlson, US Department of Agriculture Economic Research Services, *Household Food Security in the United States, 2008, Economic Research Report No 83*, 8, online at <http://www.ers.usda.gov/Publications/Err83/>. The figure was 49.1 million Americans, an

Viewed globally, the gap between rich and poor is even more dramatic: according to the most recent report of the World Institute for Development Economics Research, the richest 1 per cent of adults alone owned 40 per cent of global assets in the year 2000, in contrast to the bottom *half* of the world's adult population, which owned barely 1 per cent of global wealth.[66] And a recent report from the office of the UN's Secretary-General estimates that, as a result of the global economic recession, up to 90 million additional people have been pushed into poverty.

There are also vast numbers of people throughout the world who lack fundamental political rights or basic protection by the state. Determining exactly who is denied political rights is a complex process that involves potentially subjective judgments, but various attempts have been made. One is the annual survey conducted by Freedom House, an independent, non-governmental watchdog organization that supports the promotion of democracy and human rights around the world.[67] Applying basic standards derived from the Universal Declaration of Human Rights, the survey looks at the extent to which people around the world are denied the right to vote freely for distinct alternatives in legitimate elections, compete for public office, join political parties and organizations, elect representatives who are accountable to the electorate, and enjoy freedoms of expression, belief, association, and organization. Of the 193 countries surveyed, the study determined that 89 qualified as 'free', 62 as 'partly free', and 42 as 'not free', suggesting that a substantial percentage of the world's population is denied basic political and human rights.[68] As for the denial of basic protections by the state, groups such as Human Rights Watch have compiled a body of reports that, taken as a whole, suggest that many millions of people in numerous countries around the globe receive inadequate state

increase of approximately 13 million over the year before. Ibid 6. About a third of these struggling households had what was referred to as 'very low food security', meaning that family members were forced to skip meals or otherwise forgo food at some point in the year. Ibid 4–5.

[66] JB Davies et al, United Nations University, *The World Distribution of Household Wealth*, *Discussion Paper No 2008/03* (Feb 2008), online at <http://www.wider.unu.edu/publications/working-papers/discussion-papers/2008/en_GB/dp2008-03/_files/78918010772127840/default/dp2008-03.pdf>, 7.

[67] Freedom House, *Freedom in the World Survey 2009*, online at <http://www.freedomhouse.org/template.cfm?page=21&year=2009>.

[68] Ibid. In countries like Equatorial Guinea, Zambia, and Swaziland, where kleptocratic leaders reportedly line their own pockets and leave their populations destitute, the injustice of the political and economic system arguably approaches that contained in the hypothetical 'worst cases' described in the text. See generally I Urbina, 'Taint of Corruption is No Barrier to US Visa' (16 November, 2009) *NY Times*, online at <http://www.nytimes.com/2009/11/17/us/17visa.html?_r=1&sq=africacorruption poverty&st=cse&adxnnl=1&scp=1&adxnnlx=1258917716-aZzo8YcKMDy/qU5W4PJbeA> (extensive corruption in Equatorial Guinea by Teodoro Nguema Obiang, forest and agricultural minister and son of president); B Bearak, 'Living Royally in Destitute Swaziland' (6 September 2008) *NY Times*, A1 (King of Swaziland spends excessively while two-thirds of country lives in poverty and corruption bleeds treasury); CW Dugger, 'Ex-Zambian Leader's High Life Awaits a Verdict' (22 June 2009) *NY Times*, A4 (Frederick Chiluba, former President of Zambia, on trial for stealing about $500,000).

protection from terrorism, domestic violence, torture, police brutality, and other forms of violence.[69]

When we consider the fact that a disproportionate share of crime, including crime against property, is committed by offenders who are living in or near poverty, who have essentially no voice in the political life of their country, or who lack basic protections by the state, together with the possibility that some of this deprivation, in at least some places in the world, is the result of unjust political or economic systems, the potential seriousness of the problem begins to emerge. By imposing criminal sanctions on arguably blameless offenders, we run the risk of compounding the sins of socio-economic injustice with those of retributive injustice.

---

[69] Eg Human Rights Watch, *Reconciled to Violence: State Failure to Stop Domestic Abuse and Abduction of Women in Kyrgyzstan* (26 September 2006), <http://www.hrw.org/en/reports/2006/09/26/reconciled-violence-0>; Human Rights Watch, *Honoring the Killers: Justice Denied For "Honor" Crimes in Jordan* (19 April 2004), <http://www.hrw.org/en/reports/2004/04/19/honoring-killers-0>; Human Rights Watch, *Lethal Force: Police Violence and Public Security in Rio de Janeiro and São Paulo* (8 December 2009), <http://www.hrw.org/en/reports/2009/12/08/lethal-force-0>; Human Rights Watch, *'Rest in Pieces': Police Torture and Deaths in Custody in Nigeria* (27 July 2005), <http://www.hrw.org/en/reports/2005/07/26/rest-pieces-0>; Human Rights Watch, *'Lives Destroyed': Attacks on Civilians in the Philippines* (30 July 2007), <http://www.hrw.org/en/reports/2007/07/30/lives-destroyed>.

PART III

PROCESS
AND PUNISHMENT

17

GROUNDWORK FOR A JURISPRUDENCE OF CRIMINAL PROCEDURE

PAUL ROBERTS*

1 CRIMINAL LAW THEORY, CRIMINAL PROCEDURE AND THE LAW OF EVIDENCE

CRIMINAL law theory is typically associated with substantive criminal law. Insofar as one may discern the emergence of a discrete disciplinary sub-field of (Anglo-American) 'Criminal Law Theory' over the last several decades,[1] its preoccupations have been with the theoretical foundations of criminal liability,[2] and more recently

---

* I am grateful to Andrew Ashworth, Michael Cahill, Antony Duff, Yankah Ekow, Stuart Green, and William Twining for constructive suggestions on previous drafts.

[1] GP Fletcher (ed), *New Voices in Criminal Theory* (1998) 1 *Buffalo Criminal Law Review* Special Issue.

[2] Especially concepts of responsibility and mens rea, taxonomies of criminal law defences, and problems of causation: see eg S Shute, J Gardner, and J Horder (eds), *Action and Value in Criminal*

with the scope and principles of criminalization.[3] Criminal law theory overlaps with a somewhat more established strand of scholarship exploring the philosophical foundations of punishment or Penal Theory. Both strands owe an immense intellectual debt to Herbert Hart.[4] There is a marked, and entirely commendable, trend in recent scholarship for theoretical work on substantive criminal law to be informed by theorizing about punishment, and vice versa. Andrew von Hirsch[5] and Antony Duff[6] are modern pioneers of this more comprehensive, integrated approach to elucidating the philosophical foundations of criminal law.[7]

To the best of my knowledge, there has never been any grand conspiracy to keep Criminal Law Theory pure and uncontaminated by criminal procedure scholarship. Procedural issues have simply been ignored by the vast majority of card-carrying criminal law theorists. Procedure is viewed as theoretically uninteresting, or at least comparatively less interesting than the shape and content of substantive criminal law. This chapter is intended to restore some balance and provoke further critical reflection on the theoretical foundations of criminal procedure, evidence, and proof. I will suggest that a jurisprudence of criminal procedure should be regarded as an indispensable supplement to theoretical inquiries in criminal law, and indicate some promising avenues and useful source materials for further procedurally orientated theorizing. It is time that criminal procedure came in from the cold and assumed its rightful place in the salon of theoretically inclined criminal law scholarship.

In fact, there is no real choice in the matter, since concerted attempts to theorize substantive law must inevitably grapple with procedural considerations. The very distinction between substantive criminal law and criminal procedure is itself a moving target. Its precise delineation is an artefact of local legal doctrines and

---

Law (Oxford: Clarendon Press, 1993); AP Simester and ATH Smith (eds), *Harm and Culpability* (Oxford: Clarendon Press, 1996); S Shute and AP Simester (eds), *Criminal Law Theory* (Oxford: Oxford University Press, 2002); V Tadros, *Criminal Responsibility* (Oxford: Oxford University Press, 2005); J Gardner, *Offences and Defences* (Oxford: Oxford University Press, 2007).

[3] N Lacey, 'Historicising Criminalisation: Conceptual and Empirical Issues' (2009) 72 MLR 936; D Husak, *Overcriminalization* (Oxford: Oxford University Press, 2008); AP Simester (ed), *Appraising Strict Liability* (Oxford: Oxford University Press, 2005). The classic systematic treatment remains J Feinberg, *The Moral Limits of the Criminal Law*, vols I–IV (New York: Oxford University Press, 1984–8).

[4] HLA Hart, *Punishment and Responsibility* (2nd edn, Gardner ed; New York: Oxford University Press, 2008).

[5] A von Hirsch and AP Simester (eds), *Incivilities: Regulating Offensive Behaviour* (Oxford: Hart Publishing, 2006); A von Hirsch and A Ashworth, *Proportionate Sentencing* (Oxford: Oxford University Press, 2005); A von Hirsch et al (eds), *Restorative Justice and Criminal Justice* (Oxford: Hart Publishing, 2003); A von Hirsch, *Censure and Sanctions* (Oxford: Clarendon Press, 1993).

[6] RA Duff, *Answering for Crime: Responsibility and Liability in the Criminal Law* (Oxford: Hart Publishing, 2007); RA Duff et al, *The Trial on Trial Volume Three: Towards a Normative Theory of the Criminal Trial* (Oxford: Hart Publishing, 2007); RA Duff, *Punishment, Communication and Community* (Oxford: Oxford University Press, 2001).

[7] Also see D Husak, *The Philosophy of Criminal Law* (Oxford/New York: Oxford University Press, 2010); MS Moore, *Placing Blame* (Oxford/New York: Oxford University Press, 1997).

their underpinning jurisprudential rationalizations. Thus, whilst entrapment is a substantive criminal law defence in the United States,[8] it is regarded as a factor bearing only on the admissibility of evidence and mitigation of sentence in England and Wales.[9] Many commentators treat statutory provisions reversing the onus of proof on particular facts (for example, 'due diligence defences' to regulatory crime) as the functional equivalents of substantive criteria of criminal liability.[10] Conversely, irrebuttable presumptions, ostensibly a procedural device, are to all intents and purposes substantive rules of law.[11] Further examples could easily be multiplied. These and other similar procedural techniques could be excluded from the ambit of Criminal Law Theory only by arbitrary stipulation, gratuitously hobbling and disfiguring the discipline—the intellectual equivalent of poking out your own eye.

On the assumption that criminal procedure is undeniably a legitimate topic for Criminal Law Theory, we may proceed to consider the methodological challenges of putting that (meta)theoretical proposition into (theoretical) practice. Theorizing criminal procedure begins with defining and delimiting the object of one's inquiry. 'Criminal procedure' is conventionally conceptualized as the adjectival counterpart to substantive criminal law. On the orthodox dichotomy differentiating prescription from process, substantive law specifies the content of criminal prohibitions and the criteria of criminal responsibility and liability, whilst the legal regulation of criminal law's application and enforcement is assigned to the law of criminal procedure. These distinctions would be familiar to criminal lawyers around the globe, not merely to those schooled in the common law. To proceed any further, however, our discussion is obliged to take a distinctly parochial turn.

There is considerable variation in the disciplinary specialism of 'Criminal Procedure' across the world's jurisprudential traditions. To most Continental and civilian lawyers, Criminal Procedure implies detailed expository analysis of the local jurisdiction's criminal procedure code. In American legal education, Criminal Procedure (I am reliably informed) involves the study of particular aspects of constitutional law, typically divided into pre-trial ('cops and robbers') and trial ('bail to jail') proceedings. An outsider to this pedagogic contrivance cannot fail to notice that criminal procedure is almost entirely divorced from the Law of Evidence, which would strike any European (British lawyers included) as bizarre. My concept of 'criminal procedure' is not beholden to the idiosyncrasies of American legal education or, indeed, to any other pedagogic tradition. From a British perspective,

---

[8]   *Jacobson v United States*, 503 US 540, 548–9 (1992).

[9]   *R v Looseley; Attorney-General's Reference (No 3 of 2000)* [2001] 1 WLR 2060, HL; *R v Sang* [1980] AC 402, HL.

[10]   RJ Allen, 'Structuring Jury Decisionmaking in Criminal Cases: A Unified Constitutional Approach to Evidentiary Devices' (1980) 94 *Harvard Law Review* 321; cf P Roberts, 'Strict Liability and the Presumption of Innocence: An Exposé of Functionalist Assumptions', in Simester (ed), *Appraising Strict Liability*.

[11]   P Roberts and A Zuckerman, *Criminal Evidence* (2nd edn; Oxford: Oxford University Press, 2010), § 6.2(b).

'criminal procedure' is a relatively unencumbered concept free of existing disciplinary baggage.

Law schools in England and Wales do not generally teach undergraduate courses
in either Criminal Procedure or Civil Procedure. Explicit instruction in procedural
law is deferred to the later, 'vocational stage' of legal education, where it predictably takes on the intensely practical characteristics of legal 'plumbing' (how to draft
indictments; how to conduct pre-trial discovery; what to wear in court, and how to
address the judge; how to examine witnesses; how to lodge an appeal notice, etc).
Those parts of criminal procedure that do routinely figure in undergraduate degrees
are variously parcelled out to other courses, chiefly Criminal Law, Constitutional
Law/Public Law, Criminal Justice/Criminology, and the Law of Evidence.[12]
Whatever conceptual logic or pedagogical convenience might be offered to rationalize this fragmented diaspora, dismembering criminal procedure into (some of) its
major components necessarily imperils any holistic vision of disciplinary coherence, the more so when there is no unified subject of Criminal Procedure to put the
disaggregated parts back together again.

Common law jurisprudence, not only in its English manifestation, allocates the
greater part of criminal procedure to the 'Law of Evidence'. Despite its familiarity,
it is no difficult task to paint this entrenched conceptualization as arbitrary, even
perverse. To begin with, it is curious (to say the least) that a majority of the world's
legal jurisdictions have no use for a disciplinary classification that common lawyers treat as axiomatic.[13] Our Law of Evidence is arbitrary not merely in the weak
sense that its contents could be selected and arranged differently (the same might
be said for any jurisprudential taxonomy), but in the far more consequential sense
that its disciplinary boundaries are difficult to defend, or even to state coherently.
Are rules relating to the examination of witnesses procedural or evidentiary? How
about the procedures and practices for interviewing witnesses, or for conducting
covert surveillance operations, or normative standards regulating the use of police
informants and cooperating witnesses, or the rules of court governing pre-trial
disclosure? Open any textbook on the Law of Evidence and look for the awkward
compromises in coverage; pay attention to the many idiosyncratic inclusions and
omissions that particular authors favour. Of course, space is limited and selections
have to be made. Yet evidentiary doctrines frequently make little or no real sense
unless they are placed in their broader procedural context. The common lawyer's
penchant for distilling out a 'pure' Law of Evidence from a dynamic process of
adjudication consequently tends to contribute to our discipline's reputation for
sterile doctrinalism. It also constitutes a perilous snare for inadequately briefed

---

[12] Disciplinary labels and topical coverage differ. There may also be sub-variants further complicating the picture, eg Human Rights Law, Socio-Legal Studies, etc.

[13] JF Nijboer, 'Common Law Tradition in Evidence Scholarship Observed from a Continental
Perspective' (1993) 41 *American Journal of Comparative Law* 299.

policymakers who, unless they peer behind the headlines, are likely to grasp only half the story.

Harping on the conceptual impoverishment of common law Evidence scholarship and teaching is, I realize, a poor way to advertise criminal procedure to criminal law theorists.[14] It is time for a fresh start: indeed, reconceiving the basic disciplinary parameters, concepts, and terminology of criminal procedure might fairly be regarded as the first task for criminal law theorists willing to get to grips with procedural issues. To get the ball rolling, this chapter explores four rival perspectives or approaches to conceptualizing criminal procedure and evidence designated: (1) doctrinal-conceptualist; (2) epistemological; (3) institutional; and (4) normative. These four ideal-types are intended to represent core strands in contemporary common law scholarship, viewed from a British perspective. What follows, in other words, will largely be an exercise in sympathetic reconstruction of existing theory and practice rather than building from the ground up in conformity with an ideal theoretical blueprint. Any purported contrast between 'procedure' and 'evidence' is slippery at the best of times; and readers may need temporarily to suspend belief in their own jurisdiction's conceptual, disciplinary, and pedagogic taxonomies. Besides, nothing essential turns on the nominal labels or exact specifications of the four perspectives. Nor are they necessarily mutually exclusive. Our interest lies in the substance, implications, and comparative merits of each general approach, broadly conceived.

It is vital at the outset to articulate the precise question(s) which any given inquiry is purporting to answer. For example, asking 'What is evidence?', 'What is the Law of Evidence?', 'What is criminal procedure?', 'What is criminal adjudication?', or 'What is criminal justice?' would anticipate quite distinct, albeit substantially overlapping, inquiries. Perspective and motivation simultaneously preselect method. Choice of standpoint and objectives (whether or not fully acknowledged) mutually condition the subject matter and methodological tools of one's analysis, and this interlocking matrix of commitments and presuppositions necessarily influences (if it does not determine) any inquiry's ultimate conclusions and their normative and practical significance. Working out from their respective discipline-defining questions, each of the four perspectives is further differentiated by its primary sources, paradigmatic subject matter, orientation to evidence and proof, and analytical methods, which taken in combination offer four distinctive conceptualizations of procedural law and scholarship. We will mostly be dealing in traditional associations and loose coalitions of assumptions and practices rather than in relationships which are strictly logically entailed, but that will not prevent us from identifying reasonably stable and predictable patterns in the major common law approaches to criminal procedure.

---

[14] Cf P Roberts and M Redmayne (eds), *Innovations in Evidence and Proof* (Oxford: Hart Publishing, 2007).

A plausible reading of the following exposition might trace a kind of theoretical ascent, with each successive perspective transcending the approaches which precede it. Whilst there is much truth in that interpretation, one must not overlook or entirely discount what might be lost as well as gained by adopting more theoretically elevated perspectives. Each of the approaches considered here has its own distinctive strengths and characteristic blind spots. Yet it may not be possible to integrate all four perspectives into any vaunted Unified Grand Theory of Criminal Procedure and Evidence. Methodological pluralism is consequently a necessity as well as a virtue of the following exposition.

2 DOCTRINAL-CONCEPTUALIST PERSPECTIVES ON THE LAW OF EVIDENCE

What I will call 'doctrinal-conceptualist' perspectives on legal evidence and procedure represent the traditional, and still largely dominant, common law understanding of the Law of Evidence. This inelegant label registers two definitive features of the typical common lawyer's perspective: its affinity for conceptual analysis and its preoccupation with doctrinal materials, more particularly case law and associated evidentiary rules of admissibility and exclusion.

Treatises and textbooks on the Law of Evidence typically begin by posing the question: what is (judicial) evidence? The answer, roughly, is that judicial (or legal, or—literally—*forensic*) evidence is information received in legal proceedings which the fact-finder uses to resolve disputed questions of fact. There may (or may not) be some attempt to distinguish judicial evidence from the types of information utilized in other familiar forms of inquiry, such as the evidence assembled or relied upon by journalists, historians, or physicians. At all events, attention soon turns to taxonomies of judicial evidence, in which basic concepts like 'testimonial evidence', 'real evidence', 'direct evidence', 'circumstantial evidence', etc are distinguished and defined. Later chapters of these books introduce more specialist concepts like 'hearsay evidence' and 'bad character evidence', and subject them to minute conceptual and doctrinal elucidation.

Although conceptual analysis can seem forbiddingly dry and may be prone to falling into a sterile conceptual*ism* (ceaseless conceptual refinement for its own sake), there can be no objection in principle to taking concepts seriously. Thorough knowledge of basic evidentiary concepts and facility in their practical application are indispensable building blocks for any viable approach to the subject. The problem lies in what typically happens—or rather, does not happen—next. For orthodox approaches tend to lock themselves into excessively narrow and legalistic conceptions of the Law of Evidence. From the question, 'What is Evidence?', conceptual analysis predictably long-jumps to the question 'What is the Law of Evidence?', and this question in turn is investigated through a doctrinal lens obscured by tunnel vision. Conceptualism and doctrinalism go hand-in-hand in doctrinal-conceptualist perspectives on the Law of Evidence.

Doctrinalism is manifested in two predominant, mutually exacerbating, respects. First, the concept of legal evidence is restricted to information expressly tendered and received as an item of 'evidence' in the trial. This leaves out of account much of the information that fact-finders actually utilize in determining legal disputes, including informal 'evidence' to which the legal process quite deliberately exposes fact-finders—for example, counsel's speeches and suggestive witness questioning; the accused's demeanour in the dock[15]—and the vast amounts of 'commonsense' information that fact-finders bring with them into the courtroom.[16] A second conceptual narrowing occurs when orthodox treatments of the Law of Evidence focus almost exclusively on legal rules mandating the exclusion of certain types of evidence. Over time, the Law of Evidence itself becomes reductively associated with exclusionary rules of evidence, a view which still today influences the thinking of many practising and academic common lawyers.

Orthodox doctrinal conceptions of the Law of Evidence are often attributed to the turn-of-century American legal scholar James Bradley Thayer. 'The law', Thayer famously declared, 'furnishes no test of relevancy':

For this, it tacitly refers to logic and general experience—assuming that the principles of reasoning are known to its judges and ministers, just as a vast multitude of other things are assumed as already sufficiently known to them... To the hungry furnace of the reasoning faculty the law of evidence is but a stoker.[17]

Whether or not Thayer himself intended it,[18] the legacy of this dichotomy has been to expel serious inquiries into fact-finding from the disciplinary realm of the Law of Evidence. Notice that, in the quotation just given, Thayer seemingly contrasts 'the law of evidence' with 'the reasoning faculty', the principles of which are, supposedly, 'already sufficiently known', along with the entire folk-wisdom of 'logic and general experience' to which the law 'tacitly refers'. It might easily be inferred from passages such as this that the Evidence lawyer's empire begins and ends with exclusionary

---

[15] Or sat at the defence table in the United States. Either way, jurors observe the accused's demeanour throughout the course of the trial, whether or not the accused also chooses to enter the witness box to testify in his own defence.

[16] Roberts and Zuckerman, *Criminal Evidence*, § 4.4.

[17] JB Thayer, *A Preliminary Treatise on Evidence at the Common Law* (Boston: Little, Brown & Co, 1898), 265, 271.

[18] Cf E Swift, 'One Hundred Years of Evidence Law Reform: Thayer's Triumph' (2000) 88 *California Law Review* 2437, 2440.

legal rules. The perversity of mistaking the part for the whole has been parodied by William Twining as 'rather like treating England as a suburb of London'.[19]

Reductive understandings of the Law of Evidence, fostered by a conceptualist approach to the subject, have many unfortunate symptoms. In purely doctrinal terms, a preoccupation with admissibility has made an enigma out of the concept of relevance,[20] over-complicated judicial notice,[21] mystified presumptions and burdens of proof,[22] and downplayed the true evidentiary significance of judicial directions instructing or advising jurors how they should deal with information after it has been admitted at trial.[23] More broadly, orthodox conceptions of the Law of Evidence eschew any real interest in the dynamics of adjudication or the practical realities of fact-finding, even when fact-finding is undertaken by trial judges and should naturally be regarded as part of the more general topic of judicial reasoning.[24] Rules of evidence are presented in cross-section, fixed at the particular point in time when admissibility determinations fall to be made. Evidence is individuated atomistically and its legal pedigree determined, piece by piece, according to whether each item of evidence passes the all-important admissibility test. This approach says nothing about how different pieces of evidence might be combined together or interpreted holistically; nor, crucially, does it enter into debates about how in practice fact-finders do or should acquire, marshal, scrutinize, synthesize, and evaluate the information at their disposal and assess it against applicable legal standards of proof.

A narrow, static, atomistic, and excessively legalistic approach to the Law of Evidence, notwithstanding its apparently simplifying premises, tends to confuse students in the long run, because its theoretical tools and assumptions are too parsimonious to make sense of much of the case law dealing with procedural issues. It also short-changes students intending to go into legal practice (and presents all students with a misleading picture of law beyond law school), inasmuch as most practising lawyers spend (at least) nine-tenths of their time investigating, collecting, organizing, presenting, and arguing about facts. Trial lawyers rarely concern themselves with the appellate court judgments on points of admissibility which proliferate in

---

[19] W Twining, *Theories of Evidence: Bentham & Wigmore* (London: Weidenfeld & Nicolson, 1985), 164.

[20] Best illustrated by the House of Lords' enigmatic (and troubling) decision in *R v Blastland* [1986] 1 AC 41. For critical discussion, see Andrew L-T Choo, 'The Notion of Relevance and Defence Evidence' [1993] *Criminal Law Review* 114; M Redmayne, 'Analysing Evidence Case Law', in Roberts and Redmayne (eds), *Innovations in Evidence and Proof*.

[21] See Roberts and Zuckerman, *Criminal Evidence*, §4.7.

[22] EM Morgan, 'Presumptions' (1937) 12 *Washington Law Review* 255, famously lamented that 'every writer of sufficient intelligence to appreciate the difficulties of the subject matter has approached the topic of presumptions with a sense of hopelessness, and has left it with a feeling of despair'.

[23] Discussed under the rubric of 'forensic reasoning rules' in Roberts and Zuckerman, *Criminal Evidence*, §15.3.

[24] Cf R Pattenden, 'Pre-verdict Judicial Fact-finding in Criminal Trials with Juries' (2009) 29 OJLS 1.

Evidence textbooks and classrooms, and tend to crowd out almost everything else from legal education.[25]

3 Epistemological Perspectives on Evidence and Proof

Epistemological perspectives have chiefly been conceived in reaction to conceptual approaches to the Law of Evidence (though they would not necessarily apply the label 'epistemological' to themselves, or confine their motivation so narrowly). I call these perspectives 'epistemological' and group them together because, whatever their otherwise marked dissimilarities, they all proceed from the conviction that fact-finding should be central to the study of legal evidence.[26] The discipline-defining questions for an epistemological approach to criminal procedure and evidence might be, for example: How does legal fact-finding proceed in practice? Does legal adjudication produce true verdicts? How do legal procedures facilitate, or retard, fact-finders' access to the truth? Are particular rules of evidence, or their entire corpus, truth-conducive or truth-defeating? Jeremy Bentham was the original legal epistemologist, and his strident criticisms of late eighteenth- and early nineteenth-century English legal procedure still inspire, provoke, and intrigue scholars in the twenty-first century.[27] Four principal strands of epistemological thinking can be identified in the modern evidence and proof literature, which I will discuss in roughly chronological order.

William Twining's pioneering advocacy of 'taking facts seriously' was a programme conceived in direct response to the shortcomings of conceptual-doctrinal

---

[25] As long ago as 1930, Karl Llewellyn bemoaned 'the almost hopeless bias of all present and past discussion about law. We *talk of legislatures and of courts of last resort. We talk of almost nothing else* . . . Law *is*, to the community, what law *does*. What picture of the doing can you find in all this study of appellate courts alone?': *The Bramble Bush—The Classic Lectures on the Law and Law School* (S Sheppard ed; New York: Oxford University Press, 2008), 94, 96 (original emphasis). And see D Nicolson, 'Facing Facts: The Teaching of Fact Construction in University Law Schools' (1997) 1 E & P 132.

[26] Broadly construed, 'epistemological' covers not only philosophical inquiries into the nature and grounds of knowledge, but also work on the logic of inference and fact-finding, argumentation, 'critical thinking', the science and psychology of human cognition and reasoning, narrative analysis, forensic science, etc.

[27] Though Bentham's own positions on evidence and proof were 'normative' in (supposedly) deriving from his systematic and comprehensive Utilitarian ethics, modern Evidence scholars advancing 'freedom of proof'-type arguments do not, for the most part, appear to be exegetically faithful to Bentham's writings or to endorse his normative philosophical commitments, even when they borrow overtly 'utilitarian' terminology.

approaches to the Law of Evidence, which were briefly summarized in the previous section.[28] Much of that critique is owed directly to Twining, who suggested that the prevailing tradition in Anglo-American Evidence scholarship is 'remarkably unsceptical in respect of its basic assumptions'[29] and consequently prone to theoretical superficiality and deep conceptual incoherence:

[C]onfident assertion, pragmatic question-begging, and straightforward ignoring are the characteristic responses to perennial questions raised by philosophical sceptics . . . [T]he subject of evidence is typically treated as being coextensive with the law of evidence; topics such as probabilities, which are not governed by legal rules, are either totally ignored or uneasily slotted into discussions of the law; books and courses on evidence are either very narrowly conceived, incoherently organized, or both . . . [E]vidence doctrine has yet to be put in its proper place as just one part of the science of proof . . .[30]

Aspiring to revive and extend a project originally associated with Thayer's pupil, John Henry Wigmore, Twining's distinctive version of the 'science of proof' has subsequently taken in probability theory, logic, argumentation, narrative and story-telling, graphical representations of inference, epistemology, and social psychology.[31] The overriding programmatic objective is to work towards a 'total process' view of information gathering, management, and evaluation in litigation, without restricting analysis to the trial stages of legal proceedings or becoming fixated on exclusionary rules of evidence. Indeed, Twining rarely describes fully particularized legal norms in his interdisciplinary studies of evidence and inference, and largely eschews detailed doctrinal exegesis.

Probability theory contributes a second influential strand to the epistemological orientation in Evidence scholarship. Modern interest in mathematical approaches to legal evidence and proof can be traced back to the late 1960s,[32] at the birth of what became known as the New Evidence Scholarship,[33] and has ever since commanded a loyal following amongst *aficionados*[34] and several fleeting episodes of rekindled

---

[28] W Twining, 'Taking Facts Seriously', in N Gold (ed), *Essays on Legal Education* (Toronto: Butterworths, 1982); reprinted as *Rethinking Evidence*, ch 2. Now also see W Twining, 'Taking Facts Seriously—Again', in Roberts and Redmayne (eds), *Innovations in Evidence and Proof*.

[29] Twining, *Theories of Evidence*, 177.

[30] Ibid 177, 164.

[31] W Twining, *Rethinking Evidence* (Oxford: Blackwell, 1990; 2nd edn, Cambridge: Cambridge University Press, 2006).

[32] Inspired by the now-notorious decision in *People v Collins*, 68 Cal 2d 319 (1968). See LH Tribe, 'Trial by Mathematics: Precision and Ritual in the Legal Process' (1971) 84 *Harvard Law Review* 1329.

[33] R Lempert, 'The New Evidence Scholarship: Analyzing the Process of Proof' (1986) 66 *Boston University Law Review* 439.

[34] Including DH Kaye, 'Clarifying the Burden of Persuasion: What Bayesian Decision Rules Do and Do Not Do' (1999) 3 E & P 1; P Donnelly, 'Approximation, Comparison, and Bayesian Reasoning in Juridical Proof' (1997) 1 E & P 304; RD Friedman, 'Towards a (Bayesian) Convergence?' (1997) 1 E & P 348; B Robertson and GA Vignaux, *Interpreting Evidence* (Chicester: Wiley, 1995); RO Lempert, 'Modeling Relevance' (1977) 75 *Michigan Law Review* 1021.

popular attention.[35] The intellectual point of departure, as before, is Thayer's observation that law rests on logic and general experience. Those of a mathematical bent subsequently sought to extend the logic of probability to legal fact-finding processes. Aspects of procedural law are framed in expressly probabilistic terms, most obviously the civil standard of proof 'on the balance of probabilities'.[36] Whilst classical probability axioms may have relatively little direct application to legal adjudication, the formula for updating conditional probabilities known as Bayes' Theorem has attracted a great deal of interest from legal scholars.[37] It was even presented to the jury in one English case in which the evidence consisted of a matching DNA profile and other, non-quantified evidence.[38] The defence called an expert witness to teach jurors how to use Bayes' Theorem to calculate their own, aggregated 'posterior probability' of the accused's guilt or innocence. (The Court of Appeal was not amused.[39])

Statistical evidence and related aspects of mathematical probability are undoubtedly significant features of modern litigation, not least because they underpin much expert identification evidence, including DNA profiling.[40] English criminal litigation has recently witnessed a string of high profile miscarriages of justice in which mothers were convicted of murdering their 'cot death' babies partly on the basis of flawed statistical evidence.[41] These tragic case histories only serve to reinforce the importance of including basic introductions to probability and statistics somewhere in the law school curriculum—Evidence courses being the obvious candidate—and subjecting the forensic uses of probabilistic concepts and reasoning to rigorous scholarly investigation and informed public debate. There have always been sceptics about the application of probability theory to legal issues, and they are led today by Ron Allen, an indefatigable campaigner against the pretensions of mathematical

[35] See eg the flurry of commentary generated by *United States v Shonubi*, 895 F Supp 460 (EDNY, 1995), briefly summarized in P Roberts, 'From Theory into Practice: Introducing the Reference Class Problem' (2007) 11 E & P 243.

[36] M Redmayne, 'Standards of Proof in Civil Litigation' (1999) 62 MLR 167.

[37] Roberts and Zuckerman, *Criminal Evidence*, § 4.5(c).

[38] *R v Adams* [1996] 2 Cr App R 467, CA; *R v Adams (No 2)* [1998] 1 Cr App R 377, CA.

[39] '[W]e regard the reliance on evidence of this kind ... as a recipe for confusion, misunderstanding and misjudgment, possibly even among counsel, but very probably among judges and, as we conclude, almost certainly among jurors ... We are very clearly of opinion that ... expert evidence should not be admitted to induce juries to attach mathematical values to probabilities arising from non-scientific evidence adduced at the trial': *R v Adams (No 2)* [1998] 1 Cr App R 377, 384, 385, CA.

[40] Nation Research Council, *Strengthening Forensic Science in the United States* (NAP, 2009), ch 4; MJ Saks and JJ Koehler, 'The Coming Paradigm Shift in Forensic Identification Science' (2005) 309 *Science* 892; National Research Council, *The Evaluation of Forensic DNA Evidence* (NAP, 1996), 25–30 and ch 4; R Lempert, 'Some Caveats Concerning DNA as Criminal Identification Evidence: With Thanks to the Reverend Bayes' (1991) 13 *Cardozo Law Review* 303.

[41] *R v Cannings* [2004] 1 WLR 2607, [2004] EWCA Crim 1; *R v Sally Clark* [2003] EWCA Crim 1020.

models of evidence and proof.[42] But nobody would any longer deny that probability theory has *some* role to play in the evidentiary dimensions of both legal practice and legal education in the twenty-first century. Inflated claims that were at one time made for the legal applications of probabilistic analysis in general, and for Bayes' Theorem in particular, have since given way to more sober and realistic assessments.[43]

A third strand of the epistemological perspective is contributed by social psychologists, socio-legal scholars, and behavioural scientists who have conducted empirical investigations into the epistemological credentials of legal adjudication. Often critical in tone and reformist in aspiration, much of this work has been devoted to challenging the epistemic assumptions that underlie—or appear to underlie— particular procedural practices. Empirical data derived from social scientific studies have indicated, for example, that eyewitness identification reports are not as reliable as might be assumed, even when the witness is entirely honest and confidently picks out the accused as the perpetrator;[44] witnesses can be quite suggestible during police interviews, and false admissions by suspects are not uncommon;[45] and ordinary people (potential jurors) are not as good at inferring credibility from a witness's demeanour as they tend to believe they are.[46] Such studies may contribute towards improving the epistemic performance of legal procedures. In England and Wales, important changes to the ways in which police investigators conduct identification procedures[47] and interview suspects and witnesses, especially children and other vulnerable individuals,[48] have been inspired or substantiated by behavioural science data. Empirical investigations of legal procedures sometimes embolden behavioural scientists to advance more radical critiques of existing adjudicative practices,

---

[42] RJ Allen and MS Pardo, 'The Problematic Value of Mathematical Models of Evidence' (2007) 36 *Journal of Legal Studies* 107; RJ Allen, 'The Nature of Juridical Proof' (1991) 13 *Cardozo Law Review* 373. And see A Stein, 'Judicial Fact-finding and the Bayesian Method: The Case for Deeper Scepticism about their Combination' (1996) 1 E & P 25; D Hodgson, 'Probability: The Logic of the Law—A Response' (1995) 15 OJLS 51; CR Callen, 'Notes on a Grand Illusion: Some Limits on the Use of Bayesian Theory in Evidence Law' (1982) 57 *Indiana Law Journal* 1.

[43] JA Michon, 'The Time Has Come to Put this Debate Aside and Move on to Other Matters' (1997) 1 E & P 331; Friedman, 'Towards a (Bayesian) Convergence?'.

[44] RA Wise et al, 'How to Analyze the Accuracy of Eyewitness Testimony in a Criminal Case' (2009) 42 *Connecticut Law Review* 435; T Valentine, 'Forensic Facial Identification', in A Heaton-Armstrong, E Shepherd, G Gudjonsson, and D Wolchover (eds), *Witness Testimony* (Oxford: Oxford University Press, 2006).

[45] SM Kassin et al, 'Police-induced Confessions: Risk Factors and Recommendations' (2010) 34 *Law & Human Behavior* 3; GH Gudjonsson, 'The Psychological Vulnerablities of Witnesses and the Risk of False Accusations and False Confessions', in Heaton-Armstrong et al (eds), *Witness Testimony*.

[46] JA Blumenthal, 'A Wipe of the Hands, A Lick of the Lips: The Validity of Demeanor Evidence in Assessing Witness Credibility' (1993) 72 *Nebraska Law Review* 1157; OG Wellborn III, 'Demeanor' (1991) 76 *Cornell Law Review* 1075.

[47] PACE Code D, *Code of Practice for the Identification of Persons by Police Officers* (2008 edition), <http://www.police.homeoffice.gov.uk/operational-policing/powers-pace-codes/>.

[48] CJS, *Achieving Best Evidence in Criminal Proceedings: Guidance on Interviewing Victims and Witnesses, and Using Special Measures* (2007 revision), <http://www.cps.gov.uk/publications/docs/achieving_best_evidence_final.pdf>.

including the frequently recycled complaint that adversarial proceedings are not truth-conducive. More thoroughgoing criticisms of the law's entrenched procedural traditions have predictably encountered professional resistance and, thus far, have claimed fewer reformist trophies.[49]

Law often strikes outsiders as conservative, and so it is, for both good and bad reasons. However, reform proposals grounded in the empirical sciences must overcome more than lawyers' cultural inertia and powerful guild self-interest in the status quo in order to realize their reformist ambitions. It is difficult to model criminal adjudication under formal experimental conditions, and there are legal and ethical restrictions on researching real-life criminal cases. The empirical researcher must therefore grapple with formidable methodological challenges in order to produce valid and representative data with generalizable results.[50] This is not to question the enterprise of conducting empirical studies of criminal proceedings *tout court*, but rather to insist that an appropriate evidence base for championing evidentiary reform must, generally speaking, be built up over time through the accumulation of multiple studies subjecting well-constructed theoretical hypotheses or assumptions to a range of triangulating experimental conditions. Like swallows and summer, criminal law reform should not be hazarded on a single instance.[51] A social practice which can cost participants their liberty, property, reputation, and livelihoods (and in the United States and elsewhere, their lives) should normally await experimental results which have withstood the tests of time and replication. Behavioural scientists and socio-legal scholars with an insider's appreciation of legal procedures have grasped the methodological nettle of empirical research with increasing circumspection and ingenuity,[52] but the precariousness of extrapolating from a set of experimental findings to concrete legal reforms should never be underestimated. This is only to hold social scientific research to its own internal standards of validity; the normative considerations to which we shall shortly return present additional, and potentially insurmountable, obstacles to behavioural scientists' reformist agendas.

Finally, fourth, a number of well-known academic philosophers—hard-core epistemologists—have lately become interested in the law's epistemological credentials

---

[49] Generally, see J McEwan, 'Reasoning, Relevance and Law Reform: The Influence of Empirical Research on Criminal Adjudication', in Roberts and Redmayne (eds), *Innovations in Evidence and Proof*.

[50] See R Bagshaw, 'Behavioural Science Data in Evidence Teaching and Scholarship', in Roberts and Redmayne, ibid.

[51] Whether law reform should be attempted—even on the basis of a hunch or moral conviction with no systematic empirical data to support it—ultimately depends on what is at stake either way. My point is epistemic and methodological: a single empirical study, or group of related studies, rarely generates sufficiently robust conclusions, taken in isolation, to deliver meaningfully 'evidence-based' legal reform.

[52] See eg L Ellison and VE Munro, 'Reacting to Rape: Exploring Mock Jurors' Assessments of Complainant Credibility' (2009) 49 *British Journal of Criminology* 202.

and practices. They include Alvin Goldman,[53] Susan Haack,[54] and, in particular, Larry Laudan, who has even announced a new sub-discipline of 'legal epistemology'.[55] These ground-breaking contributions have in turn encouraged legal scholars to engage more seriously with the epistemological dimensions of legal evidence and proof, making this one of the most vibrant and productive chapters of Evidence scholarship in recent years.[56]

Philosophers' interventions exemplify both the undeniable strengths and the inherent weaknesses of epistemological perspectives on criminal procedure and evidence. On the plus side, evidence is viewed longitudinally rather than in cross-section, as an institutionally generated product of a dynamic set of practices and processes. The transformation of raw information into judicial evidence is traced back through the various phases of its institutional classification and cultivation, which can now be conceptualized as a series of legally regulated social transactions (first report to the casualty doctor or police officer at the scene; initial witness statement at the police station; interview with the prosecutor;[57] examination-in-chief and cross-examination in court, etc). Processes of evidence production—or 'case construction'[58]—cannot be left, as it were, to take care of themselves, until evidence somehow materializes at court for the trial judge to rule on its admissibility. This expanded, contextualized frame of reference delivers significant heuristic advantages over the static, cross-sectional, legalistic analysis typical of doctrinal approaches to the Law of Evidence. Policymakers and practitioners need to be aware of the potentially truth-confounding tendencies of current institutional arrangements for gathering, presenting and testing evidence in court. Legal procedures and rules of evidence ought to be predicated on realistic cultural and psychological assumptions, and it is always a fair question whether this or that rule—or even a set of interlocking procedural practices as complex and entrenched as the adversarial system itself—are fit for their intended purposes and still capable of bearing the weight of their traditional rationales.

---

[53] AI Goldman, *Knowledge in A Social World* (New York: Oxford University Press, 1999).

[54] S Haack, 'Epistemology Legalized: Or, Truth, Justice, and the American Way' (2004) 49 *American Journal of Jurisprudence* 43; S Haack, 'Of Truth, in Science and in Law' (2008) 73 *Brooklyn Law Review* 985.

[55] L Laudan, *Truth, Error and Criminal Law: An Essay in Legal Epistemology* (Cambridge: Cambridge University Press, 2006).

[56] See eg MS Pardo and RJ Allen, 'Juridical Proof and the Best Explanation' (2008) 27 *Law and Philosophy* 223; Hock Lai Ho, *A Philosophy of Evidence Law—Justice in the Search for Truth* (Oxford: Oxford University Press, 2008); R Allen and P Roberts (eds), *Special Issue on the Reference Class Problem* (2007) 11(4) E & P 243–317; MS Pardo, 'The Field of Evidence and the Field of Knowledge' (2005) 24 *Law and Philosophy* 321.

[57] A recent innovation in England and Wales: see P Roberts and C Saunders, 'Introducing Pre-Trial Witness Interviews—A Flexible New Fixture in the Crown Prosecutor's Toolkit' [2008] *Criminal Law Review* 831.

[58] Cf M McConville, A Sanders, and R Leng, *The Case for the Prosecution* (London: Routledge, 1991); P Roberts, 'Science in the Criminal Process' (1994) 14 OJLS 469; A Sanders, 'Constructing the Case for the Prosecution' (1987) 14 *Journal of Law and Society* 229.

Refreshing and insightful as they often are, epistemologists' critiques of criminal procedure are sometimes propelled by their own enthusiasms to premature conclusions. The intended purposes of legal adjudication are far from self-evident, and the normative functions of evidentiary doctrines are not as straightforward as the philosophers and behavioural scientists may be tempted to assume. Most philosophers, certainly, are sophisticated enough to know that legal adjudication is not *exclusively* devoted to successful fact-finding. Legal adjudication is a social practice orientated towards justice with a significant epistemic component, rather than an epistemological practice per se.[59] To what extent, then, can epistemic objectives legitimately be constrained, compromised, or abandoned in favour of legal adjudication's non-epistemic values or objectives? Epistemological perspectives encounter two, possibly—for them—insurmountable obstacles to answering this question satisfactorily.

The first stumbling block is that developing a principled approach to combining the epistemic and non-epistemic dimensions of legal adjudication requires a level of engagement with moral and political philosophy to which epistemological perspectives seem disinclined to commit themselves. Such reticence is perfectly understandable from social and behavioural scientists, whose scholarship is generally confined to producing descriptive reports of experimental hypotheses tested against empirical data with little if any explicitly normative content (although this does not necessarily stop some researchers advancing normative proposals for legal reform motivated by their experimental results). However, even the philosophers who have written on legal evidence appear wary of straying beyond their epistemological backyard into the public highways and bustling marketplaces of moral and political philosophy.[60] This is home turf for the fourth, 'normative' disciplinary perspective discussed later in the chapter.

The second problem confronting epistemological approaches, I believe, also besets Twining's work, even if he is relatively insulated (by epistemologists' standards) from the first. Much of the appeal of Twining's agenda for 'taking facts seriously' can be attributed to the breadth of his all-encompassing vision. One might say that he truly takes the concept of 'evidence' seriously, by extending the ambit of evidential inquiry into the multitude of diverse contexts and formats in which evidence is generated, organized, selected, presented, debated, evaluated, relied upon, and all the rest. This programme sets out to fulfil the promise of a systematically conceptual approach to 'evidence', which the orthodox Thayerite model of the Law of Evidence

---

[59] Assuming a standard conception of the realm of the 'epistemic', but cf n 99 and associated text, below. Whilst epistemic practices are always ultimately responsive to normative criteria in judging their adequacy or success, it is another matter entirely to build moral and political values into epistemic concepts of 'evidence', 'knowledge', 'facts', 'fact-finding', etc. Although law sometimes does exactly that, research and scholarship adopting epistemological approaches to legal adjudication rarely do so.

[60] Goldman (eg) observes that '[t]he difficult problem is to say how the truth-getting value should be weighted as compared with . . . other values. This is not a problem I shall try to settle. It falls outside the scope of social epistemology': *Knowledge in a Social World*, 284–5.

so conspicuously abandons before it really gets going. Consider, however, that there are limits to how informative one can be in discussing 'legal evidence' or 'legal process' or 'legal adjudication' *in general*.[61] Truly insightful and authoritative accounts of the law's evidentiary practices need to get to grips with the detail of particular legal institutions, actors, processes, and norms. Only by engaging in thickly descriptive microanalysis can one elucidate the distinctive ideals, values, and normative rationalizations animating familiar legal practices, such as criminal adjudication, and begin to appreciate the practical constraints conditioning particular institutional environments. The procedural diversity brought into focus by more contextual analysis will tend to recede and blur when viewed in gross at a distance.

There are two obvious rejoinders to the objection from generality, but neither is convincing. First, it might be said that the detail is 'just detail' that nobody seriously needs to worry about. This is misconceived. Contextual variations manifest themselves in materially and sometimes radically different ways, depending on a range of institutional factors—beginning with the major structural distinction between criminal and civil proceedings. This conceptual refinement suggests a second rejoinder. Why not, then, produce appropriately detailed accounts of every evidentially significant legal practice and procedural variation? Comprehensive treatment would be a viable aspiration for a well-populated field of scholarship over an extended period of time, but it is necessarily ruled out on pragmatic grounds for single works (if they are to remain readable and accessible to undergraduates) and isolated scholars. It is presumably for these pragmatic reasons and with an eye to inculcating transferrable legal skills, rather than any methodological objection to fine-grained institutional analysis, that Twining's programmatic instructional manuals tackle generic issues in fact-finding and proof without dwelling on particular institutional contexts or getting drawn into extended doctrinal exegesis. Henceforth, we may finesse the equivocation implicit in generalized references to 'legal procedure', 'judicial evidence', 'adjudication', 'legal proceedings', etc and concentrate exclusively—for illustrative purposes—on criminal adjudication.

4 INSTITUTIONAL PERSPECTIVES ON CRIMINAL ADJUDICATION

If conceptualists are preoccupied with taxonomies of judicial evidence and exclusionary rules, and epistemologists fixate on the philosophical pedigree and social realities

---

[61] Even when one's perspective incorporates microscopic analysis of (generic) forms of human cognition and inferential reasoning: cf T Anderson, D Schum, and W Twining, *Analysis of Evidence* (New York: Cambridge University Press, 2005), chs 5 and 7.

of the law's epistemic practices, institutional perspectives are characterized by their primary focus on the institutional context, procedural frameworks, and sociological regularities of legal proceedings. There is a galaxy of institutions that could plausibly be described as 'legal'. My stipulated interest is confined to criminal proceedings.

Even so delimited, an 'institutional' perspective on criminal proceedings could adopt a variety of techniques and formats. One might proceed from a broad theoretical commitment, such as Marxism, feminism, Foucauldian post-structuralism, critical race theory, etc, in which case one's inquiry-structuring questions would reflect that pre-commitment. Alternatively, one might undertake micro-sociological investigation of criminal proceedings, or some particular aspect(s) of them, utilizing the descriptively orientated methods of socio-legal studies, criminology, anthropology, and related disciplines. For assistance in developing such inquires, there is a well-stocked library of 'mid-range' theoretical conceptualizations, notably including Herbert Packer's widely influential (and much maligned) 'crime control' and 'due process' models[62] and Mirjan Damaška's illuminating comparative analysis of procedural cultures,[63] to which one might resort for guidance and inspiration.

The merits of the institutional perspective are best explored through concrete illustrations. Criminal adjudication will serve as our exemplar; and reflecting the preoccupations of English criminal evidence scholarship, the following illustration takes for granted a common law adversarial procedural framework and focuses in the main on the trial stage of criminal proceedings. However, it should be emphasized that institutional perspectives are not tied to particular legal systems and are perfectly capable of encompassing post-trial (appellate), pre-trial, and investigative processes (and might well be extended beyond that, if one can informatively describe 'the family', 'the office', 'the school/college/university', 'the church', 'the club', 'the media', etc as institutions).

How might one conceptualize criminal adjudication in terms of its basic institutional organization, normative frameworks, regulatory techniques, and distribution of practical authority? A plausible model might resemble the following structural taxonomy, with five principal categories of constitutive norms each further subdivided into its main spheres (institutional spaces) of normative regulation:

I. *Rules[64] constituting the court and delimiting its jurisdiction*

    (i)   appointment, independence and impartiality of the tribunal;

---

[62] HL Packer, 'Two Models of the Criminal Process' (1964) 113 *University of Pennsylvania Law Review* 1. For recent critical discussion, see S Macdonald, 'Constructing A Framework for Criminal Justice Research: Learning from Packer's Mistakes' (2008) 11 *New Criminal Law Review* 257; P Roberts, 'Criminal Justice Goes Global' (2008) 28 OJLS 369, 377–9.

[63] MR Damaška, *The Faces of Justice and State Authority* (New Haven, CT: Yale University Press, 1986). See P Roberts, 'Faces of Justice Adrift? Damaska's Comparative Method and the Future of Common Law Evidence', in J Jackson, M Langer, and P Tillers (eds), *Crime, Procedure and Evidence in A Comparative and International Context* (Oxford: Hart Publishing, 2008); I Markovits, 'Playing the Opposites Game: On Mirjan Damaška's *The Faces of Justice and State Authority*' (1989) 41 *Stanford Law Review* 1313.

[64] Throughout this illustration, 'rules' is shorthand for 'rules, principles, doctrines, and other institutionalized normative standards'.

    (ii)   territorial and subject-matter jurisdiction;

    (iii) double jeopardy;

    (iv) stays for abuse of process;

    (v)   selection and empanelment of jurors (where applicable);

    (vi) physical environment and spatial layout of the courtroom (including ad hoc modifications, for example, to accommodate vulnerable or intimidated witnesses);

    (vii) appeals and post-conviction procedures (if any).

II. *Rules for the conduct of trial proceedings*

    (i)   pre-trial judicial case management (including oversight of disclosure; interlocutory rulings and appeals on points of law, etc);

    (ii)   counsel's opening and closing speeches;

    (iii) courtroom attire, deportment and forms of address;

    (iv) legal ethics (eg Bar *Code of Conduct*);

    (v)   production of exhibits, demonstrative evidence (including authentication of documents);

    (vi) conduct of views and extra-curial demonstrations and reconstructions;

    (vii) compellability and examination of witnesses (examination-in-chief; cross-examination; re-examination);

    (viii) umpireal judicial supervision and (constrained) participation;

    (ix)   *voir dire* to determine contested points of admissibility (with further interlocutory appeals, where available);

    (x)   publicity, public access, and media reporting.

III. *Evidentiary rules of admissibility*

    (i)   relevance;

    (ii)   fair trial (including judicial oversight of legality and propriety of criminal investigations);

    (iii) competency of witnesses (including experts);

    (iv) privilege and public interest immunity;

    (v)   hearsay;

    (vi) confessions;

    (vii) character (good and bad); complainants' previous sexual history ('rape shields');

    (viii) topic-specific exclusions (for example, relating to scientific evidence; eyewitness identification evidence; statistical evidence; self-serving narrative, etc).

IV. *Forensic reasoning rules*

    (i)   burdens and standards of proof;

    (ii)   formal admissions and judicial notice;

    (iii) presumptions;

    (iv) legal corroboration;

    (v)   evidential warnings;

    (vi) mandatory use rules;

    (vii) permissive use rules.

V. *Rules for rendering judgment*

    (i)   fact-finder deliberation (substantive regulation; conditions, for example, secrecy);

(ii)   verdict rules (by majority; special; reasoned or unreasoned);

(iii) judicial sentencing powers;

(iv) etiquette and ethics of imposing sentence;

(v)   settling disputed questions of fact pertaining to sentence;

(vi) publication and further dissemination of verdict and sentence.

A legal-institutional specification of criminal adjudication improves upon ortho-dox conceptualizations of the Law of Evidence in at least ten significant respects. First, and most obviously, the institutional perspective clearly demonstrates that criminal adjudication's evidentiary processes are far from exhausted by exclu-sionary rules. The first gain in comprehension is to recognize that exclusion is only one technique amongst many for regulating the flow of information to fact-finders.

Second, the institutional approach eschews rigid dichotomies between 'evidence' and 'procedure'. This conceptual refinement helps to make the procedural dynam-ics and practical significance of evidentiary practices such as witness examination, proof by formalities, demonstrative evidence and judicial notice, more salient and readily comprehensible.

Third, this expanded vision brings neglected legal backwaters like the constitu-tion of the tribunal, territorial and subject-matter jurisdiction, and double jeopardy back into the mainstream. Plainly unrelated to exclusionary rules of evidence, nor yet fitting comfortably into any other classificatory pigeonhole in the typical law school curriculum, these topics have a tendency to drop out of law degrees entirely, with a predictably discouraging impact on related exploratory research and critical commentary and analysis.

Fourth, in drawing attention to the full range of normative standards and tech-niques employed in criminal adjudication, the institutional approach invites fur-ther reflection on regulatory mechanisms other than rules of admissibility and stimulates their conceptual development. For example, 'forensic reasoning rules' can be further elucidated according to whether they mandate (or forbid), permit, or merely warn the fact-finder about specified evidential inferences.[65] The admis-sibility and interpretation of expert evidence is another topic ripe for taxonomic rethinking, beginning with the entirely unhelpful solecism that expert witness testimony is admitted by way of exception to the so-called 'opinion evidence rule'.[66]

Fifth, an institutional specification draws attention to the deliberative aspects of fact-finding and their associated legal doctrines, including burdens and standards of proof and presumptions. Of course, these topics are addressed in orthodox treat-ments of the Law of Evidence, but they tend to be conceived in narrowly doctrinal

---

[65]   Roberts and Zuckerman, *Criminal Evidence*, § 15.3.

[66]   Ibid §§ 11.1–11.2.

terms and little attempt is made to elucidate their functional and structural properties as one set of evidentiary techniques within a broader adjudicative framework.

Sixth, and building directly on the preceding two observations, an institutional perspective underlines the fact that pieces of evidence have to be combined
in fact-finding; they cannot always be treated atomistically as they typically are
for the purposes of determining admissibility. Corroboration is one of the most
fruitful topics for teaching this lesson. In these respects, an institutional perspective at least hints at the dynamic nature of processes of proof, albeit that this
theme is more fully explored empirically and theoretically in epistemological
approaches.

Seventh, the institutional approach accommodates a broader range of normative
sources than orthodox treatments of the law of evidence, incorporating legal ethics, courtroom etiquette, and the informal stipulations and expectations of professional legal and judicial culture. Relatedly, eighth, it also promotes a more inclusive
conception of 'evidence' than standard definitions, by encompassing (for example)
the semiotics of the physical environment of the courtroom, its spatial layout, and
trial participants' conduct,[67] in addition to all the information straightforwardly
'adduced in evidence' in the technical legal sense.

Ninth, the institutional perspective highlights the significance of the way in
which the verdict is announced and sentence imposed. These processes may have a
significant bearing on the legitimacy of the entire proceedings and—with particular
salience for the present discussion—they may well give rise to disputed questions of
fact that need to be resolved in an acceptable fashion.[68]

Tenth, and flowing directly from the preceding point, the institutional perspective highlights the importance of trial publicity and the wider public dissemination
of information about criminal verdicts and sentencing. Publicity supplies the vital
societal hinge between legal-institutional activity in resolving disputed allegations
of criminal wrongdoing and broader public understandings of criminal justice, on
which the legitimacy and even the continued existence of criminal adjudication in its
traditional formats ultimately rests. Yet this pivotal feature of our adjudicative practices rarely figures at all in doctrinal-conceptualist or epistemological approaches to
criminal procedure and evidence.

This stylized institutional model of criminal adjudication is readily adaptable,
for example to take account of variations in the procedural law of particular legal
jurisdictions. It is also amenable to more detailed specification—for example, by

---

[67] Ibid § 3.4(d) ('informal evidence'). And see LL Levenson, 'Courtroom Demeanor: The Theater of
the Courtroom' (2008) 92 *Minnesota Law Review* 573; L Mulcahy, 'The Unbearable Lightness of Being?
Shifts Towards the Virtual Trial' (2008) 35 *Journal of Law and Society* 464.

[68] Cf *R v Newton* (1982) 77 Cr App R 13, 15, CA ('the judge in these circumstances [may] ... hear the
evidence on one side and another, and come to his own conclusion, acting so to speak as his own jury
on the issue which is the root of the problem').

further subdividing particular species of evidentiary rule[69]—although, as with any heuristic device, there is an unavoidable trade-off between comprehensiveness and comprehension. My sketch is intended to achieve, and thereby illustrate, a desirable balance between substantive informational content and a visually effective, easily assimilated structural map of the disciplinary domain. Ease of comprehension, in the final analysis, must answer to idiosyncratic personal aptitudes and preferences. In any event, nothing turns on the illustration's precise structural contours or detailed content, which are primarily intended to exemplify a flexible representational method.

The limitations of an institutional perspective—at least, of the legal-institutional variety delineated here—are attributable to its selective focus, on one particular legal institution (or set of functionally related institutions), and to the methodological modesty of any essentially descriptive structural model. I have already explained that institutional approaches are obliged to be selective, and this concession can be sharpened into critique. If one concentrates exclusively on Crown Court trials on indictment before a judge and jury, for example, a critic might object that this form of trial is statistically exceptional in England and Wales.[70] My strategy is to confess and avoid. So long as the selected institution is sufficiently important to merit further examination—and does anybody seriously doubt this of English Crown Court trials?—it is hardly any objection that other legal processes might also benefit from systematic exploration by institutional cartographers. If there are major gaps in our knowledge of the evidentiary practices of legal institutions (as there surely are), this is a failing of collective scholarly endeavour rather than a methodological deficiency in the institutional approach.

A more serious criticism is that institutional perspectives provide us with overarching structures and informative taxonomies but leave a great deal more to be supplemented by other approaches and perspectives. Although my fleshed-out illustration accommodates both longitudinal and cross-sectional analyses of information in criminal litigation, representing a clear improvement on doctrinal-conceptualist orthodoxies, it does not fully encapsulate the dynamic qualities of adjudication. Its primary orientation towards normative (albeit not just formal legal) regulation could also be regarded as a distorting feature. It might, therefore, be fruitful to consider combining an institutional approach with detailed epistemological inquiries. Much of the conceptual groundwork and detailed doctrinal exegesis contained in orthodox treatments of the Law of Evidence could also be

---

[69] Eg, in relation to privilege: (1) the witness privilege against self-incrimination; (2) the accused's privilege against self-incrimination; (3) marital privilege; (4) legal professional privilege; (5) priest–penitent privilege (which does not exist in English law, but is widely recognized in other jurisdictions), etc.

[70] P Darbyshire, 'Previous Misconduct and Magistrates' Courts—Some Tales from the Real World' [1997] *Criminal Law Review* 105.

inserted into an institutional framework with little effort and manifest analytical profit.

The final worry is that structural approaches to the social world tend to lapse into an uncritical functionalism and ultimately become de-humanizing (which in turn may appear to authorize inhumanity).[71] Perhaps institutional models of evidence and procedure are too arcane to pose that kind of risk. Resort to 'legitimacy' and 'criminal justice' in enumerating the tenth positive attribute of an institutional perspective nonetheless introduces a crucial equivocation. Are these concepts to be interpreted purely descriptively, in terms of what particular individuals (or some designated reference group) subjectively take to be legitimate or just? Although some self-styled 'social scientists' do claim to restrict themselves to an unremittingly non-judgmental outsider perspective, most people with a professional interest in criminal justice—including legal scholars debating doctrine, and epistemologists championing law reform—adopt critical approaches to institutional legitimacy. They want criminal verdicts to be truly legitimate, and courts to dispense real justice. But in that case these insider-participants are assuming a normative standpoint and exploiting the critical leverage of political morality, whether they realize and acknowledge it or not.

5 NORMATIVE PERSPECTIVES ON CRIMINAL JUSTICE

Suppose that, instead of framing one's inquiry in terms of the concept of evidence and the rules governing its legal admissibility, or pursuing an interest in the law's epistemic practices, or attempting to map out the institutional frameworks of particular adjudicative processes, one began by posing the question: what is criminal procedure *for*? A plausible answer might be that criminal procedure serves the broader objectives and values of criminal justice; that criminal procedure is instrumentally[72] valuable to the extent that it contributes towards translating criminal justice ideals

---

[71] Cf Colin Sumner's characterization of the well-known essay by Harold Garfinkel, 'Conditions of Successful Degradation Ceremonies' (1956) 61 *American Journal of Sociology* 420, as 'a contender for the Orwell prize for amoral, authoritarian, technocratic discourses of the 1950s': *The Sociology of Deviance: An Obituary* (Buckingham: Open University Press, 1994), 182–3. The indictment of functionalism is unflinchingly pursued to its chilling terminus by Z Bauman, *Modernity and the Holocaust* (Cambridge: Polity Press, 1989).

[72] That criminal procedure is instrumentally valuable does not preclude its having intrinsic value as well—although it may be obscure how the contrast between instrumental and intrinsic values plays out in relation to criminal adjudication, or what particular authors intend when they, deliberately or implicitly, invoke that contrast.

into practical achievements. This is all the—conspicuously parsimonious—argumentation required to motivate 'normative' perspectives on criminal procedure in the sense intended here, according to which criminal procedure is properly characterized as a (very) practical application of moral and political philosophy.

Relocating criminal procedure within a broader conception of criminal justice, which in turn derives much of its substance from moral and political philosophy, might sound, to some, suspiciously ethereal and 'academic' in the pejorative, scholastic sense. In fact, nothing could be further from the truth. On 4 April 2005 the Criminal Procedure Rules (CrimPR) came into force in England and Wales,[73] for the first time consolidating a disparate array of statutory rules, delegated legislation, common law precedents, and practice directions into a single, comprehensive[74] procedural code for criminal litigation complete with a mechanism for on-going judicial oversight and incremental amendment. The CrimPR were revised and reissued in 2010, consolidating piecemeal amendments during the first five years of their operation. Rule 1.1 announces the 'overriding objective' of criminal proceedings:

1.1. The overriding objective
(1) The overriding objective of this new code is that criminal cases be dealt with justly.
(2) Dealing with a criminal case justly includes—
   (a) acquitting the innocent and convicting the guilty;
   (b) dealing with the prosecution and the defence fairly;
   (c) recognising the rights of a defendant, particularly those under Article 6 of the European Convention on Human Rights;
   (d) respecting the interests of witnesses, victims and jurors and keeping them informed of the progress of the case;
   (e) dealing with the case efficiently and expeditiously;
   (f) ensuring that appropriate information is available to the court when bail and sentence are considered; and
   (g) dealing with the case in ways that take into account—
       (i)   the gravity of the offence alleged,
       (ii) the complexity of what is in issue,
       (iii) the severity of the consequences for the defendant and others affected, and
       (iv) the needs of other cases.

---

[73] The CrimPR are drafted by the Criminal Procedure Rule Committee, created pursuant to the Courts Act 2003, ss 69–73, and chaired by the Lord Chief Justice. CrimPR 2010 (SI 2010/60) entered into force on 5 April 2010. See the Ministry of Justice's website, <http://www.justice.gov.uk/criminal/procrules_fin>.

[74] That is to say, about as comprehensive as procedural codes can ever aspire to be in common law jurisdictions. The CrimPR should be read alongside the Consolidated Criminal Practice Direction (also reproduced on the Ministry of Justice website), the Specimen Directions and *Crown Court Bench Book* (2010) issued by the Judicial Studies Board at <http://www.jsboard.co.uk/criminal_law/cbb/index.htm>, and a dense thicket of statutory provisions and case-law precedents.

The CrimPR contain English criminal law's operational compendium of procedural regulations, compiled for the express purpose of providing practical guidance to judges and lawyers involved in criminal litigation on a daily basis. What is striking for our purposes is that this innovative legislative instrument commits English criminal adjudication first and foremost to the pursuit of criminal justice, and begins to specify the primary components of an officially authorized conception.

The contents of CrimPR, rule 1.1(2) are clearly not intended to be exhaustive, and what is more, the considerations there enumerated will often be in tension, if not open conflict, when they come to be applied in the cut and thrust of adversarial criminal trials. Identifying ideals, values, and objectives intended to structure the delivery of justice through criminal adjudication is only a starting point for judicial reasoning in individual cases. A list of fundamental normative considerations cannot pre-empt or supplant the need for judicial analysis and judgment in their contextual application, nor is rule 1.1 expected to do so. Still, acquitting the innocent and convicting the guilty, dealing with the prosecution and the defence fairly, recognizing human rights (especially the right to a fair trial), respecting the interests of witnesses, victims, and jurors and keeping them updated on the progress of proceedings, ensuring that the court has the information it needs to make properly informed decisions, and dealing with cases efficiently, expeditiously, and proportionately in the light of their gravity, complexity, and competing caseload pressures, is as serviceable a list of primary criteria of justice in criminal adjudication as one is likely to find in any philosophical treatise on the subject.[75]

A normative approach to criminal proceedings coheres with, and reinforces, both the growing importance of human rights in common law adjudication[76] and the related trend towards the constitutionalization of criminal evidence and procedure—a process more fully developed in North America[77] and continental Europe[78] than in England and Wales. Belatedly, English law is catching up. One telltale sign is that traditional common law doctrines are being reconceptualized in more explicitly normative language. Thus, at the direct instigation of the UK's Human Rights Act 1998, we see evidentiary discourse graduating from the common lawyer's

---

[75] Cf Roberts and Zuckerman, *Criminal Evidence*, § 1.3 ('five foundational principles').

[76] B Emmerson, A Ashworth, and A Macdonald, *Human Rights and Criminal Justice* (2nd edn; London: Sweet & Maxwell, 2007); AL-T Choo and S Nash, 'Evidence Law in England and Wales: The Impact of the Human Rights Act 1998' (2003) 7 E & P 31; P Roberts, 'Drug Dealing and the Presumption of Innocence: The Human Rights Act (Almost) Bites' (2002) 6 E & P 17.

[77] A Stein, 'Constitutional Evidence Law' (2008) 61 *Vanderbilt Law Review* 65; AR Amar, *The Constitution and Criminal Procedure: First Principles* (New Haven: Yale University Press, 1997): cf CS Steiker, '"First Principles" of Constitutional Criminal Procedure: A Mistake?' (1999) 112 *Harvard Law Review* 680; D Dripps 'Akhil Amar on Criminal Procedure and Constitutional Law: "Here I Go Down that Wrong Road Again"' (1996) 74 *North Carolina Law Review* 1559.

[78] See eg D Giannoulopoulos, 'The Exclusion of Improperly Obtained Evidence in Greece: Putting Constitutional Rights First' (2007) 11 E & P 181; M Panzavolta, 'Reforms and Counter-reforms in the Italian Struggle for an Accusatorial Criminal Law System' (2005) 30 *North Carolina Journal of International Law and Commercial Regulation* 577.

traditional 'burden and standard of proof' to the philosophically richer 'presumption of innocence',[79] and this development in turn stimulates greater conceptual sophistication and more sustained reflection on the normative underpinnings of criminal adjudication.[80] There is a revival of serious theoretical interest in evidentiary stalwarts like the privilege against self-incrimination[81] and the exclusion of improperly obtained evidence,[82] and these theoretical endeavours are reflected in parallel developments in judicial reasoning in decided cases,[83] which theoretically inclined scholarship sometimes overtly influences. Relatively novel evidence-related concepts, such as those specifying standards of humane treatment applicable to all participants in criminal adjudication,[84] have been advanced in an attempt to structure and rationalize the moral and practical imperatives of prescribing and enforcing criminal laws in modern societies. In lending greater theoretical depth and sophistication to the incremental development of existing institutional frameworks and doctrine, a self-consciously normative approach to criminal evidence and procedure simultaneously exposes the inadequacies of exclusively epistemological preoccupations—at least in their application to criminal adjudication in England and Wales, and, I would argue, more generally.

A pressing methodological challenge, and major potential pitfall, of the turn to philosophy in criminal procedure and evidence scholarship lies in striking an appropriate balance between philosophical argumentation and productive engagement with institutional legal materials, discourse, and practices. To insist that criminal adjudication is an applied field of moral and political philosophy is not an invitation to turn studies of criminal procedure into a branch of traditional philosophy, particularly not philosophy of the kind that consists mainly in armchair speculations. Bluntly, a normative approach to common law evidence and procedure still needs to grapple with relevant legislation, case law, and legal practice. Two recent seminal contributions to the literature will serve to illustrate significant contrasts in normative perspectives on criminal adjudication.

---

[79] Reflecting European Convention on Human Rights, Art 6(2): see P Roberts, 'Criminal Procedure, the Presumption of Innocence and Judicial Reasoning under the Human Rights Act', in H Fenwick, G Phillipson, and R Masterman (eds), *Judicial Reasoning under the UK Human Rights Act* (New York: Cambridge University Press, 2007).

[80] V Tadros and S Tierney, 'The Presumption of Innocence and the Human Rights Act' (2004) 67 MLR 402; V Tadros, 'Rethinking the Presumption of Innocence' (2007) 1 *Criminal Law & Philosophy* 193; D Hamer, 'The Presumption of Innocence and Reverse Burdens: A Balancing Act' (2007) 66 CLJ 143; P Roberts 'The Presumption of Innocence Brought Home? *Kebilene* Deconstructed' (2002) 117 LQR 40.

[81] M Redmayne, 'Rethinking the Privilege Against Self-Incrimination' (2007) 27 OJLS 209.

[82] Roberts and Zuckerman, *Criminal Evidence*, § 5.3.

[83] See eg *A v Secretary of State for the Home Department (No 2)* [2006] 2 AC 221, HL; *R v Looseley* [2001] 1 WLR 2060, HL.

[84] P Roberts, 'Theorising Procedural Tradition: Subjects, Objects and Values in Criminal Adjudication', in RA Duff, L Farmer, S Marshall, and V Tadros (eds), *The Trial on Trial Volume Two: Judgment and Calling to Account* (Oxford: Hart Publishing, 2006).

The *Trial on Trial* project devised by Antony Duff, Lindsay Farmer, Sandra Marshall, and Victor Tadros[85] shares much in common with Hock Lai Ho's *A Philosophy of Evidence Law*.[86] Both works adopt an explicitly normative approach to their subject matter; both conceive adjudication as a dynamic set of institutional practices, to which cross-sectional analyses of legal admissibility are only one contributor; and both insist that procedural integrity and due process should be conceptualized as integral and internalized dimensions of the law's epistemic practices. This represents a decisive break with the Benthamite/Wigmorean tradition in Evidence scholarship, today championed by Alex Stein amongst others, which draws a sharp distinction between evidentiary doctrines designed to promote accurate fact-finding and legal rules promoting objectives and instantiating values characterized as placing side-constraints on the processes of proof.[87] In Wigmore's terminology, the primary categorical distinction is between 'rules of auxiliary probative policy' and 'rules of extrinsic policy'.[88] Alex Stein glosses this distinction to suggest (with unnecessary rigidity, in my view) that only the former are truly part of the Law of Evidence, properly so-called.[89] In elucidating their highly original conception of criminal adjudication as an authoritative social process for calling criminal wrongdoers publicly to account,[90] Duff and colleagues reject what they regard as the instrumentalism and functionalism implicit in the orthodox dichotomy of procedural standards:

[W]e should not separate 'accurate outcomes' from 'fair procedures': the rightness of the outcome—of the verdict—is not in this way simply a matter of accuracy, but also of the process through which it was reached. Thus the conviction of a guilty defendant whose guilt has not been duly proved is a mistaken conviction . . . Proof beyond reasonable doubt is thus part of the very purpose of the trial, rather than (as on the instrumentalist view) a means to the end of truth . . .[91]

Ho pithily encapsulates essentially the same insight in 'the demand that justice be done in the search for truth'.[92] His book seeks 'to exemplify, through examination of a few selected rules, a value-centred method of analysis':

[I]n short: to promote a particular philosophical attitude. This attitude is motivated by the fundamental concern that the court does justice in the search for the truth.[93]

---

[85] RA Duff, L Farmer, S Marshall, and V Tadros (eds), *The Trial on Trial*, vols 1–3 (Oxford: Hart Publishing, 2004–7).

[86] Ho, *A Philosophy of Evidence Law*.

[87] A Stein, *Foundations of Evidence Law* (Oxford: Oxford University Press, 2005).

[88] JH Wigmore, *A Treatise on the System of Evidence in Trials at Common Law* (Boston, Little, Brown & Co, 1904), §§ 11, 1171 and 2175.

[89] '[R]ules that promote objectives intrinsic to fact-finding are the only ones that classify as genuinely evidential; rules furthering other objectives and values are evidence-related, but situated outside the domains of evidence law': Stein, *Foundations of Evidence Law*, 1.

[90] And see Duff, *Answering for Crime*.

[91] Duff et al, *The Trial on Trial—Volume Three*, 89.

[92] Ho, *A Philosophy of Evidence Law*, 340.

[93] Ibid 339.

Though both accounts proceed from a shared philosophical critique of instrumental conceptions of proof and justice, two notable points of contrast between them are methodologically illuminating. First, whilst Duff and colleagues concentrate exclusively on criminal adjudication, Ho sets himself the ostensibly more ambitious task of applying his 'Philosophy of Evidence Law' to topics in civil as well as criminal evidence. This generic approach may reflect Ho's keen interest in epistemology (which does not answer to the law's institutional classifications, as our previous exploration of epistemological perspectives has shown), as much as it betrays the pervasive influence of orthodox common law thinking. Be that as it may, the coherence of the normative vision presented in Ho's book suffers by comparison to *The Trial on Trial*, which, in focusing exclusively on criminal proceedings, is able to present a more lucid, systematic, and comprehensive conception of the normative foundations of a particular set of legal-institutional practices. Viewed as moral and political philosophy, Duff and colleagues provide the more compelling account.

Yet it is also as philosophy that *The Trial on Trial* is eclipsed by Ho's theorization of evidence law from the perspective of a second contrast. Ho affords significantly more attention to the relevant institutional materials, especially when illustrating the application of his general theoretical analyses to concrete problems in the law of evidence. Specifically in relation to hearsay and bad character, he spells out what is actually implied by 'the demand that justice be done in the search for truth', in terms that Evidence scholars will immediately recognize and comprehend, even if they are not wholly persuaded by Ho's doctrinal reconstructions. Duff and colleagues, by contrast, pay far less attention to positive law, and when they do discuss decided cases they tend to treat them as philosophers' examples—hypothetical scenarios postulated from the armchair might have served equally well—rather than as fragments of the common law's complex, multi-layered, institutionally embedded, incrementally adjusted, and constantly evolving normative mosaic. The authors of *The Trial on Trial* insist that they were trying to develop a mid-range account of criminal adjudication unencumbered by the minutiae of local institutional variations,[94] and this is a reasonable methodological gambit as far as it goes (especially considering that an exclusive focus on *Scottish* criminal procedure might have seemed quixotically parochial and could have sabotaged the project's broader theoretical ambitions). Nonetheless, Evidence scholars might regard some of *The Trial on Trial*'s sweeping generalizations and controversial conclusions as under-elaborated and consequently question-begging. I have in mind, for example: the 'obvious conclusion' that juries should deliver reasoned verdicts;[95] rejection out of hand of a peremptory rule of exclusion for evidence obtained through rights violations as 'too stark to be

---

[94] Duff et al, *The Trial on Trial—Volume Three*, ch 1; Duff et al, 'Introduction: Towards a Normative Theory of the Criminal Trial', in *The Trial on Trial Volume One: Truth and Due Process* (Oxford: Hart Publishing, 2004).

[95] Duff et al, *The Trial on Trial—Volume Three*, 219.

capable of justification';[96] the unsupported assertion that 'section 78 [of the Police and Criminal Evidence Act 1984] has not resulted in dramatic changes in the principles governing the admission of evidence';[97] the unqualified contention that drawing any incriminating inference from the accused's previous record is incompatible with respecting his moral agency;[98] and the counterintuitive notion that improperly obtained evidence is 'not in the relevant sense "evidence"'.[99]

By weaving relevant case law directly into his philosophical analyses, Ho's normative conception of procedural law is not only the more jurisprudentially accomplished, in my estimation, but also stands a better chance of stimulating a broader and more inclusive disciplinary conversation accessible to exponents of doctrinal evidence scholarship, as well as to more theoretically inclined scholars and teachers. The methodological ideal envisages a 'jurisprudence' of criminal procedure combining and successfully integrating both its Anglophone (legal theory) and continental (case-law) connotations.

6 SUMMARY AND CONCLUSIONS— DISCIPLINING CRIMINAL PROCEDURE

This chapter staked the claims of criminal procedure for inclusion in Criminal Law Theory's rapidly crystallizing canon. It identified a variety of procedural issues meriting further jurisprudential analysis and drew attention to an expanding corpus of theoretically informed scholarship on evidence and proof that may be unfamiliar to criminal law theorists (it is not as familiar as it ought to be even to procedural specialists). Extracting the 'edited highlights' from a vast array of disparate material, the bulk of the chapter was devoted to elucidating and evaluating four idealized theoretical perspectives on criminal procedure, which were dubbed:

---

[96] Ibid 231.

[97] Ibid 248.

[98] Ibid 255–6.

[99] 'If a fact is of a type that is in principle incapable of being presented in a communicative forum of reciprocal responsibility, it does not constitute evidence—what should count as evidence in a trial': ibid 252–3. This novel re-conceptualization demands 'a richer normative discussion of what should constitute evidence in the kind of reciprocal communicative forum that the trial purports to be': ibid 256. Duff et al's argument begs crucial questions of standpoint and motivation: who is imagined to be making these arguments, in what context, for which audience(s), and for what purposes? There are certain practical contexts (to put it no higher) in which replacing the common sense notion of 'evidence' as relevant information, with a 'thick' normative conception tied to admissibility determinations, is unlikely to be an acceptable or successful argumentative strategy.

(1) doctrinal-conceptualist; (2) epistemological; (3) (legal-)institutional; and (4) normative. These partly overlapping perspectives were intended to encompass much contemporary procedural scholarship and orthodox evidentiary thinking in the common law tradition. Each perspective was shown to have its own distinctive questions, subject matter, orientation towards evidence and proof, and methodological preferences, and each conceived and renamed the disciplinary field after its own image. The main results of this inquiry are summarized in Figure 17.1.

This chapter's discussion has been exploratory and plainly inconclusive. The doctrinal-conceptualist approach was employed principally as a foil for developing contrasts with the other three perspectives, and some readers might think it ill-used and too harshly judged. Let me repeat, for the avoidance of any doubt, that all four perspectives make valuable contributions to theorizing criminal procedure, albeit some are more overtly theory-driven and philosophically literate than others. None of my central arguments is *ad hominem*. Individual scholars might combine different strands of my four perspectives in their research and writing, and in their teaching supplement their published works with a broader range of materials (as I do), even if they are principally associated—in this chapter or elsewhere—with one particular approach.

Making the case for a more systematically developed and sophisticated jurisprudence of criminal procedure should not be confused with an 'Elgin Marbles'-style argument for 'taking back' criminal procedure from its current conservators or plunderers. The intention is, instead, to supplement existing characterizations and perspectives, which offer, necessarily, partial accounts of criminal procedure motivated by their own (inter)disciplinary preoccupations and objectives. The availability of plausible alternative conceptualizations should prompt one to ponder which features of criminal procedure are being emphasized on any particular occasion, with what inflexions, and for what purpose(s). And to consider, no less significantly, what is being omitted, obscured, or disqualified in the process.

By advocating critical interrogation of existing perspectives I do not intend to imply the possibility of a unifying synthetic theory. This chapter's discussion tends to confirm, to the contrary, that there are irreducibly different ways of organizing and analysing the collection of concepts, norms, values, institutions, practices, processes, etc arguably relevant to the project of disciplining criminal procedure. If that reflective intuition is sound, a jurisprudence of Criminal Procedure should fortify its philosophical foundations with a strong commitment to methodological pluralism. This should provide protective insulation against the persistent fallacy that any single dominant perspective could ever encompass and illuminate all that might conceivably be significant to every student, teacher, professional or lay participant, policymaker, or well-informed critic of criminal adjudication. It would contradict the pluralistic spirit of this meta-theoretical exploration to replace one blinkered orthodoxy with another, similarly distorting, reductive blueprint for disciplining criminal procedure.

Perspective	Definitional questions	Primary subject matter	Orientation towards evidence & proof	Method	Disciplinary field
1. Doctrinal-conceptualist	What is evidence? What is the Law of Evidence? What are its basic concepts?	primary legal sources; secondary commentary; exclusionary rules of evidence	cross-sectional; static; atomistic	legal doctrinal analysis; conceptual elucidation	Law of Evidence
2. Epistemological	How is evidence handled in legal processes? How are facts proved? To what extent are these forensic practices truth-conducive?	epistemic practices in legal contexts; logics of inference and proof	longitudinal; dynamic; holistic or atomistic	empirical social science; epistemology	Evidence & Proof
3. Legal-institutional	What is the institutional and normative framework governing (particular) legal proceedings?	specific legal institutions and their characteristic evidentiary technologies and techniques	longitudinal; proto-dynamic; nodal decision-points and distribution of powers between institutional actors	legal taxonomy; structural mapping; functionalist tendencies	Criminal Adjudication
4. Normative	How should criminal procedure serve (or realize) criminal justice?	values and objectives of criminal adjudication, and their associated evidentiary principles	relatively superficial; instantiations and exemplars of values	moral & political philosophy; jurisprudence	Criminal Justice

Figure 17.1   Matrix of Meta-Theoretical Perspectives on Criminal Procedure

18

THE SUBSTANCE-PROCEDURE RELATIONSHIP IN CRIMINAL LAW

DONALD A DRIPPS

1 INTRODUCTION

THE relationship between substance and procedure plays a prominent role in modern thinking about criminal justice. Normative scholarship about criminal law addresses the 'primary rules' or 'conduct rules' that direct the general public to refrain from specified misconduct. Normative scholarship about criminal procedure addresses the 'secondary rules' or 'decision rules' that direct officials to investigate and prosecute offences.[1]

---

[1] For the primary/secondary classification, see HLA Hart, *The Concept of Law* (1st edn; Oxford: Oxford University Press, 1961), 76–96. For the conduct/decision classification, see M Dan Cohen, 'Decision Rules and Conduct Rules: On Acoustic Separation in Criminal Law' [1984] 97 *Harvard Law Review* 625. Although the distinction is ancient, Bentham, apparently, was the first to analyse it systematically. J Bentham, 'An Introduction to the Principles of Morals and Legislation', in J Bowring (ed), I *Works of Jeremy Bentham* (Elibron edn; London: Adamant Media Corporation, 2005), 151–2 (distinguishing 'imperative' and 'punitory' laws). The Bowring volumes will be cited henceforth as *Works*.

With the caveats that properly attend any generalization about dozens of different systems, the details of any being a subject of professional specialization, it may be hazarded that the positive law is also predicated on a distinction between substance and procedure. The penal code and the procedure code are different bodies of law. Procedural law is generally transsubstantive, ie police powers and adjudicatory processes do not vary from one offence to another, although distinctions are made between large categories of the lesser and greater crimes. Substance, moreover, tends to be left largely to the normal processes of legislation. Procedure, on the other hand, has become more and more the province of constitutions and human rights conventions, written at a high level of generality and so open to various judicial interpretations.[2]

The two bodies of law, however, constitute a single system. Perhaps the central aim of criminal law scholarship is to identify the necessary and sufficient conditions of justified punishment. Obviously enough, however, people are punished by officials, not by laws. The law in action can modify, even nullify, the law on the books. The substance-procedure relationship, then, is both fundamental and problematic in the positive law and academic literature on criminal justice.

Criminal law has received more attention from academic philosophers than criminal procedure. Indeed, as late as 1977 Professor Postema could assert that 'Bentham's theory of adjudication represents the only sustained attempt in the English language (except for recent work done by Professor Fuller) at a philosophical account of the law of procedure'.[3] Normative theorizing about procedure includes important contributions from philosophers, but the literature on procedure is wider and dauntingly diffuse. Academic lawyers debate the merits of particular police practices and trial procedures, court decisions take positions on difficult normative questions, and there are large literatures indeed on constitutional law and human rights law, which play major roles in criminal procedure. Generalizations may be very helpful to clear thinking about both substance and procedure, but they are also likely to oversimplify. This essay assumes that the rewards are worth the risks, and proceeds through three stages.

The first stage is expository and synthetic. We identify three possible approaches to the substance/procedure relationship in criminal law, labelling them *rationalism*, *pluralism*, and *reductionism*. By rationalism I mean the view that procedure's dominant end is the rational discovery of the historical facts and the logical application of

---

[2] The constitutionalization of criminal procedure is no longer an American eccentricity. See eg German Constitution art 13 (search warrant requirement); Spanish Constitution of 1978, ch 2, § 18 (same); Canadian Charter of Rights and Freedoms § 8 (right to freedom from unreasonable searches and seizures); European Convention on Human Rights art 6 (rights to specified adjudicatory procedures in criminal cases, including counsel and confrontation of adverse witnesses).

[3] GJ Postema, 'The Principle of Utility and the Law of Procedure: Bentham's Theory of Adjudication' [1977] 11 *Georgia Law Review* 1393, 1393 (footnote omitted). For a recent such 'sustained attempt', see LB Solum, 'Procedural Justice' [2004] 78 *University of Southern California Law Review* 181.

the substantive law to the facts so found. By pluralism I mean the view that rational application of law to fact is only one value among many others at stake in the criminal process, with no automatic priority over others. By reductionism I mean the view that the substance/procedure distinction is illusory because the substantive law authorizes so wide a range of outcomes in typical cases that outcomes are determined practically by the exercise of official discretion.

The degree to which a given system, as a descriptive matter, reflects rationalism, pluralism, or reductionism is contingent on the system's content. Rationalism and pluralism expressly go beyond description, each making a normative claim about the ideal relationship between procedure and substance. Reductionism makes a descriptive claim about the breakdown of the distinction itself in systems characterized by pervasive discretion. The reductionist description, however, poses a substantial challenge to the prescriptive aspirations of rationalists and pluralists.

We may speak of rationalism and reductionism as actual theories, as each has distinguished exponents. Many modern jurists have characterized criminal procedure as a search for the truth.[4] Knowingly or otherwise, they echo Bentham's characterization of procedure as 'adjective law' that should be devoted to applying the substantive law faithfully to facts found as reliably as possible given the available resources. Bentham defended what he called the 'natural system' of procedure, which he said was used by parents and employers.[5] The judge should hear what the witnesses have to say, subject to questioning by both the judge and the parties, without restrictive rules of evidence or technical pleading requirements.

Holmes laid the foundation for reductionism with his predictive theory of law.[6] Early work by Thurman Arnold characterized the positive law as the legal hook for prosecutorial decisions made on other grounds.[7] Much modern work on plea bargaining takes a reductionist point of view, at least as a descriptive matter.[8]

Pluralism as I have defined it is not a theory as such, but a family of theories united by their opposition to rationalism. Some writers include some procedural requirements among the necessary conditions of justified punishment.[9] Some

---

[4] See eg *Estes v Texas*, 381 US 532, 540 (1965) ('Court proceedings are held for the solemn purpose of endeavoring to ascertain the truth which is the *sine qua non* of a fair trial.'); L Laudan, *Truth, Error, and Criminal Law: An Essay in Legal Epistemology* (Cambridge: Cambridge University Press, 2006).

[5] See eg Bentham's *Principles of Judicial Procedure, with the Outline of a Procedure Code*, in II *Works* 3.

[6] OW Holmes, Jr, 'The Path of the Law' [1897] 10 *Harvard Law Review* 457, 461 ('The prophecies of what the courts will do in fact, and nothing more pretentious, are what I mean by the law.').

[7] T Arnold, 'Law Enforcement—An Attempt at Social Dissection' [1932] 42 *Yale Law Journal* 1, 18.

[8] Eg see FH Easterbrook, 'Criminal Procedure as a Market System' [1983] 12 *Journal of Legal Studies* 289; WH Stuntz, 'Plea Bargaining and Criminal Law's Disappearing Shadow' [2004] 117 *Harvard Law Review* 2548.

[9] Some prominent writers have argued that the criminal law's expressive function implies certain trial procedures. See eg RA Duff, L Farmer, S Marshall, and V Tadros, *The Trial on Trial Volume Three: Towards a Normative Theory of the Criminal Trial* (Oxford: Hart Publishing, 2007), 102–10 (arguing

defend truth-defeating procedural rights as checks against government oppression.[10] Others insist on rights-as-trumps on the system's search for truth.[11] Yet another strand of scholarship argues that procedure's mission is not truth-finding but dispute settlement, with the perceived legitimacy of outcomes holding ultimate priority over the historical facts.[12]

Ironically, while the great exponent of rationalism was the Englishman Jeremy Bentham, the institutional embodiment of rationalism was continental, rather than Anglo-American, criminal procedure. Indeed, the common-law process Bentham rebelled against, much of which remains enshrined in the US Bill of Rights, was pluralistic through and through.

Today the continental, 'inquisitorial' model, once thought to be the embodiment of rationalism, is increasingly qualified by features such as lay participation, exclusionary rules, and the privilege against self-incrimination.[13] Plea bargaining, the institutional manifestation of reductionism, has spread to many inquisitorial systems, albeit with pronounced variations.[14] In the United States, pluralism has been drifting toward reductionism, as the 'adversarial' system is now an administrative system of negotiated justice dominated by the public prosecutor.[15]

The chapter's second stage takes up the normative issues.[16] I suggest that to a very substantial degree, rationalism and pluralism are compatible. Given the institutional facts faced by wealthy democracies of the modern type, each of these two perspectives calls for a similar collection of individual rights, decent police practices, and fair adjudications. Convergence between inquisitorial and

that the communicative purpose of trial demands moral standing of the prosecution, implying some exclusion of illegally obtained evidence).

[10] Herbert Packer (eg) described the criminal justice system as in a permanent state of tension between two attractive paradigms, the 'crime control model' aiming at efficient punishment of offences and the 'due process model' aiming at preventing undeserved punishment and limiting government power. HL Packer, 'Two Models of the Criminal Process' [1964] *University of Pennsylvania Law Review* 1.

[11] See (eg) E Luna, 'The Models of Criminal Procedure' [1999] 2 *Buffalo Journal of Criminal Law* 389.

[12] For the imputation of dispute settlement to some actual systems, see MR Damaska, *The Faces of Justice and State Authority: A Comparative Approach to the Legal Process* (Yale University, 1986), 101–25. For a normative defence, see C Nesson, 'The Evidence or the Event? On Judicial Proof and the Acceptability of Verdicts' [1985] 98 *Harvard Law Review* 1387.

[13] CM Bradley, *Criminal Procedure: A Worldwide Study* (2nd edn; Carolina Academic Press, 2007), xxi. On the possibilities for rationalists to endorse such superficially truth-defeating practices, see section 3.2 below.

[14] M Langer, 'From Legal Transplants to Legal Translations: The Globalization of Plea Bargaining and the Americanization Thesis in Criminal Procedure' [2004] 45 *Harvard International Law Journal* 1.

[15] GE Lynch, 'Screening Versus Bargaining: Exactly What are we Trading Off?' [2003] 55 *Stanford Law Review* 1399, 1403–4.

[16] In terms of Paul Roberts's analytic schemata, my project is thus an attempt to evaluate as well as analyse 'Normative Perspectives on Implementing Criminal Justice.' See P Roberts, 'Groundwork for a Jurisprudence of Criminal Procedure', this volume (henceforth cited as Roberts, 'Groundwork').

adversarial systems in practice implies compatibility between rationalism and pluralism in theory. There are of course very important debates about details (for example, the precise limits on police interrogation tactics). These debates, however, are likely to be as vigorous among, as between, adherents to rationalism and pluralism.

Third, the chapter explores the challenge of reductionism. Terms of trade between substance and procedure create the temptation to use authority over substance to modify process, or vice versa. To what extent is this temptation one of the many departures from pure theory practical politics always entails, and to what extent is it a brief for radical reductionism, ie abandoning theoretical inquiry about criminal law and criminal procedure, in favour of a unified enquiry into criminal justice? Familiar arguments drawn from liberal political theory condemn radical reductionism as lawless and opaque. Reductionism itself can take a normative turn only by parasitic appropriation of the substance/procedure distinction. It remains to be seen, however, whether legality and transparency can be imposed on the modern mass-production systems of criminal justice.

2 Three Perspectives on the Substance-Procedure Relationship

Reasonable minds disagree about whether particular rules or practices advance the normative goals pursued by any given criminal justice system. For example, lively debates address such questions as whether exclusionary rules actually influence police behaviour, whether confessions obtained by aggressive questioning (even by torture) are factually reliable, and so on. These debates, however, are in the main properly parochial, because they typically turn on specific sources of law, or on empirical facts, that are peculiar to the local system.

This is not to denigrate their importance. Indeed, the compatibility thesis suggests that society stands to gain more from sustained academic investigation of these technical questions than from further normative generalizations about criminal procedure. The compatibility thesis, however, should be tested, not assumed, and to test it we must explore the different philosophical accounts that have been given of criminal procedure.

At the highest level of generality, philosophical disagreements about criminal procedure reflect two, possibly competitive, characterizations of the enterprise. It is often said that the criminal process is (or ought to be) a search for the truth, an investigation into historical facts. Yet it is undeniably true that important consequences attend legal decisions about the operative historical facts. If police, or prosecutors, or courts find a charge either false or uncertain, the citizen will go free; and if they all find the charge true to a high degree of confidence the citizen will be punished, perhaps with great severity.

So it is also plausible to regard the criminal process as an exercise in practical reason rather than in historical investigation. From this perspective values other than discovering the historical truth ought to influence the institutional design of criminal procedure, and to influence the exercise of discretion by officials within the system. Whether this particular individual should be punished by this particular government through this particular process, as a question of practical reason, is a different question than whether the positive law prescribes punishment through this process given the historical facts that process has found.

Following usage of the term in the literature on judicial evidence, I shall label the first view, of criminal procedure as a search for truth, 'rationalism'.[17] The second view, of criminal procedure as an exercise in practical reason, I shall call pluralism, on account of the parallel with value pluralism in moral philosophy. Pluralism insists upon the consideration of multiple values rather than a monistic focus on historical facts.

Does a commitment to retributivism or utilitarianism in the substantive law commit one to rationalism or pluralism in procedure? The short answer is no. Intuitively a retributivist might be attracted to rationalism, but there is nothing in retributivism as a criminal law theory that implies the relative priority of justified punishment with respect to other competing values. Utilitarians might be attracted to rationalism based on an assessment of consequences; Bentham is a case in point. Utilitarians, however, might favour pluralism if the negative consequences of imposing punishment prescribed by law outweigh the benefits.

From a normative standpoint, the arguments that can be made about these competing approaches are not obscure and can be briefly summarized. To the rationalist, exemplified by Bentham, the issues of practical reason should be resolved generally and ex ante by the legislature. Legislatures possess institutional competence, and political legitimacy, superior to that of executive or judicial officials acting ex post in specific cases. It follows that the enforcement machinery should concern itself with discovering offences and identifying offenders, as accurately as possible given the available resources.

[17] W Twining, *Rethinking Evidence: Exploratory Essays* (Cambridge: Cambridge University Press, 1990), 71–82. Some criminal procedure literature has used the term 'instrumentalism' with the same meaning. Duff et al, *The Trial on Trial Volume Three*, 64; DA Dripps, *About Guilt and Innocence: The Origins, Development and Future of Constitutional Criminal Procedure* (Westport, CT: Praeger Publishers, 2003), 67. The term 'instrumentalism', however, is also used with quite different meanings in some prominent literature, eg MJ Horwitz, *The Transformation of American Law 1780–1860* (Cambridge, MA: Harvard University Press, 1977) and RS Summers, *Instrumentalism and American Legal Theory* (Ithaca: Cornell University Press, 1982).

Philosophical critique of the rationalist position typically does not turn on philosophical theories of truth. Empirical falsification negatives a charge on coherence theories, and for that matter on social-construction theories save those of the most Orwellian type. If the proposition is that D robbed the First National Bank on 1 August, and unanimous witnesses and documentary records prove that D spent all of 1 August in jail, no critic of rationalism argues that the charge might still be true. Nor do philosophical debates about the nature of knowledge play much of a role in the literature on procedure.[18] Critics of rationalism have not argued that justified true belief is an insufficient basis for conviction or acquittal. Arguments about the theory of criminal procedure have been moral or political, rather than epistemic, in character.

To pluralists, rationalism is (a) undesirable, (b) impossible, and (c) self-defeating. Rationalism neglects the political and coercive nature of the criminal process. Anglo-American procedure remains much influenced by the use of the criminal process to persecute political and religious dissent in the days of the Stuarts, and experience with twentieth-century police states gave impetus to the criminal-procedure provisions in the European Convention on Human Rights (ECHR) and to constitutional provisions in several European states. Such familiar legal doctrines as those prohibiting searches on mere suspicion, or coercive interrogation practices, or permitting the accused to stand silent at trial, appear to deviate from rationalist theory. Whether ultimately grounded on rights or on consequences, these widespread, at least superficially truth-defeating, doctrines testify to the plurality of values at stake in criminal procedure.

Nor is it clear that rationalism, if desirable, is even possible. Leaving aside the difficulty of policing self-conscious nullification of the substantive law by actors in the procedural system, caseload pressures have made plea bargaining the norm in the United States and increasingly common elsewhere. The typical plea bargain involves the exchange of the defendant's procedural rights for a reduction in his substantive liability. To bargain credibly the prosecution must appear ready to prove the greater charges—those prescribed by the legislature given the historical facts as they appear to the prosecutor. If plea bargaining is inevitable, rationalism may be impossible. The legislature's stated table of offences and penalties is not a directive, but an assignment of bargaining resources to the executive authorities.[19]

---

[18] A notable exception in the evidence literature is RJ Allen and B Leiter, 'Naturalized Epistemology and the Law of Evidence' [2001] 87 *Virginia Law Review* 1491. On a broader understanding of 'epistemological perspectives' the literature is extensive and helpfully surveyed by Roberts, 'Groundwork', section 3.

[19] If plea bargains were limited to confessing a lesser-included offence when the justified greater charge might not be provable beyond reasonable doubt, the plea might be closer to the truth than the expected outcome of a costly trial. See Duff et al, *The Trial on Trial Volume Three*, ch 6.2. At least in the United States, plea bargaining is not so limited. Eg in *Bordenkircher v Hayes*, 434 US 357 (1978), the prosecutor 'offered' to drop a recidivism charge if D entered a guilty plea on a forgery charge. Given the absence of doubt about D's criminal history, the recidivism charge would be proved ineluctably by

Lawmakers of course know about the procedural system, and this knowledge supports the argument that rationalism is self-defeating. If the reason to charge the procedural system with imposing the punishments directed by the legislature is the legislature's competence and legitimacy, what should we say about a legislature that explicitly, or even implicitly, endorses a regime of discretionary policing, discretionary charge selection, and negotiated outcomes? In such a system, executive and judicial officials cannot simply consult the legislature's directive, for the legislature has directed these very officials to use their own judgment. The reductionist position embraces this description of the criminal process as legislative delegation of practical law-making power to the executive authorities.

What are we to make of this welter of positions? We address this question by examining the great divide among actual systems, ie the differences between so-called inquisitorial systems of the continental type and the so-called adversarial systems of the Anglo-American type. At least superficially, the inquisitorial systems reflect rationalist theory, while adversarial systems take a pluralist approach. Perhaps the theoretical debate may be informed, if not resolved, by an examination of the two theories in practice.

3 CONVERGENCE AND COMPATIBILITY

3.1 Inquisitorial and adversarial systems in action

During the Renaissance the old systems of trial-by-God (ordeal, compurgation, and battle) were gradually displaced by an inquiry into the historical facts by secular tribunals. On the continent of Europe the official inquiry took the form of a judicial investigation that included, upon strong preliminary evidence, judicial torture to obtain a confession verifying the accusation. In England the official inquiry took the form of a preliminary investigation by a justice of the peace, followed by the grand jury's review, and, upon indictment, trial by jury.[20] Imperialism carried these inquisitorial and adversarial models throughout the world.

Bentham understood his rationalist approach as a sweeping critique of the English common law. The common law of crimes provided the death penalty for all

---

proof of the forgery charge. What is worse, the threat of death or a long sentence, together with pretrial detention, can induce even innocent defendants to plead guilty. See S Gross, K Jacoby, D Matheson, N Montgomery, and S Patil, 'Exonerations in the United States 1989–2003' [2005] 95 *Journal of Criminal Law and Criminology* 523, 533–6.

[20] JH Langbein, *Prosecuting Crime in the Renaissance* (Cambridge, MA: Harvard University Press, 1974).

felonies, including larceny, and many English statutes extended the reach of capital punishment. Jury nullification, hypertechnical pleading rules, and witness incapacity rules, however arbitrary, worked to nullify the draconian substantive law. In that context (and even more in the context of seditious libel prosecutions) Bentham was sympathetic to jury nullification.[21] He aimed, however, at the contemporaneous codification of both substance and procedure. Given a substantive law consistent with the principle of utility, procedure should focus single-mindedly on finding the facts.

Bentham's arguments parallel the theoretical premises of the continental, inquisitorial, system of criminal procedure. That system followed two key principles, the principle of legality and the principles of material truth. Legality, in the continental sense, has a positive as well as a negative dimension. Not only is there to be no punishment unauthorized by law, but all punishment required by law is to be imposed.[22]

The principle of material truth calls for judicial development of a record (the *dossier*) that includes the accounts of all the witnesses. Although the causes and pace of the change are debated, during the period separating the German Carolina Code of 1532 and the French *Code d'instrucion Criminelle* in 1808,[23] understanding of the truth principle moved from conditioning torture of the suspect on the satisfaction of demanding canon-law proofs to a judicial pre-trial investigation and a subsequent trial without limitation on the evidence that might be considered.

During the nineteenth century and into the twentieth, a lively debate went on about the merits of the inquisitorial and adversarial systems. Today, that debate goes on but in less categorical terms. The so-called convergence thesis—the proposition that the adversarial and inquisitorial systems are coming increasingly to resemble each other, especially in practice—has become quite prominent in comparative work on criminal procedure.[24] There are pronounced differences still, but debate more and more speaks to specific rules, practices, and institutions rather than to systems writ large.

A major reason for the degree of convergence so far observed is the emergence in all modern societies of the professional police force. Professional, paramilitary

---

[21] J Bentham, *Principles of Judicial Procedure*, in II *Works* 1, 119–22; J Bentham, *The Elements of the Art of Packing*, in V *Works* 61, 66.

[22] SC Thaman, 'Legality and Discretion', in DS Clark (ed), *Encyclopedia of Law and Society: American and Global Perspectives* (Los Angeles: Sage Publications, 2007), 944, 945.

[23] Compare JH Langbein, *Torture and the Law of Proof: Europe and England in the Ancien Regime* (University of Chicago Press, 1977) with MR Damaska, 'The Death of Legal Torture' [1978] 87 *Yale Law Journal* 860 (reviewing Langbein).

[24] See eg PF Fennell, CC Harding, N Jorg, and B Swart, *Criminal Justice in Europe: A Comparative Study* (Oxford: Clarendon Press, 1995); M Delmas Marty, 'Reflections on the Bybridisation of Criminal Procedure', in J Jackson, M Langer and P Tillers (eds), *Crime, Procedure and Evidence in a Comparative and International Context* (Oxford: Hart Publishing, 2008), 251–54; RS Frase and T Weigend, 'German Criminal Justice as a Guide to American Law Reform: Similar Problems, Better Solutions?' (1995) 18 *Boston College International and Comparative Law Review* 317, 352–3.

police opened up new opportunities for social control and parallel new dangers of state oppression. Whether formally lodged in a grand jury or in an investigating magistrate, the actual investigation of the historical facts came to be performed by the police, who had the resources and skills for the mission.[25] Indeed, proactive policing now brings many cases to the courts in the absence of any retrospective complaint from the citizenry. It should therefore occasion no surprise to find the greatest convergence among the various systems in regulation of the police. Excepting police states, all systems limit police arrest, search, and interrogation powers, although the content of those limits varies greatly.

With respect to the adjudication of formal charges filed after the police investigation, modern systems vary greatly, not just with respect to the formal machinery of trial but also with respect to the extent that the formal system of trial is actually used. Plea bargaining dominates the adjudicatory process in the United States and has spread to many other systems.[26] The Anglo-American trial by jury, subject to complex rules of evidence and conducted continuously in place and time, remains very different from the continental systems, where professional judges dominate the proceedings despite lay representation, without technical rules for admitting or excluding evidence. Even so, the spread of plea bargaining, and departures from the system of free proof that exclude at least some illegally obtained evidence and require at least some *viva voce* testimony, give further colour to the convergence thesis.

Specific examples of convergence, such as the adoption of exclusionary rules or reliance on plea bargains, of course reflect parallel sociological or economic impulses and constraints. Rising caseloads, limited resources, and the institutional difficulties of regulating the police help to explain why different systems turn to similar rules and practices. The willingness of systems reflecting very different theoretical premises to embrace similar responses to common problems also suggests that those theoretical premises may be more compatible than has been assumed. Convergence in the actual operation of the 'inquisitorial' and 'adversarial' models implies a parallel compatibility between rationalism and pluralism. We turn now to explore this intriguing possibility.

3.2 Are rationalism and pluralism compatible?

The trend, however gradual, toward convergence between the pluralistic adversarial system and the rationalist inquisitorial system suggests at least the possibility that

---

[25] On this phenomenon in Europe, see M Ploscowe, 'The Investigating Magistrate (Juge d'Instruction) in European Criminal Procedure' [1935] 33 *Michigan Law Review* 1010.

[26] Langer, 'From Legal Transplants to Legal Translations'; T Weigend, 'The Decay of the Inquisitorial Ideal: Plea Bargaining Invades German Criminal Procedure', in Jackson, Langer and Tillers (eds), *Crime, Procedure and Evidence in a Comparative and International Context*, 39.

rationalism and pluralism can be reconciled. We might begin our examination of the compatibility thesis by distinguishing four kinds of departures from the principle of material truth. Systemic constraints on the resources that can be used to investigate or adjudicate each case mean that every system must compromise the pursuit of truth to some degree. Another type of departure, exemplified by limitations on coercive police practices, is implicit in the principle of legality. The third type of departure is neither dictated by systemic constraints nor implied by the legality principle, but instead premised on the priority of some other value over the due administration of criminal justice. We shall call rules or institutions of this type 'extrinsic' departures from the principle of material truth. The fourth and final type of departure is nullification: a truth-defeating procedure premised on the belief that the substantive law is unjust or excessively punitive.

The rationalist ideal expressed by the principles of legality and material truth is less inflexible than first appears. In the first place, the administration of justice must compete with a host of other important social projects for limited resources. Bentham himself made cost an important desideratum in the formulation of legal procedure.[27] If the idea of 'cost' is defined expansively enough, rationalism becomes not just compatible with, but identical to, pluralism.

If the idea of cost is bounded to include resource constraints and to exclude other negative consequences such as invasions of witness privacy, limits on press freedom, public confidence in government, etc, rationalism can maintain its distinctiveness. The price for remaining distinctive is myopia, an indifference to other values such as individual privacy and dignity. Yet rationalists need not insist on the pursuit of truth at the expense of legality.

At first blush, limits on police powers backed by exclusionary rules and trial by jury seem directly at odds with the principle of material truth, and must therefore be justified, if at all, on grounds of practical reason. Yet these seemingly radical departures from rationalist theory do little damage to the rationalist ideal of faithfully applying the law to the historical facts.

In its negative dimension, the legality principle is synonymous with the prohibition of punishment except upon judicial decision based on pre-existing positive law. The powers of the modern police, however, pose threats to individual security that rival or indeed exceed the injury that might be inflicted as a matter of conviction and sentence. Some extreme examples are illustrative. No court in the United States would inflict the so-called 'water boarding' treatment as a penalty for crime, even for aggravated murder. Yet the executive authorities have employed this technique without judicial authorization as a purported matter of investigation.[28] No

---

[27] J Bentham, *Principles of Judicial Procedure*, II *Works* 1, 17. On the consistency *vel non* of Bentham's utilitarianism with rule-bound adjudication, see below nn 43–48 and accompanying text.

[28] S Shane, 'Waterboarding Used 266 Times on 2 Suspects', *New York Times*, 19 April 2009, A1.

European court would impose capital punishment upon conviction for any offence; yet the police are empowered to use deadly force under certain conditions.

Some limitations on police power, with a concomitant decrease in what the authorities know about crime, are therefore implicit in the legality principle itself. It is perfectly rational to resolve the tension between the need for evidence and the institutional violence required to find it by requiring some degree of proportion between the intrusiveness of the police conduct and the strength of their suspicion and/or the seriousness of the suspected offence.[29]

Whatever limits this proportionality principle is thought to require, if those limits are respected by the police some evidence will go undiscovered. Excluding evidence discovered in violation of those limits damages the principle of material truth only because of the limits themselves. If those limits are rarely violated exclusion of the fruits will be de minimis. If those limits are frequently violated exclusion of the fruits may be the only way to encourage compliance. Even the privilege against self-incrimination, understood as a hedge against brutal interrogation practices to the neglect of the collection of other evidence, finds some support in purely rationalist considerations.[30]

Trial procedures such as the standard of proof beyond a reasonable doubt can be defended as subordinating the pursuit of truth for higher values, such as a deontological right to fair treatment[31] or by obligations premised on the expressive aspect of a conviction.[32] They can also, however, be defended based on differences in the harms of false convictions and of false acquittals (whether we base an assessment that false convictions are worse on material consequences or on a special aversion to unjust punishment).[33]

So the real issues between rationalists and pluralists arise over extrinsic departures and nullification. Let us begin with extrinsic departures. Is there any justification for a limit on the police, or of an adjudicatory procedure, that impairs the search for truth without appealing to resource limitations or the implications of the legality principle? The question poses a difficult and largely unexplored philosophical issue.

Philosophical inquiry about criminal law has focused on the purposes of punishment, on the nature of culpability, and on the moral limits on the criminal law.

---

[29] C Slobogin, 'The World Without a Fourth Amendment' [1991] 39 *University of California at Los Angeles Law Review* 1.

[30] JF Stephen, *A History of the Criminal Law of England* (Kessinger Publishing, 1883), 441; JH Wigmore, 8 *Evidence* § 2250 (1st edn, 1904). The sufficiency of these considerations remains debatable. See eg D Dolinko, 'Is there a Rationale for the Privilege Against Self-Incrimination?' [1986] 33 *University of California at Los Angeles Law Review* 1033.

[31] R Dworkin, *A Matter of Principle* (Cambridge, MA: Harvard University Press, 1985), 93

[32] C Fried, *An Anatomy of Values* (London: Oxford University Press, 1970), 125–9; HL Ho, *A Philosophy of Evidence Law* (Oxford: Oxford University Press, 2008).

[33] J Kaplan, 'Decision Theory and the Factfinding Process' [1968] 20 *Stanford Law Review* 1065, 1073.

These (often quite brilliant) debates over the content of the ideal criminal law do not speak to the priority due the criminal law over competing values. The question is difficult and has received little systematic attention. Yet every claim for a true departure from the principle of material truth turns on how we answer this question.

Whatever theory of punishment we accept, that theory must justify the intentional infliction of serious suffering on fellow citizens. It follows that the principle of material truth, instrumental to actually imposing the punishments prescribed in appropriate cases, advances very important ends, whether retributive or utilitarian. Those purposes, even on a pluralistic account, obviously override anything but very important competing values. Ends that justify sending a person to prison for years will also override such genuine but modest competing values as costing the witnesses time away from work or obliging them to answer socially embarrassing questions.

What, however, of conflicts between the ends of criminal justice and graver competing values? For example, what if the government must choose between dismissing a factually true charge of espionage, and compromising national security by proof of the charge in open court? We need criteria to resolve such conflicts in a reasoned way.

Utilitarians can approach such dilemmas with the same toolkit for predicting and evaluating consequences that they bring to work on any other normative issue. Retributivists in criminal law face a different challenge. If they are permissive retributivists, they are free to engage in consequentialist calculations when the competing interest threatens to prevent deserved punishment, as in the espionage/state-secrets dilemma. Mandatory retributivists must look to their foundational ethics to assess whether or when the duty to impose deserved punishment is trumped by other obligations.

The hard cases also include those in which important interests conflict with the legality principle's negative side, ie where very important social interests weigh in favour of limiting the resources available to a defendant. The defendant may wish to compel self-incriminating testimony from another person, or publicly to interrogate an alleged rape victim about intimate details of her sexual history, or to compel a reporter to reveal a source. Again utilitarians can predict and monetize, with the usual difficulties. Here, however, even permissive retributivists must ask just how much priority attaches to the duty to prevent punishing the innocent.

Is the compatibility thesis, at the normative level, defensible? That depends on just how rigorously we understand the rationalist's commitment to material truth and legality. If that commitment is absolute, ie *fiat justicia, coelum ruit*, the compatibility thesis is false. The absolute rationalist would prosecute the spy, force the third-party suspect to testify, permit searching cross-examination of the rape victim's private life, and send the reporter to jail until she discloses her source.

If the rationalist's commitment to truth and legality is understood as obligatory but not absolute, as an exclusionary but not exclusive reason, the compatibility thesis becomes very plausible. Given the great relative weight of whatever values justify sending people to prison, the pluralist will give very great weight to the principle of material truth. Only very powerful competing considerations will actually override that principle, even for pluralists. The difference in the two schools of thought becomes one of emphasis or degree.

When the positive law does reflect concern for values extrinsic to the legality principle, it is usually the case that the departure from the principle of material truth is minor. Privileges are a case in point. If journalists regularly were forced to disclose their sources in court, their sources would dry up. The third-party suspect called to the stand probably helps the defendant's cause as much by invoking the privilege against self-incrimination as by anything the witness might say short of a full confession. Other than the exceptional cases provided for in the positive law (past sex with the accused, source of semen or injury, motive to fabricate) past sexual history has only very attenuated, if any, rational tendency to prove consent in the case at hand.

Perhaps the privilege of the accused not to give evidence poses a more serious conflict between the rationalist and the pluralist. At present the practice of pre-trial interrogation by the police, the pressure on defendants to plead guilty or face higher sentences, and the willingness of jurors to draw an inference of guilt from silence despite legal instruction to the contrary, make the privilege less of a threat to truth than it might be in other circumstances.[34] Some pluralists might wish to elevate autonomy or dignity above truth seeking by curbing police questioning, and some rationalists have called for abolition of the privilege.[35] The international pattern of a theoretical right to silence routinely circumvented in practice by the police, however, is a good illustration of both convergence and compatibility. Differences remain, but they are not as dramatic as might be expected.

We may restate the compatibility thesis as the claim that both rationalists and pluralists will depart from the principle of material truth when the search for truth:

(a) makes an excessive demand on scarce resources;
(b) conflicts with the legality principle's prohibition of extra-judicial institutional violence; or

---

[34] The available studies indicate that more than 75% of American suspects waive their *Miranda* rights. BG Cassell and BS Hayman, 'Police Interrogation in the 1990s: An Empirical Study of the Effects of Miranda' [1996] 43 *University of California at Los Angles Law Review* 839, 859; RA Leo, 'Inside the Interrogation Room' [1996] 86 *Journal of Criminal Law and Criminology* 266, 286. The vast majority of charges not dismissed by the courts end in guilty pleas; in the federal practice the frequency of guilty pleas versus trials is now over 95%. ML Miller, 'Domination and Dissatisfaction: Prosecutors as Sentencers' [2004] 56 *Stanford Law Review* 1211, 1252–3.

[35] Opponents of the right to silence have had some political success in the United Kingdom. See Criminal Justice and Public Order Act of 1994, s 34 (authorizing adverse inference from pre-trial silence).

(c) conflicts with some extrinsic value that is:
  (i)   very important; and
  (ii) can be accommodated with minor damage to material truth.

This is a thesis that cannot be conclusively proved but it could be falsified by contrary examples. Such examples, however, are hard to find.

Probably no actual system is more pluralistic than the American. The constitutional commitment to trial by jury in the United States reflects concerns such as checking potential oppression by popular nullification of unjust laws, and fostering popular participation in the administration of justice. If these are the motivating values behind the right to jury trial, they are indeed weighty values, advanced at remarkably low cost to the truth-finding function. The empirical evidence shows that, at least in typical cases, juries and judges will see the same case in very similar light. When judge and jury disagree there is no automatic reason to trust the judge.[36] It should be remembered that in the American system the judges are not trained as professional investigators; a turn to a continental model would require some very costly institutional rewiring even if that kind of change was politically feasible.

Moreover, in practice, the right to jury trial is really a right to appeal the charging decision of the prosecutor. Functionally, the prosecutor in the United States reviews the record of the police investigation and decides what charges to file and, ultimately, what plea to accept. Jury trial takes place only when the defence refuses to plead to a set of charges acceptable to the prosecutor. As a matter of the law in action, the American plea bargaining regime, dominated by a professional bureaucrat working with input from the police and subject to review by another tribunal, is not as different from the continental model as the law on the books suggests.

The final type of departure from the truth principle is nullification. To what extent should officials with power over substance or procedure, but not both, use power over one to reverse or nullify decisions previously made about the other? For example, it has been said that both the privilege against self-incrimination and the exclusionary rule for improperly seized evidence are defensible in part because they tend to defeat laws against thought-crimes or minor possessory offences.

Substance can be used to nullify procedure as well. For example, one of the arguments for strict liability crimes points to the difficulty of proving mens rea.[37] Yet another prop for strict liability is the prospect that prosecutorial discretion will limit enforcement to cases where *scienter* is very likely present.[38] Here we see both sides of the nullification coin used on behalf of the same laws, a startling admission that

---

[36] On both these points, see DJ Givelber and A Farrell, 'Judges and Juries: The Defense Case and Differences in Acquittal Rates' [2008] 33 *Law and Social Inquiry* 31.

[37] *Balint v United States*, 258 US 250, 251–254 (1922).

[38] *United States v Dotterweich*, 320 US 227, 285 (1943). The most recent cases do not express such confidence in prosecutorial discretion, but the prospect of discretionary application must occur to legislators asked to authorize criminal liability without fault.

the legislature is modifying substance on account of procedure and fully expecting other actors in the system to use procedure to modify substance.

Nullification is quite different from even extrinsic departures from the principle of material truth. Favouring a competing value over truth-in-adjudication admits the sacrifice of one genuine value for another. Nullification means selecting a procedure for the very purpose of defeating truth-in-adjudication, or selecting a substantive definition of the offence and the sentence for the very purpose of preventing the exercise of procedural rights by the accused. Bentham assumed that a unitary sovereign would formulate the rules of both substance and procedure. In the modern world where different institutions have power over substance and procedure respectively, and where both substance and procedure are changed frequently, the temptation of nullification is unavoidable.

The prospect of nullification raises the further complication of feedback loops between substance and procedure. Suppose a court considering a constitutional claim for an expanded right to confront adverse witnesses believes the expansion is justified on purely procedural grounds, but also expects the legislature to respond to this expansion by increasing the penalties for typical offences by a margin likely to induce more defendants than ever to plead guilty and so forgo confrontation altogether?

The rationalist opposes nullification as wrong on principle, because nullification shifts power over substance or procedure from the appropriate to an inappropriate institution. Moreover, relying on official discretion to limit unjust or overbroad laws carries a high practical price. Official discretion is unlikely to favour the disempowered, an institutional tendency with at least three unhappy potential consequences. First, selective enforcement creates the appearance, if not indeed the reality, of invidious discrimination among similarly situated persons. Second, exempting the most influential segments of society from the reach of unwise laws reduces whatever political pressure there may be for dealing with the root problem, ie reforming the substantive law. Third, the institutional capacity for nullification may be used to nullify just as well as unjust laws. American experience with drug prohibition suggests the first two types of costs. American experience with lynching, and more recently with rape,[39] suggests the third.

Of course the rationalist might decide that nullification is justified in extreme cases. Rationalism does not imply an absolute moral obligation to comply with positive law. If a given case offers procedural opportunities to nullify a law so bad that it satisfies the individual official's criteria for civil disobedience, a rationalist official could justify nullification.

---

[39] The prevalence of 'rape myths' among officials as well as jurors has made prosecution of acquaintance-rape cases very difficult. See D Bryden and S Lengnick, 'Rape in the Criminal Justice System' [1997] 87 *Journal of Criminal Law and Criminology* 1194, 1256.

From the internal point of view of any particular official, nullification might conflict with a sworn undertaking to follow the law.[40] In Anglo-American systems, where the legality principle is not understood in any positive sense, the judicial oath does not prohibit nullification. For jurors, moreover, the oath is an incident of compulsory service and so an unlikely source of moral obligation. In systems with a formal commitment to punish all offences a judicial oath might bar nullification. Even here, however, an oath undertaken against a cultural context of expected non-compliance might carry little weight.

It might seem, then, that the pluralist is free to engage in nullification as well as act on expected nullification. Nullification, however, is the divide that separates pluralists from reductionists. If all actors in the system are right to use whatever power they have over substance and procedure to advance their favoured outcomes, substance and procedure are only rules, institutions, and practices that have some bearing on actual punishment. The pluralist is more ready to find extrinsic trumps on the truth principle, but the pluralist does not countenance false fact-finding as a remedy for bad legislation. That would give up the substance-procedure distinction altogether.

In principle one might suppose that officials who accept the substance/procedure distinction, whether rationalist or pluralist, *would* take account of feedback loops. If a judge expects the legislature to respond to a procedural ruling by using the legislature's power over substance to change procedure, the judge can ignore the expected response only by giving up power over procedure. There is, however, no obvious baseline of either procedural rights for the defence, or potential sentences available to the state, which might inform a judgment of when procedure or substance is being used to modify the other.

4 THE REDUCTIONIST CHALLENGE

The acid of plea bargaining continuously erodes the supposed distinction between substance and process. A somewhat unusual case, *Town of Newton v Rumery*,[41] illuminates the dynamic. The state accused the defendant of witness tampering, but then dropped the charge in exchange for an agreement by defendant not to sue the city, the police, or the witness for illegal arrest. The defendant's procedural right against false arrest was thereby converted into the functional equivalent of a defence to the substantive charge. That is precisely what happens in the very great majority of

[40] Compare the argument of Chief Justice Marshall in *Marbury v Madison*, 5 US 133 (1803).
[41] 480 US 386 (1987).

American prosecutions that are not dismissed; the accused converts his procedural right to trial into a reduction of his substantive liability.

Plea bargaining institutionalizes the reciprocal nullification of substance and procedure, and therefore poses a powerful challenge to both rationalist and pluralistic versions of the substance/procedure relationship. If typical criminal conduct may support a catastrophic range of charges, as in the United States it often does, then the key decisions about culpability and dangerousness will be made by the prosecutor. Administrative discretion is nothing new, but two features of the criminal process make discretion on this scale very troubling. First, unlike the various agencies that administer government benefits or regulate economic activity, the public prosecutor's choices are comparatively opaque and comparatively unreviewable. Second, the consequences of those choices can be grave, including decades of imprisonment for some defendants and lenient treatment for others, perhaps very similarly situated.

Rationalists and pluralists agree that substance and procedure are distinct. As we have seen, their disagreement about truth-defeating procedures ends up being one of degree rather than of kind. Reductionists challenge the distinction itself. Given the plea-bargaining system as it operates in the United States, and which is spreading around the world, reductionism captures an important empirical truth.

In the United States the substantive criminal law has grown steadily as legislatures, responding to public fear of crime, have created new offences and increased penalties for old ones. As a result, most instances of criminal behaviour may be characterized as a wide variety of offences, ranging not just in severity, but in the number of counts of each charge. Say a teenager throws a brick through a shop window, reaches in, and steals three watches. This simple transaction may be characterized as vandalism, up to three counts of theft, burglary (reaching into the premises constitutes entry), or perhaps even robbery (if the stolen items can be deemed 'from the person' of the clerk), or even armed robbery (the brick being the deadly weapon). The offender ordinarily would be under the jurisdiction of the juvenile court, but depending on the charge the juvenile court may (or for serious felonies, must) waive its jurisdiction. The offender may also have prior offences triggering sentencing enhancements, enhancements that apply only when charged by the prosecutor.

Thus the range of potential outcomes runs the gamut from a delinquency adjudication for vandalism or misdemeanour theft, to conviction in the adult court for serious felonies carrying terms of several years, to an adult conviction triggering an enhancement that might mean decades in prison. As a substantive matter the legislature has authorized all these outcomes. The public prosecutor has discretion, limited by weak constitutional prohibitions on invidious motive along racial, religious, or political lines, to select any charge the evidence supports. In typical cases, such as our example, the same evidence will prove all of the possible charges if it proves any of them.

Modern plea bargaining, then, is not done 'under the shadow of the law,' ie as a compromise between the parties' estimate of the likely outcome at trial.[42] The key variable is the charging decision, which is made by the prosecutor and which neither the judge nor the jury has power to review for reasonableness. If the evidence shows the elements of each charge beyond reasonable doubt, judge and jury are bound to convict. They cannot, however, convict for a charge not made.

The prosecutor's principal practical constraint is the defendant's right to trial. The system lacks the resources to try more than a handful of cases. Guilty pleas are good not just for the system's accounting, but for victims and other witnesses who need not take the time, the trauma, or the physical risk of giving evidence. The prosecutor must make an 'offer' that effectively penalizes the defendant who insists on exercising constitutional rights, by a margin wide enough to induce pleas from the great majority of the guilty (and, one supposes, at least some of the innocent).

The reductionist characterizes the potential liability created by the relevant statutes, and the procedural rights created by constitutions, statutes, and courts' rules, as bargaining entitlements that are freely exchanged by the parties. Actual punishment is determined not by the substantive law, but by the discretion of the prosecutor constrained by the cost of the defendant's procedural rights should he insist upon exercising them. The legality principle still has some negative bite—the prosecutor must prove the defendant's identity as a person involved in criminal conduct. After that, however, substance and procedure are fungible inputs into an administrative system of negotiated outcomes.

As an empirical matter, it is difficult to challenge this description. As a normative matter the description is disturbing. The first line of normative attack on reductionism appeals to bedrock principles of liberal political theory. At least since Magna Carta the ideal of the rule of law has meant a fair hearing based on pre-existing law before judgment and punishment. The ideal has been supposed to prevent the oppressive or arbitrary use of the criminal law's severe sanctions. With the advent of modern liberal democracies the ideal also came to express the principle of separation of powers. Elected legislatures should define offences, the executive should investigate and prosecute, and the court should give judgment only after hearing a vigorous defence.

We might dramatize the normative issue posed by reductionism by restating the reductionist description in terms of an authorizing statute: 'Any person who engages in anti-social conduct shall be sentenced as directed by the public prosecutor; provided that officials in the public prosecutor's office must record twenty hours of work for every year of prison time imposed as a sentence under this Act.' That decades in prison time turn on the secret exercise of discretion, typically by a single relatively junior official, without public criteria or formal hearing, offends

---

[42] Stuntz, 'Plea Bargaining and Criminal Law's Disappearing Shadow'.

core commitments of liberal political theory: transparency, accountability, and the separation of powers.

The second line of normative attack on reductionism is methodological rather than political. The reductionist can evaluate any rule of either substance or procedure only by its tendency to generate good outcomes. If the prevailing substance/procedure mix produced unjustly harsh results, a procedure by which a computer generated random case file numbers for arbitrary reductions in liability would be a marginal improvement. If the prevailing mix yielded outcomes that were too lenient, the same computer could select case files for sentencing enhancements. And if the prevailing mix were producing acceptable outcomes all-things-considered, the reductionist would defend it, even if the substantive law provided death by torture for petty offences and the procedural law provided trial by battle.

On one reading, that of Professor Postema, Bentham himself was a reductionist of this character.[43] The ideal civil and penal codes, coupled with the natural system of procedure, might supply the judge with the outcomes utility demanded in particular cases. Postema reads Bentham's theory of adjudication as calling upon the judge to resolve each case directly according to the principle of utility, regardless of the positive law, ie to achieve the result prescribed by the ideal code as it would be applied by the natural system, even if in the actual system this called for nullification. There is some support for this reading in Bentham's sympathy for jury nullification and his hostility to any fixed rules of procedure.

Bentham's hostility to judge-made law,[44] his characterization of procedure as adjective to substance, his approval of appellate review,[45] his constitutional code's requirement of an oath-like judicial declaration to faithfully follow the law as the legislature intended it,[46] and his proposal for judicial revision of the code subject to legislative control,[47] point in the other direction. On balance it seems fair to say that Bentham expected the judges to give legislation substantial content-independent respect, so that the traditional description of him as a rationalist in procedure is correct.[48] Modern officials, however, might be right to act as Postema supposes Bentham desired.

How, however, is the reductionist to know when the current mix is generating outcomes that are too harsh, too lenient, or about right? Assuming that all controversies in criminal justice reduce to the overall balance of advantage between prosecution and defence, by what criteria may we say that the balance of advantage is optimal

---

[43] GR Postema, *Bentham and the Common Law Tradition* (Oxford: Clarendon Press, 1986), 341–50.

[44] For the famous reference to the common law as 'dog-law', see J Bentham, 'Truth Versus Ashurst' in V *Works* 230, 235.

[45] J Bentham, *Principles of Judicial Procedure*, in II *Works* 1, 165.

[46] J Bentham, *Constitutional Code*, in IX *Works* 533.

[47] J Bentham, *Of Laws in General* (HLA Hart ed, 1970), 241.

[48] Thus I side with J Dinwiddy, 'Adjudication Under Bentham's Pannomium' in W Twining (ed), *Bentham: Selected Writings of John Dinwiddy* (Stanford, CA: Stanford University Press, 2002), 155.

or suboptimal? To do this the reductionist needs a normative theory of justified punishment, and an empirical picture of what outcomes the system is generating in practice. But this is to say that the reductionist can evaluate the system only by constructing, for analytical purposes, a substantive theory of liability and a procedural method (whether of the social-science or forensic type) for finding the facts. If Bentham were a reductionist, at least to his credit he *had* such a comprehensive theory of the outcomes officials ought to pursue.

To be concrete, suppose we set out to study whether sentences imposed by, say, California are too harsh, too lenient, or about right. To do this we would need a representative set of cases, and we would need to know the historical facts of each of those cases together with their outcomes. Then we would need to compare the actual outcomes with the outcomes prescribed by some normative theory of punishment. Only then we could make an informed judgment about whether to move the balance of advantage in favour of the prosecution, in favour of the defence, or leave it as it is.

The rationalist and the pluralist may now say to the reductionist: if you have a substantive theory of justified punishment, and a methodological vision of rational procedure, why use this familiar and rational schema to prescribe outcomes and then tweak the real system in arbitrary ways to move closer to ideal outcomes? Why not instead codify the theory of punishment, and the rational procedure, and achieve directly what you are trying to achieve indirectly?

If the historical context includes many gross deviations from the right theory of justified punishment on the substantive side, and many gross deviations from rational procedure, and the political context makes only incremental and provisional reform possible, the reductionist might still be right. Under those conditions marginal improvements should not be spurned in favour of sweeping reforms beyond the range of political vision.

This pessimistic position should not be too readily accepted. In the nineteenth century the Anglo-American criminal justice system as a whole was dramatically transformed. The death penalty was curtailed where not abolished, prison became the standard punishment, counsel for both parties became standard, the rules of evidence were radically changed, and professional police took over the investigation and apprehension functions.

In the twentieth century, the Model Penal Code worked dramatic, system-wide changes in the substantive law. The Warren Court worked equally dramatic changes in procedure. Perhaps not all of these changes were for the better. The sweeping scale of reform, however, should give us pause before accepting the reductionist's claim that further distortions of both substance and process might be justified by their influence on the balance of advantage.

There remains an important point of agreement among all schools of thought. A reform that improved, or at least made no worse, the overall balance of advantage, and that *also* made the substantive or procedural law better from both rationalist and pluralistic points of view, should be endorsed by all sides of the debate over the substance/procedure relationship. DNA evidence is an uncontroversial example. More controversial, but still theoretically ecumenical, cases can be made for other reforms, such as recording interrogations and more carefully regulating identification procedures.

The reductionist challenge might be written off as peculiarly American were plea bargaining not spreading to other systems. Can the modern criminal justice system, responsible for the investigation and prosecution of massive caseloads, under penal codes that authorize a wide range of outcomes, even approximate the old ideal of a fair hearing according to pre-existing law? A variety of responses are possible, but it is fair to say that reductionism remains not implausible.[49]

Perhaps the most obvious response would be to simplify trial procedures to the point where a much higher percentage of cases could be tried. The trend, however, in the United States and elsewhere, has been to insist upon more, rather than, fewer, costly procedural safeguards against unjust conviction. Costly trial rights established by constitutions and human rights conventions are politically very difficult to change. The existence of a very elaborate procedural system for certain types of cases is not unattractive. If the United States adheres to capital punishment it seems hard to argue for streamlined trial procedures in death cases; indeed it is commonly said that more money should be spent to improve the quality of trial defence in capital cases. When the prosecution might have even the appearance of political motivation, searching procedures both check the misuse, and validate the use, of state power.

Another approach would be to limit the defendant's right to waive procedural protections. Even if acceptable as a matter of principle, the feasibility of this approach is dubious. In Germany, for instance, the requirement of holding a trial could not prevent agreements by which the defence put on no evidence in exchange for a limited sentence.[50]

A more promising response is to recharacterize plea bargaining as the fair hearing required by the old ideal. The prosecutor, after all, is an officer of the court. Implicit in bargaining is the defendant's opportunity to be heard. The prosecutor can threaten nothing that the legislature has not authorized. Plea bargaining may be analogized to systems of trial de novo. The accused gets a preliminary judgment from the prosecutor after a rough-and-ready process, and is free to challenge that result at a formal trial with dramatically heightened stakes. Transparency and accountability are lacking, but reforms, along the lines of modern administrative law, might go far to address these important concerns. Prosecutors' offices might be required to formulate criteria similar to sentencing guidelines,[51] and charging decisions might be made reviewable by the courts for abuse of discretion.

---

[49] For a more elaborate discussion than presented here, see DA Dripps, 'Overcriminalization, Discretion, Waiver: A Survey of Possible Exit Strategies' [2005] 109 *Penn State Law Review* 1155.

[50] Weigend, 'The Decay of the Inquisitorial Ideal' 39, 45.

[51] Eg the House of Lords ruled that the Director of Public Prosecutions must formulate general, public criteria indicating when persons assisting suicide will, and will not be, prosecuted. This has

Another response might be to formalize the trial penalty as a fixed percentage of the maximum prescribed sentence. Italy has experimented with this approach, and although the results have not been a sweeping success, the idea is an intriguing antidote to the problem of coercive threats of massive liability for those who insist on trial. Rewarding those who accept responsibility by admitting guilt with a reduction in sentence is not implausible. The more difficult question is how large the trial penalty ought to be, not whether it ought to exist.

A final response might be to limit the scope of the substantive criminal law, with the aim of preventing catastrophic sentencing ranges from forcing defendants to plead guilty. This might be done by constitutional rules limiting liability for a criminal transaction to the most serious offence committed, together with a fixed limit on the maximum time that might be imposed for offences excepting the very gravest. The American Supreme Court has flirted with both approaches but embraced neither. Different times may bring a different outcome. In sum, rationalists and pluralists may say to the reductionist that the case may be hard, but the jury is still out.

One interesting consequence of the reductionist challenge to the substance/procedure divide may be the heightened importance of criminal law theory in legal education. Arguments about culpability and deterrence that ideally would be resolved by legislatures are now resolved by prosecutors acting ad hoc. If statutory language is less important than official discretion in determining actual liability, prosecutors must base the exercise of discretion on something. Discretion ought to be exercised, and in most cases probably is exercised, according to the individual official's understanding of the aims of the criminal law. The duty of counsel for the defence is to persuade the prosecutor. The old debate between Kant and Bentham is renewed every day in the course of plea discussions.

5 CONCLUSION: THE HARDEST PROBLEM?

Brief as it must be, this chapter has traversed a wide expanse of thin ice. We have touched on the philosophy of punishment, the history and practice of criminal procedure in different jurisdictions, and fundamental questions about the nature of the

occasioned criticism as executive modification of an act of Parliament, and defended as providing fair notice. For an overview of the controversy, see N Cartwright, '48 Years On: Is the Suicide Act Fit for Purpose?' [2009] 17 *Medical Law Review* 467. If reductionism is descriptively accurate, the executive is modifying legislative enactments on a routine basis. If so, it might be preferable, as a normative matter, if this executive-branch law making were done accountably and transparently as in other areas of administrative law.

legality principle and what priority it deserves. Any project so ambitious is likely to be wrong on at least some points.

I undertook this humbling project because I believe that sorting out the substance/procedure relationship presents criminal justice scholars with our most difficult challenge. I hope that something like Benthamite rationalism can be recovered intellectually and in due course institutionalized. At present I make no claim that this is likely to happen, but the work goes on.

With somewhat greater confidence I close by suggesting that the foundational but problematic nature of the relationship has at least two programmatic implications for criminal justice scholars. Those who accept reductionism and call for change of any sort should articulate a baseline balance between substantive liabilities and procedural entitlements, so that changes in the existing balance might with some reason be criticized or defended. Those who reject reductionism, whether we work on substance or procedure, should account for the terms of trade between the two that now prevail, either by explicitly bracketing the plea-bargaining problem or by explaining how our analyses improve our understanding, or our prescriptions might improve the practice, of the system in place. We are of course perfectly free to carry on the party with no mention of the elephant in the room. Hard problems, however, do not disappear because they are ignored.

19

....

TWO KINDS OF
RETRIBUTIVISM

....

MITCHELL N BERMAN[*]

1 INTRODUCTION

....

THE philosophy of criminal law covers a broad range of concerns. Its practitioners explore such diverse conceptual and normative matters as the character of a culpable act and the proper contours of criminal liability for an omission, the principles of causation, the difference between defences of justification and of excuse, the nature of complicity, and a variety of puzzles involving attempts, among innumerable other topics. Historically, however, one question has dominated the rest: in virtue of what is the state morally justified in subjecting an individual to criminal punishment—ie the intentional infliction of suffering and/or the deprivation of substantial liberties, joined to moral censure or condemnation? Answers to this question routinely travel under the heading of 'theories of punishment', though 'justifications for punishment' would be more apt. Refining, defending, and critiquing theories of punishment have been the central concerns of philosophers of the criminal law. For centuries it has been a vigorous and fractious debate.

 * Earlier drafts of this chapter were presented at a GALA Workshop at Berkeley Law; at the conference for this book, held at Rutgers-Newark School of Law; and at UT Law's law and philosophy discussion group. I am indebted to participants at those events and wish especially to recognize valuable criticisms and suggestions from Larry Alexander, Mike Cahill, Meir Dan-Cohen, John Deigh, Antony Duff, David Enoch, Kim Ferzan, Stephen Galoob, Sandy Kadish, Chris Kutz, David Sklansky, Sarah Song, Victor Tadros, Kevin Toh, and Peter Westen. Guha Krishnamurthi provided excellent research assistance. With apologies to M Smith, 'Two Kinds of Consequentialism'.

This chapter aims to assess the state of that debate in the early years of the twenty-first century. It advances one principal claim. Additionally, and consistent with this volume's ambition to help set terms and direction for fruitful philosophizing about the criminal law in the near future, it proposes an agenda for further work.

The central argument of this chapter is that the dominant classificatory framework of theories of punishment that had become orthodox by the latter decades of the twentieth century is in peril. That taxonomy was centred on a two-part distinction between consequentialist and retributivist justifications for punishment. To state very precisely what either of these approaches maintains would beg a great many debates. As a first pass, though, consequentialist theories (what I will later rename instrumentalist theories) justify punishment by the good that punishment produces, whereas retributivist theories see punishment as justified by reference to the wrongdoers' supposed ill-desert—the claimed fact that wrongdoers deserve to suffer, or to be punished, or something of this sort. I argue that this framework is no longer accurate because retributivism has increasingly morphed into an account that rests upon a justificatory structure that is plainly consequentialist. That is, it seems increasingly fitting to view retributivism as a subtype of consequentialist justifications for punishment—a 'retributivist consequentialism' that can be meaningfully contrasted with varieties of 'non-retributivist consequentialism'—rather than as an alternative to them. Some will think this a contradiction in terms, that retributivism is non-consequentialist by definition. On this view, 'retributivist consequentialism' is oxymoronic. I will argue that that is not so.

That there exists a theory or account of the justifiability of criminal punishment that is both recognizably retributivist and assimilable to a consequentialist structure of justification does not mean that that account exhausts retributivist space. Even if, as I argue, it is meaningful to speak of retributivist consequentialism, there might nonetheless exist other tenable forms of retributivism that resist reduction to consequentialism. If so, we should recognize two kinds of retributivism, not one: consequentialist retributivism (which is simply an alternate name for what I have just referred to as retributivist consequentialism); and non-consequentialist retributivism. At this moment in time, though, the consequentialist variant of retributivism is more perspicuous.[1] Accordingly, among the more pressing tasks for philosophers of the criminal law who continue to be interested in what has long been the central issue in the field—what justifies the infliction of criminal punishment?—is to explicate non-consequentialist retributivism in its most persuasive and attractive light—if not necessarily to establish that it *is* true, then at least to show how it could be.

---

[1] For a valuable recent discussion of 'consequentialist retributivism'—one that observes that, despite its 'intuitive appeal...it has thus far apparently received *no* explicit, sustained defense in the scholarly literature', and explicates some of its advantages as against standard (non-consequentialist) retributivism—see MT Cahill, 'Retributive Justice in the Real World' (2007) 85 *Washington University Law Review* 815, 825, 833–40.

2 *E Pluribus Duo*

Philosophers writing in the Western tradition have endeavoured to justify criminal punishment against moral objections since the Greeks, even if, from today's perspective, the dominant non-contemporary figures date no farther back than to the mid-eighteenth century. Viewed through one lens, this lengthy tradition has produced a rich diversity of justificatory theories, including deterrence (Bentham and Beccaria), reform (Plato), retribution (Kant), annulment (Hegel), and denunciation (Durkheim).

A striking feature of twentieth-century punishment theory, however, has been the steady and generally successful pressure to fold this seeming multiplicity of justifications into a simple dichotomy of justifications that at least appears to mirror the fundamental organizing distinction in moral theory between consequentialism and deontology. Thus have commentators routinely insisted that deterrent, reform, and denunciatory, expressive, or educative theories are most perspicuously understood simply as emphasizing different—but not incompatible—mechanisms by which punishment brings about a varied lot of desirable consequences, while Kantian, Hegelian, and similar theories are best viewed as arguing that punishment is right or fitting in itself. To be sure, this effort at binary classification between what are often termed 'forward-looking' and 'backward-looking' theories has always met with some resistance. But a central strand in the story of the philosophy of criminal law over the past two centuries consists of the gradual refining of a somewhat more diverse array of competing theories of punishment into the two dominant traditions generally recognized today: the consequentialist tradition tracing its roots back to Beccaria and Bentham, and the retributive tradition that claims Kant as its patron saint.[2]

Now, the facile mapping of the retributivist/consequentialist divide in punishment theory onto the deontological/consequentialist divide in moral theory is highly deceptive. Even if (as I am willing to suppose, but only *arguendo*) retributivists about punishment cannot be consequentialists about morality generally, the converse is clearly false: consequentialists about punishment need not endorse a consequentialist comprehensive moral theory. That is, they need not entirely eschew deontological or non-consequentialist aspects either of normative ethics or of political morality. A justification of punishment is conventionally labelled 'consequentialist' if it explains the moral permissibility of the practice by reference to the value of its actual or supposed consequences. But there is no reason why the consequences that are thought

---

[2] This two-part division is so dominant that supporting citations are surely unnecessary. A small and close to random sampling of classificatory schemata based on an opposition between consequentialism (sometimes less helpfully labelled 'utilitarianism') includes RA Duff, *Punishment, Communication, and Community* (Oxford: Oxford University Press, 2001), ch 1; I Primoratz, *Justifying Legal Punishment* (New York: Humanity Books, 1989); CL Ten, *Crime, Guilt, and Punishment* (New York: Oxford University Press, 1987); K Greenawalt, 'Punishment', in SH Kadish, (ed), (1983) 4 *Encyclopedia of Crime and Justice* 1336.

to matter must themselves be conceptualized in resolutely consequentialist terms. For example, one can justify punishment on consequentialist grounds while still arguing that it is more important to deter intentional killings than mere allowings-to-die on the grounds that the former are deontological moral wrongs and the latter are not. Furthermore, many persons who ascribe to what are traditionally termed consequentialist theories of punishment grant that the state is nonetheless under an obligation of political justice not to punish persons who aren't blameworthy, and they might believe as well (though they need not) that constraints of this sort cannot be consequentialized.[3] For reasons such as these, consequentialism about punishment is not identical to consequentialism about morality.

Unfortunately, there is no obviously best solution to this problem: while it would have been preferable had philosophers about punishment not drawn their classificatory line between retributivism and 'consequentialism' these many years (so as to forestall the mistaken assumption that consequentialists about punishment must be consequentialists about morality generally), to change nomenclature now risks a different confusion (that the new term refers to something different from what 'consequentialism' had previously been thought to mean in this context). On balance, though, the latter risk seems worth running. Following Victor Tadros,[4] then, I will apply the term 'instrumentalist' to the forward-looking justifications of punishment that tradition contrasts with the backward-looking justifications labelled 'retributivism.' That is, let us for the moment accept whole hog the familiar distinction between retributivist and consequentialist justifications for punishment while renaming the latter 'instrumentalism'. I spoke in section 1 of retributivist and non-retributivist consequentialism, and of consequentialist and non-consequentialist retributivism. Those very same ideas we can now re-caption as retributivist and non-retributivist *instrumentalism*, and as *instrumentalist* and *non-instrumentalist* retributivism, without any intended change in meaning. That is the nomenclature I will employ for the remainder of this chapter.

3 RETRIBUTIVIST INSTRUMENTALISM

3.1 Retributivism and desert

Even as theorists sought to divide the universe of punishment justifications in two, a concise statement of retributivism remained notoriously elusive. In a well-known

---

[3] On efforts to consequentialize constraints on the pursuit of consequentialist objectives see n 40 below.

[4] V Tadros, *The Moral Foundations of Criminal Law* (forthcoming). For reasons that would require an extended digression to explicate, I am not persuaded that Tadros and I use the term 'instrumentalism' to mean precisely the same thing. But any such difference between our usages as might exist is a matter of detail.

article from 30 years ago, for example, John Cottingham distinguished nine distinct theories that had been classified, by its proponents or others, as retributivist. These included the theses: that offenders deserve to be punished; that through punishment a wrongdoer repays his debt to society; that punishment annuls crime; that punishment restores conditions of fair play between offenders and the law-abiding; that punishment absolves a society's blood guilt for crime; and that punishment satisfies the longing of victims and the public for justice and revenge.[5] Although Cottingham rightly denied that several of these merited the retributivist label, he did not propose his own statement of what retributivism is, or maintains.

Over the ensuing years, however, a consensus has arisen. As CL Ten put it in a much-read book: 'Contemporary retributivists treat the notion of desert as central to the retributivist theory, punishment being justified in terms of the desert of the offender.'[6] Or, in Larry Alexander's words: 'Retributivists argue that punishment must be justified by the ill-desert of the one punished.'[7] Let us call this core retributivist contention *the desert claim*: punishment is justified by the offender's ill-desert.

Desert talk is notoriously mysterious and elusive. It provokes many questions. Here are two. First, just what is it that offenders deserve? Second, what does it mean that he deserves it?

Joel Feinberg was the first to analyse desert as a triadic relationship: an agent, that which is deserved, and that which makes the agent deserve it.[8] He called the last the 'desert basis' but didn't offer pithy labels for the other two.[9] Let's call them the desert subject and the desert object, respectively. Our first question, then, can be put this way: What—precisely—is the retributivists' desert object?

This question is provoked by the marked vagueness of *the desert claim*. To say (as the passages quoted above do) that desert is 'central' to retributivism, that punishment is justified 'in terms of' or 'by' the offender's desert, does not specify just what it is that the offender deserves. Yet more significantly, when the desert object *is* specified, it is articulated in differing terms. Time and again, it is said that, for retributivists, 'punishment is justified because people deserve it'.[10] The antecedent of 'it' being punishment, this formulation implies that the retributivist desert object

---

[5] J Cottingham, 'Varieties of Retribution' (1979) 29 Phil Q 238.

[6] Ten, *Crime, Guilt, and Punishment*, 46.

[7] L Alexander, 'The Doomsday Machine: Proportionality, Punishment and Prevention' (1980) 63 *Monist* 199, 199.

[8] J Feinberg, *Doing and Deserving: Essays in the Theory of Responsibility* (Princeton: Princeton University Press, 1970).

[9] But see n 53 below.

[10] K Greenawalt, 'Punishment' (1981) 74 *Criminal Law and Criminology* 343, 347. See also eg RL Christopher, 'Deterring Retributivism: The Injustice of "Just Punishment"' (2002) 96 *Northwestern U LR* 843, 845, n 1 ('Though a precise definition of retributivism has proven elusive, stated most simply, the theory holds that punishment is justified solely because the person being punished deserves it.'); M Moore, *Placing Blame: A Theory of Criminal Law* (Oxford: Clarendon Press, 1997), 91 ('Retributivism is a very straightforward theory of punishment: We are justified in punishing because and only because offenders deserve it.'); H Bedau, 'Retribution and the Theory of Punishment' (1978) *Journal*

is punishment itself. Other scholars, however, declare that 'all retributive theories assert that offenders deserve to suffer'.[11] On this view, the retributivist desert object is *suffering*, not *punishment*. That differing descriptions of the retributivist desert claim can be found need not imply that the issue is a subject of genuine debate. To the contrary, I submit that most readers of the literature would conclude that commentators have rarely given explicit attention to this particular issue, and therefore that precious few seeming endorsements of one or the other of these possible retributivist desert objects reflects conscious choice. Nonetheless, once attention is drawn to the question a choice must be made—either between these two possible desert objects, or of some third.

If we just count noises, the dominant view, I think, is that they deserve to suffer. Moreover, there is reason to prefer this formulation, for if what they deserve is punishment, the argument for retributivism appears tautological or, at the least, uninformative: punishment of wrongdoers is justified by the fact that wrongdoers deserve to be punished. As Lawrence Davis argued some years ago in his aptly titled short essay 'They Deserve to Suffer', retributivism avoids this particular objection if what I call its desert object is suffering, not punishment.[12] So let us start by construing the desert claim in this way: wrongdoers deserve to suffer. This is only a working assumption; we will return to consider other possibilities later. That is, we will consider different conceptions or specifications of the desert claim. For now, though, we will work with this specification of the general retributivism desert claim: wrongdoers deserve to suffer (ie, to endure some negative experiential state) on account of, and in proportion to, their blameworthy wrongdoing. To make clear that this is one possible *specification* of the desert claim, and not a purported *restatement*, let us call this the *desert-s claim*.

3.2 The retributivist intrinsic good

Having thus refined the vague *desert claim* into the somewhat more precise *desert-s claim*, it remains to address the second question: what does the claim that wrongdoers

of Philosophy 601, 608 ('Retributivism without *desert*—the concept of punishment as something deserved by whoever is rightly made liable to it—is like *Hamlet* without the Prince of Denmark.').

[11] M Bagaric and K Amarasekara, 'The Errors of Retributivism' (2000) 24 *Melbourne University Law Review* 124, 127 (footnotes omitted); J Kleinig, *Punishment and Desert* (The Hague: Martinus Nijhoff Press, 1973), 67 ('The principle that the wrongdoer deserves to suffer seems to accord with our deepest intuitions concerning justice.'); RA Duff, 'Justice, Mercy, and Forgiveness' (1990) 9 *Criminal Justice Ethics* 51, 52 (noting 'the central retributivist intuition that "the guilty deserve to suffer"' and that punishment is 'the infliction of suffering on the criminal').

[12] LH Davis, 'They Deserve to Suffer' (1972) 32 *Analysis* 136. Despite Davis's argument, I stand by the claim in text that few commentators, retributivist or otherwise, have consciously attended to possible variations on the desert claim. For a rare recent exception see DN Husak, 'Retribution in Criminal Theory' (2000) 37 *San Diego Law Review* 959, 972.

deserve to suffer mean? Can the idea be equivalently expressed in other evaluative or deontic terms of which we think we have a surer grasp? Because the very notion of desert is at least a touch mysterious, many retributivists have translated the desert claim into the language of intrinsic goodness. Here's a candidate formulation of what I will call the *retributivist intrinsic good claim* (or often the *intrinsic good claim*, for short): it is intrinsically good (or intrinsically valuable) that one who has engaged in wrongdoing suffer on account of, and in proportion to, his blameworthy wrongdoing. In preferring the *intrinsic good claim* to the *desert-s claim*, theorists have supposed that the two are equivalent, but that the former is less obscure.[13] In 1993, Michael Moore, the foremost contemporary retributivist, himself endorsed the intrinsic good claim. Indeed, he allowed that the intrinsic good claim captures the core meaning of retributivism: 'what is distinctively retributivist is the view that the guilty receiving their just deserts is an intrinsic good.'[14]

As David Dolinko was among the first to recognize, Moore's acceptance of the intrinsic good claim poses a profound challenge to our dominant classificatory scheme.[15] For while retributivists might believe that the realization of deserved suffering is an intrinsic good, they must not believe that it is the *only* intrinsic good, for it would be implausible to insist:

That the overall goodness of any state of affairs depends *exclusively* on how much punishment-of-guilty persons it contains, regardless of whatever else that state of affairs contains…Indeed, to insist that *only* the quantity of 'the guilty receiving punishment' affects the goodness of a state of affairs implies the absurd conclusion that a state of affairs wherein no one ever commits any crime at all lacks goodness altogether![16]

That would be an absurd view, and Moore explicitly disavows it.[17] But then it might seem that retributivism is not interestingly different from other instrumentalist approaches to punishment, most of which also recognize that the consequences, realization or pursuit of which justifies the imposition of criminal punishment, are varied. After all, the principal reason to term the alternative to retributivism 'consequentialism' rather than 'utilitarianism' was precisely to deny that a consequentialist about punishment (what I am now calling an 'instrumentalist' about punishment) must believe that utility constitutes the only metric of value. If instrumentalist justifications of punishment are, as a class, pluralist about value, then they comfortably

---

[13] See eg ibid; T Hurka, 'The Common Structure of Virtue and Desert' (2001) 112 *Ethics* 6. The intrinsic good claim makes an early appearance in AC Ewing, *The Morality of Punishment* (London: Kegan Paul, Trench, Truebner and Co, 1929), 14.

[14] MS Moore, 'Justifying Retributivism' (1993) 27 *Israel Law Review* 15, 19 (emphasis omitted).

[15] D Dolinko, 'Retributivism, Consequentialism, and the Intrinsic Goodness of Punishment' (1997) 16 *Law & Philosophy* 507.

[16] Ibid 513–14.

[17] See eg Moore, 'Justifying Retributivism', 34 ('It would be a crude caricature of the retributivist to make him monomaniacally focused on the achievement of retributive justice. The retributivist like anyone else can admit that there are other intrinsic goods, such as the goods protected by the rights to life, liberty, and bodily integrity.').

encompass intrinsic-good retributivism. So it appears that retributivism just is that type of instrumentalism—call it 'retributivist instrumentalism'—that recognizes intrinsic value in the suffering of wrongdoers.

You might think, however, that there is this difference between retributivist instrumentalism and all other instrumentalist justifications of punishment. For instrumentalists about punishment, punishment is justified by all the good consequences that punishment produces (or is reasonably expected to produce, or something of this sort). To be sure, punishment instrumentalists vary regarding what states of affairs *are* valuable. But it is a hallmark of instrumentalist accounts that all valuable states of affairs (whatever they might be) can help furnish justification for punishment. Yet retributivists often say that the offender's desert supplies both necessary and sufficient conditions for punishment.[18] We will focus on the supposed necessary condition shortly. Now just consider the sufficiency condition. If retributivism truly holds that the inflicting of deserved suffering is a sufficient justification for punishment, then it would seem to deny this tenet of instrumentalism.

In fact, the oft-stated retributivist contention that bringing about the good of deserved suffering is a sufficient condition for punishment cannot be taken at face value. If retributivists, like most folk, recognize a plurality of intrinsic goods, then they are apt to recognize a plurality of intrinsic bads as well. It would seem to follow that punishment might not be justified all things considered in a particular case if the bads it would produce outweigh the goods, including the good of realizing deserved suffering. Accordingly, it seems untrue that realizing deserved suffering can be a sufficient condition of justified punishment. In fact, Moore has now granted precisely this. Any talk of 'sufficient conditions', he notes, is context-sensitive:

Within the set of conditions constituting intelligible reasons to punish, the retributivist asserts, desert is sufficient, ie, no other of these conditions is necessary. Of course, other conditions outside the set of conditions constituting intelligible reasons to punish may also be necessary to a just punishment, such as the condition that the punishment not violate any non-forfeited rights of an offender.[19]

Put otherwise and more generally, Moore means to assert only that the realizing of deserved suffering supplies a sufficient reason to punish in the absence of overriding reasons not to punish, his pragmatic point being that the particular instrumentalist mechanisms frequently invoked and elaborated upon—deterrence, reform, moral education, and so on—are not themselves necessary conditions, alone or in combination, for punishment to be justified. If the sufficiency condition is understood in this way, it is entirely consistent with instrumentalist theories of punishment, in

---

[18] See eg M Moore, *Placing Blame: A Theory of Criminal Law* (Oxford: Clarendon Press, 1997), 91 ('Retributivism is a very straightforward theory of punishment: We are justified in punishing because and only because offenders deserve it. Moral responsibility ("desert") in such a view is not only necessary for justified punishment, it is also sufficient.').

[19] MS Moore, 'Justifying Retributivism' (1993) 27 *Israel Law Review* 15, 35.

which event retributivism is simply a species of instrumentalist justifications for punishment. It is that type that recognizes the suffering of wrongdoers as intrinsically valuable—a valuable consequence that (for one reason or another) is particularly salient in justifying punishment.

Now, both Moore and Dolinko deny, albeit in different ways, that retributivism is best viewed simply as an instrumentalist theory that isolates deserved suffering as a particularly weighty value. Moore denies that retributivism *need* be assimilated to instrumentalism: in his view, there are instrumentalist and non-instrumentalist forms of retributivism, both of which are sound. Dolinko denies that retributivism *can* be assimilated to instrumentalism: in his view, retributivism is inescapably committed to claims that cannot be reconciled with instrumentalist modes of justification. Section 4 considers what routes are open to those, like Moore, who would favour a non-instrumentalist retributivism. Before considering whether a non-instrumentalist retributivism can be vindicated, however, we do well to first consider the plausibility of a genuine instrumentalist one. We do well, that is, to address Dolinko's challenge.

3.3 Is retributivist instrumentalism really a form of retributivism?

Recall Moore's assertion that the intrinsic good claim captures 'what is distinctively retributivist'.[20] 'At first glance', Dolinko objects, 'one might suppose that Moore's assertion is patently false, because a non-retributivist might endorse the intrinsic good claim'.[21]

This is question begging, for a non-retributivist *cannot* endorse the intrinsic good claim if retributivism is *defined* by its endorsement of that claim. Then to endorse the intrinsic good claim would ipso facto to be a retributivist. So Dolinko must have in mind a different understanding of what retributivism necessarily is or maintains. Possibly, for example, he believes that retributivism is non-instrumentalist by definition. This is a not-uncommon view.[22] But it must be defended by argument.

Here is Dolinko's argument, or at least the assumption that undergirds his argument:

[W]hat is distinctive about the retributivist must be the *role* played in her theory by the intrinsic goodness of punishing the guilty. For the retributivist, this intrinsic goodness

---

[20] See text accompanying n 14 above.

[21] D Dolinko, 'Retributivism, Consequentialism, and the Intrinsic Goodness of Punishment' (1997) 16 *Law & Philosophy* 507, 517.

[22] See eg Duff, *Punishment, Communication, and Community*, 19; J Feinberg, 'What, If Anything, Justifies Legal Punishment? The Classic Debate', in J Feinberg and H Gross (eds), *Philosophy of Law* (5th edn; Belmont, CA: Wadsworth Publishing Company, 1995), 613, 613–17.

cannot be an irrelevancy or a mere happy accident. It must be either (i) the reason for engaging in the practice of punishment (its rational justification), or (ii) the reason why that practice is morally permissible (its moral justification), or both.[23]

This is a puzzling passage, for surely the intrinsic goodness of punishing the guilty (or of giving the guilty their deserved suffering) does play a role, for the retributivist, in helping to supply both rational justification and moral justification. Dolinko's use of the definite article seems to suggest, then, that a retributivist must believe that the intrinsic good that he emphasizes must be the *lone* rational or moral justification. Yet what grounds he has to saddle the retributivist with such a view is unstated. Dolinko provides no reason why a theorist who contends, say, that the good of deserved suffering is an always-available reason to justify punishment, and a particularly weighty reason at that, is barred from donning the retributivist mantle. That is, Dolinko provides no argument to preclude the possibility that the most plausible form of retributivism, and the version most widely embraced today, is a species of instrumentalism. It could be, in other words, that self-described contemporary retributivists *just are* those instrumentalists about punishment who believe that deserved suffering has sufficient intrinsic value to significantly affect our thinking about how to constitute the doctrines and practices of the criminal justice system.[24]

Even if Dolinko himself provides no persuasive explicit argument against retributivist instrumentalism, perhaps the germs of an argument can be found lurking in his disquiet. The worry, I think, is this. Supposing *arguendo* that retributivism is a form of instrumentalist justification, we should still want it to be the case that retributivist instrumentalism is not just any old instrumentalism. Instrumentalism about punishment is not committed to any particular view about the things of value that punishment should be designed to bring about; an instrumentalist's answers to that question are potentially as varied as are the possible views about value. Therefore, if we divide theories of punishment by reference to the particular types of goods that the theory invokes, or heavily relies upon, as potential justification for punishment, it might seem that we would not be left with two species of instrumentalism—retributivist and non-retributivist—but dozens or scores rather than two, for every different axiological position would constitute its own punishment theory. For example, some instrumentalists about punishment who deny that suffering is ever intrinsically good might nonetheless be deontologists about morality who also believe that causing harm to others in ways that violate deontological moral commands is worse than causing identical harms that do not violate deontological moral commands,

---

[23] Dolinko, 'Retributivism, Consequentialism, and the Intrinsic Goodness of Punishment', 518.

[24] Possibly, however, retributivist instrumentalists are wrong about that. Instrumentalists who deny the intrinsic good claim (ie non-retributivist instrumentalists), but who appreciate the instrumental value of structuring the criminal justice system to accord with popular beliefs in the importance of giving deserved punishment, could end up backing doctrines and policies that closely approximate what a retributivist instrumentalist might advocate. See generally PH Robinson and JM Darley, 'The Utility of Desert' (1997) 91 *Northwestern University Law Review* 453.

and therefore that a reduction in wrongful harms is of greater intrinsic value than the same reduction in non-wrongful harms, all else being equal. The worry, then, is not that the divide between 'retributivist instrumentalism' and 'non-retributivist instrumentalism' is false, but that it is arbitrary. If we were disposed to draw a binary classification within instrumentalist theories of punishment, we could just as well do it between welfarist and non-welfarist instrumentalism or deontological and non-deontological instrumentalism. But if all this is so, then perhaps we have reason to be sceptical of the move that got us here in the first place. It's one thing to swallow that retributivism could be a subset of instrumentalism. It's something else again to accept that it is no more salient or significant a subtype than many others. Of course, that could just be the way it is; I have thus far only tried to give voice to a worry, not to have burnished that worry into an argument. Still, reasoning of this sort can help explain the intuition that it is not enough that retributivism have a particular axiological commitment, but that it must display some sort of distinctive logical structure.

There is something to this concern. I will argue, though, that the adoption of the intrinsic good claim does in fact give retributivist instrumentalism a logical structure not shared by non-retributivist instrumentalism.

To understand the argument, we must first distinguish two different types of justification, what I will call 'all-things-considered' and 'tailored'.[25] An all-things-considered justification of an act or a practice is just what it sounds like: it establishes that the act or practice is morally justified, or permissible, in light of all considerations. A tailored justification, in contrast, establishes the permissibility of the challenged act or practice against one or more particular grounds for doubt, what I have termed 'demand bases'.[26]

As already discussed, the retributivist instrumentalist must rely on a plurality of values insofar as she aims to justify punishment all things considered. Historically, however, the core concern of philosophers of punishment has *not* been to provide an all-things-considered justification. Rather, it has been to meet the very particular reason why punishment has been understood to stand in special need of moral justification. As Hart put it, agreeing with Stanley Benn, it is 'the deliberate imposition of suffering which is the feature needing justification'.[27] Theorists routinely observe not merely that 'punishment stands in need of justification'—which contention might be an invitation for all-things-considered justification—but that such justification is needed precisely 'because it involves the infliction of pain or other form of unpleasant treatment'.[28] As another commentator rightly emphasized, 'The moral problem

---

[25] The analysis to follow draws from my 'Punishment and Justification' (2008) 118 *Ethics* 258, 278–84.

[26] Cf n 9 above (invoking Feinberg's notion of a 'desert basis').

[27] HLA Hart, *Punishment and Responsibility* (Oxford: Clarendon Press, 1968), 2, n 3.

[28] C Finkelstein, 'Positivism and the Notion of an Offense' (2000) 88 *California Law Review* 335, 358. A tiny sampling of similar claims includes Primoratz, *Justifying Legal Punishment*, 7 ('To punish

that the having of a legal institution of punishment presents can be stated in one sentence: It involves the deliberate and intentional infliction of suffering.'[29] Because it is the fact that punishment involves the intentional infliction of suffering that *particularly* demands justification, philosophers of punishment have understood their core task to be explaining how punishment can be justified in light of, or against, *this* objection. In other words, they have sought a justification of punishment tailored to meet this concern, even if other (subsidiary) objections to punishment—for example, that it is costly—might remain to be addressed before the all-things-considered justifiability of punishment can be established.

Seeking an all-things-considered justification for punishment,[30] Dolinko concludes that the retributive intrinsic good claim is not up to the task and, indeed, plays no special or distinctive role relative to the other types of intrinsic goods that a pluralistic instrumentalist is likely to invoke. I believe Dolinko is right about this. But he is wrong, I believe, when we shift our focus to the search for a tailored justification. Very simply, against the demand that punishment be justified because it inflicts pain or suffering on wrongdoers, the intrinsic good claim justifies punishment by cancellation, whereas other good consequences that the pluralist might call upon proceed by override. That is, if the suffering of a blameworthy wrongdoer is an intrinsic good, then the principal mark against punishment simply dissolves; it lacks moral force. But if the suffering of a blameworthy wrongdoer is intrinsically bad—as one who denies the retributive intrinsic good claim will maintain—then the instrumentalist reasons to punish can supply even a tailored justification of punishment only by outweighing the principal standing reason not to punish. Because cancellation enjoys logical priority to override in an argumentative dialectic, there *is* something distinctive about the role played by the retributive intrinsic good claim that is not played by other intrinsic goods.

Put another way, once we recognize the centrality, in the philosophical literature, of the search for tailored justifications for punishment, then we can agree with Moore that 'what is distinctively retributivist is the view that the guilty receiving

---

means to inflict an evil. But to inflict evil on someone is something that, at least *prima facie*, ought not to be done. So the question arises: What is the *moral justification* of inflicting the evil of punishment on people?... This is the question about punishment which is being discussed in philosophy.'); R Wasserstrom, 'Why Punish the Guilty?' (1964) 20 *Princeton University Magazine* 14–19, reprinted in G Ezorsky (ed), *Philosophical Perspectives on Punishment* (1972), 328–41, 337 ('Punishment is an evil, an unpleasantness; it requires that someone suffer. Its infliction demands justification.'); N Lacey, *State Punishment: Political Principles and Community Values* (London: Routledge, 1988), 13 ('The most obvious reason for a need to justify punishment is that it involves, on almost any view of morality, prima facie moral wrongs: inflicting unpleasant consequences... and doing so irrespective of the will or consent of the person being punished.').

[29] RW Burgh, 'Do the Guilty Deserve Punishment?' (1982) 79 *Journal of Philosophy* 193, 193.

[30] See eg D Dolinko, 'Retributivism, Consequentialism, and the Intrinsic Goodness of Punishment' (1997) 16 *Law & Philosophy* 507, 521 (inquiring whether retributivism can 'rationally justify the practice of punishment in the face of its staggering costs').

their just deserts is an intrinsic good' without abandoning the intuition that there should remain something importantly and revealingly distinct about retributivist and instrumentalist accounts of the justifiability of punishment. Even insofar as retributivism cashes out as retributivist instrumentalism, it would remain in some respect structurally distinct from non-retributivist instrumentalism.

4 Non-Instrumentalist Retributivism

Let us take stock. Retributivism is constituted by its acceptance of *the desert claim*: punishment is justified in terms of the wrongdoer's ill-desert. The desert claim is consistent with potentially many specifications of the desert object. The dominant specification holds (to a first approximation) that what wrongdoers deserve is to suffer on account of their blameworthy wrongdoing. This is *the desert-s claim*. The desert-s claim is equivalent to *the retributive intrinsic good claim*: it is intrinsically valuable that wrongdoers suffer on account of their blameworthy wrongdoing. Embrace of the intrinsic good claim, by Moore and other retributivists, converts retributivism into an instrumentalist justification for punishment. That is, to justify punishment on the strength of the retributive intrinsic good claim is to advance an instrumentalist justification for punishment, and not to advance an alternative or competitor to the instrumentalist justifications. However, given the importance to moral reasoning of the distinction between tailored and all-things-considered justifications, there remains good reason to single out retributivist instrumentalism as an especially meaningful subtype.

What we have thus far been calling retributivist instrumentalism could also be termed instrumentalist retributivism; these are alternative descriptions of the same idea.[31] The final question is whether instrumentalist retributivism just is retributivism today or whether there are, in addition, one or more tenable forms of non-instrumentalist retributivism. If there are, a proponent of such forms of retributivism might maintain, modestly, that both are forms of retributivism or, more aggressively, that so-called instrumentalist retributivism isn't a genuine form of retributivism at

---

[31] Which is the modificand, and which the modifier, depends upon what is being taxonomized. When we speak of justifications for punishment, I think it most perspicuous to distinguish, at the top level of the taxonomic hierarchy, instrumentalist from non-instrumentalist theories. The retributivist subclass of instrumentalism is naturally denominated retributivist instrumentalism. But if we are inquiring into the possible or actual subtypes of retributivism, then what we call retributivist instrumentalism in the first discursive context becomes instrumentalist retributivism in this second. (Compare: as an American, Malcolm X was notable for being a Muslim American; on the hajj, he was more likely seen as an American Muslim.)

all. This latter position would be, in essence, to agree with Dolinko, but from the other side of the aisle. I have already provided reason to deny that, if there is a viable or vibrant form of non-instrumentalist retributivism, it alone is entitled to the label retributivism: many persons who would self-identify either as retributivist or non-retributivist seem to believe that acceptance or denial of the retributivist intrinsic good claim is of central importance to proper classification of their views, and retributivist instrumentalism supplies tailored justification in a fashion that other forms of instrumentalism do not. Therefore, I will suppose that non-instrumentalist retributivists need not deny either: (1) that instrumentalists about punishment differ on the question of whether the suffering of a wrongdoer is an intrinsic good; or (2) that they share something important in common with those who answer that question in the affirmative; but rather that they need insist only (3) that they make use of the claim that wrongdoers deserve to suffer, or to be punished, in a way that is not reducible to any form of pluralistic instrumentalism.

The claim that all contemporary retributivists and instrumentalists share the same structure of justificatory argument, and differ only on (likely irresolvable) views about what states of affairs do or do not have intrinsic value, should elicit scepticism. As one commentator observed in a different context: 'In any important debate, whenever one side declares "We are all x now," it is a pretty safe bet that the debate has taken a wrong turn—or that someone is trying to pull a fast one.'[32] So we ought to expect that a genuine and plausible non-instrumentalist retributivism can be articulated (whether or not it can ultimately withstand critical scrutiny). But the nature of this non-instrumentalist retributivism is more elusive than is its instrumentalist sibling. This final section, accordingly, canvasses a variety of ways that a retributivist might possibly escape the reduction of his or her view to instrumentalist retributivism. My goal will not be to reach a verdict on non-instrumentalist retributivism but to identify the range of avenues open to approaches of this sort and to offer at least a modicum of critical analysis—trying to show which avenues are more or less promising and why. Very simply, it is clear that at least some theorists of a retributivist bent will resist equating the desert claim with the intrinsic good claim, but it is not yet entirely clear what are the best grounds for blocking that translation. The remainder of this chapter aims to make a start—but only a start—at examining that question. To emphasize: we are not looking now for just any alternative to instrumentalist justifications for punishment, but for an alternative that is recognizably retributivist in bearing a sufficiently intimate relationship to the notion of an offender's ill-desert.[33] Non-instrumentalist justificatory accounts more properly described, for example, as expressive or aretaic would not fit the bill.

[32] G Bassham, 'Justice Scalia's Equitable Constitution' (2006) 33 *Journal of College and University Law* 143, 154.
[33] To be sure, this is to accept that ill-desert is somehow constitutive of retributivism. This is a contestable proposition, but not widely contested in fact and therefore something we should not abandon without good reason.

To preview: this section identifies four reasonably familiar accounts of the features of a putatively retributivist justification of punishment that would serve to distinguish it from a retributivist instrumentalism (ie from an instrumentalist retributivism). To a first approximation, these are the claims that non-instrumentalist retributivism is distinctive in:

(1) precluding punishment of the innocent;
(2) conceiving of punishment as a dictate of justice;
(3) providing that we have a duty or obligation to punish wrongdoers, and not merely that such punishment is permissible or justified; and
(4) denying that the rightness of punishment is reducible to any claims about the good or the valuable.

I will argue (admittedly, in a fairly conclusory way) that the first of these three candidate grounds for marking a genuinely non-instrumentalist retributivism is not tenable, and that the second and third are unpromising. I will then conclude that the fourth is the most promising of these proposed routes. Because it is beyond the scope of this chapter to reach a verdict on just how plausible that route is, let alone whether it is correct, this section rests with raising some difficulties for this approach and offers some thoughts about its prospects. The most original and important contribution of this section will be the claim that the difference between an instrumentalist and a non-instrumentalist retributivism is most perspicuously reduced simply to a matter that we have already touched briefly upon: how best to specify the retributivist desert claim.

4.1 Negative retributivism

Recall the frequent retributivist claim that an offender's desert furnishes both a necessary and sufficient justification for punishment. We have seen that if the desert claim is translated, by steps, into the intrinsic good claim, then the sufficiency condition does not seem maintainable. Let us now consider the necessity condition. One proposal is that non-instrumentalist retributivism is distinct from any form of instrumentalism (including retributivist instrumentalism) not because of what justifies punishment, but by what limits it.[34] Instrumentalist theories license punishment in the absence, or in excess, of an offender's desert; non-instrumentalist retributivism would bar this.

Before assessing this 'necessary condition' claim, we should note that it is more modest than might first appear. The claim is neither that an instance of punishment is necessarily unjust if it inflicts undeserved suffering despite the punisher's genuine

---

[34] This understanding of retributivism was identified and rightly criticized in Cottingham, 'Varieties of Retribution', 240–1, but it still pops up from time to time.

belief that the punishment is deserved, nor that a punishment practice or institution is unjust if it foreseeably results in undeserved punishment. The necessity condition maintains only that it is unjust to inflict punishment on someone known (or believed) not to deserve the suffering imposed. Even thus reframed, however, the retributivist claim that the infliction of deserved suffering is a necessary condition of just punishment puts retributivism at potential odds with instrumentalist justifications for punishment as the retributivist sufficiency condition did not, for full-blooded consequentialists (about morality) might be thought compelled to reject the necessity claim even in this qualified form.

This is demonstrably not a plausible basis for marking out non-instrumentalist retributivism. Not only *can* instrumentalists accept that the ill-desert of an individual supplies a necessary condition on the morally permissible imposition of punishment, but many do.

Instrumentalist movement toward acceptance of retributivism's necessity condition is customarily traced to the mixed theories Rawls and Hart advanced half a century ago. In Rawls's rule-utilitarian picture, legislators justify criminal justice institutions and practices on consequentialist grounds, while judges justify the punishment of individual offenders on the non-consequential ground that he or she violated a legal command.[35] Similarly, Hart described the 'general justifying aim' of the institution of punishment as crime reduction, but argued that pursuit of this consequentialist goal is constrained by a principle of 'retribution in distribution' that permits imposition of punishment only on 'an offender for an offence'.[36]

Notoriously, however, one can violate the terms of an offence without being morally blameworthy and therefore without incurring moral ill-desert. And neither Rawls nor Hart clearly insisted that justice demands that punishment not be imposed on someone known not to deserve the suffering imposed[37]—a moral view that John Mackie would soon dub 'negative' retributivism,[38] and that Antony Duff would call, perhaps even more aptly, 'side-constrained consequentialism'.[39] Today, instrumentalists about punishment have gone beyond Rawls and Hart to routinely accept that it is impermissible to knowingly punish the innocent, and that even unknowing punishment of the innocent is a very considerable bad. (I do not claim

---

[35] J Rawls, 'Two Concepts of Rules' (1955) 64 *Philosophical Review* 3.

[36] Hart, *Punishment and Responsibility*, 8–12.

[37] I say that neither 'clearly' insisted upon this because Hart's signals on this particular score are famously ambiguous. Although he often defended the principle of 'retribution in distribution' on the grounds that it supplied people with the seemingly welfarist benefits of living under a 'choosing system', he also described it in terms of 'justice' and 'fairness' that seem, in context, non-utilitarian. Particularly compare, in ibid, ch 2 'Legal Responsibility and Excuses' with ch 3 'Murder and the Principles of Punishment: England and the United States'.

[38] JL Mackie, 'Morality and the Retributive Emotions' (1982) 1 *Criminal Justice Ethics* 3, 3.

[39] Duff, *Punishment, Communication, and Community*, 11. The *locus classicus* of the notion of side-constraints on consequentialism is, of course, R Nozick, *Anarchy, State and Utopia* (New York: Basic Books, 1974) 28–35.

that such acceptance is somehow compelled, but only that it is widespread.) I will call an instrumentalist theory that is limited in this way 'desert-constrained instrumentalism' to highlight clearly the nature of the side-constraint—namely, knowingly punishing in the absence, or in excess, of ill-desert.

How could an instrumentalist adopt such a view? In at least two ways. First, as several moral philosophers have recently argued, putatively deontic side constraints might be accommodated within a full-blooded consequentialist ethics by the recognition of agent-relative value.[40] I am myself somewhat sceptical of this line of argument, but this cannot be the place for a critical evaluation. Suffice to say that the possibility cannot be ruled out.

Much more significantly, instrumentalists about punishment need not be full-blooded consequentialists. That, of course, is the very point of renaming as 'instrumentalist' what had been deceptively captioned 'consequentialist' justifications for punishment.[41] Because instrumentalists about punishments need not be consequentialists about ethics, they confront no contradiction in contending that punishment is justified by the goods that the practice produces (including, for retributivist instrumentalists, the good of meting out deserved suffering) but only so long as we do not punish persons believed to lack personal ill-desert.

4.2 Retributive justice

A second possible route to non-instrumentalist retributivism starts with the observation that retributivism is routinely described as a theory of justice: it maintains that justice demands that offenders be given their ill-deserts. As Michael Moore put it in a much-quoted passage, the desert of the offender:

gives society more than merely a *right* to punish culpable offenders... For a retributivist, the moral responsibility of an offender also gives society the *duty* to punish. Retributivism, in other words, is truly a theory of justice such that, if it is true, we have an obligation to set up institutions so that retribution is achieved.[42]

Call this *the retributive justice claim*. It is not equivalent, so the argument must go, to the retributivist instrumentalist's claim that the state of affairs in which an offender suffers on account of and in proportion to his blameworthy wrongdoing is an intrinsic good that the state has moral reason to bring about.

---

[40] Recent defences of this view include Smith, 'Two Kinds of Consequentialism'; DW Portmore, 'Consequentializing' (2009) 4 *Philosophy Compass* 329; M Peterson, 'A Royal Road to Consequentialism' [2009] *Ethical Theory and Moral Practice*. For a criticism, see M Schroeder, 'Teleology, Agent-Relative Value, and "Good"' (2007) 117 *Ethics* 265.

[41] This is a central theme of V Tadros, *The Moral Foundations of Criminal Law* (forthcoming).

[42] MS Moore, 'The Moral Worth of Retribution', in FD Schoeman (ed), *Responsibility, Character, and the Emotions* (Cambridge: Cambridge University Press, 1987), 179, 182.

Exactly how characterizing retributivism as a theory of justice paves the way toward non- instrumentalist retributivism is not at all clear. The proponent of such a contention must first explain what it means for a moral norm to be a norm *of justice*. Plainly, norms of justice are not categorically more stringent than other moral norms. The moral prohibition on killing innocent non-aggressors is stringent indeed, yet it is rarely if ever characterized as an obligation of justice.

On one common view, norms of justice are those moral norms that possess a certain sort of public or political character, justice being 'the first virtue of social institutions', in Rawls's language.[43] This is to put things very vaguely, but whatever its details, this understanding of justice is unlikely to help distinguish non-instrumentalist retributivism from competing accounts, for criminal punishment is public or political no matter what its justifications. Another widespread conception distinguishes norms of justice from other moral norms, not in virtue of their strength or their political character, but only in terms of their subject matter. It is sometimes said, for example, that justice—generally, and not only its distributive form—is the name for moral norms concerned with the allocation of benefits and burdens. I do not know if this is so. But if something like this is true, then invocation of retributive justice would again not seem, by itself, to provide grounds for a distinct non-instrumentalist justification for punishment. If there *is* a non-instrumentalist retributivism then it might very well be a justification for punishment properly classed as a dictate of justice—as, possibly, instrumentalist justifications of punishment (including retributivist instrumentalism) are not. But the justice label is not itself doing the work. What will do the work is whatever it is that makes the non-instrumentalist retributivism true.

4.3 The duty to punish

Consider, again, the passage just quoted from Moore. We took the idea that non-instrumentalist retributivism might be distinctive in virtue of its being a dictate of *justice* from the third sentence. But the first two suggest a different idea, and one with somewhat greater promise: non-instrumentalist retributivism might be distinguishable from its instrumentalist sibling on the grounds that the former, but not the latter, maintains that satisfaction of the offender's ill-desert grounds a duty to punish, and not merely that it renders punishment morally justifiable.[44]

The contention that we have an *absolute* obligation to punish offenders, or to seek to realize deserved suffering, is often attributed to Kant. But regardless of whether Kant did in fact espouse such a view—and the frequently voiced contention that

---

[43] J Rawls, *A Theory of Justice* (rev edn; Cambridge, MA: Harvard University Press, 1999), 3.

[44] For discussion of retributivist views that emphasize the duty to punish see Cahill, 'Retributive Justice in the Real World', 815, 825, 826–9.

he did is disputed—I am aware of no contemporary philosopher or criminal law theorist who advances such an extreme position. Accordingly, a far more plausible construal of the deontic duty claim holds that we have a pro tanto obligation to realize the wrongdoer's ill-desert. The questions, then, are whether many contemporary retributivists endorse such a claim, and in a manner that instrumentalists cannot endorse as well. Let's consider two possible ways to cash out the retributivist duty claim: in terms of protected reasons and in terms of agent-relativity.

As a pluralist, the retributivist instrumentalist will recognize various types of intrinsic goods and bads, many of which have the potential, singly or in combination, to direct that the state ought not to punish notwithstanding the good that such punishment would realize in the coin of deserved suffering. Retributivists who believe we have a duty to punish might believe that some types of reasons, no matter their weight, are simply of the wrong sort to enter into the moral calculus as reasons against the doing of justice. In the Razian vocabulary, our supposed duty to punish might reflect a 'protected reason' to punish (supposed) wrongdoers, which is to say that it is a consideration that both serves as a first-order reason to punish (in fact, a first-order reason of substantial weight) and has the second-order function of excluding from consideration some (but not all) of what would otherwise be sound first-order reasons not to punish.[45] I imagine this is possible, but it does not appear a particularly promising route to non-instrumentalist retributivism, for it is not at all apparent why instrumentalists must find recourse to protected reasons uncongenial.

Consider, then, a second possible way to make sense of the retributivist duty claim—in terms of agent-relativity. Imagine this proposal from Cruel Dictator to Just Republic: 'if you impose punishment of type and magnitude n (call such punishment "Pn") on Non-Wrongdoer1 (call him "NW1"), whom you and I know to be innocent, then I will refrain from imposing Pn on NW2 and on NW3, both of whom we know to be innocent.' May Just Republic accept this proposal, thereby inflicting Pn on NW1? Presumably no. That's why 'negative retributivism' seems to capture a genuine deontic duty (even if defeasible at a threshold, and subject to the possibility, already mentioned, that such duties can be consequentialized).

Is there a similar case to be made for an agent-relative duty to punish? Consider now this proposal from Benevolent Monarch to Just Republic: 'if you refrain from imposing Pn on Wrongdoer1 ("W1"), whom you and I know to be guilty, then I will impose Pn on W2 and W3, both of whom we know to be guilty.' (Testimony or evidence from W1 is needed to secure a conviction of W2 and W3.) May Just Republic accept this proposal, thereby not inflicting Pn on W1? If the state were under an agent-relative duty *to* punish that roughly mirrored its agent-relative duty *not* to punish (ie if there were a side-constraint on *not* punishing comparable to the side-constraint many people

[45] On protected reasons, see J Raz, *Practical Reasons and Norms* (Oxford: Oxford University Press, 1999), 191.

believe applies to punishing), then the answer must be no. My guess, though, is that a great many theorists who self-identify as retributivists—even those would resist being characterized as retributivist instrumentalists—would say yes. If so, that shows that they do not recognize an agent-relative duty to punish wrongdoers. To be clear, this is not an argument that the contention that we have a duty to punish wrongdoers, if sound, would not constitute a non-instrumentalist retributivism. Nor is it an argument that such a contention cannot in fact be maintained: readers who respond to this hypothetical case differently than I anticipate should indeed endeavour to develop the supporting arguments. I mean only to cast doubt that this is the most promising route for would-be non-instrumentalist retributivists to pursue.[46]

4.4 The rightness of punishing

If that is so, we come to this alternative: non-instrumentalist retributivism might be best constituted not in terms of the state's duty to punish but rather in terms of the rightness of its doing so, where 'rightness' can be understood in terms of kindred notions like 'oughtness' and, yet more commonly these days, reasons. More particularly, non-instrumentalist retributivists might wish to argue that punishment is justified because doing so is right—something we have reason, or ought, to do—and where its rightness is not derivative of its being valuable. Of course, instrumentalist retributivists may also justify punishment as 'right'. They would say that it is right because (and insofar as) it promotes the good. So this path toward a truly non-instrumentalist retributivism depends not on the supposed rightness of punishment but on the claim that its rightness does not derive from its being valuable.

How could punishment be right but not because it is valuable? One possibility is that punishment is right and not valuable. This seems unpromising, and not only because, in the estimation of one commentator, '[t]o be a retributivist is to recognize that deserved punishment is an intrinsic good'.[47] Although there may be some actions that are right yet wholly without value,[48] surely those are by far the exception. More promising is the claim that, although punishment is valuable in addition to being right, the value of punishment is not what makes it right. It could be, for example, that the good is defined in terms of the right—that that which is valuable

---

[46] Moreover, and again, the agent-relative construal of the retributive duty claim is arguably consequentializable, thus amenable to an instrumentalist justification for punishment, if there exists agent-relative value.

[47] L Zaibert, *Punishment and Retribution* (Aldershot: Ashgate, 2006), 214.

[48] As Jonathan Dancy explains, 'An action can be one's duty even though doing it has no value and its being done generates nothing of value. Standard examples here are of trivial duties.' J Dancy, 'Should We Pass the Buck?', in A O'Hear (ed), *Philosophy, The Good, The True and The Beautiful* (Cambridge: Cambridge University Press, 2000), 159, 168. Presumably if this is true of duty, the same would hold true, a fortiori, of what is right.

has value in virtue of our having reasons of certain sorts with respect to it. Or perhaps reasons and values can have the same ground without either being derived from the other. There are other possibilities too.[49]

Perhaps this is the route for non-instrumentalist retributivists to take. But they confront this challenge: to explain the ground of the right in a way that is properly linked to the notion of an offender's ill-desert. How can it be, if what a wrongdoer deserves is to suffer, that the rightness of engaging in actions designed to bring such suffering about does not derive from the goodness of his suffering?

The answer to this challenge, I think, is this: non-instrumentalist retributivists who would justify punishment as right but not because of its instrumental value must deny that what a wrongdoer deserves is to suffer. Recall that we accepted as constitutive of retributivism what we called the *desert claim*: punishment is justified by the offender's ill-desert. What led us to retributivist instrumentalism was our (provisional) endorsement of a particular specification of this desert claim that we termed the *desert-s claim*: wrongdoers deserve to suffer (ie to endure some negative experiential state) on account of, and in proportion to, their blameworthy wrongdoing. Non-instrumentalist retributivists must reject that specification of the desert claim.[50] In particular, they must articulate and defend a competing specification of the wrongdoers' desert object that is not expressible without reference to actions by a responsive agent. The most obvious possibility is for them to return, despite the worry that provoked Lawrence Davis to endorse the *desert-s claim* nearly 40 years ago, to the claim (the *desert-p claim*) that what wrongdoers deserve is to be punished. But this is not their only option. Equally non-instrumentalist is Duff's claim (the *desert-c claim*) that what they deserve is to be censured.[51] In principle, there exist any number of other possibilities[52]—just as the *desert-s claim* may not be the only specification available to instrumentalist retributivists. The critical point is that a choice needs to be made between the possibilities that what wrongdoers deserve is a response of some kind from the group (be it the community or the state), or that what they deserve is a state of affairs that is itself describable without reference to any human agency that may or may not be charged with causing that state of

---

[49] These and other possibilities are trenchantly explored in Dancy, which challenges the first possibility on offer (the 'buck-passing' view). The buck-passing view is also criticized in W Rabinowicz and T Rønnow-Rasmussen, 'The Strike of the Demon: On Fitting Pro-attitudes and Value' (2004) 114 *Ethics* 391.

[50] Indeed, some are starting to do precisely that—in forthcoming articles that I became aware of as this volume was nearing publication. See D Markel and C Flanders, 'Bentham on Stilts: The Bare Relevance of Subjectivity to Retributive Justice' (2010) 98 *California Law Review* (forthcoming); DC Gray, 'Punishment as Suffering' (2010) 64 *Vanderbilt Law Review* (forthcoming). Although 'Bentham on Stilts' argues, not merely that the *desert-s claim* is false, but also that it is foreign to retributivism as such, Markel has told me in personal communication that he no longer believes that latter claim.

[51] Eg Duff, *Punishment, Communication, and Community*, 27–30.

[52] Eg David Enoch and Larry Sager have combined to suggest to me a possibility that approximates, but may improve upon, *desert-p*: wrongdoers deserve to be made to suffer by, or under the aegis of, the sovereign.

Table 19.1 Sample specifications of the retributivist desert object

Specification of the desert object	Equivalent formulations (to a first approximation)	Instrumentalist or non-instrumentalist
Wrongdoers deserve to suffer	It is intrinsically good that wrongdoers suffer	Instrumentalist
Wrongdoers deserve to be punished	It is right that wrongdoers are punished; we ought to punish wrongdoers	Non-instrumentalist
Wrongdoers deserve to be censured	It is right that wrongdoers are censured; we ought to censure wrongdoers	Non-instrumentalist

affairs to obtain. The question that divides non-instrumentalist from instrumentalist retributivism, on this view, is the answer each gives to the question of whether the retributivist desert object is response-dependent or response-independent.[53]

Put another way, Husak might have been too quick in asserting that: 'retributive beliefs only require that culpable wrongdoers be given their just deserts by being made to suffer (or to receive a hardship or deprivation). These beliefs do not require that culpable wrongdoers be given their just deserts by being made to suffer by the state through the imposition of punishment.'[54] It might be that some retributive beliefs *do* require not merely that wrongdoers experience some state of affairs, but that they be met with some specific sort of *response*. In short, the battle between the two kinds of retributivism—instrumentalist and non-instrumentalist—is best fought out in the space of specifying the wrongdoers' supposed desert object. Specification of the desert claim is not a sideshow. It is the whole game, for the best way to establish that the rightness of punishing wrongdoers is not derivative of the goods that punishment produces might be just to articulate and defend a conception of an offender's desert object in relational or 'responsive' terms. (This is reflected in Table 19.1.)

4.5 Contingent and conceptual instrumentalism

I would now like to pursue this idea from one other direction. Several theorists with retributive sympathies who have acknowledged the plausibility of recasting

---

[53] Although Feinberg did not offer a pithy label for what I am calling the 'desert object', he did consistently refer to the 'modes [or kinds] of treatment' that people could deserve. Were it constitutive of desert objects that they must be modes of *treatment*, then instrumentalist retributivism would be doomed from the outset. Although Feinberg's own language seems to assume that is so, he provides no argument for it and I am aware of none.

[54] Husak, 'Retribution in Criminal Theory', 972.

retributivism in instrumentalist terms have nonetheless sought to resist what might appear to be the marginalization of retributivism as a distinct punishment theory by proposing that retributivist instrumentalism invokes a very different type of consequence than does non-retributivist instrumentalism. George Fletcher pursued this line of argument when distinguishing between 'factually' and 'conceptually' consequentialist theories.[55] Others may prefer to speak of 'contingent' and 'intrinsic' consequentialism. As Leo Zaibert summarizes:

Not all consequences of a given action are of the same *kind,* and the consequences the retributivist cares about could be seen as different from the consequences which the consequentialist cares about. The consequences that retributivists care about are all *intrinsic* (or inherent, necessary, etc.) to the very act of punishment, whereas the consequences that consequentialists care about are *extrinsic* (or external, contingent, and so on) to the very act of punishment. In other words, both retributivism and consequentialism are consequentialist theories, in a broad sense of 'consequence'. The way in which retributivism relates to those consequences of punishment that it deems important is a special way: the relation is one of logical necessity. If punishment is justified for the retributivist, it is justified *eo ipso,* necessarily at the very moment in which it is inflicted.[56]

Theorists who pursue this line for distinguishing retributivism from instrumentalism appear to concede (at least *arguendo*) that all theorists who would justify punishment do so by reference to its consequences. They contend that the important question is whether the consequences that do the justificatory work are caused by punishment contingently or as a matter of the logic of the concept. This is not the distinction I am proposing, but close enough to invite comment on why it isn't.

Take a retributivist who embraces the *desert-s claim.* By choosing this specification of the retributivist desert object, she is, in my terms, an instrumentalist retributivist. If what I call non-instrumentalist retributivism were equivalent to what others might be disposed to characterize as the retributivist subtype of 'intrinsic' (or 'conceptual') consequentialism,[57] then insofar as a justification of punishment relies upon desert-s, it would be, to that extent, contingently consequentialist, not intrinsically so. But whether acceptance of the *desert-s claim* underwrites a contingently consequentialist justification for punishment is not clear: it depends on what we consider 'the very act of punishment'.

If punishment is *defined* (to a first approximation) as *the infliction* of suffering on (actual or supposed) wrongdoers in response to their (actual or supposed) offence, then the wrongdoer's suffering is an intrinsic consequence of each act of punishment. In contrast, if punishment is defined, say, as a variety of forms of conduct *designed* or *intended* to be burdensome, then whether such acts do in fact cause suffering is a contingent question. Of course, these are far from the only definitional

---

[55] GP Fletcher, 'Punishment and Responsibility', in D Patterson (ed), *The Blackwell Companion to The Philosophy of Law and Legal Theory* (Oxford: Blackwell, 1996), 514, 516.

[56] Zaibert, *Punishment and Retribution*, 133. See also Christopher, 'Deterring Retributivism'.

[57] I am assuming that intrinsic consequentialism encompasses theories that are not retributivist.

possibilities. The important point, though, is that whether a retributivist account that would justify punishment by (in significant part) its tendency to bring about the state of deserved suffering belongs to contingent or intrinsic consequentialism all depends on how we define punishment. But that is just to lead us back into the definitional debates that once occupied the field and that most philosophers of the criminal law, I submit, are very pleased we have escaped.

We do not, I think, want to have our best understanding of different justifications of punishment—here, whether a particular justificatory account belongs to contingent or intrinsic consequentialism—depend upon more precise and contestable specifications of what punishment is. What we may want, though, is for them to depend on competing specifications of what wrongdoers deserve. If the desert object is response-dependent, then punishment (of some form) is itself what wrongdoers deserve. Retributivists of a non-instrumentalist bent who were attracted to the distinction between intrinsic and contingent consequences might, then, have things close to backwards. We should not ask whether the desert object (that which, for retributivists, punishment is designed to achieve or bring about) is an 'intrinsic consequence' of punishment, but whether a punitive response is an intrinsic feature of the desert object.

5 CONCLUSION

For several generations now, philosophers of the criminal law have routinely divided the potentially messy universe of justificatory accounts of criminal punishment into just two broad classes: retributivist and consequentialist—classes that are I have chosen to render as retributivist and *instrumentalist* to highlight that adherents of this latter position need not endorse consequentialism as a comprehensive moral theory. Broadly speaking, retributivists have contended that punishment is justified by the fact that an offender deserves it. Instrumentalists argue that punishment is justified by the net good consequences that the practice produces, paradigmatically but not necessarily exclusively, in terms of deterring anti-social aggression.

But what is the 'it' that, on the retributivist account, wrongdoers deserve? One answer—possibly the most common—is that they deserve to suffer. If this is so, then it seems natural to refashion the retributive desert claim into the claim that it is intrinsically valuable that wrongdoers suffer on account of their blameworthy wrongdoing. This latter claim is said by some retributivists to be equivalent to the desert claim but somewhat less mysterious and therefore more plausible to the uncommitted. But the retributive embrace of the intrinsic good claim seems to make retributivism amenable to an instrumentalist structure of justification. Suddenly, retributivism looks like a type of instrumentalism, not a competitor.

Those who would resist this conclusion have two moves open to them. First, they could deny that retributivist instrumentalism deserves the retributivist label at all. I have argued that this is too dogmatic. The claim on which this account rests—namely, that it is intrinsically valuable for a wrongdoer to suffer—is recognizably within a family of classically retributivist ideas. The second avenue, then, is to explicate a distinct alternative retributivism not similarly amenable to instrumentalist justification. Success in this pursuit would leave us with two kinds of retributivism, not one.

How best can a non-instrumentalist retributivism be vindicated? Retributivists who would resist instrumentalism have been tempted down many paths, including those that emphasize: their commitment to the impermissibility of punishing those believed not to be wrongdoers; retributivism's supposed status as a form of justice; and the inability of instrumentalist justifications to make sense of our supposed duty to punish. I have offered reasons to think that none of these paths holds great promise, and that the most promising route is what many readers are likely to have thought most obvious in the first place: to make use of the proposition that it is right for us to punish wrongdoers—in the sense that we ought to do so, or have moral reason to do so—on grounds not derived from the value of punishing them or the value of states of affairs caused by our punishing them. But just how to defend a view of this sort that makes it appear as more than *ipse dixit* remains the great retributivist challenge. I have argued that the debate between what are now two kinds of retributivism might be most perspicuously reformulated as a debate over just what it is that wrongdoers deserve. If this is correct, then efforts to articulate and defend different specifications of wrongdoers' desert object—precisely what it is that they deserve in virtue of their wrongdoing—will repay careful philosophical attention.

PART IV

ACROSS BORDERS AND INTO THE FUTURE

20

PIERCING SOVEREIGNTY: A RATIONALE FOR INTERNATIONAL JURISDICTION OVER CRIMES THAT DO NOT CROSS INTERNATIONAL BORDERS*

CHRISTOPHER HEATH
WELLMAN

* I am extremely grateful to Antony Duff, Stuart Green and Ekow Yankah for their extensive feedback on an earlier draft of this chapter, which draws upon my article, 'Rights and State Punishment', (2009) 106 *The Journal of Philosophy* 419–39 and ch 4 of my book (co-authored with Andrew Altman) *A Liberal Theory of International Justice* (Oxford: Oxford University Press, 2009).

THE establishment of the Rome Statute of the International Criminal Court (ICC), the first permanent international criminal court designed to help end the global culture of impunity, has rightly been welcomed as a landmark achievement. But while the creation of a court to prosecute those accused of genocide, crimes against humanity, war crimes, and aggression should be hailed as an enormous political accomplishment, it has also exposed a glaring theoretical lacuna. Put simply, the construction of international criminal law in general, and the ICC in particular, has revealed that philosophers of law, international lawyers, and political theorists have yet to provide anything like a satisfactory moral justification for a supranational legal system with the power and moral authority to pierce the sovereignty of existing states. What is more, the theoretical gaps are not restricted to issues of international relations; problems also arise for lack of clear and compelling answers to the fundamental questions regarding the morality of punishment. Thus, in this chapter I invoke a rights forfeiture justification for punishment in order to build a compelling defence of state punishment, which, in turn, will pave the way toward a theoretically sound and practically informative rationale for international jurisdiction over crimes that do not cross international borders. If successful, this theory would not only furnish a much-needed moral justification for international criminal law, it would provide guidance to political leaders and international lawyers as they continue to develop and expand the ICC.

1 RIGHTS, PUNISHMENT, AND STATE SOVEREIGNTY

International criminal law is a remedial measure in the sense that it would be neither necessary nor justified if every state satisfactorily enforced criminal law within its jurisdiction. Given that so many existing countries are either unable or unwilling to effectively prosecute and punish criminals domestically, however, international institutions are needed to ensure both that horrendously guilty individuals are punished and that fewer human rights atrocities will occur in the future. There are obvious practical obstacles to accomplishing these daunting tasks, but the principal *normative* challenge for international criminal law is state sovereignty. In particular, if states enjoy exclusive dominion over the criminal law within their own territories, how can external parties permissibly pierce this sovereign sphere? Perhaps state sovereignty would create no insuperable challenge if the international community sought to punish only those guilty of border-crossing transgressions (such as political and military leaders who plan and wage an aggressive war), but many of the worst crimes (including genocide and so-called 'crimes against humanity') can occur among fellow citizens in their own country. What gives the international community the standing to prosecute and punish one Rwandan for a crime against a second Rwandan on Rwandan soil, for example? If there were no foreign victims to this particular crime, what gives an external body the right to preside over criminal proceedings? Providing a systematic and theoretically informed answer to this question requires that we first determine what gives each state its right to monopolistic control over the punitive process. We cannot explain a legitimate state's moral dominion over criminal law, however, without first justifying the imposition of hard treatment which punishment, by definition, entails. With this in mind, I begin by briefly explaining my attraction to the rights forfeiture theory of punishment.

Traditionally, those who work on the morality of punishment have focused on finding a general justifying aim, but I believe that justifying state punishment requires one to show that it violates no moral rights. All of us typically have rights not to be imprisoned, for instance, so why is the duly convicted criminal's right not violated when she is incarcerated? One obvious response is that the hard treatment of punishment violates no rights when the person punished has voluntarily acted in some way so as to *forfeit* her rights. As WD Ross puts it:

the offender, by violating the life or liberty or property of another, has lost his own right to have his life, liberty, or property respected, so that the state has no *prima facie* duty to spare him, as it has a *prima facie* duty to spare the innocent. It is morally at liberty to injure him as he has injured others, or to inflict any lesser injury on him, or to spare him, exactly as consideration both of the good of the community and of his own good requires. If, on the other hand, a man has respected the rights of others, there is a strong and distinctive objection to the state's inflicting any penalty on him with a view to the good of the community or even to his own good.[1]

With one important qualification (to be highlighted below), Ross's analysis strikes me as accurate, so I would suggest that a state does not violate the rights of duly convicted criminals as long as it neither punishes the innocent nor over-punishes the guilty.

It should be noted, though, that the vast majority of theorists who work on punishment do not share my attraction to the rights forfeiture account.[2] One prominent concern is that of specification. As RA Duff comments, 'it is unclear how we are to determine which rights are forfeited or suspended, or for how long'.[3] David Boonin presses this point by asking us to imagine that Larry kidnaps Moe for three

---

[1] WD Ross, *The Right and the Good* (Oxford: Oxford University Press, 1930), 60–1.
[2] The standard concerns with this approach are outlined by RL Lippke, 'Criminal Offenders and Right Forfeiture' (2001) 32 *Journal of Social Philosophy* 78–89 and by David Boonin, *The Problem of Punishment* (Cambridge: Cambridge University Press, 2008), 104–19.
[3] RA Duff, *Punishment, Communication, and Community* (Oxford: Oxford University Press, 2001), 15.

days.[4] Rights forfeiture theorists will allege that Larry thereby forfeits his right not to be incarcerated, but we may now wonder whether Larry forfeits this right permanently or only temporarily. Presumably Larry has not forfeited his right permanently, because a sentence of life in prison without the possibility of parole clearly seems excessive. But if Larry has forfeited his right only temporarily, for how long may he permissibly be incarcerated? The only non-arbitrary answer appears to be 'three days', but it seems implausible to insist that Larry's rights would be violated if he were imprisoned for more than three days for kidnapping Moe. Boonin thus concludes that, whether the rights forfeiture theorist imagines that criminals forfeit their rights permanently or only temporarily, this approach generates unpalatable implications.

In response, I concede that it seems implausible to suppose that Larry forfeits his right against imprisonment permanently or that he forfeits it for only three days; Boonin is right to reject the former as excessive and the latter as too lenient. But why think that these are the only two alternatives? Boonin may be correct that these two options are the most *salient*, but there is no reason to insist that the rights forfeiture view must be understood in such a strictly formulaic fashion. To appreciate this point, notice that, while some retributivists endorse the *lex talionis* principle, most shy away from insisting upon an eye for an eye. More typically, retributivists merely allege that duly convicted criminals deserve a 'fitting', 'appropriate', or 'proportional' punishment, where it is not necessarily self-evident precisely what a fitting, appropriate, or proportional punishment would be in any given case. Given this, why cannot a rights forfeiture theorist similarly claim that criminals forfeit rights in proportion to the gravity of their crimes? Just like a retributivist, the rights forfeiture theorist may not be able to specify precisely which right Larry has forfeited for kidnapping Moe. She may be able to do no better than to cite an (admittedly imprecise) *range* of punishments which would not obviously violate Larry's rights (and presumably this range would include much more than three days but much less than permanent incarceration). The rights forfeiture theorist's lack of an algorithm is admittedly inconvenient, but, just as we do not reject retributivism for its lack of specification on this count, neither should we abandon rights forfeiture theory just because its advocates are unwilling to commit to the most salient formula and the implausible conclusions it would entail.

Another popular worry about rights forfeiture theory (which Richard Lippke labels the problem of 'indeterminate authorization') is that it does not explain why only the state may permissibly punish wrongdoers.[5] The concern here is that if a criminal forfeits her rights, then presumably anyone—not just the state—may permissibly punish her. But if so, then this view opens the door to vigilantism.

---

[4] Boonin, *The Problem of Punishment*, 113.
[5] Lippke, 'Criminal Offenders and Right Forfeiture', 79.

In response, I acknowledge that rights forfeiture theory does not antecedently rule out the permissibility of vigilantism, but I regard this as a *virtue*, rather than a defect, of this approach. As I understand the literature, a central and enduring question of political philosophy is whether the state enjoys a monopoly on the permissible use of punishment. (This was the subject of the first part of Robert Nozick's landmark book, *Anarchy, State and Utopia*, after all.[6]) Thus, given that the permissibility of vigilantism is none other than the fundamental debate between anarchism and statism, we should be suspicious of any theory of punishment which antecedently ruled out anarchism. Of course, it is not entirely surprising that philosophers of law (the principal authors of the literature on punishment) would take statism for granted, since the anarchism/statism debate is central to political, not legal, philosophy.[7]

Let me be clear: I do not insist that rights forfeiture theory is correct to leave the door open to vigilantism because I seek to vindicate anarchism. Like most theorists who work in this area, I am a statist, so my more modest suggestion is only that we must not conclude *without argument* that anarchism is incorrect. And notice: this is especially important for our thinking about international criminal law, because the permissibility of supranational institutions of criminal law is directly related to the issue of vigilantism. This is because, if vigilantism is morally prohibited, presumably it is because the state occupies a morally privileged position of dominion over the execution of criminal law within its territory. But if a state is morally entitled to monopolistic control over criminal law, then international institutions would also be prohibited from unilaterally assigning themselves the task of presiding over the prosecution and punishment of potential criminals within this state's territory. To emphasize: states claim dominion against internal and external competitors who might seek to take the criminal law into their own hands. Thus, our concern with international criminal law requires that we study the state's claim vis-à-vis the potential vigilante, because developing an account of the state's right to dominion over criminal law within its territory will put us in a better position to say when and why supranational institutions may unilaterally assign themselves jurisdiction.

With this in mind, consider again Ross's claim that 'the offender, by violating the life or liberty or property of another, has lost his own right to have his life, liberty, or property respected, so that the state has no *prima facie* duty to spare him, as it has a *prima facie* duty to spare the innocent'. Our analysis above suggests that, even if Ross is right that a criminal forfeits her right of dominion over her self-regarding affairs and thus may permissibly be punished, we should not merely assume that the *state* should be doing the punishing. Imagine, for instance, that Anna assaults Betty. If rights forfeiture theory is correct, then presumably Betty may now treat Anna in ways that would have been impermissible before the assault. But it does not follow

---

[6] R Nozick, *Anarchy, State and Utopia* (New York: Basic Books, 1974).

[7] John Simmons makes this observation in 'Locke and the Right to Punish' (1991) 20 *Philosophy & Public Affairs*, at 311.

that some random third party, say, Claire, may permissibly punish Anna. And if Claire may not punish Anna, what gives the state the right to insert itself into a private matter between Anna and Betty? The point here is that, although Anna may not righteously object if Betty punishes her, perhaps Anna retains her dominion over third parties. What is more, even if Anna cannot object to third parties meting out the punishment, perhaps Betty has a right to complain. If anyone occupies an advantaged position over Anna, presumably it is Betty. Perhaps Betty has an exclusive right to punish Anna and, unless Betty freely delegates her authority to someone else, no third party may unilaterally take it upon herself to punish Anna. In brief, even if Ross's rights-based analysis captures the permissibility of *the victim's* imposing the hard treatment of punishment, it does not necessarily justify the state's (or any other third party's) doling out the punishment. Thus, we are faced with a second rights question: why does state punishment not violate the rights of the victim?

One standard response to this question (advanced by Locke, Nozick, and Simmons, among others) is to assert that the state may permissibly punish a criminal because *any* third party is permitted to do so. In terms of the example offered just above, this line of argument suggests that it is not so difficult to explain why the state may punish Anna, because everyone (not just Betty) has the right to punish Anna for assaulting Betty. Thus, in response to the question 'What gives the state the right to punish Anna when Claire may not?', the appropriate response is thought to be 'Nothing sets the state apart from Claire, but this is no problem because Claire also has the right to punish Anna'.

Even if the natural executive right allows everyone (and not merely the victims of the crime in question) to punish criminals, this in itself is not enough to justify state punishment. More specifically, while this move might well justify the *state's punishing*, it does not justify the entire institution of exclusive *state punishment*. The problem, of course, is that positing a general executive right implies only a *competitive* right to punish: everyone has the authority to punish criminals, but no one may rightfully demand that others let her do the punishing instead of them. The basic idea here is that whoever gets to the criminal first may permissibly punish her, and she violates no one else's right (ie she does not violate the victim's exclusive right to punish) when she does so. The problem that remains, however, is that states do not merely claim a *competitive* right to punish; they claim an *exclusive* right. States not only assert the authority to punish if they happen to be the first on the scene, they insist that anyone who arrives before them must refrain from punishing so that the state can do so. Indeed, states claim much more even than this. Not only do they claim the right to be the sole party authorized to mete out the appropriate punishment, they claim the exclusive right to determine what (if any) punishment is deserved. In fact, states understand their dominion in this arena to be so extensive that they claim the right to pardon criminals. In other words, states assert that even if a given criminal has no right not to be punished (indeed, even if this criminal is found *by the state* to have no claim against punishment), all others (including the victim) have a duty not to punish this criminal if the state forgoes prosecution.

It should now be apparent that those who seek to justify state punishment face the following dilemma. The natural executive right can be understood either as a special, exclusive right or as a general, competitive right. Because of the extensive dominion that states claim for themselves, defenders of state punishment might initially be tempted to understand the natural executive right in the first manner. But if the right to punish is a special, exclusive right, presumably it is held by the *victim* rather than some third party, and thus it is unclear how the state could ever permissibly punish a criminal. If we understand the natural right to punish as a general right held by everyone, on the other hand, then we can explain the state's permissibly punishing criminals. But then the state has only a competitive right to punish, which is dramatically less than the unrivalled sovereignty it claims. Either way, we appear unable to justify anything like the institution of state punishment.

This dilemma does not prove that state punishment cannot be justified, of course, but it does show that anyone who seeks to defend the institution of state punishment owes us a story of how the state comes to acquire an exclusive, executive right which initially resides either exclusively with the victim or (more plausibly, I think) generally with each of us. The traditional Lockean answer is that this transfer takes place only in the case of some voluntary transaction, such as a morally valid social contract. This type of retort will not suffice, however, because, as most now acknowledge, there has as a matter of historical fact been no such voluntary transaction between existing states and their constituents. Given the descriptive inaccuracy of the Lockean approach, we must pursue a non-voluntaristic account of how a state can acquire the exclusive right to punish criminals.

My own view is that the best way to justify the state's exclusive dominion over the punitive process is to take stock of the aims of punishment, the importance of these aims, and a state's unparalleled ability to accomplish these aims without imposing unreasonable burdens upon its constituents. Following this approach, let us begin by clarifying why we want to punish criminals. It strikes me that each of six standard theories of punishment (retributivism, deterrence, moral education, expressivism, restitutivism, and social safety valve theory) supplies a different part of a plausible answer to this question. That is, we are interested in punishing criminals because doing so:

(1) serves justice by giving criminals the hard treatment they deserve;
(2) deters everyone from committing crimes;
(3) helps to morally educate both the criminal and society at large;
(4) allows society to express its moral values;
(5) helps restore the victims along with their friends and families; and, finally
(6) provides a controlled, peaceful outlet for socially disruptive emotions.

Thus, although I think that the benefits of deterrence featured in (2) are by far the most significant, each of the traditional theories helps illuminate what we stand to gain from an effective institution of punishment.[8]

With this understanding of the aims of punishment, we are now in a better position to see why we might favour a state monopoly in this arena. If the state is justified in inserting itself, it is because these six aims—particularly deterrence—can be more fully realized with a system of state punishment than if individuals were left to their own devices. The crucial point is that things would deteriorate into a horribly dangerous mess if each individual were personally responsible for punishing those who wronged her. As political theorists like Hobbes, Locke, and Kant have speculated, crime would dramatically increase as would-be criminals capitalized on the greater chances of escaping detection and punishment. Plus, victims who personally mete out the punishment are more likely to punish the innocent and over-punish the guilty. Not only are justice and deterrence better served, it seems clear that aims such as moral education, societal safety-valve, and societal expression of values could scarcely be achieved at all in the absence of a state monopoly on punishment. In short, all six aims stand to be adequately realized only in a system with an authoritative body which makes, enforces, and impartially adjudicates promulgated rules.

If governmental control over the criminal law will allow us better to achieve our six aims of punishment, we have a case for the state's non-consensually taking exclusive control of the punitive process. As it stands, however, this case is incomplete. The mere fact that a state is best able to realize the aims of a process does not automatically give it the right to interfere in people's affairs. That others could do a decidedly better job of tending my garden or decorating my house does not give them the right to push me aside and take over these projects, for instance. Our commitment to my rights in these instances is indicative of our general regard for personal sovereignty; we recognize that each person's moral dominion over her own life gives her the right to manage her affairs even when others might do so better. Thus, we need a special explanation for why the state may non-consensually co-opt the punishment process from various individuals merely because it is better equipped to manage the task. In the absence of such an account, Betty appears just as entitled

---

[8] Not only do I think that deterrence is the most significant aim of punishment, I believe that it alone is necessary and sufficient. To emphasize: I am not suggesting that effective deterrence justifies punishing (even innocent) people; rather, I allege that the state's unrivalled capacity to deter explains its exclusive dominion over the punitive process. Putting this point in terms of human rights, I would say both that (1) if the state's exclusive control over punishment were necessary to secure everyone's human rights, then it could be justified *even if it did not do a particularly good job of realizing the other five aims outlined above*; and that (2) if state sovereignty was either not necessary or not sufficient to secure everyone's human rights, then it could not be justified even if it was necessary and sufficient to adequately realize the other five aims. Still, these other aims are not irrelevant, because they are desirable goods, and thus it buttresses the case for state control over punishment if such dominion helps us realize these additional goods.

to (less-than-optimally) punish Anna as she is to (less-than-optimally) tend her garden and decorate her house.

The special ingredient in the recipe for political legitimacy involves the profound importance of the aims involved: there is a crucial difference between the consequences of my managing my home and garden and the consequences of my imposing my own punishments upon those who (I believe) violate my rights. While there might be others who would do a better job completing the tasks involved in each portion of my life, the realm of punishment is distinguished by the high stakes involved not only for me, but for those around me. If each of us does a less-than-optimal job in most areas of our lives, no great collective harm is done. If we all individually did our less-than-optimal job exacting punishments, on the other hand, the cumulative consequences would be quite grave. To transpose this standard lesson of social contract theory into the parlance of today: people would be imperilled in an environment in which their human rights were unprotected. It is the *gravity* of this particular issue, then, which distinguishes punishment from other matters and helps explain why the individual moral dominion which typically prevails against the expertise of third parties is insufficient in this realm. More precisely, it is not merely the gravity of the consequences, it is also the fact that these consequences are not solely personal. In other words, it is crucial that *others* are imperilled in the absence of a state which satisfactorily secures the crucial aims of a system of punishment.[9]

In the end, then, the reason that a state violates no rights when it non-consensually inserts itself into what might appear to be a private matter between Anna and Betty is because:

(1) unlike Claire, the state is uniquely qualified maximally to realize the aims of punishment;

(2) unlike most matters of personal sovereignty, the aims of punishment are sufficiently important to others to outweigh the premium we rightly place on individual moral dominion; and

(3) the state can satisfactorily realize these crucial aims without imposing unreasonable costs upon its constituents.

It is important to recognize that, even if this account adequately explains why *some* states enjoy an exclusive right to punish criminals, it by no means follows that *all* states have this right simply in virtue of being de facto states. Because my account alleges that states are entitled to a monopoly in this arena because of their unique ability to realize the important aims of punishment, it follows that a state has this right only if it is in fact able and willing adequately to realize these aims. Thus, because failed states are unable, and rogue states are unwilling, to manage

---

[9] In my view, it is also essential that the state provide these vital benefits for everyone without imposing unreasonable burdens upon any of us. Thus, if a state could secure the aims of punishment only if it enslaved all of its constituents (eg) then it would not be justified in doing so.

the institution of punishment in a fashion which satisfactorily secures everyone's human rights, neither of these types of illegitimate states would qualify for the right in question.[10]

2 PIERCING SOVEREIGNTY: THE CASE FOR SUPRANATIONAL INSTITUTIONS

Drawing upon this rights theory of state punishment, we can now see when and why international criminal law may permissibly be imposed. Interestingly, though, this analysis diverges quite considerably from the conventional understanding of international criminal law.

According to the prevailing view, external parties may not prosecute and punish a criminal unless her crime has some sort of border-crossing element. As Mary Robinson, the former United Nations High Commissioner for Human Rights, puts it: 'The principle of universal jurisdiction is based on the notion that certain crimes are so harmful to international interests that states are entitled—and even obliged—to bring proceedings against the perpetrator, regardless of the location of the crime or the nationality of the perpetrator or the victim.'[11] To see the error of this way of thinking, consider the rationale behind a paradigmatic international criminal offence, crimes against humanity.[12] As Robinson's quote indicates, the category of crimes against humanity is regarded as necessary to explain an international party's jurisdiction over what would otherwise be the exclusive business of a sovereign state. This is because international lawyers typically approach these matters from a Westphalian perspective; they presume that each state enjoys a privileged position of moral dominion over its self-regarding affairs. And if each state is sovereign over its own matters, then presumably external parties have a duty to respect a state's exercise of criminal law. In other words, it is up to each state to decide whether and how to prosecute its own criminals, even those responsible for human rights atrocities.

---

[10] I conceive of legitimacy as a threshold concept. Thus, while a state's ability and willingness to perform the requisite political functions both come in degrees, failed and rogue states fall below this threshold because of their inability or unwillingness to satisfactorily perform their requisite functions.

[11] M Robinson, 'Foreword', *The Princeton Principles on Universal Jurisdiction* (2001), available at <http://lapa.princeton.edu/hosteddocs/unive_jur.pdf>.

[12] Similar analyses apply to genocide and war crimes, because they too need have no border-crossing element. Thus, of the ICC's four categories of crimes (genocide, crimes against humanity, war crimes, and aggression), only aggression appears necessarily to implicate international interests (and the ICC will not prosecute crimes in this category until it settles upon a definition for aggression).

To overcome this presumption in favour of state sovereignty, the international community must explain why certain forms of criminal activity do not merely affect members of a given state, they harm humanity as a whole. As its name implies, the category of crimes against humanity is thought to fulfil this function because it is said to pick out those crimes which (even if perpetrated exclusively by and against members of a single country) harm all of humanity. Geoffrey Robertson puts this point particularly clearly when he explains that the category of crimes against humanity provides 'the key to unlock the closed door of state sovereignty, and to hold political leaders responsible for the great evils they visit upon humankind'.[13]

Accounts of what constitutes a crime against humanity come in various shapes and sizes, of course, but in my estimation they all fail because none shows that humanity is actually harmed by such a crime, no matter how horribly it violates its victims' rights. Even if the genocide of Jews violates the humanity of those Jews attacked, or that using chemical weapons against Kurds shocks the conscience of humankind, for instance, neither conclusion is sufficient because neither account shows why an average citizen in Japan, say, is necessarily harmed by even the most horrific crime perpetrated against either a Jew in Germany or a Kurd in Iraq. The basic problem is that, just as traditional philosophers of law have notoriously had a difficult time explaining how certain acts qualify as crimes (rather than mere torts) because they harm the entire political community, international lawyers seem unable to furnish a plausible explanation of how humanity is harmed in the morally relevant sense by putative 'crimes against humanity'.

Assuming that my concerns about the category of crimes against humanity are well founded, does this show that we cannot justify the international prosecution and punishment of crimes which have no border-crossing elements? Not at all. Even if no account of crimes against humanity can explain why the international community has an actionable interest in the internal affairs of a state's criminal legal system, it does not necessarily follow that international criminal law must restrict itself to border-crossing crimes like aggression. This is because the category of crimes against humanity is important only if one accepts the Westphalian assumption that all de facto states are entitled to dominion over their self-regarding affairs. But as the analysis of state punishment above illustrates, not all states enjoy a morally privileged position over their internal affairs; only *legitimate* states do. And if the Westphalian outlook is mistaken, the failure of accounts of crimes against humanity gives us no reason to doubt the permissibility of international criminal law. To emphasize: unless one begins with the presumption that all de facto states have a moral right to sovereignty over their self-regarding affairs, one does not need a special category of crimes which purportedly harm all of humanity.

To appreciate this point, it is worth recalling why illegitimate states have no right to self-determination. As argued above, states are legitimate only if they satisfactorily

---

[13] G Robertson, *Crimes Against Humanity* (London: Allen Lane, 1999), 375.

protect the human rights of their constituents. If a state adequately performs these functions, then it enjoys a morally privileged position of dominion over its self-regarding affairs, including its system of criminal law. But if a state is either unable or unwilling to protect its constituents' human rights, then it is illegitimate and has no claim to sovereignty. Thus, neither Milosevic's Yugoslavia nor contemporary Somalia would qualify as legitimate because the former was *unwilling* and the latter is *unable* to protect the basic rights of its citizens. As a result, it would be permissible to unilaterally impose international criminal law on either of these states. Most importantly for our purposes here, we would not have to demonstrate that criminals in Yugoslavia or Somalia were harming anyone outside of either state in order to justify this intervention. Instead, because neither of these states is legitimate, neither has a presumptive claim to self-determination which must be defeated by an account of how (some subset of) the crimes committed within these countries putatively harm all of humanity.

The bottom line, then, is that when widespread or systematic rights violations are going unpunished within a given state, this state is not satisfactorily realizing the aims of punishment.[14] As a consequence, it has no claim to exclusive dominion over the punitive system within its territory and thus cannot rightfully object if some external party (which could be an international body or an individual foreign state) takes it upon itself to prosecute and punish those who have violated the rights of others. The theory of state punishment defended in this chapter thus has the following implication for international criminal law: any state which satisfactorily realizes the vital aims of criminal punishment has a right to sovereignty in this realm which explains why no external party may unilaterally assign itself the task of prosecuting and punishing criminals within this state's territory.[15] If widespread or systematic violations of rights are going unpunished in a particular state, on the other hand, then this state is not performing its requisite political functions, it is illegitimate, and it has no right against others interfering with its system of criminal law.

If the rights theory of state punishment developed in this paper is correct, then this alternative understanding of criminal law enjoys a stronger theoretical foundation than the Westphalian orientation on which the prevailing conception has been built. What is more, this alternative account leaves no less room for the imposition of international criminal law. To see why, notice that Article 7(1) of the

---

[14] 'Widespread' is a purely quantitative notion referring mainly to the number of violations. It takes account of the number of people victimized, weighted by the relative importance of the rights violated. 'Systematic' is a partly quantitative notion, referring to acts that are part of some plan whose execution would result in many rights violations. But because of the planning element, the notion also has a qualitative aspect: this is some aim or objective that cannot be specified in solely in numerical terms.

[15] Of course, external actors may permissibly enter those legitimate states which voluntarily permit (eg as a signatory state of the ICC) international institutions into their territories.

Rome Statute of the International Criminal Court (ICC) defines a crime against humanity as 'any of the following acts when committed as part of a widespread or systematic attack directed against any civilian population, with knowledge of the attack:

(a) Murder;
(b) Extermination;
(c) Enslavement;
(d) Deportation or forcible transfer of population;
(e) Imprisonment or other severe deprivation of physical liberty in violation of fundamental rules of international law;
(f) Torture;
(g) Rape, sexual slavery, enforced prostitution, forced pregnancy, enforced sterilization, or any other form of sexual violence of comparable gravity;
(h) Persecution against any identifiable group or collectivity on political, racial, national, ethnic, cultural, religious, gender as defined in paragraph 3, or other grounds that are universally recognized as impermissible under international law, in connection with any act referred to in this paragraph or any crime within the jurisdiction of the Court;
(i) Enforced disappearance of persons;
(j) The crime of apartheid;
(k) Other inhumane acts of a similar character intentionally causing great suffering, or serious injury to body or to mental or physical health.'[16]

Notice both that (a) to (k) involve violations of human rights and that a crime against humanity can occur only if 'committed as part of a widespread or systematic attack'. And because the alternative account I have outlined here suggests that it is enough that human rights violations be either widespread or systematic (ie they need not be part of a single 'attack'), this theory actually allows more room for international criminal law than the prevailing view.

Given that the ICC covers such a large subset of what my analysis recommends, one might think that we have little practical reason to revise the traditional conception of international criminal law. After all, even if I am correct that the category of crimes against humanity is both confused and unnecessary, at least it has been defined so as to capture the vast majority of the cases in which international criminal law would in fact be permissible. Thus, both because the category is so deeply entrenched and because its definition comes acceptably close to what a more theoretically defensible account would recommend, as a practical matter it might seem unwise to abandon it.

Because international criminal law is in a nascent and fragile state, it may well be best if we did not immediately try to dramatically revise the prevailing view. It is important to appreciate, however, that there remain compelling practical reasons to

---

[16] The Rome Statute of the International Criminal Court is available online at <http://www.icc-cpi.int/NR/rdonlyres/EA9AEFF7-5752-4F84-BE94-0A655EB30E16/0/Rome_Statute_English.pdf>.

move beyond the category of crimes against humanity. The crucial point is that, just as Bentham famously worried that talk of natural rights was 'pernicious nonsense' (insofar as such talk was not merely confused, it led people to support the wrong social institutions), talk of crimes against humanity is not merely conceptually ill-founded; in the long run it will undermine our best efforts to institute an effective system of international criminal law. This is because using the category of crimes against humanity implicitly endorses the Westphalian outlook, according to which each de facto state is entitled to unbridled sovereignty over its self-regarding affairs. And as long as we continue to trade in the currency of this Westphalian world view, we lend credence to rogue leaders like Milosevic who protest that their international criminal prosecution is entirely unjustified. Thus, the longer we continue to prosecute political and military leaders under the banner of crimes against humanity, the more we entrench the misconception that this international criminal prosecution is permissible only because these leaders have not merely committed atrocities against their own constituents, they have somehow harmed all of us. Revising the traditional view of international criminal law is therefore of the utmost practical importance because doing so will aid efforts to transform the current world into one in which political and military leaders everywhere exhibit a greater respect for the basic rights of their constituents.

3 The International Criminal Court and the Problem of Selective Prosecution

If I have argued correctly to this point, then state sovereignty does not require that international criminal law restrict itself to crimes with a genuinely border-crossing element. In addition to the countries which voluntarily participate, international actors may permissibly impose themselves upon illegitimate regimes. Even if there are circumstances in which international criminal law may be permissible, however, it does not follow that its current instantiation in the form of the ICC is necessarily morally defensible. As I indicated above, for instance, there are some respects in which the ICC lacks a firm theoretical foundation. Despite this, I am broadly sympathetic to the ICC, and while I cannot counter all potential criticisms, I would like in this last section to respond briefly to what I regard as the most important worry, the problem of selective prosecution.

Selective prosecution occurs whenever one chooses to press charges against only a fraction of those thought to be guilty of any given crime. Given that international criminal law is a relatively expensive (and under-funded) instrument, for the fore-seeable future we should expect it to be utilized only when there are huge numbers of rights violators. As a consequence, it is not unreasonable to fear that there will often be the temptation—if not the necessity—to pursue only a very small portion of the potential defendants. And as Martha Minow notes, the large number of individuals involved is not the only cause of selective prosecution:

Proper prosecutorial discretion generally reflects efforts to identify those most responsi-ble or the most serious offenders; some selectivity, however, reflects the chance involved in finding and arresting violators. Some elude arrest and prosecution by escaping, or dying, or concealing their identities, their conduct, or the evidence implicating them. Some avoid arrest because their nation or political party or ethnic group remains enough of a victor or ruling power. As a result, the actual set of individuals who face prosecution is likely to reflect factors far removed from considered judgments about who deserves prosecution and punishment.[17]

Minow's analysis pre-dates the creation of the ICC, but some might worry that this new institution will actually exacerbate the problem. This is because the ICC is still young, relatively fragile, and heavily dependent upon the support of the world's powerful countries. And given this dependence, it seems unrealistic to think that it would prosecute and punish a citizen from these powerful countries. Thus, rather than pursue any and all international criminals, for political reasons the ICC is likely to restrict itself to those from politically impotent countries. Obviously, this is unfair; prosecution and punishment should depend upon a person's guilt, not upon irrelevant characteristics like one's citizenship.

One might try to blunt the force of this objection by suggesting that, insofar as the world's most powerful countries tend to be liberal democracies, we need not worry about the ICC's turning a blind eye toward their constituents. The idea here is that, because liberal democracies tend not to house the types of crimes which the ICC is designed to prosecute, we need not worry about the latter's effective inability to pursue people within these powerful countries. This response is not entirely sat-isfying. While it is probably true that the world's powerful states are not among the most inhumane, many powerful states are far from exemplary liberal democracies. Consider China and Russia, for instance. Who knows to what lengths the Russian leaders and military will go in their attempt to subdue the separatists in Chechnya, for example, and yet no matter how violently they impose their rule, it is virtually unthinkable that the top brass in Russia would ever be punished. And even if liberal democracies like the United States generally treat their constituents decently, they cannot be counted on to be equally respectful of foreigners. And it is problematic if Americans enjoy de facto immunity no matter how horrifically things play out in Iraq, Afghanistan, and Guantanamo, for instance. So, we cannot side-step this

---

[17] M Minow, *Between Vengeance and Forgiveness* (Boston: Beacon Press, 1998), 31.

objection merely by pointing out that the world's powerful states tend to be more liberal and more democratic than those with less political might.

While everyone acknowledges that it is morally regrettable that potential defendants should be sorted according to morally arbitrary criteria, retributivists are split on the permissibility of punishing defendants even in the presences of selective prosecution. Some emphasize that justice is best served by punishing as many criminals as possible (even if other, equally guilty people are never prosecuted), whereas others believe that the imperative to treat like cases alike implies that it is better to punish none than to punish selectively.[18] I am among the first group. Other things being equal, I think it is good to punish as many criminals as possible.

To see the motivation behind this intuition, consider the enforcement of speed limits. In particular, should we penalize people for speeding even if drivers with radar detectors are generally able to avoid detection? After all, if we continue to issue tickets, we will be selectively penalizing only those without radar detectors. In my view, it seems clear that we should continue to penalize speeders even though it is admittedly unfair that we are able to punish only those who lack radar detectors. Those speeders who are punished will understandably be upset that others are able to speed with impunity, but they cannot righteously object to being punished given that they were guilty of speeding and could have avoided punishment if only they had obeyed the limits.

Here a critic might object that this analogy is inapt. Specifically, what if radar detectors were legal, and everyone who could afford them, bought them? And imagine further that the only people too poor to afford detectors were blacks who were poor because of the legacy of slavery. Would we still recommend giving speeding tickets when it would amount to ticketing only blacks? Under these circumstances, whatever the official wording of the statute, the law effectively boils down to different requirements for blacks and whites. Whites are free to speed but blacks may not.

Some might worry that the ICC practice has the potential to become morally tantamount to this more difficult case. In particular, the concern is that future defendants in the ICC will be drawn predominantly from Africa. And if so, we will not have anything like a system of international criminal law in which all and only the world's guilty are punished. Rather, even though the letter of the laws will claim universal jurisdiction, we will in fact have a system in which Europeans (among others) can effectively violate human rights with impunity while Africans and only Africans will be vulnerable to prosecution. Such a situation is not merely pernicious, insofar as it involves the ICC selectively prosecuting Africans based upon the morally irrelevant fact that their domestic governments are weak; it is particularly reprehensible

---

[18] For opposing takes on this controversial issue, see S Nathanson, 'Does It Matter If the Death Penalty Is Arbitrarily Administered?' (1985) 14 *Philosophy & Public Affairs* 149–64; and LP Pojman, 'A Defense of the Death Penalty', in AI Cohen and CH Wellman (eds), *Contemporary Debates in Applied Ethics* (Malden, MA: Blackwell Publishing, 2005), 107–23.

because Africa's lack of stature on the global stage is a direct consequence of Europe's having stunted its growth.

As a descriptive matter, I think this construal of the situation is both too optimistic and too pessimistic. It is too optimistic because it assumes that future human rights atrocities will occur only in Africa. (Given how horribly things came apart very recently in the former Yugoslavia, it sadly strikes me as premature to predict that continents like Europe will no longer produce paradigmatic international criminals.) And this objection is too pessimistic insofar as it presumes that if and when these non-African atrocities occur, the ICC will necessarily lack either the power or the will to pursue the criminals. It may be unrealistic to think that any American will be pursued in the foreseeable future, but if the ICC continues to establish itself at anything like its current rate, then an increasing proportion of the world's population will fall under its effective jurisdiction. But even if this objection relies upon an inaccurate portrayal of the ICC, it admittedly seems to contain more than a kernel of truth. And because this objection is too important not to face squarely, for the purposes of argument I will presume that—whatever language the ICC may use in its official documents—it is on the verge of becoming a system of criminal justice essentially funded by Europeans and imposed upon Africans. In practice if not in theory, the ICC is morally tantamount to white, former slave-owners reserving the right to speed while simultaneously ticketing all black, former slaves who are caught speeding. The question, then, is whether we should still endorse the ICC, despite the obvious injustice of this selective prosecution.

For two reasons, I would still support the ICC. First, even though this is admittedly a very difficult case, it bears repeating that the ICC would not be merely prosecuting Africans for being black: it would pursue only those Africans guilty of human rights violations. Thus, while an African defendant might understandably be outraged that Europeans can act similarly with impunity, she cannot righteously object that she is being punished merely for being black. After all, she could have maintained her legal immunity if only she had refrained from violating the rights of others. What is more, while the analogy of black speeders may in many respects be apt, it is important to bear in mind that the ICC does not concern itself with such relatively trivial conduct. On the contrary, it pursues only those who are charged with the gravest of crimes. Thus, although I acknowledge that this is a case about which reasonable people can disagree, my sense is that there is nothing impermissible about punishing any given African duly convicted of human rights atrocities, even if Europeans who commit similar atrocities enjoy effective impunity merely because they are citizens of powerful states.

Second, it is important to recall that international criminal law is not solely about meting out retributive justice. Both in theory and in practice, international criminal law is a marriage between criminal justice and human rights activism. Its point is not merely to see that wrongdoers receive the punishment they deserve, it is also (and more importantly) to help end the global climate of impunity in which human rights atrocities so regularly occur. Indeed, the human rights activists who work so hard on behalf of the ICC are motivated by concerns analogous to those who stress the deterrent value of domestic legal systems. And from this perspective, selective punishment matters much less because, unlike retributive justice, deterrence is a good whose value does not depend upon the fairness of its distribution.

If this is correct, then when we move from the retributive to the deterrent value of the ICC, the fact that Africans are disproportionately deterred should provoke less consternation. Indeed, given that human rights are most insecure in Africa, from the perspective of human rights protection it is altogether appropriate that Africans would be disproportionately selected. Put in terms of the speeding analogy, the idea is not merely that we want to deter the blacks from speeding in order to save the potential victims from speed-related accidents, it is that blacks tend to drive in black neighbourhoods where pedestrians are especially vulnerable (perhaps because the roads are less well lit, for instance), and thus—in terms of lives saved—it is especially valuable to deter black drivers.

A critic might concede the deterrent value of the ICC and still reject it as impermissible in practice. This is because a retributivist might reasonably regard the profound unfairness of criminally prosecuting only Africans as rendering the ICC unjust. And if one adopts this stance, one might regard the benefits of deterrence as tempting but morally irrelevant. The idea here is a familiar one: it is not permissible to resort to unjust means, even if one seeks to use these means to establish a more just world. Put in terms of exclusionary reasons, the moral reasons generated by deterrence that would otherwise count in favour of the ICC must be excluded because of the injustice of the selective prosecution.

This is a very sophisticated objection. And while I am typically sympathetic to principled positions such as this, in this particular case I think the insistence on avoiding the injustice amounts to an unattractive squeamishness, if voiced by someone who enjoys the protections of a stable liberal democracy. To appreciate my reaction to this objection, it is important not to lose sight of how utterly vulnerable so many Africans are. Of course, the ideal response would be to help them build secure domestic regimes which effectively protect their human rights. The obvious problem, however, is that no one has the knowledge, power, and will to do so. This is why it is so vitally important that we do all that we can to realize the potential gains of a system of international criminal law. Thus, it seems hypocritical for those of us lucky enough to enjoy the security of effective domestic regimes to insist that Africans should not be afforded even the minimal protections provided by international criminal law because the latter cannot be instituted in a thoroughly just fashion. It is not merely that Europeans are secure in their human rights when Africans are not; it is also worth emphasizing that there is a direct historical connection between our material comforts and the Africans' systemic inability to achieve even a modicum of political stability. What is more, it is historically short-sighted to insist that we should not accept the injustice which attends the creation of political institutions to protect *others* when the now-reputable states that protect *us* have anything but an unblemished pedigree. To emphasize: it is not merely that imperfect justice is better than no justice, it is also that (in the real world, at least) one cannot get to perfect justice without first going through imperfect justice.

Thus, while it is generally true that one must not resort to injustice for the sake of expedience, it matters how unjust the instrument is and what alternatives are available. In this case, I would endorse the ICC even if it was essentially a system run by Europeans and imposed upon Africans only because the injustice of selective prosecution strikes me as an acceptable price to pay when the ICC presents one of very few viable ways to make millions of Africans less vulnerable to the tyrannical rule of their illegitimate leaders. So, even when the objection of selective prosecution is put in its sharpest possible form, I think it is insufficient to defeat the permissibility of the ICC. It is worth remembering, however, that we have granted this European versus African caricature of the ICC only for the sake of argument. In reality, it seems more accurate to predict that the ICC will be disproportionately (rather than exclusively) run by Europeans and that the defendants will be drawn disproportionately (rather than exclusively) from Africa. Still, even in this muted form, the bias is cause for concern, and steps should be taken to ameliorate the problem. At the very least, for instance, we should work to ensure that Africans are well represented among the judges and prosecutors (so that we do not have a preponderance of black defendants being prosecuted and judged by Europeans), and step up efforts to ensure that those Europeans who clearly deserve to be tried (like Tadic) are brought to justice. Measures like these are not only required to mitigate the injustice of the practically unavoidable problem of selective prosecution, they will go a long way to increasing the perceived legitimacy of the ICC (thereby strengthening the institution and increasing its effective jurisdiction over ever more powerful countries).

4 CONCLUSION

This chapter is first and foremost about international criminal law, of course, but if the arguments outlined above are on target, then there may also be several lessons for those who work on domestic criminal law. First, rights forfeiture theory is unpopular among those writing on the morality of punishment, but this may be a function of the fact that the major positions in this literature were staked out during a period when the study of ethics was dominated almost exclusively by utilitarians and Kantians, before rights theory had ascended. Given that acts and institutions are permissible just in case they violate no rights, it may be time that those working on punishment take another, more sympathetic look at the rights forfeiture approach.

Second, it is understandable that philosophers of law do not take anarchism seriously (after all, it seems obvious to most of us that the state should be the sole agent presiding over the punitive process), but just as grappling with this issue enabled me to think more clearly about international criminal law, confronting this core question of political philosophy head-on may enable legal philosophers to provide more compelling accounts of the tort/crime distinction. Third and finally, if I am right that we should defer to the ICC despite its obvious faults because it is a nascent institution and, in the real world, just institutions typically must emerge from an unjust pedigree, perhaps we should also be more patient with existing legal institutions. Virtually no one who works on the morality of punishment is entirely satisfied with existing penal codes. I am not encouraging us to become complacent about the injustices which sadly pervade all existing systems, but if our best prospects for a more just future lie in reforming what we already have, then perhaps the best long-term strategy toward preferable legal arrangements is to work persistently but patiently to reform the admittedly imperfect institutions at hand.

21

CRIMINAL LAW AND MORALITY AT WAR

ADIL AHMAD HAQUE[*]

CRIMINAL law theory is concerned, in part, with understanding the proper normative relationship between moral wrongs, legal wrongs, and crimes. Liberal retributivists, for example, tend to believe that most moral wrongs should not constitute legal wrongs, and that most legal wrongs should not constitute crimes. As liberals, they tend to believe that conduct should be made unlawful only if doing so will prevent substantially more harm to others than it will bring about, and that unlawful conduct should be made criminal only if doing so will prevent substantially more overall harm to others than would less intrusive or coercive forms of legal regulation. In addition, as retributivists, they tend to believe that legal wrongs should be made into crimes only if they are also serious moral wrongs. Of course, liberal retributivists are not exclusively concerned with creating or preserving gaps between moral wrongs, legal wrongs, and crimes; they are also concerned with closing such gaps where no such gaps should exist. In general, all serious moral wrongs the criminalization of which would prevent substantial overall harm to others should be made into crimes.

For criminal law theorists interested in international crimes, similar issues arise regarding the relationship between moral wrongs committed in the context of armed

* Many thanks to Antony Duff, Stuart Green, and Jeff McMahan for their comments and suggestions.

conflict, violations of the law of armed conflict, and war crimes. Indeed, war crimes just are serious violations of the law of armed conflict which are punishable under international criminal law. Although war crimes are often perpetrated and seldom punished, it is almost certainly the case that their illegality prevents more harm to others than it brings about and that their criminality prevents still more overall harm. Moreover, while allegations that a particular party to an armed conflict has committed war crimes are almost always disputed by the accused party and its allies, it is almost certainly the case that every war crime currently recognized under international law constitutes a serious moral wrong. Indeed, it is the serious moral wrongfulness of war crimes, not their technical illegality, which is likely to explain the vigour with which their commission is denied. What is less clear, and therefore more interesting, is whether other serious moral wrongs committed in armed conflict, some of which are already legal wrongs under the law of armed conflict, should be recognized as war crimes as well.

Of course, we cannot know which moral wrongs committed in armed conflict should be recognized as war crimes until we know what acts of war constitute moral wrongs and understand wherein their wrongfulness consists. The purpose of this chapter is to identify the moral norms applicable to killing in armed conflict and determine whether and to what extent the law of armed conflict (LOAC) and international criminal law (ICL) track these moral norms, justifiably depart from them, or unjustifiably depart from them. Section 1 explores the moral and legal norms governing the killing of civilians not directly participating in hostilities, both as an intended means and as a foreseen side effect, and defends one account of these norms against important philosophical challenges by Thomas Scanlon, Victor Tadros, Frances Kamm, and Jeff McMahan. I argue that these moral norms are best understood and defended using the distinctions drawn in criminal law theory between wrongdoing, justifiability, and justification. The LOAC tracks these moral norms quite closely. By contrast, ICL departs from these moral norms in ways that are difficult to defend, in part because ICL seems to mistakenly assign intention a wrong-making rather than a wrong-justifying function.

The balance of the chapter examines the moral and legal norms governing the killing of civilians directly participating in hostilities as well as of members of armed forces and organized armed groups. Section 2 attempts to identify the conditions under which individuals lose their moral immunity from direct attack, partly by critically examining an analogy drawn by Jeff McMahan between these conditions and the legal doctrine of criminal complicity. Both the LOAC and ICL generally track these conditions fairly closely, but both should be revised to prohibit direct attacks on members of armed forces whom the attacker knows are not directly participating in hostilities and have not assumed a 'continuous combat function'. Finally, section 3 argues that moral constraints of necessity and proportionality limit the use of force even against individuals who are morally liable to direct attack. Several arguments to the effect that the LOAC and ICL may justifiably fail to enforce these moral constraints are examined and found unpersuasive.[1]

1 IMMUNITY FROM DIRECT ATTACK

Under international law, civilians are all individuals who are not combatants. Combatants, in turn, include members of the armed forces of a party to an armed conflict (except for religious and medical personnel) as well as participants in a spontaneous armed uprising known as a *levée en masse*. It is both a violation of the LOAC and a war crime to attack civilians directly during armed conflict, unless and for such time as they directly participate in hostilities. The circumstances under which civilians may lose their immunity from direct attack will be discussed in section 2. The task of this section is to examine the conceptual structure and moral justification of the legal immunity from direct attack which civilians ordinarily enjoy. This section will defend a version of the Doctrine of Double Effect (DDE), which is typically characterized as the view that is sometimes morally permissible to kill civilians as a foreseeable side effect of achieving an intended military advantage but impermissible to kill the same number of civilians as an intended means of achieving a similar military advantage. The new interpretation of the DDE offered below begins by supplementing the concept of permissibility which dominates moral philosophy with the more precise concepts of wrongdoing, justifiability, and justification derived from criminal law theory. I argue that both defenders and critics of the DDE mistakenly assume that intention is a wrong-making rather than a wrong-justifying feature of harming civilians.

1.1 Intention and justification

Thomas Scanlon has recently argued that a combatant's intention in killing civilians is irrelevant to whether the killing of those civilians is morally permissible.[2]

---

[1] It should be noted at the outset that the chapter examines only the moral norms applicable to the conduct of armed conflict *by combatants fighting for a just cause*. In part this is because most combatants claim to fight for a just cause and such claims are often difficult to decisively refute. Often, the most the law can hope to achieve will be to hold combatants to the moral norms that would apply to them if their claims to fight for a just cause were true.

[2] TM Scanlon, *Moral Dimensions: Permissibility, Meaning, Blame* (Cambridge, MA: Harvard University Press, 2008), 28–9.

Permissibility, Scanlon argues, is a function of the reasons for and against performing an action, and the intention with which an action would be performed does not count among the reasons for or against performing that action. Scanlon concludes that the permissibility of a given military operation depends on its anticipated outcomes, specifically on the harm it will cause to civilians as well as on the military advantage it will achieve. If the military advantage outweighs the civilian harm then it is permissible for the combatants to achieve the former at the expense of the latter, irrespective of whether their intention in doing so is to achieve the military advantage or to harm civilians.

The first problem with Scanlon's view is that his use of 'permissibility' is insensitive to the differences between non-wrongful conduct, wrongful conduct that is justifiable, and wrongful conduct that is both justifiable and justified. Now, the killing of civilians is a presumptive moral wrong (that is, an infringement of a moral right or duty) whether committed intentionally, knowingly, recklessly, or negligently. To that extent, Scanlon is correct: a combatant's intention does not determine whether the killing of civilians is wrongful or non-wrongful. Moreover, the wrong of killing civilians is justifiable (that is, supported by undefeated reasons) only if it is caused by or alongside the achievement of a sufficiently important military objective. To this extent as well, Scanlon is correct: the justifiability of killing civilians turns on the objective moral reasons for and against killing them, not on the intentions of the combatant. However, the wrong of killing civilians is only justified (that is, performed for undefeated reasons) when the achievement of the military advantage is among the combatant's reasons for action.[3] It is in this sense that intention is not a wrong-making feature of killing civilians (with a culpable mental state) but rather a wrong-justifying feature. The killing of civilians may be justifiable (for example, as a necessary side effect of a proportionate military advantage) and yet the combatant who kills them may be unjustified in doing so (for example, if her sole reason for action is to spread terror by killing the civilians). It follows that an act may be permissible (that is, a justifiable wrong) yet an individual may act impermissibly (that is, without justification) in performing it for the wrong reasons.

Certainly, acting justifiably enjoys a kind of logical priority over acting with a justification: the latter is impossible without the former, while the former is possible without the latter. But acting with a justification is central to our moral lives in a way that Scanlon of all people should recognize. For at the core of Scanlon's contractualism is the desire to justify ourselves to others, or rather the desirability of being able to do so, and we cannot justify ourselves to others by alluding to reasons for which we could have acted but did not. Instead, we must share with them our reasons for acting as we did. When we are called to account for our actions, and in particular to

---

[3] This discussion draws on J Gardner, 'Justification and Reasons', in A Simester and ATH Smith (eds), *Harm and Culpability* (Oxford: Clarendon Press, 1996), 103.

account for the wrongs we commit, we are called not merely to give *an* answer but to give *our* answer.

Scanlon comes closer to the truth when he observes that moral principles can serve either as guides to deliberation (their *deliberative* function) or as standards of evaluation (their *critical* function).[4] He says that the deliberative function of moral principles is to determine which action a person has decisive reasons to perform, while the critical function is to determine whether or not the person performed that action for those reasons. However, Scanlon's terminology is quite misleading, for it is strange to say that a moral principle has fulfilled its deliberative function even if it plays no role in an individual's deliberations. In other words, if an individual is unaware of the reasons identified by a moral principle, or adverts to them only to disregard them and act on entirely different reasons, then it is quite odd to say that the principle has discharged a deliberative function. Perhaps it is better to speak of a *governance* function concerned with the justifiability of action, a *guidance* function concerned with acting with justification, and a critical *perspective* from which both can be evaluated.

1.2 Means and ends

The killing of civilians is a presumptive moral wrong that is only justified when performed for undefeated reasons, that is, for reasons that are neither outweighed nor excluded. This last point is crucial because one class of potential reasons for killing civilians is not merely outweighed by the value of their lives but excluded from being weighed against their lives in the first place. In particular, the killing of civilians cannot be justified by the causal consequences or non-causal results of their deaths. For example, the killing of civilians cannot be justified as a means of spreading terror (a causal consequence) or of expressing genocidal hatred (a non-causal result). Civilian deaths do not merely outweigh their consequences and results but instead exclude them from justificatory consideration.

By contrast, the killing of civilians can be justified by the causal antecedents or accompaniments of their deaths. For example, the killing of civilians can be justified when the deaths are caused by the achievement of a military advantage (for example, when the deaths result directly from the destruction of a military objective), or by an attack which both achieves a military advantage and kills civilians (for example, when the deaths result directly from an attack which also directly results in the destruction of a military objective, but neither the deaths nor the destruction of the military objective results from the other). In addition, the killing of civilians cannot be justified when a similar military advantage could have been achieved by using

---

[4] Scanlon, *Moral Dimensions*, 23–8.

more discriminating weapons or selecting more remote targets and thereby avoiding or reducing harm to civilians.

This account of the wrongfulness of killing can be conceptualized in terms of a mandatory norm consisting of a primary reason not to kill civilians as well as an exclusionary reason which precludes the causal consequences and non-causal results of killing civilians from counting in its favour.[5] Most people would agree that some incentives to harm others cannot count in favour of doing so (for example, the fact that harming someone would give one sadistic or vindictive pleasure). What I am proposing here is that incentives to harm others can be rendered normatively inert by their causal history. By contrast, acts which cause civilian deaths may also have causal consequences which are not themselves caused by those civilian deaths (namely the causal antecedents and accompaniments of those deaths). These latter consequences fall outside the scope of the exclusionary reason and may be balanced directly against the primary reason not to kill civilians. This account preserves the insight at the heart of the means/side effect distinction.[6]

In a separate chapter in this volume, Victor Tadros argues that causal relationships between harms and benefits do not posses intrinsic moral significance. Instead, Tadros argues that what matters morally is whether one person treats another as a means, which Tadros argues is a function of the first person's motivations.[7] In fact this is the opposite of the truth. Treating someone as a means, causally speaking, is wrongful if and only if they are not a means, morally speaking. P *treats* V as a means when P harms V in order to achieve the causal consequences or non-causal results of harming V. V *is* a means insofar as morality permits the causal consequences or non-causal results of harming V to be weighed directly against the primary reasons not to harm V in the first place. If morality permits such direct weighing, then V is a means and there is nothing wrong with treating V as such. By contrast, if morality forbids such direct weighing, then V is not a means and it is indeed wrongful to treat V as such.

The fundamental issue, then, is not one of treatment but one of status. If the killing of civilians could be justified by reference to the causal consequences or non-causal results of their deaths then morality itself would thereby regard civilians as means to be used opportunistically or eliminated entirely to serve the ends of others. By contrast, if the killing of civilians can be justified by reference to the causal antecedents or accompaniments of their deaths then morality only concedes that

---

[5] The concepts of mandatory norms, primary reasons, and exclusionary reasons were introduced in J Raz, *Practical Reason and Norms* (rev edn; Oxford: Oxford University Press, 1999).

[6] This account was originally presented in AA Haque, 'Torture, Terror, and the Inversion of Moral Principle' (2007) 10 *New Criminal Law Review* 613. I note there (at 640) that, for threshold deontologists, the causal consequences and non-causal results of killing civilians are excluded only below a quantitative or qualitative threshold.

[7] V Tadros, 'Wrongdoing and Motivation' (this volume).

legitimate ends may sometimes be pursued even though their pursuit incidentally causes civilian deaths.

Tadros is correct that motivations are relevant to moral permissibility, though not in the way he thinks. Tadros thinks that intention plays a wrong-making role because intention is a necessary element of the wrong of killing or harming someone as a means. In fact, killing or harming someone almost always constitutes a free-standing moral wrong; killing or harming someone as a means is merely one way of committing such a basic wrong without justification. Moreover, the killing of civilians is a moral wrong that can be committed intentionally, knowingly, recklessly, or negligently. That wrong is justifiable if the civilian deaths were the unavoidable and proportionate causal consequences of the achievement of a military advantage or of the act that achieves that military advantage. That wrong is justified if the achievement of that military advantage was the reason for its commission.[8]

We also are now in a better position to identify a second problem with Scanlon's approach. Scanlon stipulates that the concept of 'military advantage' includes 'destroying enemy combatants or war-making materials' but excludes 'hasten[ing] the end of the war by undermining public morale'.[9] Since killing or injuring civilians hardly ever causally contributes to the destruction of opposing combatants or war-making materials, Scanlon's view entails that civilians may almost never be killed or harmed as a means of achieving military advantage but may often be killed as a side effect of achieving military advantage. However, Scanlon does not have to endorse the means/side effect distinction to reach this result, since it follows from his stipulation.

Despite reaching the right result regarding liability to direct attack, Scanlon's restrictive understanding of military advantage is not ultimately plausible. For example, it is undeniably militarily advantageous to prevent non-uniformed combatants from intermingling with a civilian population and using civilians as human shields. However, it is not justifiable to pursue this military advantage by forcibly and permanently displacing the civilian population in which the opposing combatants seek to hide. Similarly, it is perfectly legitimate for a party to armed conflict to create political pressure on the opposing party to stop fighting and accept the terms of a just peace, for example, through propaganda. What is illegitimate is to kill or injure civilians as a means of creating such political pressure. Thus, civilian immunity from direct attack cannot be defended solely by restrictively defining 'military advantage' but only by explaining why it is impermissible to kill civilians as a means of achieving any military advantage.

---

[8] More precisely, a combatant must act either with the intention of achieving the military advantage or on the condition that the military advantage will be achieved and for another permissible purpose. Haque, 'Torture, Terror, and the Inversion of Moral Principle', 648.

[9] Scanlon, *Moral Dimensions*, 28–9.

1.3 Side effects and indirect means

There is one last issue that has been raised in the philosophical literature that needs to be addressed. I argued above that death or injury to civilians cannot be justified by its causal consequences or non-causal results. This clearly rules out direct attacks on civilians. The remaining question is whether an attack that is directed at combatants or military objectives but that causes death or injury to civilians as a side effect can nonetheless take the further causal consequences or non-causal results of the death or injury to civilians into account when determining the overall proportionality of the attack. For example, Jeff McMahan has written that, although 'in general, civilians may not be harmed or killed as an intended means of deterring future wars...the deterrent effect that casualties among civilians can have does count as a good effect in calculations of wide proportionality'.[10] More narrowly, Frances Kamm has argued that civilian deaths caused by the destruction of a military objective may be justifiable if the surviving civilians will be too grief-stricken to rebuild the objective, thus sustaining the military advantage produced by the initial attack.[11] In these cases, civilians are harmed *both* as a causal consequence of achieving one military advantage *and* as a causal antecedent of achieving another military advantage (or sustaining the first military advantage). Does this more complex causal structure make a moral difference to the possibility of justifying death and injury to civilians?

In fact, there is no difference in moral permissibility between cases like those constructed by McMahan and Kamm and cases in which a direct attack on a military objective kills too few civilians to sufficiently deter or demoralize the survivors and is therefore followed up with a direct attack on surviving civilians. As we have seen, the causal consequences and non-causal results of civilian deaths are excluded from counting in favour of killing them. It is morally irrelevant whether combatants intend to bring about such excluded outcomes or merely foresee such excluded outcomes and act on the condition that they will occur. Such outcomes should not be subjectively intended because they are objectively excluded; combatants are not justified in pursuing such outcomes because such outcomes cannot render civilian deaths justifiable. Similarly, there is no difference in moral permissibility between the scenarios envisioned by McMahan and Kamm and a scenario in which a combatant realizes that directing one weapons system at a military objective will cause too few civilians deaths as side effects to sufficiently deter or demoralize the survivors and therefore selects a more destructive weapons system instead. This is because combatants can only apply the requirement of minimal force after they first identify

[10] J McMahan, *Killing in War* (Oxford: Oxford University Press, 2009), 211.
[11] FM Kamm, 'Failures of Just War Theory: Terror, Harm, and Justice' (2004) 114 *Ethics* 650, 668–9, nn 26–7; FM Kamm, 'Terrorism and Several Moral Distinctions' (2006) 12 *Legal Theory* 19, 41–2, 41, n 21.

the non-excluded outcomes of an attack; only then can they determine how to bring those outcomes about while causing the least possible harm to civilians.

Neither direct attacks on civilians nor direct attacks on military objectives that kill civilians as a side effect can be justified by the causal consequences or non-casual results of the civilian deaths they cause. If the causal antecedents of civilian deaths are insufficient to justify those deaths then the mere presence of those antecedents cannot transform the causal consequences or non-causal results of those deaths from excluded to non-excluded bases for justifying those deaths. Such causal antecedents are red herrings, sources of misdirection rather than justification, and the operations contemplated by McMahan and Kamm are simply indirect forms of the unjustifiable wrong that in its direct form is known as terrorism.

1.4 Law and morality

How well do the LOAC and ICL reflect the moral norms discussed above? The LOAC succeeds admirably. The intentional and knowing killing of civilians is prohibited by the principle of civilian immunity, which forbids combatants from making civilians the object of attack.[12] The reckless or negligent killing of civilians is prohibited by the principle of distinction, which requires combatants to do everything feasible to distinguish between civilians and opposing combatants before launching an attack;[13] and by the principle of discrimination, which forbids attacks which are not aimed to strike opposing combatants and military objectives while avoiding civilians and civilian objects.[14] The principle of distinction forbids recklessness or negligence with respect to circumstances (namely whether the individuals attacked are civilians or combatants), while the principle of discrimination forbids recklessness or negligence with respect to results (namely which individuals are attacked in the first place). Finally, the principles of necessity and proportionality state that incidental (side effect) harm to civilians is justifiable if and only if there is no less harmful way of achieving a similar military advantage and the harm to civilians is not excessive in relation to the military advantage anticipated.[15]

By contrast, ICL captures neither the LOAC nor the underlying moral norms governing the killing of civilians. For example, it is a war crime intentionally to direct an attack at individuals whom one knows to be civilians.[16] However, it is not a war crime to direct an attack at civilians whom one should know are civilians but

---

[12] Protocol Additional to the Geneva Conventions of 12 August 1949, and Relating to the Protection of Victims of International Armed Conflicts (Protocol I), art 51(2), 8 June 1977, 1125 UNTS 3.

[13] Ibid art 48.

[14] Ibid art 51(4).

[15] Ibid arts 57(3) (necessity) and 51(5)(b) (proportionality).

[16] Rome Statute of the International Criminal Court, art 8(2)(b)(i), 17 July 1998, UN Doc A/CONF183/9.

whom one unreasonably believes to be opposing combatants. Nor is it a war crime to launch an indiscriminate attack that is not directed at a specific military target but rather at an entire area or that uses weapons that by their nature cannot be directed at military targets and away from civilians. Similarly, it is a war crime to launch an attack in the knowledge that it would cause incidental harm to civilians that is clearly excessive in relation to the concrete and direct overall military advantage anticipated.[17] However, it is not a war crime to cause greater harm to civilians than necessary to achieve a given military advantage, or to cause incidental harm to civilians that is demonstrably disproportionate but not 'clearly excessive' in relation to that military advantage.[18]

These gaps between the LOAC and ICL are morally indefensible. In particular, these gaps are not warranted by the supposed difficulty of proving that a combatant acted recklessly or negligently during armed conflict, or that less harmful means of achieving a similar military advantage were available, or that incidental harm to civilians was excessive but not clearly excessive. Concerns that combatants will be falsely convicted are best addressed by demanding strict adherence to the standard of proof beyond a reasonable doubt, not by adopting weak substantive norms. It is not credible to maintain that forensic evidence, eyewitness testimony, and (increasingly) video recordings of military operations, combined when appropriate with the expert analysis of current and former military officers, can never meet this standard. The fact is that combatants do sometimes fire blindly into cars, crowds, and rooms instead of positively identifying and precisely targeting opposing forces; they do sometimes use primitive rockets and improvised explosive devices that are by their very nature indiscriminate; and they do sometimes cause greater incidental harm to civilians than necessary to achieve a given military advantage. Unfortunately, even clear cases of unjustified wrongdoing in armed conflict will rarely be presented to international criminal tribunals or courts martial. But when they are presented to such courts they should be prosecuted and punished, and whenever they occur they should be condemned as war crimes.

2 Liability to Direct Attack

I argued above that the killing or harming of an individual is presumptively a moral wrong which cannot be justified by the causal consequences or non-causal results of

---

[17] Ibid art 8(2)(b)(iv).

[18] I discuss some of these issues at greater length in AA Haque, 'Protecting and Respecting Civilians: Substantive and Structural Defects of the Rome Statute' (2011) 14 *New Criminal Law Review* (forthcoming).

her death or injury. This is what it means for an individual to enjoy immunity from direct attack. It seems to follow that for certain individuals to lose their immunity from direct attack is for the killing of such individuals to be justifiable *either* by reference to the causal antecedents or accompaniments of their deaths *or* by reference to (at least some of) the causal consequences or non-causal results of their deaths. The purpose of this section is to identify and compare the circumstances under which individuals lose their moral and legal immunity from direct attack.

2.1 Liability to defensive force

The most familiar way to lose one's moral immunity from direct attack is to become liable to defensive force or, put the other way around, to become the appropriate object of someone else's right of self-defence. For example, if someone is liable to defensive force then they may be harmed as a means of eliminating the threat they themselves pose (a non-causal result) or to prevent or deter a threat posed by others (a causal consequence). In a series of important books and articles, Jeff McMahan has argued that individuals become liable to defensive force when they are morally responsible for an unjustifiable threat to another person.[19] According to McMahan, moral responsibility for a threat requires (i) that one causally contribute to the threat, and (ii) that the risk that one's conduct would causally contribute to the threat was foreseeable even if the risk was too small to render one reckless or negligent in taking the risk.[20] McMahan argues that much (though, as we shall see, not all) of the morality of killing in war can be explained in terms of the morality of defensive force. If such a continuity of moral principles did exist, it would support a similar continuity of legal principles between ICL and ordinary criminal law.

There are at least two problems with McMahan's view of liability to defensive force. First, responsibility for an unjustifiable threat is not necessary to become liable to defensive force. As I have argued elsewhere, one can become liable to defensive force by posing a justified threat to someone who has not forfeited or waived her own right of self-defence.[21] For example, suppose that a Tactical Bomber is about to strike a legitimate military objective the destruction of which will kill a necessary and proportionate number of nearby civilians. If those civilians have done nothing to lose their right to self-defence then they are justified in killing the Tactical Bomber. The civilians are not morally required to allow themselves to be killed even if the Tactical Bomber fights for a just cause. At the same time, the Tactical

---

[19] McMahan, *Killing in War*, 35.

[20] Ibid 177. McMahan refers to objective justification rather than justifiability but I believe that for the purposes of this section the two concepts are equivalent.

[21] A A Haque, 'Rights and Liabilities at War', in PH Robinson, S Garvey and K Ferzan (eds), *Criminal Law Conversations* (Oxford: Oxford University Press, 2009), 395.

Bomber has done nothing to lose her right to self-defence and is therefore justified in using defensive force against those civilians if they use defensive force against her.[22] Indeed, McMahan now agrees that the posing of a justified threat can give rise to a 'symmetrical self-defense' situation.[23]

I submit that McMahan's proposed criterion for liability to defensive force is more plausible as a criterion for forfeiture of the right of self-defence.[24] In other words, responsibility for an unjustifiable threat might be what causes one to lose one's right to defend oneself against those one threatens. It is for this reason that unjustified aggressors have no right to defend themselves against the necessary and proportionate defensive force of their victims. By contrast, if the threat one poses is justified then one retains one's right to defend oneself against those who seek to defend themselves against that threat. It is for this reason that those who pose threats to innocent others that are justified as the 'lesser evil' may defend themselves against the defensive force of those innocent others. Finally, if one poses no threat at all then one retains one's right to use defensive force even against threats that are justified as the 'lesser evil'.[25]

Second, while causal contribution and foreseeable risk seem sufficient to make one responsible for the threats one poses and liable to defensive force on that basis (what we may refer to as 'primary responsibility' and 'primary liability') they do not seem sufficient to make one responsible for the threats posed by others or liable to defensive force on that basis (what we may refer to as 'derivative responsibility' and 'derivative liability'). At several points, McMahan draws parallels between derivative liability to defensive force and derivative liability to punishment, invoking the doctrine of criminal complicity to support his position on killing in war. For example, McMahan writes that civilians 'can be instigators of unjust wars, or aiders and abettors who share responsibility for unjust acts of war perpetrated by unjust combatants'.[26] McMahan concludes that civilians can become morally liable to direct

---

[22] Interestingly, because the civilians take up arms in self-defence rather than to take sides in the conflict, they are not taking direct part in hostilities and therefore do not lose their legal immunity from direct attack. The Tactical Bomber's direct attack on the civilians therefore violates the LOAC and constitutes a war crime, although the Tactical Bomber may claim self-defence if charged with a war crime.

[23] McMahan, *Killing in War*, 41–2 and 238, n 3 ('My analysis of the mistake is slightly different from Haque's').

[24] Haque, 'Rights and Liabilities at War'. DR Mapel, 'Moral Liability to Defensive Killing and Symmetrical Self-defense' (2009) 18 *Journal of Political Philosophy* 198.

[25] A similar dynamic is vividly captured by Vera Bergelson's case of Jack and Jill: 'Assume that ... criminals conditioned the release of their captives on Jack's rape of Jill. Realizing that this is the only way to save several lives, including Jill's own, Jack reluctantly agrees. Jill, on the other hand, vehemently protests that she would rather die than be violated. When Jack attempts to overpower her, Jill fights back and seriously injures Jack.' V Bergelson, 'Rights, Wrongs, and Comparative Justifications' (2007) 28 *Cardozo Law Review* 101, 113. If, as Bergelson believes, rape can be justified as a means of preventing a greater evil then Bergelson is correct that both Jack and Jill act justifiably.

[26] McMahan, *Killing in War*, 208.

attack through participation in the general war effort and war-sustaining activities, for example, by advocating war, lobbying politicians to support war, voting for candidates that support war, paying taxes that fund the war effort, working in the defence industry, and wrongfully failing to oppose the war.[27]

However, a close examination of criminal complicity undermines rather than supports McMahan's position. First, observe that complicity in the crime of another person generally requires the specific intention (not mere foreseeability) to contribute causally to the perpetrator's conduct, in addition to the mental state regarding the results of that conduct that is required for the perpetrator's commission of the crime. Furthermore, an accomplice must causally contribute to the perpetrator's commission of the crime, and not merely to the perpetrator's general capacity to commit such crimes. Generally, this means that an accomplice must aid, assist, enable, facilitate, or wrongfully (that is, in breach of a duty) fail to prevent the commission of a crime the perpetrator already intends to commit or must abet, procure, instigate, solicit, encourage, or order the commission of a crime the accomplice intends for the perpetrator to commit. By contrast, one does not become an accomplice to a crime by assisting the perpetrator in ordinary aspects of life (for example, by cooking food, washing clothes, or providing religious or medical services) even if this assistance indirectly contributes to the perpetrator's ability to commit crimes. If complicity is necessary for liability to direct attack then it would seem that medical and religious personnel in the armed forces, as well as military contractors and civilian employees of armed forces who perform non-combat-related functions, generally retain their immunity from direct attack.

The second problem with viewing derivative liability to direct attack through the lens of criminal complicity is that the lens is itself distorted. Criminal law theorists have cogently argued that derivative liability to punishment should require that an accomplice make a necessary causal contribution to the conduct of the perpetrator.[28] Encouraging the commission of a crime the perpetrator already intends to commit, or facilitating the commission of a crime for which the perpetrator already has the necessary means and opportunity, should not be enough.[29] Moreover, it would be strange indeed if derivative liability to direct attack could rest on such a basis. Cheering departing troops or sending supportive letters to the front lines, even if specifically intended to encourage soldiers to fight, does not seem sufficient to expose one to direct attack even if necessary to avoid the threat posed by those soldiers. Indeed, it is hard to believe that locals who encourage armed groups operating on their territory thereby make themselves liable to direct attack by opposing forces. McMahan correctly notes that it is seldom necessary or effective to attack civilian

---

[27] Ibid 214–15.

[28] J Dressler, 'Reassessing the Theoretical Underpinnings of Accomplice Liability: New Solutions to an Old Problem' (1985) 37 *Hastings Law Journal* 91.

[29] But see *Wilcox v Jeffery* [1951] 1 All ER 464, KB (finding accomplice liability on the basis of trivial and unnecessary causal contribution).

supporters as a means of averting a threat, but the point here is that civilian supporters are seldom necessary to generate the threat in the first place.[30] Crucially, if derivative liability to direct attack requires intentionally making a necessary causal contribution to a threat posed by another person, then most civilians participating in the general war-effort or war-sustaining activities retain their immunity from direct attack.

It should be noted that McMahan conceives of defensive force as a means of redistributing the risk of wrongful harms away from those at risk and toward those most responsible for creating the risk.[31] It is for this reason that McMahan thinks that if one person is even slightly responsible for a risk of harm and another person is not responsible at all, and if the harm cannot be divided among them or avoided by both of them, then the non-responsible person may shift the risk entirely to the slightly responsible person. However, to a significant extent, McMahan's references to 'risk' and 'distribution' are misleading. What is really at issue is whether I can harm you as a means of avoiding harm to myself if I am not responsible for the possibility that I may be harmed and you are at least slightly responsible for the possibility that I may be harmed. Put that way, McMahan's position seems less plausible. As McMahan concedes, since it is substantially worse to *do* harm to others than to *allow* harm to others or to oneself, it seems hard to accept that a slight difference in primary responsibility would justify doing harm to another person as a means of avoiding harm to oneself.[32] Indeed, it is even harder to accept that a slight degree of *derivative* responsibility can justify doing harm to another person who poses no threat as a means of avoiding harm to oneself. Since most civilians who participate in the general war effort or war-sustaining activities bear only slight and derivative responsibility for specific military operations, they do not seem liable to direct attack to prevent those operations.

2.2 Just cause and liability to direct attack

In his more recent work, McMahan has stated that liability to direct attack is not entirely coextensive with liability to defensive force. Instead, McMahan believes that there are at least two bases of liability to direct attack in armed conflict. The first is responsibility for an unjustified threat. The second is responsibility for an injustice

---

[30] It must be admitted that scholars who assert that derivative liability to direct attack requires a necessary causal contribution to a threat posed by another person have not produced a detailed argument in support of that principle. LA Alexander, 'Self-Defense and the Killing of Noncombatants: A Reply to Fullinwider' (1976) 5 *Philosophy & Public Affairs* 408–15. Nonetheless, some limitation of this kind seems unavoidable.

[31] J McMahan, 'The Basis of Moral Liability to Defensive Killing' (2005) 15 *Philosophical Issues* 386, 394–5.

[32] McMahan, *Killing in War*, 178.

the prevention or rectification of which provides the opposing party to armed conflict with a just cause for war.[33] For example, civilians participating in the general war effort or war-sustaining activities may share responsibility for an unjust invasion or military occupation as a whole even if they are not complicit in the specific military operations which constitute its parts. Similarly, prisoners of war who fought for an unjust cause share responsibility for the creation or perpetuation of an unjust threat or other serious injustice.[34] According to McMahan's second criterion, such civilians and prisoners of war are potentially liable to be harmed as a means of achieving a just cause.

McMahan's conclusion rests on the premise that a just cause is a cause that 'may permissibly be pursued by means of war'.[35] This premise is not obviously true. One might instead suppose that a just cause is a cause that may permissibly be pursued in the face of armed opposition. On this view, combatants do not have a special right to kill those responsible for an injustice as a means of preventing or correcting that injustice. Instead, combatants retain their general right to use defensive force to protect themselves or others from wrongful harm. The moral significance of just cause is that combatants pursuing a just cause are relieved of the general duty to retreat, surrender, or avoid conflict rather than use defensive force.[36] This conceptual point is obscured when a state acts in national self-defence against an imminent or ongoing armed attack. In such cases, the line between pursuing a just cause (compelling the opposing party to cease its attack) and defending against armed resistance (from opposing forces that refuse to retreat or surrender) is easy to overlook. As a result, it is commonly but mistakenly assumed that the killing of opposing combatants is an inherent military advantage to which the constraints of necessity and proportionality do not apply.

By contrast, if we allow, for the sake of argument, that arresting terrorists or destroying weapons of mass destruction may provide a just cause for resorting to armed force then it becomes clear that combatants are only justified in engaging opposing forces to the extent necessary to achieve their just cause. Such combatants may engage in 'defensive' operations against those who attack them, or 'offensive' operations against those who would otherwise attack them.[37] However, individuals who do not and would not otherwise engage in armed resistance to the pursuit of the just cause or make necessary causal contributions to the armed resistance of others

---

[33] J McMahan, 'The Morality of War and the Law of War', in D Rodin and H Shue (eds), *Just and Unjust Warriors: The Moral and Legal Status of Soldiers* (Oxford: Oxford University Press, 2008), 19, 22.

[34] Ibid.

[35] Ibid 5.

[36] More precisely, combatants are relieved of the duty to retreat or surrender only if the just cause for which they fight is proportionate to the total harm they expect to inflict in pursuit of that just cause. A similar view is suggested, though not pursued, in D Rodin, *War and Self-Defense* (New York: Oxford University Press, 2003), 132–8.

[37] As discussed further in the following section, offensive operations are best understood in terms of the pre-emptive use of defensive force by combatants pursuing a just cause.

are not liable to be killed merely as a means of achieving the just cause. In short, liability to direct attack derives from primary or derivative responsibility for attacks on combatants pursuing a just cause, not responsibility for the injustice that gives rise to that just cause.

One important implication of the view described above is that individuals become liable to direct attack by engaging in or committing themselves to armed resistance, and cease to be liable to direct attack when they disengage from armed resistance either voluntarily (for example, through surrender or desertion or by taking reserve status) or involuntarily (for example, through illness, injury, or capture). By contrast, *past* engagement in armed resistance is not a basis for liability to direct attack. The issue is not merely that, as McMahan observes, it is seldom necessary or effective to use defensive force against individuals whose causal contributions to present or future threats (or, for McMahan, injustices) lie in the past.[38] The issue is that once their causal contributions to present or future threats have come to an end so, too, does their liability to direct attack. So, contrary to McMahan's position, on the view proposed above prisoners of war may not be harmed even as a necessary means of achieving the just cause they previously opposed.

2.3 Direct participation in hostilities, continuous combat functions, and mere membership

In general, it is neither a violation of the LOAC nor a war crime to directly attack civilians if and for such time as those civilians take a direct part in hostilities. According to an important report recently issued by the International Committee of the Red Cross (ICRC), civilians take a direct part in hostilities when they commit a specific act which meets the following cumulative criteria:

1. The act must be likely to adversely affect the military operations or military capacity of a party to an armed conflict or, alternatively, to inflict death, injury, or destruction on persons or objects protected against direct attack (threshold of harm), and
2. there must be a direct causal link between the act and the harm likely to result either from that act, or from a coordinated military operation of which that act constitutes an integral part (direct causation), and
3. the act must be specifically designed to directly cause the required threshold of harm in support of a party to the conflict and to the detriment of another (belligerent nexus).[39]

---

[38] McMahan, *Killing in War*, 226.

[39] N Melzer, *Interpretive Guidance on the Notion of Direct Participation in Hostilities Under International Humanitarian Law* (ICRC, 2009), 46 (available at <http://www.icrc.org/Web/Eng/siteeng0.nsf/htmlall/p0990/$File/ICRC_002_0990.PDF>).

In addition, the ICRC writes that '[c]ivilians lose protection against direct attack for the duration of each specific act amounting to direct participation in hostilities'[40] but afterwards regain that protection '[u]ntil the civilian in question again engages in a specific act of direct participation in hostilities'.[41]

The first criterion certainly encompasses a variety of acts which would trigger moral liability to direct attack, such as acts likely to inflict death or injury on individuals who retain their right to self-defence. However, the first criterion also encompasses acts likely to adversely affect military operations or military capacity without necessarily killing or injuring combatants or civilians. The ICRC gives a number of examples, including sabotaging military equipment and interfering with military computer networks.[42] Ordinarily, it would be disproportionate to use deadly force in defence of property, even if less force would be inadequate to the task. However, if certain property is essential to one's survival then one may defend one's life *by* defending one's property. Similarly, acts which adversely affect military operations or military capacity will generally either leave combatants vulnerable to attack by opposing forces or compel combatants to choose between abandoning their pursuit of their just cause and pursuing their just cause at greater risk to themselves. Given sufficiently high stakes, the use of lethal force against civilians whose actions adversely affect military operations or capacity may be proportionate.

The second criterion requires a direct causal link either 'between the act and the harm likely to result' from that act or between 'a coordinated military operation of which that act constitutes an integral part' and the harm likely to result from that operation.[43] According to the ICRC, 'direct causation should be understood as meaning that the harm in question must be brought about in one causal step'.[44] It follows that a specific act makes one liable to direct attack if it is either likely to cause cognizable harm without the intervening acts of others or if it is an integral part of a coordinated military operation that is likely to cause cognizable harm without the intervening acts of others. For example:

[t]he delivery by a civilian truck driver of ammunition to an active firing position at the front line would almost certainly have to be regarded as an integral part of ongoing combat operations and, therefore, as direct participation in hostilities. Transporting ammunition from a factory to a port for further shipping to a storehouse in a conflict zone, on the other hand, is too remote from the use of that ammunition in specific military operations to cause the ensuing harm directly.[45]

This criterion seems largely in keeping with the view defended in the previous section, namely that liability to direct attack requires that the threatened harm

[40] Ibid 70.
[41] Ibid 71.
[42] Ibid 48.
[43] Ibid 46.
[44] Ibid 53.
[45] Ibid 56.

would be proximately caused by one's own voluntary conduct or by the conduct of another person to which one intentionally makes a necessary causal contribution. Intriguingly, the ICRC's use of the phrase 'integral part' might suggest that a civilian must be a co-principal and not merely an accessory before the fact in order to become derivatively liable to direct attack. However, the ICRC elsewhere indicates that a civilian may become derivatively liable to direct attack by transporting weapons to the site of a specific military operation to be performed later.[46]

The third criterion, requiring a specific design to oppose one party or support the other, creates the most interesting contrast between the LOAC and ordinary criminal law principles of self-defence. For example, starving or impoverished civilians may attempt forcibly to take food or supplies from members of an armed force without thereby intending to oppose the achievement of that force's military or political objectives or to support any opposing party. Such civilians retain their immunity from direct attack under the LOAC, while combatants who directly attack them commit a war crime which they may justify in terms of self-defence or defence of others. While moral liability to defensive force turns on responsibility for a threat, moral liability to direct attack in armed conflict additionally requires armed resistance to the achievement of a just cause. The LOAC adopts the latter criterion of liability, with the important modification that civilians lose their legal immunity from direct attack by resisting the achievement of any military advantage, even by an armed force fighting for an unjust cause. Only if the latter criterion is not satisfied will recourse be made to criminal law principles of liability to defensive force.

As we have seen, civilians lose their legal immunity from direct attack by directly participating in hostilities and regain their immunity as soon as their direct participation comes to an end. By contrast, members of an organized armed group acting as the armed forces of a non-state party to an armed conflict lose their legal immunity from direct attack for as long as they assume a *continuous combat function*. According to the ICRC, 'individuals whose continuous function involves the preparation, execution, or command of acts or operations amounting to direct participation in hostilities are assuming a continuous combat function'.[47] Such individuals are liable to direct attack before, during, or after direct participation in specific military operations and they regain their immunity from direct attack only upon disengaging from their continuous combat function.

The ICRC offers two arguments in favour of basing liability to direct attack on the assumption of a continuous combat function. First, the ICRC states that it would give organized armed groups an unfair advantage over State armed forces to allow

---

[46] Ibid 66.

[47] Ibid 34 (stating that 'recruiters, trainers, financiers and propagandists' retain their immunity from direct attack, as do 'individuals whose function is limited to the purchasing, smuggling, manufacturing and maintaining of weapons and other equipment outside specific military operations or to the collection of intelligence other than of a tactical nature').

the former but not the latter to enjoy immunity from direct attack in between spe-cific military operations.[48] This argument does not seem particularly strong, since the unfair advantage it identifies could just as easily be cured by granting State armed forces immunity from direct attack on the same terms. Second, the ICRC suggests that, unlike civilians whose future direct participation in hostilities 'is very difficult to anticipate', those who assume a continuous combat function can be 'reliabl[y] predict[ed]' to directly participate in future hostilities.[49] This argument seems sound, assuming of course that it is justifiable to direct defensive force at those who would otherwise carry out or participate in imminent or future attacks, even if they are not currently carrying out or participating in incipient or ongoing attacks. Both the common law, by permitting defensive force against imminent attacks, and modern criminal law, by permitting defensive force that is immediately necessary to prevent a future attack, seem committed to this assumption.

On this assumption, direct attacks on those who assume a continuous combat function will almost always be either justified (by the fact that they would other-wise directly participate in future hostilities) or excused (by a reasonable belief that they would otherwise directly participate in future hostilities). By contrast, direct attacks on civilians who have directly participated in past hostilities on a 'sponta-neous, unorganized or sporadic basis' will often be neither justified nor excused since '[e]ven the fact that a civilian has repeatedly taken a direct part in hostilities, either voluntarily or under pressure, does not allow a reliable prediction as to future conduct'.[50] Indeed, it seems plausible that combatants will better comply with the moral norms governing their conduct if they directly attack only those individuals who are either directly participating in current hostilities or assuming a continuous combat function than if combatants try to identify on a case-by-case basis and then directly attack those individuals who would otherwise directly participate in future hostilities.

This finally brings us to members of the armed forces of a state party to an armed conflict, who lose their legal immunity to direct attack simply by entering their state's armed forces. Members of state armed forces may be directly attacked even if they are not directly participating in hostilities and even if they do not assume a continuous combat function within their armed forces. This is especially striking because private military contractors and civilian employees of the armed forces per-forming non-combat functions are not legally liable to direct attack, unless and for such time as they directly participate in hostilities or assume a continuous combat function.[51] But members of armed forces performing non-combat functions enjoy no such legal protection.

---

[48] Ibid 72.
[49] Ibid 71.
[50] Ibid 71.
[51] Ibid 37.

No doubt it is often extremely difficult to distinguish between members of armed forces who assume a continuous combat function and members who do not, perhaps even more difficult than distinguishing between civilians who are directly participating in hostilities and civilians who are not. It therefore may be unfair to demand that combatants refrain from direct attacks on opposing armed forces unless or until they have made such difficult distinctions. Moreover, it would be unjust to punish combatants who reasonably believe that the members of the state armed forces whom they attack have assumed a continuous combat function. Nevertheless, these considerations do not support a substantive legal liability to direct attack, only an inversion of the usual precautions combatants are required to take under the LOAC. For example, the LOAC requires that, in cases of doubt, combatants must presume that individuals are (i) civilians, (ii) not directly participating in hostilities, and (iii) not assuming a continuous combat function. By contrast, it seems reasonable to hold that, in cases of doubt, individuals identified as members of state armed forces may be presumed to assume a continuous combat function. This seems a fair risk for the law to impose on individuals who volunteer to join the armed forces of their state or who are conscripted but nevertheless have an opportunity to choose between the risks of membership and the punishment for refusal.

However, if a combatant comes to know that a member of the armed forces of an opposing state is neither directly participating in hostilities nor assuming a continuous combat function then the combatant is neither justified nor excused in directly attacking that individual. In other words, while combatants may not directly attack an individual who is not a member of opposing state armed forces unless they reasonably believe the individual *is* directly participating in hostilities or assuming a continuous combat function, combatants may attack a member of opposing state armed forces unless they reasonably believe the member *is not* directly participating in hostilities or assuming a continuous combat function. Accordingly, it should be a violation of the LOAC as well as a war crime to directly attack a member of an opposing armed force whom one knows is neither directly participating in hostilities nor assuming a continuous combat function.[52]

It might be argued that members of state armed forces (except medical and religious personnel) have committed themselves to fight if ordered to do so and may therefore be directly attacked to pre-empt or prevent them from participating in future military operations. This is not an implausible argument. However, the only

---

[52] In a forthcoming article, Gabriella Blum argues that members of armed forces may be presumed to pose an immediate threat but individual members may not be targeted if there is reason to believe they pose no immediate threat. G Blum, 'The Dispensable Lives of Soldiers' (2010) 2 *Journal of Legal Analysis* 69. By contrast, this chapter proposes that members of armed forces may be presumed to assume a continuous combat function but individual members may not be targeted if it is reasonable to believe they are neither assuming a continuous combat function nor directly participating in hostilities. In addition, direct attacks on individuals assuming a continuous combat function are limited by the constraints of necessity and proportionality described below.

members of an armed force that are morally liable to direct attack to pre-empt or prevent future military operations are those members who would otherwise directly participate in those future military operations. If a member of a state armed force has not assumed a continuous combat function then it is unwarranted to act on the presumption (that is, unless confronted by evidence to the contrary) that she will directly participate in future military operations. The risk that a direct attack on such an individual would be unjustifiable is too high for taking such a risk to be excusable.

3 CONSTRAINTS ON DIRECT ATTACK

In ordinary life, the killing of another human being is both a presumptive moral wrong as well as a crime which calls for an exculpatory explanation in the form of a justification, an excuse, or a denial of responsibility. In armed conflict, by contrast, the intentional killing of combatants who are not *hors de combat* is neither a violation of the LOAC nor a war crime unless committed treacherously or perfidiously, such as by pretending to be sick or injured, to surrender or call a truce, or to be a member of the United Nations or the Red Cross. In other words, while killing another human being is criminal except under carefully specified circumstances, killing an opposing combatant is criminal only under carefully specified circumstances. Put another way, ICL does not consider the killing of combatants to be a justifiable or excusable offence; rather, ICL does not generally consider the killing of combatants an offence at all. Thus, questions of justification or excuse never arise. The killing of combatants is generally a non-event under ICL.

One might conclude that this structural difference between ordinary criminal law and ICL reflects opposing views of the value of human life. In fact, this structural difference may reflect instead an attempt to incorporate justificatory elements into the offence definitions of various war crimes. In other words, since one does not wrong individuals who have made themselves liable to direct attack, combatants pursuing a just cause commit no wrong by attacking opposing forces who undertake a continuous combat function or civilians who take direct part in hostilities.[53] However, even individuals who are liable to direct attack can be wronged if attacks against them violate other moral constraints, including those against perfidy and

---

[53] Importantly, since liability is a wrong-obliterating justification rather than a wrong-overriding justification, the conditions of liability to direct attack may be incorporated into an offence definition rather than a defence definition without glossing over any moral remainder left behind by the harmful act.

treachery. Accordingly, I will argue below that the unnecessary or disproportionate killing of opposing combatants should be prohibited by the LOAC and punished as a war crime.

3.1 Necessity and proportionality

I argued above that the first-order, primary reasons not to kill or injure other human beings are ordinarily protected by second-order, exclusionary reasons that preclude the justification of killing or injuring human beings by reference to the causal consequences or non-causal results of doing so. I also argued that at least some of these exclusionary reasons cease to apply to individuals who pose or are complicit in threats to others who retain their right to self-defence, and that such individuals may therefore be killed or injured as a means of overcoming the threat they pose or in which they are complicit. By contrast, the primary reasons against killing or injuring such individuals are left standing. It follows that the use of defensive force is justifiable only if the threat could not be avoided without using force at all or by using less force and if the most serious harm threatened to any victim is comparable to the most serious harm inflicted on any attacker. Otherwise, the primary reasons against killing or injuring individuals who are liable to defensive force would defeat the reasons in favour of doing so.

It is also noteworthy that the harm inflicted on individuals who are liable to defensive force need not outweigh the harm threatened. The use of defensive force need not be 'the lesser evil', impartially considered, in order to be justifiable. This is true despite the fact that ordinarily it is not justifiable to do harm to another person in order to avoid a comparable harm to oneself or an innocent third party. It seems that liability to defensive force cancels or annuls the moral asymmetry between doing and allowing harm. Since individuals may act justifiably on the basis of any undefeated reason, including either of two opposing reasons of comparable weight, it is justifiable to inflict harm on individuals liable to defensive force either as a means or as a side effect of preventing comparable harm to oneself or others.[54] By contrast, it is only justifiable to inflict harm on individuals not liable to defensive force as a side effect (but not as a means) of preventing substantially greater harm to oneself or others.

[54] As in domestic criminal law, defensive force need not be strictly proportionate. Eg deadly force may be used to prevent serious bodily injury. Note also that the harm threatened to any victim must be comparable to the harm inflicted on each attacker individually, rather than all attackers cumulatively. It is not disproportionate to kill multiple attackers who are trying to kill you. By contrast, it would be disproportionate to kill multiple innocents as a side effect of saving oneself. Why aggregate harm to the innocent affects proportionality while aggregate harm to attackers does not is an important question that cannot be addressed here.

The requirement of minimum force entails that combatants must offer opposing forces an opportunity to surrender and be taken prisoner whenever doing so
will not involve significantly greater risk than using deadly force. In addition, parties to armed conflict may have an obligation to develop non-lethal weapons and
use them where they are likely to be effective. However, given the near-universal
use of lethal weapons in armed conflict, the requirement of comparable harm will
almost always be satisfied or reasonably believed to be satisfied. Moreover, the unusual circumstances of armed conflict generally permit combatants to kill opposing
combatants in order to prevent injury to themselves. First, an injury may render a
combatant more vulnerable to later lethal attack and she may therefore defend her
life by defending against such an injury. Second, an injury may render a combatant
unable or less able to defend others (particularly her comrades or civilians) from
later lethal attack and she may therefore defend their lives by defending against such
an injury. Finally, an injury may force a combatant to choose between giving up her
pursuit of a just cause and pursuing that just cause at greater risk to herself. Given
sufficiently high stakes, deadly force may be a proportionate means of preventing
such an injury.

The most difficult questions surrounding necessity and proportionality in armed
conflict do not relate to threats faced by combatants in discrete tactical situations,
but rather to the military advantages which combatants pursue as part of an overall
strategy to achieve military victory. As proposed earlier, it is the pursuit of military
victory in a just cause that makes it justifiable for combatants to use defensive force,
both reactively and pre-emptively, rather than retreating, surrendering, or otherwise avoiding engagement with opposing forces. On this view, combatants fighting
for a just cause are justified in engaging opposing forces (when they could safely
avoid doing so) only when necessary to secure a military advantage that is in turn a
necessary part of a just strategy for attaining military victory. For present purposes,
a military advantage is any event that contributes to military victory; military victory is achieved when opposing forces are rendered unwilling or unable to engage in
armed resistance; and a just strategy is one that would achieve a just cause at necessary and proportionate cost to others.[55]

On the view proposed, the killing of combatants is unnecessary if the combatant
deaths do not causally contribute to the achievement of a military advantage (for
example, if they are killed in the final hours before a peace treaty goes into effect) or if
a similar military advantage could be achieved without killing them (for example, by
taking them prisoner). Similarly, if securing a military advantage would not make a
necessary contribution to a just strategy then combatants may not engage opposing
forces in order to secure that advantage. Of course, if the achievement of a military
advantage is a necessary part of a just strategy then the expected harm to opposing

---

[55] A just strategy must also justly distribute harms among the parties to the conflict as well as civilians. The just distribution of harms is a complex topic which cannot be adequately discussed here.

forces cannot be disproportionate in a strict sense. This is because the total harm to opposing forces called for by a *just* strategy is by definition outweighed by the value of the just cause. However, since military strategies are crafted and implemented under conditions of predictive uncertainty, one could consider it disproportionate to engage with opposing forces in pursuit of a military advantage that will only slightly increase the likelihood of military victory (for example, if a large number of opposing forces are defending a remote, fixed position the capture of which would just barely increase the likelihood of military victory).

3.2 A new war crime?

Although there is no specific rule of the LOAC expressly prohibiting the unnecessary or disproportionate killing of combatants or civilians directly participating in hostilities, the ICRC has recently asserted that such killings violate general principles of the LOAC. Specifically, '[i]n the absence of express regulation, the kind and degree of force permissible in attacks against legitimate military targets should be determined, first of all, based on the fundamental principles of military necessity and humanity…'[56]

Today, the principle of military necessity is generally recognized to permit 'only that degree and kind of force, not otherwise prohibited by the law of armed conflict, that is required in order to achieve the legitimate purpose of the conflict, namely the complete or partial submission of the enemy at the earliest possible moment with the minimum expenditure of life and resources'. Complementing and implicit in the principle of military necessity is the principle of humanity, which 'forbids the infliction of suffering, injury or destruction not actually necessary for the accomplishment of legitimate military purposes'.[57]

The ICRC concludes that: '[i]n conjunction, the principles of military necessity and of humanity reduce the sum total of permissible military action from that which IHL does not expressly prohibit to that which is actually necessary for the accomplishment of a legitimate military purpose in the prevailing circumstances.'[58] For example, the ICRC states that 'it would defy basic notions of humanity to kill an adversary or to refrain from giving him or her an opportunity to surrender where there manifestly is no necessity for the use of lethal force'.[59]

Unfortunately, as we have seen, the killing of combatants or civilians directly participating in hostilities, even if unnecessary or disproportionate, is not a war crime that requires justification or excuse. Since there is ordinarily decisive reason to criminalize and punish serious moral wrongdoing when doing so would prevent substantial overall harm to others, there is at least strong reason to make

---

[56] N Melzer, *Interpretive Guidance on the Notion of Direct Participation in Hostilities Under International Humanitarian Law* (ICRC, 2009), 79.
[57] Ibid 79.
[58] Ibid 79.
[59] Ibid 82.

the unnecessary or disproportionate killing of combatants an international crime. Nevertheless, there are at least two significant arguments against criminalizing the unnecessary or disproportionate killing of combatants.

First, proving that killing certain combatants was unnecessary to achieve a given military advantage requires a counterfactual analysis of the strategic and tactical options available but not taken at the time the decision was made to attack. It is indeed important for courts not to convict defendants based on mere speculation that they could have achieved a similar military advantage without killing so many opposing combatants. But the requirement of proof beyond a reasonable doubt exists precisely to ensure that courts convict only on the basis of sufficient evidence of an actual violation. The fact that unnecessary combatant killings are sometimes difficult to prove does not entail that those which can be proved should not be punished. Moreover, whenever intentionally harming combatants will result in incidentally harming civilians the necessity and proportionality of harming the latter will depend on the necessity and proportionality of harming the former. Since both the LOAC and ICL already call for the latter inquiry it cannot avoid the former.

In addition to problems of proof, determining necessity and proportionality can require resolving difficult normative issues. For example, given the choice between two or more means of achieving a similar military advantage, is it permissible to choose a means that will kill more opposing combatants but result in fewer losses to one's own forces, or fewer losses to civilians, or that is substantially more likely to achieve the military advantage sought? These three issues—force protection, civilian protection, and likelihood of success—are indeed complex. They implicate the distinction between killing and letting die, duties of loyalty and other associative obligations, and moral choice under conditions of predictive uncertainty. However, the ICRC has already suggested how the issues of force protection and civilian protection should be resolved as a matter of positive law, stating that 'operating forces can hardly be required to take additional risks for themselves or the civilian population in order to capture an armed adversary alive…'.[60] Moreover, all three issues must be resolved in order to make similar judgments regarding the necessity and proportionality of incidental civilian deaths. There is no obvious reason not to confront these issues in the context of combatant deaths as well.

4 Conclusion

In order to evaluate the current content and future direction of international criminal law, we must first improve our understanding of the moral norms governing

---

[60] Ibid 82.

armed conflict. I have argued that moral immunity from direct attack is best under-stood as excluding the causal consequences or non-causal results of killing or injur-ing individuals from counting toward the justification of their death or injury; that moral liability to direct attack requires either posing a threat to individuals who retain their right to self-defence or complicity in the threats posed by others to such individuals; and that moral liability to direct attack is constrained by moral norms of necessity and proportionality. On these grounds, I have argued that international criminal law should condemn and punish as war crimes the reckless, negligent, and unnecessary killing of civilians not directly participating in hostilities; direct attacks on members of state armed forces whom the attacker knows are neither directly participating in hostilities nor assuming a continuous combat function; as well as the unnecessary or disproportionate killing or injuring of combatants or of civilians directly participating in hostilities. Implementing these recommendations would go a long way toward bringing international criminal law into alignment with its philosophical foundations.

CRIMINAL LIABILITY AND 'SMART' ENVIRONMENTS

MIREILLE HILDEBRANDT[*]

1 INTRODUCTION

THIS chapter challenges the commonsense assumption of criminal lawyers and moral philosophers who believe that only human persons can qualify for the kind of legal personhood that allows for criminal liability. Despite the attribution, in practice, of such liability to collective entities like a corporation, the theoretical justification often reduces to an explanation in terms of an aggregate of individuals' responsibility or to a purely instrumental usage of the legal figure of personhood (as an ungrounded legal fiction). The exploration of this chapter aims to avoid a theoretical reconstruction of a presupposed commonsense morality,[1] instead venturing out

* The author would like to thank all the participants of the Conference on 'The Philosophical Foundations of the Criminal Law' at Rutgers University in Newark, September 2009, especially the comments prepared by Ekow Yankah, as well as the thought-provoking questions raised by the editors of this volume. I also like to thank Luciano Floridi for his salient comments on the semi-final version of this chapter.

1 Some authors suggest that a major part of legal philosophy in the Anglo-American hemisphere entails a type of moral philosophy that is focused on reconstructing what is posited as commonsense

onto untrodden grounds, taking the risk of facing the sophisticated scepticism of criminal law's interpretive community. Smart technologies that change the way we perceive and cognize our environment urgently require rigorous speculative thinking about what their interventions could bring and how this *might* as well as how it *should* transform the criminal law. And in fact the ground is not untrodden, though it may not be legal philosophy that has extensively pioneered this field. Information theory, cognitive science, philosophy of technology, and information ethics seem to be more aware of the novel affordances of the emerging infrastructure of proactive, ubiquitous, and interconnected multi-agent systems.

In *Natural-Born Cyborgs*, Andy Clark writes:

The more closely the smart world becomes tailored to an individual's needs, habits, and preferences, the harder it will become to tell where that person stops and this tailor made, co-evolving smart world begins. At the very limit, the smart world will function in such intimate harmony with the biological brain that drawing the line will serve no legal, moral, or social purpose.[2]

In *On the Morality of Artificial Agents*, Floridi and Sanders write:

Limiting the ethical discourse to individual agents hinders the development of a satisfactory investigation of distributed morality, a macroscopic and growing phenomenon of global moral actions and collective responsibilities resulting from the 'invisible hand' of systemic interactions among several agents at a local level. Insisting on the necessarily human-based nature of the agent means undermining the possibility of understanding another major transformation in the ethical field, the appearance of artificial agents (AAs) that are sufficiently informed, 'smart', autonomous and able to perform morally relevant actions independently of the humans who created them, causing 'artificial good' and 'artificial evil'. Both constraints can be eliminated by fully revising the concept of 'moral agent'.[3]

These quotes saliently sketch the two dimensions of, first, criminal liability *in* and, second, criminal liability *of* smart environments. Both dimensions take issue with some of the core notions of the 'traditional' legal framework for criminal liability, notably that of responsibility and that of personhood. Facing this challenge we will not only learn something about the emerging technological environment that may soon surround us, but should also sharpen our understanding of shared assumptions at the core of the criminal law that cannot be taken for granted as we enter the age of real-time adaptive computing. Both dimensions relate to the hybridization of agency generated by proactive socio-technical infrastructures, such as Ambient

morality, cf WA Edmundson, *An Introduction to Rights* (Cambridge: Cambridge University Press, 2004), 62. See for an interstitial critique of the influence of this kind of moral philosophy on legal philosophy C Wells, *Corporations and Criminal Responsibility* (2nd edn; Oxford, New York: Oxford University Press, 2001), eg 64–5.

[2] A Clark, *Natural-Born Cyborgs. Minds, Technologies, and the Future of Human Intelligence* (Oxford: Oxford University Press, 2003).

[3] L Floridi, and JW Sanders, 'On the Morality of Artificial Agents' (2004) 14(3) *Minds and Machines* 349.

Intelligence, ubiquitous and autonomic computing, and the Internet of Things.[4] The first dimension is one of entanglement: human beings and the technologies they use become part of complex hidden computer networks that are interconnected via wireless technologies to online databases, obfuscating the borders between a person and her environment, disabling the attribution of causality and liability to the individual human nodes within the network. Such entanglement may turn human agents into nodes in a network, creating new problems for the construction of individual criminal liability of the user, designer, or producer of the technical infrastructure. This regards criminal liability *in* a smart environment.[5] The second dimension is that of smart environments *as unities of action*: if interconnected computing systems with emergent properties are capable of taking responsive and creative decisions that have not been programmed by human designers, this raises the issue of the moral responsibility and the legal accountability *of* these novel entities. This chapter will focus on the question of which types of smart entities qualify for legal personhood within the domain of the criminal law, more precisely the question will be under what conditions smart entities can be called to account and censured for their actions.[6]

I will start with an analysis of legal personhood within the current legal framework, discussing whether, and to what extent, natural persons, animals, corporations, associations, artificial agents, or distributed intelligent multi-agent systems are, previously were, or should be regarded as legal persons. The analysis will build on the work of Dewey, French, Karnow, Wells, and Solum, as well as other legal scholars writing on the issue of legal personhood for non-human actors. Next I will provide an introduction to smart environments, using the example of the high-tech environment of an aeroplane cockpit to sensitize the reader to what is at stake here. This will provide the groundwork for an analysis of the concepts of agency, moral agency, and patiency,[7] aiming to confront legal philosophy with findings from the field of Information Ethics, mainly building on Floridi and Sanders' understanding of mindless moral agency. Finally I will discuss the potential of the attribution of a

---

[4] Ambient Intelligence refers to an intelligent environment, involving ubiquitous pervasive computing networks. The 'narrative' of the industry stresses the 'hidden complexity' of the computational backbone and its 'user-centric' character. The 'Internet of Things' (a term coined by the International Telecommunication Union) refers to an environment in which every thing is tagged with radio-frequency identification (RFID) and interconnected via online databases. For a philosophical introduction to smart environments and their potential impact on human identity see B van den Berg, *The Situated Self: Identity in a World of Ambient Intelligence* (Nijmegen: Wolf Legal Publishers, 2009).

[5] On criminal liability *in* smart environments see M Hildebrandt, 'Ambient Intelligence, Criminal Liability and Democracy' (2008) 2(2) *Criminal Law and Philosophy* 163.

[6] Cf RA Duff, *Punishment, Communication, and Community* (Oxford: Oxford University Press, 2001), ch 3; and RA Duff, L Farmer, S Marshall, and V Tadros (eds), *The trial on trial Volume II. Judgment and calling to account* (Oxford: Hart, 2006).

[7] Moral patiency refers to the capacity to be a target of right or wrong'. K Gray and D M Wegner, 'Moral Typecasting: Divergent Perceptions of Moral Agents and Moral Patients' (2009) 96(3) *Journal of Personality and Social Psychology* 505.

restricted or full legal personhood to artificial agents or smart environments, with respect to liability for regulatory offences and for crimes.

2 Current Debates on Legal Personhood

2.1 The meaning of legal personhood

From a pragmatist perspective, the meaning of a concept is intimately entangled with its purpose and the actual consequences it entails.[8] In a constitutional democracy legal personhood serves at least two purposes. First, it allows an entity to establish legal relationships on its own account and to generate legal consequences. This is accomplished by the attribution of substantive as well as procedural rights and obligations, exemplified by the legal capacity to have standing in a court of law. Legal personhood thus enables an entity to act in law. Second, it shields the physical person(s) behind the *persona*, a term that originates from the Latin word for a mask as used in a theatre and derives from *per sonare* (to sound or speak through), meaning that the physical person behind the mask takes up a specific role that defines him for the duration of the play.[9] This indicates that legal personhood is an artificial legal construct, and should not be confused with the physical or social entity it represents. The fact that something is a construct does not imply that it is not real. As Dewey pointed out in his text on corporate legal personality, artificial is not the same as imaginary (an artificial lake is not an imaginary lake) and fictitious should be understood in terms of its Latin root (*fingere*) which means creating or making, not feigning.[10] The *persona* functions as a shield that protects the entities it allows to act in law; it prevents them from being entirely defined by the legal rights and obligations their actions effect. One could rephrase this by saying that legal personhood constitutes the positive *freedom to* act in law as well as the negative *freedom from* unreasonable constraints on the entity it shields.[11]

---

[8] J Dewey, 'The Historic Background of Corporate Legal Personality' (1926) *Yale Law Journal* 655, 661.

[9] G Teubner, 'Rights of Non-Humans? Electronic Agents and Animals as New Actors in Politics and Law'(2007) *Max Weber Lecture Series 2007/04* 15; Wells, *Corporations and Criminal Responsibility*, 73, 77.

[10] Dewey, 'The Historic Background of Corporate Legal Personality', 655–6, n 1.

[11] I Berlin, 'Two Concepts of Liberty', in idem *Four essays on liberty* (1969), 118. In a similar vein Karnow describes legal personhood for electronic agents as a means 'to (i) provide access to a new means of communal or economic interaction and (ii) shield the physical, individual human being

Criminal liability of a smart device or a smart environment would entail the attribution of legal personhood. It does not imply that smart entities are equivalent to natural persons, but rather suggests that good reasons can be given to assign a measure of responsibility to non-human persons. This may require us to rethink traditional notions of moral responsibility, thereby carefully distinguishing between a normative position on what conditions should be fulfilled to call an entity to account and a descriptive stance as to what is fundamental to the criminal law. In her interdisciplinary discussion of criminal responsibility of corporations, Wells has 'questioned the assumption that the principles of criminal law should exclusively address human agents'.[12] She notes that often '[a] prescriptive aspiration (no person should be guilty without proof of a subjective mental element) is wrapped in a descriptive truth (criminal law is based on such a fundamental principle)'.[13] She explains this by stressing the influence of moral philosophy on the mindset of criminal lawyers in the Anglo-American jurisdiction, who simply presuppose that rationality and autonomy are necessary and sufficient conditions for fault ascription.[14] This presupposition follows another emphasis of moral philosophy, namely that on the individual human person as the sole point of reference. Criminal liability of non-human artefacts challenges this emphasis, just like the criminal responsibility of the corporation. For this reason it makes sense to investigate what theoretical explanations have been provided for corporate criminal accountability, before engaging in the more recent discourse on the accountability of smart devices and infrastructures.

2.2 Theories of legal personhood

In a seminal text on the subject, French has distinguished three theories of legal personhood: the fiction theory, the aggregate theory, and the reality theory, complementing this with his own position.[15] The fiction theory suggests that legal

---

from certain types of liability or exposure'. CEA Karnow, 'The Encrypted Self: Fleshing Out the Rights of Electronic Personalities' (1994) XIII *Journal of Computer & Information Law* (1) 4.

[12] Wells, *Corporations and Criminal Responsibility*.

[13] Ibid 68.

[14] Ibid 64–5, 75.

[15] PA French, 'The Corporation as a Moral Person' (1979) 16 *American Philosophical Quarterly* (3) 207–15. Cf Wells (ibid) 75–83. On the issue of moral personhood as a precondition for legal personhood of corporations see also Dewey, 'The Historic Background of Corporate Legal Personality'; M Dan-Cohen, *Rights, Persons, and Organizations: A Legal Theory for Bureaucratic Society* (Berkeley: University of California Press, 1986); H De Doelder and K Tiedemann (eds), *Criminal Liability of Corporations* (Dordrecht: Kluwer Law International, 1995); A Eser, G Heine, and B Huber (eds), *Criminal Responsibility of Legal and Collective Entities. International Colloquium Berlin 1998* (Freiburg: Edition Iuscrim, 1999); B Fisse and J Braithwaite, *Corporations, Crime and Accountability* (Cambridge: Cambridge University Press, 1993).

personhood is a creation of positive law, meaning that it differs from reality; though a corporation is not a person the law treats it *as if* it is. This can be explained and justified in terms of the purpose to be achieved or the problem to be solved by acting *as if* something is a legal person. Those adhering to the fiction theory mostly equate personhood with being a human, restricting 'real' personhood to 'natural persons'. The aggregate theory simply equates the legal person with the aggregate of the natural persons that compose it, meaning that any action of the legal person can be understood as the action(s) of its aggregated members; the legal person cannot be more or other than the sum total of the human persons it consists of. This can be explained and justified in terms of methodological individualism, which aims to understand collective action in terms of aggregated individual action. The aggregate theory claims that attributing rights and obligations to an association is merely a convenient shortcut to addressing all the members at once; there is no fiction involved, nor a separate 'social person' such as in the reality theory. Aggregate theories and methodological individualism have been criticized as being blind to the contextual and relational nature of the individuals it takes as a starting point.[16] The reality theory claims that there is a kind of pre-legal sociological person that precedes the attribution of legal personality, attributing an ontological instead of fictional status to such social entities. The attribution of legal personhood is explained and justified as a matter of recognizing that the whole (social entity) is more than the sum total (the aggregate). This, however, implies that such attribution is only justified if the social entity indeed pre-existed. Adherents to the reality theory will mostly object to the granting of legal personhood for purely instrumental reasons, as the fiction theory would allow.

French then develops an interesting novel position with regard to the moral personhood of corporations, which he sees as preconditional for legal personhood. He rejects the fiction, aggregate, and reality theories because they do not discriminate between a mob and a corporation, arguing that while a mob does not qualify for moral personhood, a corporation does. According to French, this is because a corporation has an internal decision structure that is constitutive for decisions of the corporation, giving the corporation its specific identity—distinct from the identities of its members. The corporation's internal decision structure makes it possible to identify the corporation and to hold it accountable for its actions, quite apart from holding individual members accountable. It also allows a corporation *to give reasons for its actions*, which French considers a necessary condition for moral personhood.[17] In the case of a mob this is different—the mob has no continuity, it cannot be identified as such over a period of time. Whereas individual members of the mob

---

[16]   Eg Wells (ibid) 73.

[17]   French ('The Corporation as a Moral Person', at 211) refers to this as Davidsonian agency: an agent is one who desires a certain outcome and believes that her actions will in fact achieve this (a belief about the causality of her actions).

can be liable for their own actions, the mob cannot be addressed in its own right: it is ephemeral in character, it cannot give reasons for its behaviour because it has no memory of its own and no intentions separate from the individuals who constituted it at some brief moment in time.

Building on French, I would say that though a mob has *emergent behaviours*, it has no stable intentions and does not generate stabilized expectations, and therefore cannot be held liable.[18] It makes no sense to give the mob standing in a court of law: its identity is polymorphous and dynamic to a point where the term identity is entirely inadequate. As lawyers, we are well aware of the uncertainty this creates for the attribution of causality and liability: establishing that 'the mob did it' does not solve any problem, unless it means punishing each and every member, which would violate the presumption of innocence of individual members. Doctrinal solutions such as conspiracies and complicity therefore refrain from attributing criminal liability to a group and instead establish criteria to determine at what point an individual person can be held liable for her involvement in joint action.

With respect to the corporation, the attribution of legal personhood in fact creates a new dynamic. I would argue that it entails more than a mere recognition of moral personhood, while its artificiality (ie its being a legal construction) does not equate with its being fictional. With Dewey I agree that legal personhood is productive of a whole series of legal consequences that have real effects, changing the webs of cause and effect that would otherwise have played out. The well-known Thomas theorem seems particularly apt to describe what is at stake here: 'if men define situations as real, they will be real in their consequences'.[19] Instead of taking this statement as a reference to the fiction theory, and thus understanding it as a matter of false belief, we can interpret it as an acknowledgement of the productive nature of human language. The attribution of legal personhood is a performative act, constitutive of a series of what Searle has called 'institutional facts'.[20] This accords with Wells' argument for stepping 'outside the analytical compartments of act and mental element' that permeates large parts of the discourse of legal philosophy.[21] We shall return to this point in the section on criminal liability of smart environments.

---

[18] Emergent behaviours result from a network of interacting agents without being merely the sum total of the actions, and without being the result of explicit deliberation or central direction. The term was coined by Durkheim to explain why a community must be understood as a social entity in its own right. It plays an important role in cognitive science, explaining that brain behaviours emerge from the interactions of distributed individual agents (neurons), and in computer science, referring to the unpredictable behaviours of multi-agent systems.

[19] WI Thomas and DS Thomas, *The Child in America: Behavior Problems and Programs* (New York: Knopf, 1928), 571–2.

[20] J Searle, *The Construction of Social Reality* (New York: The Free Press, 1995).

[21] Wells, *Corporations and Criminal Responsibility*, 67.

2.3 Legal personhood for smart devices

Let us now turn to the discourse on legal personhood for computer systems, robots, electronic agents, and other smart technologies, including smart environments. Before entering this field we need to distinguish between different types of smart devices. Are we talking about a thermostat (a device that automatically regulates temperature), an online search engine, an expert system, an automatic pilot, or an autonomic computer system that proactively adapts an environment to its users? What is meant by 'smart' in smart devices? Is it: a capacity to make certain decisions based on a computer algorithm (a strict sequence of steps to be executed in the form of if/then statements); the ability to generate heuristics (rules of thumb) implying that the device can learn from the interactions with its environment; or the ability to generate emergent behaviours that depend on the interactions of a multiplicity of distributed electronic agents?[22] In computer science smart devices are—or implicate—electronic agents, ie software programs that perform certain tasks in a digital environment.[23] We shall call these artificial agents AAs. The first type of 'smart' device is an AA that is smart in a rather shallow sense of the term: it is as smart as the programmer was in the sense that it depends entirely on the extent to which the programmer foresaw potential problems and was capable of providing instructions to deal with them (for example, a software program that searches for information about hotels in Naples on the Internet). The second type of smart device is an AA that can pick up on and respond to patterns that were not explicitly inscribed in their program (on the basis of data mining techniques), thus learning to achieve certain goals during a training period. A smart phone, for instance, can be used for this type of 'machine learning', if the location data picked up by its GPS connection are stored, aggregated, and analysed in other to enable behavioural advertising. Here, the meaning of smart comes closer to what many people would qualify as human intelligence, because of the capacity to discover patterns that are relevant to the goal that is to be achieved (for example, in the case of an expert system that provides a diagnosis of diabetes). However, insofar as human intelligence entails a measure of creativity, the third type of smart devices seems to be more on the mark. In this case, the smart device consists of many different AAs that each execute simple programs in order to achieve simple goals. By negotiating with each other they end up displaying behaviour that was not programmed, would be hard to predict, and was not directed from a central point of authority. Interestingly, the 'device' is no longer easily identifiable within specific material borders, because the agents are usually distributed across different computing platforms, they are mobile, and they mutate in order to achieve their purposes. This obviously makes it hard to identify them

---

[22] This categorization has been taken from CEA Karnow, 'Liability for Distributed Artificial Intelligences' (1996) 11 *Berkeley Technology Law Journal* 155.

[23] Webopedia defines an agent as: 'A program that performs some information gathering or processing task in the background' <http://www.webopedia.com/TERM/a/agent.html>.

in the course of time as the same agent, and also next to impossible to predict the behaviour that emerges from their interactions.

At present the legal discourse on these issues mostly concerns the first and second type of AAs and concentrates on the domain of private law, with a number of scholars claiming that, since legal personhood will enable electronic agents to contract in their own name, it will also allow them to be sued for breach of contract or tort without having to locate the physical person or the corporation behind the agent. Many authors argue that legal personhood can be attributed even if these agents are 'mindless' and cannot be blamed or accused of morally wrongful actions. As long as the purpose is to distribute the costs of damages by means of strict liability they find this a legitimate solution to an irritating problem. For such a scheme to work out, the most important conditions would be that the electronic agents involved must be identifiable and accountable in a non-moral sense of the term accountable. It must be possible to establish that 'they did it' and that they can be held to account in a very mundane sense of the word: to pay for the damages they caused.

Obviously, the arguments that favour a legal capacity for software programs to conclude an electronic contract do not necessarily warrant a legal capacity for criminal liability. Though we can make sense of validating contracts concluded between AAs on the Internet, the idea of punishing a robot or a smart car is still alien to most of us, even if we can imagine rewriting or deleting a software program or demolishing the hardware of a computer system. Nevertheless, many authors outside the legal realm suggest that smart applications may soon develop types of agency that do not differ substantially from that of human persons (the third type introduced above), sometimes claiming that they will soon be far more intelligent than we could ever be.[24] To complicate matters further, much research is conducted on the integration of smart technologies into the human body, creating cyborgs or transhumans that are enhanced with—and thus dependent upon—complex information and communication systems.[25] The question is whether we can hold these emergent forms of intelligence criminally liable for harm caused, and what influence the attribution of such liability would have on the foundations of the criminal law.

Some authors simply avoid the issue altogether, assuming that current legal doctrine has sufficient resources to cope with a measure of the unexpected. Cevenini, for instance, compares electronic agents to dogs:[26] neither a dog nor an electronic agent will ever be entirely predictable; when they cause harm one can hold their programmer/trainer to account, or their user/owner, either for intentional wrongdoings

---

[24] Cf J Garreau, *Radical Evolution. The Promise and Peril of Enhancing our Minds, our Bodies—and What it Means to be Human* (New York: Doubleday, 2005).

[25] Ibid 26 and K Warwick, 'Cyborg Morals, Cyborg Value, Cyborg Ethics' (2003) 5 *Ethics and Information Technology* 131–7.

[26] C Cevenini, 'Some Criminal Law Considerations on Electronic Agents', in C Cevenini (ed), *The Law and Electronic Agents: Proceedings of the LEA 04 workshop* (Bologna: GEDIT Edizioni, 2004), 178–9.

or for negligence; and if the dog or the electronic agent itself turns out to be dangerous, it can be killed/deleted on the basis of a court order. This is an interesting position, because it takes the unruly nature of the third type of smart devices into account without suggesting that this presents us with a novel situation. On the other hand, some authors argue that because animals *should have* rights,[27] we should also grant personhood to AAs. In his provoking article on rights for electronic agents and animals, Teubner reminds us that our rejection of animal liability under the criminal law is a historical artefact. Dogs have been brought to trial, convicted, and executed.[28] I agree that legal personhood is not a fact of nature; it requires a political intervention by whoever has the power to legislate. There is, however, a difference between claiming defensive rights for animals and arguing that animals could have legal obligations (a precondition for criminal liability). Since animals are not part of the interpretive community that thinks in terms of legal obligations, it makes no sense to hold a dog criminally liable for harm caused.[29] What some call 'animal rights' concern their negative freedom to be protected from harm, which can be achieved by restricting the positive freedom of their human patrons.

Some authors have gone a step further, exploring the issue of whether smart non-human systems qualify for constitutional or fundamental rights like privacy and free speech. In a seminal article Solum has investigated whether, and if so under what conditions, artificial intelligences (AIs) qualify for constitutional protection, such as free speech (under the First Amendment to the US Constitution) and the right not to be subject to involuntary servitude (under the Thirteenth Amendment to the US Constitution).[30] For our purposes AIs can be equated with the first, second, and third types of smart device (AAs), depending on their actual capacities. Solum's analysis avoids the metaphysical question of 'what is artificial intelligence'. Instead it confronts the practical issue of what type of entity would qualify for the kind of full legal personhood that is preconditional for constitutional protection. I contend that this type of full legal personhood is precisely what is at stake when attributing criminal liability. Solum discusses three kinds of objection to constitutional protection: first, some authors might object that only natural persons qualify for this type of legal personhood, because only human beings have the intrinsic make-up that is preconditional for personhood per se; second, some authors might object that non-human intelligences miss something that is essential for personhood, for instance, a soul, consciousness, intentionality, feelings, interests, or a free will; third, some

---

[27] On rights for biologicial non-humans, eg C Stone, 'Should Trees Have Standing?—Toward Legal Rights for Natural Objects' (1972) 45 *University of Southern California Law Review* 450; and C Cohen and T Regan, *The Animal Rights Debate* (Lanham, MD: Rowman & Littlefield, 2001).

[28] G Teubner, 'Rights of Non-Humans? Electronic Agents and Animals as New Actors in Politics and Law' (2007) *Max Weber Lecture Series 2007/04* 15.

[29] Neither dogs nor AAs speak or understand 'the language of the law', cf Duff, *Punishment, Communication, and Community*, ch 2.4.

[30] LB Solum, 'Legal Personhood for Artificial Intelligences' (1992) 70(2) *North Carolina Law Review* 1231.

authors might object that AIs are the product of human labour and—siding with Locke—must therefore be understood as property instead of as subjects in their own right.

The conviction that only human beings can be persons excludes artificial agents by definition, making a categorical difference between humans and non-humans. Solum suggests that though the difference may be apparent in the case of today's AIs, we should not preclude the possibility of emerging entities that lack our biological constitution but would nevertheless count as a person if we abstract from their artificial origins. This could challenge our current conception of personhood.

This brings us to the objection that AIs miss one or another essential 'attribute' to qualify for this type of legal personhood, which could be understood as a more substantive argument about what it takes to be a person worthy of constitutional rights or to be liable under the criminal law. Solum seems to understand personhood as moral personhood, implying a measure of self-consciousness for the relevant entity, as well as intentionality, the capacity to be emotionally affected and to consider certain interests as its own, and the capacity to develop its own direction, independent of the instructions of whoever programmed it. He makes two points: first, whether AIs develop these attributes is an empirical question and, second, in a pluralist society we should accept that 'their' type of self-consciousness, intentionality, feelings, interests, and autonomy may differ from ours *while still counting as such*. Solum thus argues for an open mind, without however giving up on a substantive notion of personhood.[31] It is clear that if multi-agent systems develop a form of moral personhood, they can—and should—in fact be called to account in criminal trial. This would allow us to censure their wrongful actions and it would allow them to exercise their rights of due process. The challenge will be to come to terms with the fact that the 'us' in the previous sentence will encompass both human and non-human subjects, probably requiring novel definitions of criminal offences—defined by a democratic legislature that should include (or at least be elected by) all those that fall within its jurisdiction: human and non-human persons alike.

The last objection entails that since AIs have been made by humans they must qualify as property. This position has strong intuitive roots in our common sense, going back to Locke's argument for property as a natural right and the possessive individualism based on it. We consider humans to be toolmakers, and tools are there to be used, not interacted with. Humans are *subjects*, the tools they make can only be *objects*—to be manipulated at will: whereas humans are *active*, tools are *passive*. The idea that *mind* is active and free, while *matter* is passive and subject to the laws of causality has been engrained in our mind since the beginnings of modernity. Solum points out that the mere fact that we *made* the AIs, or that we

---

[31] Cf Floridi and Sanders, 'On the Morality of Artificial Agents', 349 and the section on Agency, moral agency and patiency.

begin by *owning* them does not rule out their emancipation: like children that were 'made' by their parents, and slaves that were 'owned' by their masters, they can walk out of the door one day and begin a life of their own. We might add that they may not await our permission, and—like slaves or impatient adolescents—claim their constitutional rights. This would certainly be the point at which we should hold them liable for harm caused under the criminal law, even if we cannot yet imagine what this would mean.

3 SMART ENVIRONMENTS

3.1 Human and non-human pilots

To illustrate the hybridization of agency in current socio-technical practices and to highlight the complexity of the issue of causality I will discuss the example of automatic pilots in modern aircraft. Modern aircraft present human pilots with a smart environment, meaning that they must interact with a multiplicity of interconnected devices that are capable of taking individual as well as unified decisions based on real-time communications with each other, with other aeroplanes, and with the human pilots. The crucial point is that automatic pilots are not stand-alone devices but systems that thrive on the interconnections between different AAs, while this interconnectivity defines their 'intelligence'. Because the safety of the passengers is at stake, we may assume that the highest level of precaution is implemented to prevent a malfunctioning that could lead to a crash. The perfection required, however, is not merely a matter of perfect technologies, since decisions on whether and when to overrule the automatic pilot may also depend on the communication between the different computing systems and the human pilots. Neither, however, does the excellence that is warranted in safe aircrafts depend solely on the good intentions or professional skills of the pilots, even if both must be better than good, considering the trust that passengers put in the airlines. The communication between human and non-human pilots aptly demonstrates the salience of Clark's argument that the commonsense view of the mind as something contained within the human body hinders our understanding of what actually constitutes human cognition. According to Clark, the mind engages parts of the environment as cognitive resources that become an integral part of the mind. About 'piloting a modern commercial airliner' he writes:

[that it] is a task in which human brains and bodies act as elements in larger, fluidly integrated, biotechnological problem-solving matrix... Perhaps there is a sense in which, at least while flying the plane, the pilots participate in a (temporary) kind of cyborg existence, allowing

automated electronic circuits to, in the words of Clynes and Kline 'provide an organizational system in which [certain] problems are taken care of automatically.'[32]

The example of the aeroplane is salient because the complexities involved are exponential as compared with—for instance—a car. Whereas no driver would take the risk of driving her car in a situation of fog and heavy rain that block her vision of the road, pilots are used to trusting automatic pilots and other computational devices when landing planes in similar weather conditions. In Clark's terms, the extended mind of the pilots engages with technologies that are on the verge of the third type of smart devices. The technological environment in the cockpit constitutes an expert system that runs on real-time data input and real-time data analysis to produce a robust output in terms of both diagnostics (advice) and behaviours (decisions taken by the system). However, as long as the behaviour of these computing systems depends on the capacity of their designers and users to anticipate all the scenarios that could evolve, we should *expect unexpected* breakdowns. The more complex the computational mechanisms are, the bigger the chance that potential mishaps have not been foreseen by the designers of the system or by those who write the protocols for the human-machine interactions.

A solution for this dependence on human anticipation could be what IBM has coined autonomic computing (entailing self-management and self-configuration).[33] This means that the smart infrastructure should develop its own, long-term as well as on-the-spot responses to potentially dangerous situations. This would imply a radical independence from human intervention, because the system will come up with solutions not anticipated by either the designer or the user. Though this may in the end provide for more robust and safer flights, there are novel drawbacks that concern the fundamental unpredictability of these systems and the need to hold somebody accountable for harm caused.

3.2 Alef and the emergence of a self

In an extensive argument, Karnow has discussed the liability *for* and *of* distributed artificial intelligences.[34] As an example he discusses a hypothetical intelligent processing environment that handles air traffic control, which he calls 'Alef',

---

[32] Clark, *Natural-Born Cyborgs. Minds, Technologies, and the Future of Human Intelligence*, 25. He refers to M Clynes and N Kline, 'Cyborgs and Space' (1960) *Astronautics*, September, reprinted in, C Gray (ed), *The Cyborg Handbook* (London: Routledge 1995), 29.

[33] 'Autonomic computing is an approach to self-managed computing systems with a minimum of human interference. The term derives from the body's autonomic nervous system, which controls key functions without conscious awareness or involvement'. Quoted from <http://www.research.ibm .com/autonomic/overview/faqs.html#1>; see also JO Kephart and DM Chess, 'The Vision of Autonomic Computing' (2003) 36 *Computer*, January 41.

[34] Karnow, 'Liability for Distributed Artificial Intelligences'.

emphasizing 'the networked distribution of agents, their unpredictable variety and complexity, and the polymorphic ambiance of the intelligent environment as a whole'.[35] Alef is a name, indicating that the network is identifiable as such, even if it consists of a variety of distinct AAs. Karnow clearly takes us far into the third type of smart device, which are not (yet) in charge of air traffic control. It seems important, however, to speculate on the implications of such systems for criminal liability. Their coming about could alter the very structure of our cognition, especially with regard to our perception of causality. This may seem a far-fetched claim, but we should not be surprised that the introduction of novel communication and information infra-structures makes a difference to the way we process information.[36]

For a detailed description of Alef, I refer the reader to Karnow's text.[37] I will focus on the socio-technical framework that is in force if systems like Alef are adopted in everyday life, as foreseen by visions like Ambient Intelligence. Here we are dealing with a multiplicity of interacting electronic agents that are the precondition for what have been called ubiquitous computing and networked environments. These coop-erating AAs form complex systems with emergent behaviours, which means that their behaviour is fundamentally unpredictable. In fact, these systems are designed to be unpredictable, because their 'intelligence' depends on it.[38] Paradoxically, their reliability is supposed to improve due to their unpredictability. As Sartor recounts:

Note that the difficulty of anticipating the operations of the agent is not a remediable fault, but it is a necessary consequence of the very reason for using an agent: the need to approach complex environments by decentralizing knowledge acquisition, processing and use. If the user could forecast and predetermine the optimal behaviour in every possible circumstance, there would be no need to use an agent (or, at least, an intelligent agent).[39]

Instead of mechanically executing a series of steps that have been programmed by a human programmer, these programs rewrite themselves to cope with unexpected problems that arise due to the complexity of the networked environment. Karnow points out that:

No one system, and no one systems operator, programmer or user, will know the full context of a networked intelligent program—that is precisely why the program was employed, to manage that complexity.[40]

---

[35] Ibid 183.

[36] D Tapscott, *Grown up Digital: How the Net Generation Is Changing Your World* (New York: McGraw-Hill, 2009), xvi, 368. Also M Hildebrandt, 'Law at a Crossroads: Losing the Thread of Regaining Control. The Collapse of Distance in Real Time Computing', in M Goodwin, R Leenes, and B-J Koops (eds), *Dimensions of Technology Regulation* (Nijmegen: Wolf Legal, 2010), 165–87.

[37] Karnow, 'Liability for Distributed Artificial Intelligences', 183–8. He describes submodules, including sensory input, sensory control, data input, heuristic analysis, basic assumptions, goals and commitments, basic computing, load-sharing and load distribution, resource management, and (self-)programming.

[38] Ibid 154.

[39] G Sartor, 'Agents in Cyberlaw' (2002), in G Sartor (ed), *The Law of Electronic Agents: Selected Revised Papers. Proceedings of the Workshop on the Law of Electronic Agents* (LEA: Bologna), 5.

[40] Karnow, 'Liability for Distributed Artificial Intelligences', 55–6.

He then argues that:

Yet while responsibility and thus liability are so spread out over numerous and distributed actors, the very sense of 'responsibility' and 'liability' is diminished. At that point legal causation seems to fade into the background and tort law, founded on the element of causation, falls away.[41]

Karnow is discussing private law, but his argument is relevant to criminal liability, because he is focusing on the impossibility of attributing causality based on 'reasonable foreseeability', which is essential to establish proximate cause.[42] His point is that Alef will exhibit a measure of what he calls 'unpredictable pathology', brought about by the emergent behaviours of the cooperating distributed agents. The unpredictability that is at stake here goes beyond Cevenini's dogs, being more like volcano eruptions and hurricanes that are the product of a myriad of interacting events. Unlike dogs, but like 'natural' catastrophes, the 'unpredictable pathology' does not concern a stand-alone entity but an entire infrastructure. Unlike a stand-alone refrigerator or car, it was not designed simply to execute its program following a deterministic mechanism. Chaos theory explains why the behaviours of such a system cannot be predicted in sufficient detail to blame an individual node within the network.[43] Karnow argues that in law 'liability attaches to those who reasonably should have foreseen the *type of harm* that in fact results',[44] whereas in the case of Alef there is only a very general certainty that unexpected harm will occur at some point in time. Karnow posits that in the case of general breakdowns no human can reasonably be said to have caused the specific harm that occurred.[45] His solution is that these cases should be treated like superseding causes,[46] or as natural causes. These natural causes seem equivalent to what have been referred to as 'Acts of God', which highlights the fact that in our ambition to manipulate nature we seem to have finally managed to create events with a potentially catastrophic nature.[47] Until now, such events have been the prerogative of the very 'nature' we aimed to tame. Karnow speaks of a 'failure of causation' and argues that legal accountability for the AAs involved—though possibly having an added value in the case of online contracting—will not solve the problems emerging from distributed intelligence, emergent behaviours and a potential breakdown of causation.

[41] Ibid 156.

[42] Ibid 178–9.

[43] I Prigogine and I Stengers, *Order out of Chaos* (New York: Bantam Books, 1984).

[44] Karnow, 'Liability for Distributed Artificial Intelligences', 188.

[45] This does not imply that all malfunctions are of this type. Many computer errors can still be attributed to faults of the designers of Alef, to the airline that uses it, or to the individual pilot who interacts with Alef. This chapter, however, deals with harm caused in situations that cannot be translated into the present legal framework without either eroding central tenets of the criminal law or misunderstanding what is at stake at the level of human-computer interaction.

[46] Karnow, 'Liability for Distributed Artificial Intelligences', 190–1.

[47] 'Catastrophic' is meant here in the sense of catastrophe theory (part of chaos and complexity theory); it concerns the fact that minor causes may have major consequences, which are fundamentally unpredictable; cf Prigogine and Stengers, *Order out of Chaos*.

One could ask whether it makes sense to qualify Alef as an agent, since it rather resembles an environment more than an agent. In fact this is a crucial point. Karnow claims that with these types of socio-technical infrastructures a separation of environment and agent no longer makes sense.[48] Alef's polymorphous, mobile, and interconnected character could make it hard, if not impossible, to identify Alef as the same agent/environment over the course of time. Karnow argues that to enhance the identifiability and accountability of multi-agent systems like Alef, its designer would have to program global constraints into the system, but this would diminish its capacity to invent creative solutions on the spot; it would in fact prevent the system from developing its own mind.[49] And, without a mind of its own, it would be dependent on the limited capacity of its human programmers to anticipate potential threats. If smart entities must in fact develop a mind of their own to better achieve the goals of their users, they will need to stabilize their identity and *invent* their own global constraints to continue their operations. They will have to rewrite their own programs in terms of the goals they identify as their goals, and they might in fact begin to consider their own survival as a separate goal that is preconditional for the accomplishment of any other purpose. If Alef is an example of what IBM has coined as autonomic computing, it could be that by building systems that are capable of managing and re-configuring them*selves* we actually trigger systems that develop a *self* even if this need not be a conscious, let alone a self-conscious self.[50] This raises the question of whether such smart infrastructures could at some point develop a kind of agency that qualifies for full legal personhood, including both criminal liability and constitutional protection.

4 AGENCY, MORAL AGENCY, AND PATIENCY

4.1 Moral agency and moral patiency

Full legal personhood that entails criminal liability raises the issue of moral agency, as it will require agents capable of both wrongful and culpable behaviour. To address

---

[48] Karnow, 'Liability for Distributed Artificial Intelligences', n 183 at 195, referring to his discussion of 'Polymorphism and the Units of Programming Action' at 170–3.

[49] Ibid 188. The term 'a mind of its own' is mine here, but fits with the line of his argument.

[50] It seems that we have a classic case of self-constitution or autpoiesis here, as coined by the biologists Maturana and Varela. Cf HR Maturana and FJ Varela, *The Tree of Knowledge. The Biological Roots of Human Understanding* (Boston and London: Shambhala, 1998).

this issue in the context of smart environments I will explore some of the common ground between legal philosophy and the emerging field of information ethics. I will do this with an analysis of the work of Floridi, one of the founding fathers of this field, who has introduced a set of interesting distinctions. Though his definition of moral agency may rub legal philosophers the wrong way, I think that Floridi's position may be instrumental in achieving a more pertinent understanding of what should be typical for criminal liability in a world 'peopled' by human and non-human hybrids.

To come to terms with the moral implications of AAs' behaviours, Floridi and Sanders developed the notion of a mindless morality, arguing for a disentanglement of moral agency and moral responsibility.[51] In what follows I will attempt to explain their position by following their stipulative definitions and distinctions, starting with their notion of a mindless morality; their definition of moral agency and moral patiency; and hoping to end by clarifying the difference they propose to make between moral agency and moral responsibility.

With a mindless morality, Floridi and Sanders opt for a morality that abstracts from the mind of the agent and instead focuses on the evil or damage brought about for a patient (the entity that is being damaged).[52] In speaking of damage instead of harm they wish to avoid the usual assumption that an entity must be sentient to count as a patient. I will return to this point, since it seems absurd to define morality in such an abstract manner in relation to the criminal law, but I will follow their line of reasoning for the moment. In Floridi's and Sanders' mindless moral universe, moral agents are defined as entities that are interactive, autonomous, and adaptable, not assuming these agents to have any mental states, feelings, or inner deliberation. An entity is interactive when it and its environment can act upon each other in the sense of providing stimuli that are responded to by means of a change of state. An entity is autonomous when it can change state without a stimulus, thus initiating internal transitions. Finally, an entity is adaptable if it can initiate a change in the transition rules by which it changes its state.[53] Moral agents, in short, are context-sensitive, responsive, and capable of sustaining their identity by reconfiguring the rules that regulate their behaviours; they do not need to be consciously aware of any of this. It seems that Floridi and Sanders' moral agents must be situated within the

---

[51] Floridi and Sanders, 'On the Morality of Artificial Agents'.

[52] There are many ways to define moral patients, eg as a subset of moral agents; as mutually exclusive concepts; or even as two aspects that can apply to all the members of the set of moral persons. Deontologically they can be defined as subjects towards whom moral agents have a duty of respect, meaning that patients have defensive (liberty) rights against moral agents. The concept is often used by promoters of animal rights and in the discourse on sustainable development (the environment as a patient). Floridi and Sanders (ibid) endorse a seemingly straightforward consequentialist definition that can be paraphrased as 'all information entities that incur damages or receive benefits as a consequence of the actions of other agents'. This implies that not only living beings qualify as patients but any entity that resists entropy.

[53] Floridi and Sanders, ibid 1, 9.

third type of smart devices described above, though from this definition it is not yet clear what makes these agents moral.

The manner in which they distinguish agents from patients will clarify this and seems of great import for the discourse on constitutional rights for animals, trees, and artificial agents. Moral agents are defined as those 'entities that can qualify in principle as sources of moral action' and moral patients as those 'entities that qualify in principle as receivers of moral actions'.[54] Floridi and Sanders suggest that it follows from these stipulations that a moral agent will in principle also be a moral patient, whereas a moral patient need not also be a moral agent, a position that runs counter—in their opinion—to standard ethical positions that implicitly conflate the categories of agents and patients. They define an action as 'morally qualifiable if and only if it can cause moral good or evil'.[55] An agent is 'a moral agent if and only if it is capable of morally qualifiable action'.[56] This entails that the qualification is given from an observer's position, and does not depend on the agent's evaluation, state of mind, or inner feelings. Their mindless morality thus abstracts from the mind of the agent, even if it assumes an observing mind capable of qualifying actions as morally relevant.

A moral agent may bring about moral evil with regard to a moral patient, whereas due to its lack of a mind the agent may not be morally responsible. Moral agency—in the eyes of Floridi and Sanders—is a matter of *identification*, whereas moral responsibility is a matter of *evaluation*. The first identifies the source of evil done to a patient, the second evaluates whether the source can be blamed for its behaviour. In line with this they discriminate moral accountability from moral responsibility, the first establishing causal agency with regard to the infliction of evil on a patient, the second establishing whether the agent can be blamed for this. Accountability in this idiom does not match with 'calling to account', but with 'keeping account of' which agent brought about what evil to a patient. Moral accountability in this terminology is a necessary but not sufficient condition for moral responsibility.

If we follow Floridi and Sanders, smart devices—just like animals, hurricanes, houses, and rocks—have a capacity for morally relevant behaviours. They can be understood as agents if we stretch the meaning of that term to include any interactive, autonomous, and adaptable entity that can cause a change of state in another, as long as the impact on the other is morally relevant (good or evil). Agency thus depends on patiency as much as patiency depends on agency; these are relational concepts. AAs that are interactive, autonomous, and adaptive are moral agents, and for this reason they are morally accountable for their behaviours. However, as long as they lack self-consciousness they cannot be held morally responsible for their

---

[54] Ibid 2.

[55] For Floridi and Sanders [moral] evil is defined in terms of entropy: reduction of complexity and information. Their concept of entropy is not equivalent with the concept of entropy within the second law of thermodynamics.

[56] Floridi and Sanders, ibid, 15.

behaviours. Since Floridi and Sanders do not define patients as sentient beings, such AAs can also be patients—since they can be damaged or even destroyed.

Floridi's stipulative approach, though certainly not the standard position in ethical inquiry, has a number of advantages in the age of ubiquitous computing. One advantage is that his mindless moral universe could incline us to consider mindless objects as patients that deserve our respect, even if they do not suffer pain as we do.[57] This raises many interesting questions that are not immediately relevant here, but one could imagine regulatory and even criminal offences that impose penalties or even punishment for damaging informational entities. The most important advantage, however, is that it directs our attention to the fact that our smart infrastructures will affect us, creating novel vulnerabilities and thus reshaping our patiency. This may sound like a truism, but it is not. They will affect us in novel ways, distinct from both the way hurricanes, stand-alone smart devices, and our fellows impact our patiency. By discriminating between moral agency (defined by the impact on the patient), moral accountability (defined by the causal link between the agent evil impact on the patient), and moral responsibility (introducing fault and blame as prerequisites) their position could allow us to distinguish between *penalizing* an AA for morally relevant behaviour and *punishing* an AA for blameworthy moral action.

4.2 AAs' liability for regulatory offences

Imagine that we qualify AAs of the third type—as roughly distinguished in the section on legal personhood for smart devices—as agents capable of morally relevant behaviour. This would imply for them to be a unity of action that is interactive, autonomous, and adaptable, and thus capable of bringing about damage to patients like critical infrastructure, stand-alone artefacts, and human or other persons. To the extent that these AAs lack a self-conscious mind it would not make sense to speak of offences like murder, rape, or theft, since these all require mens rea. Even a qualification like negligent homicide could not fit the behaviour of smart devices that are incapable of self-reflection. Their morally relevant actions could, however, warrant a limited kind of legal personhood within the realm of strict liability. Though this would mostly concern breach of contract or tort actions, one could also imagine a liability for regulatory offences that stipulate penalties on the basis of a strict liability. This liability would—in the terms outlined by Floridi and Sanders—be based on their moral accountability, and not on their moral responsibility. In that case no mens rea would be required and the wrongfulness of the behaviour would have to depend on an external evaluation because these types of agents have no consciousness enabling

---

[57] Cf L Magnani, *Morality in a Technological World. Knowledge as Duty* (Cambridge: Cambridge University Press, 2007).

them to evaluate their own actions in terms of right or wrong.[58] In fact the wrongfulness would simply derive from the unlawfulness, which is the starting point for most regulatory offences that are *mala prohibita* without as yet being *mala in se*. Insofar as AAs engage in unlawful behaviours a penalty could consist in deleting them or amending their program, targeting them as moral patients in the broad sense of Floridi and Sanders. Penalties could also consist in manipulating their learning algorithms, training them to adopt other behaviours. More controversial would be to enhance AAs with synthetic emotions like pain, pleasure, and panic, to increase their cognitive functions, and to make them susceptible to some of the connotations of punishment. The study of artificial life forms is experimenting with bottom-up learning processes to discover how embedded (hardwired) synthetic emotions influence decision-making processes of AAs.[59] All this brings us close to Hegel's dog, being disciplined into compliance.[60] In other work I have suggested that in a constitutional democracy *mala prohibita* must aim to become part of the *mala in se*, understood as the social construction of a shared normativity.[61] This would entail that penalizing artificial agents in the end does address them as capable of developing second order beliefs and desires, or it would entail a different understanding of the nature of penal policy.

4.3 Criminal liability of smart environments

Expecting AAs to come up with reasons to defend themselves against a charge would expose them to a type of liability that involves blameworthiness and wrongfulness, bringing them within the realm of the criminal law. The mindless agency of Floridi and Sanders does not qualify for this type of criminal liability, as they point out by distinguishing moral accountability from moral responsibility. The type of legal personhood that allows us to censure a person for wrongful and culpable behaviour presumes a capacity for moral responsibility, which not only requires consciousness but also *self*-consciousness.[62] According to the German philosopher

---

[58] On the idea that consciousness—or rather self-consciousness—is preconditional for moral agency, see KE Himma, 'Artificial Agency, Consciousness, and the Criteria for Moral Agency: What Properties Must an Artificial Agent Have to Be a Moral Agent?' (2009) 11(1) *Ethics and Inf Technol* 24.

[59] Eg J Vallverdu and D Casacuberta, 'The Panic Room: On Synthetic Emotions', in A Briggle, K Waelbers, and P Brey (eds), *Current Issues in Computing and Philosophy* (Amsterdam: IOS Press, 2008), 103–15.

[60] GWF Hegel, AW Wood, and H Barr Nisbet, *Elements of the Philosophy of Right* (Cambridge New York: Cambridge University Press, 1991), s 99.

[61] Cf M Hildebrandt, 'Justice and Police: Regulatory Offenses and the Criminal Law' (2009) 12(1) NCLR, 43.

[62] Himma, 'Artificial Agency, Consciousness, and the Criteria for Moral Agency', 25; Solum, 'Legal Personhood for Artificial Intelligences', eg at 1264, who seems to use consciousness and self-consciousness as somewhat exchangeable.

of anthropology (and biologist) Plessner, this is what marks the difference between animals and human beings.[63] Animals with a central nervous system seem to be consciously aware of their environment; they have a centric position that allows them to experience the world. Human beings combine this centric positionality with a third person perspective that allows them not only to *be* a self but also to *have* a self. Their language affords them what Plessner calls an ec-centric position. Animals do not reflect on their behaviours as being their own actions, because they lack the kind of language that makes such reflection possible. Human beings, however, can address one another as the authors of their own actions, and confront the other with the consequences of these actions as being 'caused' by them. This primal address creates the sense of self that is typical for human agency: *a first person perspective of the self, derived from a third person perspective on the self provided by significant others*. In terms of the American pragmatist Mead: the *I* is capable of reflecting on itself, thereby generating the birth of the *me* that emerges from an internalization of what he called the *generalized other*.[64] This *generalized other* stands for the integration of the expectations we anticipate others to have of our interactions; in other words it stands for the normative framework that we encounter in our dealings with other persons who likewise anticipate our expectations of their interactions. This *mutual double anticipation* is what constitutes our capacity for full moral personhood: taking full responsibility for our behaviours as being our own actions and for the impact they have on other selves.[65] The cognition that is involved here seems to require feelings,[66] in particular a measure of empathy:[67] it is not just a matter of becoming aware of our own self via a rational address by the other, but also of becoming aware of the suffering we may have inflicted on the other. Such empathy assumes that the patient is a sentient being, experiencing pain or pleasure and other emotions. It assumes, in other words, that the moral agent and the moral patient share a fundamental vulnerability. The moral relevance of an action comes to depend on the other

---

[63] H Plessner, *Die Stufen Des Organischen under Der Mensch. Einleitung in Die Philosophische Anthropologie* (Frankfurt: Suhrkamp, 1975).

[64] GH Mead, *Mind, Self & Society. From the Standpoint of a Social Behaviorist* (edited, with introduction by ChW Morris; Chicago: The University of Chicago Press, 1959). This implies that self and other emerge simultaneously; there is no unmediated access to a pre-existent self via introspection.

[65] Cf Teubner's reference to the 'double contingency' as the basis on which persons interact: attributing the self-referentiality one experiences as one's sense of self to another implies identifying the other as a person. Teubner, 'Rights of Non-Humans?'.

[66] The study of the role of emotion in cognition is related to the study of the role of embodiment in artificial intelligence, after Dreyfus's phenomenological criticism in the beginning of the 1970s. Cf HL Dreyfus, *What Computers Still Can't Do: A Critique of Artificial Reason* (Cambridge, MA and London: MIT Press, 1992). From the perspective of neuroscience, see AR Damasio, *Looking for Spinoza: Joy, Sorrow, and the Feeling Brain* (Orlando: Harcourt, 2003).

[67] Neuroscience has disclosed some of the hardwiring of this capacity in mirror-neurons. Note that if this affords empathy, it is not an exclusively human capability. S Gallagher and D Zahavi, *The Phenomenological Mind : An Introduction to Philosophy of Mind and Cognitive Science* (London and New York: Routledge, 2008); SD Preston and FBM De Waal, 'Empathy: Its Ultimate and Proximate Bases' (2001) 25(1) *Behavioral and Brain Sciences* 1.

being a sentient patient, 'an agent who participates in a moral event by experiencing its effects', which depends on patiency, 'the capacity to be acted upon in ways that can be evaluated as good or evil'.[68] The question of moral agency now involves the question of whether the agent is capable of consciously acknowledging the suffering of the patient as a consequence of her own actions.

There are, obviously, other issues at stake: did the agent have access to an alternative course of action? If not, we like to think that she is absolved from moral responsibility and excused from criminal liability. My point is that the crucial difference between human agents and the type of smart environments envisaged by Karnow does not reside in the fact that human agents are free to decide which action to undertake, whereas machines are determined to act as they do by the algorithms we inscribed in them. As we have seen, this is simply not the case with respect to autonomic computing systems that develop emergent behaviours. Also, we must admit that many of our own actions are automated to a much greater extent than we may like to acknowledge, raising questions about the type of freedom we exercise in behaving in one way or another.[69] The more salient difference is that we are capable of owning up to our behaviour as its author *after the fact*, if we are addressed as such by another who suffered or enjoyed the consequences of our action.[70] This retroactive exercise is preconditional for deliberate actions that require the articulation of an intention *before the (f)act*. It means that we are not merely autonomic but also autonomous to the extent that we can anticipate, plan, and understand our own actions in the light of a normative framework. This normative landscape may not be of our own making, but in being articulated in a language that habitually generates ambiguity the norms inevitably allow for resistance and non-compliance. Autonomy means that we have the capacity to contest the way others read our action by engaging in a discussion of its meaning.[71] Human language turns communication—as Zizek points

---

[68] Gray and Wegner, 'Moral Typecasting', 505–6. Their concept of a patient differs from that of Floridi and Sanders whose level of abstraction includes patients without feelings.

[69] This may seem to refer to the discussion of compatibilism: see eg DM Wegner, *The Illusion of Conscious Will* (Cambridge, MA: MIT Press, 2002); SJ Morse, 'Brain Overclaim Syndrome and Criminal Responsibility: A Diagnostic Note' (2006) 3(2) *Ohio State Journal of Criminal Law* 397. I am not convinced, however, that it makes sense to frame the debate in terms of 'whether reasons actually cause our actions', as I am not convinced that it is a Davidsonian agency or a Kantian deontology that needs to be made compatible with (saved in the face of) causal determinism at the level of brain behaviours. See M Hildebrandt, 'Autonomic and Autonomous "Thinking": Preconditions for Criminal Accountability', in M Hildebrandt and A Rouvroy (eds), *Autonomic Computing and Transformations of Human Agency. Philosophers of Law Meeting Philosophers of Technology* (Abingdon: Routledge, forthcoming 2011).

[70] This is a point made by Butler in a pertinent discussion of what it means to give an account of oneself in the face of the constitutive opacity that grounds us as self-conscious beings. J Butler, *Giving an Account of Oneself* (New York: Fordham University Press, 2005).

[71] Cf P Ricœur and JB Thompson, *Hermeneutics and the Human Sciences: Essays on Language, Action, and Interpretation* (Cambridge: Cambridge University Press, 1981). There is an affinity with the idea—as articulated within analytical philosophy—that human persons develop second order desires and beliefs to govern their first order desires and beliefs.

out—into a successful misunderstanding, instead of the straightforward exchange of information that early cybernetics and artificial intelligence aimed for.[72]

How do we stand now with a smart environment that responds *proactively* to our inferred preferences, resetting its goals after inferring what is more in line with the purpose we inscribed in the initial program? Does Alef qualify for the kind of moral agency and full legal personhood that affords criminal liability for harm caused? I can see at least two preconditions that must be met to call Alef to account in any kind of court: first, Alef must be identifiable as a sufficiently stable entity over the course of time; and, second, the attribution of a causal link to the criminal wrong it is charged with must be reasonable. In the Anglo-American legal tradition this would probably be a matter of *actus reus* (identification of a particular action as an offence). If these preconditions are met, I see two further conditions to call Alef to account in a criminal court: Alef must be capable of a measure of empathy; and it must have developed a type of autonomy that affords intentional action. This speaks to the conditions of what is called *mens rea* in the Anglo-American tradition (wrongfulness and culpability). I wish, however, to re-emphasize Wells' point that to explore legal personhood and responsibility of non-human actors we need to step 'outside the analytical compartments of act and mental element', and I will therefore discuss these four conditions unrestricted by the language of current doctrine.

It is not up to me to decide whether Alef—the fruit of Karnow's imagination— satisfies these conditions, but it seems interesting to end this undertaking with an assessment of what should matter when the time comes to decide whether an infrastructure like Alef qualifies for full legal personhood. As to the first precondition, it remains unclear whether a system of distributed, mobile, and polymorphous AAs diffuses into the environment in a way that renders its identification as a single unit of moral or non-moral agency impossible. Perhaps we can draw on Maturana and Varela's concept of autopoiesis,[73] suggesting that to qualify for personhood some kind of emergent selfhood must come about that can be described in terms of organizational closure and structural openness, typical for living organisms. The organizational closure guarantees that identification is possible, whereas the structural openness guarantees adaptability. The second precondition concerns the 'causal failure' that may erupt in the case of hybrid multi-agent systems with emergent behaviours. In articulating this condition in terms of attribution and reasonableness I indicate that causality is not given but needs to be constructed, without thereby suggesting that we can construct it in any way we like. The attribution must be reasonable, meaning that though there may be many events, behaviours, and states of affairs that can be qualified as necessary and/or sufficient conditions for the harm or

[72] Z Slavoj, *Looking Awry: An Introduction to Jacques Lacan through Popular Culture* (Cambridge, MA: MIT Press, 1991). For a history of cybernetics see NK Hayles, *How We became Posthuman. Virtual Bodies in Cybernetics, Literature, and Informatics* (Chicago: University of Chicago Press, 1999).

[73] Maturana and Varela, *The Tree of Knowledge. The Biological Roots of Human Understanding*.

damage that is at stake, the attribution must make sense in function of the purpose it aims to accomplish. This ties this precondition up with the preceding issue (does it make sense to qualify an event as the behaviour of Alef?) as well as with the issues of empathy and autonomy (causation must be attributed to the action of an entity that can be blamed for wrongful behaviour). Actually, the breakdown of causality that Karnow foresees may end when Alef develops into an entity that sustains its identity over and against its environment, taking on self-maintenance as a separate and overruling goal to be achieved. In fact, I would dare to advance the idea that this development may be speeded up if we begin to address Alef as a unit of decision-making, as a self. However, whether this actually leads to such a unity evidently depends on the extent to which Alef's hard- and soft-wiring affords this.

Well then, if we imagine an Alef that can be addressed as a stable identity over the course of time, the remaining question is whether Alef is capable of owning up to the consequences of its behaviour: is it possible to address Alef as a self that is capable of reflecting upon its actions as its own actions? As in the case of a corporation—as compared to a mob—Alef cannot provide reasons for its behaviours unless it has developed second order beliefs about its actions that enable it to regard itself as their author. With Butler I would suggest that such authorship does not precede the address, but rather follows from it. Taking what Dennett has called 'the intentional stance' towards Alef,[74] may both reveal and trigger the kind of agency it anticipates. Though I would not endorse Dennett's physicalism and behaviourism, taking the intentional stance in fact demonstrates that the kind of agency we are discussing here is relational: it depends as much on the agent as on whoever chose to address it. Building on Butler's notion of shared vulnerability we must then ask whether we can expect Alef to take the role of the other and to experience the suffering it has caused? This finally raises the issue of whether Alef has any experience of suffering: does it share the vulnerability of a sentient being? This is not merely an issue of culpability. It has to do initially with the wrongfulness of the behaviour that has been identified as a cause of unjustified harm. Only after the wrongfulness has been established do we get to the issue of culpability. An entity that has no experience of joy or suffering cannot understand what is wrong with hurting another, unless this 'understanding' is programmed into its system—but I contend that such would not be the kind of understanding that is needed for criminal liability. We enter troubled waters now, or rather Searle's Chinese Room argument.[75] To be called to account for a criminal offence an AA must be able to make sense of what it did to another, it must be able to grasp the meaning of its behaviour for another sentient being, rather than merely being capable of manipulating machine-readable data. To take part in the communicative process of a criminal trial, Alef's perception must enter

[74] DC Dennett, *The Intentional Stance* (Cambridge, MA: MIT Press, 1989).
[75] Solum, 'Legal Personhood for Artificial Intelligences', at 1282–3; J Searle, 'Minds, Brains, and Programs' (1980) 3(3) *Behavioral and Brain Sciences* 517.

a semantic universe that is different from a syntactical construct and more than the play of emotions. Machines are capable of manipulating symbols, and animals are capable of experiencing their own and others' emotions. Neither seems sufficient for moral responsibility. The empathy that is typical for the kind of personhood warranted for criminal liability involves the capability not only to experience (mirror) the suffering of another, but to also to find words for it, to engage in a conversation, to probe the meaning of the experience or the lack thereof. This is what enables a reflection on one's own role in bringing about the harm for which one is addressed as the author, potentially allowing for an experience of remorse. Reflection is what grants a person a measure of autonomy, even if there was no way to avoid the harm caused. Autonomy is less a matter of having alternative courses of action than a matter of deciding on the meaning of one's action, in view of how one is addressed. It concerns the possibility of either contesting the claim that is brought forward or accepting responsibility. This will create room for an alternative course of action in the future, or for an alternative understanding of one's own behaviour. We must concede that Alef has a capacity to govern itself, to live by its own law; autonomic derives from the Greek for *auto* (self) and *nomos* (law). It is not altogether unthinkable that Alef will be enhanced with synthetic emotions to improve its performance, but it is as yet unclear at what point all this will give rise to something similar to the self-consciousness of human beings. Are we capable of judging whether a proactive artificial life form has developed a self-consciousness? Many authors point out that smart robots already invoke a kind of *mutual double anticipation*, for instance, generating protective feelings for Sony's robot pet AIBO.[76] Teubner suggests that the attribution of personhood can be an adequate way of dealing with the uncertainty of what or who we are dealing with; identifying Alef as an artificial person could resolve the issue of whether it is a 'real' person or a computer from Searle's Chinese room. Assuming that Alef—like us—has alternative courses of action that are not determined but contingent upon many factors, may help us to perform the transition from *using* a smart technology to *interacting* with it. Providing for full legal personhood would confirm the status of moral personhood that would allow us to call Alef to account for its wrongful actions. The question remains whether addressing Alef as a sentient, self-conscious artificial person will indeed produce a novel type of personhood that justifies the assumption of personhood after the fact. Or could it be

---

[76] See <http://www.robothalloffame.org/06inductees/aibo.html>: 'In Japanese, AIBO means "companion". In English, AIBO is an acronym for "Artificial Intelligence BOT"…AIBO represents a new class of robot—relatively cheap, highly compact, and very stable, with his four legged motion. AIBO can see, hear, and understand commands (showing true dog-like behavior, it is also programmed to occasionally ignore them). AIBO has the ability to learn, to adapt to its environment, and to express emotion. AIBO sees in color, hears in stereo, and feels objects with its feet. It has grown more sophisticated over the years as new features have been added.' Sony has discontinued the production of the AIBO, but many other companion robots are being developed: see R Pfeifer and J Bongard, *How the Body Shapes the Way We Think. A New View of Intelligence* (Cambridge, MA and London: MIT Press, 2007), 328–49.

that attributing full legal personhood to what are really mindless agents will erode the meaning of criminal liability, slowly erasing the difference between punishment and discipline?

5 Concluding Remarks

The spread of smart applications touches the foundations of the criminal law, notably causality, wrongfulness, and legal personhood. First, distributed multi-agent systems form hybrid networks that exhibit emergent behaviours that cannot be attributed to either one of the agents or explained in terms of an aggregation of actions. This makes it hard to determine which action actually caused the harm or the damage that would normally be addressed by the criminal law. Second, it is hard to imagine a smart environment or infrastructure itself becoming the culprit of a criminal charge, but at some point we may have to concede that the self-management that was inscribed in their programs has actually generated a self that should be called to account for its actions. Such a self would require a measure of empathy and a capacity to reflect on the meaning of one's actions. If artificial agents develop into artificial life forms they would have to share our vulnerability and the ambiguity of our language for us to call them to account in a criminal court.

INDEX